NEW PERSPECTIVES ON
Microsoft® Office 2013

SECOND COURSE

NEW PERSPECTIVES ON

Microsoft® Office 2013

SECOND COURSE

Ann Shaffer
Katherine T. Pinard
Roy Ageloff

Patrick Carey
Joseph J. Adamski
June Jamrich Parsons
Dan Oja

Sharon Scollard
Mohawk College

Carol A. DesJardins
St. Clair County Community College

S. Scott Zimmerman
Brigham Young University

Beverly B. Zimmerman
Brigham Young University

CENGAGE
Learning·

Australia • Brazil • Japan • Korea • Mexico • Singapore • Spain • United Kingdom • United States

CENGAGE
Learning®

New Perspectives on Microsoft Office 2013, Second Course

Director of Development: Marah Bellegarde

Executive Editor: Donna Gridley

Associate Acquisitions Editor: Amanda Lyons

Product Development Manager: Leigh Hefferon

Senior Product Manager: Kathy Finnegan

Product Manager: Julia Leroux-Lindsey

Developmental Editors: Kim T. M. Crowley, Robin M. Romer, Mary Pat Shaffer, Sasha Vodnik

Editorial Assistant: Melissa Stehler

Brand Manager: Elinor Gregory

Market Development Managers: Kristie Clark, Gretchen Swann

Senior Content Project Managers: Jennifer Feltri-George, Jennifer Goguen McGrail

Composition: GEX Publishing Services

Art Director: GEX Publishing Services

Text Designer: Althea Chen

Cover Art: ©Michael Adendorff/Flickr Open/Getty Images

Copyeditors: Suzanne Huizenga, Michael Beckett

Proofreader: Lisa Weidenfeld

Indexer: Alexandra Nickerson

Some of the product names and company names used in this book have been used for identification purposes only and may be trademarks or registered trademarks of their respective manufacturers and sellers.

Microsoft and the Office logo are either registered trademarks or trademarks of Microsoft Corporation in the United States and/or other countries. Cengage Learning is an independent entity from the Microsoft Corporation, and not affiliated with Microsoft in any manner.

Disclaimer: Any fictional data related to persons or companies or URLs used throughout this book is intended for instructional purposes only. At the time this book was printed, any such data was fictional and not belonging to any real persons or companies.

Library of Congress Control Number: 2013943473

ISBN-13: 978-1-285-16775-6

ISBN-10: 1-285-16775-9

Cengage Learning
200 First Stamford Place, 4th Floor
Stamford, CT 06902
USA

Cengage Learning is a leading provider of customized learning solutions with office locations around the globe, including Singapore, the United Kingdom, Australia, Mexico, Brazil, and Japan. Locate your local office at: **www.cengage.com/global**

Cengage Learning products are represented in Canada by Nelson Education, Ltd.

For your course and learning solutions, visit **www.cengage.com**

Purchase any of our products at your local college store or at our preferred online store **www.cengagebrain.com**

ProSkills Icons © 2014 Cengage Learning.

Printed in the United States of America
2 3 4 5 6 7 19 18 17 16 15 14

Preface

The New Perspectives Series' critical-thinking, problem-solving approach is the ideal way to prepare students to transcend point-and-click skills and take advantage of all that Microsoft Office 2013 has to offer.

In developing the New Perspectives Series, our goal was to create books that give students the software concepts and practical skills they need to succeed beyond the classroom. We've updated our proven case-based pedagogy with more practical content to make learning skills more meaningful to students.

With the New Perspectives Series, students understand *why* they are learning *what* they are learning, and are fully prepared to apply their skills to real-life situations.

About This Book

This book provides complete coverage of introductory-to-advanced concepts and skills for Microsoft Office 2013, and includes the following:

- Three Word 2013 tutorials on working with templates, themes, and styles; performing a mail merge; and collaborating with others
- Four Excel 2013 tutorials plus two appendices that cover creating Excel tables and PivotTables; managing multiple workbooks; developing an Excel application; and working with advanced functions, custom formats, and advanced filters
- Four Access 2013 tutorials plus one appendix that cover creating advanced queries and enhancing table design; creating custom forms and reports; sharing, integrating, and analyzing data; and understanding relational databases and database design
- Two PowerPoint 2013 tutorials on applying advanced formatting to objects; creating advanced animations; and distributing presentations

New for this edition!

- Each tutorial has been updated with new case scenarios throughout, which provide a rich and realistic context for students to apply the concepts and skills presented.
- A new Troubleshoot type of Case Problem, in which certain steps of the exercise require students to identify and correct errors—which are intentionally placed in the files students work with—promotes problem solving and critical thinking.
- The content has been developed so that students and instructors can work seamlessly on either the Windows 7 or Windows 8 operating system.

System Requirements

This book assumes a typical installation of Microsoft Office 2013 and Microsoft Windows 8. (You can also complete the material in this text using another version of Windows 8, or using Windows 7. You may see only minor differences in how some windows look.) The browser used for any steps that require a browser is Internet Explorer 10.

The New Perspectives Approach

Context

Each tutorial begins with a problem presented in a "real-world" case that is meaningful to students. The case sets the scene to help students understand what they will do in the tutorial.

Hands-on Approach

Each tutorial is divided into manageable sessions that combine reading and hands-on, step-by-step work. Colorful screenshots help guide students through the steps. **Trouble?** tips anticipate common mistakes or problems to help students stay on track and continue with the tutorial.

VISUAL OVERVIEW

Visual Overviews

Each session begins with a Visual Overview, a two-page spread that includes colorful, enlarged screenshots with numerous callouts and key term definitions, giving students a comprehensive preview of the topics covered in the session, as well as a handy study guide.

PROSKILLS

ProSkills Boxes and Exercises

ProSkills boxes provide guidance for how to use the software in real-world, professional situations, and related ProSkills exercises integrate the technology skills students learn with one or more of the following soft skills: decision making, problem solving, teamwork, verbal communication, and written communication.

KEY STEP

Key Steps

Important steps are highlighted in yellow with attached margin notes to help students pay close attention to completing the steps correctly and avoid time-consuming rework.

INSIGHT

InSight Boxes

InSight boxes offer expert advice and best practices to help students achieve a deeper understanding of the concepts behind the software features and skills.

TIP

Margin Tips

Margin Tips provide helpful hints and shortcuts for more efficient use of the software. The Tips appear in the margin at key points throughout each tutorial, giving students extra information when and where they need it.

REVIEW

APPLY

Assessment

Retention is a key component to learning. At the end of each session, a series of Quick Check questions helps students test their understanding of the material before moving on. Engaging end-of-tutorial Review Assignments and Case Problems have always been a hallmark feature of the New Perspectives Series. Colorful bars and headings identify the type of exercise, making it easy to understand both the goal and level of challenge a particular assignment holds.

REFERENCE

TASK REFERENCE

GLOSSARY/INDEX

Reference

Within each tutorial, Reference boxes appear before a set of steps to provide a succinct summary and preview of how to perform a task. In addition, a complete Task Reference at the back of the book provides quick access to information on how to carry out common tasks. Finally, each book includes a combination Glossary/Index to promote easy reference of material.

www.cengage.com/series/newperspectives

Our Complete System of Instruction

BRIEF

INTRODUCTORY

COMPREHENSIVE

Coverage To Meet Your Needs

Whether you're looking for just a small amount of coverage or enough to fill a semester-long class, we can provide you with a textbook that meets your needs.

- Brief books typically cover the essential skills in just 2 to 4 tutorials.
- Introductory books build and expand on those skills and contain an average of 5 to 8 tutorials.
- Comprehensive books are great for a full-semester class, and contain 9 to 12+ tutorials.

So if the book you're holding does not provide the right amount of coverage for you, there's probably another offering available. Go to our Web site or contact your Cengage Learning sales representative to find out what else we offer.

COURSECASTS

CourseCasts – Learning on the Go. Always available…always relevant.

Want to keep up with the latest technology trends relevant to you? Visit http://coursecasts. course.com to find a library of weekly updated podcasts, CourseCasts, and download them to your mp3 player.

Ken Baldauf, host of CourseCasts, is a faculty member of the Florida State University Computer Science Department where he is responsible for teaching technology classes to thousands of FSU students each year. Ken is an expert in the latest technology trends; he gathers and sorts through the most pertinent news and information for CourseCasts so your students can spend their time enjoying technology, rather than trying to figure it out. Open or close your lecture with a discussion based on the latest CourseCast.

Visit us at http://coursecasts.course.com to learn on the go!

Instructor Resources

We offer more than just a book. We have all the tools you need to enhance your lectures, check students' work, and generate exams in a new, easier-to-use and completely revised package. This book's Instructor's Manual, ExamView testbank, PowerPoint presentations, data files, solution files, figure files, and a sample syllabus are all available on a single CD-ROM or for downloading at http://www.cengage.com.

SAM: Skills Assessment Manager

Get your students workplace-ready with SAM, the premier proficiency-based assessment and training solution for Microsoft Office! SAM's active, hands-on environment helps students master computer skills and concepts that are essential to academic and career success.

Skill-based assessments, interactive trainings, business-centric projects, and comprehensive remediation engage students in mastering the latest Microsoft Office programs on their own, allowing instructors to spend class time teaching. SAM's efficient course setup and robust grading features provide faculty with consistency across sections. Fully interactive MindTap Readers integrate market-leading Cengage Learning content with SAM, creating a comprehensive online student learning environment.

www.cengage.com/series/newperspectives

BRIEF CONTENTS

TABLE OF CONTENTS

EXCEL TUTORIALS

ACCESS TUTORIALS

OBJECTIVES

Session 5.1
- Create a new document from a template
- Move through a document using Go To
- Use the thesaurus to find synonyms
- Customize a document theme
- Save a custom theme
- Select a style set
- Customize a style
- Change character spacing

Session 5.2
- Create a new style
- Inspect styles
- Reveal and compare text formatting details
- Review line and page break settings
- Generate and update a table of contents
- Create and use a template
- Create a Quick Part

Working with Templates, Themes, and Styles

Creating a Summary Report

Case | *Department of Cultural Affairs*

In the small city of Westphal, Minnesota, citizen committees often work with city departments to make recommendations regarding municipal issues. A new committee led by Jonah Freiburg, a senior member of the Department of Cultural Affairs, is responsible for recommending a new site for the increasingly popular Blue Spruce Folk Festival. Jonah has asked you to help prepare the report summarizing the committee's preliminary recommendations. He's also interested in learning more about Word templates, so he'd like you to do some research by opening a few templates and examining the styles they offer. Next, he wants you to modify the formatting currently applied to his report document, including modifying the theme and one of the styles, creating a new style, and adding a table of contents. Then he wants you to create a template that can be used for all reports produced by the department, as well as a reusable text box containing the department's address and phone number, which department members can insert into any Word document via the Quick Part gallery.

STARTING DATA FILES

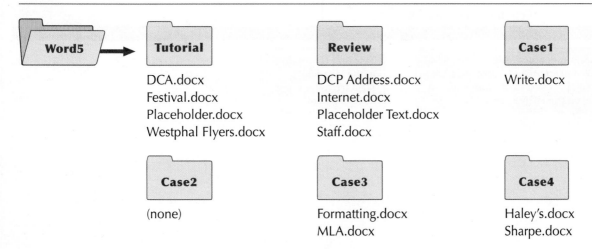

Word5 → Tutorial

DCA.docx
Festival.docx
Placeholder.docx
Westphal Flyers.docx

Review

DCP Address.docx
Internet.docx
Placeholder Text.docx
Staff.docx

Case1

Write.docx

Case2

(none)

Case3

Formatting.docx
MLA.docx

Case4

Haley's.docx
Sharpe.docx

Session 5.1 Visual Overview:

The **theme colors** are the colors you see in the Theme Colors section of any color gallery, such as the Font Color gallery. Theme colors are used in the document's styles to format headings, body text, and other elements.

Every document has two **theme fonts**, which are used in the document's styles. The theme fonts appear at the top of the font list when you click the Font arrow in the Font group on the HOME tab.

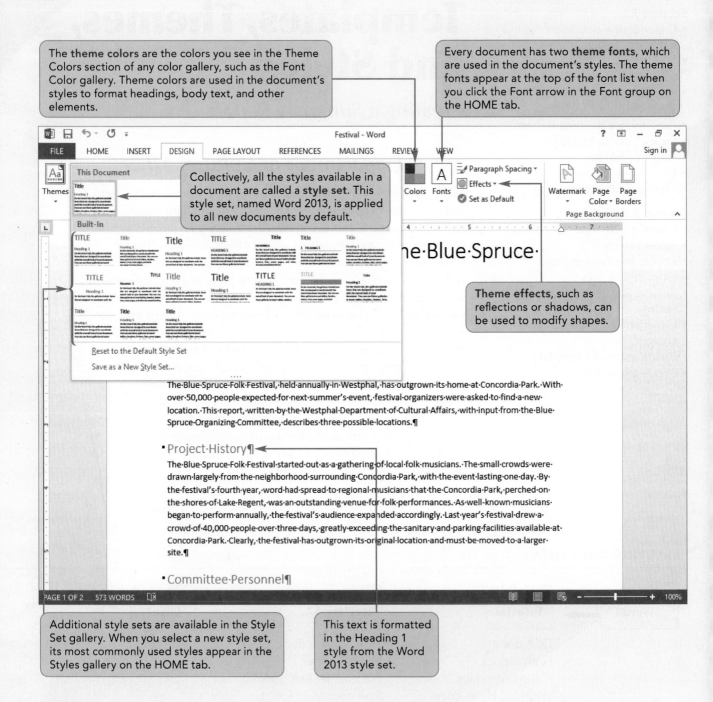

Collectively, all the styles available in a document are called a **style set**. This style set, named Word 2013, is applied to all new documents by default.

Theme effects, such as reflections or shadows, can be used to modify shapes.

The·Blue·Spruce·Folk·Festival,·held·annually·in·Westphal,·has·outgrown·its·home·at·Concordia·Park.·With· over·50,000·people·expected·for·next·summer's·event,·festival·organizers·were·asked·to·find·a·new· location.·This·report,·written·by·the·Westphal·Department·of·Cultural·Affairs,·with·input·from·the·Blue· Spruce·Organizing·Committee,·describes·three·possible·locations.¶

Project·History¶

The·Blue·Spruce·Folk·Festival·started·out·as·a·gathering·of·local·folk·musicians.·The·small·crowds·were· drawn·largely·from·the·neighborhood·surrounding·Concordia·Park,·with·the·event·lasting·one·day.·By· the·festival's·fourth·year,·word·had·spread·to·regional·musicians·that·the·Concordia·Park,·perched·on· the·shores·of·Lake·Regent,·was·an·outstanding·venue·for·folk·performances.·As·well-known·musicians· began·to·perform·annually,·the·festival's·audience·expanded·accordingly.·Last·year's·festival·drew·a· crowd·of·40,000·people·over·three·days,·greatly·exceeding·the·sanitary·and·parking·facilities·available·at· Concordia·Park.·Clearly,·the·festival·has·outgrown·its·original·location·and·must·be·moved·to·a·larger· site.¶

Committee·Personnel¶

Additional style sets are available in the Style Set gallery. When you select a new style set, its most commonly used styles appear in the Styles gallery on the HOME tab.

This text is formatted in the Heading 1 style from the Word 2013 style set.

TASK	PAGE #	RECOMMENDED METHOD
Total, calculate in a report	AC 393	In Layout view, click any value in the column to calculate, click the DESIGN tab, in the Grouping & Totals group, click Totals, click the desired function
Total row, add or remove from an Excel table	EX 267	On TABLE TOOLS DESIGN tab, in the Table Style Options group, click the Total Row check box
Total row, select a summary statistics	EX 288	In the Total row cell, click the arrow button, click a summary function
Track Changes, turn on or off	WD 356	Click REVIEW tab, click the Track Changes button in the Tracking group
Trusted folder, create	AC 291	Click the FILE tab, click Options, click Trust Center, click Trust Center Settings, click Trusted Locations, click Add new location, click Browse, navigate to the desired folder, click OK four times
Validation circle, clear from a cell	EX 421	Enter valid data in the circled cell
Validation circles, clear all	EX 421	On the DATA tab, in the Data Tools group, click the Data Validation button arrow, click Clear Validation Circles
Validation Rule field or table property, set	AC 284	Display the table in Design view, select the field or table, enter the rule in the Validation Rule box
Validation Text property, set	AC 284	Display the table in Design view, select the field, enter the text in the Validation Text box
Webpage, open in Internet Explorer	WD 403	Start Internet Explorer, click File on the menu bar, click Open, select a webpage, click OK
Webpage, save document as	WD 394	*See* Reference box: Saving a Word Document as a Webpage
WordArt shape, change	PPT 158	Click DRAWING TOOLS FORMAT tab, in WordArt Styles group, click Text Effects, point to Transform, click style
WordArt styles, apply	PPT 157	Click INSERT tab, in Text group, click WordArt, click style, type text
Workbook, save with macros	EX 453	On the Quick Access Toolbar, click the Save button, click No, select the save location, enter the filename, click the Save as type button, click Excel Macro-Enabled Workbook, click Save
Workbooks, link	EX 352	Enter a formula in the format =[*WorkbookName*]*WorksheetName!CellRange*
Workbooks, switch between	EX 354	On the VIEW tab, in the Window group, click the Switch Windows button, click the workbook to make active
Worksheet, unprotect	EX 427	Go to the worksheet, on the REVIEW tab, in the Changes group, click the Unprotect Sheet button
Worksheet group, print	EX 347	Create a worksheet group, apply page layout settings, print as usual
Worksheet window, split into panes or remove split	EX 290	On the VIEW tab, in the Window group, click the Split button

Custom Themes and Style Sets

The Themes gallery displays the available themes on your computer, including any custom themes you have created and saved in the Document Themes folder.

This style set, named Shaded, is applied to the Festival document, shown below. In the Shaded style set, the Heading 1 style formats text with blue paragraph shading and a white font color.

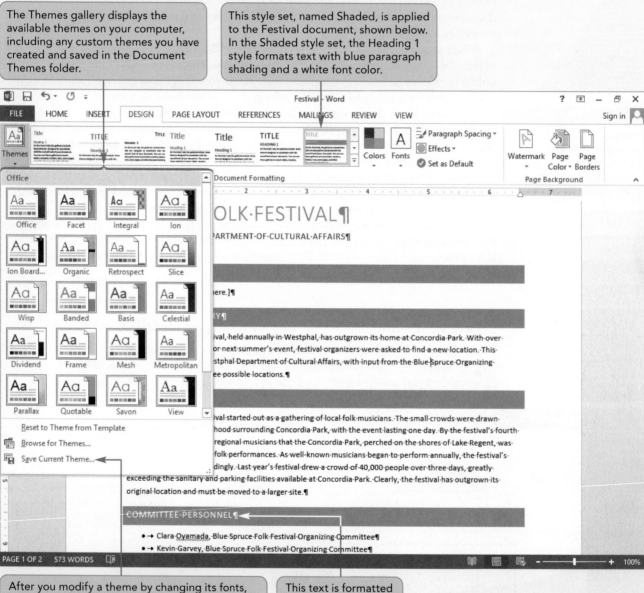

After you modify a theme by changing its fonts, colors, and effects, you can save it as a new theme using the Save Current Theme command. Your custom theme will be saved in the Document Themes subfolder inside Word's Template folder unless you specify another location.

This text is formatted in the Heading 1 style from the Shaded style set.

Creating a New Document from a Template

A template is a file that you use as a starting point for a series of similar documents so that you don't have to re-create formatting and text for each new document. A template can contain customized styles, text, graphics, or any other element that you want to repeat from one document to another. In this tutorial, you'll customize the styles and themes in a Word document, and then save the document as a template to use for future documents. Before you do that, however, you will investigate some of the ready-made templates available at Office.com.

When you first start Word, the Recent screen in Backstage view displays a variety of templates available from Office.com. You can also enter keywords in the Search for online templates box to find templates that match your specific needs. For example, you could search for a calendar template, a birthday card template, or a report template.

Every new, blank document that you open in Word is a copy of the Normal template. Unlike other Word templates, the **Normal template** does not have any text, formatting, or graphics, but it does include all the default settings that you are accustomed to using in Word. For example, the default theme in the Normal template is the Office theme. The Office theme, in turn, supplies the default body font (Calibri) and the default heading font (Calibri Light). The default line spacing and paragraph spacing you are used to seeing in a new document are also specified in the Normal template.

Jonah would like you to review some templates designed for reports. As you'll see in the following steps, when you open a template, Word actually creates a document that is an exact copy of the template. The template itself remains unaltered, so that you can continue to use it as the basis for other documents.

To review some report templates available on Office.com:

1. On the ribbon, click the **FILE** tab to open Backstage view, and then click **New** in the navigation bar. The New screen in Backstage view displays thumbnail images of the first page of a variety of templates. See Figure 5-1.

Figure 5-1 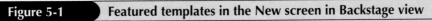 Featured templates in the New screen in Backstage view

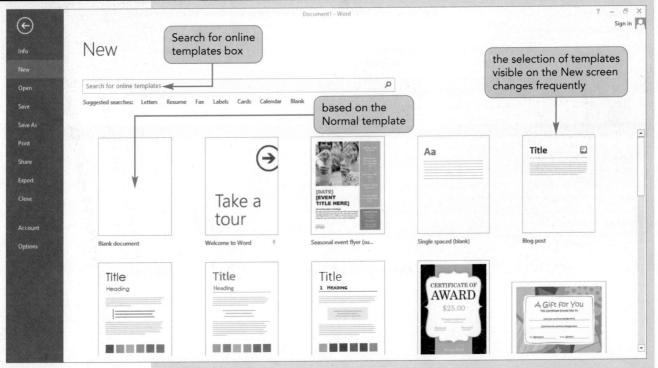

Trouble? If you just started Word, you'll see the list of templates on the Recent screen. You'll be able to complete the next step using the Search for online templates box on the Recent screen.

Below the Search for online templates box are template options available from Office.com. You've already used the Blank document template to open a new, blank document that is based on the Normal template. The list of templates changes frequently as new templates become available, so your screen probably won't match Figure 5-1 exactly.

If your computer has been used to create customized templates, two additional links are displayed below the Search for online templates box—FEATURED and PERSONAL. You can ignore those links for now. In this case, you want to open a document based on a template designed specifically for reports.

▶ **2.** Click the **Search for online templates** box, type **report** and then press the **Enter** key. The New screen displays thumbnail images for a variety of report templates. If you scroll down to the bottom, you'll see options for searching for templates to use in other Office applications. The Category pane on the right displays a list of report categories. You could click any category to display only the templates in that category.

▶ **3.** Click the first template in the top row. A window opens with a preview of the template. Figure 5-2 shows the Report (Essential design) template. The template that opens on your computer might be different.

| Figure 5-2 | Previewing a template |

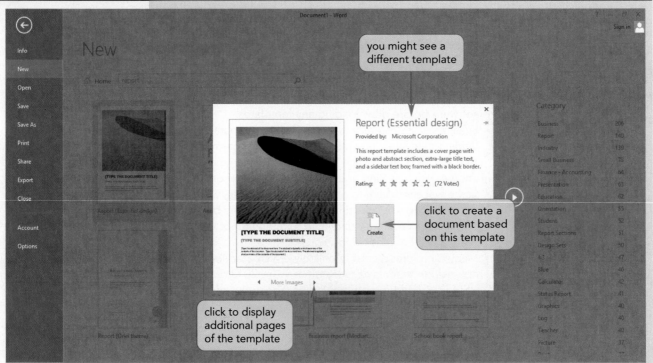

You could click the Close button to close the preview window and browse other report templates, but Jonah asks you to continue investigating the current template.

◗ **4.** Click the **Create** button. A new document opens. A document based on the Essential design report template begins with a cover page and contains a number of content controls designed specifically for the template, similar to the content controls you've seen in other documents. It also contains some placeholder text, a header, a footer, and graphics.

At this point, you could save the document with a new name and then begin revising it to create an actual report. But since your goal now is to review various templates, you'll close the document.

◗ **5.** Close the document without saving any changes.

◗ **6.** On the ribbon, click the **FILE** tab, and then click **New** in the navigation bar.

◗ **7.** Search online for newsletter templates, open a document based on one of the templates, and then review the document, making note of the various elements it includes.

◗ **8.** Close the newsletter document without saving it.

◗ **9.** Return to the New screen, and search for templates for flyers. Open a new document based on one of the templates, review the document, and then close it without saving it.

PROSKILLS

Decision Making: Using Templates from Other Sources

The Office.com website offers a wide variety of templates that are free to registered Microsoft Office users. Countless other websites offer templates for free, for individual sale, as part of a subscription service, or a combination of all three. However, you need to be wary when searching for templates online. Keep in mind the following when deciding which sites to use:

- Files downloaded from the Internet can infect your computer with viruses and spyware, so make sure your computer has up-to-date antivirus and antispyware software before downloading any templates.
- Evaluate a site carefully to verify that it is a reputable source of virus-free templates. Verifying the site's legitimacy is especially important if you intend to pay for a template with a credit card. Search for the website's name and URL using different search engines (such as Bing and Google) to see what other people say about it.
- Some websites claim to offer templates for free, when in fact the offer is primarily a lure to draw visitors to sites that are really just online billboards, with ads for any number of businesses completely unrelated to templates or Word documents. Avoid downloading templates from these websites.
- Many templates available online were created for earlier versions of Word that did not include themes or many other Word 2013 design features. Make sure you know what you're getting before you pay for an out-of-date template.

Now that you are finished reviewing report templates, you will open the document containing the report about the Blue Spruce Folk Festival.

To open Jonah's report document:

1. Open the document **Festival** from the Word5 ▶ Tutorial folder included with your Data Files, and then save it as **Festival Report** in the location specified by your instructor.

2. Display nonprinting characters and the rulers, switch to Print Layout view, and then change the Zoom level to **120%**, if necessary. See Figure 5-3.

Figure 5-3   **Festival Report document**

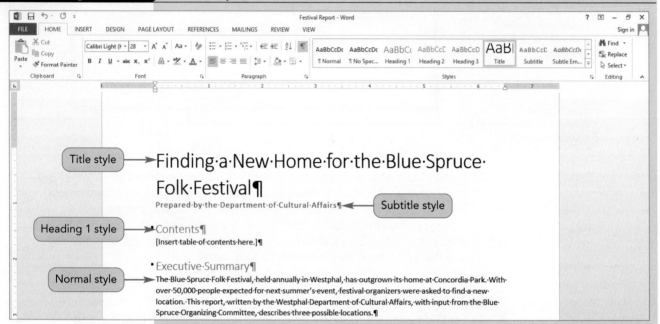

The report is formatted using the default settings of the Normal template, which means its current theme is the Office theme. Text in the report is formatted using the Title, Subtitle, Heading 1, Heading 2, and Normal styles. The document includes a footer containing the department name and a page number field.

Before you begin revising the document, you should review its contents. To get a quick overview of a document, it's helpful to use the Go To feature.

Using Go To

The Go To tab in the Find and Replace dialog box allows you to move quickly among elements in a document. For example, you can use it to move from heading to heading, from graphic to graphic, or from table to table. In a long document, this is an efficient way to review your work. Although the Festival Report document is not very long, you can still review its contents using Go To.

To use the Go To feature to review the Festival Report document:

1. If necessary, press the **Ctrl+Home** keys to move the insertion point to the beginning of the document.

2. On the ribbon, make sure the HOME tab is displayed.

3. In the Editing group, click the **Find button arrow** to display the Find menu, and then click **Go To**. The Find and Replace dialog box opens, with the Go To tab displayed. See Figure 5-4.

| Figure 5-4 | Go To tab in the Find and Replace dialog box |

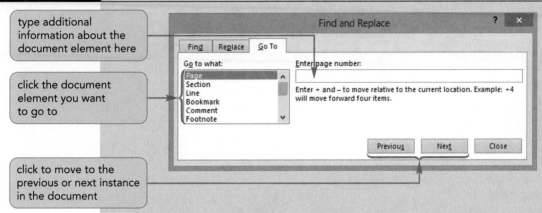

type additional information about the document element here

click the document element you want to go to

click to move to the previous or next instance in the document

In the Go to what box, you can click the document element you want to go to. Then click the Next or Previous buttons to move back and forth among instances of the selected element in the document. You can also enter more specific information in the box on the right. For instance, when Page is selected in the Go to what box, you can type a page number in the box, and then click Next to go directly to that page.

Right now, Jonah would like to review all the headings in the document—that is, all the paragraphs formatted with a heading style.

4. Scroll down to the bottom of the Go to what box, click **Heading**, and then click the **Next** button. The document scrolls down to position the first document heading, "Contents," at the top of the document window.

5. Click the **Next** button again. The document scrolls down to display the "Executive Summary" heading at the top of the document window.

6. Click the **Next** button six more times to display the last heading in the document, "Framingham Park," at the top of the document window.

7. Click the **Previous** button to display the "Metcalfe Farm" heading at the top of the document window, and then close the Find and Replace dialog box.

INSIGHT

Choosing Between Go To and the Navigation Pane

Both the Go To tab in the Find and Replace dialog box and the Navigation pane allow you to move through a document heading by heading. Although you used Go To in the preceding steps, the Navigation pane is usually the better choice for working with headings; it displays a complete list of the headings, which helps you keep an eye on the document's overall organization. However, the Go To tab is more useful when you want to move through a document one graphic at a time, or one table at a time. In a document that contains a lot of graphics or tables, it's a good idea to use the Go To feature to make sure you've formatted all the graphics or tables similarly.

Next, before you begin formatting the document, Jonah asks you to help him find a synonym for a word in the text.

Using the Thesaurus to Find Synonyms

In any kind of writing, choosing the right words to convey your meaning is important. If you need help, you can use Word's thesaurus to look up a list of synonyms, or possible replacements, for a specific word. You can right-click a word to display a shortcut menu with a short list of synonyms, or open the Thesaurus task pane for a more complete list.

Jonah is not happy with the word "sheds" in the paragraph about the Metcalfe Farm site because he thinks it suggests the buildings on the property are shabby or in need of repair. He asks you to find a more appropriate synonym.

To look up a synonym in the thesaurus:

1. In the first line after the "Metcalfe Farm" heading, right-click the word **sheds**. A shortcut menu opens.

2. Point to **Synonyms**. A menu with a list of synonyms for "sheds" is displayed, as shown in Figure 5-5.

Figure 5-5   **Shortcut menu with list of synonyms**

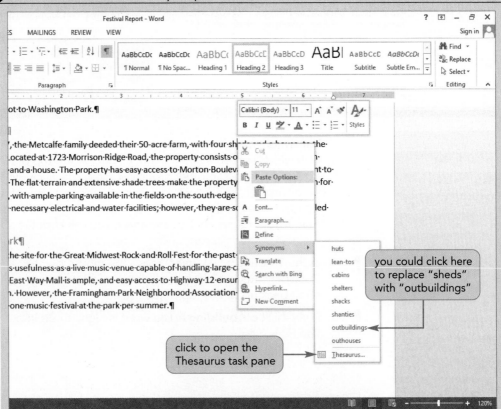

One word in the list, "outbuildings," is a good replacement for "sheds." You could click "outbuildings" to insert it in the document in place of "sheds," but Jonah asks you to check the Thesaurus task pane to see if it suggests a better option.

3. At the bottom of the shortcut menu, click **Thesaurus**. The Thesaurus task pane opens on the right side of the document window, with the word "sheds" at the top, and a more extensive list of synonyms below. The word "sheds" is also selected in the document, ready to be replaced. See Figure 5-6.

Figure 5-6 Thesaurus task pane

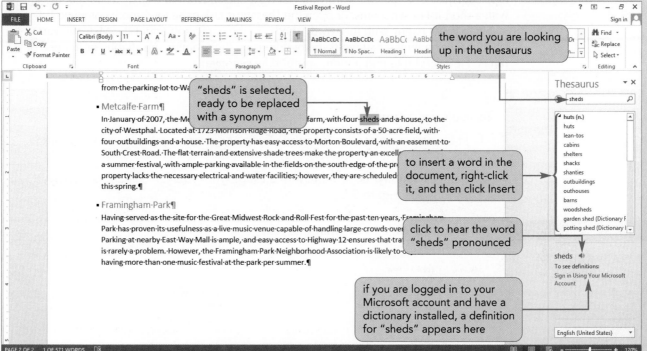

The synonym list in the task pane is organized by different shades of meaning, with words related to the idea of a "hut" at the top of the list. You can scroll down the list to see other groups of synonyms, including some that are synonyms for "sheds" when it is used as a verb rather than a noun. Below the list of synonyms, the word "sheds" appears in blue, with a speaker icon next to it. If your computer has a speaker, you can click the speaker icon to hear the word "sheds" pronounced correctly.

4. In the Thesaurus task pane, move the mouse pointer over the list of synonyms to display the scroll bar, scroll down to display other synonyms, and then scroll back up to the top of the list.

5. Right-click **outbuildings**. The word is highlighted in blue, and a menu opens. See Figure 5-7.

| Figure 5-7 | Selecting a synonym in the Thesaurus task pane |

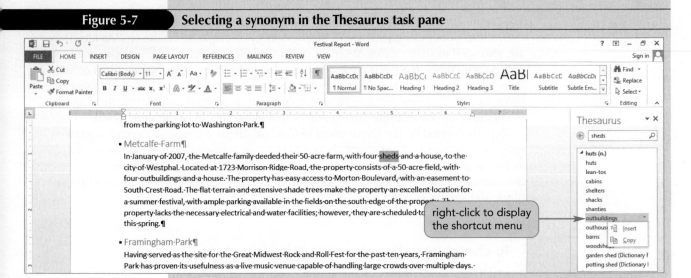

Trouble? If the Thesaurus task pane changes to display a set of synonyms for the word "outbuildings," you clicked the word "outbuildings" with the left mouse button instead of the right. Click the Back button ⊝ to redisplay the synonyms for "sheds," and then begin again with Step 5.

▶ **6.** Click **Insert** to replace "sheds" with "outbuildings" in the document, and then close the Thesaurus task pane.

▶ **7.** Save the document.

Now that the document text is finished, you can get to work on the formatting. You'll start by customizing the document theme.

Customizing the Document Theme

A document theme consists of three main components—theme colors, theme fonts, and theme effects. A specific set of colors, fonts, and effects is associated with each theme, but you can mix and match them to create a customized theme for your document. The theme fonts are the fonts used in a document's styles. You see them at the top of the font list when you click the Font arrow in the Font group on the HOME tab. The theme colors are displayed in the Theme Colors section of any color gallery. The colors used to format headings, body text, and other elements are all drawn from the document's theme colors. Theme effects alter the appearance of shapes. Because they are generally very subtle, theme effects are not a theme element you will typically be concerned with.

When you change the theme colors, fonts, or effects for a document, the changes affect only that document. However, you can also save the changes you make to create a new, custom theme, which you can then use for future documents.

The Festival Report document, which was based on the Normal template, is formatted with the Office theme—which applies a blue font color to the headings by default, and formats the headings in the Calibri Light font. Jonah wants to select different theme colors and theme fonts. He doesn't plan to include any graphics, so there's no need to customize the theme effects. You'll start with the theme colors.

Changing the Theme Colors

The theme colors, which are designed to coordinate well with each other, are used in the various document styles, including the text styles available on the HOME tab. They are also used in shape styles, WordArt styles, and picture styles. So when you want to change the colors in a document, it's always better to change the theme colors rather than selecting individual elements and applying a new color to each element from a color gallery. That way you can be sure colors will be applied consistently throughout the document—for example, the headings will all be shades of the same color.

Reports created by the Department of Cultural Affairs are typically emailed to many recipients, some of whom might choose to print the reports. To keep printing costs as low as possible for all potential readers of his report, Jonah wants to format his document in black and white. He asks you to apply a set of theme colors consisting of black and shades of gray.

To change the theme colors in the document:

1. Press the **Ctrl+Home** keys to display the beginning of the document.

2. On the ribbon, click the **DESIGN** tab.

3. In the Document Formatting group, move the mouse pointer over the **Colors** button. A ScreenTip is displayed, indicating that the current theme colors are the Office theme colors.

4. Click the **Colors** button. A gallery of theme colors opens, with the Office theme colors selected at the top of the gallery. See Figure 5-8.

| Figure 5-8 | Theme Colors gallery |

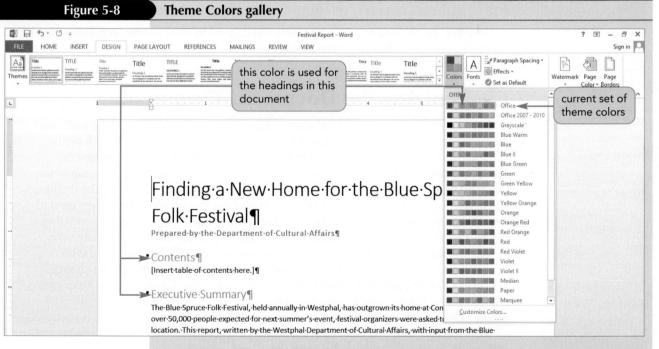

Each set of colors contains eight colors, with each assigned to specific elements. For example, the third color from the left is the color used for headings. The remaining colors are used for other types of elements, such as hyperlinks, page borders, shading, and so on.

Trouble? If you see additional theme colors at the top of the gallery under the "Custom" heading, then custom theme colors have been created and stored on your computer.

> **5.** Move the mouse pointer over the options in the gallery to observe the Live Preview of the colors in the document.

> **6.** Near the top of the gallery, click the **Grayscale** color set, which is the third from the top. The document headings are now formatted in gray.

> **7.** Save the document.

The new colors you selected affect only the Festival Report document. Your changes do not affect the Office theme that was installed with Word. Next, Jonah asks you to customize the document theme further by changing the theme fonts.

Changing the Theme Fonts

As with theme colors, you can change the theme fonts in a document to suit your needs. Each theme uses two coordinating fonts—one for the headings and one for the body text. In some themes, the same font is used for the headings and the body text. When changing the theme fonts, you can select from all the font combinations available in any of the themes installed with Word.

To select a different set of theme fonts for the document:

> **1.** In the Document Formatting group, move the mouse pointer over the **Fonts** button. A ScreenTip is displayed, indicating that the current fonts are Calibri Light for headings and Calibri for body text.

> **2.** Click the **Fonts** button. The Theme Fonts gallery opens, displaying the heading and body font combinations for each theme.

> **3.** Scroll down to review the fonts. Jonah prefers the Franklin Gothic set of theme fonts, which includes Franklin Gothic Medium for headings and Franklin Gothic Book for the body text.

> **4.** In the Theme Fonts gallery, point to **Franklin Gothic** to display a Live Preview in the document. See Figure 5-9.

Figure 5-9	**Theme Fonts gallery**

point to this set of theme fonts to display a Live Preview in the document

5. Click **Franklin Gothic**. The Theme Fonts gallery closes, and the new fonts are applied to the document.
6. Save the document.

The changes you have made to the theme fonts for the Festival Report document do not affect the original Office theme that was installed with Word and that is available to all documents. To make your new combination of theme fonts and theme colors available to other documents, you can save it as a new, custom theme.

INSIGHT

Creating Custom Combinations of Theme Colors and Fonts

The theme color and font combinations installed with Word were created by Microsoft designers who are experts in creating harmonious-looking documents. It's usually best to stick with these preset combinations rather than trying to create your own set. However, in some situations you might need to create a customized combination of theme colors or fonts. When you do so, that set is saved as part of Word so that you can use it in other documents.

To create a custom set of theme colors, you click the Colors button in the Document Formatting group on the DESIGN tab, and then click Customize Colors to open the Create New Theme Colors dialog box, in which you can select colors for different theme elements, and enter a descriptive name for the new set of theme colors. The custom set of theme colors will be displayed as an option in the Themes Colors gallery. To delete a custom set of colors from the Theme Colors gallery, right-click the custom color set in the gallery, click Delete, and then click Yes.

To create a custom set of heading and body fonts, you click the Fonts button in the Document Formatting group on the DESIGN tab, click Customize Fonts, select the heading and body fonts, and then enter a name for the new set of fonts in the Name box. The custom set of theme fonts is displayed as an option in the Theme Fonts gallery. To delete a custom set of fonts from the Theme Fonts gallery, right-click the custom font set in the gallery, click Delete, and then click Yes.

Saving a Custom Theme

TIP

To delete a custom theme saved in the Document Themes folder, click the Themes button on the DESIGN tab, right-click the theme, click Delete, and then click Yes.

You can save a custom theme to any folder, but when you save a custom theme to the default location—the Document Themes subfolder inside the Templates folder—it is displayed as an option in the Themes gallery.

Jonah asks you to save his combination of theme fonts and theme colors as a new custom theme, using "DCA," the acronym for "Department of Cultural Affairs," as part of the filename.

To save the new custom theme:

1. In the Document Formatting group, click the **Themes** button, and then click **Save Current Theme**. The Save Current Theme dialog box opens. See Figure 5-10.

Figure 5-10   **Save Current Theme dialog box**

a theme saved to this location appears as an option in the Themes gallery

default theme name

file will be saved as an Office Theme file type

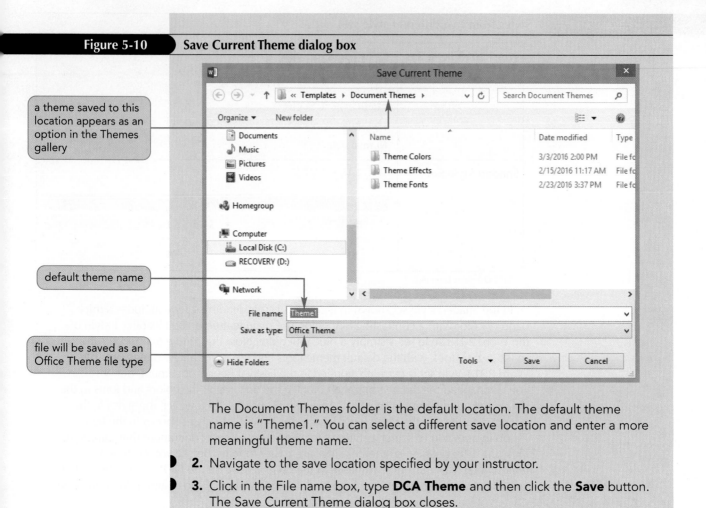

The Document Themes folder is the default location. The default theme name is "Theme1." You can select a different save location and enter a more meaningful theme name.

▶ **2.** Navigate to the save location specified by your instructor.

▶ **3.** Click in the File name box, type **DCA Theme** and then click the **Save** button. The Save Current Theme dialog box closes.

Jonah plans to use the new theme to help standardize the look of all documents created in his department. When he is ready to apply it to a document, he can click the Themes button in the Document Formatting group on the DESIGN tab, click Browse for Themes, navigate to the folder containing the custom theme, and then select the theme. If he wants to be able to access his theme from the Themes gallery instead, he will need to save it to the Document Themes folder first.

Jonah likes the document's new look, but he wants to make some additional changes. First, he wants to select a different style set.

Selecting a Style Set

Recall that a style is a set of formatting options that you can apply to a specific text element in a document, such as a document's title, heading, or body text. So far, you have used only the set of styles available in the Style gallery on the HOME tab. However, 16 additional style sets, or groups of styles, are available in the Style Set gallery accessed via the Document Formatting group on the DESIGN tab.

Each style set has a Normal style, a Heading 1 style, a Heading 2 style, and so on, but the formatting settings associated with each style vary from one style set to another. See Figure 5-11.

Figure 5-11   **Styles from two different style sets**

Word 2013 Style Set	Title Style
	Heading 1 style
	Heading 2 style
	Normal style
Shaded Style Set	TITLE STYLE
	HEADING 1 STYLE
	HEADING 2 STYLE
	Normal style

© 2014 Cengage Learning

In the Shaded style set shown in Figure 5-11, the Heading 1 style includes a thick band of color with a contrasting font color. The main feature of the Heading 1 style of the Word 2013 style set is simply a blue font color. Note that Figure 5-11 shows the styles as they look with the default theme fonts and colors for a new document. The Word 2013 style set is currently applied to the Festival Report document; but because you've changed the theme fonts and colors in the document, the colors and fonts in the document are different from what is shown in Figure 5-11. However, the styles in the document still have the same basic look as the Word 2013 styles shown in the figure.

Jonah asks you to select a style set for the Festival Report document that makes the Heading 1 text darker, so the headings are easier to read. Before you do that, you'll review the styles currently available in the Style gallery on the HOME tab. Then, after you select a new style set, you'll go back to the Style gallery to examine the new styles.

To review the styles in the Style gallery and select a new style set for the document:

1. On the ribbon, click the **HOME** tab.

2. In the Styles group, click the **More** button and then review the set of styles currently available in the Style gallery. Note that the icon for the Heading 1 style indicates that it applies a light gray font color.

3. On the ribbon, click the **DESIGN** tab.

4. In the Document Formatting group, click the **More** button to open the Style Set gallery. Move the mouse pointer across the icons in the gallery to display their ScreenTips and to observe the Live Previews in the document.

5. Point to the **Lines (Stylish)** style set, which is second from the right in the top row. In the Lines (Stylish) style set, the Heading 1 style applies a dark gray font color, with a light gray line that spans the width of the document. See Figure 5-12.

Figure 5-12   Live Preview of the Lines (Stylish) style set

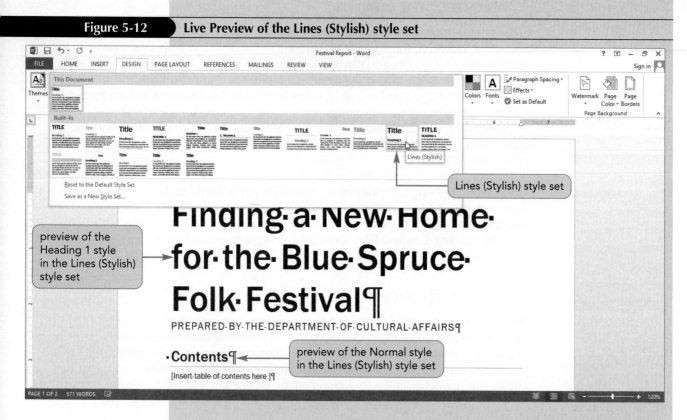

Notice that the theme fonts you specified earlier—Franklin Gothic Medium for headings and Franklin Gothic Book for body text—are still applied, as are the Grayscale theme colors.

6. Click the **Lines (Stylish)** style set. The styles in the document change to reflect the styles in the Lines (Stylish) style set. You can verify this by looking at the Style gallery on the HOME tab.

7. On the ribbon, click the **HOME** tab.

8. In the Styles group, click the **More** button to review the styles available in the Style gallery. The icon for the Heading 1 style indicates that it now applies a black font color. The style also applies a light gray underline, although that is not visible in the Style gallery icon.

9. Click anywhere in the document to close the Style gallery, and then save the document.

The Set as Default Button: A Note of Caution

INSIGHT

The Set as Default button in the Document Formatting group on the DESIGN tab saves the document's current formatting settings as the default for any new blank documents you create in Word. In other words, it saves the current formatting settings to the Normal template. You might find this a tempting option, but, as you will learn in Session 5.2, when working with styles, modifying the Normal template is almost never a good idea. Instead, a better option is to save a document with the formatting you like as a new template. You can then use the template for documents that you want to match your current document.

Customizing Styles

The ability to select a new style set gives you a lot of flexibility when formatting a document. However, sometimes you will want to customize an individual style to better suit your needs. To do so, you can modify or update the style. When you modify a style, you open the Modify Style dialog box, where you then select formatting attributes to add to the style. When you update a style, you select text in the document that is already formatted with the style, apply new formatting to the text, and then update the style to incorporate the new formatting. Updating a style is usually the better choice because it allows you to see the results of your formatting choices in the document, before you change the style itself.

Jonah asks you to update the Heading 1 style for the report by expanding the character spacing and applying italic formatting. You will begin by applying these changes to a paragraph that is currently formatted with the Heading 1 style. Then you can update the Heading 1 style to match the new formatting. As a result, all the paragraphs formatted with the Heading 1 style will be updated to incorporate expanded character spacing and italics.

Changing Character Spacing

The term **character spacing** refers to the space between individual characters. To add emphasis to text, you can expand or contract the spacing between characters. As with line and paragraph spacing, space between characters is measured in points, with one point equal to 1/72 of an inch. To adjust character spacing for selected text, click the Dialog Box Launcher in the Font group on the HOME tab, and then click the Advanced tab in the Font dialog box. Of the numerous settings available on this tab, you'll find two especially useful.

First, the Spacing box allows you to choose Normal spacing (which is the default character spacing for the Normal style), Expanded spacing (with the characters farther apart than with the Normal setting), and Condensed spacing (with the characters closer together than with the Normal setting). With both Expanded and Condensed spacing, you can specify the number of points between characters.

Second, the Kerning for fonts check box allows you to adjust the spacing between characters to make them look like they are spaced evenly. Kerning is helpful when you are working with large font sizes, which can sometimes cause evenly spaced characters to appear unevenly spaced. Selecting the Kerning for fonts check box ensures that the spacing is adjusted automatically.

To add expanded character spacing and italics to a paragraph formatted with the Heading 1 style:

1. In the document, scroll down if necessary and select the **Executive Summary** heading, which is formatted with the Heading 1 style.

2. Make sure the HOME tab is selected on the ribbon.

3. In the Font group, click the **Dialog Box Launcher**. The Font dialog box opens.

4. Click the **Advanced** tab. The Character Spacing settings at the top of this tab reflect the style settings for the currently selected text. The Spacing box is set to Normal. The more advanced options, located in the OpenType Features section, allow you to fine-tune the appearance of characters.

5. Click the **Spacing** arrow, and then click **Expanded**. See Figure 5-13.

Figure 5-13   **Changing character spacing in the Font dialog box**

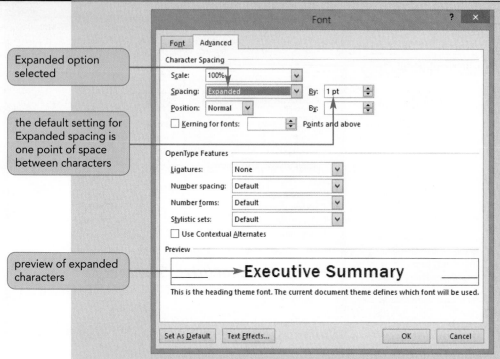

Expanded option selected

the default setting for Expanded spacing is one point of space between characters

preview of expanded characters

The By box next to the Spacing box indicates that each character is separated from the other by one point of space. You could increase the point setting; but in the current document, one point is fine. The Preview section shows a sample of the expanded character spacing.

Next, you need to apply italic formatting, which you could do from the Font group on the HOME tab. But since you have the Font dialog box open, you'll do it from the Font tab in the Font dialog box instead.

6. In the Font dialog box, click the **Font** tab.

Here you can apply most of the settings available in the Font group on the HOME tab, and a few that are not available in the Font group—such as colored underlines and **small caps** (smaller versions of uppercase letters). You can also hide text from view by selecting the Hidden check box.

7. In the Font style box, click **Italic**. The Preview section of the Font tab shows a preview of the italic formatting applied to the "Executive Summary" heading. See Figure 5-14.

Figure 5-14	Applying italic formatting to text using the Font dialog box

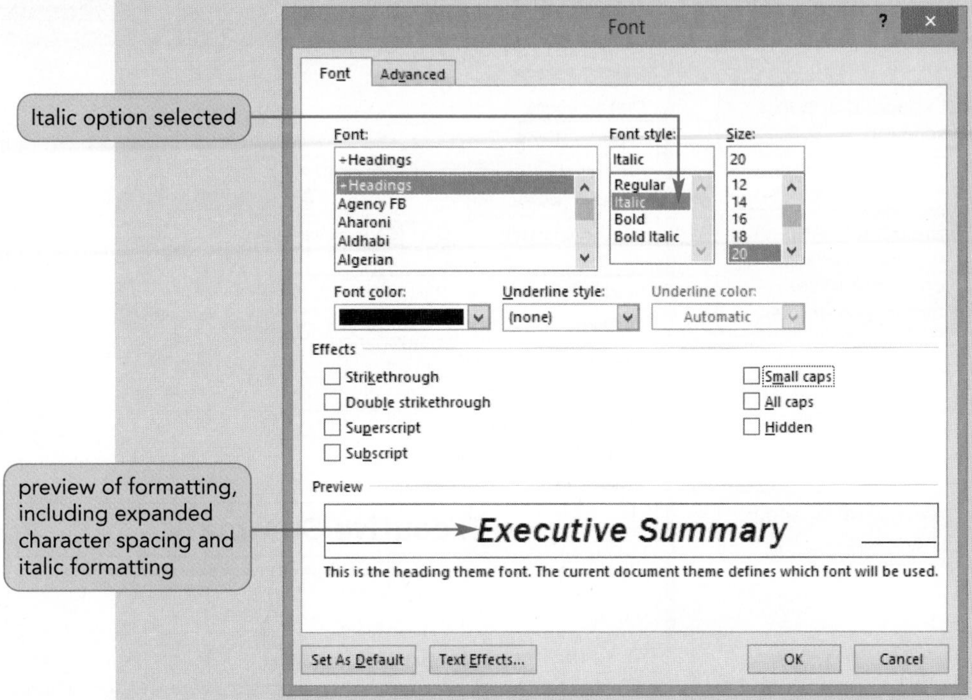

Italic option selected

preview of formatting, including expanded character spacing and italic formatting

The other font attributes associated with the Heading 1 style are also visible on the Font tab.

▶ **8.** Click the **OK** button to close the Font dialog box. The selected heading is now italicized, with the individual characters spread slightly farther apart.

▶ **9.** Click anywhere in the "Executive Summary" heading to deselect the text, and then save the document.

Now that the selected heading is formatted the way you want, you can update the Heading 1 style to match it. When working with styles, it's helpful to open the Styles pane to see more information about the styles in the current style set, so you'll do that next.

Displaying the Styles Pane

The Styles pane shows you more styles than are displayed in the Style gallery. You can click a style in the Styles pane to apply it to selected text, just as you would click a style in the Style gallery.

The Styles pane provides detailed information about each style. In particular, it differentiates between character styles, paragraph styles, and linked styles. A **character style** contains formatting options that affect the appearance of individual characters, such as font style, font color, font size, bold, italic, and underline. When you click a character style, it formats the word that contains the insertion point, or, if text is selected in the document, any selected characters.

A **paragraph style** contains all the character formatting options as well as formatting options that affect the paragraph's appearance—including line spacing, text alignment, tab stops, and borders. When you click a paragraph style, it formats the entire paragraph that contains the insertion point, or, if text is selected in the document, it formats all selected paragraphs (even paragraphs in which just one character is selected).

A **linked style** contains both character and paragraph formatting options. If you click in a paragraph or select a paragraph and then apply a linked style, both the paragraph

styles and character styles are applied to the entire paragraph. If you apply a linked style to a selected word or group of words rather than to an entire paragraph, only the character styles for that linked style are applied to the selected text; the paragraph styles are not applied to the paragraph itself. All of the heading styles in Word are linked styles.

To open the Styles pane to review information about the styles in the current style set:

▶ **1.** Make sure the HOME tab is selected on the ribbon.

▶ **2.** In the Styles group, click the **Dialog Box Launcher**. The Styles pane opens on the right side of the document window. See Figure 5-15.

| Figure 5-15 | Styles pane |

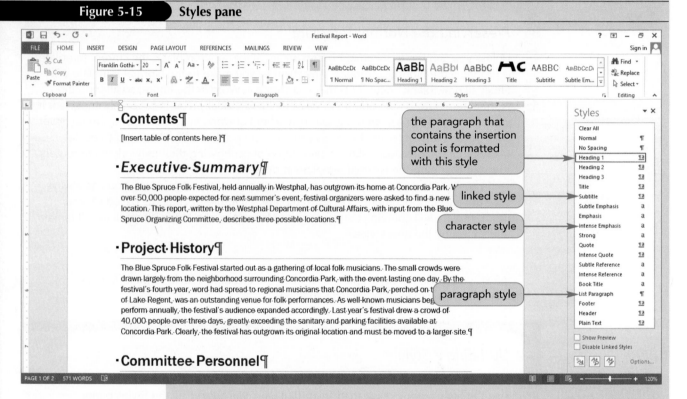

Trouble? If the Styles pane on your computer is floating over the top of the document window, double-click the pane's title bar to dock the Styles pane on the right side of the document window.

The outline around the Heading 1 style in the Styles pane indicates that the insertion point is currently located in a paragraph formatted with the Heading 1 style. A paragraph symbol to the right of a style name indicates a paragraph style, a lowercase letter "a" indicates a character style, and a combination of both a paragraph symbol and a lowercase letter "a" indicates a linked style. You can display even more information about a style by moving the mouse pointer over the style name in the Styles pane.

▶ **3.** In the Styles pane, move the mouse pointer over **Heading 1**. An arrow is displayed to the right of the Heading 1 style name, and a ScreenTip with detailed information about the Heading 1 style opens below the style name.

The information in the ScreenTip relates only to the formatting applied by default with the Heading 1 style; it makes no mention of italic formatting or expanded character spacing. Although you applied these formatting changes to the "Executive Summary" heading, they are not yet part of the Heading 1 style.

You'll incorporate the new formatting into the Heading 1 style in the next section, when you update the style.

Updating a Style

Word is set up to save all customized styles to the current document by default. In fact, when you update a style, you don't even have a choice about where to save it—the updated style is automatically saved to the current document, rather than to the current template. If for some reason you needed to save a customized style to the current template instead, you would need to modify the style using the Modify Style dialog box, where you could then select the New documents based on this template button to save the modified style to the current template.

Next, you'll use the Styles pane to update the Heading 1 style to include italic formatting with expanded character spacing.

To update the Heading 1 style:

1. In the document, make sure the insertion point is located in the paragraph containing the "Executive Summary" heading, which is formatted with the Heading 1 style.

The insertion point must be located in the "Executive Summary" heading to ensure that you update the Heading 1 style with the correct formatting.

> **2.** In the Styles pane, right-click **Heading 1**. A menu opens with options related to working with the Heading 1 style. See Figure 5-16.

Figure 5-16   **Heading 1 style menu**

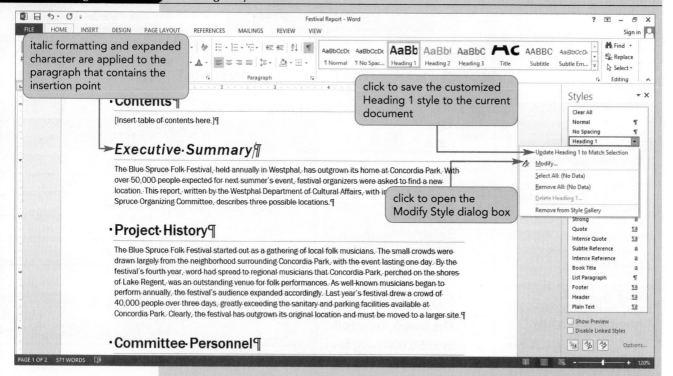

> **3.** Click **Update Heading 1 to Match Selection**. The Heading 1 style is updated to reflect the changes you made to the "Executive Summary" heading. As a result, all the headings in the document formatted in the Heading 1 style now have italic formatting with expanded character spacing.

> **4.** Save the document. The updated Heading 1 style is saved along with the document. No other documents are affected by this change to the Heading 1 style.

You can also use the Styles pane to create a new style for a document. You will do that in the next session.

Session 5.1 Quick Check

REVIEW

1. By default, all new, blank documents are based on which template?
2. Which dialog box contains the Go To tab?
3. What are the three components of a document theme?
4. Explain how to select a new style set.
5. Explain how to display the dialog box tab where you can adjust the character spacing for selected text.
6. What is the difference between a character style and a paragraph style?
7. By default, are updated styles saved to the current document or the current template?

Session 5.2 Visual Overview:

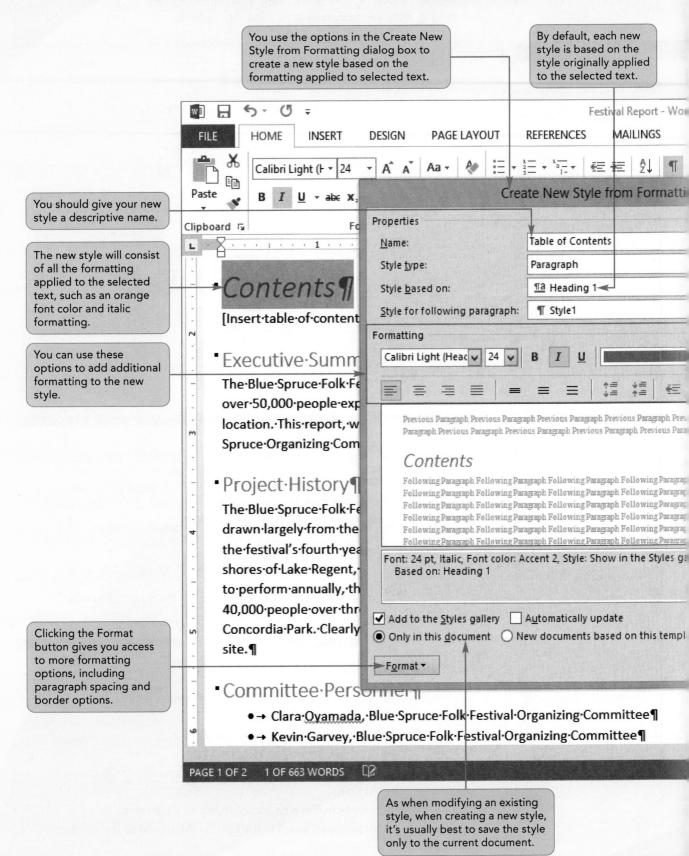

You use the options in the Create New Style from Formatting dialog box to create a new style based on the formatting applied to selected text.

By default, each new style is based on the style originally applied to the selected text.

You should give your new style a descriptive name.

The new style will consist of all the formatting applied to the selected text, such as an orange font color and italic formatting.

You can use these options to add additional formatting to the new style.

Clicking the Format button gives you access to more formatting options, including paragraph spacing and border options.

As when modifying an existing style, when creating a new style, it's usually best to save the style only to the current document.

Creating a New Style

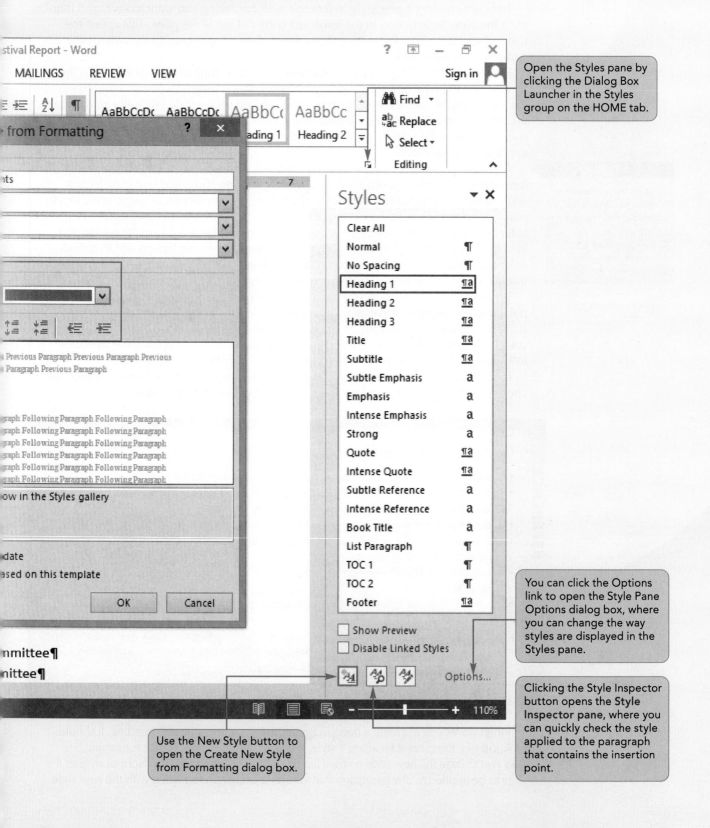

Open the Styles pane by clicking the Dialog Box Launcher in the Styles group on the HOME tab.

You can click the Options link to open the Style Pane Options dialog box, where you can change the way styles are displayed in the Styles pane.

Clicking the Style Inspector button opens the Style Inspector pane, where you can quickly check the style applied to the paragraph that contains the insertion point.

Use the New Style button to open the Create New Style from Formatting dialog box.

Creating a New Style

Creating a new style is similar to updating a style, except that instead of updating an existing style to match the formatting of selected text, you save the text's formatting as a new style. By default a new style is saved to the current document. You can choose to save a new style to the current template, but, as explained earlier, that is rarely advisable.

To begin creating a new style, select text with formatting you want to save, and then click the New Style button in the lower-left corner of the Styles pane. This opens the Create New Style from Formatting dialog box, where you can assign the new style a name and adjust other settings.

Remember that all text in your document has a style applied to it, whether it is the default Normal style or a style you applied. When you create a new style based on the formatting of selected text, the new style is based on the style originally applied to the selected text. That means the new style retains a connection to the original style, so that if you make modifications to the original style, these modifications will also be applied to the new style.

For example, suppose you need to create a new style that will be used exclusively for formatting the heading "Budget" in all upcoming reports. You could start by selecting text formatted with the Heading 1 style, then change the font color of the selected text to purple, and then save the formatting of the selected text as a new style named "Budget." Later, if you update the Heading 1 style—perhaps by adding italic formatting—the text in the document that is formatted with the Budget style will also be updated to include italic formatting because it is based on the Heading 1 style. Note that the opposite is not true—changes to the new style do *not* affect the style on which it is based.

When creating a new style, you also must consider what will happen when the insertion point is in a paragraph formatted with your new style, and you then press the Enter key to start a new paragraph. Typically, that new paragraph is formatted in the Normal style, but you can choose a different style if you prefer. You make this selection using the Style for following paragraph box in the Create New Style from Formatting dialog box.

In most cases, any new styles you create will be paragraph styles. However, you can choose to make your new style a linked style or a character style instead.

> **TIP**
>
> To break the link between a style and the style it is based on, click the Style based on arrow in the Create New Style from Formatting dialog box, and then click (no style).

REFERENCE

Creating a New Style

- Select the text with the formatting you want to save as a new style.
- In the lower-left corner of the Styles pane, click the New Style button to open the Create New Style from Formatting dialog box.
- Type a name for the new style in the Name box.
- Make sure the Style type box contains the correct style type. In most cases, Paragraph style is the best choice.
- Verify that the Style based on box displays the style on which you want to base your new style.
- Click the Style for following paragraph arrow, and then click the style you want to use. Normal is usually the best choice.
- To save the new style to the current document, verify that the Only in this document option button is selected; or to save the style to the current template, click the New documents based on this template option button.
- Click the OK button.

Jonah wants you to create a new paragraph style for the "Contents" heading. It should look just like the current Heading 1 style, with the addition of small caps formatting. He asks you to base the new style on the Heading 1 style, and to select the Normal style as the style to be applied to any paragraph that follows a paragraph formatted with the new style.

To format the "Contents" heading in small caps:

▶ **1.** If you took a break after the last session, make sure the Festival Report document is open in Print Layout view with the nonprinting characters and the ruler displayed. Confirm that the document Zoom level is set at 120% and that the Styles pane is docked on the right side of the document window.

▶ **2.** Make sure the HOME tab is selected on the ribbon.

▶ **3.** In the document, select the **Contents** heading.

▶ **4.** In the Font group, click the **Dialog Box Launcher** and then, in the Font dialog box, click the **Font** tab, if necessary.

▶ **5.** In the Effects section, click the **Small caps** check box to add a check. See Figure 5-17.

Figure 5-17   Formatting the "Contents" heading

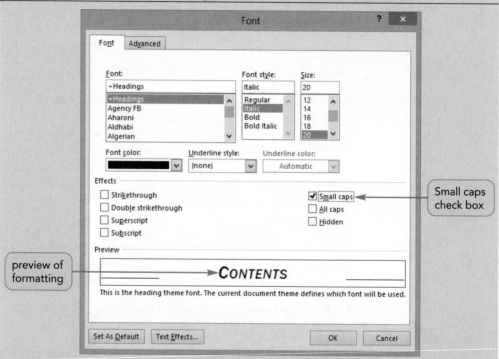

▶ **6.** Click the **OK** button. The Font dialog box closes, and the "Contents" heading is formatted in small caps.

Now that the text is formatted the way you want, you can save its formatting as a new style.

To save the formatting of the "Contents" heading as a new style:

▶ **1.** Verify that the **Contents** heading is still selected.

▶ **2.** In the lower-left corner of the Styles pane, click the **New Style** button ⊞. The Create New Style from Formatting dialog box opens. A default name for the new style, "Style1," is selected in the Name box. The name "Style1" is also displayed in the Style for following paragraph box.

3. Type **Contents** to replace the default style name with the new one. The Style type box contains Paragraph by default, which is the type of style you want to create. The Style based on box indicates that the new Contents style is based on the Heading 1 style, which is also what you want. Notice that the Style for following paragraph box is now blank. You need to select the Normal style.

4. Click the **Style for following paragraph** arrow, and then click **Normal**. See Figure 5-18.

Figure 5-18 **Creating a new style**

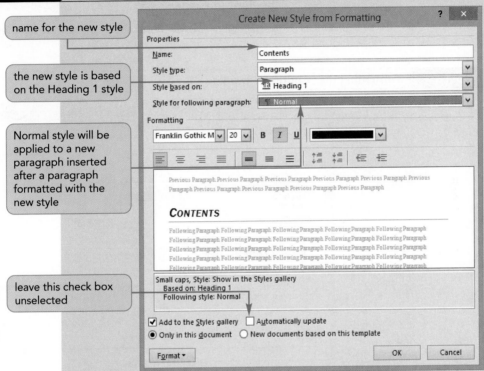

name for the new style

the new style is based on the Heading 1 style

Normal style will be applied to a new paragraph inserted after a paragraph formatted with the new style

leave this check box unselected

---

5. In the bottom-left corner of the dialog box, verify that the Only in this document button is selected.

Note that, by default, the Automatically update check box is *not* selected. As a general rule, you should not select this check box because it can produce unpredictable results in future documents based on the same template.

If you plan to use a new style frequently, it's helpful to assign a keyboard shortcut to it. Then you can apply the style to selected text simply by pressing the keyboard shortcut.

6. In the lower-left corner of the Create New Style from Formatting dialog box, click the **Format** button, and then click **Shortcut key** to open the Customize Keyboard dialog box. If you wanted to assign a keyboard shortcut to the Contents style, you would click in the Press new shortcut key box, press a combination of keys not assigned to any other function, and then click the Assign button. For now, you can close the Customize Keyboard dialog box without making any changes.

7. Click the **Close** button. You return to the Create New Style from Formatting dialog box.

TIP

To assign a keyboard shortcut to an existing style, right-click the style in the Styles pane, click Modify, click the Format button, and then click Shortcut key.

8. Click the **OK** button. The Create New Style from Formatting dialog box closes. The new Contents style is added to the Style gallery and to the Styles pane. See Figure 5-19.

| Figure 5-19 | Contents style added to Quick Styles gallery and Styles pane |

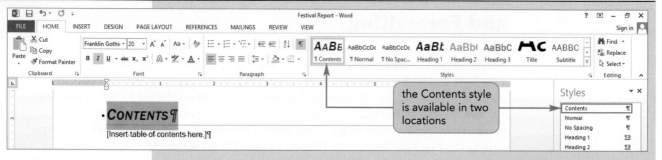

After you update a style or create a new one, you can create a custom style set that contains the new or updated style.

9. On the ribbon, click the **DESIGN** tab.

10. In the Document Formatting group, click the **More** button, and then click Save as a New Style Set. The Save as a New Style Set dialog box opens, with the QuickStyles folder selected as the save location by default. Only style sets saved to the QuickStyles folder will appear in the Style Set gallery.

In this case, you don't actually want to create a new style set, so you can close the Save as a New Style Set dialog box.

11. Click the **Cancel** button, and then save the document.

INSIGHT

Managing Your Styles

If you create a lot of styles, the Style gallery can quickly become overcrowded. To remove a style from the Style gallery without deleting the style itself, right-click the style in the Styles gallery and then click Remove from Style Gallery.

To delete a style entirely, open the Styles pane, and then right-click the style. What happens next depends on the type of style you are trying to delete. If the style was based on the Normal style, you can click Delete Style (where *Style* is the name of the style you want to delete), and then click Yes. If the style was based on any other style, you can click Revert to *Style* (where *Style* is the style that the style you want to delete was based on), and then click Yes.

If you create a new style and then paste text formatted with your style in a different document, your new style will be displayed in that document's Style gallery and Styles pane. This means that a document containing text imported from multiple documents can end up with a lot of different styles. In that case, you'll probably reformat the document to use only a few styles of your choosing. But what do you do about the remaining, unused styles? You could delete them, but that can be time-consuming. It's sometimes easier to hide the styles that are not currently in use in the document. At the bottom of the Styles pane, click the Options link to open the Style Pane Options dialog box, click the Select styles to show arrow, and then click In current document.

The styles used in the Festival Report document are relatively simple. However, in a long document with many styles, it's easy to lose track of the style applied to each paragraph and the formatting associated with each style. In that case, it's important to know how to display additional information about the document's formatting.

Displaying Information About Styles and Formatting

When you need to learn more about a document's formatting—perhaps because you're revising a document created by someone else—you should start by opening the Styles pane. To quickly determine which style is applied to a paragraph, you can click a paragraph (or select it), and then look to see which style is selected in the Styles pane. To display a brief description of the formatting associated with that style, you can point to the selected style in the Styles pane. However, if you need to check numerous paragraphs in a long document, it's easier to use the Style Inspector pane, which remains open while you scroll through the document and displays only the style for the paragraph that currently contains the insertion point. To see a complete list of all the formatting applied to a paragraph, you can use the **Reveal Formatting pane**. Within the Reveal Formatting pane, you can also choose to compare the formatting applied to two different paragraphs.

Inspecting Styles

You can use the Style Inspector to examine the styles attached to each of the paragraphs in a document. When you are using the Style Inspector, it's also helpful to display the HOME tab on the ribbon so the Style gallery is visible.

To use the Style Inspector pane to examine the styles in the document:

▶ **1.** On the ribbon, click the **HOME** tab.

▶ **2.** On page 1, click anywhere in the **[Insert table of contents here.]** paragraph. The Normal style is selected in both the Style gallery and the Styles pane, indicating that the paragraph is formatted with the Normal style.

▶ **3.** At the bottom of the Styles pane, click the **Style Inspector** button [icon]. The Style Inspector pane opens, and is positioned next to the Styles pane. See Figure 5-20.

Figure 5-20 **Style Inspector pane**

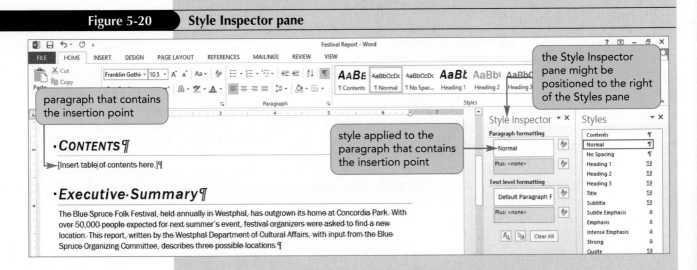

Trouble? If the Style Inspector pane on your computer is floating over the top of the document window, double-click the pane's title bar to dock the Style Inspector pane next to the Styles pane.

In the Style Inspector pane, the top box under "Paragraph formatting" displays the name of the style applied to the paragraph that currently contains the insertion point.

▶ **4.** Press the **Ctrl+↓** keys. The insertion point moves down to the next paragraph, which contains the "Executive Summary" heading. The Style Inspector pane tells you that this paragraph is formatted with the Heading 1 style.

▶ **5.** Press the **Ctrl+↓** keys as necessary to move the insertion point down through the paragraphs of the document, observing the style names displayed in the Style Inspector pane as well as the styles selected in the Styles pane. Note that the bulleted paragraphs below the "Committee Personnel" heading are formatted with the List Paragraph style. This style is applied automatically when you format paragraphs using the Bullets button in the Paragraph group on the HOME tab.

▶ **6.** Scroll up and select the paragraph **[Insert table of contents here.]**.

Finding Styles

Suppose you want to find all the paragraphs in a document formatted with a specific style. One option is to right-click the style in the Styles pane, and then click Select All *Number* Instances, where *Number* is the number of paragraphs in the document formatted with the style.

Another way to find paragraphs formatted with a particular style is by using the Find tab in the Find and Replace dialog box. If necessary, click the More button to display the Format button in the lower-left corner of the Find tab. Click the Format button, click Style, select the style you want in the Find Style dialog box, and then click the OK button. If you want to find specific text formatted with the style you selected, you can type the text in the Find what box on the Find tab, and then click Find Next to find the first instance. If, instead, you want to find any paragraph formatted with the style, leave the Find what box blank.

You can also use the Find and Replace dialog box to find paragraphs formatted with one style and then apply a different style. On the Replace tab, click in the Find what box and use the Format button to select the style you want to find. Then, click in the Replace with box and use the Format button to select the style you want to use as a replacement. Click Find Next to find the first instance of the style, and then click Replace to apply the replacement style. As you've probably guessed, you can also type text in the Find what and Replace with boxes to find text formatted with a specific style and replace it with text formatted in a different style.

Next, Jonah wants you to use the Reveal Formatting panes to learn more about the formatting applied by the Normal and Heading 2 styles.

Examining and Comparing Formatting in the Reveal Formatting Pane

You access the Reveal Formatting pane by clicking a button in the Style Inspector pane. Because the Reveal Formatting pane only describes formatting details without mentioning styles, it's helpful to keep the Style Inspector pane open while you use the Reveal Formatting pane.

To examine formatting details using the Reveal Formatting pane:

> **1.** At the bottom of the Style Inspector pane, click the **Reveal Formatting** button. The Reveal Formatting pane opens, displaying detailed information about the formatting applied to the selected paragraph. See Figure 5-21.

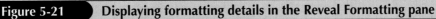

Figure 5-21   **Displaying formatting details in the Reveal Formatting pane**

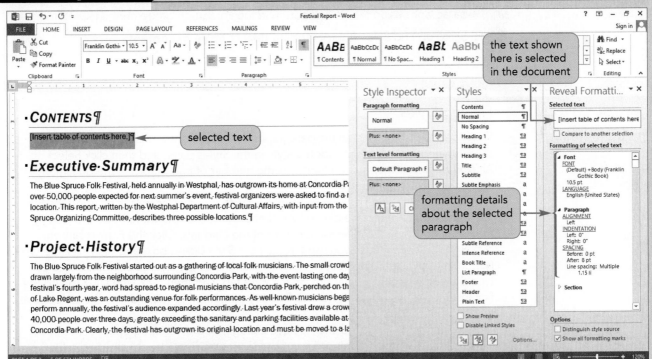

Trouble? If the Reveal Formatting pane on your computer is floating over the top of the document window, double-click the pane's title bar to dock the Reveal Formatting pane next to the other two task panes.

The Formatting of selected text box displays information about the formatting applied to the paragraph that contains the insertion point. Note that this information includes no mention of the style used to apply this formatting, but you can still see the style's name, Normal, displayed in the Style Inspector pane.

Now that you have the Reveal Formatting pane open, you can use it to compare one paragraph's formatting to another's. Jonah asks you to compare text formatted with the Normal style to text formatted with the Heading 2 style.

To compare the formatting of one paragraph to another:

▶ **1.** In the Reveal Formatting pane, click the **Compare to another selection** check box to select it. The options in the Reveal Formatting pane change to allow you to compare the formatting of one paragraph to that of another. Under Selected text, both text boxes display the selected text, "[Insert table of contents here.]" This tells you that, currently, the formatting applied to the selected text is being compared to itself.

Now you'll compare this paragraph to one formatted with the Heading 2 style.

▶ **2.** In the document, scroll down to page 2 and select the text **Washington Park**, which is formatted with the Heading 2 style. The text "Washington Park" is displayed in the Reveal Formatting pane, in the text box below "[Insert table of contents here.]" The Formatting differences section displays information about the formatting applied to the two different paragraphs. See Figure 5-22.

Figure 5-22	Comparing one paragraph's formatting with another's

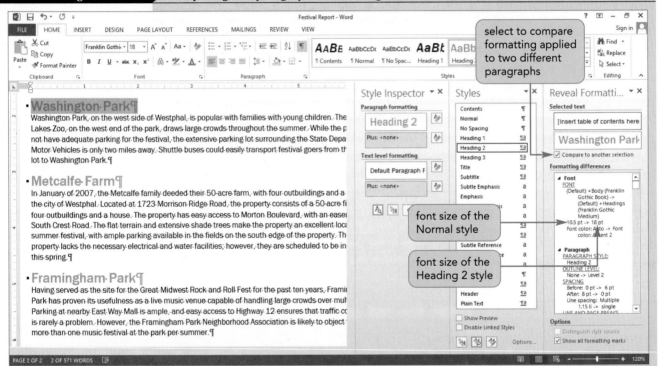

The information in the Reveal Formatting pane is very detailed. But, generally, if you see two settings separated by a hyphen and a greater than symbol, the item on the right relates to the text in the bottom box. For example, in the Font section, you see "10.5 pt -> 18 pt." This tells you that the text in the top text box, "[Insert table of contents here.]," is formatted in a 10.5-point font, whereas the text in the bottom text box, "Washington Park," is formatted in an 18-point font.

The Paragraph section of the Reveal Formatting pane provides some information about two important default settings included with all of Word's heading styles—line and page break settings.

Reviewing Line and Page Break Settings

By default, all of Word's heading styles are set up to ensure that a heading is never separated from the paragraph that follows it. For example, suppose you have a one-page document that includes a heading with a single paragraph of body text after it. Then suppose you add text before the heading that causes the heading and its paragraph of body text to flow down the page so that, ultimately, the entire paragraph of body text moves to page 2. Even if there is room for the heading at the bottom of page 1, it will move to page 2, along with its paragraph of body text. The setting that controls this is the **Keep with next** check box on the Line and Page Breaks tab in the Paragraph dialog box. By default, the Keep with next check box is selected for all headings.

A related setting on the same tab is the **Keep lines together** check box, which is also selected by default for all headings. This setting ensures that if a heading paragraph consists of more than one line of text, the lines of the heading paragraph will never be separated by a page break. This means that if one line of a heading moves from page 1 to page 2, all lines of the heading will move to page 2.

A nonprinting character in the shape of a small black square is displayed next to any paragraph for which either the Keep lines together setting or the Keep with next setting is selected. Because both settings are selected by default for all the heading styles (Heading 1 through Heading 9), you always see this nonprinting character next to text formatted with a heading style. By default, the Keep lines together setting and the Keep with next setting are deselected for all other styles. However, if you have a paragraph of body text that you want to prevent from breaking across two pages, you could apply the Keep lines together setting to that paragraph.

One helpful setting related to line and page breaks—Widow/Orphan control—is selected by default for all Word styles. The term **widow** refers to a single line of text alone at the top of a page. The term **orphan** refers to a single line of text at the bottom of a page. When selected, the **Widow/Orphan control** check box, which is also found on the Line and Page Breaks tab of the Paragraph dialog box, ensures that widows and orphans never occur in a document. Instead, at least two lines of a paragraph will appear at the top or bottom of a page.

You can see evidence of the line and page break settings in the formatting information displayed in the Reveal Formatting pane. Jonah asks you to check these settings for the Festival Report document. You'll start by displaying information about only the paragraph formatted with the Heading 2 style.

To review line and page break settings in the Reveal Formatting pane:

1. In the Reveal Formatting pane, click the **Compare to another selection** check box to deselect it. The Reveal Formatting pane changes to display only information about the formatting applied to "Washington Park," which is currently selected in the document.

   The Style Inspector pane tells you that "Washington Park" is formatted with the Heading 2 style, so all the information in the Reveal Formatting pane describes the Heading 2 style.

2. In the Formatting of selected text box, scroll down to display the entire Paragraph section.

3. Review the information below the blue heading "LINE AND PAGE BREAKS." The text "Keep with next" and "Keep lines together" tells you that these two settings are active for the selected text. The blue headings in the Reveal Formatting pane are actually links that open a dialog box with the relevant formatting settings.

4. In the Formatting of selected text box, click **LINE AND PAGE BREAKS**. The Paragraph dialog box opens, with the Line and Page Breaks tab displayed. See Figure 5-23.

Figure 5-23 Line and Page Breaks tab in the Paragraph dialog box

The settings on the tab are the settings for the selected paragraph, which is formatted with the Heading 2 style. The Widow/Orphan control, Keep with next, and Keep lines together check boxes are all selected, as you would expect for a heading style.

You are finished reviewing formatting information, so you can close the Paragraph dialog box and the Reveal Formatting pane.

5. In the Paragraph dialog box, click the **Cancel** button; and then, in the Reveal Formatting pane, click the **Close** button ☒.

6. In the Style Inspector pane, click the **Close** button ☒; and then, in the Styles pane, click the **Close** button ☒.

7. Click anywhere in the document to deselect the "Washington Park" heading.

You are almost finished working on the Festival Report document. Your next task is to add a table of contents.

Generating a Table of Contents

TIP

To delete a table of contents, click the Table of Contents button, and then click Remove Table of Contents.

You can use the Table of Contents button in the Table of Contents group on the REFERENCES tab to generate a table of contents that includes any text to which you have applied heading styles. A **table of contents** is essentially an outline of the document. By default, in a table of contents, Heading 1 text is aligned on the left, Heading 2 text is indented slightly to the right below the Heading 1 text, Heading 3 text is indented slightly to the right below the Heading 2 text, and so on.

The page numbers and headings in a table of contents in Word are hyperlinks that you can click to jump to a particular part of the document. When inserting a table of contents, you can insert one of several predesigned formats. If you prefer to select from more options, open the Table of Contents dialog box where, among other settings, you can adjust the level assigned to each style within the table of contents.

REFERENCE

Generating a Table of Contents

- Apply heading styles, such as Heading 1, Heading 2, and Heading 3, to the appropriate text in the document.
- Move the insertion point to the location in the document where you want to insert the table of contents.
- On the ribbon, click the REFERENCES tab.
- In the Table of Contents group, click the Table of Contents button.
- To insert a predesigned table of contents, click one of the Built-In styles in the Table of Contents menu.
- To open a dialog box where you can choose from a variety of table of contents settings, click Custom Table of Contents to open the Table of Contents dialog box. Click the Formats arrow and select a style, change the Show levels setting to the number of heading levels you want to include in the table of contents, verify that the Show page numbers check box is selected, and then click the OK button.

The current draft of Jonah's report is fairly short, but the final document will be much longer. He asks you to create a table of contents for the report now, just after the "Contents" heading. Then, as Jonah adds sections to the report, he can update the table of contents.

To insert a table of contents into the document:

▶ **1.** Scroll up to display the "Contents" heading on page 1.

▶ **2.** Below the heading, delete the placeholder text **[Insert table of contents here.]**. Do not delete the paragraph mark after the placeholder text. Your insertion point should now be located in the blank paragraph between the "Contents" heading and the "Executive Summary" heading.

▶ **3.** On the ribbon, click the **REFERENCES** tab.

▶ **4.** In the Table of Contents group, click the **Table of Contents** button. The Table of Contents menu opens, displaying a gallery of table of contents formats. See Figure 5-24.

Figure 5-24	Table of Contents menu

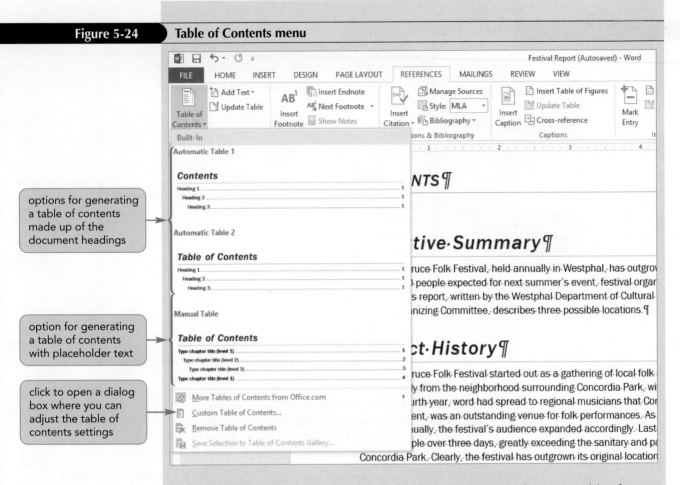

options for generating a table of contents made up of the document headings

option for generating a table of contents with placeholder text

click to open a dialog box where you can adjust the table of contents settings

The Automatic Table 1 and Automatic Table 2 options each insert a table of contents made up of the first three levels of document headings in a predefined format. Each of the Automatic options also includes a heading for the table of contents. Because Jonah's document already contains the heading "Contents," you do not want to use either of these options.

The Manual option is useful only in specialized situations, when you need to type the table of contents yourself—for example, when creating a book manuscript for an academic publisher that requires a specialized format.

You'll use the Custom Table of Contents command to open the Table of Contents dialog box.

5. Below the Table of Contents gallery, click **Custom Table of Contents**. The Table of Contents dialog box opens, with the Table of Contents tab displayed. See Figure 5-25.

Figure 5-25   **Table of Contents dialog box**

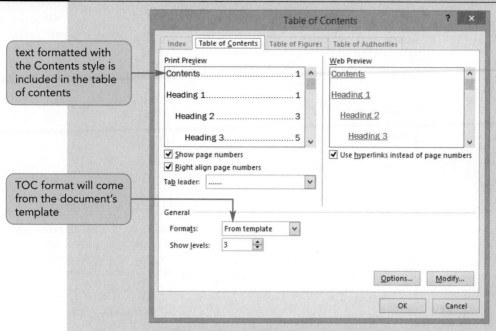

text formatted with the Contents style is included in the table of contents

TOC format will come from the document's template

The Print Preview box on the left shows the appearance of the table of contents in Print Layout view, while the Web Preview box on the right shows what the table of contents would look like if you displayed it in Web Layout view. The Formats box shows the default option, From template, which applies the table of contents styles provided by the document's template.

In the Print Preview section, notice that the Contents heading style, which you created in Session 5.1, appears in the table of contents at the same level as the Heading 1 style.

▶ **6.** In the lower-right corner of the Table of Contents dialog box, click the **Options** button. The Table of Contents Options dialog box opens. The Styles check box is selected, indicating that Word will compile the table of contents based on the styles applied to the document headings.

▶ **7.** In the TOC level list, review the priority level assigned to the document's styles, using the vertical scroll bar, if necessary. See Figure 5-26.

Figure 5-26   **Checking the styles used in the table of contents**

Contents style is assigned the same TOC level as the Heading 1 style

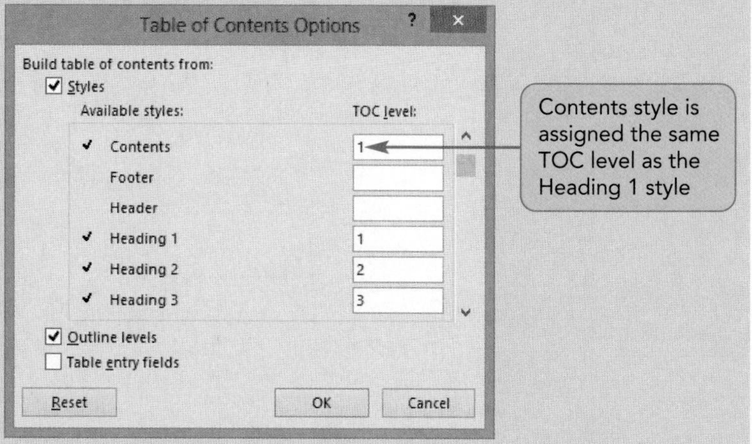

If the box next to a style name is blank, then text formatted with that style does not appear in the table of contents. The numbers next to the Contents, Heading 1, Heading 2, and Heading 3 styles tell you that any text formatted with these styles appears in the table of contents. Heading 1 is assigned to level 1, and Heading 2 is assigned to level 2.

Like Heading 1, the Contents style is assigned to level 1; however, you don't want to include the "Contents" heading in the table of contents itself. To remove any text formatted with the Contents style from the table of contents, you need to delete the Contents style level number.

8. Delete the **1** from the TOC level box for the Contents style, and then click the **OK** button. "Contents" is no longer displayed in the sample table of contents in the Print Preview and Web Preview sections of the Table of Contents dialog box.

9. Click the **OK** button to accept the remaining default settings in the Table of Contents dialog box. Word searches for text formatted with the Heading 1, Heading 2, and Heading 3 styles, and then places those headings and their corresponding page numbers in a table of contents. The table of contents is inserted at the insertion point, below the "Contents" heading. See Figure 5-27.

Figure 5-27 **Table of contents inserted into document**

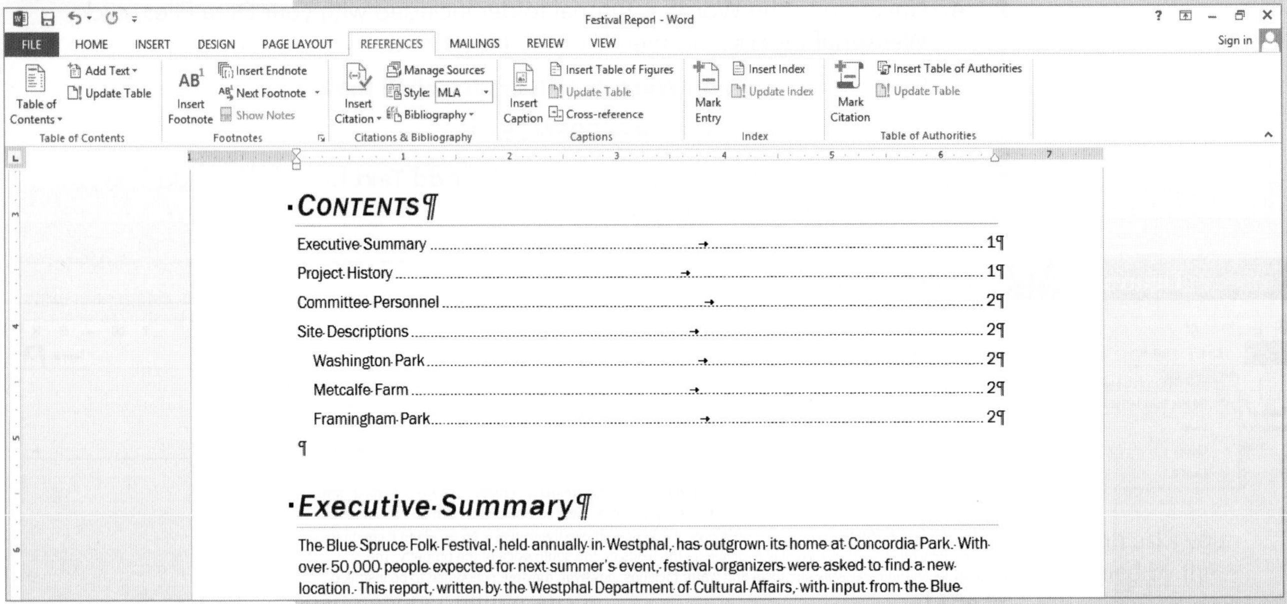

The text in the table of contents is formatted with the TOC styles for the current template. Depending on how your computer is set up, the table of contents might appear on a light gray background.

You can check the hyperlink formatting to make sure the headings really do function as links.

10. Press and hold the **Ctrl** key while you click **Metcalfe Farm** in the table of contents. The insertion point moves to the beginning of the "Metcalfe Farm" heading near the bottom of page 2.

11. Save the document.

REFERENCE

Saving a Document as a Template

- On the ribbon, click the FILE tab, and then click Export in the navigation bar.
- Click Change File Type, click Template, and then click the Save As button to open the Save As dialog box with Word Template selected in the Save as type box.
- Navigate to the folder in which you want to save the template. To save the template to the Custom Office Templates folder that is installed with Word, click the Documents folder in the Navigation pane of the Save As dialog box, and then click Custom Office Templates.
- In the File name box, type a name for the template.
- Click the Save button.

You will save the new Department of Cultural Affairs template in the location specified by your instructor; however, you'll also save it to the Custom Office Templates folder so you can practice opening a new document based on your template from the New screen in Backstage view.

To save the Festival Report document as a new template:

1. Save the **Festival Report** document to ensure that you have saved your most recent work.

2. On the ribbon, click the **FILE** tab, and then click **Export** in the navigation bar.

3. Click **Change File Type**. The Export screen displays options for various file types you can use when saving a file. For example, you could save a Word document as a Plain Text file that contains only text, without any formatting or graphics. See Figure 5-30.

Figure 5-30	Export screen with Change File Type options in Backstage view

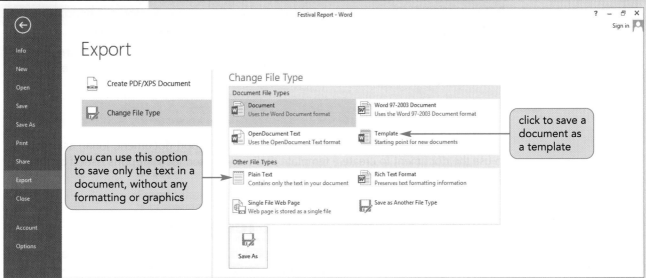

TIP

You can also click the FILE tab, click Save As, and then select Template as the file type.

4. Under Change File Type, click **Template**, and then click the **Save As** button. The Save As dialog box opens with Word Template selected in the Save as type box.

5. If necessary, navigate to the location specified by your instructor. Next, you'll replace the selected, default filename with a new one.

6. In the File name box, type **DCA Report**. See Figure 5-31.

Figure 5-31	Saving a document as a template

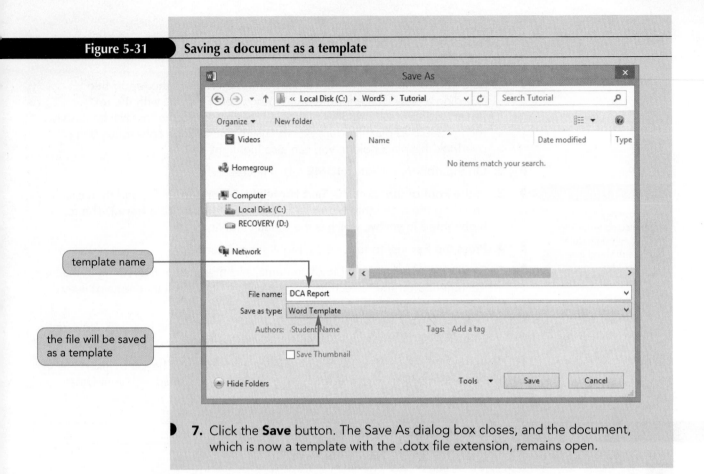

template name

the file will be saved as a template

7. Click the **Save** button. The Save As dialog box closes, and the document, which is now a template with the .dotx file extension, remains open.

PROSKILLS

Written Communication: Standardizing the Look of Your Documents

Large companies often ask their employees to use a predesigned template for all corporate documents. If you work for an organization that does not require you to use a specific template, consider using one anyway in order to create a standard look for all of your documents. A consistent appearance is especially important if you are responsible for written communication for an entire department because it ensures that colleagues and clients will immediately recognize documents from your department.

Be sure to use a professional-looking template. If you decide to create your own, use document styles that make text easy to read, with colors that are considered appropriate in your workplace. Don't try to dazzle your readers with design elements. In nearly all professional settings, a simple, elegant look is ideal.

To make the new DCA Report template really useful to Jonah's colleagues, you need to delete the specific information related to the music festival and replace it with place-holder text explaining the type of information required in each section. In the following steps, you will delete the body of the report and replace it with some placeholder text. Jonah wants to use the current subtitle, "Prepared by the Department of Cultural Affairs," as the subtitle in all department reports, so there's no need to change it. However, the title will vary from one report to the next, so you need to replace it with a suitable placeholder. You'll retain the table of contents. When Jonah's colleagues use the template to create future reports, they can update the table of contents to include any headings they add to their new documents.

To replace the information about the music festival with placeholder text:

1. Scroll up to the top of the document, and then replace the report title "Finding a New Home for the Blue Spruce Folk Festival" with the text **[Insert title here.]**. Be sure to include the brackets so the text will be readily recognizable as placeholder text. To ensure that Jonah's colleagues don't overlook this placeholder, you can also highlight it.

2. On the ribbon, click the **HOME** tab, if necessary.

3. In the Font group, click the **Text Highlight Color** button 🔲, and then click and drag the highlight pointer 🖌 over the text **[Insert title here.]**. The text is highlighted in yellow, which is the default highlight color.

TIP

To remove highlighting from selected text, click the Text Highlight Color button arrow, and then click No Color.

4. Press the **Esc** key to turn off the highlight pointer.

5. Scroll down below the table of contents, and then delete everything in the document after the "Executive Summary" heading so all that remains is the "Executive Summary" heading.

6. Press the **Enter** key to insert a blank paragraph below the heading. Now you can insert a file containing placeholder text for the body of the template.

7. In the blank paragraph under the "Executive Summary" heading, insert the **Placeholder** file from the Word5 ▸ Tutorial folder included with your Data Files. See Figure 5-32.

Figure 5-32   **Template with placeholder text**

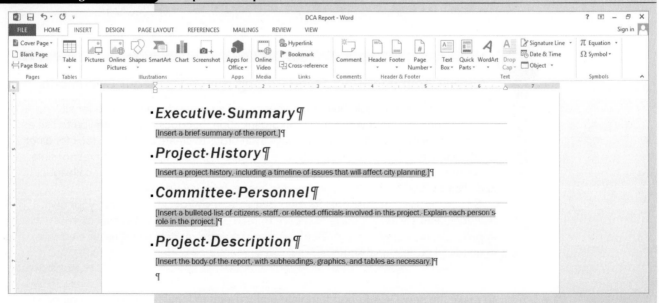

Scroll up to review the document, and notice that the inserted placeholder text is highlighted and the headings are all correctly formatted with the Heading 1 style. When Jonah created the Placeholder document, he formatted the text in the default Heading 1 style provided by the Office theme. But when you inserted the file into the template, Word automatically applied your updated Heading 1 style. Now you can update the table of contents.

8. On the ribbon, click the **REFERENCES** tab.

9. In the Table of Contents group, click the **Update Table** button. The table of contents is updated to include the new headings.

▶ **10.** On the Quick Access Toolbar, click the **Save** button 🖫 to save your changes to the template just as you would save a document.

At this point, you have a copy of the template stored in the location specified by your instructor. If you closed the template, clicked the FILE tab, and then opened the template again from the same folder, you would be opening the template itself, and not a new document based on the template. If you want to be able to open a new document based on the template from the New screen, you have to save the template to the Custom Office Templates folder. You'll do that next. You can also open a new document based on a template by double-clicking the template file from within File Explorer. You'll have a chance to try that in the Case Problems at the end of this tutorial.

To save the template to the Custom Office Templates folder:

▶ **1.** On the ribbon, click the **FILE** tab, and then click **Save As** in the navigation bar.

▶ **2.** Click **Computer** if necessary, and then click the **Browse** button to open the Save As dialog box.

▶ **3.** In the Navigation pane of the Save As dialog box, click the **Documents** folder, and then, in the file list on the right, double-click **Custom Office Templates**. See Figure 5-33.

Figure 5-33   **Saving a template in the Custom Office Templates folder**

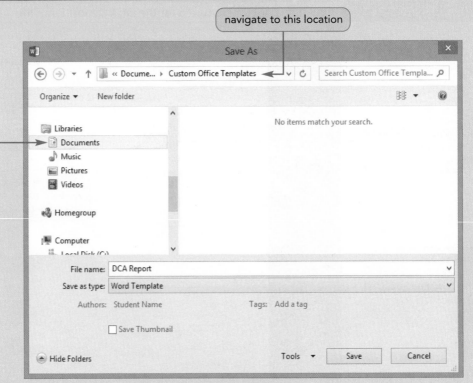

the Custom Office Templates folder is a subfolder of the Documents folder

navigate to this location

▶ **4.** Click the **Save** button to save the template to the Custom Office Templates folder and close the Save As dialog box.

▶ **5.** On the ribbon, click the **FILE** tab, and then click **Close** in the navigation bar to close the template, just as you would close a document.

The template you just created will simplify the process of creating new reports in Jonah's department.

Opening a New Document Based on Your Template

Documents created using a template contain all the text and formatting included in the template. Changes you make to this new document will not affect the template file, which remains unchanged in the Custom Office Templates folder.

Jonah would like you to use the DCA Report template to begin a report on a new literacy program.

To open a new document based on the DCA Report template:

▶ **1.** On the ribbon, click the **FILE** tab, and then click **New** in the navigation bar.

Because you have created and saved a template, the New tab in Backstage view now includes two links—FEATURED and PERSONAL. The FEATURED link is selected by default, indicating that the templates currently featured by Office.com are displayed. To open the template you just saved to the Custom Office Templates folder, you need to display the personal templates instead.

▶ **2.** Click **PERSONAL**. The DCA Report template is displayed as an option on the New screen. See Figure 5-34.

Figure 5-34	Opening a document based on the DCA Report template

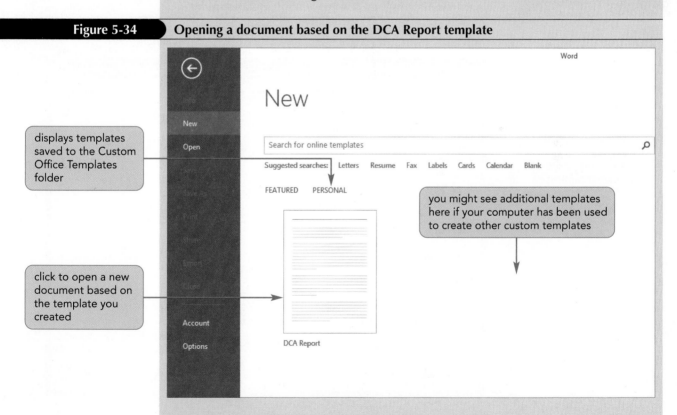

displays templates saved to the Custom Office Templates folder

you might see additional templates here if your computer has been used to create other custom templates

click to open a new document based on the template you created

▶ **3.** Click **DCA Report**. A new document opens containing the text and formatting from the DCA Report template.

▶ **4.** Delete the placeholder **[Insert title here.]** and type **Start Again Literacy Project** in its place.

> Jonah and his colleagues will add new material to this report later. For now, you can close it.
>
> ▶ **5.** Save the document as **Literacy Project** in the location specified by your instructor, and then close the document.
>
>   Next, to ensure that you can repeat the steps in this tutorial, you will delete the DCA Report template from the Custom Office Templates folder. You can delete it from within the Open dialog box.
>
> ▶ **6.** On the ribbon, click the **FILE** tab, and then in the navigation bar, click **Open**.
>
> ▶ **7.** Click **Computer** if necessary, and then click the **Browse** button.
>
> ▶ **8.** In the navigation pane of the Save As dialog box, click the **Documents** folder, and then double-click **Custom Office Templates**. The DCA Report template is displayed in the file list.
>
> ▶ **9.** Right-click **DCA Report** to display a shortcut menu, and then click **Delete**. The template file is removed from the file list.
>
> ▶ **10.** Click **Cancel** to close the Open dialog box, and then close Backstage view.

Creating a template makes it easy to create a series of similar documents. But what if you want to insert specific text such as an address or email address, or a graphic such as a logo, in many different documents? In that case, you can save the item as a Quick Part.

Creating a New Quick Part

A **Quick Part** is reusable content that you create and that you can then insert into any document later with a single click in the Quick Part gallery. For example, you might create a letterhead with your company's address and logo. To save the letterhead as a Quick Part, you select it and then save it to the Quick Part gallery. Later, you can insert the letterhead into a document by clicking it in the Quick Part gallery.

By default, a new Quick Part appears as an option in the Quick Part gallery. However, you can assign a Quick Part to any gallery you want. For example, you could assign a text box Quick Part to the Text Box gallery so that every time you click the Text Box button on the INSERT tab, you see your text box as one of the options in the Text Box gallery.

Quick Parts are just one type of a larger category of reusable content known as **building blocks**. All of the ready-made items that you can insert into a document via a gallery are considered building blocks. For example, preformatted headers, preformatted text boxes, and cover pages are all examples of building blocks. Some reference sources use the terms "building block" and "Quick Part" as if they were synonyms, but in fact a Quick Part is a building block that you create.

When you save a Quick Part, you always save it to a template; you can't save a Quick Part to an individual document. Which template you save it to depends on what you want to do with the Quick Part. If you want the template to be available to all new documents created on your computer, you should save it to the Building Blocks template. The **Building Blocks template** is a special template that contains all the building blocks installed with Word on your computer, as well as any Quick Parts you save to it. If you want to restrict the Quick Part to only documents based on the current template, or if you want to be able to share the Quick Part with someone else, you should save it to the current template. To share the Quick Part, you simply distribute the template to anyone who wants to use the Quick Part.

Creating and Using Quick Parts

- Select the text, text box, header, footer, table, graphic, or other item you want to save as a Quick Part. If you want to save only a formatted structure as a Quick Part (such as a formatted text box), delete any text in the item before selecting it.
- On the ribbon, click the INSERT tab.
- In the Text group, click the Quick Parts button, and then click Save Selection to Quick Part Gallery.
- In the Create New Building Block dialog box, replace the text in the Name box with a descriptive name for the Quick Part.
- Click the Gallery arrow, and then choose the gallery to which you want to save the Quick Part.
- To make the Quick Part available to all documents on your computer, select Building Blocks in the Save in box. To restrict the Quick Part to the current template, select the name of the template on which the current document is based.
- Click the OK button.

Jonah has created a text box containing the address and phone number for the Department of Cultural Affairs. He asks you to show him how to save the text box as a Quick Part. He wants the Quick Part to be available to all new documents created on his computer, so you'll need to save it to the Building Blocks template.

To save a text box as a Quick Part:

1. Open the document **DCA** from the Word5 ▸ Tutorial folder included with your Data Files, and then save it as **DCA Address** in the location specified by your instructor.

2. Display nonprinting characters and the rulers, switch to Print Layout view, and then change the Zoom level to **120%**, if necessary.

3. Click the **text box** to select it, taking care to select the entire text box and not the text inside it. When the text box is selected, you'll see the anchor symbol in the left margin.

4. On the ribbon, click the **INSERT** tab.

5. In the Text group, click the **Quick Parts** button. If any Quick Parts have been created on your computer, they will be displayed in the gallery at the top of the menu. Otherwise, you will see only the menu shown in Figure 5-35.

| Figure 5-35 | Quick Parts menu, with no Quick Part gallery visible |

6. At the bottom of the menu, click **Save Selection to Quick Part Gallery**. The Create New Building Block dialog box opens. The name of this dialog box is appropriate because a Quick Part is a type of building block. See Figure 5-36.

Figure 5-36   **Create New Building Block dialog box**

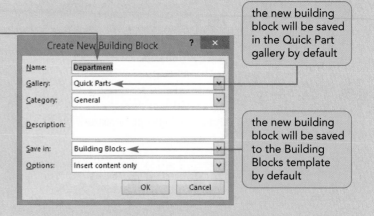

the first word in the text box is used as the name of the new building block by default

the new building block will be saved in the Quick Part gallery by default

the new building block will be saved to the Building Blocks template by default

By default, the first word in the text box, "Department," is used as the default name for the new building block. Also, the default setting in the Gallery box tells you that the new building block will be saved in the Quick Part gallery. You could change this by selecting a different gallery name. The Save in box indicates that the Quick Part will be saved to the Building Blocks template, which means it will be available to all documents on your computer.

Jonah asks you to accept the default settings.

▶ **7.** Click the **OK** button to accept your changes and close the Create New Building Block dialog box.

You've finished creating the new Quick Part. Now you can try inserting it in the current document.

To insert the new Quick Part into the current document:

▶ **1.** Press the **Ctrl+End** keys to move the insertion point to the end of the document.

▶ **2.** In the Text group, click the **Quick Parts** button. This time, the Quick Part gallery is displayed at the top of the menu. See Figure 5-37.

Figure 5-37   **New Quick Part in the Quick Part gallery**

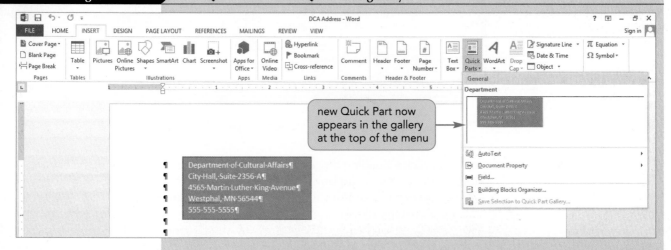

new Quick Part now appears in the gallery at the top of the menu

> **3.** Click the **Department** Quick Part. A copy of the blue text box is inserted at the end of the document, at the insertion point.

> **4.** In the newly inserted text box, replace the phone number with your first and last names, and then save the document.

The new Quick Part is stored in the Quick Part gallery, ready to be inserted into any document. However, after reviewing the Quick Part, Jonah has decided he wants to reformat the address text box and save it as a new Quick Part later. So you'll delete the Quick Part you just created.

To delete a Quick Part:

> **1.** In the Text group, click the Quick Parts button, and then click Building Blocks Organizer to open the Building Blocks Organizer dialog box. Here you see a list of all the building blocks available in your copy of Word, including Quick Parts. See Figure 5-38.

Figure 5-38   **Building Blocks Organizer dialog box**

click to sort by the gallery to which each building block is saved

click to sort the building blocks alphabetically by name

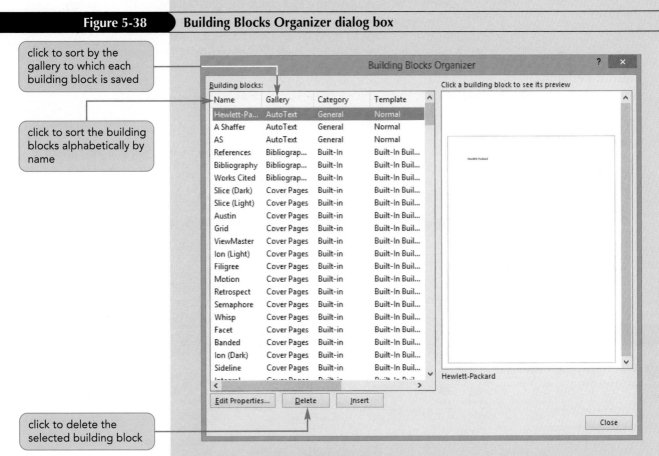

click to delete the selected building block

The list on your computer will be somewhat different from the list shown in Figure 5-38.

You can click a building block in the list, and then click the Edit Properties button to open a dialog box where you can rename the building block and make other changes. You can also use the Building Blocks Organizer to delete a building block.

2. Click the **Name** column header to sort the building blocks alphabetically by name, scroll down and click **Department**, click the **Delete** button, and then click the **Yes** button in the warning dialog box. The Department Quick Part is deleted from the list in the Building Blocks Organizer.

3. Click the **Close** button.

4. In the Text group, click the **Quick Parts** button, and then verify that the Department Quick Part is no longer displayed in the Quick Part gallery.

   Finally, to completely delete the Quick Part from the Building Blocks template, you need to save the current document. In the process of saving the document, Word will save your changes to the Building Blocks template, which controls all the building blocks available in your copy of Word. If you don't save the document now, you'll see a warning dialog box later, when you attempt to close the document. It's easy to get confused by the wording of this warning dialog box, and you might end up restoring your Quick Part rather than deleting it. To avoid seeing this warning dialog box entirely, remember to save the current document after you delete a Quick Part.

5. Save the **DCA Address** document and then close it.

Jonah is happy to know how to save Quick Parts to the Building Blocks template. He'll create a new Quick Part later, and save it to a custom template so he can make it available to everyone in his department.

REVIEW

Session 5.2 Quick Check

1. Explain how to create a new style.
2. Is it possible to remove a style from the Style gallery without deleting the style itself?
3. What is the difference between the Style Inspector pane and the Reveal Formatting pane?
4. What must you do if you want to be able to open a new document based on a template you created?
5. What must you do to your document before you can create a table of contents for it?
6. What button can you click to revise a table of contents, and where is that button located?
7. What term is used to refer to all the ready-made items that you can insert into a document via a gallery, such as preformatted headers, preformatted text boxes, and cover pages?
8. What is the relationship between Quick Parts and building blocks?

ASSESS

SAM Projects

Put your skills into practice with SAM Projects! SAM Projects for this tutorial can be found online. If you have a SAM account, go to www.cengage.com/sam2013 to download the most recent Project Instructions and Start Files.

PRACTICE

Review Assignments

Data Files needed for the Review Assignments: DCP Address.docx, Internet.docx, Placeholder Text.docx, Staff.docx

Jonah's DCA Report template is now used for all reports created by employees of the Westphal Department of Cultural Affairs. Inspired by Jonah's success with the template, a project manager in the Department of City Planning (DCP), Suzanne Hansen, wants you to help with a report on expanding high-speed Internet access for city residents. After you format the report, she'd like you to save the document as a new template, and then create a Quick Part. Complete the following steps:

1. Create a new document based on the Oriel report template from Office.com. Replace the [TYPE THE DOCUMENT TITLE] placeholder with your name, and then save the document as **Document from Oriel Template** in the location specified by your instructor. If you see a dialog box explaining that the document is being upgraded to the newest file format, click the OK button.

2. Close the document.

3. Open the document **Internet** from the Word5 ▸ Review folder included with your Data Files, and then save it as **Internet Report** in the location specified by your instructor.

4. Use the Go To feature to review all the headings in the document.

5. In the second line of the "Project Background" section, use the Thesaurus task pane to replace "vital" with a synonym. Use the third synonym in the list of words related to "fundamental."

6. Change the theme colors to Grayscale, and then change the theme's fonts to the Georgia fonts.

7. Save the new colors and fonts as a theme named **DCP Theme** in the location specified by your instructor.

8. Change the style set to Minimalist.

9. Change the formatting of the "Project Background" heading by adding italic formatting and by changing the character spacing so that it is expanded by 1 point between characters.

10. Update the Heading 1 style to match the newly formatted "Project Background" heading.

11. Revise the "Likely Challenges" heading by changing the font size to 16 points, and then update the Heading 2 style to match the newly formatted "Likely Challenges" heading.

12. Create a new paragraph style for the "Contents" heading that is based on the Heading 1 style, but that also includes Gray-25%, Accent 2 paragraph shading and the White, Background 1 font color. Name the new style TOC (short for "Table of Contents"), select Normal as the style for the following paragraph, and then save the new style to the current document.

13. Open the Style Inspector pane, and check the style applied to each paragraph in the document. Then use the Reveal Formatting pane to compare the formatting applied to the "Contents" heading with the formatting applied to the "Project Background" heading.

14. Delete the placeholder below the "Contents" heading, and then insert a custom table of contents that does not include the TOC style. Except for excluding the TOC style, use the default settings in the Table of Contents dialog box.

15. Insert a blank paragraph at the end of the document, and then insert the Word file **Staff** from the Word5 ▸ Review folder included with your Data Files. Add the text **Contributing Staff Members** to the table of contents as a Level 1 heading, and then delete the blank paragraph at the end of the document.

16. At the end of the report, replace "Student Name" with your first and last names.

17. Save your changes to the Internet Report document.

18. Save the Internet Report document as a Word Template named **DCP Report** in the location specified by your instructor.

19. On page 1, replace the title "HIGH-SPEED INTERNET ACCESS FOR ALL RESIDENTS" with the placeholder text **[INSERT TITLE HERE.]**, and then highlight the placeholder in the default yellow color.

20. Delete everything in the report after the table of contents.

21. In the blank paragraph below the table of contents, insert the Word file **Placeholder Text** from the Word5 ▶ Review folder included with your Data Files.

22. At the end of the template, replace "Student Name" with your first and last names, and then update the table of contents.

23. Save the template, save it again to the Custom Office Templates folder, and then close it.

24. Open a new document based on the DCP Report template, enter **New South Side Bike Path** as the document title, save the new document as **Bike Path** in the location specified by your instructor, and then close it.

25. Delete the DCP Report template from the Custom Office Templates folder.

26. Open the document **DCP Address** from the Word5 ▶ Review folder included with your Data Files, and then save it as a Word Template named **DCP Address Box** in the location specified by your instructor.

27. Save the green text box as a Quick Part named **Address**. Save it to the DCP Address Box template, not to the Building Blocks template.

28. Save the template and close it.

Case Problem 1

Data File needed for this Case Problem: Write.docx

Write and Wrong Quality Assurance   Arshia Husain is the founder and owner of Write and Wrong Quality Assurance, a consulting firm that reviews book manuscripts from a variety of fields for technical accuracy. When one of Arshia's consultants reviews a book, he or she must fill out a report consisting of tables that detail various issues. By the time a consultant finishes reviewing an entire book, the report can be quite long. Therefore, it's important that each report include a table of contents on the first page. Your job is to create a template that Arshia and her consultants can use when reviewing manuscripts. Complete the following steps:

1. Open the document **Write** from the Word5 ▶ Case1 folder included with your Data Files, and then save it as **Write and Wrong** in the location specified by your instructor.

2. Use Go To to review all the tables in the document.

3. Change the document's theme to the View theme, and then change the theme colors to Red Orange. Change the style set to Basic (Simple).

4. Highlight in yellow the four instances of placeholder text below the company name and above the "Contents" heading.

5. Format the "Contents" heading by changing the character spacing to Expanded, with the default amount of space between the expanded characters. Increase the font size to 18 points, add italic formatting, and then change the font color to one shade darker, using the Red, Accent 1, Darker 50% font color. Update the Heading 1 style for the current document to match the newly formatted heading.

6. Create a new paragraph style for the company name at the top of the document that is based on the Heading 1 style, but that also includes Red, Accent 3, Darker 25% paragraph shading; White, Background 1 font color; 20-point font size; and center alignment. Add 16 points of paragraph spacing before the paragraph and 6 points after. Name the new style **Company**. Select the Normal style as the style for the following paragraph, and save the style to the current document.

7. Remove the Company style from the Style Gallery.

8. Below the "Contents" heading, replace the yellow highlighted placeholder text with a custom table of contents that does not include the Company style.

9. In the document, delete the paragraph containing the "Contents" heading, and then update the table of contents to remove "Contents" from it.

10. Click in the paragraph before the table of contents, and increase the spacing after it to 24 points.

11. Add the "General Recommendations" heading, which is above the last table, to the table of contents at the same level as the "Organization" heading.

12. Above the second table, replace "Illustrations" with a synonym. In the Thesaurus task pane, use the fourth synonym in the list of words related to "artworks," and then update the table of contents to include the revised heading.

13. Save your changes to the Write and Wrong document, and then save the Write and Wrong document as a template named **Issue Report** in the location specified by your instructor.

14. Save one of the blank tables as a Quick Part named **Additional Table**. Save the Quick Part to the Issue Report template.

15. Save the template to its current location, and then save the template again to the Custom Office Templates folder. Close the template.

16. Open a document based on your new template, and then save the new document as **System** in the location specified by your instructor.

17. Replace the publication title placeholder with the text **System Management: Theory and Practice**.

18. At the end of the document, insert the text **Special Issues**, format it with the Heading 1 style, and then insert the Additional Table Quick Part in a new paragraph after the heading.

19. Update the table of contents to include the new heading.

20. Save and close the document, and then delete the Issue Report template from the Custom Office Templates folder.

Case Problem 2

There are no Data Files needed for this Case Problem.

Blooming Town Beekeepers   Paula Spalding is president of Blooming Town Beekeepers, an association of people interested in raising bees in urban settings. The group plans to have a booth at an upcoming gardening exposition, and Paula is preparing a series of handouts to share with people who are interested in becoming beekeepers. Your job is to create a sample handout for Paula based on an Office.com template. In the handout, you'll use drawings from Office.com, which Paula will eventually replace with her own photos. Your completed handout should look like the one shown in Figure 5-39.

Figure 5-39   **Handout for Blooming Town Beekeepers**

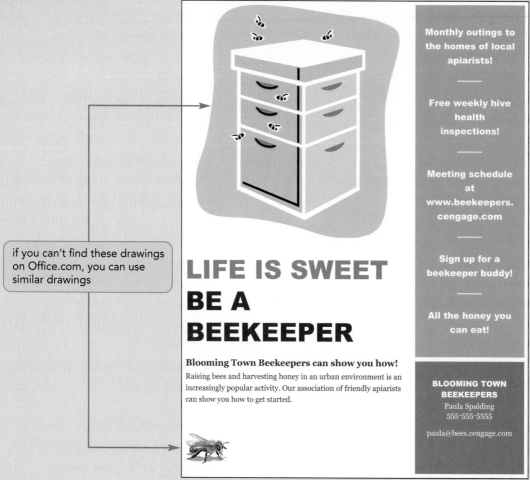

if you can't find these drawings on Office.com, you can use similar drawings

© 2014 Cengage Learning; Images used with permission of Microsoft Corporation

After you finish the handout, Paula would like you to use it as the basis for a new template that she can use for future handouts. Complete the following steps:

1. Open a new document based on the Office.com template named "Seasonal event flyer (summer)."
2. Save the new document as **Beekeepers** in the location specified by your instructor. Notice that the left side of the document is laid out using a table structure. The two colored boxes on the right side are laid out using a separate table structure.
3. Replace the [DATE] placeholder with the text **LIFE IS SWEET**.
4. Replace the [EVENT TITLE HERE] placeholder with the text **BE A BEEKEEPER**.
5. Replace the [Event Description Heading] placeholder with the text **Blooming Town Beekeepers can show you how!**
6. Replace the placeholder text below "Blooming Town Beekeepers can show you how!" with the following text: **Raising bees and harvesting honey in an urban environment is an increasingly popular activity. Our association of friendly apiarists can show you how to get started**.
7. Delete the "replace with LOGO" picture in the lower-left corner of the page, and then replace it with the clip art drawing of a bee shown in Figure 5-39. Find the image by going to Office.com and searching for the keyword **bee**. If you cannot find the image shown in Figure 5-39, choose a similar image. If necessary, resize the inserted picture to make it approximately one-inch square.

8. Replace the remaining placeholder text as follows:
   - [Add Key Event Info Here!]: **Monthly outings to the homes of local apiarists!**
   - [Don't Be Shy—Tell Them Why They Can't Miss It!]: **Free weekly hive health inspections!**
   - [One More Point Here!]: **Meeting schedule at www.beekeepers.cengage.com**
   - [Add More Great Info Here!]: **Sign up for a beekeeper buddy!**
   - [You Have Room for Another One Here!]: **All the honey you can eat!**
   - [COMPANY NAME]: **BLOOMING TOWN BEEKEEPERS**
   - [Street Address][City, ST ZIP Code][Telephone]: **Paula Spalding 555-555-5555**
   - [Web Address]: **paula@bees.cengage.com**

9. Insert a manual line break after Paula's last name, and then delete the extra space before her phone number so the phone number is centered under her name.

10. Replace Paula's first and last names with your name. If you can't fit your entire name, abbreviate it, perhaps by using only your first initial and your last name, so that it fits on one line.

11. Delete the [Dates and Times] placeholders.

12. At the top of the document, replace the photo of the girls holding ice cream cones with a drawing of a beehive from Office.com. Use the beehive drawing shown earlier in Figure 5-39, which you can find by searching for the keyword **hive**. If you cannot locate the image shown in Figure 5-39, choose a similar image. Change its text wrap setting to In Front of Text, and then resize and position it appropriately within the table cell.

13. Attach a comment to the first paragraph in the green column that reads: **This document contains *number* paragraph styles, *number* linked styles, and *number* character styles**. For each type of style, replace *number* with the correct number.

14. Save the document, and then save it again as a template named **Beekeepers Flyer** in the location specified by your instructor.

15. Delete the comment.

16. In the green shaded column, replace the four paragraphs of text with four instances of the placeholder text **[Insert beekeeper information.]**.

17. Save the bee picture as a Quick Part named **Bee** to the Beekeepers Flyer template.

18. Save and close the template.

Case Problem 3

RESEARCH

Data Files needed for this Case Problem: Formatting.docx, MLA.docx

MLA-Style Research Paper Template   You are a research assistant for Jasper Leff, a professor of history at a local college. Professor Leff requires his students to write three MLA-style research papers each semester. To ensure that his students use the proper format, he wants to provide them with a Word template for an MLA-style research paper. He asks you to create the template for him. You'll start by doing some research on specifications for the MLA style. Complete the following steps:

1. Open the document **Formatting** from the Word5 ▶ Case3 folder included with your Data Files, and then save it as **MLA Formatting** in the location specified by your instructor.

2. Change the document's theme to the Slice theme, and then change the theme colors to Violet II. Change the style set to Lines (Simple).

3. Using a source on the web or an up-to-date print publication, research the characteristics of an MLA-style research paper.

4. In the MLA Formatting document, fill in the table with the necessary information about MLA-style research papers.

5. Save the MLA Formatting document, and then use it for reference as you complete the remaining steps in this Case Problem.

6. Open the document **MLA** from the Word5 ▶ Review folder included with your Data Files, and then save it as a Word template named **MLA Paper** in the location specified by your instructor.

7. Review the template, which contains three paragraphs that Professor Leff generated by typing =lorem() and pressing the Enter key. You can use this text as body text to separate placeholder headings in the template.

8. Edit the comment to insert the appropriate examples after each colon. Format the examples in the comment with yellow highlighting.

9. Add your name in the appropriate location for an MLA-style research paper, and then add placeholder text in square brackets for any missing document elements. For example, for the paper title, you should insert [**Title**]. Format all the placeholder text as it would be formatted if it were text in an actual MLA-style research paper. Include one [**Heading**] placeholder after the first paragraph of body text, and one more after the second paragraph of body text. Include the appropriate title for the bibliography. For the bibliography itself, include the left-aligned placeholder text [**Insert bibliography using Word's bibliography feature.**].

10. Format the body text appropriately, and then apply the appropriate line and paragraph spacing to the entire template.

11. Save the MLA Paper template, and then close it.

Case Problem 4

Data File needed for this Case Problem: Haley's.docx, Sharpe.docx

CHALLENGE

Sharpe Sustainability Designs   You are the assistant to Haley Sachjten, the publications director at Sharpe Sustainability Designs, an engineering firm in New York City. Sharpe specializes in projects that minimize a building's impact on the environment by using as many recycled materials as possible and by maximizing energy efficiency. Haley often uses Word styles in the reports and other publications she creates for the company, and she wants to learn more about managing styles. In particular, she wants to learn how to copy styles from one document to another. She's asked you to help her explore the Style Pane Options, Manage Styles, and Organizer dialog boxes. She would also like your help creating a Quick Part for a memo header. Complete the following steps:

1. Open the document **Sharpe** from the Word5 ▸ Case4 folder included with your Data Files, and then save it as **Sharpe Memo** in the location specified by your instructor. This document contains the text you will eventually save as a Quick Part. It contains all the default styles available in any new Word document, as well as one style, named Memo Header, which Haley created earlier. In the following steps, you will copy styles from another document to this document. For now, you can close it.

2. Close the Sharpe Memo document.

3. Open the document **Haley's** from the Word5 ▸ Case4 folder included with your Data Files, and then save it as **Haley's Styles** in the location specified by your instructor. This document contains styles created by Haley, which you will copy to the Sharpe Memo document. It also includes sample paragraphs formatted with Haley's styles, and one paragraph that you will format with a style later in this Case Problem.

✪ **Explore** 4. Open the Style Pane Options dialog box, and then change the settings so the Styles pane displays only the styles currently used in the document, in alphabetical order. Before closing this dialog box, verify that these settings will only be applied to the current document rather than to new documents based on this template.

5. Press the Print Screen button on your keyboard to capture a screenshot that shows the Styles pane displaying only the styles used in the current document, in alphabetical order.

6. Paste the screenshot at the end of the document, just as you would paste text that you had previously copied to the Clipboard.

✪ **Explore** 7. At the bottom of the Styles pane, click the Manage Styles button, and then click the Import/Export button to open the Organizer dialog box. Close the Normal template and open the Sharpe Memo document instead. (*Hint*: On the right, under the In Normal box, click the Close File button, and then click the Open File button. In the Open dialog box, you'll need to display all files.)

✦ **Explore** 8. Copy the following styles from the Haley's Styles document to the Sharpe Memo document: Company Name, Department, Energy, and Product Description. Then copy the Memo style from the Sharpe Memo document to the Haley's Styles document.

9. Close the Organizer dialog box, and then save your changes to the Sharpe Memo document.

10. In the Haley's Styles document, apply the Memo style to the "Sample of Memo style" paragraph at the end of the document.

11. Save the Haley's Styles document, and then close it.

12. Open the **Sharpe Memo** document, and then review the list of styles in the Styles pane to locate the styles you just copied to this document from the Haley's Styles document.

13. Apply the Company Name style to "Sharpe Sustainability Designs" in the second paragraph.

14. Save the Sharpe Memo document, and then save it again as a template named **Sharpe Memo Template** in the location specified by your instructor.

15. Select all of the text in the document, and then save it as a Quick Part named **Green Memo**. Save the Quick Part to the current template, not to the Building Blocks template.

16. Change the Paragraph shading for the first paragraph to blue, using the Blue, Accent 5 color in the top row of the Shading gallery, and then save the document text as a new Quick Part named **Blue Memo**. Again, save the Quick Part to the current template.

17. Delete all the text from the document, save the Sharpe Memo Template file, and then close it.

✦ **Explore** 18. Open a File Explorer window, and then navigate to the location where you saved the Sharpe Memo Template file. Open a new document based on the template by double-clicking the template's filename in File Explorer.

19. Save the new document as **Sample Memo** in the location specified by your instructor, insert the Blue Memo Quick Part in the document, and then save and close the document.

Using Mail Merge

Creating a Form Letter, Mailing Labels, and a Telephone Directory

WORD

OBJECTIVES

Session 6.1
- Insert a date field
- Select a main document
- Create a data source
- Insert mail merge fields into a main document
- Edit a main document
- Preview a merged document
- Complete a mail merge

Session 6.2
- Reopen a main document
- Edit a data source
- Sort and filter records
- Create mailing labels
- Create a phone directory
- Convert a table to text

Case | *Candlestick Artisan Bakery*

Maiya Kandel owns Candlestick Artisan Bakery in Carlyle, Louisiana. The bakery has just moved to a new, expanded location with an attached coffee shop. Maiya hopes to encourage customers to visit the coffee shop by offering a free cup of coffee and pastry. She plans to send a form letter to regular customers announcing the new location and the opening of the coffee shop.

The form letter will also contain specific details for individual customers, such as name, address, and each customer's favorite type of bread and pastry. Maiya has already written the text of the form letter. She plans to use the mail merge process to add the personal information for each customer to the form letter. She asks you to revise the form letter by inserting a date field in the document that will display the current date. Then she wants you to use the Mail Merge feature in Word to create customized letters for her customers. After you create the merged letters, she'd like you to create mailing labels for the envelopes and a directory of employee phone numbers. Finally, you'll convert some text to a table so that it can be used in a mail merge.

STARTING DATA FILES

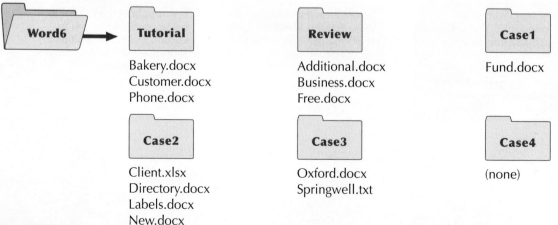

Word6 → **Tutorial**
Bakery.docx
Customer.docx
Phone.docx

Review
Additional.docx
Business.docx
Free.docx

Case1
Fund.docx

Case2
Client.xlsx
Directory.docx
Labels.docx
New.docx

Case3
Oxford.docx
Springwell.txt

Case4
(none)

Microsoft product screenshots used with permission from Microsoft Corporation.

Session 6.1 Visual Overview:

Use the Start Mail Merge button to select the type of main document you are creating. Possible types include letters, envelopes, emails, labels, and directories.

The Select Recipients button allows you to select an existing data source or create a new one in the New Address List dialog box.

The MAILINGS tab contains four groups of options that, working left to right, walk you through the process of creating a mail merge.

To complete the mail merge, you click the Finish & Merge button. This creates a new document, the **merged document**, which contains a separate copy of the main document for each record in the data source.

The Edit Recipient List button allows you to make changes to a data source.

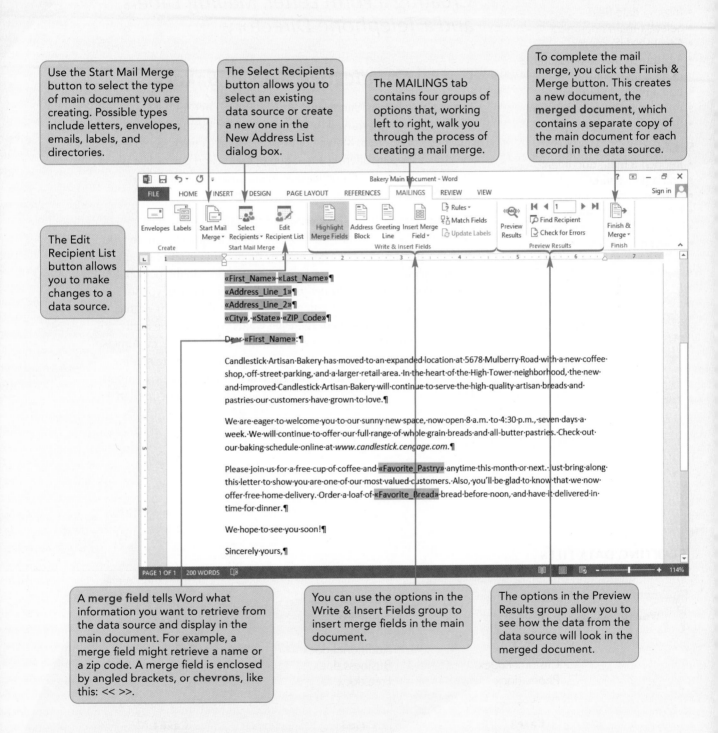

A **merge field** tells Word what information you want to retrieve from the data source and display in the main document. For example, a merge field might retrieve a name or a zip code. A merge field is enclosed by angled brackets, or **chevrons**, like this: << >>.

You can use the options in the Write & Insert Fields group to insert merge fields in the main document.

The options in the Preview Results group allow you to see how the data from the data source will look in the merged document.

Mail Merge

A **data source** is a file that contains information, such as names and addresses, that is organized into fields and records; the merge fields cause the information in the data source to be displayed in the main document. You can use a Word table, an Excel spreadsheet, or other types of files as data sources, or you can create a new data source using the New Address List dialog box.

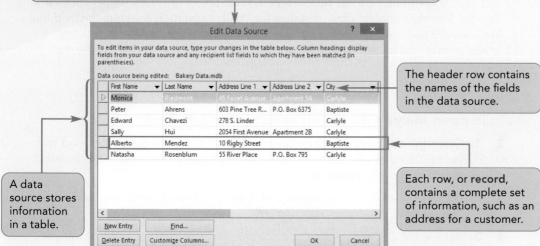

Edit Data Source ? ×

To edit items in your data source, type your changes in the table below. Column headings display fields from your data source and any recipient list fields to which they have been matched (in parentheses).

Data source being edited: Bakery Data.mdb

First Name	Last Name	Address Line 1	Address Line 2	City
Monica	Piedmont	45 Fairet Avenue	Apartment 5A	Carlyle
Peter	Ahrens	603 Pine Tree R...	P.O. Box 6375	Baptiste
Edward	Chavezi	278 S. Linder		Carlyle
Sally	Hui	2054 First Avenue	Apartment 2B	Carlyle
Alberto	Mendez	10 Rigby Street		Baptiste
Natasha	Rosenblum	55 River Place	P.O. Box 795	Carlyle

New Entry   Find...

Delete Entry   Customize Columns...   OK   Cancel

The header row contains the names of the fields in the data source.

Each row, or **record**, contains a complete set of information, such as an address for a customer.

A data source stores information in a table.

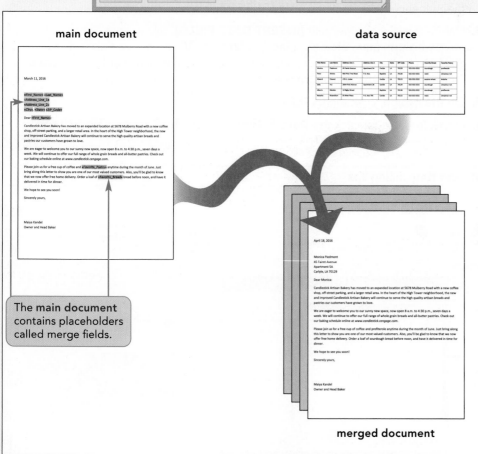

main document

March 11, 2016

«First_Name» «Last_Name»
«Address_Line_1»
«Address_Line_2»
«City», «State» «ZIP_Code»

Dear «First_Name»:

Candlestick Artisan Bakery has moved to an expanded location at 5678 Mulberry Road with a new coffee shop, off-street parking, and a larger retail area. In the heart of the High Tower neighborhood, the new and improved Candlestick Artisan Bakery will continue to serve the high quality artisan breads and pastries our customers have grown to love.

We are eager to welcome you to our sunny new space, now open 8 a.m. to 4:30 p.m., seven days a week. We will continue to offer our full range of whole grain breads and all-butter pastries. Check out our baking schedule online at www.candlestick.cengage.com.

Please join us for a free cup of coffee and «Favorite_Pastry» anytime during the month of June. Just bring along this letter to show you are one of our most valued customers. Also, you'll be glad to know that we now offer free home delivery. Order a loaf of «Favorite_Bread» bread before noon, and have it delivered in time for dinner.

We hope to see you soon!

Sincerely yours,

Maiya Kandel
Owner and Head Baker

data source

April 18, 2016

Monica Piedmont
45 Fairet Avenue
Apartment 5A
Carlyle, LA 70129

Dear Monica:

Candlestick Artisan Bakery has moved to an expanded location at 5678 Mulberry Road with a new coffee shop, off-street parking, and a larger retail area. In the heart of the High Tower neighborhood, the new and improved Candlestick Artisan Bakery will continue to serve the high quality artisan breads and pastries our customers have grown to love.

We are eager to welcome you to our sunny new space, now open 8 a.m. to 4:30 p.m., seven days a week. We will continue to offer our full range of whole grain breads and all-butter pastries. Check out our baking schedule online at www.candlestick.cengage.com.

Please join us for a free cup of coffee and profiterole anytime during the month of June. Just bring along this letter to show you are one of our most valued customers. Also, you'll be glad to know that we now offer free home delivery. Order a loaf of sourdough bread before noon, and have it delivered in time for dinner.

We hope to see you soon!

Sincerely yours,

Maiya Kandel
Owner and Head Baker

The **main document** contains placeholders called merge fields.

merged document

Inserting a Date Field

A **date field** is an instruction that tells Word to display the current date in a document. Although a date field is not a merge field, it's common to use date fields in mail merge documents to ensure that the main document always includes the current date. Every time you open a document containing a date field, it updates to display the current date. To insert a date field, you use the Date and Time dialog box to select from a variety of date formats. In addition to displaying the date with the current day, month, and year, you can include the current time and the day of the week. Word inserts a date field inside a content control; unless the content control is selected, the field looks like ordinary text.

Maiya asks you to insert a date field in her document before beginning the mail merge process.

To open Maiya's document and insert a date field:

▶ 1. Open the document **Bakery** from the Word6 ▶ Tutorial folder included with your Data Files, and then save it as **Bakery Main Document** in the location specified by your instructor.

▶ 2. Display nonprinting characters, switch to Print Layout view, display the rulers, and then set the Zoom level to **120%**.

▶ 3. Review the contents of the letter. Notice that the fourth paragraph includes the placeholder text "[INSERT DATE FIELD]."

▶ 4. Delete the placeholder text **[INSERT DATE FIELD]**, taking care not to delete the paragraph mark after the placeholder text. When you are finished, the insertion point should be located in the second blank paragraph of the document, with two blank paragraphs below it.

▶ 5. On the ribbon, click the **INSERT** tab.

▶ 6. In the Text group, click the **Date & Time** button. The Date and Time dialog box opens. See Figure 6-1.

Figure 6-1   **Date and Time dialog box**

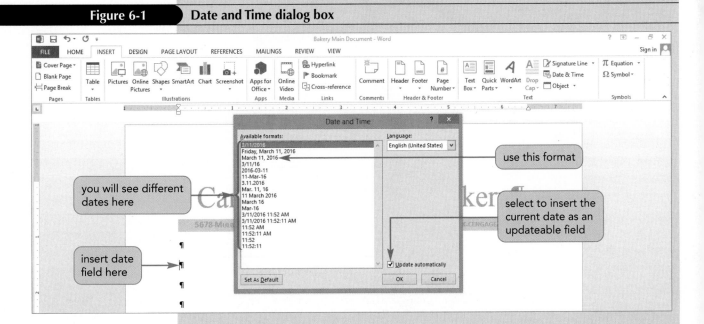

The Available formats list provides options for inserting the current date and time. In this case, you want to insert the date as a content control in a format that includes the complete name of the month, the date, and the year (for example, March 11, 2016).

▶ **7.** In the Available formats list, click the third format from the top, which is the month, date, and year format.

▶ **8.** Make sure the **Update automatically** check box is selected so the date is inserted as a content control that updates every time you open the document.

▶ **9.** Click the **OK** button. The current date is inserted in the document. At this point, it looks like ordinary text. To see the content control, you have to click the date.

▶ **10.** Click the date to display the content control. If you closed the document and then opened it a day later, the content control would automatically display the new date. See Figure 6-2.

Figure 6-2   **Date field inside content control**

current date is displayed inside a content control

▶ **11.** Scroll down to display the letter's closing, change "Maiya Kandel" to your first and last names, and then scroll back up to the beginning of the letter.

▶ **12.** Save the document.

Now that the document contains the current date, you can begin the mail merge process.

Performing a Mail Merge

When you perform a mail merge, you insert individualized information from a data source into a main document. A main document can be a letter or any other kind of document containing merge fields that tell Word where to insert names, addresses, and other variable information from the data source. When you **merge** the main document with information from the data source, you produce a new document called a merged document. The Session 6.1 Visual Overview summarizes mail merge concepts.

Maiya's main document is the letter shown in the Session 6.1 Visual Overview. In this session, you will insert the merge fields shown in this letter. You'll also create Maiya's data source, which will include the name and address of each customer. The data source will also include information about each customer's favorite bread and pastry.

You can perform a mail merge by using the Mail Merge task pane, which walks you through the steps of performing a mail merge. You access the Mail Merge task pane by clicking the Start Mail Merge button in the Start Mail Merge group, and then clicking the Step-by-Step Mail Merge Wizard command on the menu. You can also use the options on the MAILINGS tab, which streamlines the process and offers more tools. In this tutorial, you'll work with the MAILINGS tab to complete the mail merge for Maiya. The MAILINGS tab organizes the steps in the mail merge process so that you can move from left to right across the ribbon using the buttons to complete the merge.

Starting the Mail Merge and Selecting a Main Document

The first step in the mail merge process is selecting the type of main document. Your choice of main document type affects the commands that are available to you later as you continue through the mail merge process, so it's important to make the correct selection at the beginning. In this case, you will use a letter as the main document.

To start the mail merge process and select a main document:

1. On the ribbon, click the **MAILINGS** tab.

   Notice that most of the buttons in the groups on the MAILINGS tab are grayed out, indicating the options are unavailable. These options only become available after you begin the mail merge process and select a data source.

2. In the Start Mail Merge group, click the **Start Mail Merge** button. The Start Mail Merge menu opens, as shown in Figure 6-3.

Figure 6-3 **Start Mail Merge menu**

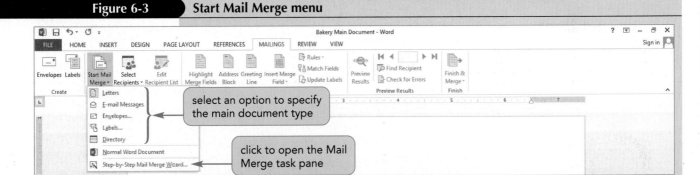

The first five options on the menu allow you to specify the type of main document you will create. Most of the options involve print items, such as labels and letters, but you can also select an email message as the type of main document. In this case, you'll create a letter.

3. Click **Letters**. The Start Mail Merge menu closes.

   Next, you need to select the list of recipients for Maiya's letter; that is, you need to select the data source.

▶ **4.** In the Start Mail Merge group, click the **Select Recipients** button. The Select Recipients menu allows you to create a new recipient list, use an existing list, or select from Outlook Contacts (the address book in Outlook).

Because Maiya hasn't had a chance to create a data source yet, she asks you to create one.

▶ **5.** Click **Type a New List**. The New Address List dialog box opens, as shown in Figure 6-4.

Figure 6-4	New Address List dialog box

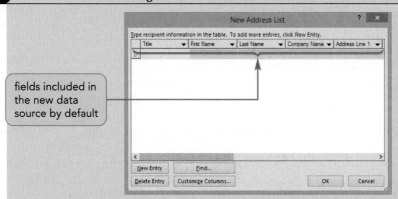

fields included in the new data source by default

The default fields for a data source are displayed in this dialog box. Before you begin creating the data source, you need to identify the fields and records Maiya wants you to include.

Creating a Data Source

As described in the Session 6.1 Visual Overview, a data source is a file that contains information organized into fields and records. Typically, the data source for a mail merge contains a list of names and addresses, but it can also contain email addresses, telephone numbers, and other data. Various kinds of files can be used as the data source, including several types of files from Office applications, such as a Word table stored in a document file, an Excel workbook, or an Access database. You can also use a file from another kind of database, such as one created by a corporation to store its sales information.

When performing a mail merge, you'll usually select an existing data source file—created in another application—that already contains the necessary information. However, in this tutorial, you'll create a new data source in Word and then enter the data into it so you can familiarize yourself with the basic structure of a data source. After creating the new data source, you'll save the file in its default format as an Access database file, with an .mdb file extension. Microsoft Outlook also uses MDB files to store contact information—in which case they are referred to as Microsoft Office Address Lists files.

When you create a new data source, Word provides a number of default fields, such as First Name, Last Name, and Company. You can customize the data source by adding new fields and removing the default fields that you don't plan to use. When creating a data source, keep in mind that each field name must be unique; you can't have two fields with the same name.

The Microsoft Office Address Lists file you will create in this session will contain information about Maiya's customers, including each customer's name, address, preferred type of bread, and favorite pastry. Maiya collected all the necessary information by asking customers to sign up for the bakery's mailing list. Figure 6-5 shows one of the forms she used to collect the information.

Figure 6-5   Customer comment card

© 2014 Cengage Learning

The information on each form will make up one record in the data source. Each blank on the form translates into one field in the data source as shown in Figure 6-6.

Figure 6-6   Fields to include in the data source

Field Names	Description
First Name	Customer's first name
Last Name	Customer's last name
Address Line 1	Customer's street address
Address Line 2	Additional address information, such as an apartment number
City	City
State	State
ZIP Code	Zip code
E-mail Address	Customer's email address
Phone	Customer's home or cell phone number
Favorite Bread	Customer's favorite type of bread
Favorite Pastry	Customer's favorite pastry

© 2014 Cengage Learning

Even though you won't need the customers' email addresses or phone numbers to complete the mail merge, you can still include them in the data source. That way, Maiya can reuse the data source in future mail merges to send emails to her customers, or when creating a directory of phone numbers for home delivery customers.

REFERENCE

Creating a Data Source for a Mail Merge

- On the ribbon, click the MAILINGS tab.
- In the Start Mail Merge group, click the Select Recipients button, and then click Type a New List to open the New Address List dialog box.
- To select the fields for your data source, click the Customize Columns button to open the Customize Address List dialog box.
- To delete an unnecessary field, select it, click the Delete button, and then click the Yes button.
- To add a new field, click the Add button, type the name of the field in the Add Field dialog box, and then click the OK button.
- To rearrange the order of the field names, click a field name, and then click the Move Up button or the Move Down button.
- To rename a field, click a field name, click the Rename button to open the Rename Field dialog box, type a new field name, and then click the OK button to close the Rename Field dialog box.
- Click the OK button to close the Customize Address List dialog box.
- In the New Address List dialog box, enter information for the first record, click the New Entry button, and then enter the information for the next record. Continue until you are finished entering all the information for the data source, and then click the OK button to open the Save Address List dialog box.
- Type a name for the data source in the File name box. By default, Word will save the file to the My Data Sources folder unless you specify another save location. Click the Save button. The file is saved with the .mdb file extension.

You're ready to create the data source for the form letter using information Maiya has given you for three of her customers. However, before you begin entering information, you need to customize the list of fields to include only the fields Maiya requires.

To customize the list of fields before creating the data source:

▶ 1. In the New Address List dialog box, click the **Customize Columns** button. The Customize Address List dialog box opens. Here you can delete the fields you don't need, add new ones, and arrange the fields in the order you want. You'll start by deleting fields.

▶ 2. In the Field Names box, verify that **Title** is selected, and then click the **Delete** button. A message is displayed asking you to confirm the deletion.

▶ 3. Click the **Yes** button. The Title field is deleted from the list of field names.

▶ 4. Continue using the Delete button to delete the following fields: **Company Name**, **Country or Region**, and **Work Phone**.

Next, you need to add some new fields. When you add a new field, it is inserted below the selected field, so you'll start by selecting the last field in the list.

▶ 5. In the Field Names box, click **E-mail Address**, and then click the **Add** button. The Add Field dialog box opens, asking you to type a name for your field. See Figure 6-7.

Figure 6-7 Add Field dialog box

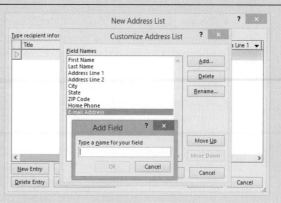

6. Type **Favorite Bread** and then click the **OK** button. The field "Favorite Bread" is added to the Field Names list.

7. Use the Add button to add the **Favorite Pastry** field below the Favorite Bread field.

Next, you need to move the E-mail Address field up above the Home Phone field, so that the fields are in the same order as they appear on the form shown in Figure 6-5.

8. Click **E-mail Address**, and then click the **Move Up** button. The E-mail Address field moves up, so it is now displayed just before the Home Phone field.

Finally, because Maiya's form asks customers to fill in a home or cell phone number, you need to change "Home Phone" to simply "Phone."

9. Click **Home Phone**, and then click the **Rename** button to open the Rename Field dialog box.

10. In the To box, replace "Home Phone" with **Phone** and then click the **OK** button to close the Rename Field dialog box and return to the Customize Address List dialog box. See Figure 6-8.

Figure 6-8 Customized list of field names

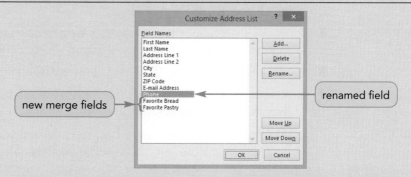

11. Click the **OK** button in the Customize Address List dialog box to close it and return to the New Address List dialog box. This dialog box reflects the changes you just made. For instance, it no longer includes the Title field. The fields are listed in the same order as they appeared in the Customize Address List dialog box.

▶ **12.** Use the horizontal scroll bar near the bottom of the New Address List dialog box to scroll to the right to display the Favorite Bread and Favorite Pastry fields. See Figure 6-9.

| Figure 6-9 | Changes made to New Address List dialog box |

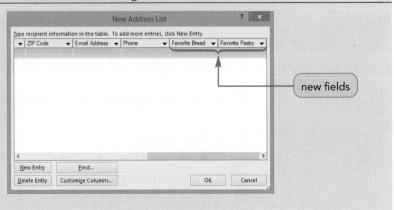

new fields

Organizing Field Names

Although the order of field names in the data source doesn't affect their placement in the main document, it's helpful to arrange field names logically in the data source so you can enter information quickly and efficiently. For example, you'll probably want the First Name field next to the Last Name field. To make it easier to transfer information from a paper form to a data source, it's a good idea to arrange the fields in the same order as on the form, just like you did in the preceding steps. Also, note that if you include spaces in your field names, Word will replace the spaces with underscores when you insert the fields into the main document. For example, Word transforms the field name "First Name" into "First_Name."

Now that you have specified the fields you want to use, you are ready to enter the customer information into the data source.

Entering Data into a Data Source

Maiya has given you three completed customer information forms and has asked you to enter the information from the forms into the data source. You'll use the New Address List dialog box to enter the information. As you press the Tab key to move right from one field to the next, the dialog box will scroll to display fields that are not currently visible.

To enter data into a record using the New Address List dialog box:

▶ **1.** In the New Address List dialog box, scroll to the left to display the First Name field.

▶ **2.** Click in the **First Name** field, if necessary, and then type **Monica** to enter the first name of the first customer.

Do not press the spacebar after you finish typing an entry in the New Address List dialog box.

TIP

You can press the Shift+Tab keys to move the insertion point to the previous field.

3. Press the **Tab** key to move the insertion point to the Last Name field.

4. Type **Piedmont** and then press the **Tab** key to move the insertion point to the Address Line 1 field.

5. Type **45 Fairet Avenue** and then press the **Tab** key to move the insertion point to the Address Line 2 field.

6. Type **Apartment 5A** and then press the **Tab** key to move the insertion point to the City field.

7. Type **Carlyle** and then press the **Tab** key to move the insertion point to the State field.

8. Type **LA** and then press the **Tab** key to move the insertion point to the ZIP Code field.

9. Type **70129** and then press the **Tab** key to move the insertion point to the E-mail Address field.

10. Type **piedmont@sample.cengage.com** and then press the **Tab** key to move the insertion point to the Phone field.

11. Type **555-555-5555** and then press the **Tab** key to move the insertion point to the Favorite Bread field.

12. Type **sourdough** and then press the **Tab** key. The insertion point is now in the Favorite Pastry field, which is the last field in the data source.

13. Type **profiterole** and then stop. Do *not* press the Tab key.

14. Use the horizontal scroll bar to scroll to the left, and then review the data in the record. See Figure 6-10.

Figure 6-10   **Completed record**

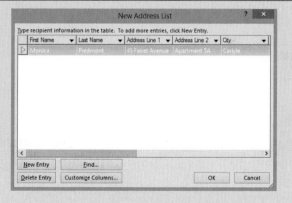

You have finished entering the information for the first record of the data source. Now you're ready to enter information for the next two records. You can create a new record by clicking the New Entry button, or by pressing the Tab key after you have finished entering information into the last field for a record. Note that within a record, you can leave some fields blank. For example, only two of Maiya's three customers included information for the Address Line 2 field.

To add additional records to the data source:

 1. In the New Address List dialog box, click the **New Entry** button. A new, blank record is created.

 2. Enter the information shown in Figure 6-11 for the next two records. To start the Edward Chavezi record, press the **Tab** key after entering the Favorite Pastry field for the Peter Ahrens record.

Figure 6-11		Information for records 2 and 3								
First Name	Last Name	Address Line 1	Address Line 2	City	State	ZIP Code	E-mail Address	Phone	Favorite Bread	Favorite Pastry
Peter	Ahrens	603 Pine Tree Road	P.O. Box 6375	Baptiste	LA	70128	ahrens@sample.cengage.com	555-555-5555	raisin	cinnamon roll
Edward	Chavezi	278 S. Linder		Carlyle	LA	70123	chavezi@sample.cengage.com	555-555-5555	sesame wheat	kolache

© 2014 Cengage Learning

Note that the Address Line 2 field should be blank in the Edward Chavezi record.

Trouble? If you start a fourth record by mistake, click the Delete Entry button to remove the blank fourth record.

You have entered the records for three customers. Maiya's data source eventually will contain hundreds of records for Candlestick Artisan Bakery customers. The current data source, however, contains the records Maiya wants to work with now. Next, you need to save the data source.

Saving a Data Source

TIP

Within File Explorer, the file type for a Microsoft Office Address Lists file is listed as "Microsoft Access Database."

After you finish entering data for your new data source, you can close the New Address List dialog box. When you do so, the Save Address List dialog box opens, where you can save the data source using the default file type, Microsoft Office Address Lists.

To save the data source:

 1. In the New Address List dialog box, click the **OK** button. The New Address List dialog box closes, and the Save Address List dialog box opens, as shown in Figure 6-12.

Figure 6-12 Saving the data source

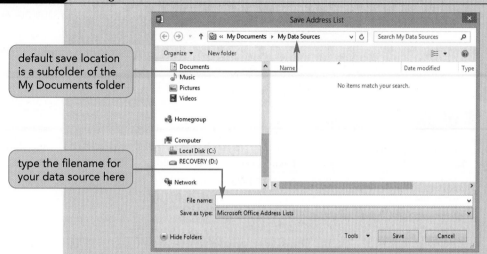

default save location is a subfolder of the My Documents folder

type the filename for your data source here

The Save as type box indicates that the data source will be saved as a Microsoft Office Address Lists file. The File name box is empty; you need to name the file before saving it.

2. Click the **File name** box, if necessary, and then type **Bakery Data**.

Unless you specify another save location, Word will save the file to the My Data Sources folder, which is a subfolder of the My Documents folder.

In this case, you'll save the data source in the same location in which you saved the main document.

3. Navigate to the location in which you saved the main document, and then click the **Save** button. The Save Address List dialog box closes, and you return to the main document.

The next step in the mail merge process is to add the necessary merge fields to the main document. For Maiya's letter, you need to add merge fields for the inside address, for the salutation, and for each customer's favorite type of pastry and bread.

Decision Making: Planning Your Data Source

When creating a data source, think beyond the current mail merge task to possible future uses for your data source. For example, Maiya's data source includes both an E-mail Address field and a Phone field—not because she wants to use that information in the current mail merge project, but because she can foresee needing these pieces of information at a later date to communicate with her customers. Having all relevant customer information in one data source will make it easier to retrieve and use the information effectively.

In some cases, you'll also want to include information that might seem obvious. For example, Maiya's data source includes a State field even though all of her current customers live in or around Carlyle, Louisiana. However, she included a State field because she knows that her pool of addresses could expand sometime in the future to include residents of other states.

Finally, think about the structure of your data source before you create it. Try to break information down into as many fields as seems reasonable. For example, it's always better to include a First Name field and a Last Name field, rather than simply a Name field, because including two separate fields makes it possible to alphabetize the information in the data source by last name. If you entered first and last names in a single Name field, you could only alphabetize by first name.

If you're working with a very small data source, breaking information down into as many fields as possible is less important. However, it's very common to start with a small data source, and then, as time goes on, find that you need to continually add information to the data source, until you have a large file. If you failed to plan the data source adequately at the beginning, the expanded data source could become difficult to manage.

Another important issue is what type of file you use to store your data source. In this session, you created a data source from within Word and saved it as a Microsoft Office Address Lists file. However, in most situations, you should save your data source in a spreadsheet or database file so that you can utilize the data manipulation options a spreadsheet program or database program provides.

Inserting Merge Fields

When inserting merge fields into the main document, you must include proper spacing around the fields so that the information in the merged document will be formatted correctly. To insert a merge field, you move the insertion point to the location where you want to insert the merge field, and then click the Insert Merge Field button arrow in the Write & Insert Fields group.

For Maiya's letter, you will build an inside address by inserting individual merge fields for the address elements. The letter is a standard business letter, so you'll place merge fields for the customer's name and address below the date.

To insert a merge field in the main document:

▶ **1.** Click in the second blank paragraph below the date.

▶ **2.** In the Write & Insert Fields group, click the **Insert Merge Field button arrow**. A menu opens with the names of all the merge fields in the data source. Note that the spaces in the merge field names have been replaced with underscores. See Figure 6-13.

Figure 6-13 Insert Merge Field menu

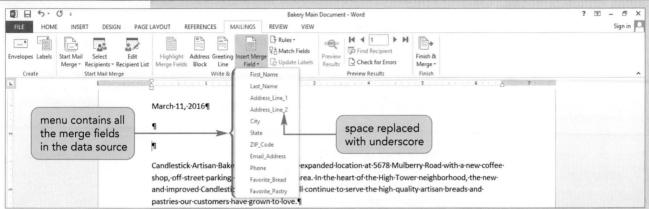

menu contains all the merge fields in the data source

space replaced with underscore

Trouble? If the Insert Merge Field dialog box opens, you clicked the Insert Merge Field button instead of the Insert Merge Field button arrow. Close the dialog box and repeat Step 2.

3. Click **First_Name**. The Insert Merge Field menu closes, and the merge field is inserted into the document.

The merge field consists of the field name surrounded by double angled brackets << >>, also called chevrons.

Trouble? If you make a mistake and insert the wrong merge field, click to the left of the merge field, press the Delete key to select the field, and then press the Delete key again to delete it.

4. In the Write & Insert Fields group, click the **Highlight Merge Fields** button. The First_Name merge field is displayed on a gray background, making it easier to see in the document. See Figure 6-14.

TIP

You can only insert merge fields into a main document using the tools on the MAILINGS tab or in the Mail Merge task pane. You cannot type merge fields into the main document—even if you type the angled brackets.

Figure 6-14 First_Name merge field highlighted in main document

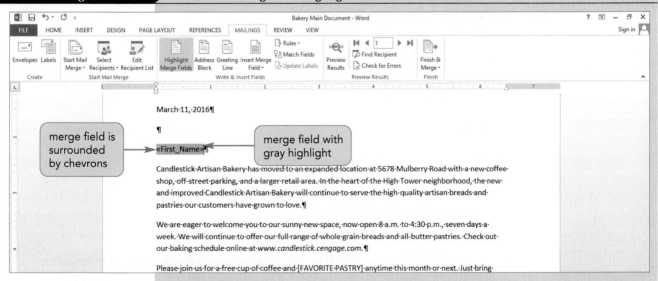

merge field is surrounded by chevrons

merge field with gray highlight

Later, when you merge the main document with the data source, Word will replace the First_Name merge field with information from the First Name field in the data source.

Now, you're ready to insert the merge fields for the rest of the inside address. You'll add the necessary spacing and punctuation between the merge fields as well. You might be accustomed to pressing the Shift+Enter keys to start a new line in an inside address without inserting paragraph spacing. However, because your data source includes a record in which one of the fields (the Address Line 2 field) is blank, you need to press the Enter key to start each new line. As you will see later in this tutorial, this ensures that Word hides the Address Line 2 field in the final merged document whenever that field is blank. To maintain the proper spacing in the main document, you'll adjust the paragraph spacing after you insert all the fields.

To insert the remaining merge fields for the inside address:

▶ **1.** Press the **spacebar** to insert a space after the First_Name merge field, click the **Insert Merge Field button arrow**, and then click **Last_Name**.

▶ **2.** Press the **Enter** key to start a new paragraph, click the **Insert Merge Field button arrow**, and then click **Address_Line_1**. Word inserts the Address_Line_1 merge field into the form letter.

▶ **3.** Press the **Enter** key, click the **Insert Merge Field button arrow**, and then click **Address_Line_2**. Word inserts the Address_Line_2 merge field into the form letter.

▶ **4.** Press the **Enter** key, insert the **City** merge field, type **,** (a comma), press the **spacebar** to insert a space after the comma, and then insert the **State** merge field.

▶ **5.** Press the **spacebar**, and then insert the **ZIP_Code** merge field. The inside address now contains all the necessary merge fields. See Figure 6-15.

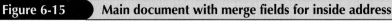
Figure 6-15   **Main document with merge fields for inside address**

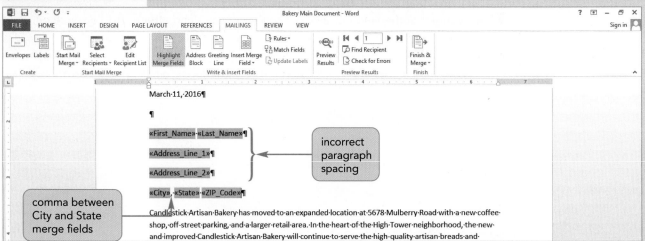

Next, you will adjust the paragraph spacing for the inside address.

▶ **6.** Select the first three paragraphs of the inside address.

▶ **7.** On the ribbon, click the **HOME** tab.

▶ **8.** In the Paragraph group, click the **Line and Paragraph Spacing** button, and then click **Remove Space After Paragraph**. The paragraph spacing is removed, so that the paragraphs of the inside address are now correctly spaced.

You can now add the salutation of the letter, which will contain each customer's first name.

To insert the merge field for the salutation:

▶ **1.** Insert a new paragraph after the ZIP_Code field, type **Dear** and then press the **spacebar**.

▶ **2.** On the ribbon, click the **MAILINGS** tab.

▶ **3.** In the Write & Insert Fields group, click the **Insert Merge Field button arrow**, click **First_Name** to insert this field into the document, and then type **:** (a colon).

▶ **4.** Save the document.

You'll further personalize Maiya's letter by including merge fields that will allow you to reference each customer's favorite type of pastry and bread.

To add merge fields for each customer's favorite type of pastry and bread:

▶ **1.** Scroll down to display the third paragraph in the body of the letter, which begins "Please join us...."

▶ **2.** In the third paragraph in the body of the letter, select the placeholder text **[FAVORITE PASTRY]**, including the brackets. You'll replace this phrase with a merge field. Don't be concerned if you also select the space following the closing bracket.

▶ **3.** Insert the **Favorite_Pastry** merge field. Word replaces the selected text with the Favorite_Pastry merge field.

▶ **4.** Verify that the field has a single space before it and after it. Add a space on either side if necessary.

▶ **5.** Replace the placeholder text "[FAVORITE BREAD]" in the third paragraph in the body of the letter with the **Favorite_Bread** merge field, and adjust the spacing as necessary. See Figure 6-16.

| Figure 6-16 | Main document after inserting merge fields |

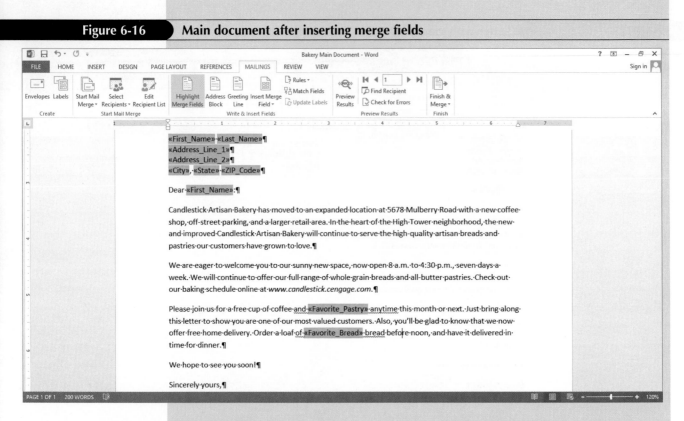

Trouble? The text before and after the inserted merge fields might be marked with a wavy blue underline because Word mistakenly identifies the text as a grammatical error. You can ignore the wavy underlines.

6. Save the document.

The main document now contains all the necessary merge fields.

Previewing the Merged Document

Your next step is to preview the merged document to see how the letter will look after Word inserts the information for each customer. When you preview the merged document, you can check one last time for any missing spaces between the merge fields and the surrounding text. You can also look for any other formatting problems, and, if necessary, make final changes to the data source.

To preview the merged document:

1. In the Preview Results group, click the **Preview Results** button. The data for the first record (Monica Piedmont) replaces the merge fields in the form letter. On the ribbon, the Go to Record box in the Preview Results group shows which record is currently displayed in the document. See Figure 6-17.

Figure 6-17   **Letter with merged data for first record**

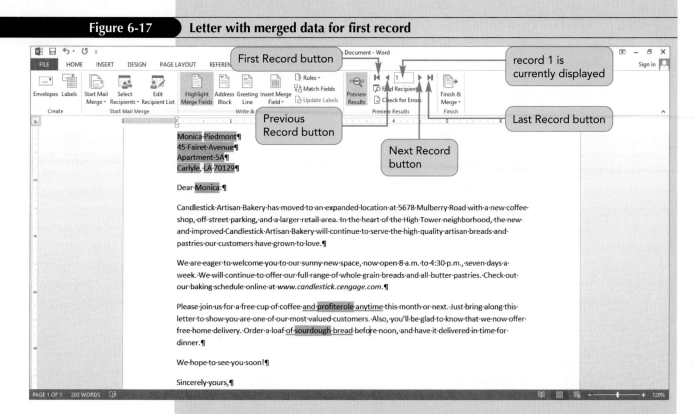

Note that the inside address, which includes information from the Address Line 2 field, contains a total of four lines.

▶ **2.** Carefully check the Monica Piedmont letter to make sure the text and formatting are correct, and make any necessary corrections. In particular, make sure that the spacing before and after the merged data is correct; it is easy to accidentally omit spaces or add extra spaces around merge fields.

▶ **3.** In the Preview Results group, click the **Next Record** button ▶. The data for Peter Ahrens is displayed in the letter. As with the preceding record, the inside address for this record includes four lines of information.

▶ **4.** Click the **Next Record** button ▶ again to display the data for Edward Chavezi in the letter. In this case, the inside address includes only three lines of information. See Figure 6-18.

Figure 6-18   **Address for third record**

▶ **5.** In the Preview Results group, click the **First Record** button ◀ to redisplay the first record in the letter (with data for Monica Piedmont).

The main document of the mail merge is complete. Now that you have previewed the merged documents, you can finish the merge.

Merging the Main Document and the Data Source

When you finish a merge, you can choose to merge directly to the printer. In other words, you can choose to have Word print the merged document immediately without saving it as a separate file. Alternatively, you can merge to a new document, which you can save using a new filename. If your data source includes an E-mail Address field, you can also create a mail merge in email format, generating one email for every email address in the data source.

Maiya wants to save an electronic copy of the merged document for her records, so you'll merge the data source and main document into a new document.

To complete the mail merge:

▶ **1.** In the Finish group, click the **Finish & Merge** button. The Finish & Merge menu displays the three merge options. See Figure 6-19.

| Figure 6-19 | Finishing the merge |

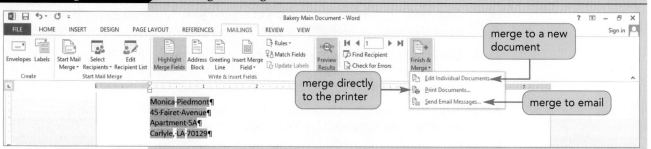

▶ **2.** In the Finish & Merge menu, click **Edit Individual Documents**. The Merge to New Document dialog box opens. Here, you need to specify which records to include in the merge. You want to include all three records from the data source.

▶ **3.** Verify that the **All** option button is selected, and then click the **OK** button. Word creates a new document named Letters1, which contains three pages—one for each record in the data source. See Figure 6-20.

Figure 6-20   Merged document

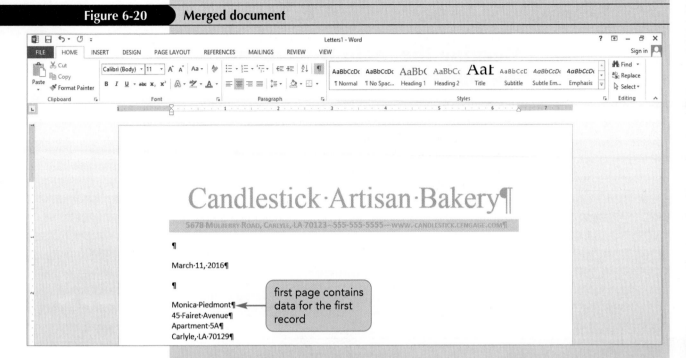

In this new document, the merge fields have been replaced by the specific names, addresses, and so on from the data source.

4. Scroll down and review the contents of the document. Note that each letter is addressed to a different customer, and that the favorite bread and pastry vary from one letter to the next.

5. Scroll back to the first page of the document, and as you scroll, notice that the letters are separated by Next Page section breaks.

6. Save the merged document in the location specified by your instructor, using the filename **Bakery Merged Letters 1**.

7. Close the **Bakery Merged Letters 1** document. The document named "Bakery Main Document" is now the active document.

After completing a merge, you need to save the main document. That ensures that any changes you might have made to the data source during the course of the mail merge are saved along with the main document.

8. Save and close the **Bakery Main Document** file.

Note that if you need to take a break while working on a mail merge, you can save the main document and close it. The data source and field information are saved along with the document. When you're ready to work on the merge again, you can open the main document and update the connection to the data source. You'll see how this works at the beginning of the next session, when you will learn how to use additional mail merge features.

REVIEW

Session 6.1 Quick Check

1. Define the following:
   a. data source
   b. record
   c. date field
2. What is the first step in performing a mail merge?
3. List at least three types of files that you can use as data sources in a mail merge.
4. Explain how to use the options on the MAILINGS tab to insert a merge field into a main document.
5. What are the two ways to start a new record in the New Address List dialog box?
6. List the three different ways to complete a merge.

Session 6.2 Visual Overview:

The Edit Recipient List button opens the Mail Merge Recipients dialog box.

In the Mail Merge Recipients dialog box, you can make changes that affect individual records or the structure and organization of the data source itself.

To sort a data source according to the contents of a particular field, click that field's column header. To sort in ascending order, click the field header once. To sort in descending order, click it twice.

A checkmark indicates that a record will be included in the merge. By default, all records are checked. To omit a record from the merge, click its check box to delete the checkmark.

To make changes to the contents of individual records, select the data source in the Data Source box, and then click the Edit button to open the Edit Data Source dialog box.

To sort by more than one field, click the Sort command.

You can click the Filter command to further customize a data source. When you filter data, you temporarily display only records that contain a particular value in a particular field.

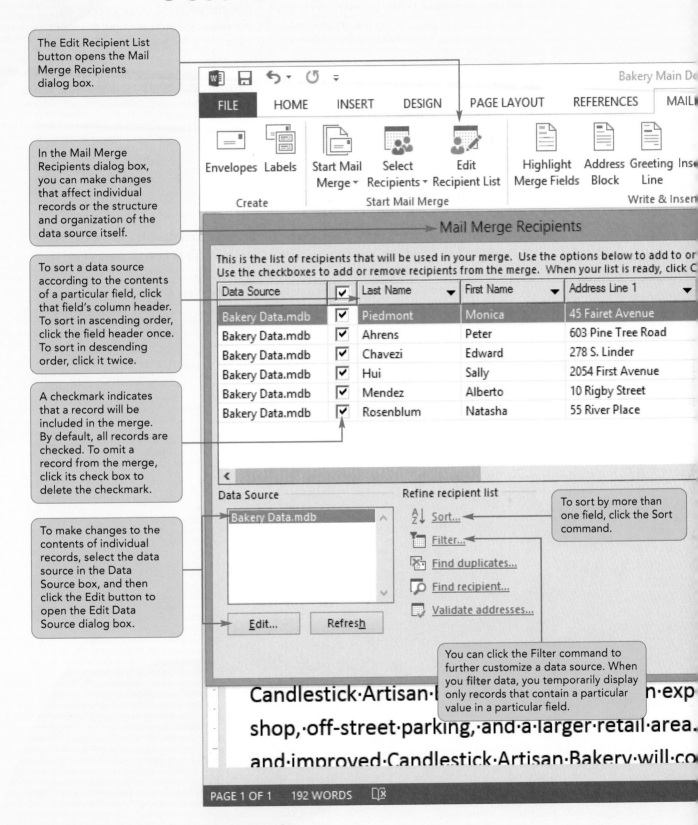

Editing a Data Source

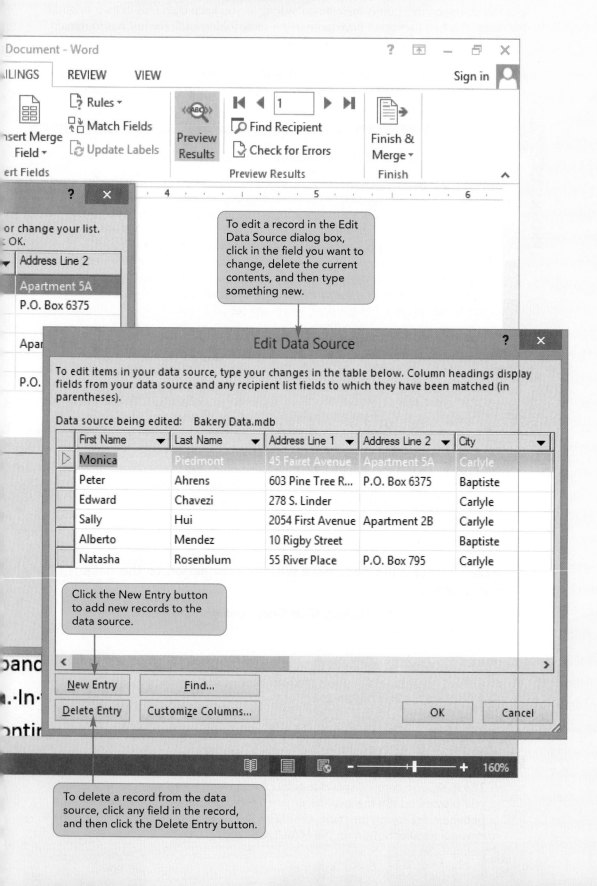

Document - Word

MAILINGS   REVIEW   VIEW   Sign in

Insert Merge Field ▾   Rules ▾   Match Fields   Update Labels   Preview Results |◀ ◀ 1 ▶ ▶| Find Recipient   Check for Errors   Finish & Merge ▾

Insert Fields   Preview Results   Finish

To edit a record in the Edit Data Source dialog box, click in the field you want to change, delete the current contents, and then type something new.

or change your list. OK.

Address Line 2
Apartment 5A
P.O. Box 6375

Apar

P.O.

Edit Data Source

To edit items in your data source, type your changes in the table below. Column headings display fields from your data source and any recipient list fields to which they have been matched (in parentheses).

Data source being edited: Bakery Data.mdb

First Name	Last Name	Address Line 1	Address Line 2	City
Monica	Piedmont	45 Fairet Avenue	Apartment 5A	Carlyle
Peter	Ahrens	603 Pine Tree R...	P.O. Box 6375	Baptiste
Edward	Chavezi	278 S. Linder		Carlyle
Sally	Hui	2054 First Avenue	Apartment 2B	Carlyle
Alberto	Mendez	10 Rigby Street		Baptiste
Natasha	Rosenblum	55 River Place	P.O. Box 795	Carlyle

Click the New Entry button to add new records to the data source.

New Entry   Find...

Delete Entry   Customize Columns...   OK   Cancel

160%

To delete a record from the data source, click any field in the record, and then click the Delete Entry button.

Reopening a Main Document

Performing a mail merge creates a connection between the main document file and the data source file. This connection persists even after you close the main document and exit Word. The connection is maintained as long as you keep both files in their original locations. The two files don't have to be in the same folder; each file just has to remain in the folder it was in when you first performed the mail merge.

When you reopen a main document, you see a warning dialog box explaining that data from a database (that is, the data source) will be placed in the document you are about to open. You can click Yes to open the document with its connection to the data source intact.

PROSKILLS

Teamwork: Sharing Main Documents and Data Sources

In professional settings, a mail merge project often involves files originating from multiple people. The best way to manage these files depends on your particular situation. For instance, at a small office supply company, the marketing manager might supply the text of a main document introducing monthly sales on printer supplies, while the sales manager might supply an updated list of names and addresses of potential customers every month. Suppose that you are the person responsible for performing the mail merge on the first of every month. You'll be able to work more efficiently if you, the marketing manager, and the sales manager agree ahead of time on one storage location for the project. For example, you might set up a special folder on the company network for storing these files.

In large companies that maintain massive databases of customer information, a data source is typically stored at a fixed network location. In those situations, you'll probably need to work with the technical staff who manage the databases to gain access to the data sources you need for your mail merge projects. Maintaining the security of such data sources is extremely important, and you usually can't access them without a password and the appropriate encryption software.

Maiya has new customer information she wants you to add to the data source that you used in the previous mail merge, and she wants to perform another merge with the new data. To add the new customer information, you will start by opening the Bakery Main Document, which is linked to the data source.

To reopen the main document with its connection to the data source intact:

1. Open the document **Bakery Main Document** from the location in which you stored it in Session 6.1.

   Word displays a warning message indicating that opening the document will run a SQL command. SQL (usually pronounced *sequel*) is the database programming language that controls the connection between the main document and the data source.

2. Click the **Yes** button to open the main document with its link to the data source intact.

3. On the ribbon, click the **MAILINGS** tab.

   The main document displays the data for the last record you examined when you previewed the merged document (Monica Piedmont). You can alternate between displaying the merge fields and the customer data by toggling the Preview Results button on the MAILINGS tab.

Trouble? If you see the merge fields instead of the data for one of the bakery customers, skip to Step 5.

4. In the Preview Results group, click the **Preview Results** button to deselect it. The merge fields are displayed in the main document. At the beginning of the letter, the date field, which is not a merge field, continues to display the current date.

5. If necessary, highlight the merge fields by clicking the **Highlight Merge Fields** button in the Write & Insert Fields group.

Maintaining, Breaking, and Reestablishing the Connection to a Data Source

As you have seen, when you reopen a main document, Word displays a warning dialog box, where you can click Yes to open the document with its connection to the data source intact. But what if you want to break the connection between the main document and the data source? One option is to click No in the warning dialog box. In that case, the main document opens with no connection to the data source. If the main document is currently open and already connected to the data source, you can break the connection by clicking Normal Word Document on the Start Mail Merge menu. You can reestablish the connection at any time by starting the mail merge over again and using the Select Recipients button to select the data source.

Keep in mind that you could also break the connection between a main document and its data source if you move one or both of the files to a different folder. Exactly what happens in this case depends on how your computer is set up and where you move the files. In the case of a broken connection, when you open the main document, you'll see a series of message boxes informing you that the connection to the data source has been broken. Eventually, you will see a Microsoft Word dialog box with a button labeled Find Data Source, which you can click, and then use the Select Data Source dialog box to locate and select your data source.

If you are creating mail merges for personal use, it's a good idea to either store the data source in the default My Data Sources folder and keep it there, or store the data source and the main document in the same folder (a folder other than the My Data Sources folder). The latter option is best if you think you might need to move the files to a different computer. That way, if you do need to move them, you can move the entire folder.

Editing a Data Source

After you complete a mail merge, you might need to make some changes to the data source and redo the merge. You can edit a data source in two ways—from within the program used to create the data source, or via the Mail Merge Recipients dialog box in Word. If you are familiar with the program used to create the data source, the simplest approach is to edit the file from within that program. For example, if you were using an Excel worksheet as your data source, you could open the file in Excel, edit it (perhaps by adding new records), save it, and then reselect the file as your data source. To edit the Microsoft Office Address Lists file that you created as a data source for this project, you can use the Mail Merge Recipients dialog box.

Editing a Microsoft Office Address Lists Data Source in Word

- Open the main document for the data source you want to edit.
- On the ribbon, click the MAILINGS tab.
- In the Start Mail Merge group, click the Edit Recipient List button.
- In the Data Source box in the Mail Merge Recipients dialog box, select the data source you want to edit, and then click the Edit button.
- To add a record, click the New Entry button, and then enter the data for the new record.
- To delete a record, click any field in the record, and then click the Delete Entry button.
- To add or remove fields from the data source, click the Customize Columns button, click Yes in the warning dialog box, make any changes, and then click the OK button. Remember that if you remove a field, you will delete any data entered into that field for all records in the data source.
- Click the OK button in the Edit Data Source dialog box, click the Yes button in the Microsoft Office Word dialog box, and then click the OK button in the Mail Merge Recipients dialog box.

Maiya would like you to add information for three new customers to the data source.

To edit the data source by adding records:

1. In the Start Mail Merge group, click the **Edit Recipient List** button. The Mail Merge Recipients dialog box opens, displaying the contents of the data source that is currently connected to the main document—the Bakery Data file.

   This dialog box is designed to let you edit any data source, not just the one currently connected to the main document. To edit the Bakery Data file, you first need to select it in the Data Source box in the lower-left corner. If you had multiple data sources stored in the same folder as the Bakery Data file, you would see them all in this list box.

2. In the Data Source box, click **Bakery Data.mdb**. The filename is selected.

   Note that the file has the extension .mdb, which is the file extension for an Access database file—the default format for a data source created in Word. See Figure 6-21.

Figure 6-21   **Bakery Data.mdb file selected in the Mail Merge Recipients dialog box**

data source is an Access database file with an .mdb file extension

click to select the data source

Edit button

Mail Merge Recipients

This is the list of recipients that will be used in your merge. Use the options below to add to or change your list. Use the checkboxes to add or remove recipients from the merge. When your list is ready, click OK.

Data Source	✓	Last Name	First Name	Address Line 1	Address Line 2
Bakery Data.mdb	✓	Piedmont	Monica	45 Fairet Avenue	Apartment 5A
Bakery Data.mdb	✓	Ahrens	Peter	603 Pine Tree Road	P.O. Box
Bakery Data.mdb	✓	Chavezi	Edward	278 S. Linder	

Data Source

Bakery Data.mdb

Refine recipient list

Sort...
Filter...
Find duplicates...
Find recipient...
Validate addresses...

Edit...   Refresh

OK

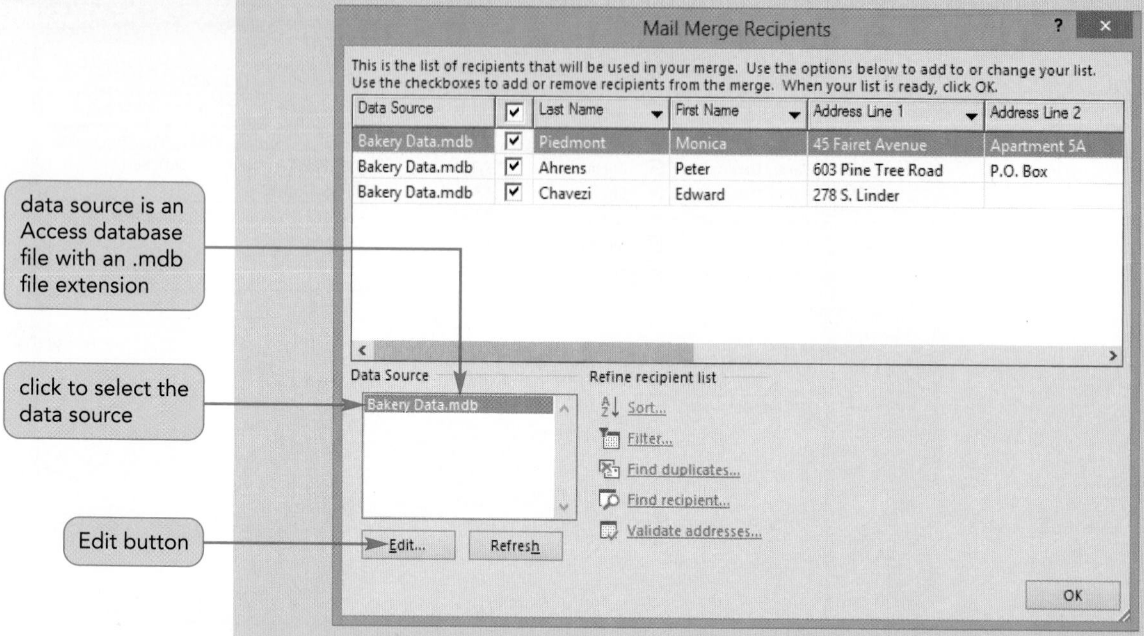

3. Click the **Edit** button. The Edit Data Source dialog box opens.

4. Click the **New Entry** button, and then enter the information for the three new records shown in Figure 6-22.

Figure 6-22   **New customer data**

First Name	Last Name	Address Line 1	Address Line 2	City	State	Zip Code	E-Mail Address	Phone	Favorite Bread	Favorite Pastry
Sally	Hui	2054 First Avenue	Apartment 2B	Carlyle	LA	70129	hui@sample.cengage.com	555-555-5555	sourdough	cinnamon roll
Alberto	Mendez	10 Rigby Street		Baptiste	LA	70128	mendez@sample.cengage.com	555-555-5555	sourdough	profiterole
Natasha	Rosenblum	55 River Place	P.O. Box 795	Carlyle	LA	70123	rosenblum@sample.cengage.com	555-555-5555	raisin	cinnamon roll

© 2014 Cengage Learning

When you are finished, you will have a total of six records in the data source. Notice that the record for Alberto Mendez contains no data in the Address Line 2 field.

5. Click the **OK** button, and then click the **Yes** button in the message box that asks if you want to update the Bakery Data.mdb file. You return to the Mail Merge Recipients dialog box, as shown in Figure 6-23.

Figure 6-23   New records added to data source

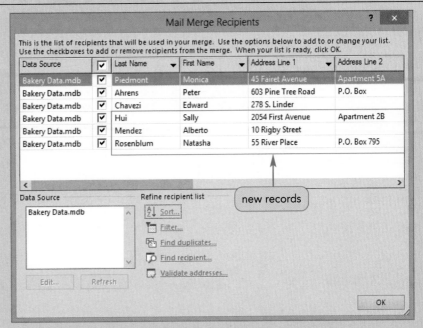

Trouble? If your records look different from those in Figure 6-23, select the data source, click the Edit button, edit the data source, and then click the OK button.

You'll leave the Mail Merge Recipients dialog box open so you can use it to make other changes to the data source.

Sorting Records

You can sort, or rearrange, information in a data source table just as you can sort information in any other table. To quickly sort information in ascending order (*A* to *Z*, lowest to highest, or earliest to latest) or in descending order (*Z* to *A*, highest to lowest, or latest to earliest), click a field's heading in the Mail Merge Recipients dialog box. The first time you click the heading, the records are sorted in ascending order. If you click it a second time, the records are sorted in descending order.

To perform a more complicated sort, you can click the Sort command in the Mail Merge Recipients dialog box to open the Filter and Sort dialog box, where you can choose to sort by more than one field. For example, you could sort records in ascending order by last name, and then in ascending order by first name. In that case, the records would be organized alphabetically by last name, and then, in cases where multiple records contained the same last name, those records would be sorted by first name.

REFERENCE

Sorting a Data Source by Multiple Fields

- On the ribbon, click the MAILINGS tab.
- In the Start Mail Merge group, click the Edit Recipient List button to open the Mail Merge Recipients dialog box.
- Click Sort to open the Sort Records tab in the Filter and Sort dialog box.
- Click the Sort by arrow, select the first field you want to sort by, and then select either the Ascending option button or the Descending option button.
- Click the Then by arrow, select the second field you want to sort by, and then select either the Ascending option button or the Descending option button.
- If necessary, click the Then by arrow, select the third field you want to sort by, and then select either the Ascending option button or the Descending option button.
- Click the OK button to close the Filter and Sort dialog box.
- Click the OK button to close the Mail Merge Recipients dialog box.

As Maiya looks through the letters to her customers in the merged document, she notices one problem—the letters are not grouped by zip codes. Currently, the letters are in the order in which customers were added to the data source file. Maiya plans to use business mail (also known as bulk mail) to send her letters, and the U.S. Postal Service offers lower rates for mailings that are separated into groups according to zip code. She asks you to sort the data file by zip code and then by last name, and then merge the main document with the sorted data source.

To sort the data source by zip code:

1. In the Mail Merge Recipients dialog box, click **Sort**. The Filter and Sort dialog box opens, with the Sort Records tab displayed.

2. Click the **Sort by** arrow to display a menu, scroll down in the menu, and then click **ZIP Code**. The Ascending button is selected by default, which is what you want.

3. In the Then by box, directly below the Sort by box, click the **Then by** arrow, and then click **Last Name**. See Figure 6-24.

Figure 6-24   Sorting by zip code and by last name

4. Click the **OK** button. Word sorts the records from lowest zip code number to highest; and then, within each zip code, it sorts the records by last name.

   In the Mail Merge Recipients dialog box, the record for Edward Chavezi, with zip code 70123, is now at the top of the data source list. The record for Natasha Rosenblum, which also has a zip code of 70123, comes second. The remaining records are sorted similarly, with the record for Monica Piedmont the last in the list. When you merge the data source with the form letter, the letters will appear in the merged document in this order.

5. Click the **OK** button. The Mail Merge Recipients dialog box closes.

6. On the MAILINGS tab, in the Preview Results group, click the **Preview Results** button. The data for Edward Chavezi is displayed in the main document.

7. In the Finish group, click the **Finish & Merge** button, and then click **Edit Individual Documents**.

8. In the Merge to New Document dialog box, verify that the **All** option button is selected, and then click the **OK** button. Word generates the new merged document with six letters—one letter per page as before, but this time the first letter is addressed to Edward Chavezi.

9. Scroll down and verify that the letters in the newly merged document are arranged in ascending order by zip code and then in ascending order by last name.

10. Save the new merged document in the location specified by your instructor, using the filename **Bakery Merged Letters 2**, and then close it. You return to the Bakery Main Document.

11. Save the **Bakery Main Document** file and keep it open for the next set of steps.

Next, Maiya would like you to create a set of letters to send to customers who listed "cinnamon roll" as their favorite pastry.

Filtering Records

TIP

To omit an individual record from a merge, you can deselect the corresponding check box in the Mail Merge Recipients dialog box rather than using a filter.

Maiya wants to inform customers that cinnamon rolls are now available with or without pecans. She asks you to modify the form letter and then merge it with the records of customers who have indicated that cinnamon rolls are their favorite pastry. To select specific records in a data source, you filter the data source to temporarily display only the records containing a particular value in a particular field.

To filter the data source to select specific records for the merge:

1. In the Preview Results group, click the **Preview Results** button to deselect it and display the merge fields in the Bakery Main Document file instead of the data from the data source.

2. Save the Bakery Main Document with the new name **Cinnamon Main Document** in the location specified by your instructor.

3. In the document, scroll down to the third paragraph in the body of the letter, and then click to the right of the Favorite_Pastry merge field.

4. Insert a space, type **(now available with or without pecans)** and then verify that the sentence reads "Please join us for a free cup of coffee and <<Favorite_Pastry>> (now available with or without pecans) anytime this month or next."

5. In the Start Mail Merge group, click the **Edit Recipient List** button to open the Mail Merge Recipients dialog box, and then scroll to the right so you can see the Favorite Pastry field.

6. In the header row, click the **Favorite Pastry** arrow. A menu opens, listing all the entries in the Favorite Pastry field as well as a few other options. See Figure 6-25.

Figure 6-25   Filtering records in a data source

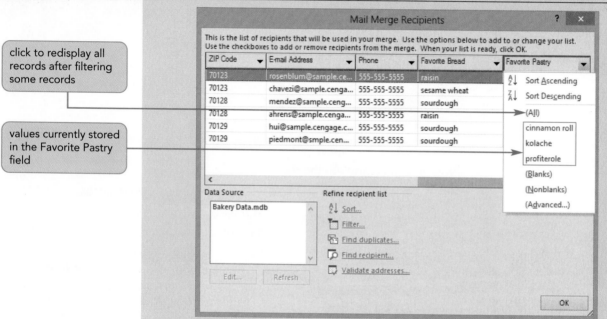

click to redisplay all records after filtering some records

values currently stored in the Favorite Pastry field

Trouble? If the records sort by Favorite Pastry, with all the records for cinnamon rolls at the top, you clicked the Favorite Pastry column header instead of the arrow. That's not a problem; you don't need to undo the sort. Repeat Step 6, taking care to click the arrow.

You can use the "(All)" option to redisplay all records after previously filtering a data source. The "(Advanced)" option takes you to the Filter Records tab in the Filter and Sort dialog box, where you can perform complex filter operations that involve comparing the contents of one or more fields to a particular value to determine if a record should be displayed or not. In this case, however, you can use an option in this menu.

7. Click **cinnamon roll**. Word temporarily hides all the records in the data source except those that contain "cinnamon roll" in the Favorite Pastry field. See Figure 6-26.

| Figure 6-26 | Filtered data source |

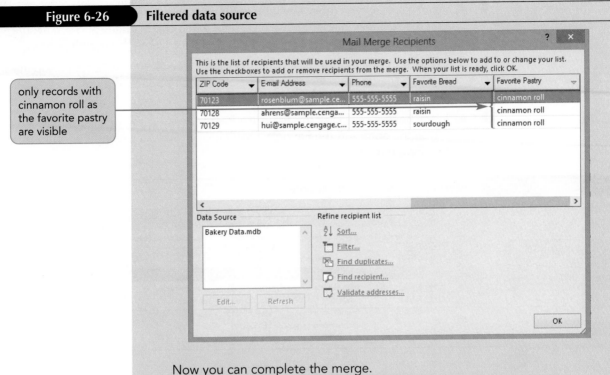

only records with cinnamon roll as the favorite pastry are visible

Now you can complete the merge.

8. Click the **OK** button. The Mail Merge Recipients dialog box closes.

9. In the Preview Results group, click the **Preview Results** button, and then review the three records for Natasha Rosenblum, Peter Ahrens, and Sally Hui as they appear in the main document.

10. In the Finish group, click the **Finish & Merge** button, and then click **Edit Individual Documents**. In the Merge to New Document dialog box, verify that the **All** option button is selected, and then click the **OK** button. Word generates the merged document with three letters—one letter per page.

11. Save the merged document with the filename **Bakery Merged Letters 3** in the location specified by your instructor, and then close it.

12. Save the **Cinnamon Main Document** file, and then close it.

Next, you'll create and print mailing labels for the form letters.

Creating Mailing Labels

Maiya could print the names and addresses for the letters directly on envelopes, or she could perform a mail merge to create mailing labels. The latter method is easier because she can print 14 labels at once rather than printing one envelope at a time.

Maiya has purchased Avery® Laser Printer labels, which are available in most office-supply stores. Word supports most of the Avery label formats, allowing you to choose the layout that works best for you. Maiya purchased labels in 8 1/2 × 11-inch sheets that are designed to feed through a printer. Each label measures 4 × 1.33 inches. Each sheet contains seven rows of labels, with two labels in each row, for a total of 14 labels. See Figure 6-27.

TIP

It is a good idea to print one page of a label document on regular paper so you can check your work before printing on the more expensive sheets of adhesive labels.

Figure 6-27   **Layout of a sheet of Avery® labels**

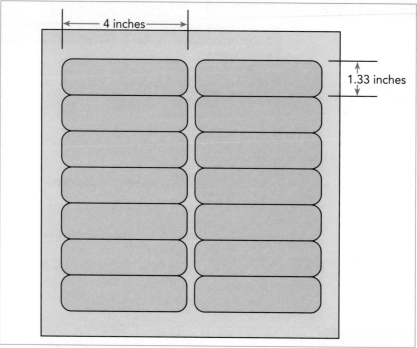

© 2014 Cengage Learning

Performing a mail merge to create mailing labels is similar to performing a mail merge to create a form letter. You begin by selecting Labels as the type of main document, and then you specify the brand and product number for the labels you are using. You will also need to specify a data source file. In this case, you'll use the Microsoft Office Address Lists data source file, Bakery Data.mdb, which you created and used in the form letter mail merges.

To specify the main document for creating mailing labels:

1. Open a new, blank document, and then save the document as **Bakery Labels Main Document** in the location specified by your instructor.

2. Make sure nonprinting characters are displayed, and zoom out so you can see the whole page.

3. On the ribbon, click the **MAILINGS** tab.

4. In the Start Mail Merge group, click the **Start Mail Merge** button.

    At this point, if you wanted to merge to envelopes instead of labels, you could click Envelopes to open the Envelope Option dialog box, where you could select the envelope size you wanted to use. In this case, however, you want to merge to labels.

5. Click **Labels**. The Label Options dialog box opens.

6. Click the **Label vendors** arrow to display a list of vendors, scroll down, and then click **Avery US Letter**.

7. Scroll down the Product number box, and then click **5162 Easy Peel Address Labels**. See Figure 6-28.

Figure 6-28   **Label Options dialog box**

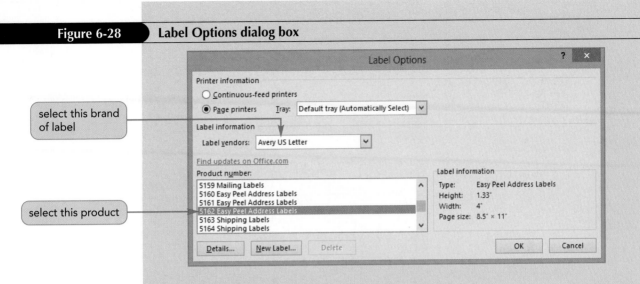

select this brand of label

select this product

8. Click the **OK** button. The Label Options dialog box closes, and Word inserts a table structure into the document, with one cell for each of the 14 labels on the page, as shown in Figure 6-29.

Figure 6-29   **Document ready for labels**

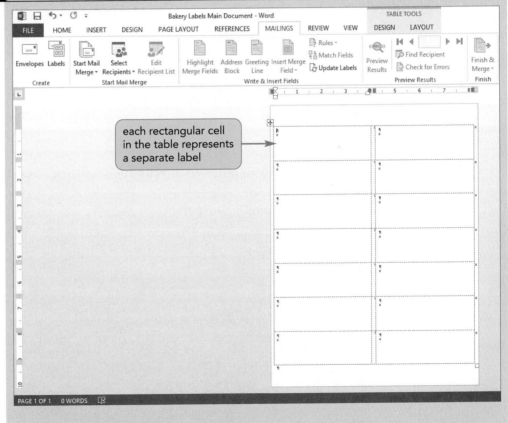

each rectangular cell in the table represents a separate label

As with all table gridlines, these gridlines are visible only on the screen; they will not be visible on the printed labels.

Trouble? If you don't see the table gridlines, click the TABLE TOOLS LAYOUT tab, and then, in the Table group, click the View Gridlines button to select it.

You have finished setting up the document. Next, you need to select the data source you created earlier. Note that the changes you made to the data source as a whole earlier in this session (sorting the records and selecting only some records) have no effect on the data source in this new mail merge. However, the changes you made to individual records (such as editing individual records or adding new records) are retained.

To continue the mail merge for the labels:

1. In the Start Mail Merge group, click the **Select Recipients** button, and then click **Use an Existing List**. The Select Data Source dialog box opens.

2. Navigate to the location where you stored the Bakery Data file, select the **Bakery Data** file, and then click the **Open** button. The Select Data Source dialog box closes and you return to the main document.

3. Change the Zoom level to **120%** so you can read the document.

   In each label except the first one, the code <<Next Record>> is displayed. This code tells Word to retrieve the next record from the data source for each label.

4. Verify that the insertion point is located in the upper-left label, and make sure the MAILINGS tab is still selected on the ribbon.

TIP

You can only use the AddressBlock merge field if you include a State field in your data source.

5. In the Write & Insert Fields group, click the **Address Block** button. The Insert Address Block dialog box opens. The left pane displays possible formats for the name in the address block. The default format, "Joshua Randall Jr.," simply inserts the first and last name, which is what Maiya wants. The Preview pane on the right currently shows the first address in the data source, which is the address for Monica Piedmont.

6. In the Preview section of the Insert Address Field dialog box, click the **Next** button ▷. The record for Peter Ahrens is displayed in the Preview pane, as shown in Figure 6-30.

Figure 6-30 **Previewing addresses in the Insert Address Block dialog box**

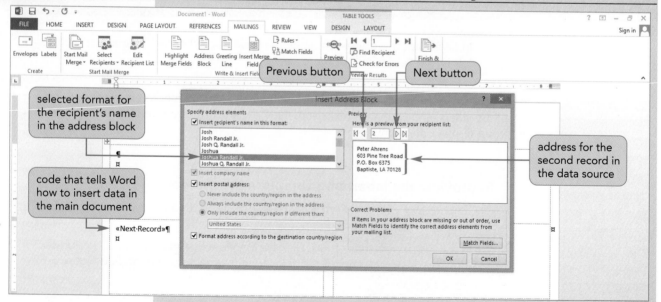

7. Click the **OK** button. The Insert Address Block dialog box closes, and an AddressBlock merge field is displayed in the upper-left label on the page. Next, you need to update the remaining labels to match the one containing the AddressBlock merge field.

8. In the Write & Insert Fields group, click the **Update Labels** button. The AddressBlock merge field is inserted into all the labels in the document, as shown in Figure 6-31.

Figure 6-31   **Field codes inserted into document**

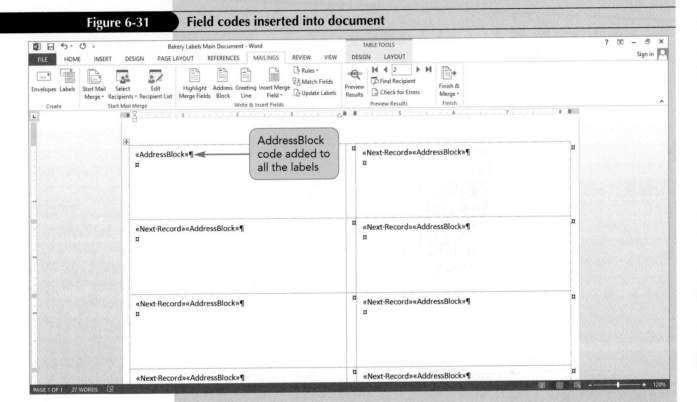

In all except the upper-left label, the Next Record code is displayed to the left of the AddressBlock merge field.

You are ready to preview the labels and complete the merge. To ensure that you see all the labels in the preview, make sure the Go to Record box in the Preview Results group displays the number "1".

To preview the labels and complete the merge:

1. If necessary, click the **First Record** button [K] in the Preview Results group to display "1" in the Go to Record box.

2. In the Preview Results group, click the **Preview Results** button. The addresses for Maiya's six customers are displayed in the main document. See Figure 6-32.

| Figure 6-32 | Previewing addresses in labels |

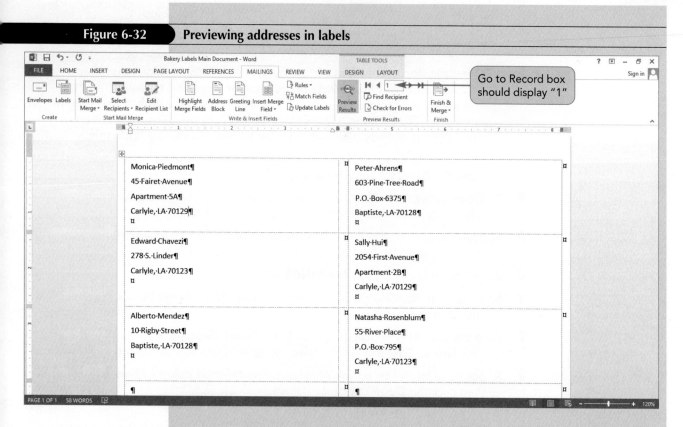

3. In the Finish group, click the **Finish & Merge** button, and then click **Edit Individual Documents**.

4. In the Merge to New Document dialog box, verify that the **All** option button is selected, and then click the **OK** button. The finished labels are inserted into a new document named Labels1.

5. Scroll through the document. The document contains space for 14 labels; but because the data source contains only six records, the new document only contains addresses for six labels.

6. In the upper-left label, change "Monica Piedmont" to your first and last names, and then save the merged document as **Bakery Merged Labels** in the location specified by your instructor.

7. Close the **Bakery Merged Labels** document, then save and close the **Bakery Labels Main Document** file.

Creating a Telephone Directory

Next, Maiya wants you to create a telephone directory for all bakery employees. Maiya has already created a Word document containing the phone numbers; you will use that document as the data source for the merge. You'll set up a mail merge as before, except this time you will select Directory as the main document type. You'll start by examining the Word document that Maiya wants you to use as the data source, and then you'll create the main document.

To review the data source and create the main document for the directory:

▶ 1. Open the document **Phone** from the Word6 ▶ Tutorial folder, and then save it as **Bakery Phone Data** in the location specified by your instructor. The information in this document is arranged in a table with three column headings—"First Name," "Last Name," and "Phone." The information in the table has already been sorted in alphabetical order by last name.

▶ 2. Replace "Maiya Kandel" with your first and last names, and then save and close the **Bakery Phone Data** document.

▶ 3. Open a new, blank document, display nonprinting characters and the rulers, if necessary, and then change the Zoom level to **120%**.

▶ 4. Save the main document as **Bakery Directory Main Document** in the location in which you saved the Bakery Phone Data document.

▶ 5. On the ribbon, click the **MAILINGS** tab.

▶ 6. In the Start Mail Merge group, click the **Start Mail Merge** button, and then click **Directory**.

▶ 7. In the Start Mail Merge group, click the **Select Recipients** button, and then click **Use an Existing List** to open the Select Data Source dialog box.

▶ 8. Navigate to and select the Word document named **Bakery Phone Data**, and then click the **Open** button.

You're ready to insert the fields in the main document. Maiya wants the directory to include the names at the left margin of the page and the phone numbers at the right margin, with a dot leader in between. Recall that a dot leader is a dotted line that extends from the last letter of text on the left margin to the beginning of the nearest text aligned at a tab stop.

To set up the directory main document with dot leaders:

▶ 1. With the insertion point in the first line of the document, insert the **First_Name** merge field, insert a space, and then insert the **Last_Name** merge field.

▶ 2. In the Write & Insert Fields group, click the **Highlight Merge Fields** button. The First_Name and Last_Name merge fields are displayed on a gray background. Now you'll set a tab stop at the right margin (at the 6-inch mark on the horizontal ruler) with a dot leader.

▶ 3. On the ribbon, click the **HOME** tab.

TIP

You can click the Clear All button in the Tabs dialog box to delete all the tab stops in the document.

▶ 4. In the Paragraph group, click the **Dialog Box Launcher** to open the Paragraph dialog box, and then in the lower-left corner of the Indents and Spacing tab, click the **Tabs** button. The Tabs dialog box opens.

▶ 5. In the Tab stop position box, type **6**, and then click the **Right** option button in the Alignment section.

▶ 6. Click the **2 ....** option button in the Leader section. See Figure 6-33.

Figure 6-33   Creating a tab with a dot leader

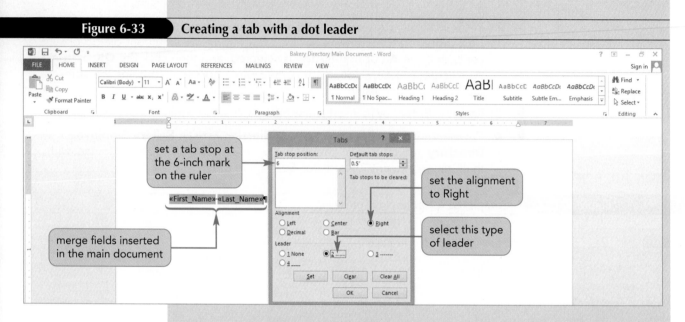

7. Click the **OK** button. Word clears the current tab stops and inserts a right-aligned tab stop at the 6-inch mark on the horizontal ruler.

8. Press the **Tab** key to move the insertion point to the new tab stop. A dotted line stretches across the page, from the Last_Name merge field to the right margin.

9. On the ribbon, click the **MAILINGS** tab.

> Be sure to press the Enter key here to ensure that each name and telephone number is displayed on a separate line.

10. Insert the **Phone** merge field at the insertion point. The dot leader shortens to accommodate the inserted merge fields.

11. Press the **Enter** key. The completed main document should look like the one shown in Figure 6-34.

Figure 6-34   Completed main document for the telephone directory

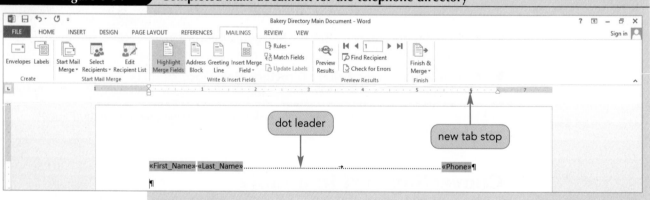

You are now ready to merge this file with the data source.

To finish the merge for the telephone directory:

1. In the Preview Results group, click the **Preview Results** button, and then review the data for the first record in the document.

▶ **2.** In the Finish group, click the **Finish & Merge** button, and then click **Edit Individual Documents**. In the Merge to New Document dialog box, verify that the **All** option button is selected, and then click the **OK** button. Word creates a new document named Directory1 that contains the completed telephone list.

▶ **3.** Press the **Enter** key to insert a new paragraph at the beginning of the document.

▶ **4.** Click in the new paragraph, type **Candlestick Artisan Bakery Employee Directory** and then format the new text in 22-point, Times New Roman, with the Orange, Accent 2 font color. See Figure 6-35.

| Figure 6-35 | Completed telephone directory |

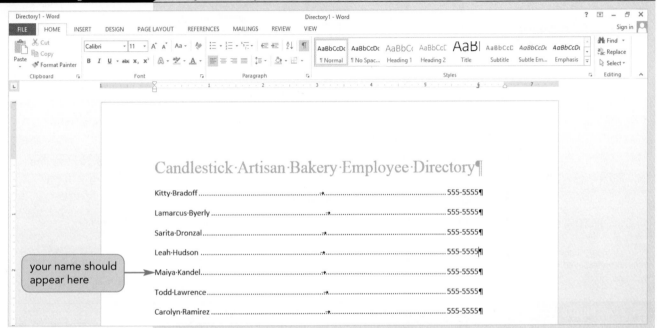

> your name should appear here

▶ **5.** Save the document as **Bakery Merged Directory** in the location in which you saved the main document, and then close it.

▶ **6.** Save and close the **Bakery Directory Main Document** file.

Maiya needs your help with one other task related to managing information about the bakery's customers and employees.

Converting Text to a Table

TIP

To convert a table to text, click in the table, click the TABLE TOOLS LAYOUT tab, click Convert to Text in the Data group, click the separator you prefer, and then click OK.

To be completely proficient in mail merges, you should be able to take information from a variety of sources and set it up for use as a data source. In particular, it's helpful to be able to convert text to a table. For example, address information exported from email and contact management programs often takes the form of a **CSV (comma-separated value) file**, a text file in which each paragraph contains one record, with the fields separated by commas. CSV files can have a .txt or .csv file extension. The commas in a CSV file are known as **separator characters**, or sometimes **delimiters**.

You can use the Convert Text to Table command on the Table menu to transform text from a Word document or a CSV file into a table. But first you need to make sure the text is set up correctly; that is, you need to make sure that separator characters are used

consistently to divide the text into individual fields. In a CSV file, commas are used as separator characters, but you might encounter a Word document that uses tab characters, or other characters, as separator characters. After you verify that separator characters are used consistently within a document, you need to make sure each paragraph in the document contains the same number of fields.

Upon conversion, each field is formatted as a separate cell in a column, and each paragraph mark starts a new row, or record. Sometimes a conversion might not turn out the way you expect. In that case, undo it and then review the text to make sure each paragraph contains the same number of data items, with the items divided by the same separator character.

Maiya's assistant, who isn't familiar with Word tables, typed some information about new customers as text in a Word document. She forgot to include an email address and phone number for each customer. Maiya wants to convert the text to a table, and then add columns for the missing information. The next time the customers visit the bakery, she can ask them for the missing information and then add it to the table.

To convert text into a table:

1. Open the document named **Customer** from the Word6 ▸ Tutorial folder, and then save it as **Customer Table** in the location specified by your instructor.

2. Display nonprinting characters, if necessary, and then change the Zoom level to **120%**. See Figure 6-36.

Figure 6-36	Text with inconsistent separator characters

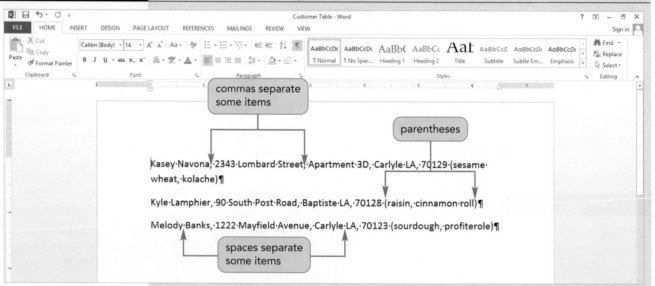

The document consists of three paragraphs, each of which contains a customer's name, address, city, state, zip code, favorite bread, and favorite pastry. Some of the fields are separated by commas and spaces (for example, the address and the city), but some are only separated by spaces, with no punctuation character (for example, the first and last names). Also, the favorite bread and favorite pastry are enclosed in parentheses. You need to edit this information so that fields are separated by commas, with no parentheses enclosing the last two items.

3. Edit the document to insert a comma after each first name, city, and zip code, and then delete the parentheses in each paragraph.

Before you can convert the text into a table, you also need to make sure each paragraph includes the same fields. Currently, the first paragraph includes two pieces of address information—a street address and an apartment number, which is equivalent to an Address Line 1 field and an Address Line 2 field. However, the other paragraphs only include an Address Line 1 field.

▶ **4.** In the second paragraph, click to the right of the comma after "Road," press the **spacebar**, and then type **,** (a comma).

▶ **5.** In the third paragraph, click to the right of the comma after "Avenue," press the **spacebar**, and then type **,** (a comma). Now the second and third paragraphs each contain a blank field. See Figure 6-37.

Figure 6-37 **Text set up for conversion to a table**

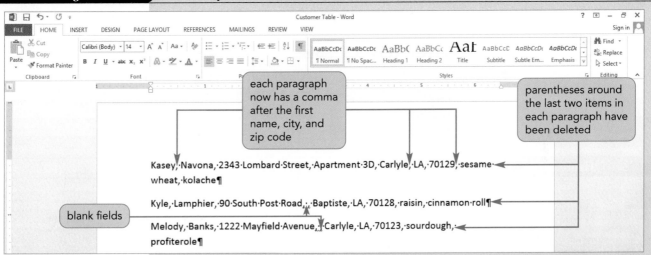

> each paragraph now has a comma after the first name, city, and zip code

> parentheses around the last two items in each paragraph have been deleted

Kasey,·Navona,·2343·Lombard·Street,·Apartment·3D,·Carlyle,·LA,·70129,·sesame·wheat,·kolache¶

Kyle,·Lamphier,·90·South·Post·Road,·,·Baptiste,·LA,·70128,·raisin,·cinnamon·roll¶

> blank fields

Melody,·Banks,·1222·Mayfield·Avenue,·,·Carlyle,·LA,·70123,·sourdough,·profiterole¶

▶ **6.** Press the **Ctrl+A** keys to select the entire document.

▶ **7.** On the ribbon, click the **INSERT** tab.

▶ **8.** In the Tables group, click the **Table** button, and then click **Convert Text to Table**. The Convert Text to Table dialog box opens. See Figure 6-38.

Figure 6-38 **Converting text to a table**

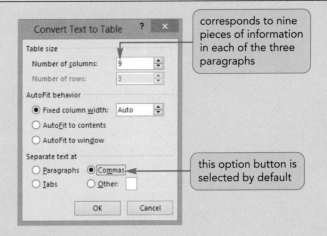

> corresponds to nine pieces of information in each of the three paragraphs

> this option button is selected by default

Note that the Number of columns setting is 9, and the Number of rows setting is 3. This corresponds to the nine fields in each of the three paragraphs.

In the Separate text at section of the dialog box, you can choose from three possible separator characters—paragraphs, commas, and tabs. If the text in your document was separated by a character other than paragraphs, commas, or tabs, you could type the character in the box to the right of the Other button. In this case, though, the default option, Commas, is the correct choice because the information in each paragraph is separated by commas.

9. Click the **OK** button. The Convert Text to Table dialog box closes, and the text in the document is converted into a table consisting of nine columns and three rows.

10. Save the document.

Now that you have converted the text to a table, you need to finish the table by adding the columns for the phone numbers and email addresses, and adding a header row to identify the field names.

To finish the table by adding columns and a header row:

1. Switch to **Landscape** orientation, and then select the column containing the zip codes.

2. On the ribbon, click the **TABLE TOOLS LAYOUT** tab.

3. In the Rows & Columns group, click the **Insert Right** button twice to add two blank columns to the right of the column containing zip codes.

4. Select the table's top row, and then in the Rows & Columns group, click the **Insert Above** button.

5. Enter the column headings shown in Figure 6-39 and format them in bold.

Figure 6-39	Table with new columns and column headings

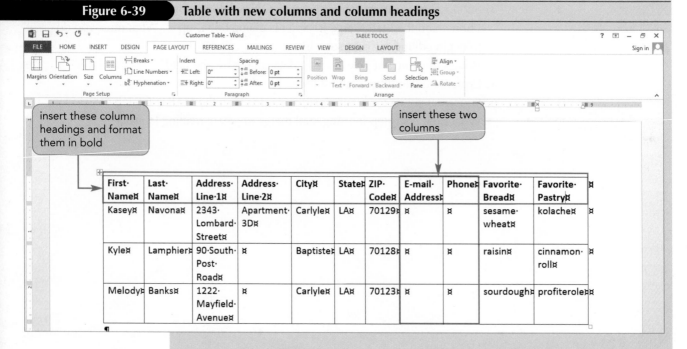

First Name	Last Name	Address Line 1	Address Line 2	City	State	ZIP Code	E-mail Address	Phone	Favorite Bread	Favorite Pastry	
Kasey	Navona	2343 Lombard Street	Apartment 3D	Carlyle	LA	70129			sesame wheat	kolache	
Kyle	Lamphier	90 South Post Road		Baptiste	LA	70128			raisin	cinnamon roll	
Melody	Banks	1222 Mayfield Avenue		Carlyle	LA	70123			sourdough	profiteroles	

insert these column headings and format them in bold

insert these two columns

6. Save the **Customer Table** document, and then close it.

You have finished converting text into a table. Maiya can use the table later as the data source for another mail merge. As her business expands, she plans to continue to use Word's mail merge feature to inform her customers about new products and specials.

Combining Data with a Microsoft Office Address Lists File

If you have data in a Word file that you want to combine with data in a Microsoft Office Address Lists file, or any other Microsoft Access file, start by setting up the Word document as a table. That way, you can be sure that each record includes the same fields. You can also review the table quickly to confirm that you have entered data in the various fields in a consistent format. Once you are confident that you have set up the table correctly, you can begin the process of combining it with the Microsoft Office Address Lists file.

First, delete the heading row, and then convert the table back to text, separating the fields with commas. Next, save the Word file as a Plain Text file with the .txt file extension. Finally, open the Microsoft Office Address Lists file in Access, click the EXTERNAL DATA tab, and then click the Text File button in the Import & Link group to begin importing the text file into the Microsoft Office Address Lists file. In the Get External Data - Text File dialog box, click the Append a copy of the records to the table button, and then click the Browse button to select the plain text file.

Session 6.2 Quick Check

1. What must you do to maintain the connection between a main document and its data source after you close the main document?
2. Assuming Word is running but no documents are open, what's the first step in editing a Microsoft Office Address Lists data source that you created in Word?
3. Suppose you want to edit a Microsoft Office Address Lists data source named Phone, and the Mail Merge Recipients dialog box is open. What must you do to begin editing the data source?
4. What's the quickest way to sort a data source by one field?
5. Explain how to filter a data source.
6. Suppose you have a blank document open with the MAILINGS tab selected. What's the next step in using mail merge to create mailing labels?

SAM Projects

Put your skills into practice with SAM Projects! SAM Projects for this tutorial can be found online. If you have a SAM account, go to www.cengage.com/sam2013 to download the most recent Project Instructions and Start Files.

Review Assignments

Data Files needed for the Review Assignments: Additional.docx, Business.docx, Free.docx

The new and improved Candlestick Artisan Bakery is a big hit. Maiya has greatly expanded her customer base, and she now has a thriving home delivery business. Customers sign up for weekly deliveries with the promise of a free dessert every six months. On the home delivery sign-up form, customers can choose between a free apple tart or chocolate cake. Now she wants to send a letter inviting weekly home delivery customers to reserve their free dessert three days before they want it delivered. She also needs to create a directory of other businesses she deals with frequently. Finally, she needs to convert some additional customer information into a table that she can use as a data source. Complete the following steps:

1. Open the document **Free** from the Word6 ▸ Review folder included with your Data Files, and then save the document as **Free Dessert Main Document** in the location specified by your instructor.
2. In the letter's closing, replace Maiya's first and last names with your own.
3. In the first paragraph, replace the placeholder text "[INSERT DATE FIELD]" with a date field that displays the current month, day, and year—in the format March 11, 2016.
4. Begin the mail merge by selecting Letters as the type of main document.
5. Create a data source with the following fields in the following order: First Name, Last Name, Address Line 1, Address Line 2, City, State, ZIP Code, E-mail Address, Phone, and Free Dessert. Remove any extra fields, and rename fields as necessary.
6. Create four records using the information shown in Figure 6-40.

Figure 6-40   Information for new data source

First Name	Last Name	Address Line 1	Address Line 2	City	State	ZIP Code	E-mail Address	Phone	Free Dessert
Jeane	Cutler	299 Allen Boulevard	Apartment 8D	Carlyle	LA	70129	cutler@sample.cengage.com	555-555-5555	apple tart
Kent	Hesse	933 Chilton Avenue		Beatty	LA	70120	hesse@sample.cengage.com	555-555-5555	chocolate cake
Tyrell	Greely	52 Eton Place	P.O. Box 9080	Carlyle	LA	70128	greely@sample.cengage.com	555-555-5555	apple tart
Katya	Pushkin	821 Ruby Road		Carlyle	LA	70129	pushkin@sample.cengage.com	555-555-5555	chocolate cake

© 2014 Cengage Learning

7. Save the data source as **Dessert Data** in the location in which you saved the main document.
8. Edit the data source to replace "Kent Hesse" with your first and last names.
9. Sort the data source in ascending order by zip code and then by last name.
10. Replace the placeholder text "[INSERT INSIDE ADDRESS]" with an inside address consisting of the necessary separate merge fields. Adjust the paragraph spacing in the inside address as necessary.

11. In the salutation, replace the placeholder text "[INSERT FIRST NAME]" with the First_Name merge field.

12. In the body of the letter, replace the placeholder text "[INSERT FREE DESSERT]" with the Free_Dessert merge field.

13. Save your changes to the main document, and then preview the merged document. Correct any formatting or spacing problems.

14. Merge to a new document, save the merged document as **Merged Free Dessert Letters** in the location in which you saved the main document, and then close the file.

15. Filter the data source to display only records for customers who requested a free apple tart, and then complete a second merge. Save the new merged document as **Merged Apple Tart Letters** in the location in which you saved the main document. Close all documents, saving all changes.

16. Open a new, blank document, and create a set of mailing labels using the vendor Avery US Letters and product number 5162. Save the main document as **Dessert Labels Main Document** in the location in which you saved the Dessert Data file.

17. Select the Dessert Data file you created earlier in this assignment as the data source.

18. Insert an AddressBlock merge field in the "Joshua Randall Jr." format, and then update the labels.

19. Preview the merged labels, merge to a new document, and then save the new document as **Merged Dessert Labels** in the location in which you saved the main document. Save and close all open documents.

20. Open the document **Business** from the Word6 ▸ Review folder, and then save it as **Business Data** in the location specified by your instructor.

21. Open a new, blank document, and then save it as **Business Directory Main Document** in the location in which you saved the Business Data file. Create a directory main document. Select the Business Data file as the data source.

22. Set a right tab at 6 inches with a dot leader and insert the necessary merge fields. At the top of the merged document, insert the heading **Candlestick Artisan Bakery Business Contacts** and format the heading in 22-point, Times New Roman, with the Orange, Accent 2 font color. Save the merged document as **Merged Business Directory** in the location in which you saved the main document. Save and close all open documents.

23. Open the document **Additional** from the Word6 ▸ Review folder, and then save it as **Additional Data** in the location specified by your instructor. Convert the data in the document to a table with eight columns. Insert a header row with the following column headers formatted in bold—**First Name**, **Last Name**, **Address Line 1**, **Address Line 2**, **City**, **State**, **ZIP Code**, and **Free Dessert**. Replace "David Essenberg" with your first and last names. Save and close the document.

Case Problem 1

Data File needed for this Case Problem: Fund.docx

New Morning Children's Theater   Nancy Ortega is the business manager for New Morning Children's Theater in Morning View, Colorado. As part of a new fund-raising campaign for the theater, Nancy plans to send out customized letters to last year's donors, asking them to consider donating the same amount or more this year. She asks you to help her create the letters and the envelopes for the campaign. Complete the following steps:

1. Open the document **Fund** from the Word6 ▸ Case1 folder, and then save it as **Fund-Raising Main Document** in the location specified by your instructor. In the closing, replace "Nancy Ortega" with your first and last names.

2. In the first paragraph, replace the placeholder text "[INSERT DATE FIELD]" with a date field that displays the current month, day, and year—in the format March 11, 2016.

3. Begin the mail merge by selecting Letters as the type of main document.

APPLY

4. Create a data source with the following field names, in the following order—Title, First Name, Last Name, Address Line 1, Address Line 2, City, State, ZIP Code, E-mail Address, and Donation Amount.

5. Enter the four records shown in Figure 6-41.

Figure 6-41   Four records for new data source

Title	First Name	Last Name	Address Line 1	Address Line 2	City	State	ZIP Code	E-mail Address	Donation Amount
Mr.	Bennie	Fuhrman	1577 Shanley Boulevard	Unit 2A	Denver	CO	80332	fuhrman@ sample. cengage.com	$500
Mr.	Arwen	Saiz	633 Kennelworth		Denver	CO	80332	saiz@sample. cengage.com	$125
Ms.	Kathy	Royal	4424 Gatehouse Lane		Morning View	CO	80015	royal@sample. cengage.com	$250
Ms.	Laxmi	Sung	844 Winter Way	Apartment 6	Morning View	CO	80311	sung@sample. cengage.com	$1,000

© 2014 Cengage Learning

6. Save the data source as **Fund-Raising Data** in the location in which you saved the main document.

7. Edit the data source to replace "Laxmi Sung" with your first and last names. Change the title to **Mr.** if necessary.

8. Sort the data source alphabetically by last name.

9. Build an inside address using separate merge fields. Include the Title field before the First_Name field.

10. Add a salutation using the Title and Last_Name merge fields, as indicated in the document. Adjust paragraph spacing as necessary, and take care to delete all placeholder text.

11. In the paragraph that begins "In order to produce…," insert the Donation_Amount merge field where indicated. Delete the placeholder text.

12. Save your changes to the Fund-Raising Main Document file. Preview the merged document, and then merge to a new document.

13. Save the merged letters document as **Merged Fund-Raising Letters** in the location in which you saved the main document, and then close it.

14. Save the Fund-Raising Main Document file, and then close it.

15. Open a new, blank document, and then save it as **Fund-Raising Envelopes Main Document** in the location in which you saved the Fund-Raising Data file. The theater has envelopes with a pre-printed return address, so you don't need to type a return address. Select Envelopes as the type of main document, and then select Size 10 (4 1/8 × 9 1/2 in) as the envelope size in the Envelope Options dialog box.

16. Use the Fund-Raising Data file you created earlier as the data source. In the recipient address area of the envelope, insert an AddressBlock merge field in the format "Mr. Joshua Randall Jr.".

17. Filter the records in the Fund-Raising Data file so that only records with Morning View addresses are included in the merge.

18. Merge to a new document.

19. Save the merged document as **Merged Fund-Raising Envelopes** in the location in which you saved the main document, and then close it. Save the main document and close it.

Case Problem 2

Data Files needed for this Case Problem: Client.xlsx, Directory.docx, Labels.docx, New.docx

Golden Day Wealth Management   As an account manager at Golden Day Wealth Management, you need to send letters to potential clients asking them to consider meeting with an investment adviser. Your data for the mail merge is saved as an Excel file. The data file includes names and addresses, as well as information about each potential client's preferred type of investment and the name of the adviser you think would be the best match for each client. To ensure that you can maintain the connection between the data source and the main document files, you will first start Excel, and then save the data source file to the location specified by your instructor. Complete the following steps:

1. Start Excel. In the Recent screen, click Open Other Workbooks. Navigate to the Word6 ▸ Case2 folder included with your Data Files, and then open the Excel workbook **Client**.

2. Click the FILE tab, click Save As, save the Excel workbook as **Client Data** in the location specified by your instructor, and then close Excel.

3. Open the document **New** from the Word6 ▸ Case2 folder included with your data files.

4. Save the Word document as **New Client Main Document** in the location in which you saved the Client Data file.

5. In the letter's closing, replace "Student Name" with your first and last names.

6. Replace the field that displays the date and time with a date field that displays the current month, day, and year—in the format March 11, 2016.

7. Begin the mail merge by selecting Letters as the type of main document.

8. For the data source, select the Excel workbook Client Data that you just saved. Click the OK button in the Select Table dialog box.

9. From within Word, edit the data source to replace "StudentFirstName" and "StudentLastName" with your first and last names.

10. Delete the placeholder text for the inside address, and then insert an Address Block merge field for the inside address in the format "Joshua Randall Jr.".

11. In the salutation, insert the First_Name merge field where indicated.

12. In the body of the letter, replace the placeholders "[INSERT INVESTMENT TYPE]" and "[INSERT ADVISER NAME]" with the appropriate merge fields.

13. Sort the records in the data source in ascending order by Investment Type.

⚙ **Troubleshoot** 14. Preview the merged document, and note that the lines of the inside address (inserted by the AddressBlock merge field) are spaced too far apart. Make any changes necessary so the inside address and the salutation include the appropriate amount of paragraph and line spacing.

15. Preview all the records in the document.

16. Merge to a new document. Save the merged document as **Merged New Client Letters** in the location in which you saved the main document.

17. Close all open documents, saving all changes.

⚙ **Troubleshoot** 18. Open the document **Labels** from the Word6 ▸ Case2 folder included with your Data Files, and save it as **Problem Labels** in the location specified by your instructor. Attach a comment to the Zip code in the first label that explains what error in the main document would result in a set of labels that includes information for only one record. Save and close the document.

19. Create a main document for generating mailing labels on sheets of Avery US Letter Address labels, product number 5162, using the Client Data file as your data source. Use the AddressBlock merge field in the format "Joshua Randall Jr.". Save the main document as **New Client Labels Main Document** in the location in which you saved the Client Data file.

20. Preview the merged document, merge to a new document, and then save the merged document as **Merged New Client Labels** in the location in which you saved the main document. Close all open documents, saving any changes.

21. Re-open the **New Client Main Document**, maintaining the connection to its data source, and then save it as **New Client Main Document, Filtered** in the same folder. Filter out all records in the data source except records for clients interested in municipal bonds and then, if necessary, sort the filtered records so the one containing your name is displayed first.

⚙ **Troubleshoot** 22. Preview the merged document, fix any problems with line and paragraph spacing in the inside address and salutation, and then complete the merge to a new document. Save the merged document as **Merged Municipal Bonds** in the location in which you saved the main document.

23. Close all open documents, saving any changes.

⚙ **Troubleshoot** 24. Open the document **Directory** from the Word6 ▸ Case2 folder included with your Data Files and save it as **Problem Directory** in the location specified by your instructor. This directory is supposed to list each client, along with his or her preferred investment type. Attach a comment to the first name in the directory that explains what error in the main document would result in a directory formatted like the one in the Problem Directory file.

25. Save and close the document.

Case Problem 3

Data Files needed for this Case Problem: Oxford.docx, Springwell.txt

Oxford Fitness and Health Club Christina Oates is the membership manager for Oxford Fitness and Health, a chain of 24-hour health clubs in Columbus, California. Oxford has just bought out a competitor, Springwell Health Club. Christina needs to send a letter to Springwell members explaining that their memberships will be transferred to Oxford. In the letter, she also wants to remind Springwell members when their current memberships will expire. The customer data has been saved in a text file, with the data fields separated by commas. Christina needs your help to convert the text file to a Word table, which she can then use as the data source for a mail merge. Complete the following steps:

1. In Word, open the text file **Springwell.txt** from the Word6 ▸ Case3 folder included with your Data Files. (*Hint*: If the file is not listed in the Open dialog box, make sure All Files is selected in the box to the right of the File name box.)

2. Save the Springwell.txt file as a Word document named **Springwell Data** in the location specified by your instructor. (*Hint*: In the Save As dialog box, remember to select Word Document as the file type.)

3. Format the document text using the Normal style, and then switch to Landscape orientation.

4. Convert the text to a table with eight columns. Insert a header row with the following column headers formatted in bold—**First Name**, **Last Name**, **Address Line 1**, **Address Line 2**, **City**, **State**, **ZIP Code**, and **Expiration**.

5. Replace "Tom Dylan" with your first and last names, save the document, and then close it.

6. Open the document **Oxford** from the Word6 ▸ Case3 folder, and then save it as **Oxford Main Document** in the location in which you saved the Springwell Data file.

7. In the letter's closing, replace "Christina Oates" with your first and last names.

8. In the first paragraph, replace the placeholder text "[INSERT DATE FIELD]" with a date field that displays the current month, day, and year—in the format 3/11/16.

9. Select Letters as the type of main document.

10. Select the Springwell Data document as the data source.

11. Replace the placeholder text "[INSERT INSIDE ADDRESS]" with an AddressBlock merge field in the format "Joshua Randall Jr.". Format the paragraph containing the AddressBlock merge field using the No Spacing style.

✦ **Explore** 12. Delete the placeholder text "[INSERT SALUTATION]." Insert a salutation using the Greeting Line button in the Write & Insert Fields group on the MAILINGS tab. In the Insert Greeting Line dialog box, create a salutation that includes "Dear" and the customer's first name followed by a colon. For invalid recipient names (that is, recipients for which the First Name field in the data source is blank), select the "(none)" option. Add 12 points of paragraph spacing before the salutation paragraph.

13. In the body of the letter, replace the placeholder text "[INSERT EXPIRATION]" with the Expiration merge field.

✦ **Explore** 14. Use the Rules button in the Write & Insert Fields group on the MAILINGS tab to replace the placeholder text "[SEE YOU SOON]" with a merge field that displays the message **We hope to see you soon at our new downtown location, opening early next year!** if the value in the ZIP Code field is equal to 90849; otherwise, the field should display **We hope to see you soon!** (*Hint*: In the Rules menu, click If…Then…Else…, select ZIP_Code as the Field name, select Equal to as the Comparison, and type **90849** in the Compare to box. Insert the appropriate text in the Insert this text box and in the Otherwise insert this text box.)

✦ **Explore** 15. In the Mail Merge Recipients dialog box, use the Filter command to display only the records that include either April 1 or May 1 in the Expiration field. (*Hint*: On the Filter Records tab of the Query Options dialog box, you need to fill in two rows. Select Expiration in the Field box in both rows; select Equal to in the Comparison box for both rows; type the correct dates in the Compare to boxes; and in the first list box on the far left, select Or instead of And.)

16. In the Mail Merge Recipients dialog box, sort the displayed records alphabetically by last name.

17. Preview the merged documents, adjust spacing around the merge fields as necessary, and then merge to a new document. Save the merged document as **Merged Oxford Letters** in the location in which you saved the main document.

18. Close all open documents, saving any changes.

Case Problem 4

There are no data files needed for this Case Problem.

Bureau of Labor Statistics   Tracy Sheehan is a professor of economics at a large university. She is beginning research for an article on the country's fastest growing occupations, as listed in a report issued by the United States Department of Labor's Bureau of Labor Statistics. Before she can get started, Professor Sheehan needs to organize a great deal of printed information into file folders. As her student intern, it's your job to create labels for the file folders, with one label for each of the occupations. You will retrieve the list of occupations from the Bureau of Labor Statistics website, and then use it as the data source for a mail merge. Complete the following steps:

1. Open a new, blank document, and then save it as **Occupations Data from the US BLS** in the location specified by your instructor.

2. Open a browser and go to the Bureau of Labor Statistics website at www.bls.gov.

3. Use the Search BLS.gov box to search for **Table 1.3: Fastest growing occupations, 2010 and projected 2020**.

4. In the search results, click the Fastest growing occupations link, and then verify that the table named "Table 1.3: Fastest growing occupations, 2010 and projected 2020" is displayed in your browser.

5. Click and drag the mouse to select the entire table, and then use the appropriate keyboard shortcut to copy the table. Do not include the Source row at the bottom of the table.

6. Switch to the **Occupations Data from the US BLS** document in Word, and then paste the table in the Word document.

7. Click and drag the mouse to select the gray-shaded header row and the "Total, All Occupations" row, and then delete the selected rows.

8. Delete the first column on the left, which contains the numeric codes.

9. On the right side of the table, delete all the columns of numbers except for the last one, which contains the median annual wage. When you are finished, the table should contain two columns. In the top row, you should see "Personal Care Aides" in the left column and "19,640" in the right column.

10. Insert a header row in the table with the boldface column headers **Occupation** and **Median Annual Wage**.

11. Save and close the Occupations Data from the US BLS file.

12. Open a new, blank document, and then save it as **File Labels Main Document** in the location in which you saved the Occupations Data from the US BLS file.

13. Select Labels as the type of main document, using the Avery product 5966 Filing Labels.

14. Select the Occupations Data from the US BLS file as your data source.

15. In the first label, insert the Occupation merge field, type **,** (a comma), insert a space, type **$** (a dollar sign), and then insert the Median_Annual_Wage merge field.

16. Format the Occupation merge field in bold.

17. Update the labels and preview the merge results. The first label should read "Personal Care Aides, $19,640". "Personal Care Aides" should be formatted in bold.

18. In the "Veterinarians" label at the end of the document, type **,** (a comma) after the median annual wage, and then type your first and last names.

19. Merge to a new document, and then save the new document as **Merged File Labels** in the location in which you saved the main document.

20. Close the Merged File Labels document and any other open documents, saving any changes.

OBJECTIVES

Session 7.1
- Track changes in a document
- Compare and combine documents
- Accept and reject tracked changes
- Embed an Excel worksheet
- Modify an embedded Excel worksheet

Session 7.2
- Link an Excel chart
- Modify and update a linked Excel chart
- Create bookmarks
- Insert and edit hyperlinks
- Save a Word document as a webpage
- Format a web document
- View a web document in a web browser
- Create and publish a blog post

Collaborating with Others and Integrating Data

Preparing an Information Sheet and a Webpage

Case | *Rain Gardens for Carrel Springs*

Anya Pathak is the community outreach coordinator for the Carrel Springs Watershed Foundation, an environmental organization based in Carrel Springs, Kansas, devoted to improving water quality throughout the Carrel Springs area. Anya is currently working on an information sheet about rain gardens, a special type of garden designed to retain and absorb polluted rain runoff. She has asked Oliver Miller, the foundation's publicity director, to review a draft of her document. While Oliver is revising the document, Anya has asked you to work on another copy, making additional changes. When you are finished with your review, Anya wants you to merge Oliver's edited version of the document with your most recent draft.

After you create a new version of the document for Anya, she wants you to add some budget figures from an Excel workbook. She also needs you to add a pie chart Oliver created. To make the document available to the organization's members, Anya asks you to help distribute it in electronic form and publish it on the organization's website. Finally, Anya wants you to help her create a blog post in Word discussing potential sites for rain gardens.

STARTING DATA FILES

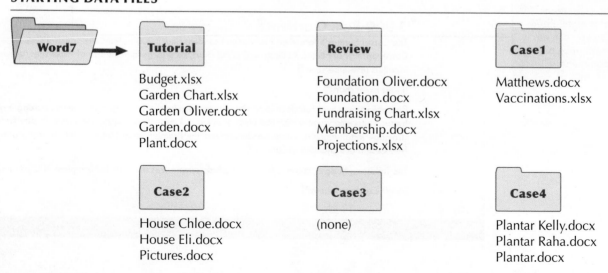

Word7 → **Tutorial**
Budget.xlsx
Garden Chart.xlsx
Garden Oliver.docx
Garden.docx
Plant.docx

Review
Foundation Oliver.docx
Foundation.docx
Fundraising Chart.xlsx
Membership.docx
Projections.xlsx

Case1
Matthews.docx
Vaccinations.xlsx

Case2
House Chloe.docx
House Eli.docx
Pictures.docx

Case3
(none)

Case4
Plantar Kelly.docx
Plantar Raha.docx
Plantar.docx

Session 7.1 Visual Overview:

When you point to a tracked change in the document, a ScreenTip displays the name of the reviewer who made the change, when the change was made, and what the change was.

When you click this button to turn on Track Changes, Word marks the changes you make to the document with revision marks, or **tracked changes**.

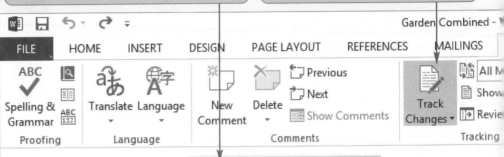

Anya Pathak, 4/14/2016 2:35:00 PM
inserted:
perennials

A vertical line appears in the left margin next to text that has been changed in any way.

Inserted text appears with an underline and a contrasting color, with a different color for each person, or reviewer, who edits the document. Here, text inserted by Anya is red, and text inserted by Oliver is orange.

Text with a comment attached is highlighted in color so you can easily see the reference point for the comment.

Rain·Gar[den]···[Sp]rings¶

Planted·with·colorful·perennials,·a·rain·garden·is·beautiful,·low-maintenance,·relatively·inexpensive what·is·a·rain·garden,·exactly?·It's·a·garden·in·a·shallow,·bowl-shaped·depression·that·allows·it·to runoff·from·buildings,·driveways,·roads,·and·lawns.·The·rain·is·then·absorbed·into·the·garden,·prev pollutant-laden·runoff·from·flowing·into·storm·sewers,·and·from·there·into·lakes,·rivers,·and·stream

A·rain·garden·transforms·the·water·it·absorbs,·replenishing·the·aquifer·with·fresh,·pollutant-free·w estimate·that·a·well-designed·rain·garden·can·remove·up·to·95%·of·fertilizers chemicals·from·rainwater·runoff,·and·up·to·85%·of·sediment.·Preven contaminants·from·reaching·the·Carrel·Springs·watershed·is·esse the·area's·plants·and·wildlife·healthy·and·vibrant.·For·examp nutrient-rich·fertilizer·from·flowing·into·the·watershed·reduce algal·bloom,·in·which·algae·spreads·throughout·lakes·and·str available·oxygen·and,·eventually,·killing·native·fish.¶

Over·the·past·five·years,·the·Carrel·Springs·Watershed·Foun with·the·Carrel·Springs·Department·of·Streets·and·Maintenar scale·rain·gardens·on·public·lands·that·link·directly·to·major· Homeowners·can·do·their·part·by·installing·their·own·rain·gar terraces·between·sidewalks·and·city·streets.¶

▪ 3,000·Rain·Gardens¶

The·Carrel·Springs·Watershed·Foundation·has·identified·3,000·potential·residential·sites·for·rain·g Carrel·Springs·city·limits.·As·illustrated·in·this·chart,·on·a·large·percentage·of·these·sites,·gardens·h installed·or·will·be·soon.¶

[Insert·Excel·chart]¶

Except·for·an·annual·fall·cleanup,·a·rain·garden·requires·no·ongoing·maintenance,·making·it·an·at homeowners·who·want·to·minimize·outdoor·upkeep.·Residents·can·apply·for·grants·to·pay·for·exce drainage·installation.·Volunteer·gardeners·from·the·Prairie·Friends·Native·Plant·Society·are·availa free·design·and·planting·assistance.¶

The·following·budget,·created·by·Anya·Pathak,·summarizes·the·costs·for·a·typical·200-square-foo

[Insert·Excel·worksheet]¶

PAGE 1 OF 1   406 WORDS

Tracking Changes

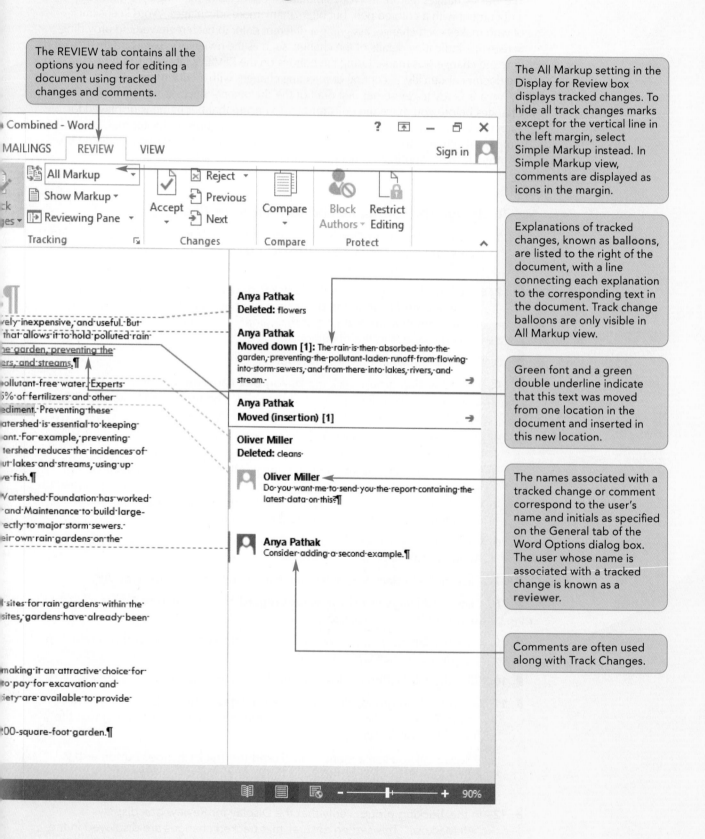

The REVIEW tab contains all the options you need for editing a document using tracked changes and comments.

The All Markup setting in the Display for Review box displays tracked changes. To hide all track changes marks except for the vertical line in the left margin, select Simple Markup instead. In Simple Markup view, comments are displayed as icons in the margin.

Explanations of tracked changes, known as **balloons**, are listed to the right of the document, with a line connecting each explanation to the corresponding text in the document. Track change balloons are only visible in All Markup view.

Green font and a green double underline indicate that this text was moved from one location in the document and inserted in this new location.

The names associated with a tracked change or comment correspond to the user's name and initials as specified on the General tab of the Word Options dialog box. The user whose name is associated with a tracked change is known as a **reviewer**.

Comments are often used along with Track Changes.

Editing a Document with Tracked Changes

The Track Changes feature in Word simulates the process of marking up a hard copy of a document with a colored pen, but offers many more advantages. Word keeps track of who makes each change, assigning a different color to each reviewer and providing ScreenTips indicating details of the change, such as the reviewer's name and the date and time the change was made. Using the buttons on the REVIEW tab, you can move through the document quickly, accepting or rejecting changes with a click of the mouse.

Anya is ready to revise her first draft of the document. She asks you to turn on Track Changes before you make the edits for her. To ensure that her name is displayed for each tracked change, and that your screens match the figures in this tutorial, you will temporarily change the username on the General tab of the Word Options dialog box to "Anya Pathak." You'll also change the user initials to "AP."

To change the username and turn on Track Changes:

1. Open the document **Garden** located in the Word7 ▸ Tutorial folder included with your Data Files, and then save it as **Garden Anya** in the location specified by your instructor.

2. Switch to Print Layout view if necessary, display the rulers and nonprinting characters, and change the document Zoom level to **110%**. You'll use this zoom setting for the first part of this tutorial to ensure that you can see all the tracked changes in the document.

3. On the ribbon, click the **REVIEW** tab.

4. In the Tracking group, click the **Dialog Box Launcher** to open the Track Changes Options dialog box, and then click **Change User Name**. The Word Options dialog box opens, with the General tab displayed.

5. On a piece of paper, write down the current username and initials, if they are not your own, so you can refer to it when you need to restore the original username and initials later in this tutorial. Although the user initials do not appear on the Word screen, in a printed document, the username is replaced with the user initials to save space. Therefore, you should always change the user initials whenever you change the username.

6. Click in the **User name** box, delete the current username, and then type **Anya Pathak**.

7. Click in the **Initials** box, delete the current initials, and then type **AP**.

8. Click the **Always use these values regardless of sign in to Office** checkbox to insert a check, if necessary.

9. Click the **OK** button. The Word Options dialog box closes, and you return to the Track Changes Options dialog box.

10. Click the **OK** button to close the Track Changes Options dialog box.

11. In the Tracking group, click the **Track Changes** button. Blue highlighting on the Track Changes button tells you that it is selected, indicating that the Track Changes feature is turned on.

    Trouble? If you see a menu, you clicked the Track Changes button arrow rather than the button itself. Press the Esc key to close the menu, and then click the Track Changes button to turn on Track Changes.

12. In the Tracking group, verify that the Display for Review box displays "All Markup." This setting ensures that tracked changes are displayed in the document as you edit it.

Trouble? If the Display for Review box does not display "All Markup," click the Display for Review arrow, and then click All Markup.

▶ **13.** In the Tracking group, click the **Show Markup** button, and then point to **Balloons**. See Figure 7-1.

Figure 7-1   Track Changes turned on

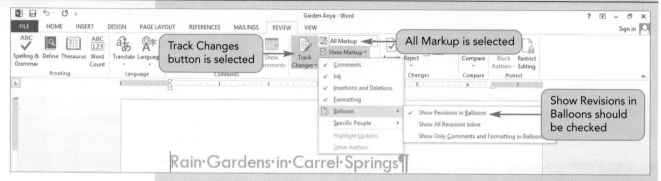

▶ **14.** If you do not see a checkmark next to Show Revisions in Balloons, click **Show Revisions in Balloons** now to select it and close the menu. Otherwise, click anywhere in the document to close the menu.

Now that Track Changes is turned on, you can begin editing Anya's document. First, Anya needs to change the word "flowers" in the first sentence to "perennials."

To edit Anya's document and view the tracked changes:

▶ **1.** In the line below the "Rain Gardens in Carrel Springs" heading, select the word **flowers** and then type **perennials**. The new word, "perennials," is displayed in color, with an underline. A vertical line is displayed in the left margin, drawing attention to the change. To the right of the document, the username associated with the change (Anya Pathak) is displayed, along with an explanation of the change. See Figure 7-2.

Figure 7-2   Edit marked as tracked change

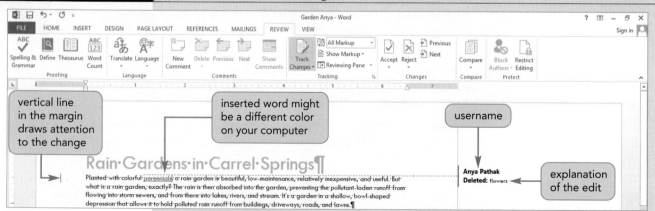

▶ **2.** Move the mouse pointer over the newly inserted word "perennials." A ScreenTip displays information about the edit, along with the date and time the edit was made.

▶ **3.** Move the mouse pointer over the explanation of the change to the right of the document. The explanation is highlighted, and the dotted line connecting the change in the document to the explanation turns solid. In a document with many tracked changes, this makes it easier to see which explanation is associated with which tracked change.

Next, Anya wants you to move the second-to-last sentence in this paragraph to the end of the paragraph.

▶ **4.** Press the **Ctrl** key, and then click in the sentence that begins "The rain is then absorbed into the garden...." The entire sentence is selected.

▶ **5.** Drag the sentence to insert it at the end of the paragraph, and then click anywhere in the document to deselect it. See Figure 7-3.

Figure 7-3   **Tracked changes showing text moved to a new location**

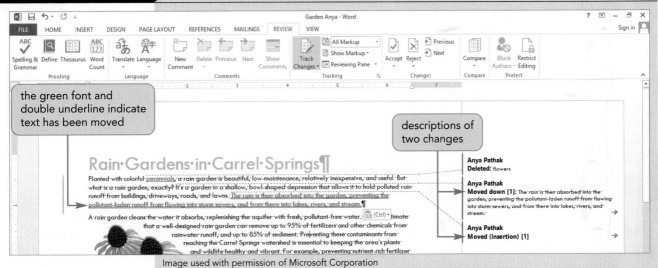

Image used with permission of Microsoft Corporation

The sentence is inserted with a double underline in green, which is the color Word uses to denote moved text. Word also inserts a space before the inserted sentence, and marks the nonprinting space character as a tracked change. A vertical bar in the left margin draws attention to the moved text.

To the right of the document, descriptions of two new changes are displayed. The "Moved down [1]" change shows the text of the sentence that was moved. The "Moved (insertion) [1]" change draws attention to the sentence in its new location at the end of the paragraph.

A blue, right-facing arrow next to a tracked change explanation indicates that the change is related to another change. You can click the arrow to select the related change.

▶ **6.** Next to the "Moved (insertion) [1]" change, click the blue, right-facing arrow ➡ to select the moved sentence in the "Moved down [1]" balloon. See Figure 7-4.

Figure 7-4   Selecting a related change

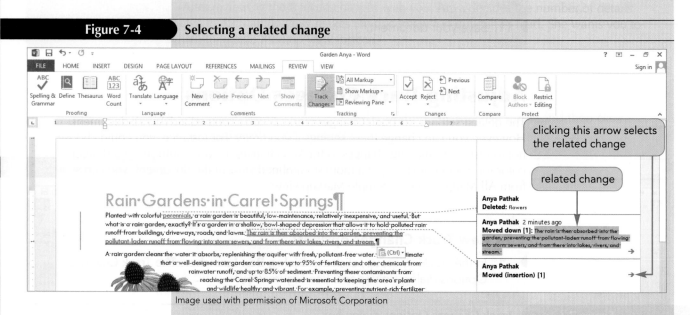

Image used with permission of Microsoft Corporation

After reviewing the sentence in its new location at the end of the paragraph, Anya notices that she needs to add an "s" to the end of the word "stream."

7. In the sentence you moved in Step 5, click to the right of the "m" in "stream," and then type the letter **s**. The newly inserted letter is displayed in the same color as the word "perennials" at the beginning of the paragraph.

Finally, Anya asks you to insert a comment reminding her to consider adding a second example of the damage caused by rain runoff. Comments are commonly used with tracked changes. In All Markup view, they are displayed, along with other edits, to the right of the document.

8. In the line of text above the "3,000 Rain Gardens" heading, double-click the word **streets**.

9. In the Comments group, click the **New Comment** button. The word "streets" is highlighted in the same color used for the word "perennials," and the insertion point moves to the right of the document, ready for you to type the comment text.

10. Type **Consider adding a second example.** See Figure 7-5.

Figure 7-5   Comment added to document

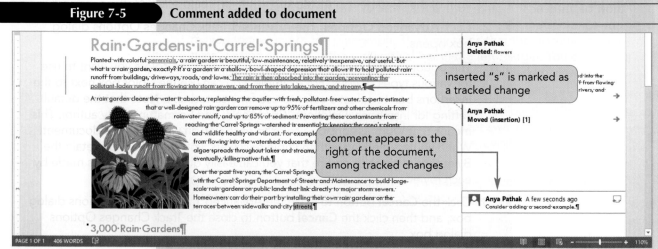

Image used with permission of Microsoft Corporation

▶ **8.** Click the **OK** button. The Combine Documents dialog box closes.

Trouble? If you see a dialog box alerting you to a formatting conflict, click the "Your document (Garden Anya)" button is selected, if necessary, and then click the continue with Merge button.

A new document opens. It contains the tracked changes from both the original document and the revised document.

At this point, depending on the previous settings on your computer, you might see only the new, combined document, or you might also see the original and revised documents open in separate windows. You might also see the Reviewing pane, which includes a summary of the number of revisions in the combined document along with a list of all the changes, as shown in Figure 7-9.

Figure 7-9	Two documents combined

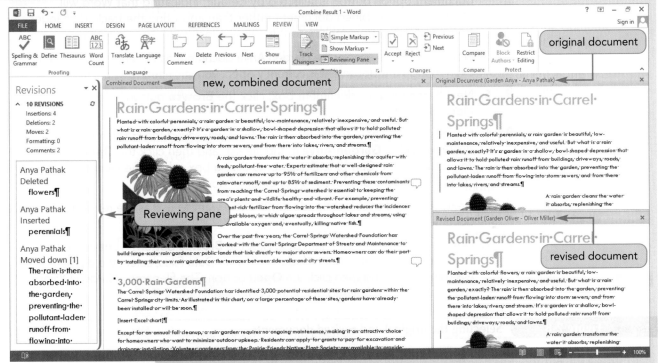

Image used with permission of Microsoft Corporation

Note that your combined document might have a different name than shown in Figure 7-9. For instance, it might be named "Document 1," instead of "Combine Result 1."

▶ **9.** In the Compare group, click the **Compare** button, and then point to **Show Source Documents**.

▶ **10.** If a checkmark appears next to Show Both, press the **Esc** key twice to close both menus; otherwise, click **Show Both**. Your screen should now match Figure 7-9.

Trouble? If the Reviewing pane is still not displayed, click the Reviewing Pane button in the Tracking group to display the Reviewing pane.

Trouble? If your Reviewing pane is displayed horizontally rather than vertically, as shown in Figure 7-9, click the Reviewing Pane button arrow in the Tracking group, and then click Reviewing Pane Vertical.

Note that the combined document and the two source documents are all displayed in Simple Markup view. Instead of Print Layout view, which you typically use when working on documents, the three documents are displayed in Web Layout view. You'll learn more about Web Layout view later in this tutorial. For now, all you need to know is that in Web Layout view, the line breaks change to suit the size of the document window, making it easier to read text in the small windows.

It's helpful to have the source documents displayed when you want to quickly compare the two documents. For example, right now Anya wants to scroll down the documents to see how they differ. When you scroll up or down in the Revised Document pane, the other documents scroll as well.

To scroll the document panes simultaneously:

▶ **1.** Click in the Revised Document (Garden Oliver - Oliver Miller) pane to display its scroll bar, and then drag the scroll bar down to display the text "3,000 Rain Gardens." The text in the Combined Document pane and in the Original Document (Garden Anya - Anya Pathak) pane scrolls down to match the text in the Revised Document (Garden Oliver - Oliver Miller) pane. See Figure 7-10.

| Figure 7-10 | Document panes scrolled to compare versions |

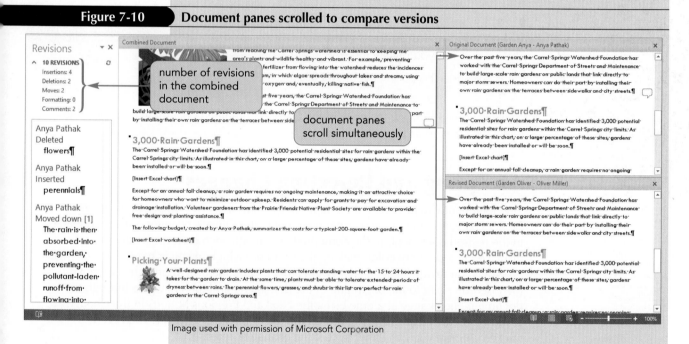

Image used with permission of Microsoft Corporation

Now that you've reviewed both documents, you can hide the source documents to make the combined document easier to read. After you hide the source documents, you can review the edits in the Reviewing pane.

To hide the source documents and review the edits in the Reviewing pane:

▶ **1.** In the Compare group, click the **Compare** button, point to the **Show Source Documents** button, and then click **Hide Source Documents**. The panes displaying the original and revised documents close, and the combined document window switches to Print Layout view.

TIP

To hide a reviewer's edits, click the Show Markup button in the Tracking group, point to Specific People, and then click the person's name.

Trouble? If the combined window does not switch to Print Layout view, click the Print Layout view button 🔲 on the status bar.

▶ **2.** Move the mouse over the list of edits in the Reviewing pane to display the vertical scroll bar, and then scroll down and review the list of edits. Notice that the document contains the edits you made earlier (under Anya's name) as well as edits made by Oliver Miller.

Anya prefers to review changes using All Markup view instead of the Reviewing pane.

▶ **3.** In the Tracking group, click the **Reviewing Pane** button to deselect it. The Reviewing pane closes.

▶ **4.** In the Tracking group, click the **Display for Review** arrow, and then click **All Markup**.

▶ **5.** In the Tracking group, click the **Show Markup** arrow, point to Balloons, and then make sure **Show Revisions in Balloons** is selected.

▶ **6.** Save the document as **Garden Combined** in the location specified by your instructor.

▶ **7.** In the Tracking group, click the **Track Changes** button to turn off Track Changes. This ensures that you won't accidentally add any additional edit marks as you review the document.

▶ **8.** Change the Zoom level to **120%**.

Next, you will review the edits in the Garden Combined document to accept and reject the changes as appropriate.

Accepting and Rejecting Changes

The document you just created contains all the edits from two different reviewers—Anya's changes made in the original document, and Oliver's changes as they appeared in the revised document. In the combined document, each reviewer's edits are displayed in a different color, making it easy to see which reviewer made each change.

When you review tracked changes in a document, the best approach is to move the insertion point to the beginning of the document, and then navigate through the document one change at a time using the Next and Previous buttons in the Changes group on the REVIEW tab. This ensures you won't miss any edits. As you review a tracked change, you can either accept the change or reject it.

REFERENCE

Accepting and Rejecting Changes

- Move the insertion point to the beginning of the document.
- On the ribbon, click the REVIEW tab.
- In the Changes group, click the Next button to select the first edit or comment in the document.
- To accept a selected change, click the Accept button in the Changes group.
- To reject a selected change, click the Reject button in the Changes group.
- To accept all the changes in the document, click the Accept button arrow, and then click Accept All Changes.
- To reject all the changes in the document, click the Reject button arrow, and then click Reject All Changes.

To accept and reject changes in the Garden Combined document:

1. Press the **Ctrl+Home** keys to move the insertion point to the beginning of the document.

2. In the Changes group, click the **Next** button. To the right of the document, in a tracked change balloon, the deleted word "flowers" is selected, as shown in Figure 7-11.

Figure 7-11	First change in document selected

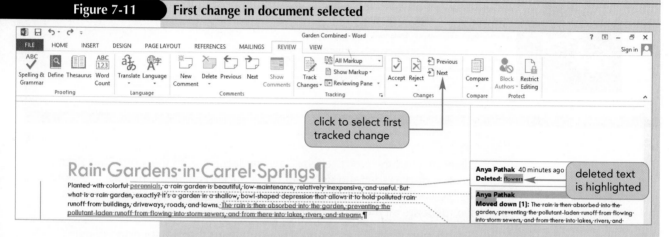

Trouble? If a style-related change is selected instead, click the Accept button in the Changes group, and then continue with Step 3.

Trouble? If the insertion point moves to Oliver's comment, you clicked the Next button in the Comments group instead of the Next button in the Changes group. Repeat Steps 1 and 2.

3. In the Changes group, click the **Accept** button. The tracked change balloon is no longer displayed, indicating that the change has been accepted. The inserted word "perennials" is now selected in the document.

Trouble? If you see a menu below the Accept button, you clicked the Accept button arrow by mistake. Press the Esc key to close the menu, and then click the Accept button.

4. Click the **Accept** button. To the right of the document, in a tracked change balloon, the sentence that you moved is now selected.

5. Click the **Accept** button. The tracked change balloon containing the moved sentence and the related "Moved (insertion) [1]" tracked change balloon are no longer displayed. In the document, the sentence itself is displayed in black, like the surrounding text, indicating that the change has been accepted. Now the space before the moved sentence, which Word automatically inserted when you moved the sentence, is selected.

6. Click the **Accept** button to accept the insertion of the space, and then click the **Accept** button again to accept the insertion of the letter "s" at the end of "stream." In a tracked change balloon to the right of the document, Oliver's deletion of the word "cleans" is selected. See Figure 7-12.

Figure 7-12 **Reviewing Oliver's changes**

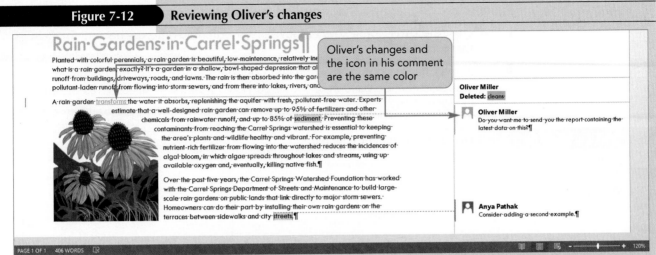

Image used with permission of Microsoft Corporation

Oliver deleted the word "cleans" and replaced it with the word "transforms," which is displayed in the document as a tracked change. The inserted word, the tracked change balloon for the deleted word, and the icon in Oliver's comment are all the same color.

Anya prefers to keep the original word, "cleans," so you need to reject Oliver's change.

▶ **7.** In the Changes group, click the **Reject** button to reject the deletion of the word "cleans." The tracked change balloon is no longer displayed, and the word "cleans" is restored in the document, to the left of the inserted word "transforms," which is now selected. See Figure 7-13.

Figure 7-13 **Document after rejecting change**

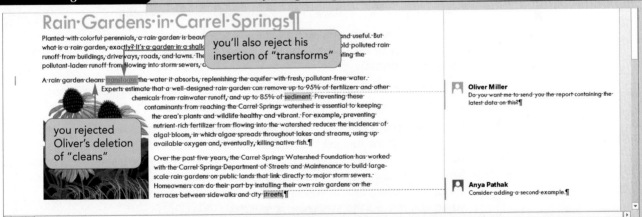

Image used with permission of Microsoft Corporation

Next, you need to reject the insertion of this word.

▶ **8.** Click the **Reject** button. The inserted word "transforms" is removed from the document, and the insertion point moves to the beginning of Oliver's comment. Anya has already talked to Oliver about the report mentioned in his comment, so you can delete the comment.

▶ **9.** In the Comments group, click the **Delete** button to delete the comment.

▶ **10.** In the Changes group, click the **Next** button. (You could also click the Next button in the Comments group since the next item is a comment.) The insertion point moves to Anya's comment. Anya has decided not to add a second example, so you can delete her comment, too.

▶ **11.** In the Comments group, click the **Delete** button.

▶ **12.** In the Changes group, click the **Next** button. A Microsoft Word dialog box opens with a message indicating that there are no more comments or tracked changes in the document.

▶ **13.** Click the **OK** button to close the dialog box.

▶ **14.** In the fourth paragraph from the end of the document, replace "Anya Pathak" with your first and last names, and then save the document.

Now that you have finished editing and reviewing the document with tracked changes, you need to restore the original username and initials settings. Then you can close Anya's original document, which you no longer need.

To restore the original username and initials settings and close Anya's original document:

▶ **1.** In the Tracking group, click the **Dialog Box Launcher** to open the Track Changes Options dialog box.

▶ **2.** Click the **Change User Name** button, and then change the username and initials back to their original settings on the General tab of the Word Options dialog box.

▶ **3.** Click the **OK** button to close the Word Options dialog box, and then click the **OK** button again to close the Track Changes Options dialog box.

▶ **4.** On the taskbar, click the **Word** button ▣, and then click the **Garden Anya - Word** thumbnail to display the document.

▶ **5.** Close the Garden Anya document.

▶ **6.** Save the **Garden Combined** document, and then display the rulers.

▶ **7.** On the ribbon, click the **HOME** tab.

INSIGHT

Checking for Tracked Changes

Once a document is finished, you should make sure it does not contain any tracked changes or comments. This is especially important in situations where comments or tracked changes might reveal sensitive information that could jeopardize your privacy, or the privacy of the organization you work for.

You can't always tell if a document contains comments or tracked changes just by looking at it because the comments or changes for some or all of the reviewers might be hidden. Also, the Display for Review box in the Tracking group on the REVIEW tab might be set to No Markup, in which case all tracked changes would be hidden. To determine whether or not a document contains any tracked changes or comments, open the Reviewing pane and verify that the number of revisions for each type is 0. You can also use the Document Inspector to check for a variety of issues including leftover comments and tracked changes. To use the Document Inspector, click the FILE tab, click Info, click Check for Issues, click Inspect Document, and then click the Inspect button.

Now that you have combined Oliver's edits with Anya's, you are ready to add the budget and the pie chart to the document.

Embedding and Linking Objects from Other Programs

The programs in Office 2013 are designed to accomplish specific tasks. As you've seen with Word, you can use a word-processing program to create, edit, and format documents such as letters, reports, newsletters, and proposals. On the other hand, Microsoft Excel, a **spreadsheet program**, allows you to organize, calculate, and analyze numerical data in a grid of rows and columns, and to illustrate data in the form of charts. A spreadsheet created in Microsoft Excel is known as a **worksheet**. Each Excel file—called a **workbook**—can contain multiple worksheets. Throughout this tutorial, a portion of an Excel worksheet is referred to as a **worksheet object**, and a chart is referred to as a **chart object**.

Sometimes it is useful to combine information created in the different Office programs into one file. For her document, Anya wants to use budget data from an Excel worksheet. She also wants to include an Excel chart that shows the percentage of completed rain gardens. You can incorporate the Excel data and chart into Anya's Word document by taking advantage of **object linking and embedding**, or **OLE**, a technology that allows you to share information among the Office programs. This process is commonly referred to as **integration**.

Before you start using OLE, you need to understand some important terms. Recall that in Word, an object is anything that can be selected and modified as a whole, such as a table, picture, or block of text. Another important term, **source program**, refers to the program used to create the original version of an object. The program into which the object is integrated is called the **destination program**. Similarly, the original file that contains the object you are integrating is called the **source file**, and the file into which you integrate the object is called the **destination file**.

You can integrate objects by either embedding or linking. **Embedding** is a technique that allows you to insert a copy of an object into a destination document. You can double-click an embedded object in the destination document to access the tools of the source program, allowing you to edit the object within the destination document using the source program's tools. Because the embedded object is a copy, any changes you make to it are not reflected in the original source file, and vice versa. For instance, you could embed data from a worksheet named Itemized Expenses into a Word document named Travel Report. Later, if you change the Itemized Expenses file, those revisions would not be reflected in the Travel Report document. The opposite is also true; if you edit the embedded object from within the Travel Report file, those changes will not be reflected in the source file Itemized Expenses. The embedded object retains no connection to the source file.

Figure 7-14 illustrates the relationship between an embedded Excel worksheet object in Anya's Word document and the source file.

| Figure 7-14 | Embedding an Excel worksheet object in a Word document |

source file is an Excel workbook named Budget; changes made to this file will *not* be reflected in the destination file

source program is Excel

destination file is the Garden Combined Word document; changes made to this file will *not* be reflected in the source file

destination program is Word

embedded worksheet object

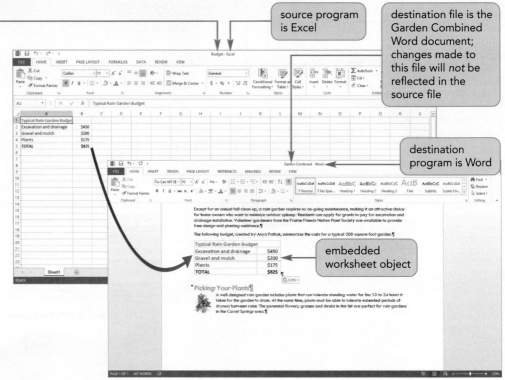

© 2014 Cengage Learning; Image used with permission of Microsoft Corporation

Linking is similar to embedding, except that the object inserted into the destination file maintains a connection to the source file. Just as with an embedded object, you can double-click a linked object to access the tools of the source program. However, unlike with an embedded object, changes to a linked object show up in both the destination file and the source file. The linked object in the destination document is not a copy; it is a shortcut to the original object in the source file.

Figure 7-15 illustrates the relationship between the data in Oliver's Excel chart and the linked object in Anya's Word document.

Figure 7-15 **Linking an Excel chart object to a Word document**

source file is an Excel workbook named Rain Garden Chart; changes made to this file will be reflected in the destination file

source program is Excel

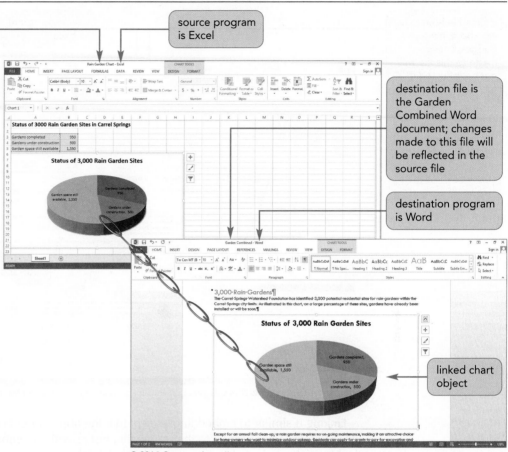

destination file is the Garden Combined Word document; changes made to this file will be reflected in the source file

destination program is Word

linked chart object

© 2014 Cengage Learning

PROSKILLS

Decision Making: Choosing Between Embedding and Linking

Embedding and linking are both useful when you know you'll want to edit an object after inserting it into Word. But how do you decide whether to embed or link the object? Create an embedded object if you won't have access to the original source file in the future, or if you don't need (or want) to maintain the connection between the source file and the document containing the linked object. Two advantages of embedding are that the source file is unaffected by any editing in the destination document, and the two files can be stored separately. You could even delete the source file from your disk without affecting the copy embedded in your Word document. A disadvantage is that the file size of a Word document containing an embedded object will be larger than the file size of a document containing a linked object.

Create a linked object whenever you have data that is likely to change over time, and when you want to keep the object in your document up to date. In addition to the advantage of a smaller destination file size, both the source file and the destination file can reflect recent revisions when the files are linked. A disadvantage to linking is that you have to keep track of two files (the source file and the destination file) rather than just one.

Embedding an Excel Worksheet Object

To embed an object from an Excel worksheet into a Word document, you start by opening the Excel worksheet (the source file) and copying the Excel object to the Office Clipboard. Then, in the Word document (the destination file), you open the Paste Special dialog box. In this dialog box, you can choose to paste the copied Excel object in a number of different forms. To embed it, you select Microsoft Office Excel Worksheet Object.

Anya wants to include the budget for a typical rain garden in her document. If she needs to adjust numbers in the budget later, she will need access to the Excel tools for recalculating the data. Therefore, you'll embed the Excel object in the Word document. Then you can use Excel commands to modify the embedded object from within Word.

To embed the Excel data in the Word document:

▶ 1. Scroll down to the paragraph above the "Picking Your Plants" heading, and then delete the placeholder text **[Insert Excel worksheet]**, taking care not to delete the paragraph mark after it. The insertion point should now be located in a blank paragraph above the "Picking Your Plants" heading.

   Now you need to open Oliver's Excel file and copy the budget.

▶ 2. Start Microsoft Excel 2013, open the file **Budget** located in the Word7 ▶ Tutorial folder included with your Data Files, and then maximize the Excel program window if necessary. See Figure 7-16.

Figure 7-16 **Budget file open in Excel**

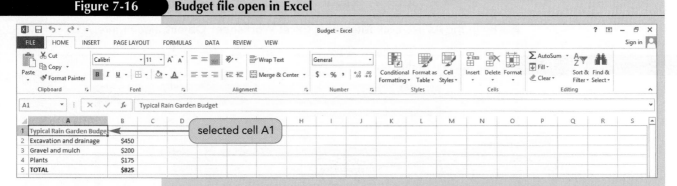

An Excel worksheet is arranged in rows and columns, just like a Word table. The intersection between a row and a column is called a **cell**; an individual cell takes its name from its column letter and row number. For example, the intersection of column A and row 1 in the upper-left corner of the worksheet is referred to as cell A1. Currently, cell A1 is selected, as indicated by its dark outline.

To copy the budget data to the Office Clipboard, you need to select the entire block of cells containing the budget.

▶ 3. Click cell **A1** (the cell containing the text "Typical Rain Garden Budget"), press and hold the **Shift** key, and then click cell **B5** (the cell containing "$825"). See Figure 7-17.

Figure 7-17 **Budget data selected in worksheet**

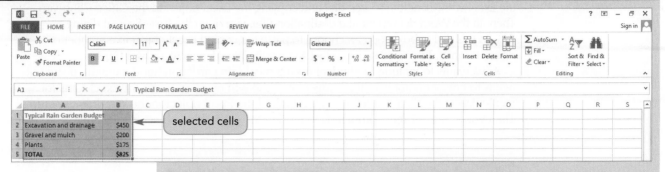

Now that the data is selected, you can copy it to the Office Clipboard.

Be sure to keep Excel open; otherwise you won't have access to the commands for embedding the data in Word.

▶ **4.** Press the **Ctrl+C** keys. The border around the selected cells is now flashing, indicating that you have copied the data in these cells to the Office Clipboard. Next, you will switch to Word without closing Excel.

▶ **5.** On the taskbar, click the **Word** button to return to the Garden Combined document. The insertion point is still located in the blank paragraph above the "Picking Your Plants" heading.

▶ **6.** On the ribbon, click the **HOME** tab.

▶ **7.** In the Clipboard group, click the **Paste button arrow**, and then click **Paste Special** to open the Paste Special dialog box.

▶ **8.** In the As list, click **Microsoft Excel Worksheet Object**. See Figure 7-18.

Figure 7-18 **Paste Special dialog box**

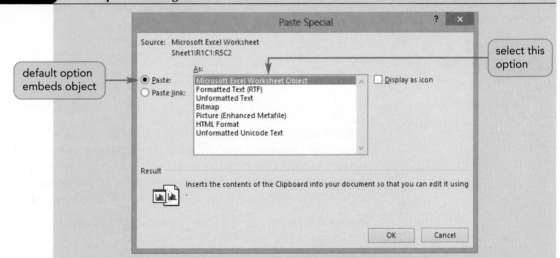

Next, you can choose to embed the Excel object or link it, depending on whether you select the Paste button (for embedding) or the Paste link button (for linking). The Paste button is selected by default, which is what you want in this case.

▶ **9.** Click the **OK** button. The Excel worksheet object is inserted in the Word document, as shown in Figure 7-19.

Figure 7-19   **Excel worksheet object embedded in Word document**

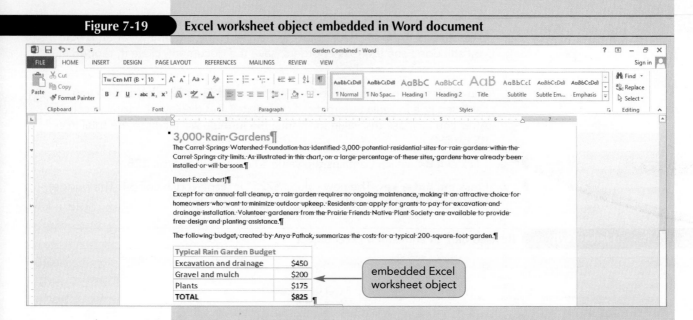

Trouble? If you don't see the top or bottom horizontal gridline in the embedded Excel object, don't be concerned. It won't affect the rest of the steps.

At this point, the Excel data looks like an ordinary table. But because you embedded it as an Excel worksheet object, you can modify it from within Word, using Excel tools and commands.

Modifying an Embedded Worksheet Object

After you embed an object in Word, you can modify it in two different ways. First, you can click the object to select it, and then move or resize it just as you would a graphic object. Second, you can double-click the object to display the tools of the source program on the Word ribbon, and then edit the contents of the object. After you modify the embedded object using the source program tools, you can click anywhere else in the Word document to deselect the embedded object and redisplay the usual Word tools on the ribbon.

Anya would like to center the Excel object on the page. Also, the value for Plants is incorrect, so she asks you to update the budget with the new data.

To modify the embedded Excel object:

▶ **1.** Click anywhere in the Excel object. Selection handles and a dotted outline are displayed around the Excel object, indicating that it is selected. With the object selected, you can center it as you would center any other selected item.

▶ **2.** Make sure the HOME tab is selected on the ribbon.

▶ **3.** In the Paragraph group, click the **Center** button ☰. The Excel object is centered between the left and right margins of the document.

▶ **4.** Double-click anywhere inside the Excel object. The object's border changes to resemble the borders of an Excel worksheet, with horizontal and vertical scroll bars, row numbers, and column letters. The Word tabs on the ribbon are replaced with Excel tabs.

Trouble? If you don't see the Excel borders around the worksheet object, click outside the worksheet object to deselect it, and then repeat Step 4. If you still don't see the Excel borders, save the document, close it, reopen it, and then repeat Step 4.

You need to change the value for Plants from $175 to $225. Although you can't see it, a formula automatically calculates and displays the total in cell B5. After you increase the value for Plants, the formula will increase the total in cell B5 by $50.

▶ **5.** Click cell **B4**, which contains the value $175, and then type **225**.

▶ **6.** Press the **Enter** key. The new value "$225" is displayed in cell B4. The budget total in cell B5 increases from $825 to $875. See Figure 7-20.

Figure 7-20   **Revised data in embedded Excel object**

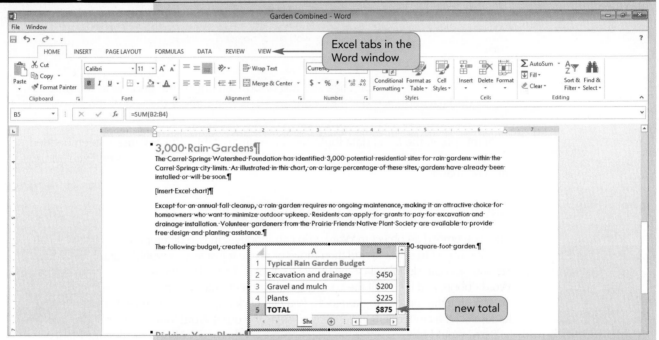

▶ **7.** In the document, click outside the borders of the Excel object to deselect it. The Word tabs are now visible on the ribbon again.

▶ **8.** On the taskbar, click the **Microsoft Excel** button [x] to display the Excel window.

Because you embedded the Excel object rather than linking it, the Plant value of $175 and the Total of $825 remain unchanged.

▶ **9.** On the ribbon, click the **FILE** tab, and then click **Close** in the navigation bar. The Budget workbook closes, but Excel remains open.

In this session, you worked with tracked changes in a document. You learned how to combine and compare documents, and you accepted and rejected tracked changes in a combined document. You also embedded an Excel Worksheet object in a Word document and modified the embedded worksheet object from within Word. In the next session, you'll learn how to link an object instead of embedding it. You'll also create bookmarks, and insert and edit hyperlinks in a document. You'll save a Word document as a webpage, format the webpage, and then view it in a web browser. Finally, you'll learn how to create and publish a blog post.

REVIEW

Session 7.1 Quick Check

1. Explain how to turn on Track Changes.
2. How do you open the Track Changes Options dialog box?
3. If you have two documents that contain tracked changes, should you use the Compare feature or the Combine feature?
4. Explain the difference between a linked object and an embedded object.
5. What button do you use in Word to embed an object that you've copied to the Clipboard?
6. How do you start editing an embedded Excel object in Word?

Session 7.2 Visual Overview:

To link an Excel chart object to a Word document, you first need to open the Excel workbook that contains the chart.

The two paste buttons with chain links on them allow you to paste the chart as a linked object. Here, the mouse is pointing to the Use Destination Theme & Link Data button, which pastes the chart using the green theme colors of the Word document, which is the destination file.

The Keep Source Formatting & Link Data button pastes the chart using the blue theme colors of the Excel workbook, which is the source file.

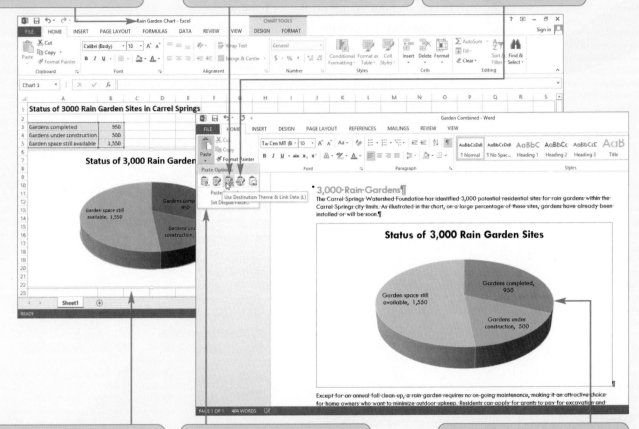

Linking an Excel chart to a Word document is essentially a copy-and-paste operation. You need to click the chart to select it, and then copy it to the Office Clipboard. The border around this chart tells you it is selected. To quickly copy the chart to the Office Clipboard, you can press the Ctrl+C keys.

In the Word document, you need to click where you want to insert the chart, and then click the Paste button arrow to display the Paste Options menu. Remember to keep Excel open when you switch to the Word document; otherwise, the linking options you need won't be visible in this menu.

Word displays a Live Preview of the pasted chart when you place the mouse pointer over a button in the Paste Options menu. In this Live Preview, the green chart matches the theme colors of the Word document because the mouse pointer is currently positioned over the Use Destination Theme & Link Data button.

Linking an Excel Chart Object

You can edit a linked chart object from within the Word document.

After you select the chart in the Word document, you click the Edit Data button on the CHART TOOLS DESIGN tab. This opens a spreadsheet window with the Excel source file displayed.

If the chart in the Word window does not change to reflect changes made to data in the spreadsheet window, you can click the Refresh Data button to update the chart in the Word window.

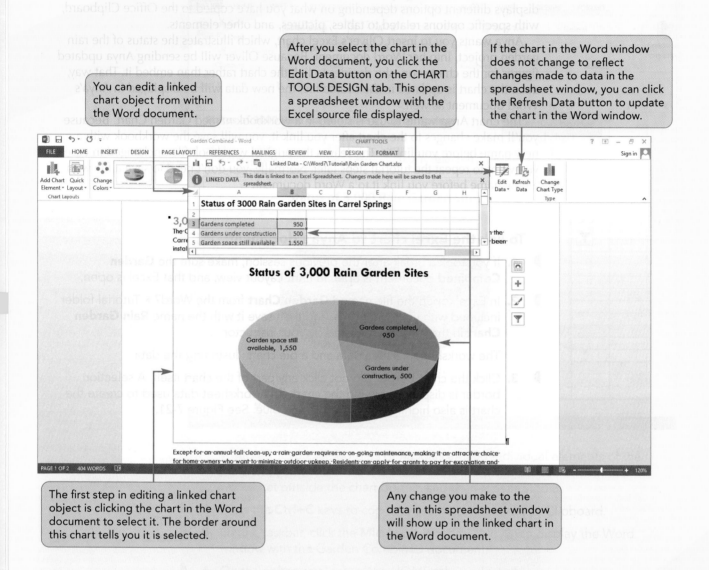

The first step in editing a linked chart object is clicking the chart in the Word document to select it. The border around this chart tells you it is selected.

Any change you make to the data in this spreadsheet window will show up in the linked chart in the Word document.

Figure 7-24   **Spreadsheet window with chart data**

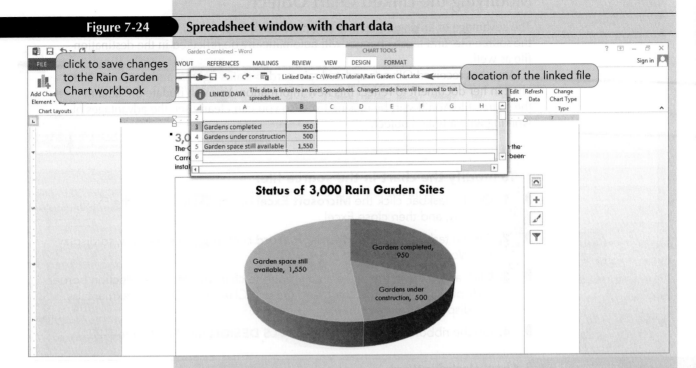

The file path at the top of the spreadsheet window shows the location of the linked file you are about to edit.

6. In the Excel window, click cell **B3**, which contains the value "950," and then type **975**.

7. Press the **Enter** key. The new value is entered in cell B3, and the label in the "Gardens completed" section of the pie chart changes from 950 to 975 in the linked chart in the Word document. Although you can't see the pie chart in the Excel spreadsheet window, it has also been updated to display the new value.

   Trouble? If the chart in the Word document does not change to show the new value, click anywhere in the white area inside the chart border, and then click the Refresh Data button in the Data group on the CHART TOOLS DESIGN tab in the Word window. Then, click cell B4 in the spreadsheet window.

8. In the Excel window, type **475** in cell B4, and then press the **Enter** key. The new number is entered in cell B4, and the value in the "Gardens under construction" section of the pie charts in both the Excel and Word windows changes to match. See Figure 7-25.

Figure 7-25 **Modifying the linked chart data**

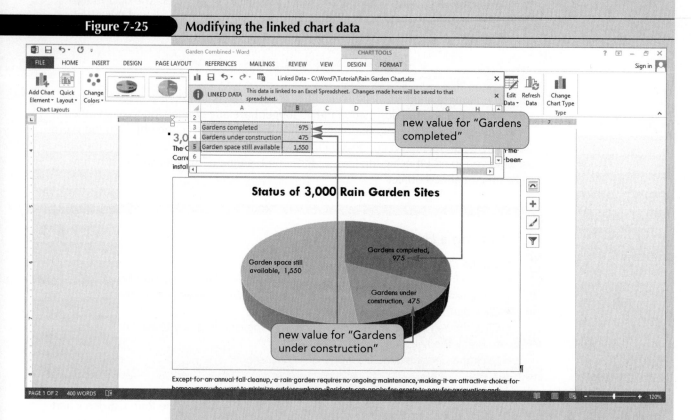

9. At the top of the spreadsheet window, click the **Save** button 🖫, and then click the **Close** button ✕ to close the spreadsheet window.

10. In the Word document, click anywhere outside the chart to deselect it, and then save the Garden Combined document.

When you edited the data in the spreadsheet window, you were actually editing the Rain Garden Chart workbook. If you wanted, you could start Excel and open the Rain Garden Chart workbook to verify that it contains the new values.

INSIGHT

Editing a Linked Worksheet Object

The steps for editing a linked worksheet object are slightly different from the steps for editing a linked chart object. Instead of editing a linked worksheet object from within Word, you need to start Excel, open the workbook, and then edit the worksheet in Excel. You can quickly open the workbook in Excel by right-clicking the linked worksheet object in Word, pointing to Linked Worksheet Object on the shortcut menu, and then clicking Edit Link. This opens the workbook in Excel, where you can edit the data and save your changes. When you are finished, close the workbook, and then return to the Word document. Finally, to update the data within the Word document, right-click the linked worksheet object in the Word document to open a shortcut menu, and then click Update Link.

Anya is finished with her work on the chart. She does not expect the data in it to change, so she wants to break the link between the Excel workbook and the Word document.

Breaking Links

If you no longer need a link between files, you can break it. When you break a link, the source file and the destination file no longer have any connection to each other, and changes made in one file do not affect the other. However, the object in the Word document still retains its connection to the source program. Double-clicking the object allows you to edit it using the tools of the source program. In other words, it behaves like an embedded object.

Breaking a Link to a Source File

- On the ribbon, click the FILE tab.
- On the Info screen, click Edit Links to Files to open the Links dialog box.
- In the list of links in the document, click the link that you want to break.
- Click the Break Link button.
- Click the Yes button in the dialog box that opens asking you to confirm that you want to break the link.
- Click the OK button to close the Links dialog box.

Now, you will break the link between Anya's document and the Rain Garden Chart workbook.

To break the link between the Word document and the Excel workbook:

1. On the ribbon, click the **FILE** tab. Backstage view opens with the Info screen displayed.

2. On the Info screen, click **Edit Links to Files**. The Links dialog box opens with the only link in the document (the link to the Rain Garden Chart workbook) selected. See Figure 7-26.

Figure 7-26   The Links dialog box

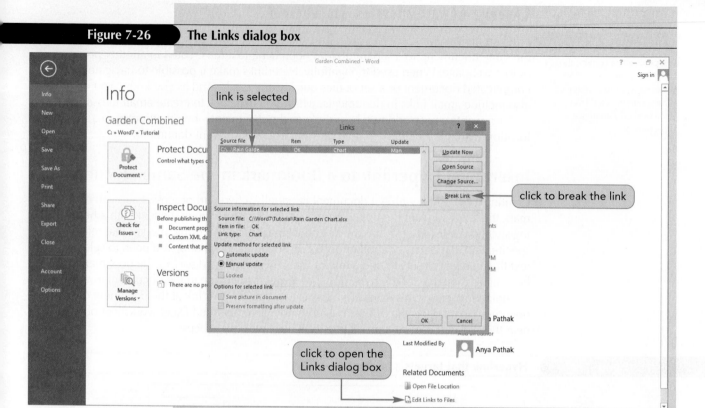

3. In the Links dialog box, click the **Break Link** button, and then click **Yes** in the dialog box that opens asking if you are sure you want to break the link. The list in the Links dialog box now indicates there is no source file for the chart in the document.

4. Click the **OK** button to close the dialog box. You return to the Info screen in Backstage view.

   With the link broken, you can no longer edit the Excel data from within Word. You can verify this by looking at the CHART TOOLS DESIGN tab.

5. At the top of the navigation bar, click the **Back** button ⬅ to close Backstage view and return to the document.

6. Click anywhere inside the chart border to select the chart.

7. On the ribbon, click the **CHART TOOLS DESIGN** tab, if necessary. Notice that the Edit Data button in the Data group is grayed out, indicating this option is no longer available.

8. Click anywhere outside the chart border to deselect it, and then save the document.

Next, Anya asks you to turn your attention to adding hyperlinks to her document. Although hyperlinks are widely used in webpages, you can also use them in ordinary Word documents.

Using Hyperlinks in Word

A hyperlink is a word, phrase, or graphic that you can click to jump to another part of the same document, to a separate Word document, to a file created in another program, or to a webpage. When used thoughtfully, hyperlinks make it possible to navigate a complicated document or a set of files quickly and easily. And as you know, you can also include email links in documents, which you can click to create email messages.

Anya wants you to add two hyperlinks to the document—one that jumps to a location within the document, and one that opens a different document.

Inserting a Hyperlink to a Bookmark in the Same Document

Creating a hyperlink within a document is actually a two-part process. First, you need to mark the text you want the link to jump to—either by formatting the text with a heading style, or by inserting a bookmark. A **bookmark** is an electronic marker that refers to specific text, a picture, or another object in a document. Second, you need to select the text that you want users to click, format it as a hyperlink, and specify the bookmark or heading as the target of the hyperlink. The **target** is the place in the document to which the link connects. In this case, Anya wants to create a hyperlink at the beginning of the document that targets the budget (which is now an embedded Excel worksheet object) near the end of the document. Figure 7-27 illustrates this process.

Figure 7-27	Hyperlink that targets a bookmark

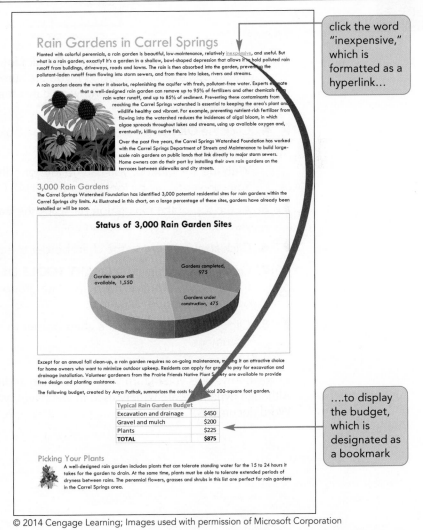

click the word "inexpensive," which is formatted as a hyperlink…

….to display the budget, which is designated as a bookmark

To create a hyperlink in Anya's document, you'll first need to designate the budget as a bookmark.

To insert a bookmark:

▶ **1.** Scroll down and click the budget worksheet object, at the top of page 2. A dotted outline and handles are displayed around the budget, indicating that it is selected.

▶ **2.** On the ribbon, click the **INSERT** tab.

▶ **3.** In the Links group, click the **Bookmark** button. The Bookmark dialog box opens. You can now type the bookmark name, which cannot contain spaces.

▶ **4.** In the Bookmark name box, type **Budget**. See Figure 7-28.

Figure 7-28	Creating a bookmark

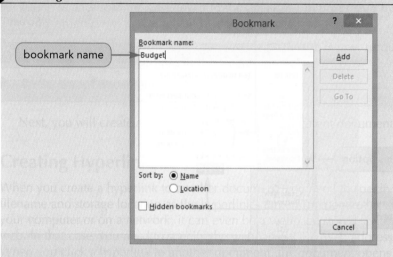

TIP

To delete a bookmark, click it in the Bookmark dialog box, and then click the Delete button.

▶ **5.** Click the **Add** button. The Bookmark dialog box closes. Although you can't see any change in the document, the budget worksheet object has been designated as a bookmark.

The bookmark you just created will be the target of a hyperlink, which you will create next.

Creating a Hyperlink to a Location in the Same Document

- Select the text, graphic, or other object that you want to format as a hyperlink.
- On the ribbon, click the INSERT tab.
- In the Links group, click the Hyperlink button to open the Insert Hyperlink dialog box.
- In the Link to pane, click Place in This Document.
- In the Select a place in this document list, click the bookmark or heading you want to link to, and then click the OK button.

Anya wants you to format the word "inexpensive" at the beginning of the document as a hyperlink that will target the bookmark you just created.

Anya wants to insert a hyperlink that, when clicked, will open a Word document containing a list of plants that grow well in rain gardens. You'll start by opening the document containing the plant list and saving it with a new name.

To create a hyperlink to the Plant List document:

▶ **1.** Open the document **Plant** located in the Word7 ▶ Tutorial folder included with your Data Files, save it as **Plant List** in the location specified by your instructor, and then close it.

▶ **2.** In the Garden Combined document, scroll down to the end of the document, and then select the word **list** in the second-to-last line.

▶ **3.** On the ribbon, click the **INSERT** tab.

▶ **4.** In the Links group, click the **Hyperlink** button. The Insert Hyperlink dialog box opens.

▶ **5.** In the Link to pane, click **Existing File or Web Page**. The dialog box displays options related to selecting a file or a webpage.

▶ **6.** Click the **Look in** arrow, navigate to the location where you stored the Plant List file, if necessary, and then click **Plant List** in the file list. See Figure 7-31.

Figure 7-31 | **Inserting a hyperlink to a different document**

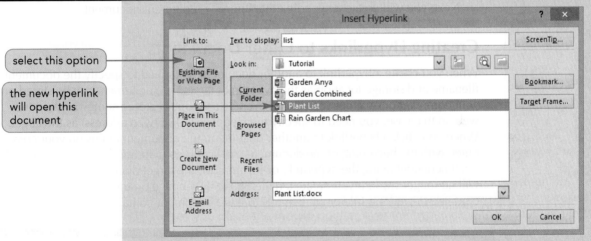

▶ **7.** Click the **OK** button. The new "list" hyperlink is formatted in green with an underline. Now, you will test the hyperlink.

▶ **8.** Press and hold the **Ctrl** key, and then click the **list** hyperlink. The Plant List document opens. See Figure 7-32.

Figure 7-32	Plant List document

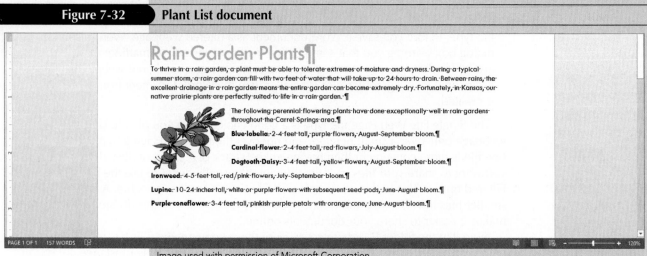

Image used with permission of Microsoft Corporation

9. Close the Plant List document, and then return to the Garden Combined document. The link is now turquoise because you clicked it.

10. Save your document.

Now that you have finalized the document and added the necessary hyperlinks, your next step is to save the document as a webpage.

Saving a Word Document as a Webpage

Webpages are special documents designed to be viewed in a program called a **browser**. One widely used browser is Internet Explorer. Because webpages include code written in **Hypertext Markup Language**, or **HTML**, they are often referred to as **HTML documents**.

To create sophisticated webpages (or a complete website), you'll probably want to use a dedicated HTML editor, such as Adobe Dreamweaver. However, in Word you can create a simple webpage from an existing document by saving it as a webpage. When you do so, Word inserts HTML codes that tell the browser how to format and display the text and graphics. Fortunately, you don't have to learn Hypertext Markup Language to create webpages with Word. When you save the document as a webpage, Word creates all the necessary HTML codes (called tags); however, you won't actually see the HTML codes in your webpage.

You can choose from three different webpage file types in Word. The main differences among these file types are file size and the way special elements, such as WordArt or embedded or linked objects, are treated when they are displayed in a browser:

- **Single File Web Page**—Saves the document as an MHTML file, which is similar to an HTML file, with all graphics stored in the file along with the text; a Single File Web Page file also retains the formatting of the original Word document. A document saved as a Single File Web Page can be more than three or four times the size of the original Word document. In the file name for a Single File Web Page file, avoid including spaces and special characters such as exclamation marks or percent signs, because they can prevent the browser from displaying the page correctly.
- **Web Page**—Saves the document as an HTML file, with a separate folder containing graphics and other elements that control the page's formatting. The HTML file created using the Web Page file type is approximately the same size as the original Word document, but the accompanying files can be two or three times the size of the Word document.

- **Web Page, Filtered**—Saves the document as an HTML file, with graphics stored in a separate folder. This file type retains less information than the other two formats, so some of the document formatting might change or disappear when you use this file type. Before you save a Word document as a filtered webpage, Word displays a dialog box warning you that some Office features (typically formatting) may not be available when you reopen the page. The total file size of a filtered webpage and its accompanying graphics files is smaller than the Word document from which it is created.

The Single File Web Page file type is a good choice when you plan to share your webpage only over a small network and not over the Internet. Having to manage only one file is more convenient than having to keep track of a group of files. But when you want to share your files over the Internet, it's usually better to use the Web Page, Filtered option. This will keep your overall file size as small as possible. A group of smaller files travels across the web faster than one large file, so this division of files makes it easier to share your documents online.

Note that the folder Word creates to store the accompanying files has the same name as your webpage, plus an underscore and the word "files." For instance, a webpage saved as Finance Summary would be accompanied by a folder named Finance Summary_files.

REFERENCE

Saving a Word Document as a Webpage

- Open the Save As dialog box and navigate to the location where you want to save the webpage.
- Click the Save as type arrow, and then click Single File Web Page; Web Page; or Web Page, Filtered.
- If desired, type a new filename in the File name box.
- Click the Change Title button to open the Enter Text dialog box.
- In the Page title box, type a title, which will be displayed at the top of the browser window, and then click the OK button.
- In the Save As dialog box, click the Save button. If you saved the document using the Web Page, Filtered option, click Yes in the warning dialog box.

After you save a document as a webpage, Word displays it in **Web Layout view**, which displays the document similarly to the way it would be displayed in a web browser. In Web Layout view, the text spans the width of the screen, with no page breaks, and without any margins or headers and footers. Also, text wrapping around graphics often changes in Web Layout view, as the text expands to fill the wider area of the screen.

To save the Garden Combined document as a webpage:

1. On the ribbon, click the **FILE** tab, and then click **Save As** in the navigation bar.

2. In the Save As dialog box, navigate to the location specified by your instructor.

   Because Anya wants to retain the document formatting, she asks you to use the Single File Web Page type.

3. Click the **Save as type** arrow, and then click **Single File Web Page**.

4. In the File name box, change the filename to **Rain_Garden_Webpage**.

5. At the bottom of the Save As dialog box, click the **Change Title** button to open the Enter Text dialog box, and then type **Rain Gardens in Carrel Springs** in the Page title box. This title will be displayed at the top of the browser window. See Figure 7-33.

Figure 7-33   ▶ **Webpage title in Enter Text dialog box**

this title will appear at the top of the browser window

name of the webpage file

file type

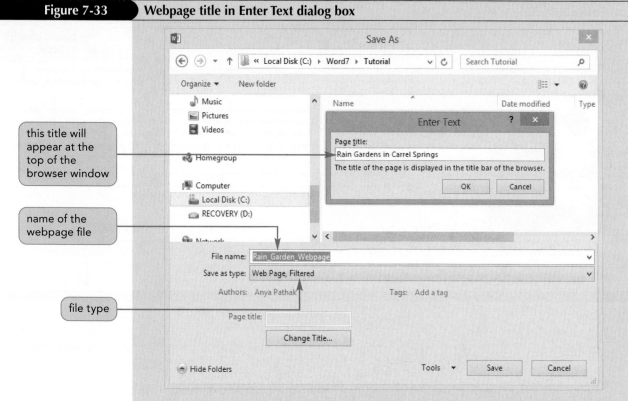

6. In the Enter Text dialog box, click the **OK** button.

7. In the Save As dialog box, click the **Save** button. The document is converted into a webpage and displayed in Web Layout view. The text spans the document window and is no longer constrained by the page margins. The filename Rain_Garden_Webpage is displayed in the Word title bar. The title you specified in Step 5 won't be visible until you open the webpage in a browser, at which point it will be displayed in the browser's title bar.

8. Scroll up to the beginning of the document.

Because the text spans the entire document window, it's often necessary to increase the Zoom level in Web Layout view to make the text easier to read.

9. Change the Zoom level to **200%**. Unlike in Print Layout view, when you zoom in on the document in Web Layout view, the line breaks adjust to ensure that as much text as possible remains visible in the document window.

10. Change the Zoom level to **140%**. The line breaks readjust to accommodate the new Zoom level. See Figure 7-34.

Figure 7-34   **New webpage displayed in Web Layout view**

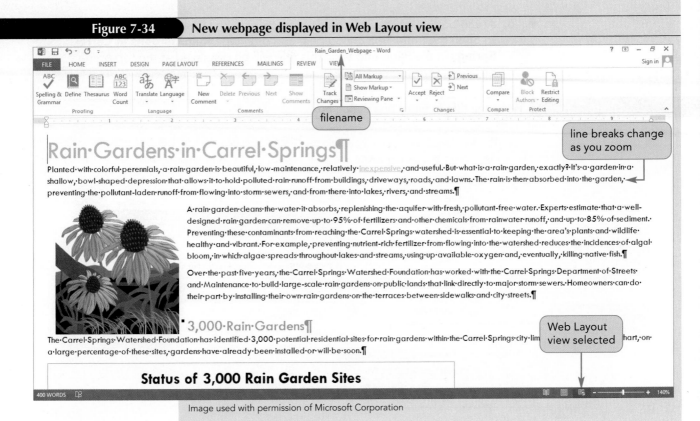

Image used with permission of Microsoft Corporation

Next, Anya asks you to adjust the document's formatting to improve its appearance in Web Layout view.

Formatting a Webpage

You can edit and format text, colors, and graphics in a webpage the same way you edit and format a normal Word document. Anya asks you to start by adjusting the webpage's graphics and text.

Modifying Graphics and Text for Web Layout View

After you convert a Word document into a webpage, you might need to adjust the position, size, and formatting settings for the graphics to make them look better as the user zooms in or out on the page.

To adjust the graphics in the Rain_Garden_Webpage file:

1. Drag the picture of the pink flowers up and to the left slightly to position it directly below the "Rain Gardens in Carrel Springs" heading, with its anchor symbol next to the picture's upper-left corner.

2. Change the picture's height to **1.5** inches. The picture's width adjusts to 1.48 inches automatically.

3. Scroll down in the document, and then click the chart object.

4. Make sure the HOME tab is displayed on the ribbon.

5. In the Paragraph group, click the **Center** button.

▶ **6.** Scroll down in the document, click the bluebell picture at the bottom of the webpage, and change its height to **1** inch. Its width automatically changes to 0.87 inches.

After you convert a Word document to a webpage, you typically also need to adjust the text's formatting to accommodate the wider text, which spans the width of the viewer's screen. In particular, it's often helpful to use a larger font size for headings. Anya asks you to increase the font size for the title and headings.

To increase the font size for the title and headings:

▶ **1.** Select the title **Rain Gardens in Carrel Springs** at the top of the webpage.

▶ **2.** In the Font group, click the **Increase Font Size** button $\boxed{\text{A}^{^\cdot}}$ twice to increase the font size from 28 points to 48 points.

▶ **3.** Change the font size for the "3,000 Rain Gardens" heading and the "Pick Your Plants" heading to 28 points, and then deselect any selected text.

▶ **4.** Save your work.

Next, you'll make more changes to the Rain_Garden_Webpage file to improve its online appearance.

Applying a Background Fill Effect

When formatting a webpage, you can focus on how the page will look on the screen, without having to consider how it will look when printed. This means you can take advantage of some formatting options that are only visible on the screen, such as a background page color or a background fill effect. A **fill effect** is a repeating graphic element, such as a texture, a photo, or a color gradient. It's essential to use fill effects judiciously. In the hands of a trained graphic designer, they can be striking; if used carelessly, they can be garish and distracting. As a general rule, you should avoid using photos and textures, and instead stick with simple colors or color gradients.

Anya decides to use a gradient background in shades of green.

To apply a background fill effect to the document:

▶ **1.** On the ribbon, click the **DESIGN** tab.

▶ **2.** In the Page Background group, click the **Page Color** button. The Page Color gallery opens, with a menu at the bottom. You could click a color in the gallery to select it as a background color for the page. To select another type of background effect, you need to click Fill Effects.

▶ **3.** Click **Fill Effects** to open the Fill Effects dialog box, and then click the **Gradient** tab, if necessary. Note that you could use other tabs in this dialog box to add a textured, patterned, or picture background.

▶ **4.** In the Colors section, click the **Two colors** button. The Color 1 and Color 2 boxes and arrows are displayed.

▶ **5.** Click the **Color 1** arrow, and then click **Lime, Accent 1, Lighter 80%**, the fifth color from the left in the second row of the Theme Colors section.

▶ **6.** Click the **Color 2** arrow, and then click **Sky Blue, Background 2, Lighter 60%**, the third color from the left in the third row of the Theme Colors section.

▶ **7.** In the Shading styles section, click the **Vertical** option button to change the gradient pattern so it stretches vertically up and down the page. Compare your dialog box to Figure 7-35.

Figure 7-35 **Selecting a gradient background**

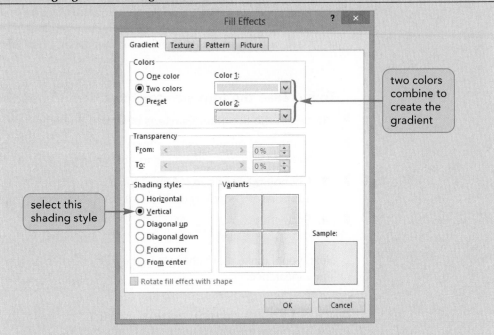

▶ **8.** Click the **OK** button. The document's background is now a gradient that varies between lime green and sky blue.

▶ **9.** Scroll down so you can see the budget near the bottom of the webpage.

The gradient background is light enough to make the document text easy to read. However, it's now hard to see the gridlines of the budget worksheet object. You can fix that by changing the object's background color.

To change the background for the budget worksheet object:

▶ **1.** Right-click the budget worksheet object to display a shortcut menu, and then click **Format Object**. The Format Object dialog box opens, with the Picture tab displayed.

▶ **2.** Click the **Colors and Lines** tab to display settings related to the colors used in the worksheet object. In the Fill section, the Color box currently displays "No Color," indicating that the object's background is the same as the webpage's background.

▶ **3.** In the Fill section, click the **Color** arrow, and then click **White, Background 1**, the first square in the top row of the Theme Colors section. See Figure 7-36.

Figure 7-36   **Format Object dialog box**

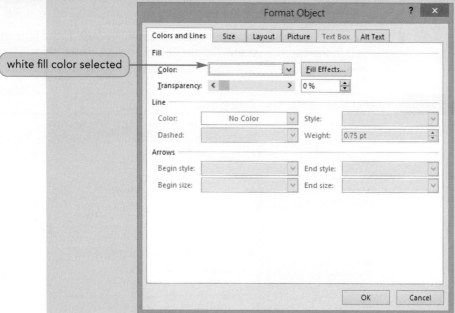

white fill color selected

> **4.** Click the **OK** button to close the Format Object dialog box. The budget now has a white background, which makes the gridlines easier to see.

> **5.** Click outside the budget to deselect it, and then save the document.

Next, you will add horizontal lines to separate the various sections of the webpage.

Inserting Horizontal Lines

Horizontal lines allow you to see at a glance where one part of a webpage ends and another begins. You can also add horizontal lines to regular Word documents.

Anya wants you to add a horizontal line before the "3,000 Rain Gardens" heading and before the "Picking Your Plants" heading.

To insert horizontal lines into the webpage:

> **1.** Scroll up and click at the beginning of the "3,000 Rain Gardens" heading.

> **2.** On the ribbon, click the **HOME** tab.

> **3.** In the Paragraph group, click the **Borders button arrow** to open the Borders gallery, and then click **Horizontal Line** to insert a default gray line.

   Anya wants to change the line's color. She also wants to make the line shorter, so it doesn't span the full page.

> **4.** Right-click the horizontal line to display a shortcut menu, and then click **Format Horizontal Line**. The Format Horizontal Line dialog box opens, with settings for changing the line's width, height, alignment, and color. The current Width setting is 100%, meaning that the line spans the entire page from left to right. To leave a little space on each side, you need to lower the percentage.

5. Triple-click the **Width** box, and then type **75**. Because the Center alignment option at the bottom of the dialog box is selected by default, the shorter line will be centered on the page, with space to its left and its right.

6. Click the **Color** arrow, and then click **Lime, Accent 1**, the fifth square from the left in the top row of the Theme Colors section. The Color gallery closes, and the Use solid color (no shade) check box is now selected. See Figure 7-37.

Figure 7-37	Format Horizontal Line dialog box

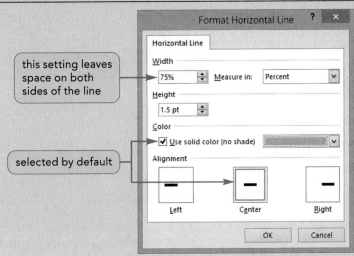

this setting leaves space on both sides of the line

selected by default

7. Click the **OK** button, and then click anywhere in the document to deselect the horizontal line. Your webpage should look similar to Figure 7-38.

Figure 7-38	Newly inserted horizontal line

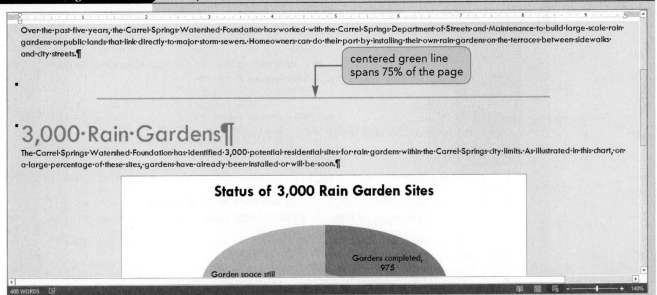

Now, you can copy the line, and then insert it before the other heading.

TIP

To remove a horizontal line, click the line to select it, and then press the Delete key.

▶ **8.** Click the horizontal line to select it, and then press the **Ctrl+C** keys to copy it to the Clipboard.

▶ **9.** Scroll down, click to the left of the "P" in the "Picking Your Plants" heading, and then press the **Ctrl+V** keys to insert the horizontal line before the heading.

▶ **10.** Save the document.

You've finished formatting the webpage. Next, you'll create a new hyperlink and edit the existing one.

Editing Hyperlinks

Anya's webpage contains two hyperlinks—the "inexpensive" link, which jumps to the budget, and the "list" link, which jumps to a Word document containing a list of plants suitable for rain gardens. You originally created these hyperlinks in Anya's Word document, and they are still functional, even after you saved the document as a webpage. However, before Anya can publish her page on the web, she needs to save the Plant List document as a webpage, format it to match the Rain_Garden_Webpage file, and then edit the hyperlink that connects the two pages.

To save the Plant List document as a webpage:

▶ **1.** Scroll down, if necessary, to the end of the webpage, press and hold the **Ctrl** key, and then click the **list** hyperlink. The Plant List document opens.

▶ **2.** Save the document using the Single File Web Page file type, in the location specified by your instructor. Name the webpage **Plant_List_Webpage** and use **Recommended Plants** as the title.

You need to adjust the font size for the headings in this document, and then change the page's background.

▶ **3.** Select the **Rain Garden Plants** heading, increase its font size to **48** points, and then deselect the heading.

▶ **4.** On the ribbon, click the **DESIGN** tab.

▶ **5.** In the Page Background group, click the **Page Color** button, and then click **Fill Effects**.

▶ **6.** In the Fill Effects dialog box, click the **Two colors** button.

▶ **7.** Click the **Color 1** arrow, and then click **Lime, Accent 1, Lighter 80%**, the fifth color from the left in the second row of the Theme Colors section.

▶ **8.** Click the **Color 2** arrow, and then click **Sky Blue, Background 2, Lighter 60%**, the third color from the left in the third row of the Theme Colors section.

▶ **9.** In the Shading styles section, click the **Vertical** button, and then click the **OK** button.

▶ **10.** Save the webpage file, and then close it. You return to the Rain_Garden_Webpage file in Word.

Now, you need to edit the hyperlink in the Rain_Garden_Webpage file so it targets the new webpage file named Plant_List_Webpage, instead of the old Word document named Plant List.

To edit the list hyperlink:

▶ **1.** Position the pointer over the **list** hyperlink at the end of the webpage to display a ScreenTip, which indicates that the link will jump to a document named Plant List.docx.

▶ **2.** Right-click the **list** hyperlink to open a shortcut menu, and then click **Edit Hyperlink**. The Edit Hyperlink dialog box opens. It looks just like the Insert Hyperlink dialog box, which you have already used. To edit the hyperlink, you simply select a different target file.

▶ **3.** In the Link to pane, verify that the **Existing File or Web Page** option is selected.

▶ **4.** Navigate to the location where you saved the Plant_List_Webpage file, if necessary, and then click **Plant_List_Webpage** in the file list.

▶ **5.** Click the **OK** button. You return to the Rain_Garden_Webpage file.

▶ **6.** Place the mouse pointer over the **list** hyperlink to display a ScreenTip, which indicates that the link will now jump to a webpage named Plant_List_Webpage.mht.

The edited hyperlink now correctly targets the webpage containing the plant list. After users read the plant list, they most likely will want to return to the main webpage. Therefore, Anya asks you to insert a hyperlink in the Plant_List_Webpage file that will take readers back to the Rain_Garden_Webpage file.

To open the Plant_List_Webpage file, you might be tempted to click the "list" hyperlink in the Rain_Garden_Webpage file. However, if you do, the webpage would open in Internet Explorer. To open a webpage in Word, you need to use the Open command in Backstage view.

To insert a hyperlink in the Plant_List_Webpage file:

▶ **1.** On the ribbon, click the **FILE** tab, and then click **Open** in the navigation bar.

▶ **2.** Navigate to and click the **Plant_List_Webpage** file, and then click the **Open** button. The Plant_List_Webpage file opens.

▶ **3.** Press the **Ctrl+End** keys to move the insertion point to the end of the document, and then press the **Enter** key.

▶ **4.** Type **Return to main page.**

▶ **5.** Select the text **Return to main page.**

▶ **6.** On the ribbon, click the **INSERT** tab.

▶ **7.** In the Links group, click the **Hyperlink** button, and then click **Existing File or Web Page**, if necessary.

▶ **8.** Navigate to the location where you stored the Rain_Garden_Webpage file, if necessary, and then click **Rain_Garden_Webpage** in the file list.

▶ **9.** Click the **OK** button. Word formats the selected text as a hyperlink.

▶ **10.** Save the Plant_List_Webpage file, and then close it. You return to the Rain_Garden_Webpage file.

▶ **11.** Save and close the **Rain_Garden_Webpage** file, but do not exit Word.

Now, after a user reviews the list of plants, he or she can click the hyperlink to return to the main webpage.

Keeping Track of Documents Containing Hyperlinks

When your documents or webpages include hyperlinks to other documents or webpages, you must keep track of where you store the target files. If you move a target file to a different location, hyperlinks to it will not function properly. In this case, you created a hyperlink in the Rain_Garden_Webpage file that links to the Plant_List_Webpage file, and vice versa. To ensure that these hyperlinks continue to function, you must keep both webpages in the folder they were in when you created the link. If you have to move a target webpage, you must edit the hyperlink to select the target webpage in its new location.

Now, Anya suggests you view both webpages in a browser and test the hyperlinks.

Viewing the Webpage in a Browser

You're now ready to view the finished webpages in Internet Explorer, a web browser. In the browser, you can test the hyperlinks and verify that the formatting looks the way you intended. In a browser, you don't have to press the Ctrl key to use a hyperlink. Instead, you simply click the link.

To view the webpages in a web browser:

▶ **1.** Start Internet Explorer.

▶ **2.** On the Internet Explorer title bar, click the **Maximize** button ☐, if necessary, so that the program window fills the entire screen.

▶ **3.** On the menu bar, click **File**, and then click **Open**. The Open dialog box opens.

  Trouble? If you do not see a menu bar below the title bar in the browser window, right-click the title bar to open the shortcut menu, and then click Menu bar to place a checkmark next to this option.

▶ **4.** Click the **Browse** button, navigate to the location where you saved the Rain_Garden_Webpage file, click the **Rain_Garden_Webpage** file, and then click the **Open** button. You return to the Open dialog box.

▶ **5.** Click the **OK** button. The Open dialog box closes, and Anya's webpage is displayed in the browser window. The title "Rain Gardens in Carrel Springs" is displayed in the tab above the Internet Explorer menu bar. See Figure 7-39.

Figure 7-39   **Webpage displayed in a browser window**

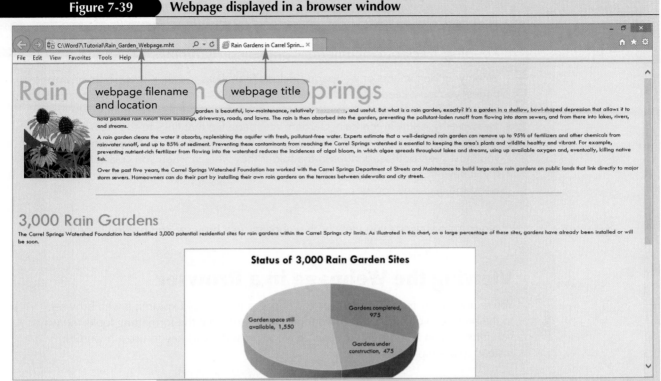

Image used with permission of Microsoft Corporation

6. Scroll down and review the webpage. Anya points out that the font size is too small to read easily in the browser window. You can fix this by zooming in.

7. In the menu bar, click **View**, point to **Zoom**, and then click **150%**. The browser window zooms in, making the text easier to read.

8. Scroll back up and click the **inexpensive** hyperlink. The budget is displayed in the browser window. Note that the font in the budget looks different in the browser than it did in Word. Fonts often appear less sharply delineated in a browser than they do in the Word window.

9. In the last paragraph of the document, click the **list** hyperlink. The browser opens the Plant_List_Webpage file.

10. At the bottom of the page, click the **Return to main page.** hyperlink to display the Rain_Garden_Webpage file in your browser.

11. Close Internet Explorer.

PROSKILLS

Teamwork: Emailing Word Documents

Creating and publishing webpages is a powerful way to share documents among colleagues. But sometimes emailing a document as an attachment is the simplest way to share a file. To get started emailing a document, first make sure you have set up Microsoft Outlook as your email program. Then, in Word, open the document you want to email. On the ribbon, click the FILE tab, and then click Share in the navigation bar. On the Share screen, click Email, and then select the email option you want. When you email documents, keep in mind the following:

- Many email services have difficulty handling attachments larger than 4 MB. Consider storing large files in a compressed (or zipped) folder to reduce their size before emailing them.
- Other word-processing programs and early versions of Word might not be able to open files created in Word 2013. To avoid problems with conflicting versions, you have two options. You can save the Word document as a rich text file (using the Rich Text File document type in the Save As dialog box) before emailing it; all versions of Word can open rich text files. Another option is to save the document as a PDF.
- If you plan to email a document that contains links to other files, remember to email all the linked files.
- Attachments, including Word documents, are sometimes used maliciously to spread computer viruses. Remember to include an explanatory note with any email attachment so that the recipient can be certain the attachment is legitimate. Also, it's important to have a reliable virus checker program installed if you plan to receive and open email attachments.

The new webpages are just one way to share information about rain gardens. Anya also wants to write a blog post discussing the potential rain garden sites the foundation has identified. She asks you to help her create a blog post in Word.

Creating and Publishing a Blog Post

Creating a blog post in Word is similar to creating a new Word document except that instead of clicking Blank document in Backstage view, you click Blog post. Note that before you can publish your blog post using Word, you need to register a blog account with an Internet blog provider that is compatible with Microsoft Word 2013.

Anya asks you to help her create a blog post about the new webpages.

To create and publish a blog post:

1. On the ribbon, click the **FILE** tab, and then click **New** in the navigation bar to display the icons for the various document templates.

2. Scroll down if necessary, and then click **Blog post**.

3. In the Blog post window, click the **Create** button. A blank blog post opens. Assuming you have not previously registered for a blog account, you also see the Register a Blog Account dialog box.

To register a blog account, you could click the Register Now button to open the New Blog Account dialog box. From there, you could follow the prompts to register your blog account. Anya will register her blog account later, so you can skip the registration step for now.

▶ **4.** Click the **Register Later** button to close the dialog box.

▶ **5.** At the top of the blog post, click the **[Enter Post Title Here]** placeholder, and then type **Rain Gardens in Carrel Springs**.

▶ **6.** Click in the blank paragraph below the blog title, and then type **The Carrel Springs Watershed Foundation has identified 3,000 potential residential sites for rain gardens within the Carrel Springs city limits.** See Figure 7-40.

| Figure 7-40 | Blog post |

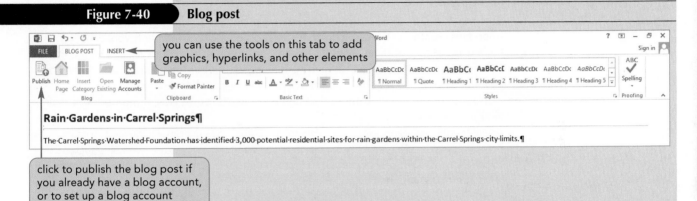

you can use the tools on this tab to add graphics, hyperlinks, and other elements

Rain·Gardens·in·Carrel·Springs¶

The·Carrel·Springs·Watershed·Foundation·has·identified·3,000·potential·residential·sites·for·rain·gardens·within·the·Carrel·Springs·city·limits.¶

click to publish the blog post if you already have a blog account, or to set up a blog account

At this point, you could use the tools on the INSERT tab to add hyperlinks, graphics, and other items to your blog post. Anya plans to add more text and some graphics to her blog post later. For now, you can save the post, and then explore options for publishing it.

▶ **7.** Save the blog post as **Rain Garden Blog Post** in the location specified by your instructor. Note that a blog post is a regular Word document file, with a .docx extension.

▶ **8.** On the BLOG POST tab, in the Blog group, click the **Publish** button.

Assuming you have not previously registered for a blog account, you see the Register a Blog Account dialog box again. At this point, you could click the Register an Account button and then follow the on-screen instructions to register a blog account and publish your blog. Because Anya plans to do that later, you can close the blog post for now.

Trouble? If you see a menu below the Publish button, you clicked the Publish button arrow instead of the Publish button. Press the Esc key, and then click the Publish button.

TIP

To add, remove, or change blog accounts, click the Manage Accounts button in the Blog group on the BLOG POST tab.

9. Click the **Cancel** button to close the Register a Blog Account dialog box, and then click the **OK** button in the Microsoft Word dialog box.

10. Close the blog post.

Anya plans to write weekly blog posts describing the foundation's progress with the rain garden projects. Combined with the new webpages, they will help generate interest in the foundation's work.

Session 7.2 Quick Check

REVIEW

1. Explain how to break a link between a Word file and another file.
2. What is the first step in creating a hyperlink to a location in the same document?
3. Are page backgrounds displayed on a printed page?
4. What is the difference between the way text is displayed in Web Layout view and the way it is displayed in Print Layout view?
5. What file type should you use if you want to share a webpage over the Internet?
6. Explain how to edit a hyperlink.
7. What is the file extension for a blog post file?

ASSESS

SAM Projects

Put your skills into practice with SAM Projects! SAM Projects for this tutorial can be found online. If you have a SAM account, go to www.cengage.com/sam2013 to download the most recent Project Instructions and Start Files.

PRACTICE

Review Assignments

Data Files needed for the Review Assignments: Foundation Oliver.docx, Foundation.docx, Fundraising Chart.xlsx, Membership.docx, Projections.xlsx

Anya is working on a new document about the Carrel Springs Watershed Foundation. She has written a draft of the document and has emailed it to Oliver. While he reviews it, Anya asks you to turn on Track Changes and continue working on the document. Then, she can combine her edited version of the document with Oliver's, accepting or rejecting changes as necessary. She also needs you to insert some data from an Excel worksheet as an embedded object and insert an Excel chart as a linked object. She then wants you to create a version of the document with hyperlinks, format the document for viewing as a webpage, save it as a webpage, and view it in a browser. Complete the following steps:

1. Open the document **Foundation** from the Word7 ▸ Review folder included with your Data Files. Save the file as **Foundation Anya** in the location specified by your instructor.
2. Change the username to **Anya Pathak** and the user initials to **AP**, and then turn on Track Changes.
3. In the second paragraph, move the sentence that begins "Over the years…" to the end of the paragraph, and then add an **s** to the last word in the sentence.
4. In the third paragraph, in the first sentence, change "Harrison Paulson" to your first and last names, and then change "south" to **west** so the sentence reads "…west of Carrel Springs."
5. In the fourth paragraph, in the first line, attach a comment to the phrase "Since that day" that reads **Consider inserting exact date?**
6. Save your changes to the Foundation Anya document.
7. Combine the Foundation Anya document with Oliver's edited version, which is named **Foundation Oliver**, located in the Word7 ▸ Review folder included with your Data Files. Use the Foundation Anya document as the original document.
8. Save the combined document as **Foundation Combined** in the location specified by your instructor.
9. Turn off Track Changes, and then reject Oliver's deletion of "five" and his insertion of "seven." Accept all the other changes in the document. Delete all comments.
10. Change the username and initials back to their original settings, and then save the Foundation Combined document. Close the Foundation Anya document, saving changes if you didn't save them earlier.
11. In the Foundation Combined document, replace the placeholder "[Insert Excel worksheet]" with the fundraising projections in the **Projections.xlsx file**, which is located in the Word7 ▸ Review folder included with your Data Files. Include everything from cell A1 through cell B6. Insert the worksheet as an embedded object, and then close the Projections.xlsx file.
12. Center the embedded object, and then change the "Spring native plant sale" value in the embedded worksheet object from $70,000 to **$80,000**. Don't be concerned if you see pound symbols (#) in some of the cells.
13. Open the workbook **Fundraising Chart.xlsx** in the Word7 ▸ Review folder included with your Data Files, and then save it as **CSWF Fundraising Chart.xlsx** in the location specified by your instructor. Copy the chart to the Office Clipboard.

14. Return to the Foundation Combined document, and then replace the placeholder "[Insert Excel chart]" with a linked copy of the chart using the destination theme. Save the Foundation Combined document, and then close it.

15. Return to the CSWF Fundraising Chart workbook in Excel. Edit the data in the workbook by changing the percentage for state and federal grants to **35%**, and the percentage for private donations to **45%**. Save the workbook, and then close Excel.

16. Open the **Foundation Combined** document and review the chart. If it doesn't contain the new percentages, click the chart, and use the Refresh Data button to update the chart.

17. Save the Foundation Combined document, and then save the document with the new name **Foundation No Links** in the location specified by your instructor.

18. Break the link to the Excel workbook, and then save the document.

19. Format the Excel worksheet object as a bookmark named **Projections**. In the third line of the second paragraph, format the word "funds" as a hyperlink that targets the "projections" bookmark. Test the hyperlink to make sure it works. Save the document.

20. Open the document **Membership** from the Word7 ▸ Review folder included with your Data Files, and then save the file as **Membership Levels** in the location specified by your instructor. Close the Membership Levels document and return to the Foundation No Links document.

21. Format the last word in the document, "here," as a hyperlink that targets the Membership Levels document. Test the hyperlink to make sure it works, and then close the Membership Levels document. Save the Foundation No Links document.

22. Save the Foundation No Links document as a webpage in the location specified by your instructor using the Single File Web Page file type. Use **Foundation_Webpage** for the filename and **CSWF Main Page** as the page title.

23. Add a two-color gradient page color using Turquoise, Accent 1, Lighter 60% as Color 1 and White, Background 1 as Color 2—with the shading style set to Diagonal up.

24. Change the background color for the worksheet object to white, and center the chart.

25. Insert a horizontal line before the "Fundraising for the Future" heading. Keep the default color, but change the width to 75%. Insert an identical horizontal line before the "Become a Member" heading.

26. At the beginning of the page, change the font size for the "Carrel Springs Watershed Foundation" title to 36 points. Save the webpage.

27. Open the document **Membership Levels**, and then save it as a webpage using the Single File Web Page type. Use **Membership_Levels_Webpage** for the filename and **CSWF Membership Page** as the page title.

28. Format the new webpage to match the Foundation_Webpage file by adding the same white and turquoise gradient page color with the Diagonal up shading style, and by changing the font size for the text "Join the Carrel Springs Watershed Foundation" to 36 points.

29. At the end of the Membership_Levels_Webpage document, insert a new paragraph that is not part of the bulleted list, and then insert the text **Click to return to main page**.

30. Format the new text as a hyperlink that targets the Foundation_Webpage file, save the Membership_Levels_Webpage file, and then close it.

31. In the Foundation_Webpage file, edit the "here" hyperlink at the end of the page to target the Membership_Levels_Webpage. Save the Foundation_Webpage document, close the document, and then close it.

32. Start Internet Explorer, and then open the **Foundation_Webpage** file in the browser window. Review the webpage in the browser, note the differences in the gradient style and fonts, test the hyperlinks, and then, if necessary, open the webpages in Word again, correct any problems with the hyperlinks, and then test them again in Internet Explorer.

33. When you are certain all the links work, close the browser, and then close any open Word documents.

34. Create a new blog post without attempting to register a blog account. Save the blog post as **Foundation Blog Post** in the location specified by your instructor. Insert **Fundraising for the Future** as the post title, and then type the following as the text of the blog post: **The Carrel Springs Watershed Foundation finances water improvement programs throughout the Carrel Springs area**.

35. Save and close the Foundation Blog Post file.

Case Problem 1

Data Files needed for this Case Problem: Matthews.docx, Vaccinations.xlsx

Big Bay Veterinary Clinic   You recently started working as a veterinary assistant at Big Bay Veterinary Clinic in Coleton, Alaska. A client just called the clinic and asked you to send a summary of her dog's current vaccinations. The vaccination information is stored in an Excel workbook. You need to respond with a letter that contains the vaccination information embedded as an Excel worksheet object. After you embed the worksheet object, you need to make some edits to the document using Track Changes. Finally, the clinic manager is considering using Word to create posts for the clinic's new blog, so she asks you to create a sample blog post. Complete the following steps:

1. Open the document **Matthews** from the Word7 ► Case1 folder included with your Data Files. Save the file as **Matthews Letter** in the location specified by your instructor.

2. In the signature line, replace "Student Name" with your name.

3. Delete the placeholder "[Insert Excel worksheet]."

4. Start Excel, open the workbook **Vaccinations** from the Word7 ► Case1 folder included with your Data Files, and then save it as **Vaccinations Summary** in the location specified by your instructor.

5. Select the two-column list of vaccination types and dates, from cell A7 through cell B11, and then copy the selection to the Clipboard.

6. Insert the worksheet data into the Word document in the blank paragraph that previously contained the placeholder text. Insert the data as a linked object that uses the destination styles.

7. Save the Word document, and then return to the Vaccinations Summary workbook and close Excel.

8. Starting from within the Word window, edit the linked worksheet object to change the date for the Distemper vaccination to **7/20/2016**. (*Hint*: Remember that the steps for editing a linked worksheet object are different from the steps for editing a linked chart.) Save the workbook, close Excel, and then update the link in Word.

9. Save the Matthews Letter document, and then save it again as **Matthews Letter No Links** in the location specified by your instructor.

10. Break the link in the Matthews Letter No Links document.

11. If necessary, change the username to your first and last names, change the initials to your initials, and then turn on Track Changes.

12. At the beginning of the letter, delete the date, and then type the current date using the format 3/1/16.

13. In the inside address, change "Road" to **Lane**.

14. At the end of the paragraph that reads "Please call if you have any questions." add the sentence **In the future, I can send you summaries by email if you prefer**.

15. Open the Reviewing pane and note the total number of revisions, the number of insertions, and the number of deletions in the document. Attach a comment to the word "Clinic" in the first paragraph that reads **This document contains x insertions and x deletions. It contains a total of x revisions**. Replace the three instances of *x* with the correct numbers. (*Hint*: The total number of revisions will change when you insert the comment. The number that you type in the comment should reflect this updated total.)

16. Close the Reviewing pane, save your changes to the Matthews Letter No Links document, and then save it with the new name **Matthews Letter Changes Accepted** in the location specified by your instructor.

17. Turn off Track Changes, delete the comment, and then reject the replacement of "Lane" for "Road." Accept all the other changes in the document.

18. Return the username and initials to their original settings.

19. Save the Matthews Letter Changes Accepted document, and then close it.

20. Create a new blog post without attempting to register a blog account. Save the blog post as **Clinic Blog Post** in the location specified by your instructor. Insert **News from Big Bay Veterinary Clinic** as the post title, and then type the following as the text of the blog post: **Lyme disease is on the rise in this area, so make sure your pets are fully protected from ticks**.

21. Save and close the blog post.

Case Problem 2

TROUBLESHOOT

Data Files needed for this Case Problem: House Chloe.docx, House Eli.docx, Pictures.docx

Kensington Financial, Department of Human Resources   Chloe Zimmer is an assistant in the Human Resources Department at Kensington Financial, an investment firm with offices in Chicago, New York, and London. When a Kensington employee is transferred to a new city, the Human Resources Department helps with the transition—in some cases, by helping the employee sell his or her home. Right now, Chloe is working at the Chicago office with Eli Ravenna, who has been transferred to London. He is hoping to sell his house himself so he doesn't have to pay a real estate agent fee. It's Chloe's job to help publicize Eli's house by creating a flyer to post around the office, and a webpage for a neighborhood newsletter. She's already edited the house description using Track Changes. Now, she asks for your help in combining her copy of the edited file with Eli's. Then, you'll save and format the documents as webpages so Chloe can post them on the company's network. Complete the following steps:

1. Open the document **House Eli** from the Word7 ▸ Case2 folder included with your Data Files, review its contents, and then close it.

2. Open the document **House Chloe** from the Word7 ▸ Case2 folder included with your Data Files, and then review its contents.

3. Combine the House Chloe and House Eli documents, using the House Chloe file as the original document. If you see a dialog box alerting you to a formatting conflict, use the formatting in the House Chloe file. Save the resulting new document as **House Combined** in the location specified by your instructor. Close the House Chloe document.

4. In the House Combined document, review the tracked changes. Reject Eli's deletion of "Square." Accept the rest of the changes in the document, and then delete the comment.

5. Change the username and initials to yours, and then turn on Track Changes, if necessary.

6. Change the street address in the second paragraph to **2245**, and then add a new sentence at the end of the document that reads **Click here to see pictures of this charming residence**.

7. Save the House Combined document, and then save it again as **House For Sale** in the location specified by your instructor.

8. Accept all changes in the House For Sale document, turn off Track Changes, and then change the username and initials back to their original settings.

9. Open the document **Pictures** from the Word7 ▸ Case2 folder included with your Data Files, and then save it as **House Pictures** in the location specified by your instructor.

⚙ Troubleshoot 10. Because the House for Sale and House Pictures documents will be linked when the documents are posted online, the theme and styles of both documents should match. Make any necessary changes to the theme and the style set in the House Pictures document to match the settings in the House For Sale document.

⚙ **Troubleshoot** 11. The House Pictures document contains an erroneous hyperlink that jumps to an unrelated external website. Remove that hyperlink from the document. Check the two remaining hyperlinks to make sure they jump to the appropriate targets—either a spot in the current document, or the House for Sale document. Make any necessary edits to the hyperlink to correct any errors.

12. In the House for Sale document, format the last sentence as a hyperlink that jumps to the House Pictures document. Save both documents.

13. Save the House for Sale document as a Single File Web Page file using **House_for_Sale_Webpage** as the filename and **2245 Cinnamon Trail** as the title. Save the webpage in the location specified by your instructor.

14. Save the House Pictures document as a Single File Web Page file using **House_Pictures_Webpage** as the filename and **Pictures** as the title. Save the webpage in the location specified by your instructor.

15. Edit the hyperlinks so they target the correct files, and then save and close both files.

16. Close Word, open the **House_For_Sale_Webpage** file in a browser, and then test the hyperlinks. If necessary, open the webpages in Word and make corrections to ensure that all the hyperlinks work correctly. Then save your changes and test the hyperlinks in a browser again. When you're finished, close your browser.

Case Problem 3

CREATE

There are no Data Files needed for this Case Problem.

Fabricante Tech   You have just started an internship at Fabricante Tech, a company that designs and hosts webpages for businesses of all sizes. Before you begin learning how to use a full-blown web design program, your supervisor asks you to demonstrate your understanding of hyperlinks by creating a set of linked pages using Microsoft Word. The pages should focus on a topic of interest to you, and should include multiple graphics and links to live webpages accessible via the Internet. Your supervisor asks you to use all your formatting skills to create an attractive set of pages. Complete the following steps:

1. Select a topic that interests you, such as your favorite hobby, your school, a sports team, a vacation destination, or a company you'd like to work for some day. Because you are creating sample webpages for your work supervisor, choose a topic that is appropriate for a professional setting.

2. Open a new, blank Word document and save it as a Web Page, Filtered file using **Main Page** as the filename and a title that describes your topic. Save the webpage in the location specified by your instructor.

3. Create two more new, blank webpages, using the Web Page, Filtered file type. Name these files **Linked Page 1** and **Linked Page 2**, with appropriate titles, and save them in the location specified by your instructor.

4. In the Main Page file, add text and at least three pictures that introduce the reader to your topic. Use your own pictures or download some from Office.com. Include at least three headings.

5. In the Linked Page 1 file, add text that provides more detail about one aspect of your topic. The text should mention one external webpage available via the Internet. Include at least one picture and at least one heading at the beginning of the page. Do the same in the Linked Page 2 file.

6. In the Linked Page 1 file, format the text that refers to an external webpage as a hyperlink that jumps to that page. Do the same in the Linked Page 2 file. (*Hint*: Use Internet Explorer to display the external webpage, right-click the URL in the box at the top of the browser window, and then click Copy. In the Insert Hyperlink dialog box, use the appropriate keyboard shortcut to paste the URL into the Address box.)

7. In the Main Page file, add hyperlinks that jump to the Linked Page 1 file and to the Linked Page 2 file.

8. In the Linked Page 1 and Linked Page 2 files, add hyperlinks that jump back to the Main Page file.

9. Format the three pages identically, using a theme, heading styles, and a style set of your choice. Use horizontal lines to separate the different sections on each page, and add a two-color gradient page background to all three files.

10. Close Word, open the **Main Page** file in a browser, and then test the hyperlinks. If necessary, open the webpage files in Word and make corrections to ensure that all the hyperlinks work correctly. Then save your changes and test the hyperlinks in a browser again. When you're finished, close your browser and close any open Word documents.

Case Problem 4

Data Files needed for this Case Problem: Plantar Kelly.docx, Plantar Raha.docx, Plantar.docx

CHALLENGE

Idaho Valley Physical Therapy Clinic   Ethan Henderson is a physical therapist at Idaho Valley Physical Therapy, in Taylorville, Idaho. He is creating a series of fact sheets that he can email to clients. The fact sheets will summarize treatments for many common ailments diagnosed by Ethan and his colleagues at the clinic. Each fact sheet will also include a link to an Internet video that clients can view when they need a reminder about how to do their prescribed exercises. Ethan has already emailed a draft of his first fact sheet to his two colleagues, Kelly and Raha, and he now needs to combine their copies with his to create a final draft. However, because Kelly forgot to turn on Track Changes before she edited the document, he'll need to compare her draft with his so that he can see her changes marked as tracked changes.

After he finishes accepting and rejecting changes, Ethan wants you to show him how to add a video to the document. The clinic is preparing a series of videos that he will eventually incorporate into his fact sheets before distributing them; but for now, he asks you to show him how to insert any video from the Internet. Finally, after the fact sheet is finished, Ethan would like you to help him create a chart that illustrates the average distance each client travels to the clinic. Complete the following steps:

1. Open the document **Plantar** from the Word7 ▸ Case4 folder included with your Data Files, save it as **Plantar Ethan** in the location specified by your instructor, review the document to familiarize yourself with its contents, and then close it.

2. Open the document **Plantar Kelly** from the Word7 ▸ Case4 folder, review its contents, and then close it.

⊕ **Explore** 3. Compare the Plantar Ethan document with the Plantar Kelly document, using Plantar Ethan as the original document, and show the changes in a new document.

4. Review the new document to verify that Kelly's changes to Ethan's draft are now displayed as tracked changes, and then save the document as **Plantar Kelly Tracked Changes** in the location specified by your instructor.

5. Combine the Plantar Kelly Tracked Changes document with the Plantar Raha document, using the Plantar Kelly Tracked Changes file as the original document.

6. Save the new document as **Plantar Fasciitis Fact Sheet** in the location specified by your instructor.

7. Accept all changes in the document, and then turn off Track Changes, if necessary.

⊕ **Explore** 8. Use Word Help to learn how to insert an Internet video in a document. In the blank paragraph at the end of the document, insert a video of someone demonstrating Achilles tendon stretches. Take care to choose a video that is appropriate for a professional setting. After you insert the video in the document, click the Play button on the video image to test it. Press the Esc button to close the video window when you are finished watching it.

⊕ **Explore** 9. In the Word document, size the video image just as you would an ordinary picture so that it fits on the first page.

10. Save the Plantar Fasciitis Fact Sheet document and close it.

11. Open a new, blank document, and then save it as **Client Travel Time Chart** in the location specified by your instructor.

⊕ **Explore** 12. Use Word Help to learn how to create a chart using Word's Chart tool. Create a bar chart using the 3-D Stacked Bar type. Include the data shown in Figure 7-41. For the chart title, use **Miles Driven by Clients for Weekly, Monthly, and Annual Appointments**.

Figure 7-41   **Data for bar chart**

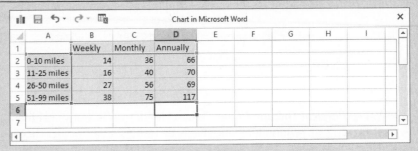

⊕ **Explore** 13. Format the chart with the Style 8 chart style.

14. Change the document's theme to Celestial.

15. Save and close all documents.

Teamwork

Collaborating with Others to Create Documents

Collaboration means working together to achieve a specific goal through teamwork.

Organizations establish collaborative teams for completing a wide variety of tasks, with long- or short-term goals. Sometimes team members collaborate on projects by working side by side. However, it's increasingly common for the members of a team to collaborate from different geographical locations, using telecommunications technologies and social networks to complete tasks.

When forming a team, it is important to understand the skills each team member has, and how those skills can best be used as the team collaborates to achieve its goals. An effective team is made up of people with abilities and talents that are complementary and well suited to the tasks at hand. It's also essential that each team member understand his or her responsibilities. On a truly integrated team, team members support each other and agree to share new responsibilities when they arise, rather than waiting around for someone else to pick up the slack.

The Structure of a Team

When structuring a team, it is important to identify team leaders, work coordinators, idea people, and critics. Each member must recognize the significance of his or her individual contributions to the team's overall success in meeting its goals. Some team members will serve specific roles on the team. For example, task specialists spend a lot of time and effort ensuring that the team achieves its goals by presenting ideas, sharing opinions, collecting information, sorting details, and motivating the team to stay on track. When stresses occur due to time constraints or heavy workloads, positive team morale and a sense of shared focus and camaraderie become essential. Some team members hold the role of managing social satisfaction by strengthening the team's social bonds through encouragement, empathy, conflict resolution, compromise, and tension reduction—the latter can be accomplished through humor or organizing social activities outside of the work environment. Often, individual team members will serve more than one role on the team. For example, the task specialist might also be the team leader, and the idea person might also fill the social satisfaction role.

In this exercise, you will work with a team to create documents. As you structure your team to complete these tasks, consider the roles team members must fill. Before beginning, you should discuss the roles each member is comfortable assuming, and determine how complementary your collective abilities are.

To ensure your team works effectively to complete tasks and achieve its goals:

- Recognize that everyone brings something of value to the team.
- Respect and support each other as you work toward the common goal.
- Try to see things from the other person's perspective when conflicts or criticisms arise.
- Encourage or support team members who might need assistance.
- Address negative or unproductive attitudes immediately so they don't damage team energy and morale.
- Seek outside help if the team gets stuck and can't move forward.
- Provide periodic positive encouragement or rewards for contributions.

Using Technology in Teamwork

Team members often work together from separate locations. Also, most of the time, teams need to produce work on accelerated schedules, and therefore need to work efficiently. In these instances, teams depend on technology to accomplish work tasks. Corporate intranets and networks, email and voice mail, texting

and instant messaging, teleconferencing and software collaboration tools, social networks, and cell phones can all support teamwork. Before beginning a team project, identify the technology tools the team will use to communicate and document work activities. Then, determine how the team will organize, combine, and make available the documents and files it produces.

PROSKILLS

Create a Report Template, a Directory, and a Webpage

At this point, you should feel confident that you have the word-processing skills required to create, revise, and distribute useful documents in your professional and personal life. But there's no need to wait to use these new skills. You can create some practical documents right now, starting with a template for a report that you need to create routinely. In the following exercise, work with your team members to create documents using the Word skills and features presented in Tutorials 5 through 7.

Note: Please be sure *not* to include any personal information of a sensitive nature in the documents you create to be submitted to your instructor for this exercise. Later on, you can update the documents with such information for your own personal use.

1. Meet with your team to plan a new document template to use for school reports or another type of report that you might have to create on a regular basis. Work with your group to select an appropriate template installed with Word, delete or edit document controls as necessary, insert placeholder text as necessary, and customize the theme. Select an appropriate style set, and create at least one new style that will be useful in your report. As a group, take the time to plan your template to ensure that it will be useful for a series of similar documents.

2. Use your template as the basis for a new report. Insert a file containing the text of a report you or a team member wrote for one of your classes, or insert appropriate text of your choosing, and then format the text using the template styles. Remember to include a table of contents in the report. At the end of the report, include a hyperlink that jumps to the beginning of the report.

3. If you or a team member are familiar with Excel, open a new workbook, enter some data that supports one of the points in the team's report, and then embed the worksheet data in the report. If you don't know how to enter data in Excel, you can embed the data from the Budget file in the Word7 ► Tutorial folder included with your Data Files, and then edit the data as necessary. Note that you can widen a column in Excel by dragging the right border of the column's header (the letter at the top of the column).

4. Email a copy of your report to a team member. Have him or her edit the document with Track Changes turned on, and then send the report back to you.

5. Combine your edited copy of the document with the copy edited by your team member. Accept or reject changes as necessary. Save the new, combined document with a new name.

6. Meet with your team and choose a type of information, such as email addresses or birthdays, that the group would like to organize in a single document. Create a Word table, and then enter fictitious information into the table. You can replace this with real information later for your personal use, after you've handed in your assignments. Sort the information based on one of the columns.

7. Create a main document for a directory that includes a dot leader. Use the group's Word table from Step 6 as the data source. Insert the necessary merge codes into the main document and complete the merge.

8. Format the merged document with a two-color gradient page color and add a title. Format the title appropriately. Save the document as a webpage that consists of only one file.

OBJECTIVES

Session 5.1
- Explore a structured range of data
- Freeze rows and columns
- Plan and create an Excel table
- Rename and format an Excel table
- Add, edit, and delete records in an Excel table
- Sort data

Session 5.2
- Filter data using filter buttons
- Filter an Excel table with a slicer
- Insert a Total row to summarize an Excel table
- Split a worksheet into two panes
- Insert subtotals into a range of data
- Use the Outline buttons to show or hide details

Session 5.3
- Create and modify a PivotTable
- Apply PivotTable styles and formatting
- Filter a PivotTable
- Insert a slicer to filter a PivotTable
- Insert a recommended PivotTable
- Create a PivotChart

Working with Excel Tables, PivotTables, and PivotCharts

Tracking Cash Receipts

Case | *Laurie's Coffeehouse*

Laurie Kye's dream of opening Laurie's Coffeehouse became a reality three months ago. Laurie's Coffeehouse serves coffee blends and specialty drinks, along with breakfast and lunch items. To keep the shop interesting, Laurie sells unique handcrafted gifts at the counter. The coffeehouse is located in Cave Creek, Arizona, which is a popular tourist attraction and close to a community college campus, so it attracts heavy foot traffic. Recently, the coffeehouse has become a weekend meeting place for many motorcyclists and bikers.

Now that Laurie's Coffeehouse has settled into a smooth routine, Laurie wants to analyze her business operations more carefully. She wants to determine what is working best, and what is selling most each day. In addition, Laurie wants information to help her make ordering and staffing decisions. She has entered the January cash receipts data into an Excel workbook, and has asked you to help her analyze the data. You'll work with the data as an Excel table so you can easily edit, sort, and filter the data. You'll also summarize the data using the Subtotals command, a PivotTable, and a PivotChart.

STARTING DATA FILES

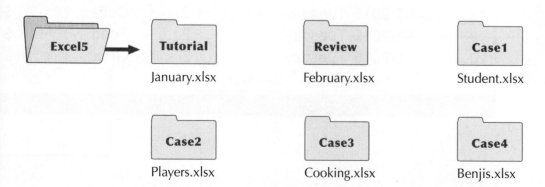

Excel5 → Tutorial
January.xlsx

Review
February.xlsx

Case1
Student.xlsx

Case2
Players.xlsx

Case3
Cooking.xlsx

Case4
Benjis.xlsx

Microsoft product screenshots used with permission from Microsoft Corporation.

Session 5.1 Visual Overview:

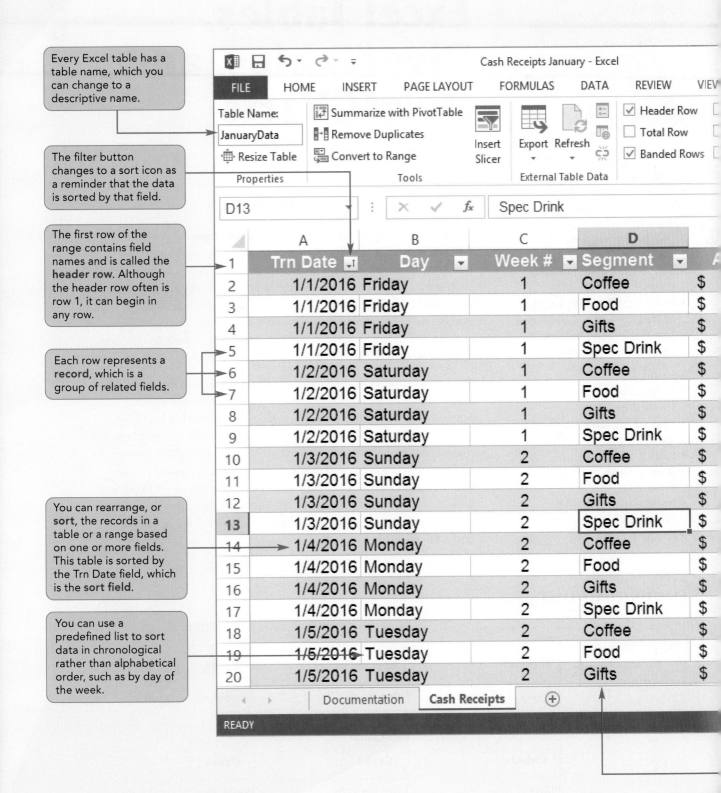

Every Excel table has a table name, which you can change to a descriptive name.

The filter button changes to a sort icon as a reminder that the data is sorted by that field.

The first row of the range contains field names and is called the **header row**. Although the header row often is row 1, it can begin in any row.

Each row represents a **record**, which is a group of related fields.

You can rearrange, or **sort**, the records in a table or a range based on one or more fields. This table is sorted by the Trn Date field, which is the **sort field**.

You can use a predefined list to sort data in chronological rather than alphabetical order, such as by day of the week.

	A	B	C	D	
1	**Trn Date**	**Day**	**Week #**	**Segment**	A
2	1/1/2016	Friday	1	Coffee	$
3	1/1/2016	Friday	1	Food	$
4	1/1/2016	Friday	1	Gifts	$
5	1/1/2016	Friday	1	Spec Drink	$
6	1/2/2016	Saturday	1	Coffee	$
7	1/2/2016	Saturday	1	Food	$
8	1/2/2016	Saturday	1	Gifts	$
9	1/2/2016	Saturday	1	Spec Drink	$
10	1/3/2016	Sunday	2	Coffee	$
11	1/3/2016	Sunday	2	Food	$
12	1/3/2016	Sunday	2	Gifts	$
13	1/3/2016	Sunday	2	Spec Drink	$
14	1/4/2016	Monday	2	Coffee	$
15	1/4/2016	Monday	2	Food	$
16	1/4/2016	Monday	2	Gifts	$
17	1/4/2016	Monday	2	Spec Drink	$
18	1/5/2016	Tuesday	2	Coffee	$
19	1/5/2016	Tuesday	2	Food	$
20	1/5/2016	Tuesday	2	Gifts	$

Table Name: JanuaryData

Cash Receipts January - Excel

FILE   HOME   INSERT   PAGE LAYOUT   FORMULAS   DATA   REVIEW   VIEW

Summarize with PivotTable
Remove Duplicates
Resize Table   Convert to Range
Properties   Tools

Insert Slicer   Export   Refresh   External Table Data

☑ Header Row   ☐
☐ Total Row
☑ Banded Rows

D13   Spec Drink

Documentation   **Cash Receipts**   +

READY

Elements of an Excel Table

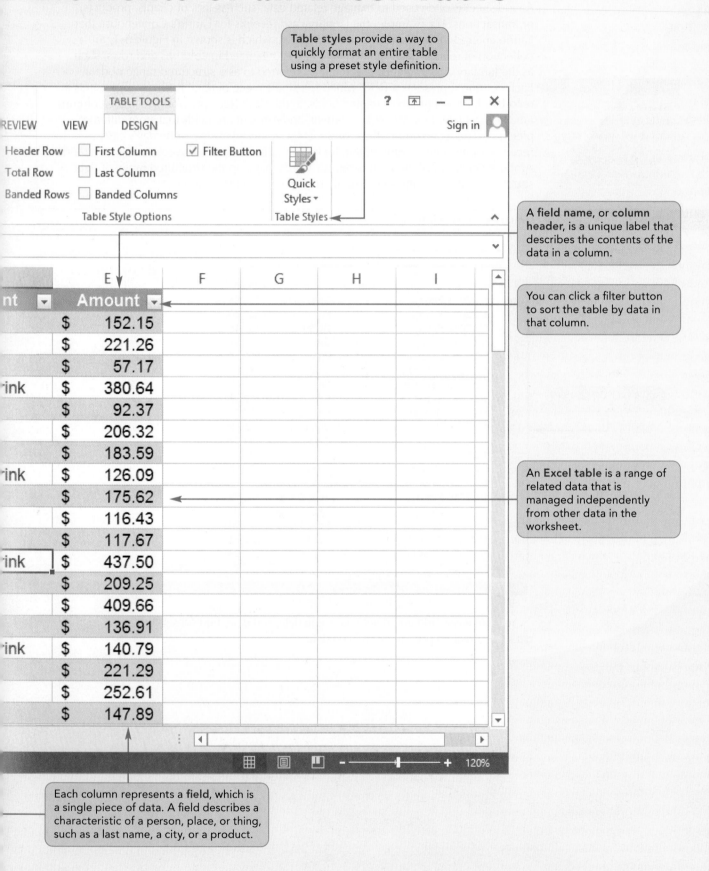

Table styles provide a way to quickly format an entire table using a preset style definition.

A **field name**, or **column header**, is a unique label that describes the contents of the data in a column.

You can click a filter button to sort the table by data in that column.

An **Excel table** is a range of related data that is managed independently from other data in the worksheet.

Each column represents a **field**, which is a single piece of data. A field describes a characteristic of a person, place, or thing, such as a last name, a city, or a product.

Planning a Structured Range of Data

A worksheet is often used to manage related data, such as lists of clients, products, or transactions. For example, the January cash receipts for Laurie's Coffeehouse that Laurie entered in the Cash Receipts worksheet, which is shown in Figure 5-1, are a collection of related data. Related data that is organized in columns and rows, such as the January cash receipts, is sometimes referred to as a structured range of data. Each column represents a field, which is a single piece of data. Each row represents a record, which is a group of related fields. In the Cash Receipts worksheet, the columns labeled Trn Date, Day, Week #, Segment, and Amount are fields that store different pieces of data. Each row in the worksheet is a record that stores one day's cash receipts for a specific segment that includes the Trn Date, Day, Week #, Segment, and Amount fields. All of the cash receipts records make up the structured range of data. A structured range of data is commonly referred to as a list or table.

> **TIP**
>
> In Excel, a range of data is any block of cells, whereas a structured range of data has related records and fields organized in rows and columns.

Figure 5-1   January cash receipts data

each column is a field

each row is a record

	A	B	C	D	E	F	G	H	I
1	Trn Date	Day	Week #	Segment	Amount				
2	1/1/2016	Friday	1	Spec Drink	380.64				
3	1/1/2016	Friday	1	Food	221.26				
4	1/1/2016	Friday	1	Coffee	152.15				
5	1/1/2016	Friday	1	Gifts	57.17				
6	1/2/2016	Saturday	1	Food	206.32				
7	1/2/2016	Saturday	1	Gifts	183.59				
8	1/2/2016	Saturday	1	Spec Drink	126.09				
9	1/2/2016	Saturday	1	Coffee	92.37				
10	1/3/2016	Sunday	2	Spec Drink	437.50				
11	1/3/2016	Sunday	2	Coffee	175.62				
12	1/3/2016	Sunday	2	Gifts	117.67				
13	1/3/2016	Sunday	2	Food	116.43				
14	1/4/2016	Monday	2	Food	309.66				
15	1/4/2016	Monday	2	Coffee	209.25				
16	1/4/2016	Monday	2	Spec Drink	140.79				
17	1/4/2016	Monday	2	Gifts	136.91				
18	1/5/2016	Tuesday	2	Spec Drink	262.04				
19	1/5/2016	Tuesday	2	Food	252.61				
20	1/5/2016	Tuesday	2	Coffee	221.29				

Documentation   **Cash Receipts**   ⊕

READY

You can easily add and delete data, edit data, sort data, find subsets of data, summarize data, and create reports about related data.

PROSKILLS

Decision Making: The Importance of Planning

Before you create a structured range of data, you should create a plan. Planning involves gathering relevant information about the data and deciding your goals. The end results you want to achieve will help you determine the kind of data to include in each record and how to divide that data into fields. Specifically, you should do the following to create an effective plan:

- Spend time thinking about how you will use the data.
- Consider what reports you want to create for different audiences (supervisors, customers, directors, and so forth) and the fields needed to produce those reports.
- Think about the various questions, or *queries*, you want answered and the fields needed to create those results.

This information is often documented in a **data definition table**, which lists the fields to be maintained for each record, a description of the information each field will include, and the type of data (such as numbers, text, or dates) stored in each field. Careful and thorough planning will help you avoid having to redesign a structured range of data later.

Before creating the list of cash receipts, Laurie carefully considered what information she needs and how she wants to use it. Laurie plans to use the data to track daily cash receipts for each segment of business activity, which she has identified as coffee, specialty drinks, food, and gifts. She wants to be able to create reports that show specific lists of cash receipts, such as all the cash receipts for a specific date, day of the week, or week of the year. Based on this information, Laurie developed the data definition table shown in Figure 5-2.

| Figure 5-2 | Data definition table for the cash receipts |

Data Definition Table			
Field	Description	Data Type	Notes
Trn Date	Date of the cash receipts	Date	Transaction Date (abbreviated to Trn Date) Use the *mm/dd/yyyy* format
Day	Day of the week	Text	Sunday, Monday, Tuesday, ...
Week #	Week of the year	Number	1–52
Segment	Business category for the cash receipts	Text	Coffee, Spec Drink, Food, Gifts
Amount	Cash receipts total for a specific transaction date and segment	Number	Use the Accounting format and show two decimal places

After you determine the fields and records you need, you can enter the data in a worksheet. You can then work with the data in many ways, including the following common operations:

- Add, edit, and delete data in the range.
- Sort the data range.
- Filter to display only rows that meet specified criteria.
- Insert formulas to calculate subtotals.
- Create summary tables based on the data in the range (usually with PivotTables).

You'll perform many of these operations on the cash receipts data.

Creating an Effective Structured Range of Data

INSIGHT

For a range of data to be used effectively, it must have the same structure throughout. Keep in mind the following guidelines:

- **Enter field names in the top row of the range.** This clearly identifies each field.
- **Use short, descriptive field names.** Shorter field names are easier to remember and enable more fields to appear in the workbook window at once.
- **Format field names.** Use formatting to distinguish the header row from the data. For example, apply bold, color, and a different font size.
- **Enter the same kind of data in a field.** Each field should store the smallest bit of information and be consistent from record to record. For example, enter Los Angeles, Tucson, or Chicago in a City field, but do not include states, such as CA, AZ, or IL, in the same column of data.
- **Separate the data from the rest of the worksheet.** The data, which includes the header row, should be separated from other information in the worksheet by *at least* one blank row and one blank column. The blank row and column enable Excel to accurately determine the range of the data.

Laurie created a workbook and entered the cash receipts data for January based on the plan outlined in the data definition table. You'll open this workbook and review its structure.

To open and review Laurie's workbook:

1. Open the **January** workbook located in the Excel5 ▶ Tutorial folder included with your Data Files, and then save the workbook as **Cash Receipts January** in the location specified by your instructor.

2. In the Documentation sheet, enter your name in cell B3 and the date in cell B4.

3. In the range A7:D13, review the data definition table. This table, which was shown in Figure 5-2, describes the different fields that are used in the Cash Receipts worksheet.

4. Go to the **Cash Receipts** worksheet. This worksheet, which was shown in Figure 5-1, contains data about the coffeehouse's cash receipts. Currently, the worksheet includes 121 cash receipts. Each cash receipt record is a separate row (rows 2 through 122) and contains five fields (columns A through E). Row 1, the header row, contains labels that describe the data in each column.

5. Scroll the worksheet to row **122**, which is the last record. The column headers in row 1 are no longer visible. Without seeing the column headers, it is difficult to know what the data entered in each column represents.

Freezing Rows and Columns

You can select rows and columns to remain visible in the workbook window as you scroll the worksheet. **Freezing** a row or column lets you keep the headers visible as you work with the data in a large worksheet. You can freeze the top row, freeze the first column, or freeze the rows and columns above and to the left of the selected cell. If you freeze the top row, row 1 remains on the screen as you scroll, leaving column headers visible and making it easier to identify the data in each record.

Laurie wants to see the column headers as she scrolls the cash receipts data. You'll freeze row 1, which contains the column headers.

To freeze row 1 of the worksheet:

1. Press the **Ctrl+Home** keys to return to cell A1. You want to freeze row 1.

2. On the ribbon, click the **VIEW** tab.

3. In the Window group, click the **Freeze Panes** button, and then click **Freeze Top Row**. A horizontal line appears below the column labels to indicate which row is frozen.

4. Scroll the worksheet to row **122**. This time, the column headers remain visible as you scroll. See Figure 5-3.

TIP
To freeze the columns and rows above and to the right of the selected cell, click the Freeze Panes button, and then click Freeze Panes.

Figure 5-3   Top row of the worksheet is frozen

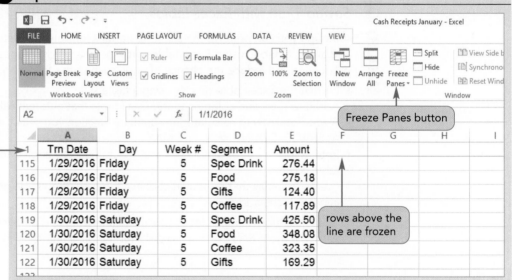

5. Press the **Ctrl+Home** keys. Cell A2, the cell directly below the frozen row, becomes the active cell.

After you freeze panes, the first option on the Freeze Panes button menu changes to Unfreeze Panes. This option releases the frozen panes so that all the columns and rows in the worksheet shift when you scroll. Laurie wants you to use a different method to keep the column headers visible, so you will unfreeze the top row of the worksheet.

To unfreeze the top row of the worksheet:

1. On the VIEW tab, in the Window group, click the **Freeze Panes** button. The first Freeze Panes option is now Unfreeze Panes.

2. Click **Unfreeze Panes**. The headers are no longer frozen, and the dark, horizontal line below the column headers is removed. You can now scroll all the rows and columns in the worksheet.

Creating an Excel Table

You can convert a structured range of data, such as the cash receipts data in the range A1:E122, to an Excel table. An Excel table makes it easier to identify, manage, and analyze the groups of related data. When a structured range of data is converted into an Excel table, you see the following:

- A filter button in each cell of the header row
- The range formatted with a table style
- A sizing handle (a small triangle) in the lower-right corner of the last cell of the table
- The TABLE TOOLS DESIGN tab on the ribbon

You can create more than one Excel table in a worksheet. Although you can leave the cash receipts data as a structured range of data and still perform all of the tasks in this section, creating an Excel table helps you to be more efficient and accurate.

INSIGHT

Saving Time with Excel Tables

Although you can perform the same operations for both a structured range of data and an Excel table, using Excel tables provides many advantages to help you be more productive and reduce the chance of error, such as the following:

- Format the Excel table quickly using a table style.
- Add new rows and columns to the Excel table that automatically expand the range.
- Add a Total row to calculate the summary function you select, such as SUM, AVERAGE, COUNT, MIN, and MAX.
- Enter a formula in one table cell that is automatically copied to all other cells in that table column.
- Create formulas that reference cells in a table by using table and column names instead of cell addresses.

These Excel table features let you focus on analyzing and understanding the data, leaving the more time-consuming tasks for the program to perform.

Laurie wants you to create an Excel table from the cash receipts data in the Cash Receipts worksheet. You'll be able to work with the Excel tables to analyze Laurie's data effectively.

To create an Excel table from the cash receipts data:

1. If necessary, select any cell in the range of cash receipts data to make it the active cell.

2. On the ribbon, click the **INSERT** tab.

3. In the Tables group, click the **Table** button. The Create Table dialog box opens. The range of data you want to use for the table is selected in the worksheet, and a formula with its range reference, =$A$1:$E$122, is entered in the dialog box.

4. Verify that the **My table has headers** check box is selected. The headers are the field names entered in row 1. If the first row did not contain field names, the My table has headers check box would be unchecked and Excel would insert a row of headers with the names Column1, Column2, and so on.

▶ **5.** Click the **OK** button. The dialog box closes, and the range of data is converted to an Excel table, which is selected. Filter buttons appear in the header row, the sizing handle appears in the lower-right corner of the last cell of the table, the table is formatted with a predefined table style, and the TABLE TOOLS DESIGN tab appears on the ribbon. See Figure 5-4.

Figure 5-4	Excel table with the cash receipts data

▶ **6.** Select any cell in the table, and then scroll down the table. The field names in the header row replace the standard lettered column headers (A, B, C, and so on) as you scroll, so you don't need to freeze panes to keep the header row visible. See Figure 5-5.

Figure 5-5	Cash receipts table scrolled

▶ **7.** Press the **Ctrl+Home** keys to make cell A1 the active cell. The column headers return to the standard display, and the Excel table header row scrolls back into view as row 1.

Renaming an Excel Table

Each Excel table in a workbook must have a unique name. Excel assigns the name Table1 to the first Excel table created in a workbook. Any additional Excel tables you create in the workbook are named consecutively as Table2, Table3, and so forth. You can assign a more descriptive name to a table, making it easier to identify a particular table by its content. Descriptive names are especially useful when you create more than one Excel table in the same workbook because they make it easier to reference the different Excel tables. Table names must start with a letter or an underscore but can use any combination of letters, numbers, and underscores for the rest of the name. Table names cannot include spaces, but you can use an underscore or uppercase letters instead of spaces to separate words in a table name, such as January_Data or JanuaryData.

Laurie wants you to rename the Excel table you just created from the January cash receipts data.

TIP

If you copy a worksheet that contains a table, Excel adds the next consecutive number at the end of the table name to create a unique table name.

To rename the Table1 table:

▶ **1.** On the TABLE TOOLS DESIGN tab, in the Properties group, select **Table1** in the Table Name box. See Figure 5-6.

Figure 5-6	Table Name box

enter a descriptive table name

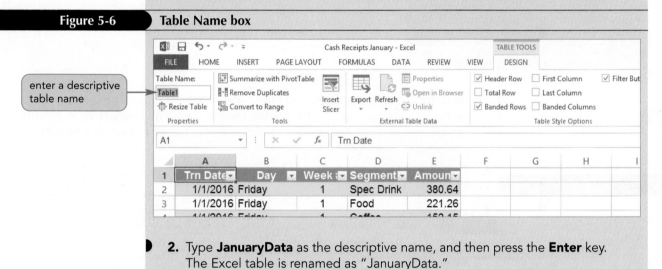

▶ **2.** Type **JanuaryData** as the descriptive name, and then press the **Enter** key. The Excel table is renamed as "JanuaryData."

Modifying an Excel Table

You can modify an Excel table by adding or removing table elements or by changing the table's formatting. For every Excel table, you can display or hide the following elements:

- **Header row**—The first row of the table that includes the field names
- **Total row**—A row at the bottom of the table that applies a function to the column values
- **First column**—Formatting added to the leftmost column of the table
- **Last column**—Formatting added to the rightmost column of the table
- **Banded rows**—Formatting added to alternating rows so that even and odd rows are different colors, making it simpler to distinguish records
- **Banded columns**—Formatting added to alternating columns so they are different colors, making it simpler to distinguish fields
- **Filter buttons**—Buttons that appear in each column of the header row and open a menu with options for sorting and filtering the table data

You can also modify a table by applying a table style. As with other styles, a table style formats all of the selected table elements with a consistent, unified design. You can change the font, fill, alignment, number formats, column widths and row heights, and other formatting of selected cells in the table the same way you would for other cells in the worksheet.

Laurie wants the JanuaryData table to have a format that makes the table easier to read. You will apply a table style and make other formatting changes to the table.

To format the JanuaryData table:

1. On the TABLE TOOLS DESIGN tab, in the Table Styles group, click the **More** button. A gallery of table styles opens.

2. In the Table Styles gallery, in the Medium section, click **Table Style Medium 3**. The table now has an orange style.

3. In the Table Style Options group, click the **Banded Rows** check box. The alternating row colors disappear. The table is more challenging to read this way, so you will reapply the banded rows formatting.

4. In the Table Style Options group, click the **Banded Rows** check box to select it. The alternating row colors reappear.

5. Change the width of columns A through E to **12** characters. The entire column headers and all values will now be visible.

6. Select the **Amount** column, and then change the values to the **Accounting** format. See Figure 5-7.

TIP

To display or hide alternating column colors, click the Banded Columns check box in the Table Style Options group.

| Figure 5-7 | Modified JanuaryData table |

columns A through E widened to 12 characters

table formatted with Table Style Medium 3

Amount column formatted with the Accounting format

7. Select cell **A1** to make it the active cell.

Maintaining Data in an Excel Table

As you develop a worksheet with an Excel table, you may need to add new records to the table, find and edit existing records in the table, and delete records from the table. Laurie wants you to make several changes to the data in the JanuaryData table.

Adding Records

As you maintain data in an Excel table, you often need to add new records. You add a record to an Excel table in a blank row. The simplest and most convenient way to add a record to an Excel table is to enter the data in the first blank row below the last record. You can then sort the data to arrange the table in the order you want. If you want the record in a specific location, you can also insert a row within the table for the new record.

The cash receipts records for January 31 are missing from the JanuaryData table. Laurie asks you to add to the table four new records that contain the missing data.

To add four records to the JanuaryData table:

▶ 1. Press the **End** key, and then press the ↓ key to make cell A122 the active cell. This cell is in the last row of the table.

▶ 2. Press the ↓ key to move the active cell to cell A123, which is in the first blank row below the table.

> **TIP**
>
> You can drag the sizing handle to add columns or rows to the Excel table or delete them from it.

▶ 3. In cell A123, type **1/31/2016**, and then press the **Tab** key. Cell B123 in the Day column becomes the active cell. The table expands to include a new row with the same formatting as the rest of the table. The AutoCorrect Options button appears so you can undo the table formatting if you hadn't intended the new data to be part of the existing table. The sizing handle moves to the lower-right corner of cell E123, which is now the cell in the lower-right corner of the table. See Figure 5-8.

Figure 5-8   New row added to the JanuaryData table

120	1/30/2016	Saturday	5	Food	$	348.08	
121	1/30/2016	Saturday	5	Coffee	$	323.35	sizing handle
122	1/30/2016	Saturday	5	Gifts	$	169.29	
123	1/31/2016						

AutoCorrect Options button

‹ › | Documentation | **Cash Receipts** | ⊕

READY

Trouble? If cell A124 is the active cell, you probably pressed the Enter key instead of the Tab key. Click cell B123 and then continue entering the data in Step 4.

▶ 4. In the range **B123:E123**, enter **Sunday** as the Day, **6** as the Week #, **Food** as the Segment, and **164.50** as the Amount, pressing the **Tab** key after each entry. Cell A124 becomes the active cell and the table expands to include row 124.

▶ 5. In the range **A124:E126**, enter the following cash receipts:

1/31/2016	**Sunday**	**6**	**Coffee**	**278.98**
1/31/2016	**Sunday**	**6**	**Gifts**	**178.17**
1/31/2016	**Sunday**	**6**	**Spec Drink**	**345.88**

▶ 6. Press the **Enter** key. The records are added to the table. See Figure 5-9.

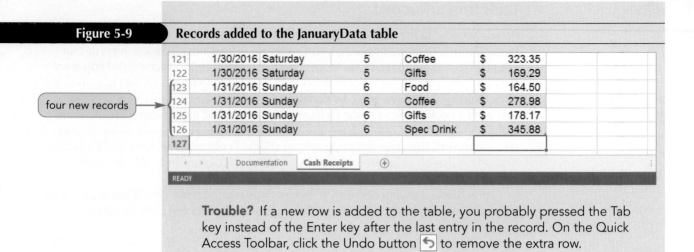

| Figure 5-9 | Records added to the JanuaryData table |

121	1/30/2016	Saturday	5	Coffee	$	323.35
122	1/30/2016	Saturday	5	Gifts	$	169.29
123	1/31/2016	Sunday	6	Food	$	164.50
124	1/31/2016	Sunday	6	Coffee	$	278.98
125	1/31/2016	Sunday	6	Gifts	$	178.17
126	1/31/2016	Sunday	6	Spec Drink	$	345.88
127						

four new records

Documentation **Cash Receipts** (+)

READY

Trouble? If a new row is added to the table, you probably pressed the Tab key instead of the Enter key after the last entry in the record. On the Quick Access Toolbar, click the Undo button ⟲ to remove the extra row.

Finding and Editing Records

Although you can manually scroll through the table to find a specific record, often a quicker way to locate a record is to use the Find command. When using the Find or Replace command, it is best to start at the top of a worksheet to ensure that all cells in the table are searched. You edit the data in a table the same way as you edit data in a worksheet cell.

Laurie wants you to update the January 20 cash receipts for the Gifts segment. You'll use the Find command to locate the record, which is currently blank. Then, you'll edit the record in the table to change the amount to $154.25.

To find and edit the record for Gifts on 1/20/2016:

▶ **1.** Press the **Ctrl+Home** keys to make cell A1 the active cell so that all cells in the table will be searched.

▶ **2.** On the HOME tab, in the Editing group, click the **Find & Select** button, and then click **Find** (or press the **Ctrl+F** keys). The Find and Replace dialog box opens.

▶ **3.** In the Find what box, type **1/20/2016**, and then click the **Find Next** button. Cell A79, which contains the Coffee segment, is selected. This is not the record you want.

▶ **4.** Click the **Find Next** button three times to display the record for Gifts on 1/20/2016.

▶ **5.** Click the **Close** button. The Find and Replace dialog box closes.

▶ **6.** Press the **Tab** key four times to move the active cell to the Amount column, type **154.25**, and then press the **Enter** key. The record is updated.

▶ **7.** Press the **Ctrl+Home** keys to make cell A1 the active cell.

Deleting a Record

As you work with the data in an Excel table, you might find records that are outdated or duplicated. In these instances, you can delete the records. To delete records that are incorrect, out of date, or no longer needed, select a cell in each record you want to delete, click the Delete button arrow in the Cells group on the HOME tab, and then click Delete Table Rows. You can also delete a field by selecting a cell in the field you want to delete, clicking the Delete button arrow, and then clicking Delete Table Columns. In addition, you can use the Remove Duplicates dialog box to locate and remove records that have the same data in selected columns. The Remove Duplicates dialog box lists all columns in the table. Usually, all columns in a table are selected to identify duplicate records.

Laurie thinks that one of the cash receipts was entered twice. You'll use the Remove Duplicates dialog box to locate and delete the duplicate record from the table.

To find and delete the duplicate record from the JanuaryData table:

▶ **1.** Scroll to row **64**, and observe that the entries in row 64 and row 65 are exactly the same. One of these records needs to be deleted.

▶ **2.** On the ribbon, click the **TABLE TOOLS DESIGN** tab.

▶ **3.** In the Tools group, click the **Remove Duplicates** button. The Remove Duplicates dialog box opens, and all of the columns in the table are selected. Excel looks for repeated data in the selected columns to determine whether any duplicate records exist. If duplicates are found, all but one of the records are deleted. See Figure 5-10.

Figure 5-10	Remove Duplicates dialog box

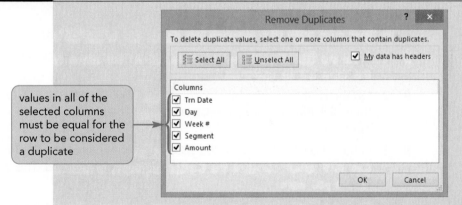

values in all of the selected columns must be equal for the row to be considered a duplicate

You want to search all columns in the table for duplicated data so that you don't inadvertently delete a record that has duplicate values in all of the selected fields but a unique value in the deselected field.

▶ **4.** Click the **OK** button. A dialog box opens, reporting "1 duplicate values found and removed; 124 unique values remain."

▶ **5.** Click the **OK** button.

Trouble? If you deleted records you did not intend to delete, you can reverse the action. On the Quick Access Toolbar, click the Undo button, and then repeat Steps 3 through 5.

▶ **6.** Press the **Ctrl+Home** keys to make cell A1 the active cell.

Sorting Data

The records in an Excel table initially appear in the order they were entered. As you work, however, you may want to view the same records in a different order. For example, Laurie might want to view the cash receipts by segment or day of the week. You can sort data in ascending or descending order. **Ascending order** arranges text alphabetically from A to Z, numbers from smallest to largest, and dates from oldest to newest. **Descending order** arranges text in reverse alphabetical order from Z to A, numbers from largest to smallest, and dates from newest to oldest. In both ascending and descending order, blank cells are placed at the end of the table.

Sorting One Column Using the Sort Buttons

You can quickly sort data with one sort field using the Sort A to Z button or the Sort Z to A button. Laurie wants you to sort the cash receipts in ascending order by the Segment column. This will rearrange the table data so that the records appear in alphabetical order by Segment.

To sort the JanuaryData table in ascending order by the Segment column:

1. Select any cell in the Segment column. You do not need to select the entire JanuaryData table, which consists of the range A1:E125. Excel determines the table's range when you click any cell in the table.

TIP

You can also use the Sort & Filter button in the Editing group on the HOME tab.

2. On the ribbon, click the **DATA** tab.

3. In the Sort & Filter group, click the **Sort A to Z** button. The data is sorted in ascending order by Segment. The Segment filter button changes to show that the data is sorted by that column. See Figure 5-11.

| Figure 5-11 | JanuaryData table sorted by the Segment field |

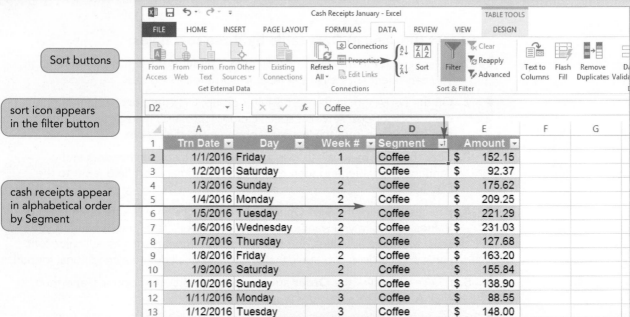

Sort buttons

sort icon appears in the filter button

cash receipts appear in alphabetical order by Segment

	A	B	C	D	E	F	G
1	Trn Date	Day	Week #	Segment	Amount		
2	1/1/2016	Friday	1	Coffee	$ 152.15		
3	1/2/2016	Saturday	1	Coffee	$ 92.37		
4	1/3/2016	Sunday	2	Coffee	$ 175.62		
5	1/4/2016	Monday	2	Coffee	$ 209.25		
6	1/5/2016	Tuesday	2	Coffee	$ 221.29		
7	1/6/2016	Wednesday	2	Coffee	$ 231.03		
8	1/7/2016	Thursday	2	Coffee	$ 127.68		
9	1/8/2016	Friday	2	Coffee	$ 163.20		
10	1/9/2016	Saturday	2	Coffee	$ 155.84		
11	1/10/2016	Sunday	3	Coffee	$ 138.90		
12	1/11/2016	Monday	3	Coffee	$ 88.55		
13	1/12/2016	Tuesday	3	Coffee	$ 148.00		

Trouble? If the data is sorted in the wrong order, you might have clicked in a different column than the Segment column. Repeat Steps 1 through 3.

Sorting Multiple Columns Using the Sort Dialog Box

Sometimes one sort field is not adequate for your needs. For example, Laurie wants to arrange the JanuaryData table so that the cash receipts are ordered first by Day (Sunday, Monday, and so forth), then by Segment for each day of the week, and then by Amount (highest to lowest). You must sort by more than one column to accomplish this. The first sort field is called the **primary sort field**, the second sort field is called the **secondary sort field**, and so forth. Although you can include up to 64 sort fields in a single sort, you typically will use one to three sort fields. In this case, the Day field is the primary sort field, the Segment field is the secondary sort field, and the Amount field is the tertiary sort field. When you have more than one sort field, you should use the Sort dialog box to specify the sort criteria.

Sorting Data Using Multiple Sort Fields

- Select any cell in a table or range.
- On the DATA tab, in the Sort & Filter group, click the Sort button.
- If necessary, click the Add Level button to insert the Sort by row.
- Click the Sort by arrow, select the column heading for the primary sort field, click the Sort On arrow to select the type of data, and then click the Order arrow to select the sort order.
- For each additional column to sort, click the Add Level button, click the Then by arrow, select the column heading for the secondary sort field, click the Sort On arrow to select the type of data, and then click the Order arrow to select the sort order.
- Click the OK button.

Laurie wants to see the cash receipts sorted by day, and then within day by segment, and then within segment by amount, with the highest amounts appearing before the smaller ones for each segment. This will make it easier for Laurie to evaluate business on specific days of the week in each segment.

To sort the JanuaryData table by three sort fields:

1. Select cell **A1** in the JanuaryData table. Cell A1 is the active cell—although you can select any cell in the table to sort the table data.

2. On the DATA tab, in the Sort & Filter group, click the **Sort** button. The Sort dialog box opens. Any sort specifications (sort field, type of data sorted on, and sort order) from the last sort appear in the dialog box.

3. Click the **Sort by** arrow to display the list of the column headers in the JanuaryData table, and then click **Day**. The primary sort field is set to the Day field.

4. If necessary, click the **Sort On** arrow to display the type of sort, and then click **Values**. Typically, you want to sort by the numbers, text, or dates stored in the cells, which are all values. You can also sort by formats such as cell color, font color, and cell icon (a graphic that appears in a cell due to a conditional format).

5. If necessary, click the **Order** arrow to display sort order options, and then click **A to Z**. The sort order is set to ascending.

6. Click the **Add Level** button. A Then by row is added below the primary sort field.

7. Click the **Then by** arrow and click **Segment**, and then verify that **Values** appears in the Sort On box and **A to Z** appears in the Order box.

8. Click the **Add Level** button to add a second Then by row.

9. Click the second **Then by** arrow, click **Amount**, verify that **Values** appears in the Sort On box, click the **Order** arrow, and then click **Largest to smallest** to specify a descending sort order for the Amount values. See Figure 5-12.

Figure 5-12 | **Sort dialog box with three sort fields**

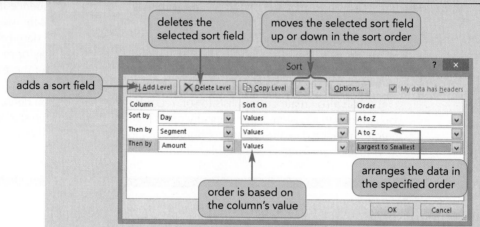

10. Click the **OK** button. Excel sorts the table records first in ascending order by the Day field, then within each Day in ascending order by the Segment field, and then within each Segment in descending order by the Amount field. For example, the first 20 records are Friday cash receipts. Of these records, the first five are Coffee, the next five are Food, and so on. Finally, the Friday Coffee receipts are arranged from highest to lowest in the Amount column. See Figure 5-13.

Figure 5-13 | **Cash receipts sorted by Day, then by Segment, and then by Amount**

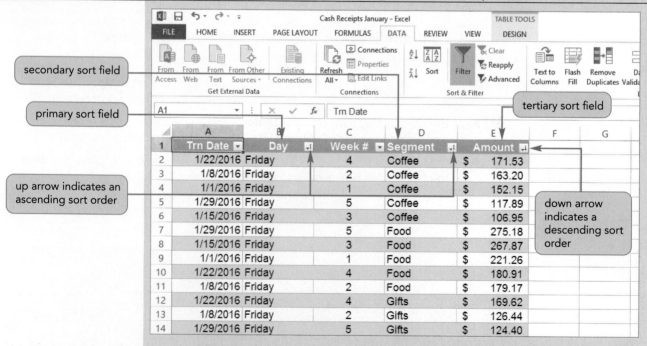

11. Scroll the table to view the sorted table data.

The table data is sorted in alphabetical order by the day of the week: Friday, Monday, Saturday, and so forth. This default sort order for fields with text values is not appropriate for days of the week. Instead, Laurie wants you to base the sort on chronological rather than alphabetical order. You'll use a custom sort list to set up the sort order Laurie wants.

Sorting Using a Custom List

Text is sorted in ascending or descending alphabetical order unless you specify a different order using a custom list. A **custom list** indicates the sequence in which you want data ordered. Excel has two predefined custom lists—day-of-the-week (Sun, Mon, Tues, ... and Sunday, Monday, Tuesday, ...) and month-of-the-year (Jan, Feb, Mar, Apr, ... and January, February, March, April, ...). If a column consists of day or month labels, you can sort them in their correct chronological order using one of these predefined custom lists.

You can also create custom lists to sort records in a sequence you define. For example, you can create a custom list to logically order high-school or college students based on their admittance date (freshman, sophomore, junior, and senior) rather than alphabetical order (freshman, junior, senior, and sophomore).

REFERENCE

Sorting Using a Custom List

- On the DATA tab, in the Sort & Filter group, click the Sort button.
- Click the Order arrow, and then click Custom List.
- If necessary, in the List entries box, type each entry for the custom list (in the desired order) and press the Enter key, and then click the Add button.
- In the Custom lists box, select the predefined custom list.
- Click the OK button.

You'll use a predefined custom list to sort the records by the Day column in chronological order rather than alphabetical order.

To use a predefined custom list to sort the Day column:

▶ **1.** Make sure the active cell is in the JanuaryData table.

▶ **2.** On the DATA tab, in the Sort & Filter group, click the **Sort** button. The Sort dialog box opens, showing the sort specifications from the previous sort.

▶ **3.** In the Sort by Day row, click the **Order** arrow to display the sort order options, and then click **Custom List**. The Custom Lists dialog box opens.

▶ **4.** In the Custom lists box, click **Sunday, Monday, Tuesday, ...** to place the days in the List entries box. See Figure 5-14.

Figure 5-14	Custom Lists dialog box

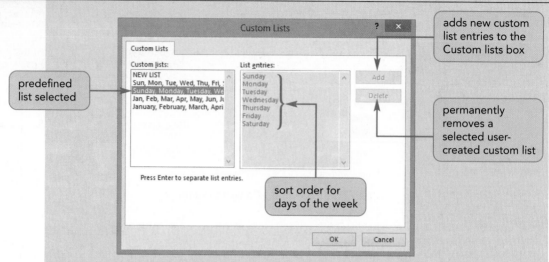

predefined list selected

adds new custom list entries to the Custom lists box

permanently removes a selected user-created custom list

sort order for days of the week

▶ **5.** Click the **OK** button to return to the Sort dialog box. The custom sort list—Sunday, Monday, Tuesday, ...—appears in the Order box.

▶ **7.** Click the **OK** button. The table is sorted based on the predefined custom list.

▶ **8.** Scroll the sorted table to verify that the cash receipts are sorted by their chronological day order—Sunday, Monday, Tuesday, Wednesday, Thursday, Friday, Saturday.

So far, you created an Excel table for the cash receipts, and then named and formatted the table. You updated the table by adding, editing, and deleting records. You also sorted the records and used a predefined custom list to sort the Day field by its chronological order. In the next session, you will continue to work with the JanuaryData table.

Session 5.1 Quick Check

REVIEW

1. In Excel, what is the difference between a range of data and a structured range of data?
2. Explain the difference between a field and a record.
3. What is the purpose of the Freeze Panes button in the Window group on the VIEW tab? Why is this feature helpful?
4. What three elements indicate that a range of data is an Excel table?
5. How can you quickly find and delete duplicate records from an Excel table?
6. If you sort table data from the most recent purchase date to the oldest purchase date, in what order have you sorted the data?
7. An Excel table of college students tracks each student's first name, last name, major, and year of graduation. How can you order the table so that students graduating in the same year appear together in alphabetical order by the student's last name?
8. An Excel table of sales data includes the Month field with the values Jan, Feb, Mar, ... Dec. How can you sort the data so the sales data is sorted by Month in chronological order (Jan, Feb, Mar, ... Dec)?

Session 5.2 Visual Overview:

Filtering is the process of displaying a subset of rows in an Excel table or a structured range of data that meets the criteria you specify. In this case, the table is filtered to show the cash receipts for Week 2.

If you want to change an Excel table back to a structured range of data, you click the Convert to Range button.

The filter button opens the Filter menu, which includes options to sort and filter the table based on the data in that column.

As a reminder that the records are filtered, only the row numbers of the records that match the filter appear (leaving gaps in the consecutive numbering) and are blue. Rows of records that don't match the filter are hidden.

The selection list displays the unique items in the selected column. You can select one item or multiple items from the list to filter the table by.

The Total row is used to calculate summary statistics (including sum, average, count, maximum, and minimum) for any column in an Excel table.

The status bar indicates that the table is filtered.

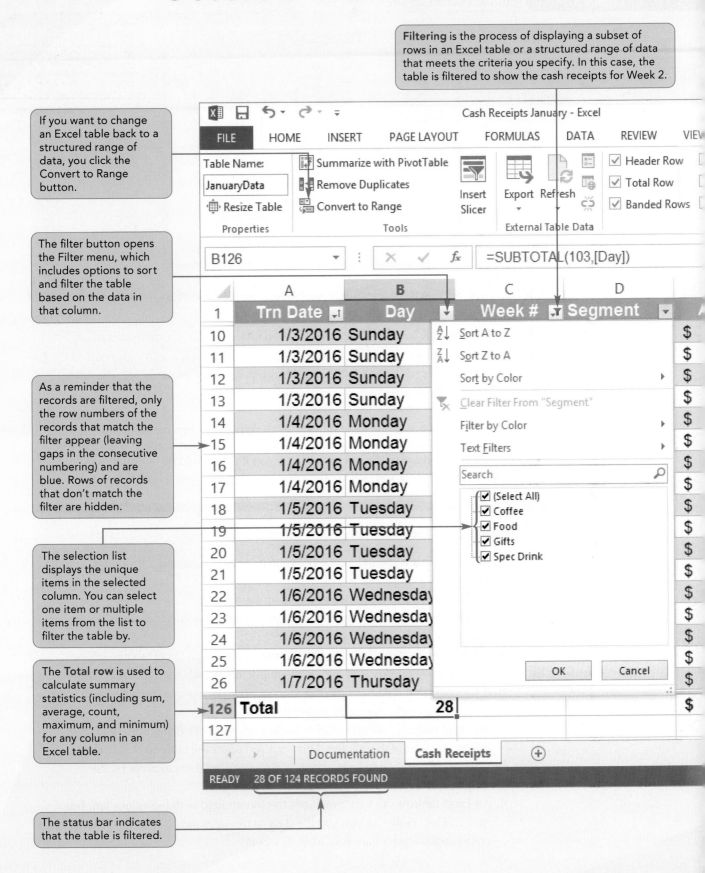

Filtering Table Data

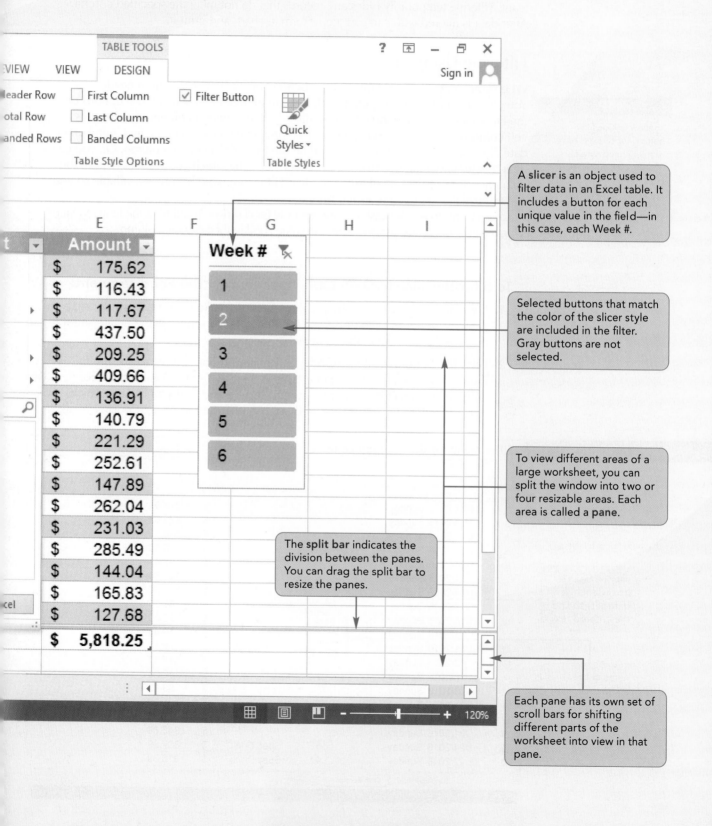

A **slicer** is an object used to filter data in an Excel table. It includes a button for each unique value in the field—in this case, each Week #.

Selected buttons that match the color of the slicer style are included in the filter. Gray buttons are not selected.

To view different areas of a large worksheet, you can split the window into two or four resizable areas. Each area is called a **pane**.

The **split bar** indicates the division between the panes. You can drag the split bar to resize the panes.

Each pane has its own set of scroll bars for shifting different parts of the worksheet into view in that pane.

Filtering Data

Laurie needs to determine if she should increase food orders on Saturdays, her busiest day. She wants to see a list of all Food receipts on Saturdays. Although you could sort the receipts by Segment and Day to group the records of interest to Laurie, the entire table would still be visible. A better solution is to display only the specific records you want. Filtering temporarily hides any records that do not meet the specified criteria. After data is filtered, you can sort, copy, format, chart, and print it.

Filtering Using One Column

TIP

To show or hide filter buttons for an Excel table or a structured range of data, click the Filter button in the Sort & Filter group on the DATA tab.

When you create an Excel table, a filter button appears in each column header. You click a filter button to open the Filter menu for that field. You can use options on the Filter menu to create three types of filters. You can filter a column of data by its cell colors or font colors. You can filter a column of data by a specific text, number, or date filter, although the choices depend on the type of data in the column. Or, you can filter a column of data by selecting the exact values by which you want to filter in the column. After you filter a column, the Clear Filter command becomes available so you can remove the filter and redisplay all the records.

Laurie wants to see the cash receipts for only Food orders. You'll filter the JanuaryData table to show only those records with the value Food in the Segment column.

To filter the JanuaryData table to show only the Food segment:

▶ 1. If you took a break after the previous session, make sure the Cash Receipts January workbook is open, the Cash Receipts worksheet is the active sheet, and the JanuaryData table is active.

▶ 2. Click the **Segment** filter button ⌄. The Filter menu opens, as shown in Figure 5-15, listing the unique entries in the Segment field—Coffee, Food, Gifts, and Spec Drink. All of the items are selected, but you can set which items to use to filter the data. In this case, you want to select Food.

| **Figure 5-15** | **Filter menu for the Segment column** |

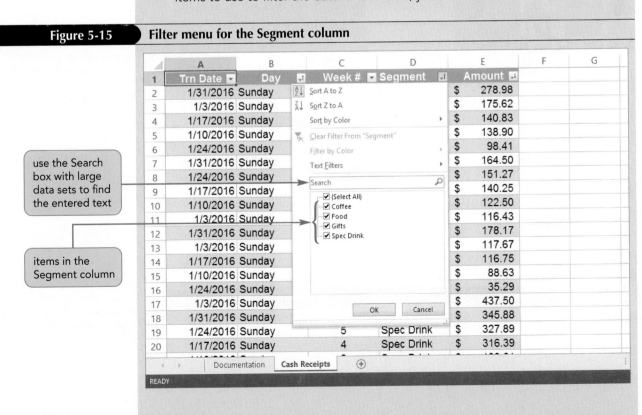

use the Search box with large data sets to find the entered text

items in the Segment column

3. Click the **(Select All)** check box to remove the checkmarks from all of the Segment items.

4. Click the **Food** check box to insert a checkmark. The filter will show only records that match the checked item, and will hide records that contain the unchecked items.

5. Click the **OK** button. The filter is applied. The status bar lists the number of Food rows found in the entire table—in this case, 31 of the 124 records in the table are displayed. See Figure 5-16.

Figure 5-16	JanuaryData table filtered to show only Food

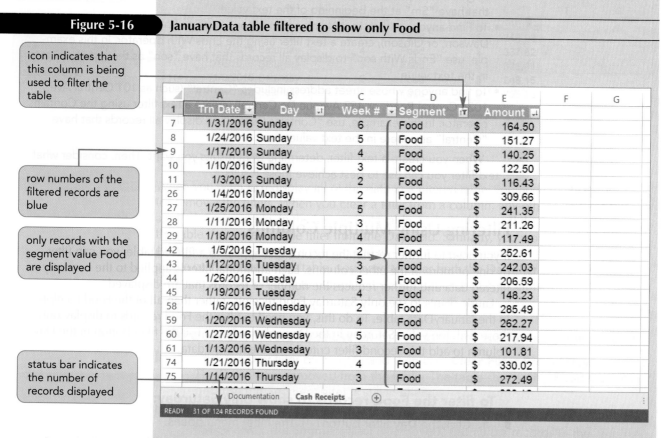

icon indicates that this column is being used to filter the table

row numbers of the filtered records are blue

only records with the segment value Food are displayed

status bar indicates the number of records displayed

READY   31 OF 124 RECORDS FOUND

6. Review the records to verify that only records with Food in the Segment column are visible. All other records in this column are hidden, leaving gaps in the row numbers.

7. Point to the **Segment** filter button ⏹. A ScreenTip—Segment: Equals "Food"—describes the filter applied to the column.

The Filter menu includes options to Sort by Color and Filter by Color. These options enable you to filter and sort data using color, one of many cell attributes. Laurie could use specific cell background colors for certain receipts in the JanuaryData table. For example, she might want to highlight the dates when the coffeehouse could have used an additional employee. So cells in the Trn Date column for busy days would be formatted with yellow as a reminder. You could click the Sort by Color option to display a list of available colors by which to sort, and then click the specific color so that all the records for the days when she needed more help in the store (formatted with yellow) would appear together. Similarly, you could click the Filter by Color option to display a submenu with the available colors by which to filter, and then click a color.

Figure 5-19 Custom AutoFilter dialog box

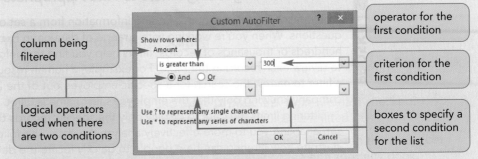

column being filtered

operator for the first condition

criterion for the first condition

logical operators used when there are two conditions

boxes to specify a second condition for the list

Custom AutoFilter

Show rows where:
Amount

is greater than ▾ 300 ◀

● And ○ Or

▾

Use ? to represent any single character
Use * to represent any series of characters

OK   Cancel

▶ **4.** Click the **OK** button. The status bar indicates that 17 of 124 records were found. The 17 records that appear in the JanuaryData table are either Coffee or Spec Drink, and have an Amount greater than $300.

Next, you'll sort the filtered data to show the largest Amount first. Although you can sort the data using Sort buttons, as you did earlier, these sort options are also available on the Filter menu. If you want to perform a more complex sort, you still need to use the Sort dialog box.

To sort the filtered table data:

▶ **1.** Click the **Amount** filter button. The Filter menu opens. The sort options are at the top of the menu.

▶ **2.** Click **Sort Largest to Smallest**. The filtered table now displays Coffee and Spec Drink categories with daily receipts greater than $300 sorted in descending order. See Figure 5-20.

Figure 5-20 Filtered and sorted JanuaryData table

icon shows that this column is filtered

Spec Drink or Coffee with daily amount greater than $300 sorted in descending order by Amount

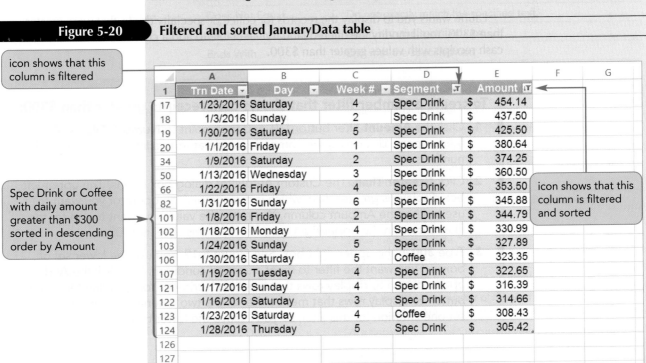

	A	B	C	D	E	F	G
1	Trn Date ▾	Day ▾	Week # ▾	Segment ▾	Amount ▾		
17	1/23/2016	Saturday	4	Spec Drink	$ 454.14		
18	1/3/2016	Sunday	2	Spec Drink	$ 437.50		
19	1/30/2016	Saturday	5	Spec Drink	$ 425.50		
20	1/1/2016	Friday	1	Spec Drink	$ 380.64		
34	1/9/2016	Saturday	2	Spec Drink	$ 374.25		
50	1/13/2016	Wednesday	3	Spec Drink	$ 360.50		
66	1/22/2016	Friday	4	Spec Drink	$ 353.50		
82	1/31/2016	Sunday	6	Spec Drink	$ 345.88		
101	1/8/2016	Friday	2	Spec Drink	$ 344.79		
102	1/18/2016	Monday	4	Spec Drink	$ 330.99		
103	1/24/2016	Sunday	5	Spec Drink	$ 327.89		
106	1/30/2016	Saturday	5	Coffee	$ 323.35		
107	1/19/2016	Tuesday	4	Spec Drink	$ 322.65		
121	1/17/2016	Sunday	4	Spec Drink	$ 316.39		
122	1/16/2016	Saturday	3	Spec Drink	$ 314.66		
123	1/23/2016	Saturday	4	Coffee	$ 308.43		
124	1/28/2016	Thursday	5	Spec Drink	$ 305.42		
126							
127							

icon shows that this column is filtered and sorted

◀ ▶   Documentation   **Cash Receipts**   ⊕

READY   17 OF 124 RECORDS FOUND

Laurie will use this data to help her decide on which days she may hire additional workers. You need to restore the entire table of cash receipts, which you can do by clearing all the filters at one time.

To clear all the filters from the JanuaryData table:

1. On the ribbon, click the **DATA** tab, if necessary.

2. In the Sort & Filter group, click the **Clear** button. All of the records are redisplayed in the table.

Creating a Slicer to Filter Data in an Excel Table

Another way to filter an Excel table is with slicers. You can create a slicer for any field in the Excel table. You also can create more than one slicer for a table. Every slicer consists of an object that contains a button for each unique value in that field. For example, a slicer created for the Day field would include seven buttons—one for each day of the week. One advantage of a slicer is that it clearly shows what filters are currently applied—the buttons for selected values are a different color. However, a slicer can take up a lot of space or hide data if there isn't a big enough blank area near the table. You can format the slicer and its buttons, changing its style, height, and width.

Laurie wants to be able to quickly filter the table to show cash receipts for a specific week. You will add a slicer for the Week # field so she can do this.

To add the Week # slicer to the JanuaryData table:

1. On the ribbon, click the **TABLE TOOLS DESIGN** tab.

2. In the Tools group, click the **Insert Slicer** button. The Insert Slicers dialog box opens, listing every available field in all tables in the workbook. You can select any or all of the fields.

3. Click the **Week #** check box to insert a checkmark, and then click the **OK** button. The Week # slicer appears on the worksheet. All of the slicer buttons are selected, indicating that every Week # is included in the table.

4. Drag the **Week #** slicer to the right of the JanuaryData table, placing its upper-left corner in cell G1.

5. If necessary, click the **Week #** slicer to select it. The SLICER TOOLS OPTIONS tab appears on the ribbon and is selected.

6. In the Size group, enter **2.2"** in the Height box and **1"** in the Width box. The slicer is resized, eliminating the extra space below the buttons and to the right of the labels.

7. In the Slicer Styles group, click the **More** button, and then click **Slicer Style Dark 2**. The slicer colors now match the formatting of the Excel table. See Figure 5-21.

Figure 5-21 JanuaryData table with the Week # slicer

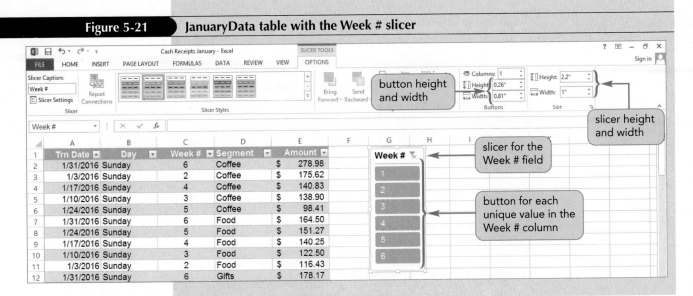

You can use the slicer to quickly filter records in an Excel table. Just click the slicer button corresponding to the data you want to display in the table. If you want to show more than one week, hold down the Ctrl key as you click the buttons that correspond to the additional data you want to show.

Laurie wants you to filter the JanuaryData table to display cash receipts for Week 1 and Week 5. You will use the Week # slicer to do this.

To filter the JanuaryData table using the Week # slicer:

▶ 1. On the Week # slicer, click the **1** button. Only Week 1 data appears in the JanuaryData table. All of the other buttons are gray, indicating that these weeks are not included in the filtered data.

▶ 2. Press and hold the **Ctrl** key, click the **5** button, and then release the **Ctrl** key. Cash receipts for Week 5 are now added to the JanuaryData filtered table. See Figure 5-22.

Figure 5-22 **JanuaryData table filtered to show Weeks 1 and 5**

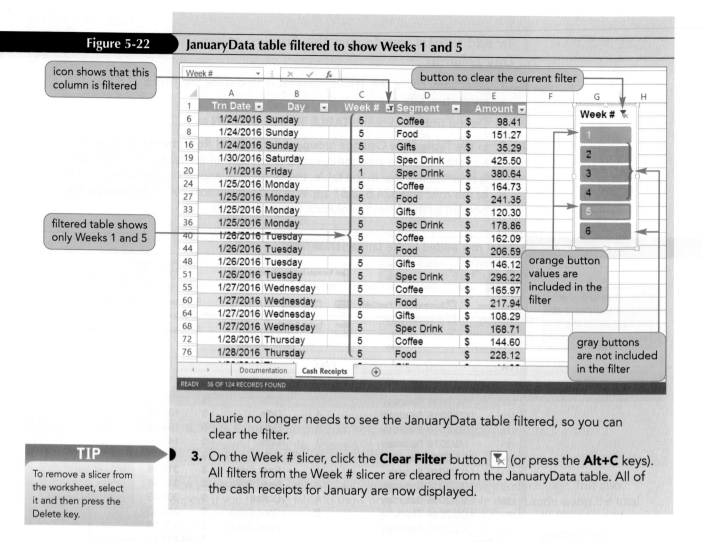

icon shows that this column is filtered

button to clear the current filter

filtered table shows only Weeks 1 and 5

orange button values are included in the filter

gray buttons are not included in the filter

READY 36 OF 124 RECORDS FOUND

Laurie no longer needs to see the JanuaryData table filtered, so you can clear the filter.

3. On the Week # slicer, click the **Clear Filter** button ![clear filter icon] (or press the **Alt+C** keys). All filters from the Week # slicer are cleared from the JanuaryData table. All of the cash receipts for January are now displayed.

TIP

To remove a slicer from the worksheet, select it and then press the Delete key.

Using the Total Row to Calculate Summary Statistics

The Total row is used to calculate summary statistics (including sum, average, count, maximum, and minimum) for any column in an Excel table. The Total row is inserted immediately after the last row of data in the table. A double-line border is inserted to indicate that the following row contains totals, and the label Total is added to the leftmost cell of the row. By default, the Total row adds the numbers in the last column of the Excel table or counts the number of records if the data in the last column contains text. When you click in each cell of the Total row, an arrow appears that you can click to open a list of the most commonly used functions. You can also select other functions by opening the Insert Functions dialog box.

Laurie wants to see the total amount of cash receipts in January and the total number of records being displayed. You will add a Total row to the JanuaryData table, and then use the SUM and COUNT functions to calculate these statistics for Laurie.

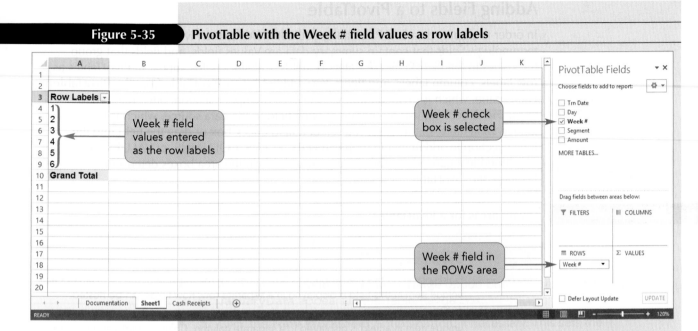

Figure 5-35   PivotTable with the Week # field values as row labels

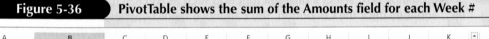

Trouble? If the Week # field appears in the VALUES area, you probably checked the Week # field, which places fields with numeric values in the VALUES area. Drag the Week # field from the VALUES area to the ROWS area.

▶ **2.** In the PivotTable Fields pane, click the **Amount** check box. The Sum of Amount button is placed in the VALUES box because the field contains numeric values. The PivotTable groups the items from the JanuaryData table by Week # and calculates the total Amount for each week. The grand total appears at the bottom of the PivotTable. See Figure 5-36.

Figure 5-36   PivotTable shows the sum of the Amounts field for each Week #

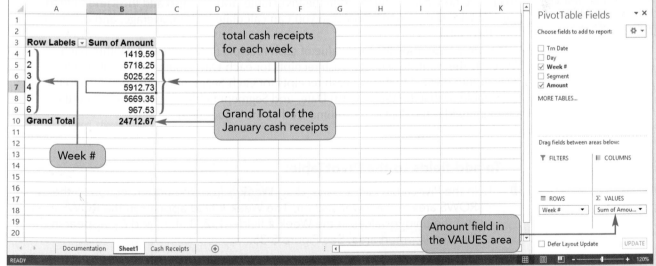

Next, you'll add the Trn Date and Segment fields to the PivotTable.

▶ **3.** In the PivotTable Fields pane, click the **Trn Date** check box. The Trn Date field appears in the ROWS area box below the Week # field, and the unique items in the Trn Date field are indented below each Week # field item in the PivotTable report.

Trouble? If the PivotTable Fields pane is not visible, the active cell is probably not in the PivotTable. Click any cell within the PivotTable to redisplay the PivotTable Fields pane. If the PivotTable Fields pane is still not visible, click the PIVOTTABLE TOOLS ANALYZE tab, and then click the Field List button in the Show group.

▶ **4.** In the PivotTable Fields pane, click the **Segment** check box. The Segment field appears in the ROWS area below the Trn Date field, and its unique items are indented below the Week # and Trn Date fields already in the PivotTable. See Figure 5-37.

Figure 5-37   PivotTable with Week #, Trn Date, and Segment field items as row labels

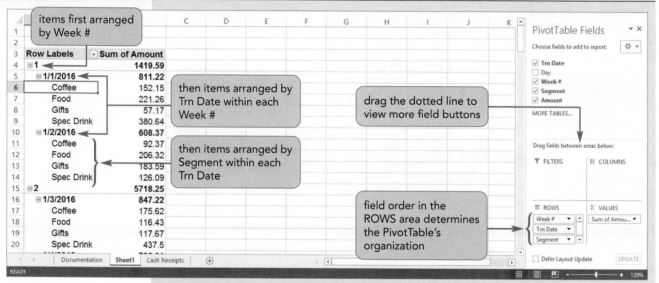

Trouble? If the Segment field button is not visible in the ROWS area, drag the dotted line above the "Drag fields between areas below" label up until the Segment field button is visible.

If a PivotTable becomes too detailed or confusing, you can always remove one of its fields. In the PivotTable Fields pane, click the check box of the field you want to remove. The field is then deleted from the PivotTable and the area box.

Changing the Layout of a PivotTable

You can add, remove, and rearrange fields to change the PivotTable's layout. Recall that the benefit of a PivotTable is that it summarizes large amounts of data into a readable format. After you create a PivotTable, you can view the same data in different ways. Each time you make a change in the areas section of the PivotTable Fields pane, the PivotTable layout is rearranged. This ability to "pivot" the table—for example, change row headings to column positions and vice versa—makes the PivotTable a powerful analytical tool.

Based on Laurie's PivotTable plan that was shown in Figure 5-31, the Segment field items should be positioned as columns instead of rows in the PivotTable. You'll move the Segment field now to produce the layout Laurie wants.

To move the Segment field to the COLUMNS area:

▶ **1.** In the PivotTable Fields pane, locate the **Segment** field button in the ROWS area.

▶ **2.** Drag the **Segment** field button from the ROWS area to the COLUMNS area. The PivotTable is rearranged so that the Segment field is a column label instead of a row label. See Figure 5-38.

Figure 5-38   PivotTable rearranged with Segment as a column label

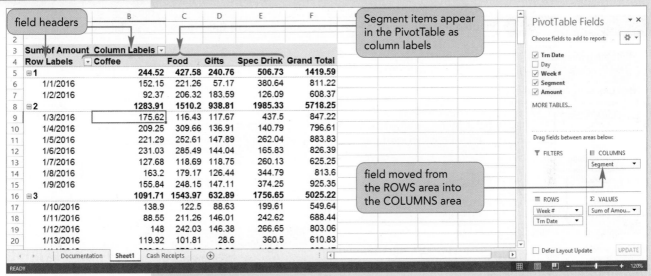

The PivotTable now has the layout that Laurie wants.

INSIGHT

Choosing a Report Layout

There are three different report layouts available for PivotTables. The report layout shown in Figure 5-38, which is referred to as the Compact Form, is the default layout. It places all fields from the ROWS area in a single column, and indents the items from each field below the outer fields. In the Outline Form layout, each field in the ROWS area takes a column in the PivotTable. The subtotal for each group appears above every group. The Tabular Form layout displays one column for each field and leaves space for column headers. A total for each group appears below each group. To select a different report layout, click the Report Layout button in the Layout group on the PIVOTTABLE TOOLS DESIGN tab.

Formatting a PivotTable

Like worksheet cells and Excel tables, you can quickly format a PivotTable report using one of the built-in styles available in the PivotTable Styles gallery. As with cell and table styles, you can point to any style in the gallery to see a Live Preview of the PivotTable with that style. You also can modify the appearance of PivotTables by adding or removing banded rows, banded columns, row headers, and column headers.

Laurie wants you to apply the Pivot Style Medium 10 style, which makes each group in the PivotTable stand out and makes subtotals in the report easier to find.

To apply the Pivot Style Medium 10 style to the PivotTable:

▶ **1.** Make sure the active cell is in the PivotTable.

▶ **2.** On the ribbon, click the **PIVOTTABLE TOOLS DESIGN** tab.

▶ **3.** In the PivotTable Styles group, click the **More** button ⏷ to open the PivotTable Styles gallery.

▶ **4.** Move the pointer over each style to see the Live Preview of the PivotTable report with that style.

▶ **5.** Click the **Pivot Style Medium 10** style (the third style in the second row of the Medium section). The style is applied to the PivotTable.

You can format cells in a PivotTable the same way that you format cells in a worksheet. This enables you to further customize the look of the PivotTable by changing the font, color, alignment, and number formats of specific cells in the PivotTable. Laurie wants the numbers in the PivotTable to be quickly recognized as dollars. You'll change the total Amount values in the PivotTable to the Currency style.

To format the Amount field in the PivotTable as currency:

▶ **1.** In the VALUES area of the PivotTable Fields pane, click the **Sum of Amount** button. A shortcut menu opens with options related to that field.

▶ **2.** Click the **Value Field Settings** button on the shortcut menu. The Value Field Settings dialog box opens. See Figure 5-39.

Figure 5-39 ▶ **Value Field Settings dialog box**

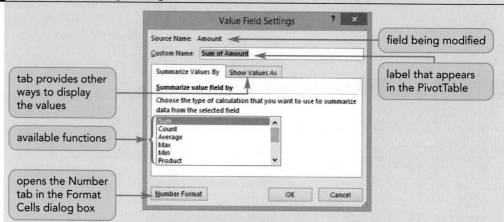

- field being modified
- label that appears in the PivotTable
- tab provides other ways to display the values
- available functions
- opens the Number tab in the Format Cells dialog box

▶ **3.** In the Custom Name box, type **Total Cash Receipts** as the label for the field. You will leave Sum as the summary function for the field; however, you could select a different function.

▶ **4.** Click the **Number Format** button. The Format Cells dialog box opens. This is the same dialog box you have used before to format numbers in worksheet cells.

TIP

You can also right-click in the PivotTable data area and click Number Format or Format Cells to quickly format the PivotTable.

▶ **5.** In the Category box, click **Currency**. You will use the default number of decimal places, currency symbol, and negative number format.

▶ **6.** Click the **OK** button. The numbers in the PivotTable will be formatted as currency with two decimal places.

▶ **7.** Click the **OK** button. The Value Field Settings dialog box closes. The PivotTable changes to reflect the label you entered, and the number format for the field changes to currency.

Filtering a PivotTable

As you analyze the data in a PivotTable, you might want to show only a portion of the total data. You can do this by filtering the PivotTable. Filtering a field lets you focus on a subset of items in that field.

Adding a Field to the FILTERS Area

You can drag one or more fields to the FILTERS area of the PivotTable Fields pane to change what values are displayed in the PivotTable. A field placed in the FILTERS area provides a way to filter the PivotTable so that it displays summarized data for one or more items or all items in that field. For example, placing the Week # field in the FILTERS area allows you to view or print the total cash receipts for all weeks, a specific week such as Week 1, or multiple weeks such as Weeks 2 through 5.

Laurie wants you to move the Week # field from the ROWS area to the FILTERS area so that she can focus on specific subsets of the cash receipts.

To add the Week # field to the FILTERS area:

▶ **1.** In the PivotTable Fields pane, drag the **Week #** button from the ROWS area to the FILTERS area. By default, the Filter field item shows "(All)" to indicate that the PivotTable displays all the summarized data associated with the Week # field. See Figure 5-40.

Figure 5-40   **PivotTable with the Week # filter**

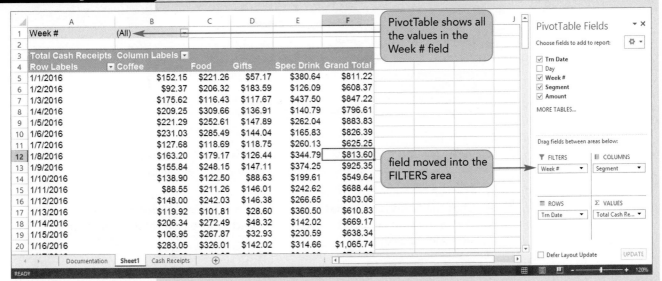

Next, you'll filter the summarized report to show only cash receipts for Week 2.

▶ **2.** In cell B1, click the **filter** button ⬇. The Filter menu opens, showing the field items displayed.

▶ **3.** In the Filter menu, click **2**, and then click the **OK** button. The PivotTable displays the total Amount of cash receipts for the dates in Week 2. The filter button changes to indicate the PivotTable is currently filtered. See Figure 5-41.

| Figure 5-41 | Week # filter set to show cash receipts in Week 2 |

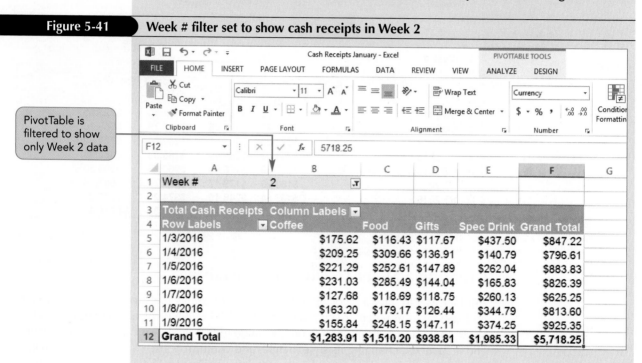

PivotTable is filtered to show only Week 2 data

Filtering PivotTable Fields

Another way that you can filter field items in the PivotTable is by using the Filter menu, which you open by clicking the Row Labels filter button or the Column Labels filter button. You then check or uncheck items to show or hide them, respectively, in the PivotTable.

Laurie wants to exclude Gifts from her analysis. She asks you to remove the cash receipts for Gifts from the PivotTable.

To filter Gifts from the Segment column labels:

▶ **1.** In the PivotTable, click the **Column Labels** filter button ⬇. The Filter menu opens, listing the items in the Segment field.

▶ **2.** Click the **Gifts** check box to remove the checkmark. The Select All check box is filled with black indicating that all items are not selected.

▶ **3.** Click the **OK** button. The Gifts column is removed from the PivotTable. The PivotTable includes only cash receipts from Coffee, Food, and Spec Drink (specialty drinks). See Figure 5-42. You can show the hidden objects by clicking the Column Labels filter button and checking the Gifts check box.

Figure 5-42 | **PivotTable report filtered by Segment**

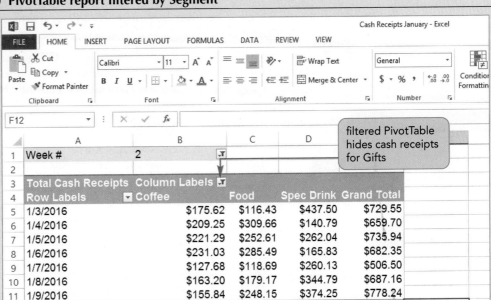

Creating a Slicer to Filter a PivotTable

Another way to filter a PivotTable is with a slicer just like the slicer you created to filter an Excel table. You can create a slicer for any field in the PivotTable Fields pane. The slicer contains a button for each unique value in that field. You can format the slicer and its buttons, changing its style, height, and width. You also can create more than one slicer at a time. For example, you can have a slicer for Week # that has a button for each unique Week # value, and a second slicer for Segment. This allows you to filter a PivotTable report so that it displays the cash receipts for Week 2 sales of coffee, food, and specialty drinks by clicking the corresponding slicer buttons.

Laurie wants flexibility in how she views the data in the PivotTable, so she asks you to add a slicer for the Week # field to the current PivotTable.

To add the Week # slicer to the PivotTable:

▸ 1. On the ribbon, click the **PIVOTTABLE TOOLS ANALYZE** tab.

▸ 2. In the Filter group, click the **Insert Slicer** button. The Insert Slicers dialog box opens, displaying a list of available PivotTable Fields. You can select any or all of the fields.

▸ 3. Click the **Week #** check box to insert a checkmark, and then click the **OK** button. The Week # slicer appears on the worksheet. Because the PivotTable is already filtered to display only the results for Week # 2, the 2 button is selected. The other slicer buttons are white because those weeks have been filtered and are not part of the PivotTable.

▸ 4. If necessary, click the **Week #** slicer to select it. The SLICER TOOLS OPTIONS tab appears on the ribbon.

▸ 5. On the SLICER TOOLS OPTIONS tab, in the Size group, change the height to **2.2"** and change the width to **1"**. The slicer object is resized, eliminating the extra space below the buttons and to the right of the labels.

▶ **6.** In the Slicer Styles group, click the **More** button, and then click **Slicer Style Dark 2**. The slicer colors now match the PivotTable.

▶ **7.** Drag the **Week #** slicer to the right of the PivotTable, placing its upper-left corner in cell G3. See Figure 5-43.

Figure 5-43 ▶ **Week # slicer**

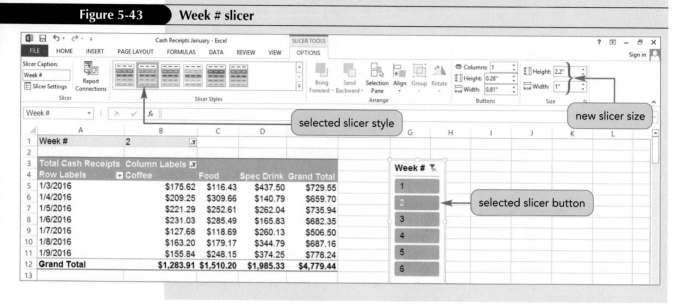

Laurie wants you to display the results of the PivotTable for all the full weeks in January—Weeks 2, 3, 4, and 5. You can do this quickly using the Week # slicer.

To filter the PivotTable using the Week # slicer:

▶ **1.** Press and hold the **Ctrl** key, click the **3** button, and then release the **Ctrl** key. Week 3 data also appears in the PivotTable.

▶ **2.** Press and hold the **Ctrl** key, click the **4** button, click the **5** button, and then release the **Ctrl** key. Data for Weeks 4 and 5 is added to the PivotTable.

TIP

To remove all filters from the PivotTable, click the Clear Filter button in the upper-right corner of the slicer.

▶ **3.** Click the **Week # 2** slicer button. Only the cash receipts for Week 2 are displayed in the PivotTable.

After you have finished creating a PivotTable, you can hide the PivotTable Fields pane so that it won't appear when a cell is selected in the PivotTable. You can also assign more descriptive names to the PivotTable as well as the worksheet that contains the PivotTable.

To hide the PivotTable Fields pane and rename the PivotTable and worksheet:

▶ **1.** Click in the PivotTable to display the PIVOTTABLE TOOLS contextual tabs on the ribbon.

▶ **2.** Click the **PIVOTTABLE TOOLS ANALYZE** tab.

▶ **3.** In the Show group, click the **Field List** button. The PivotTable Fields pane is hidden and won't reappear when a cell in the PivotTable is selected.

▶ **4.** In the PivotTable group, select the default name in the PivotTable Name box, type **WeeklySummary** as the descriptive PivotTable name, and then press the **Enter** key.

▶ **5.** Rename the worksheet as **Weekly Summary PivotTable**.

Refreshing a PivotTable

You cannot change data directly in a PivotTable. Instead, you must edit the data source on which the PivotTable is created. However, PivotTables are not updated automatically when the source data for the PivotTable is updated. After you edit the underlying data, you must **refresh**, or update, the PivotTable report to reflect the revised calculations.

Displaying the Data Source for a PivotTable Cell

As you have seen, PivotTables are a great way to summarize the results of an Excel table. However, at some point, you may question the accuracy of a specific calculation in your PivotTable. In these cases, you can "drill down" to view the source data for a summary cell in a PivotTable. You simply double-click a summary cell, and the corresponding source data of the records for the PivotTable cell is displayed in a new worksheet.

The cash receipts entry for Food on 1/4/2016 should have been $409.66 (not $309.66 as currently listed). You'll edit the record in the JanuaryData table, which is the underlying data source for the PivotTable. This one change will affect the PivotTable in several locations—the Grand Total value of receipts in Week 2 is $1,510.20 for the Food, $659.70 for 1/4/2016, and $4,779.44 overall.

To update the JanuaryData table and refresh the PivotTable:

▶ **1.** Go to the **Cash Receipts** worksheet, and then find the Food cash receipts for 1/4/2016. The amount is $309.66.

▶ **2.** Click the record's **Amount** cell, and then enter **409.66**. The receipt's Amount is updated in the table. You'll return to the PivotTable report to see the effect of this change.

▶ **3.** Go to the **Weekly Summary PivotTable** worksheet. The Amount for Food on 1/4/2016 is still $309.66, the Grand Total for Food is still $1,510.20, the Grand Total for 1/4/2016 is still $659.70, and the overall Grand Total is still $4,779.44. The PivotTable was not automatically updated when the data in its source table changed, so you need to refresh the PivotTable.

▶ **4.** Click any cell in the PivotTable.

▶ **5.** On the ribbon, click the **PIVOTTABLE TOOLS ANALYZE** tab.

▶ **6.** In the Data group, click the **Refresh** button. The PivotTable report is updated. The totals are now $409.66, $1,610.20, $759.70, and $4,879.44. See Figure 5-44.

| Figure 5-44 | Refreshed PivotTable |

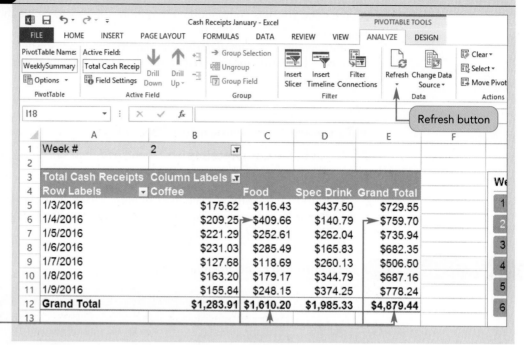

updated cash receipts values

Creating Different Types of PivotTables

This tutorial only scratched the surface of the variety of PivotTables you can create. Here are a few more examples:

- Most PivotTable summaries are based on numeric data; Excel uses SUM as the default calculation. If your analysis requires a different calculation, you can select any of the 11 built-in summary calculations. For example, you could build a report that displays the minimum, maximum, and average receipts for each week in January.
- You can use PivotTables to combine row label and column label items into groups. If items are numbers or dates, they can be grouped automatically using the Grouping dialog box, or they can be grouped manually using the Ctrl key to select items in a group and then clicking Group Selection from the shortcut menu. For example, you can manually combine Saturday and Sunday receipts into a Weekend group, and combine Monday through Friday receipts into a Weekday group, and then display total receipts by these groups within the PivotTable. Over time, you will also be able to group the Trn Date field to summarize daily cash receipts by month, quarter, and year.
- You can develop PivotTables that use the percent of row, percent of column, or percent of total calculation to view each item in the PivotTable as a percent of the total in the current row, current column, or grand total. For example, you can display the total weekly receipts as a percent of the total monthly receipts.
- You can develop PivotTables that display how the current month/quarter/year compares to the previous month/quarter/year. For example, you can compare this month's receipts for each category to the corresponding receipts for the previous month to display the difference between the two months.

Being able to enhance PivotTables by changing summary calculations, consolidating data into larger groups, and creating custom calculations based on other data in the VALUES area gives you flexibility in your analysis.

Creating a Recommended PivotTable

The Recommended PivotTables dialog box shows previews of PivotTables based on the source data. This lets you see different options for how to create the PivotTable, and you can choose the one that best meets your needs.

Laurie wants to summarize sales by days-of-the-week so she can gain insights into staffing and ordering for each day. You will see if a recommended PivotTable meets Laurie's request.

To create a recommended PivotTable:

▶ **1.** Go to the **Cash Receipts** worksheet, and then select any cell in the Excel table.

▶ **2.** On the ribbon, click the **INSERT** tab.

▶ **3.** In the Tables group, click the **Recommended PivotTables** button. The Recommended PivotTables dialog box opens. You can select from several PivotTables. See Figure 5-45.

Figure 5-45	Recommended PivotTable dialog box

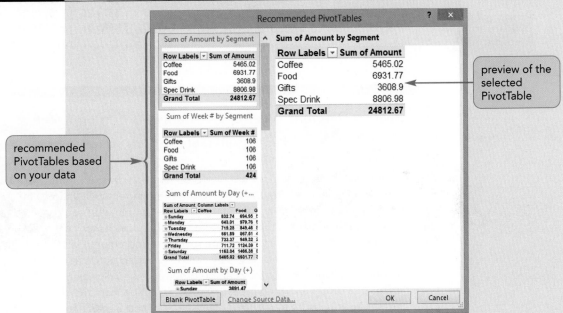

The Sum of Amount by Day PivotTable meets Laurie's request.

▶ **4.** Click **Sum of Amount by Day** (the fourth PivotTable in the left pane). An enlarged version of the selected PivotTable is displayed in the right pane of the dialog box.

▶ **5.** Click the **OK** button. A PivotTable of the cash receipts by day appears in a new worksheet. See Figure 5-46.

Figure 5-46   **PivotTable of cash receipts by day**

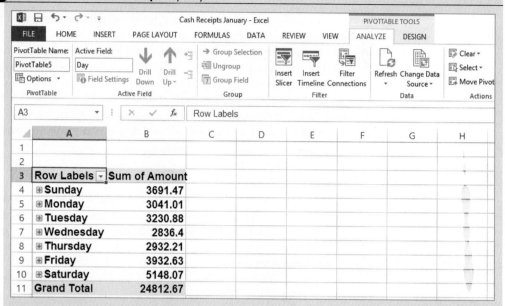

6. In the PivotTable Fields pane, in the VALUES area, click the **Sum of Amount** button, and then click **Value Field Settings** on the shortcut menu. The Value Field Settings dialog box opens.

7. Click the **Number Format** button. The Format Cells dialog box opens.

8. In the Category box, click **Currency**, and then click the **OK** button.

9. Click the **OK** button. The numbers in the PivotTable are formatted as currency with two decimal places.

10. On the ribbon, click the **PIVOTTABLE TOOLS DESIGN** tab.

11. In the PivotTable Styles group, click the **More** button to open the PivotTable Styles gallery, and then click the **Pivot Style Medium 10** style. The style is applied to the PivotTable.

12. Rename the worksheet as **Daily Receipts PivotTable**.

Laurie will use the summary of sales by days-of-the-week in the Daily Receipts PivotTable worksheet to evaluate staffing and ordering for each day.

INSIGHT

Adding a Calculated Field to a PivotTable Report

Occasionally, you might need to display more information than a PivotTable is designed to show, but it doesn't make sense to alter your data source to include this additional information. For example, you might want to include a field that shows an 8 percent sales tax on each value in an Amount field. In these instances, you can add a calculated field to the PivotTable. A **calculated field** is a formula you define to generate PivotTable values that otherwise would not appear in the PivotTable. The calculated field formula looks like a regular worksheet formula.

To add a calculated field to a PivotTable, complete the following steps:

1. Select any cell in the PivotTable report.
2. On the ANALYZE tab, in the Calculations group, click Fields, Items & Sets, and then click Calculated Field.
3. In the Name box, type a name for the field, such as Sales Tax.
4. In the Formula box, enter the formula for the field. To use data from another field, click the field in the Fields box, and then click Insert Field. For example, to calculate an 8 percent sales tax on each value in the Amount field, enter =Amount*8%.
5. Click the Add button.
6. Click the OK button. The calculated field is added PivotTable's data area and to the PivotTable Field List

As you can see, you can use calculated fields to include additional information in a PivotTable.

Creating a PivotChart

A PivotChart is a graphical representation of the data in a PivotTable. You can create a PivotChart from a PivotTable. A PivotChart allows you to interactively add, remove, filter, and refresh data fields in the PivotChart similar to working with a PivotTable. PivotCharts can have all the same formatting as other charts, including layouts and styles. You can move and resize chart elements, or change formatting of individual data points.

Laurie wants you to add a PivotChart next to the Sum of Amount by Day PivotTable. You will prepare a clustered column chart next to the PivotTable.

TIP

You can also create a PivotChart based directly on an Excel table, which creates both a PivotTable and a PivotChart.

To create and format the PivotChart:

1. Select any cell in the PivotTable.

2. On the ribbon, click the **PIVOTTABLE TOOLS ANALYZE** tab.

3. In the Tools group, click the **PivotChart** button. The Insert Chart dialog box opens.

4. If necessary, click the **Clustered Column** chart (the first chart in the Column charts section), and then click the **OK** button. A PivotChart appears next to the PivotTable along with the PivotChart Fields pane.

   Trouble? If you selected the wrong PivotChart, delete the PivotChart you just created, and then repeat Steps 1 through 4.

5. On the ribbon, click the **PIVOTCHART TOOLS DESIGN** tab.

6. In the Chart Layouts group, click the **Add Chart Element** button, point to **Legend**, and then click **None**. The legend is removed from the PivotChart. You do not need a legend because the PivotChart has only one data series.

▶ **7.** In the PivotChart, right-click the chart title, and then click **Edit Text** on the shortcut menu. The insertion point appears in the title so you can edit it.

▶ **8.** Select the title, type **Cash Receipts by Day** as the new title, and then click the chart area to deselect the title.

▶ **9.** Right-click any column to select the series, and then use the **Fill** button on the Mini toolbar above the shortcut menu to change its fill color to the **Orange, Accent 2** theme color.

▶ **10.** Drag the PivotChart so its upper-left corner is in cell **D3**. The PivotChart is aligned with the PivotTable. See Figure 5-47.

Figure 5-47   PivotChart added to the PivotTable report

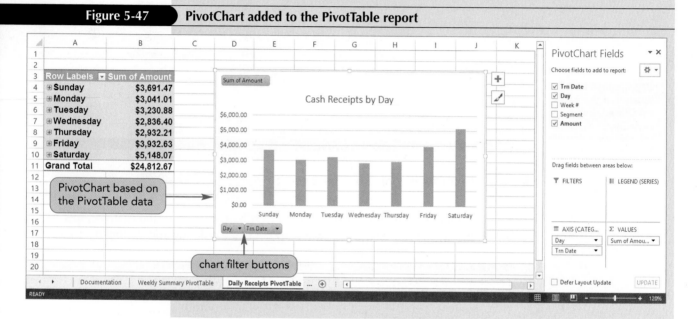

The PIVOTCHART TOOLS contextual tabs enable you to work with and format the selected PivotChart the same way as an ordinary chart. A PivotChart and its associated PivotTable are linked. When you modify one, the other also changes. You can quickly display different views of the PivotChart by using the chart filter buttons on the PivotChart to filter the data.

Laurie wants you to display cash receipts for only Monday through Friday. You will filter the PivotChart to display only those items.

To filter the PivotChart to display cash receipts for Monday through Friday:

▶ **1.** Make sure the PivotChart is selected, and then click the **Day** axis field button in the PivotChart. The Filter menu opens.

▶ **2.** Click the **Sunday** and **Saturday** check boxes to remove their checkmarks.

▶ **3.** Click the **OK** button. The PivotChart displays only cash receipts for the weekdays. The PivotTable is automatically filtered to display the same results.

▶ **4.** Select cell **A1**. See Figure 5-48.

Figure 5-48   **Filtered PivotChart**

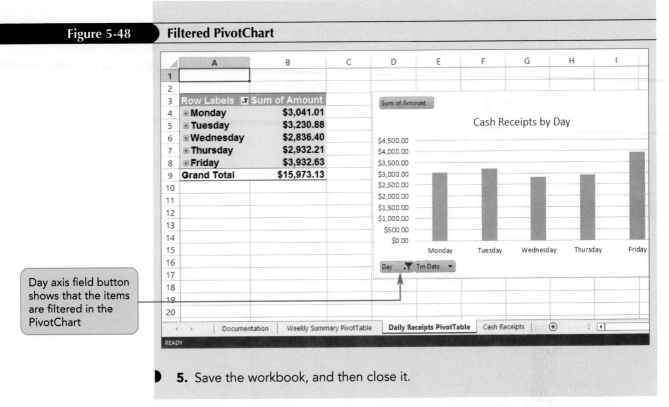

Day axis field button shows that the items are filtered in the PivotChart

5. Save the workbook, and then close it.

Laurie is pleased with the PivotTable and PivotChart. Both show the cash receipts arranged by day of the week, which will help her make ordering and staffing decisions.

Session 5.3 Quick Check

REVIEW

1. What is a PivotTable?
2. How do you add fields to a PivotTable?
3. How are fields such as region, state, and country most likely to appear in a PivotTable?
4. How are fields such as revenue, costs, and profits most likely to appear in a PivotTable?
5. A list of college students includes a code to indicate the student's gender (male or female) and a field to identify the student's major. Would you use a filter or a PivotTable to (a) create a list of all females majoring in history, and (b) count the number of males and females in each major?
6. An Excel table of professional baseball player data consists of team name, player name, position, and salary. What area of a PivotTable report would be used for the Team name field if you wanted to display the average salaries by position for all teams or an individual team?
7. After you update data in an Excel table, what must you do to a PivotTable based on that Excel table?
8. What is a PivotChart?

Review Assignments

PRACTICE

Data File needed for the Review Assignments: February.xlsx

Laurie wants to analyze the cash receipts data for February. She entered this data into a new workbook and wants you to sort and filter the data, as well as create summary reports using the Subtotal command, PivotTables, and PivotCharts. Complete the following:

1. Open the **February** workbook located in the Excel5 ▶ Review folder included with your Data Files, and then save the workbook as **Cash Receipts February**.
2. In the Documentation worksheet, enter your name and the date.
3. In the Cash Receipts worksheet, freeze the top row so the headers remain on the screen as you scroll.
4. Make a copy of the Cash Receipts worksheet, and then rename the copied worksheet as **Feb Data**. (*Hint*: To make a copy of the worksheet, press and hold the Ctrl key as you drag the sheet tab to the right of the Cash Receipts sheet tab.)
5. In the Feb Data worksheet, unfreeze the top row.
6. Create an Excel table for the cash receipts data.
7. Format the Excel table with Table Style Medium 25, and then change the Amount field to the Accounting format with two decimal places.
8. Rename the Excel table as **FebruaryData**.
9. Make the following changes to the FebruaryData table:
   a. Add a record for **2/29/2016**, **Monday**, **10**, **Spec Drink**, **353.11**.
   b. Edit the record for Coffee on 2/27/2016 by changing the Amount from 219.71 to **269.71**.
   c. Delete any duplicate records.
10. Make a copy of the Feb Data worksheet, and then rename the copied worksheet as **Sort Trn Date**. In the Sort Trn Date worksheet, sort the cash receipts by Trn Date, displaying the newest receipts first, and then by Amount displaying the largest amounts first.
11. Make a copy of the Feb Data worksheet, and then rename the copied worksheet as **Sort By Day**. In the Sort By Day worksheet, sort the cash receipts by Day (use the custom list order of Sunday, Monday, …), then by Segment (A to Z), and then by Amount (smallest to largest).
12. Make a copy of the Feb Data worksheet, and then rename the copied worksheet as **Filter Omit Gifts**. In the Filter Omit Gifts worksheet, filter the FebruaryData table to display the cash receipts for all items except Gifts.
13. In the Filter Omit Gifts worksheet, insert the Total row to calculate the average amount of the cash receipts for the filtered data. Change the label in the Total row to **Average**. Sort the filtered data by descending order by Amount.
14. Split the Filter Omit Gifts worksheet into two panes above the last row of the table. Display the cash receipt records in the top pane, and display only the Total row in the bottom pane.
15. Make a copy of the Feb Data worksheet, and then rename the copied worksheet as **Filter By Day**. In the Filter By Day worksheet, insert a slicer for the Day column. Move the slicer to row 1. Format the slicer with Slicer Style Light 3. Change the slicer's width to 1.2" and its height to 2.5". Use the slicer to display cash receipts for Saturday and Sunday.
16. Make a copy of the Feb Data worksheet, and then rename the copied worksheet as **Subtotals**. In the Subtotals worksheet, convert the FebruaryData table to a range, and then sort the range by the Segment column.
17. In the Subtotals worksheet, use the Subtotal command to calculate the total cash receipts for each segment in the Amount column. Display only the subtotal results.
18. Based on the data in the Feb Data worksheet, create a PivotTable in a new worksheet that shows the total receipts by Day. Format the data area with the Currency format. Rename the worksheet with the PivotTable as **PivotTable By Day**.

9. Make a copy of the Sales Data worksheet, and then rename the copied worksheet as **Subtotals 2016**. Filter the list to display only data for 2016, and then include subtotals that calculate the total Sales by Region and Month. (*Hint*: You need two sets of subtotals.)

10. Make a copy of the Sales Data worksheet, and then rename the copied worksheet as **Bottom 15**. Display the 15 lowest periods based on sales (each row represents a period). Sort the sales so that the lowest sales appear first.

11. Based on the data in the Sales Data worksheet, create the PivotTable and PivotChart shown in Figure 5-49, summarizing sales by year and month. Rename the worksheet as **PivotChart**.

Figure 5-49 PivotTable and PivotChart summarizing sales by year and month

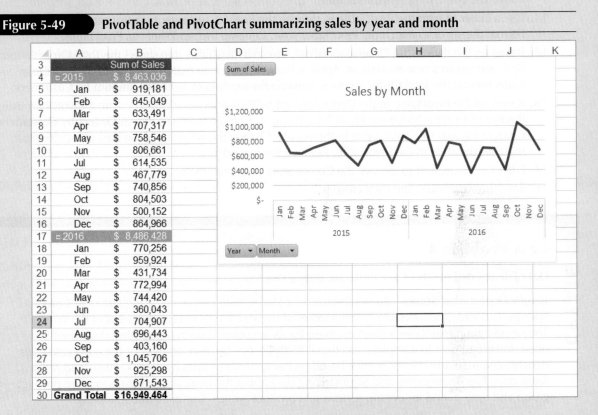

12. Based on the data in the Sales Data worksheet, create the PivotTable shown in Figure 5-50 to calculate the sum, average, minimum, and maximum sales categorized by region and product group. Insert a Year slicer and use it to show sales in 2016. Rename the worksheet as **Region Statistics**.

Figure 5-50   PivotTable displaying sales categorized by region and product group

	A	B	C	D	E	F	G
2							
3	Row Labels	Sum of Sales	Average Sales	Minimum Sales	Maximum Sales		Year
4	⊟ Colorado	$ 3,330,178	$ 55,503	$ 7	$ 167,539		
5	Automotive	$ 564,908	$ 47,076	$ 7	$ 130,405		2015
6	Electronics	$ 499,670	$ 41,639	$ 1,738	$ 147,135		
7	Gardening	$ 782,519	$ 65,210	$ 5,607	$ 167,539		2016
8	Housewares	$ 788,597	$ 65,716	$ 21,017	$ 147,298		
9	Sporting	$ 694,484	$ 57,874	$ 2,522	$ 135,193		
10	⊟ Oklahoma	$ 2,636,197	$ 43,937	$ 175	$ 176,220		
11	Automotive	$ 916,489	$ 76,374	$ 969	$ 170,688		
12	Electronics	$ 452,901	$ 37,742	$ 1,154	$ 176,220		
13	Gardening	$ 405,111	$ 33,759	$ 175	$ 119,667		
14	Housewares	$ 333,699	$ 27,808	$ 1,176	$ 107,097		
15	Sporting	$ 527,997	$ 44,000	$ 5,441	$ 105,933		
16	⊟ Utah	$ 2,520,053	$ 42,001	$ 684	$ 168,339		
17	Automotive	$ 499,020	$ 41,585	$ 684	$ 168,220		
18	Electronics	$ 520,268	$ 43,356	$ 7,544	$ 145,865		
19	Gardening	$ 358,252	$ 29,854	$ 2,148	$ 78,942		
20	Housewares	$ 469,331	$ 39,111	$ 1,770	$ 127,490		
21	Sporting	$ 673,182	$ 56,099	$ 3,089	$ 168,339		

13. Based on the data in the Sales Data worksheet, create the PivotTable and slicers shown in Figure 5-51 displaying total sales by Year, Product Group, and Region. Include a second value calculation that displays each Product Group and Region as a percentage of the total company sales. (*Hint:* In Excel Help, read about how to calculate a percentage for subtotals in a PivotTable.) Rename the worksheet as **Percent of Company Sales**.

Figure 5-51   PivotTable displaying sales by Year, Product Group, and Region

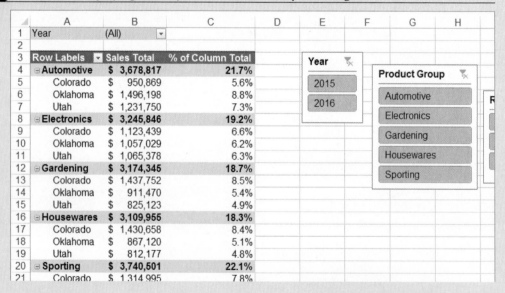

	A	B	C	D	E	F	G	H
1	Year	(All)						
2								
3	Row Labels	Sales Total	% of Column Total		Year			
4	⊟ Automotive	$ 3,678,817	21.7%				Product Group	
5	Colorado	$ 950,869	5.6%		2015			
6	Oklahoma	$ 1,496,198	8.8%		2016		Automotive	
7	Utah	$ 1,231,750	7.3%				Electronics	
8	⊟ Electronics	$ 3,245,846	19.2%					
9	Colorado	$ 1,123,439	6.6%				Gardening	
10	Oklahoma	$ 1,057,029	6.2%				Housewares	
11	Utah	$ 1,065,378	6.3%					
12	⊟ Gardening	$ 3,174,345	18.7%				Sporting	
13	Colorado	$ 1,437,752	8.5%					
14	Oklahoma	$ 911,470	5.4%					
15	Utah	$ 825,123	4.9%					
16	⊟ Housewares	$ 3,109,955	18.3%					
17	Colorado	$ 1,430,658	8.4%					
18	Oklahoma	$ 867,120	5.1%					
19	Utah	$ 812,177	4.8%					
20	⊟ Sporting	$ 3,740,501	22.1%					
21	Colorado	$ 1,314,995	7.8%					

14. Format the PivotTable and slicers with matching styles, and adjust the height and width of the slicers as needed to improve their appearance.

15. Filter the Product Group to display sales in 2016 for the Automotive and Electronics product groups in all Regions except Utah.

16. Save the workbook, and then close it.

EXCEL

Managing Multiple Worksheets and Workbooks

Summarizing Recycling Data

OBJECTIVES

Session 6.1
- Create a worksheet group
- Format and edit multiple worksheets at once
- Create cell references to other worksheets
- Consolidate information from multiple worksheets using 3-D references
- Create and print a worksheet group

Session 6.2
- Create a link to data in another workbook
- Create a workbook reference
- Learn how to edit links

Session 6.3
- Insert a hyperlink in a cell
- Create a workbook based on an existing template
- Create a custom workbook template

Case | *Better World Recycling*

In 2010, Maria Guzman and Edward McKay, a couple of college friends, opened Better World Recycling, a collection site for recyclable plastics. Since then, they have expanded the business to accept other types of recyclable items, including paper, glass, metal, Styrofoam, and plastic. The company also expanded from the original location in Columbia, Kansas, to two additional locations—Richmond, Indiana, and Marion, Iowa. With the expansion, Maria assumed the duties and title of COO (Chief Operating Officer) and Edward became the CEO (Chief Executive Officer).

Maria, working in Columbia, is responsible for analyzing collections at all locations. Each recycling site tracks the amount of each material it collects during each quarter. Each site enters this information in a workbook, which is sent to Maria to consolidate and analyze. Maria has received the workbooks with the quarterly collections data for the past year from all three locations—Columbia, Richmond, and Marion. She wants you to create a worksheet in each workbook that summarizes the collection totals.

STARTING DATA FILES

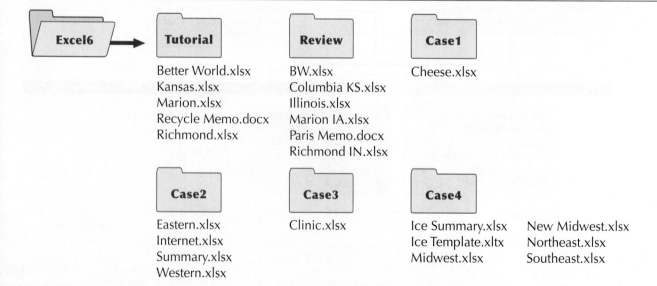

Excel6 → Tutorial
Better World.xlsx
Kansas.xlsx
Marion.xlsx
Recycle Memo.docx
Richmond.xlsx

Review
BW.xlsx
Columbia KS.xlsx
Illinois.xlsx
Marion IA.xlsx
Paris Memo.docx
Richmond IN.xlsx

Case1
Cheese.xlsx

Case2
Eastern.xlsx
Internet.xlsx
Summary.xlsx
Western.xlsx

Case3
Clinic.xlsx

Case4
Ice Summary.xlsx
Ice Template.xltx
Midwest.xlsx

New Midwest.xlsx
Northeast.xlsx
Southeast.xlsx

Session 6.1 Visual Overview:

Anything you do in the active sheet—such as entering formulas, adding labels, and formatting—is automatically done to all sheets in the worksheet group, saving you time and ensuring consistency.

When worksheets are grouped, the workbook is in group-editing mode and "[Group]" appears in the title bar.

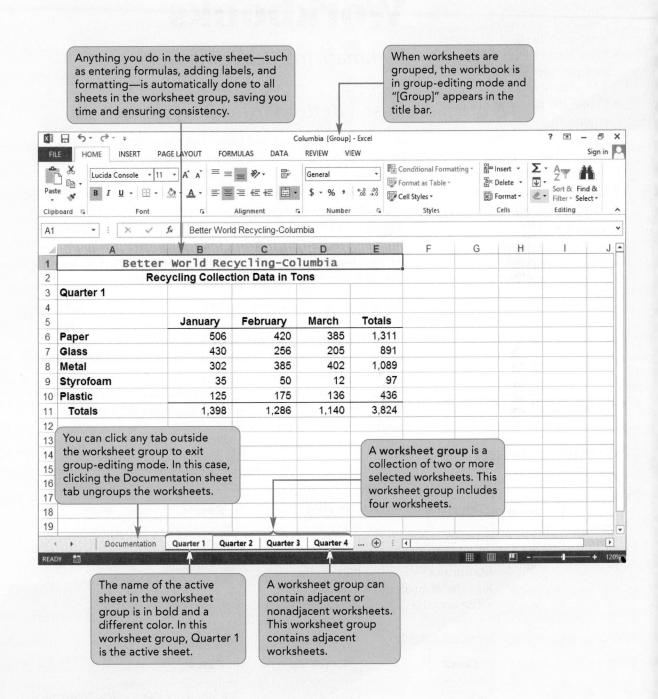

You can click any tab outside the worksheet group to exit group-editing mode. In this case, clicking the Documentation sheet tab ungroups the worksheets.

A worksheet group is a collection of two or more selected worksheets. This worksheet group includes four worksheets.

The name of the active sheet in the worksheet group is in bold and a different color. In this worksheet group, Quarter 1 is the active sheet.

A worksheet group can contain adjacent or nonadjacent worksheets. This worksheet group contains adjacent worksheets.

Worksheet Groups and 3-D References

A **3-D reference** is a reference to the same cell or range in multiple worksheets in the same workbook. This 3-D reference refers to cell E10 in the Quarter 1, Quarter 2, Quarter 3, and Quarter 4 worksheets.

When two or more worksheets have identical row and column layouts, as the quarterly worksheets in this workbook do, you can enter formulas with 3-D references to summarize those worksheets in another worksheet.

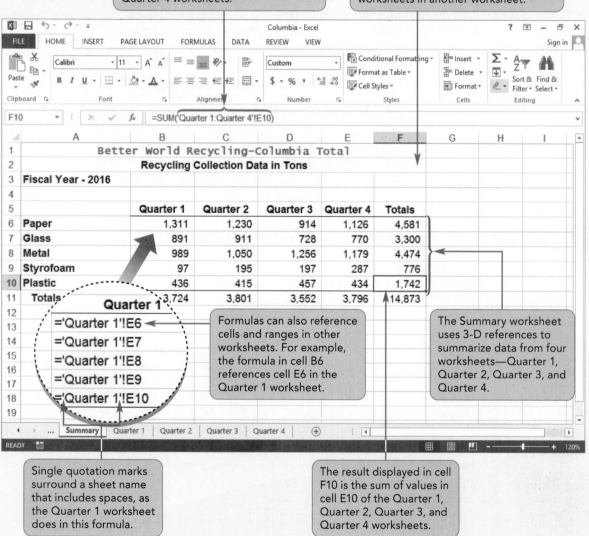

Formula bar: =SUM('Quarter 1:Quarter 4'!E10)

	A	B	C	D	E	F
1	Better World Recycling–Columbia Total					
2	Recycling Collection Data in Tons					
3	Fiscal Year - 2016					
4						
5		Quarter 1	Quarter 2	Quarter 3	Quarter 4	Totals
6	Paper	1,311	1,230	914	1,126	4,581
7	Glass	891	911	728	770	3,300
8	Metal	989	1,050	1,256	1,179	4,474
9	Styrofoam	97	195	197	287	776
10	Plastic	436	415	457	434	1,742
11	Totals	3,724	3,801	3,552	3,796	14,873

Quarter 1
='Quarter 1'!E6
='Quarter 1'!E7
='Quarter 1'!E8
='Quarter 1'!E9
='Quarter 1'!E10

Formulas can also reference cells and ranges in other worksheets. For example, the formula in cell B6 references cell E6 in the Quarter 1 worksheet.

The Summary worksheet uses 3-D references to summarize data from four worksheets—Quarter 1, Quarter 2, Quarter 3, and Quarter 4.

Sheet tabs: Summary | Quarter 1 | Quarter 2 | Quarter 3 | Quarter 4

Single quotation marks surround a sheet name that includes spaces, as the Quarter 1 worksheet does in this formula.

The result displayed in cell F10 is the sum of values in cell E10 of the Quarter 1, Quarter 2, Quarter 3, and Quarter 4 worksheets.

Grouping Worksheets

Workbook data is often placed in several worksheets. Using multiple worksheets makes it easier to group and summarize data. For example, a company such as Better World Recycling with branches in different geographic regions can place collection information for each region in separate worksheets. Rather than scrolling through one large and complex worksheet that contains data for all regions, users can access collection information for a specific region simply by clicking a sheet tab in the workbook.

Using multiple worksheets enables you to place summarized data first. Managers interested only in an overall picture can view the first worksheet of summary data without looking at the details available in the other worksheets. Others, of course, might want to view the supporting data in the individual worksheets that follow the summary worksheet. In the case of Better World Recycling, Maria used separate worksheets to summarize the amount of each item collected at the Columbia location for each quarter of the 2016 fiscal year.

You will open Maria's workbook and review the current information.

To open and review the Better World Recycling workbook:

1. Open the **Kansas** workbook located in the Excel6 ▶ Tutorial folder included with your Data Files, and then save the document as **Columbia** in the location specified by your instructor.

2. In the Documentation worksheet, enter your name and the date.

3. Go to the **Quarter 1** worksheet, and then view the recycling data for the first quarter of the year. See Figure 6-1.

| Figure 6-1 | Quarter 1 worksheet for Better World Recycling-Columbia |

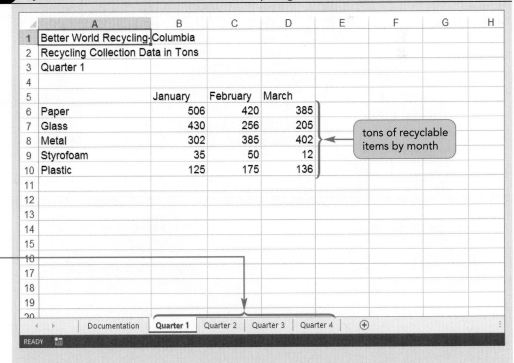

4. Review the **Quarter 2**, **Quarter 3**, and **Quarter 4** worksheets. The layout for all four worksheets is identical.

Maria didn't enter any formulas in the workbook. You need to enter formulas to calculate the total number of tons of collected recyclables for each column (columns B through D) in all four worksheets. Rather than retyping the formulas in each worksheet, you can enter them all at once by creating a worksheet group. A worksheet group, like a range, can contain adjacent or nonadjacent worksheets. In group-editing mode, most editing tasks that you complete in the active worksheet also affect the other worksheets in the group. By forming a worksheet group, you can:

- **Enter or edit data and formulas.** Changes made to content in the active worksheet are also made in the same cells in all the worksheets in the group. You can also use the Find and Replace commands with a worksheet group.
- **Apply formatting.** Changes made to formatting in the active worksheet are also made to all the worksheets in the group, including changing row heights or column widths and applying conditional formatting.
- **Insert or delete rows and columns.** Changes made to the worksheet structure in the active worksheet are also made to all the worksheets in the group.
- **Set the page layout options.** Changes made to the page layout settings in one worksheet also apply to all the worksheets in the group, such as changing the orientation, scaling to fit, and inserting headers and footers.
- **Apply view options.** Changes made to the worksheet view such as zooming, showing and hiding worksheets, and so forth are also made to all the worksheets in the group.
- **Print all the worksheets.** You can print all of the worksheets in the worksheet group at the same time.

Worksheet groups save you time and help improve consistency among the worksheets because you can perform an action once, yet affect multiple worksheets.

REFERENCE

Grouping and Ungrouping Worksheets

- To select an adjacent group, click the sheet tab of the first worksheet in the group, press and hold the Shift key, click the sheet tab of the last worksheet in the group, and then release the Shift key.
- To select a nonadjacent group, click the sheet tab of one worksheet in the group, press and hold the Ctrl key, click the sheet tabs of the remaining worksheets in the group, and then release the Ctrl key.
- To ungroup the worksheets, click the sheet tab of a worksheet that is not in the group (or right-click the sheet tab of one worksheet in the group, and then click Ungroup Sheets on the shortcut menu).

In the Columbia workbook, you'll group an adjacent range of worksheets—the Quarter 1 worksheet through the Quarter 4 worksheet.

To group the quarterly worksheets:

1. Click the **Quarter 1** sheet tab to make the worksheet active. This is the first worksheet you want to include in the group.

2. Press and hold the **Shift** key, and then click the **Quarter 4** sheet tab. This is the last worksheet you want to include in the group.

3. Release the **Shift** key. The sheet tabs are white, the green border at the bottom of the sheet tab extends across all the tabs, and the sheet tab labels, Quarter 1 through Quarter 4, are in bold, indicating they are all selected. The text "[Group]" appears in the title bar to remind you that a worksheet group is selected in the workbook. See Figure 6-2.

TIP

If you cannot see the sheet tab of a worksheet you want to include in a group, use the sheet tab scroll buttons to display it.

| Figure 6-2 | Grouped worksheets |

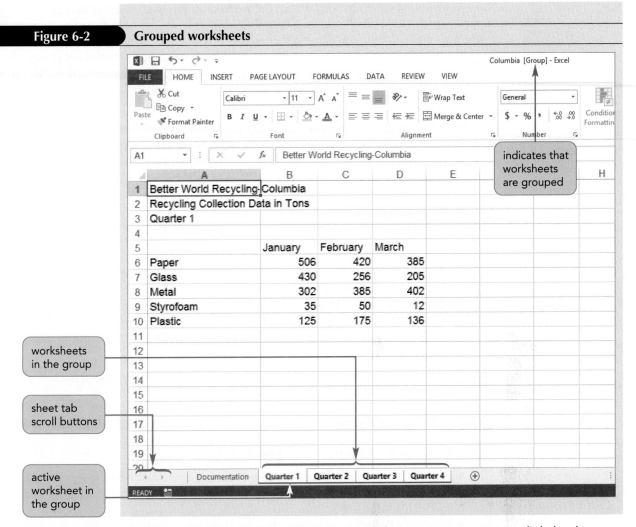

worksheets in the group

sheet tab scroll buttons

active worksheet in the group

You can change which worksheet in a worksheet group is active. Just click the sheet tab of the worksheet you want to make active. If a worksheet group includes all the worksheets in a workbook, you cannot change which worksheet is the active sheet because clicking a sheet tab ungroups the worksheets.

To change the active sheet in the grouped quarterly worksheets:

▶ 1. Click the **Quarter 2** sheet tab to make the worksheet active. The Quarter 2 worksheet is now the active worksheet in the group.

▶ 2. Click the **Quarter 4** sheet tab. The Quarter 4 worksheet is now the active worksheet in the group.

Entering Headings and Formulas in a Worksheet Group

When you enter a formula in the active worksheet (in this case, the Quarter 1 worksheet), the formula is entered in the same cells in all the worksheets in the group. The grouped worksheets must have the exact same organization and layout (rows and columns) in order for this to work. Otherwise, any formulas you enter in the active worksheet will be incorrect in the other worksheets in the group and could overwrite existing data.

With the quarterly worksheets grouped, you will enter the formulas to calculate the collection totals for each month.

To enter formulas to calculate the collection totals in the worksheet group:

▶ 1. Select cell **B11**. You want to enter the formula in cell B11 in each of the four worksheets in the group.

▶ 2. On the HOME tab, in the Editing group, click the **AutoSum** button, and then press the **Enter** key. The formula =SUM(B6:B10) is entered in cell B11 in each worksheet, adding the total tons of recyclable items collected at the Columbia site for the first month of the quarter. For Quarter 4, the October total of collected items shown in cell B11 is 1194.

▶ 3. Copy the formula in cell B11 to the range **C11:D11**. The formula calculates the total tons of recyclable items collected for the other months in the quarter. For Quarter 4, the other collection totals are 1209 tons in November and 1413 tons in December.

▶ 4. In cell **E6**, enter a formula with the SUM function to add the total tons of paper collected for each quarter at the Columbia site. The formula =SUM(B6:D6) adds the monthly totals of the tons of paper collected. In Quarter 4, 1126 tons of paper were collected.

▶ 5. Copy the formula in cell E6 to the range **E7:E11** to calculate the total tons of glass, metal, Styrofoam, and plastic, as well as the total tons of all recyclable items, collected at the Columbia site for each quarter. For Quarter 4, the Columbia site collected 770 tons of glass, 1179 tons of metal, 287 tons of Styrofoam, 454 tons of plastic, and 3816 tons of recyclables overall.

▶ 6. In cell **A11** and in cell **E5**, enter the label **Totals**.

▶ 7. Select cell **B11**. The formula =SUM(B6:B10) appears in the formula bar, and the formula result 1194 appears in the cell. See Figure 6-3.

| Figure 6-3 | Formulas entered in all of the worksheets in the group |

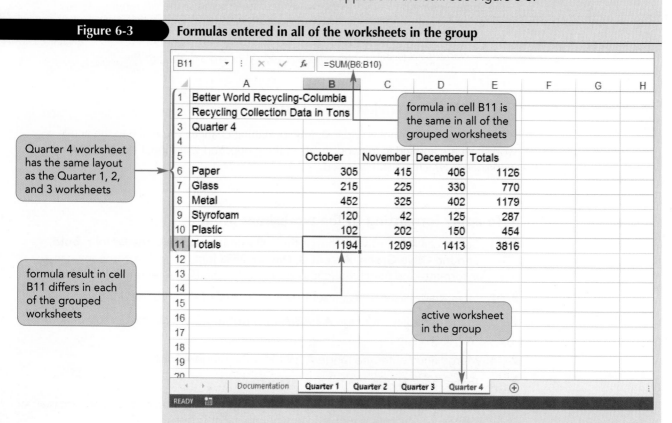

The formulas and labels you entered in the Quarter 4 worksheet were entered in the Quarter 1, 2, and 3 worksheets at the same time.

▶ 8. Click the **Quarter 3** sheet tab, and then make sure that cell **B11** is the active cell. The formula =SUM(B6:B10), which adds the number of tons collected in Quarter 3, appears in the formula bar, and the formula result 1111 appears in the cell.

▶ 9. Click the **Quarter 2** sheet tab, and then make sure cell **B11** is the active cell. The formula =SUM(B6:B10), which adds the number of tons collected in Quarter 2, appears in the formula bar, and the formula result 1395 appears in the cell.

▶ 10. Click the **Quarter 1** sheet tab, and then make sure cell **B11** is the active cell. The formula =SUM(B6:B10), which adds the number of tons collected in Quarter 1, appears in the formula bar, and the formula result 1398 appears in the cell.

The grouped worksheets made it quick to enter the formulas needed to calculate the monthly and recyclable item totals for each quarter.

Editing Grouped Worksheets

When you enter, edit, or format cells in a worksheet group, the changes you make to one worksheet are automatically applied to the other worksheets in the group. For example, if you delete a value from one cell, the content is also deleted from the same cell in all the worksheets in the group. Be cautious when editing a worksheet that is part of a group. If the layout and structure of the other grouped worksheets are not exactly the same, you might inadvertently overwrite data in some of the worksheets. Also, remember to ungroup the worksheet group after you finish entering data, formulas, and formatting. Otherwise, changes you intend to make in one worksheet will be made to all the worksheets in the group, potentially producing incorrect results.

Formatting a Worksheet Group

As when inserting formulas and text, any formatting changes you make to the active worksheet are applied to all worksheets in the group. You will format the quarterly worksheets, which are still grouped.

To apply formatting to the worksheet group:

▶ 1. Select cell **A1**, and then format the cell with the **Lucida Console** font, **bold**, and the **Olive Green, Accent 3, Darker 25%** font color. The company name is formatted to match the company name on the Documentation worksheet.

▶ 2. Increase the indent of cell **A11** by one. The label shifts to the right.

▶ 3. In the nonadjacent range **A2:A3;A6:A11;B5:E5**, bold the text in the headings.

▶ 4. Merge and center the range **A1:E1** and the range **A2:E2**.

▶ 5. In the range **B5:E5**, center the text.

▶ 6. In the range **B6:E11**, apply the **Comma Style** number format with no decimal places. No change is visible in any number that is less than 1000.

7. In the range **B5:E5** and the range **B10:E10**, add a bottom border.

8. Select cell **A1**. All the worksheets in the group are formatted.

9. Go to each worksheet in the group and review the formatting changes, and then go to the **Quarter 1** worksheet. See Figure 6-4.

Figure 6-4   **Formatting applied to the worksheet group**

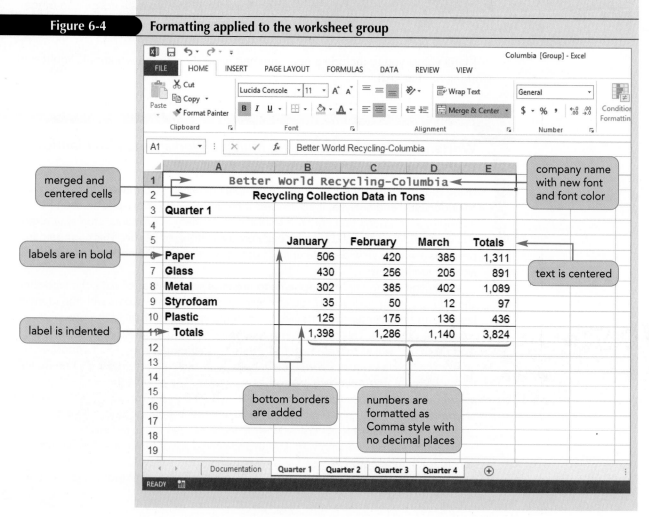

Ungrouping Worksheets

When you ungroup the worksheets, each worksheet functions independently again. If you forget to ungroup the worksheets, any changes you make in one worksheet will be applied to all the worksheets in the group. So be sure to ungroup worksheets when you are finished making changes that apply to multiple worksheets. To ungroup worksheets, click the sheet tab of a worksheet that is not part of the group. If a worksheet group includes all of the sheets in a workbook, click any of the sheet tabs to ungroup the worksheets.

You will ungroup the quarterly worksheets so you can work in each worksheet separately.

To ungroup the quarterly worksheets:

Be sure to ungroup the worksheets; otherwise, any changes you make will affect all worksheets in the group.

▶ **1.** Click the **Documentation** sheet tab. The worksheets are ungrouped because the Documentation worksheet was not part of the worksheet group. The text "[Group]" no longer appears in the Excel title bar.

▶ **2.** Verify that the worksheets are ungrouped and the word "[Group]" no longer appears in the title bar.

Maria wants you to include a new Summary worksheet in the workbook. You'll start working on that next.

PROSKILLS

Written Communication: Using Multiple Worksheets with Identical Layouts

Using multiple worksheets to organize complex data can help make that data simpler to understand and analyze. It also makes it easier to navigate to specific data. For example, a workbook that contains data about a variety of products, stores, or regions could use a different worksheet for each product, store, or region. This arrangement provides a way to view discrete units of data that can be combined and summarized in another worksheet.

When you use multiple worksheets to organize similar types of data, the worksheets should have identical layouts. You can quickly group the worksheets with the identical layouts, and then enter the formulas, formatting, and labels in all of the grouped worksheets at once. This helps to ensure consistency and accuracy among the worksheets as well as make it faster to create the different worksheets needed.

Using multiple worksheets with identical layouts enables you to use 3-D references to quickly summarize the data in another worksheet. The summary worksheet provides an overall picture of the data that is detailed in the other worksheets. Often, managers are more interested in this big picture view. However, the supporting data is still available in the individual worksheets when a deeper analysis is needed.

So, when you are working with a large and complex worksheet filled with data, consider the different ways to organize it in multiple worksheets. Not only will you save time when entering and finding data, but also the data becomes more understandable, and connections and results become clearer.

Working with Multiple Worksheets

As you develop a workbook, you might need to add a worksheet that has the same setup as an existing worksheet. Rather than starting from scratch, you can copy that worksheet as a starting point. For example, Maria wants the workbook to include a Summary worksheet that adds the annual totals of tons of recyclable materials collected from quarterly worksheets. The formulas you create in the Summary worksheet will reference cells in each quarterly worksheet using 3-D references. You can then group the completed worksheets to develop a consistent page setup in all worksheets and then print them all at once.

Copying Worksheets

Often, after spending time developing a worksheet, you can use it as a starting point for creating another, saving you time and energy compared to developing a new worksheet from scratch. Copying a worksheet duplicates all the values, formulas, and formats into

the new worksheet, leaving the original worksheet intact. You can then edit, reformat, and enter new content as needed to create the exact worksheet you need.

REFERENCE

Copying Worksheets

- Select the sheet tabs of the worksheets you want to copy.
- Right-click the sheet tabs, and then click Move or Copy on the shortcut menu.
- Click the To book arrow, and then click the name of an existing workbook or click (new book) to create a new workbook for the worksheets.
- In the Before sheet box, click the worksheet before which you want to insert the new worksheet.
- Click the Create a copy check box to insert a checkmark to copy the worksheets.
- Click the OK button.

or

- Select the sheet tabs of the worksheets you want to copy.
- Press and hold the Ctrl key as you drag the selected sheet tabs to a new location in the sheet tabs, and then release the Ctrl key.

Maria wants you to create the Summary worksheet to provide an overall picture of the data in the detailed quarterly worksheets. The Summary worksheet needs the same formatting and structure as the quarterly worksheets. To ensure consistency among worksheets, you will copy the Quarter 1 worksheet to the beginning of the workbook, and then modify its contents.

To copy the Quarter 1 worksheet and create the Summary worksheet:

1. Click the **Quarter 1** sheet tab, and then press and hold the **Ctrl** key as you drag the worksheet to the left of the Documentation worksheet. The pointer changes to ⬚ and a triangle indicates the drop location.

2. Release the mouse button, and then release the **Ctrl** key. An identical copy of the Quarter 1 worksheet appears in the new location. The sheet tab shows "Quarter 1 (2)" to indicate that this is the copied sheet.

3. Rename the Quarter 1 (2) worksheet as **Summary**.

4. Move the **Summary** worksheet between the Documentation worksheet and the Quarter 1 worksheet.

> **TIP**
>
> To move a worksheet or a worksheet group to another location in the same workbook, drag its sheet tab and drop it in its new location.

Maria wants the Summary worksheet to show the collection data for each product by quarter, and the total collections for each product and quarter. You will modify the Summary worksheet to do this now.

To modify the Summary worksheet:

1. Make sure the **Summary** worksheet is the active sheet.

2. In cell **A3**, enter **2016**. This is the year to which the summary refers.

3. In cell **A1**, enter **Better World Recycling–Columbia Total**. The new title reflects this worksheet's content. The formatting should remain intact.

4. Delete the collection data from the range **B6:E10**. The formatting remains intact. See Figure 6-5.

| Figure 6-5 | Summary worksheet created from the Quarter 1 worksheet |

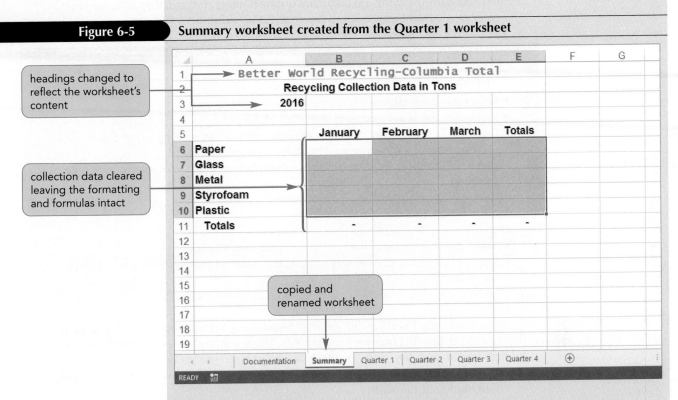

headings changed to reflect the worksheet's content

collection data cleared leaving the formatting and formulas intact

copied and renamed worksheet

▶ **5.** Insert a new **column C** into the worksheet. The column appears between the January and February labels with the same formatting as January.

▶ **6.** In the range **B5:E5**, enter **Quarter 1**, **Quarter 2**, **Quarter 3**, and **Quarter 4** in each respective cell.

▶ **7.** Copy the formula in cell B11 to cell **C11**. See Figure 6-6.

| Figure 6-6 | Summary worksheet modified |

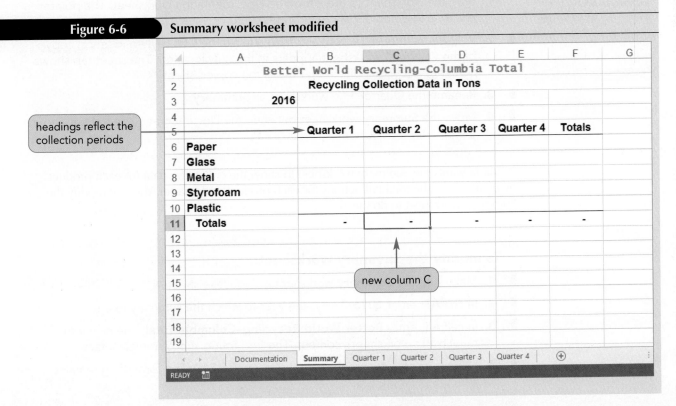

headings reflect the collection periods

new column C

Referencing Cells and Ranges in Other Worksheets

When you use multiple worksheets to organize related data, you can reference a cell or a range in another worksheet in the same workbook. For example, the Summary worksheet references cells in the four quarterly worksheets to calculate the total collections for the entire year. The syntax to reference a cell or a range in a different worksheet is

> `=SheetName!CellRange`

where `SheetName` is the worksheet's name as listed on the sheet tab and `CellRange` is the reference for the cell or range in that worksheet. An exclamation mark (!) separates the worksheet reference from the cell or range reference. For example, you could enter the following formula in the Summary worksheet to reference cell D10 in the Quarter1 worksheet:

> `=Quarter1!D10`

If the worksheet name contains spaces, you must enclose the name in single quotation marks. For example, the following formula references cell D10 in the Quarter 1 worksheet:

> `='Quarter 1'!D10`

You can use these references to create formulas that reference cells in different locations in different worksheets. For example, to add collections from two worksheets—cell C9 in the Quarter 1 worksheet and cell C9 in the Quarter 2 worksheet—you would enter the following formula:

> `='Quarter 1'!C9+'Quarter 2'!C9`

You could type the formula directly in the cell, but it is faster and more accurate to use your mouse to select cells to enter their references to other worksheets.

REFERENCE

Entering a Formula with References to Another Worksheet

- Select the cell where you want to enter the formula.
- Type = and begin entering the formula.
- To insert a reference from another worksheet, click the sheet tab for the worksheet, and then click the cell or select the range you want to reference.
- When the formula is complete, press the Enter key.

Maria wants you to enter a formula in cell A4 in each quarterly worksheet that displays the fiscal year entered in cell A3 in the Summary worksheet. All four quarterly worksheets will use the formula =Summary!A3 to reference the fiscal year in cell A3 of the Summary worksheet.

To enter the formula that references the Summary worksheet:

1. Click the **Quarter 1** sheet tab, press and hold the **Shift** key, and then click the **Quarter 4** worksheet. The Quarter 1 through Quarter 4 worksheets are grouped.

2. Select cell **A4**. This is the cell in which you want to enter the formula to display the fiscal year.

3. Type **=** to begin the formula, click the **Summary** sheet tab, and then click cell **A3**. The reference to cell A3 in the Summary worksheet is added to the formula in cell A4 in the grouped worksheets.

▶ **6.** Click the **Custom Footer** button to open the Footer dialog box, type your name in the Left section box, click in the Right section box, click the **Insert Date** button 🗓 to add the &[Date] code in the section box (which inserts the current date in the right section of the footer), and then click the **OK** button.

▶ **7.** Click the **Print Preview** button. The preview of the Summary worksheet, the first worksheet in the group, appears on the Print screen in Backstage view. See Figure 6-14.

| Figure 6-14 | Preview of the worksheet group |

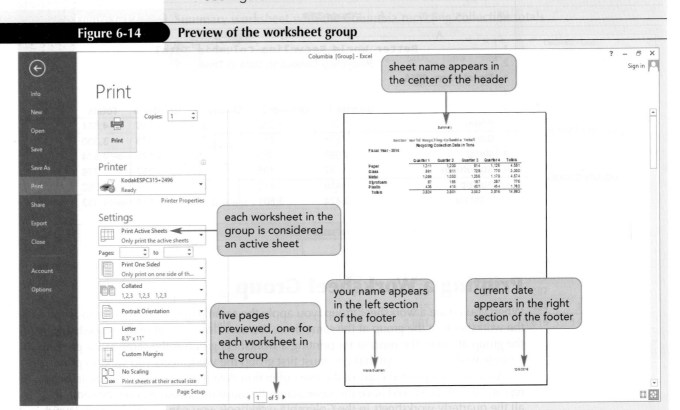

▶ **8.** Below the preview, click the **Next Page** button ▶ four times to view the other worksheets in the group. Each page has the same page layout but the header shows the sheet tab names.

   Trouble? If only one page appears in the preview, the worksheets are not grouped. Click the Back button to exit Backstage view, and then repeat Steps 1 through 8.

▶ **9.** Click the **Back** button ← to exit Backstage view without printing the worksheet group.

▶ **10.** Go to the **Documentation** worksheet to ungroup the worksheets, and then go to the **Summary** worksheet.

In this session, you consolidated the data in Better World Recycling's Columbia workbook into a Summary worksheet so that Maria can quickly see the collection totals for the recyclable items. In the next session, you will help Maria determine the annual totals for the other Better World Recycling collection sites—Richmond and Marion.

Session 6.1 Quick Check

REVIEW

1. What is a worksheet group?
2. How do you select an adjacent worksheet group? How do you select a nonadjacent worksheet group? How do you deselect a worksheet group?
3. What formula would you enter in the Summary worksheet to reference cell C8 in the Quarter 2 worksheet?
4. What is the 3-D reference to cell E6 in the adjacent Summary 1, Summary 2, and Summary 3 worksheets?
5. Explain what the formula =AVERAGE(Sheet1:Sheet4!B1) calculates.
6. If you insert a new worksheet named Sheet5 after Sheet4, how would you change the formula =MIN(Sheet1:Sheet4!B1) to include Sheet5 in the calculation?
7. If you insert a new worksheet named Sheet5 before Sheet4, how would you change the formula =SUM(Sheet1:Sheet4!B1) to include Sheet5 in the calculation?
8. How do you apply the same page layout to all of the worksheets in a workbook at one time?

4. In cell **F6**, enter the SUM function to add the range B6:E6. A total of 13,819 tons of paper were collected at all sites in 2016.

5. Copy the formula in cell F6 to the range **F7:F11**. The total recyclable materials collected in 2016 were 10,626 tons of glass, 13,430 tons of metal, 2,043 tons of Styrofoam, and 6,069 tons of plastic, with a grand total of 45,987 tons collected for the year.

6. Format the range B6:F11 with the **Comma style** and no decimal places.

7. Format the range B10:F10 with a **bottom border**, and then select cell **A1** to deselect the range. See Figure 6-20.

Figure 6-20	Completed summary of collection data

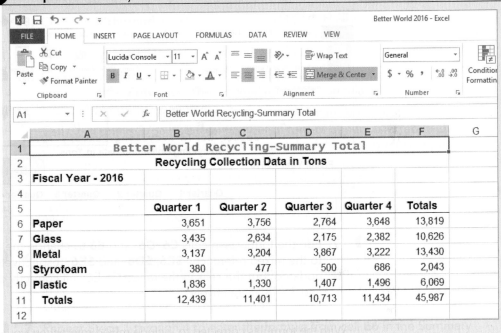

Maria is pleased; the regional summary results match her expectations.

INSIGHT

Managing Linked Workbooks

As you work with a linked workbook, you might need to replace a source file or change where you stored the source and destination files. However, replacing or moving a file can affect the linked workbook. Keep in mind the following guidelines to manage your linked workbooks:

- If you rename a source file, the destination workbook won't be able to find it. A dialog box opens, indicating "This workbook contains one or more links that cannot be updated." Click the Continue button to open the workbook with the most recent values, or click the Change Source button in the Edit Links dialog box to specify the new name of that linked source file.
- If you move a source file to a different folder, the link breaks between the destination and source files. Click the Change Source button in the Edit Links dialog box to specify the new location of the linked workbook.
- If you receive a replacement source file, you can swap the original source file with the replacement file. No additional changes are needed.
- If you receive a destination workbook but the source files are not included, Excel will not be able to find the source files, and a dialog box opens with the message "This workbook contains one or more links that cannot be updated." Click the Continue button to open the workbook with the most recent values, or click the Break Link button in the Edit Links dialog box to replace the external references with the existing values.
- If you change the name of a destination file, you can open that renamed version destination file without affecting the source files or the original destination file.

Updating Linked Workbooks

When workbooks are linked, it is important that the data in the destination file accurately reflects the contents of the source file. When data in a source file changes, you want the destination file to reflect those changes. If both the source and destination files are open when you make a change, the destination file is updated automatically. If the destination file is closed when you make a change in a source file, you choose whether to update the link to display the current values, or continue to display the older values from the destination file when you open the destination file.

Updating a Destination Workbook with Source Workbooks Open

When both the destination and source workbooks are open, any changes you make in a source workbook automatically appear in the destination workbook. Maria tells you that Columbia actually collected 100 fewer tons of metal in March than was recorded. After you correct the March value in the Quarter 1 worksheet, the amount in the Summary worksheet of the Columbia workbook and the regional total in the Better World 2016 workbook will also change if both the source and destination files are open.

To update the source workbook with the destination file open:

1. Make the **Columbia** workbook active, and then go to the **Quarter 1** worksheet. You'll update the total for metal collected in March.

2. If the ribbon is still collapsed, pin the ribbon so you can see both the tabs and the groups.

| Figure 6-25 | Edit Links dialog box |

your paths will match the location where you save your workbooks

replaces the links to source files with the current values of the linked cells

updates the destination file with data from the latest saved version of the selected course file

The Edit Links dialog box lists all of the files to which the destination workbook is linked so that you can update, change, open, or remove the links. You can see that the destination workbook—Better World 2016 Audited—has links to the Richmond, Columbia, and Marion workbooks. The dialog box shows the following information about each link:

- **Source**—indicates the file to which the link points. The Better World 2016 Audited workbook contains three links pointing to the Columbia.xlsx, Richmond.xlsx, and Marion.xlsx workbooks.
- **Type**—identifies the type of each source file. In this case, the type is an Excel worksheet, but it could also be a Word document, a PowerPoint presentation, or some other type of file.
- **Update**—specifies the way values are updated from the source file. The letter *A* indicates the link is updated automatically when you open the workbook, or when both the source and destination files are open simultaneously. The letter *M* indicates the link must be updated manually by the user, which is useful when you want to see the older data values before updating to the new data. To manually update the link and see the new data values, click the Update Values button.
- **Status**—shows whether Excel successfully accessed the link and updated the values from the source document (status is OK), or Excel has not attempted to update the links in this session (status is Unknown). The status of the three links in the Better World 2016 Audited workbook is Unknown.

Maria wants you to break the links so that the Better World 2016 Audited workbook contains only the updated values (and is no longer affected by changes in the source files). Then she wants you to save the Better World 2016 Audited workbook for her to archive. This allows Maria to store a "snapshot" of the data at the end of the fiscal year.

To convert all external reference formulas to their current values:

> **TIP**
> You cannot undo the break link action. To restore the links, you must reenter the external reference formulas.

> 1. In the Edit Links dialog box, click the **Break Link** button. A dialog box opens, alerting you that breaking links in the workbook permanently converts formulas and external references to their existing values.

> 2. Click the **Break Links** button. No links appear in the Edit Links dialog box.

> 3. Click the **Close** button. The Better World 2016 Audited workbook now contains values instead of formulas with external references.

> 4. Select cell **B6**. The value 3,651 appears in the cell and the formula bar; the link (the external reference formula) was replaced with the data value. All of the cells in the range B6:E10 contain values rather than external reference formulas.

You ca
to cells
enter c
them f
the wo

▶ **5.** Save the Better World 2016 Audited workbook, and then close it. The Better World 2016 workbook contains external reference formulas, and the Better World 2016 Audited workbook contains current values.

In this session, you worked with multiple worksheets and workbooks, summarizing data and linking workbooks. This ensures that the data in the summary workbook is accurate and remains updated with the latest data in the source files. In the next session, you will create templates and hyperlinks.

REVIEW

Session 6.2 Quick Check

1. What is the external reference to the range B6:F6 in the Grades worksheet in the Grade Book workbook located in the Course folder on drive D?
2. What is a source file?
3. What is a destination file?
4. How are linked workbooks updated when both the destination and source files are open?
5. How are linked workbooks updated when the source file is changed and the destination file is closed?
6. How would you determine to what workbooks a destination file is linked?
7. What are the layouts that you can use to arrange multiple workbooks?
8. When you have broken the links for a cell, what appears in the formula bar when you select that cell?

▶ **7.** In cell **B3**, enter **[Site Name Here]**, and then merge and center the range **B3:C3**.

▶ **8.** Go to the **Summary** worksheet. The quarterly worksheets are ungrouped, and dashes, representing zeros, appear in the cells in the ranges B6:F11, which contain formulas.

▶ **9.** In cell **A1**, enter **Better World Recycling**. This text will remind users to enter the correct site name.

▶ **10.** In cell **B3**, enter **[Site Name Here]**, and then merge and center **B3:C3**.

▶ **11.** In cell **A3**, enter **[Enter Fiscal Year - yyyy]**. This text will remind users to enter the year.

▶ **12.** Group the **Summary** through **Quarter 4** worksheets, and then increase the width of column A so you can see the entire contents of cell A3. See Figure 6-31.

Figure 6-31	Worksheet modified to be used as the basis of a custom template

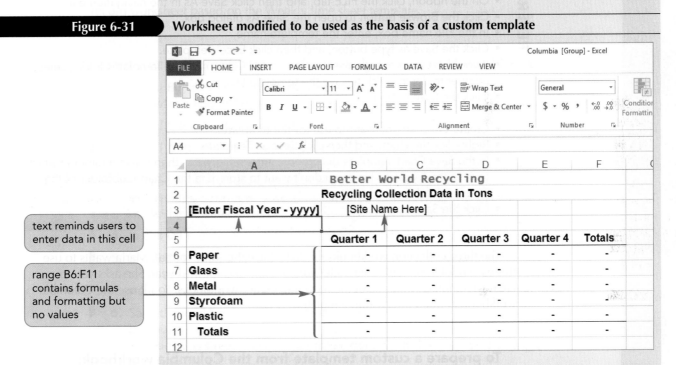

text reminds users to enter data in this cell

range B6:F11 contains formulas and formatting but no values

▶ **13.** Go to the **Documentation** worksheet, and then delete your name and the date from the range B3:B4.

▶ **14.** In cell **A6**, enter **To compile the recycling collection data for:**.

▶ **15.** In cell **B6**, enter **[Site Name Here]**, and then select cell **A1**. The Documentation worksheet is updated to reflect the purpose of the workbook.

By default, Excel looks for template files in the Templates folder. This location opens when you save a workbook as a template and is where custom templates are often stored. However, you can change in which folder a template is saved. All template files have the .xltx file extension. This extension differentiates template files from workbook files, which have the .xlsx file extension. After you have saved a workbook in a template format, you can make the template accessible to other users.

The Columbia workbook no longer contains any specific data, but the formulas and formatting will still be in effect when new data is entered. Maria asks you to save this workbook as a template.

To save the Columbia workbook as a template:

▶ **1.** On the ribbon, click the **FILE** tab to open Backstage view, and then in the navigation bar, click **Save As**. The Save As screen appears.

▶ **2.** Select the location where you are saving the files for this tutorial. If you are saving files to your hard drive, select **Computer**, and then click the **Browse** button. The Save As dialog box opens.

  Trouble? If you are saving your files in your SkyDrive, select **SkyDrive**, click **Sign In** to sign in to your account if necessary, and then follow the instructions for saving a document in SkyDrive.

▶ **3.** In the File name box, type **Better World Recycling Template** as the template name.

▶ **4.** Click the **Save as type** button, and then click **Excel Template**. The save location changes to the Custom Office Templates folder on your computer. You want to save the template in the same location as the other files you created in this tutorial.

Make sure you change the save location so you can easily find and use the template file later in the next set of steps.

▶ **5.** Navigate to the location where you are storing the files you create in this tutorial.

▶ **6.** Click the **Save** button. The Better World Recycling Template is saved in the location you specified.

▶ **7.** Close the Better World Recycling Template workbook template.

Maria will use the Better World Recycling Template file to create the workbooks to track next year's collections for each site, and then distribute the workbooks to each site manager. By basing these new workbooks on the template file, Maria has a standard workbook with identical formatting and formulas for each manager to use. She also avoids the risk of accidentally changing the workbook containing the 2016 data when preparing for 2017.

INSIGHT

Copying Styles from One Template to Another

Consistency is a hallmark of professional documents. If you have already created a template with a particular look, you can easily copy the styles from that template into a new template. This is much faster and more accurate than trying to recreate the same look by performing all of the steps you used originally. Copying styles from template to template guarantees uniformity. To copy styles from one template to another:

1. Open the template with the styles you want to copy.
2. Open the workbook or template in which you want to place the copied styles.
3. On the HOME tab, in the Styles group, click the Cell Styles button, and then click Merge Styles. The Merge Styles dialog box opens, listing the currently open workbooks and templates.
4. Select the workbook or template with the styles you want to copy, and then click the OK button to copy those styles into the current workbook or template.
5. If a dialog box opens, asking if you want to "Merge Styles that have the same names?", click the YES button.
6. Save the workbook with the new styles as the Excel Template file type.

Creating a New Workbook from a Template

A template file has special properties that allow you to open it, make changes, and save it in a new location. Only the data must be entered because the formulas are already in the template file. The original template file is not changed by this process. After you have saved a template, you can access the template from the New screen in Backstage view or in the location you saved it.

Maria wants all Better World Recycling locations to collect data in the same format and submit the workbooks to the central office for analysis. She wants you to create a workbook for fiscal year 2017 based on the Better World Recycling Template file. You will enter Columbia as the site name where indicated on all of the worksheets, and then enter test data for January.

To create a new workbook based on the Better World Recycling Template file:

> **TIP**
>
> To create a copy of work-book based on a template stored in the Custom Office Templates folder, click the FILE tab, click New in the navigation bar, click PERSONAL below the Search for online templates box, and then click the template.

1. On the taskbar, click the **File Explorer** button. The Libraries window opens.

2. Navigate to the location where you stored the template file.

3. Double-click the **Better World Recycling Template** file. A new workbook opens named "Better World Recycling Template1" to indicate this is the first copy of the Better World Recycling workbook created during the current Excel session.

4. Go to the **Summary** worksheet, enter **Columbia Total** in cell B3, and then enter **Fiscal Year - 2017** in cell A3.

5. Group the **Quarter 1** through **Quarter 4** worksheets, and then in cell **B3**, enter **Columbia** as the site name in the Site Name Here box.

6. Go to the **Documentation** worksheet to ungroup the worksheets.

7. In cell **B6**, enter **Columbia**.

8. Go to the **Quarter 1** worksheet. The text "Fiscal Year - 2017" appears in cell A4.

9. Enter the following test data in the range **B6:B10**, which has the orange fill color:

   cell B6: **150**

   cell B7: **50**

   cell B8: **123**

   cell B9: **45**

   cell B10: **23**

10. Review the totals in the range E6:E11 (the cells that contain formulas to sum each column). See Figure 6-32.

Figure 6-32   New workbook based on the Better World Recycling Template file

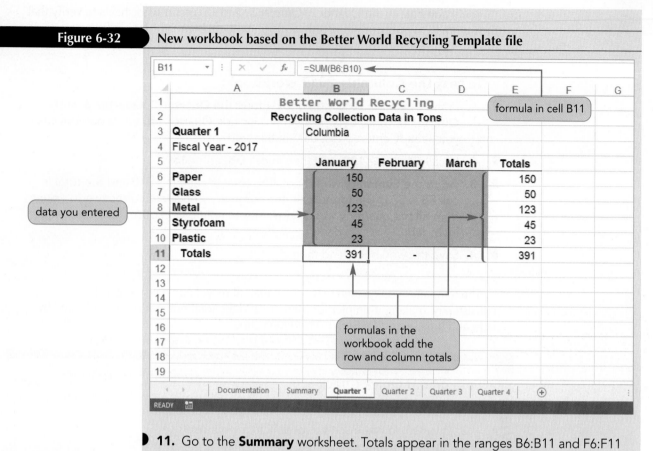

data you entered

formula in cell B11

formulas in the workbook add the row and column totals

11. Go to the **Summary** worksheet. Totals appear in the ranges B6:B11 and F6:F11 as a result of the formulas in this worksheet. See Figure 6-33.

Figure 6-33   Summary worksheet with test data

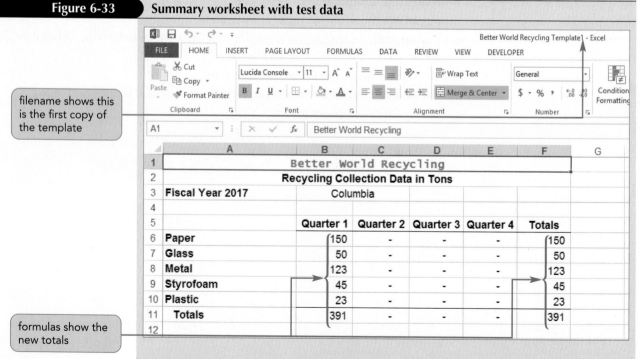

filename shows this is the first copy of the template

formulas show the new totals

12. Save the workbook as **Columbia 2017** in the location specified by your instructor. The copy of the template is saved as a workbook with the .xlsx file extension. The original template file is not changed.

You'll add data to the Quarter 2, Quarter 3, and Quarter 4 worksheets to verify that the Summary worksheet is correctly adding numbers from the four worksheets.

To test the Columbia 2017 workbook:

1. In the Columbia 2017 workbook, group the **Quarter 2**, **Quarter 3**, and **Quarter 4** worksheets. You did not include Quarter 1 in this group because you already entered test data in this worksheet.

2. In cell **C6**, enter **120**, and then in cell **D8**, enter **150**.

3. Go to the **Summary** worksheet. The total in cell F6 is 510 and the total in cell F8 is 573. The formulas in the Summary worksheet correctly add values from all the quarterly worksheets. The template workbook is functioning as intended.

4. Save the workbook, and then close it.

The templates you created will ensure that all recycling centers enter data consistently, making it simpler for Maria to add the total number of tons recycled by item and time period for Better World Recycling.

Session 6.3 Quick Check

REVIEW

1. How do you insert a hyperlink into a worksheet cell?
2. Why would you insert a hyperlink in a worksheet?
3. What is a template?
4. What is a custom template?
5. What is one advantage of using a custom template rather than simply using the original workbook file to create a new workbook?
6. What are some examples of task-specific templates available from the Office.com site?
7. How do you save a workbook as a template?
8. How do you create a workbook based on a template that is not saved in the Custom Office Templates folder?

Review Assignments

Data Files needed for the Review Assignments: Illinois.xlsx, Paris Memo.docx, BW.xlsx, Columbia KS.xlsx, Marion IA.xlsx, Richmond IN.xlsx

Based on its success in Columbia, Richmond, and Marion, Better World Recycling expanded to Paris, Illinois. The new site opened on January 1, 2016. Willa Jaworska, the manager of the Paris site, collected the center's recycling data in a workbook provided by Maria Guzman at the central office. Before Willa can send the completed workbook to Maria for the year-end reporting, she needs to summarize the results and format the worksheets. Complete the following:

1. Open the **Illinois** workbook located in the Excel6 ▸ Review folder included with your Data Files. Save the workbook as **Paris IL** in the location specified by your instructor.
2. In the Documentation worksheet, enter your name and the date, and then review the worksheets in the workbook.
3. Create a worksheet group that contains the Quarter 1 through Quarter 4 worksheets.
4. In the worksheet group, enter formulas in the range B11:D11 to total each column, and then enter formulas in the range E6:E11 to total each row.
5. Format the quarterly worksheets as specified below:
   a. In cell E5 and cell A11, enter **Totals**.
   b. In the range A2:A3;A6:A11;B5:E5, bold the text.
   c. Merge and center the range A1:E1 and the range A2:E2.
   d. In the range B5:E5, center the text.
   e. Add a bottom border to the range B5:E5 and the range B10:E10.
   f. Format the range B6:E11 with the Comma style and no decimal places.
6. Ungroup the worksheets, make a copy of the Quarter 1 worksheet, rename it as **Summary**, and then place it after the Documentation worksheet.
7. In the Summary worksheet, make the following changes:
   a. In cell A1, change the heading to **Better World Recycling - Paris Total**.
   b. Change cell A3 to **Fiscal Year - 2016**.
   c. Insert a column between columns B and C.
   d. In the range B5:E5, change the headings to **Quarter 1**, **Quarter 2**, **Quarter 3**, and **Quarter 4**, respectively.
   e. In the range B5:F5, center the text.
   f. Clear the data from the range B6:F11.
8. Complete the formulas in the Summary worksheet using the following steps. Remember to use the Fill Without Formatting so that you can keep the bottom border on the range B10:F10.
   a. Create formulas referencing cells in other worksheets to collect the quarterly totals for the recyclable products in the range B6:E10 in your Summary worksheet.
   b. Create 3-D cell references in the range F6:F10 to calculate totals for each type of recyclable product.
   c. Total the data in columns B through F using the SUM function.
9. The March collection total for metal should have been **164**. Make that correction, and then verify that the total metal collected in Quarter 1 in the Summary worksheet has changed to 384 tons, the total recyclables collected in Quarter 1 has changed to 2,065 tons, and the total metal collected in 2016 has changed to 2,111 tons.
10. Group the Quarter 1 through Quarter 4 worksheets, and then enter a formula in cell A4 to reference cell A3 in the Summary worksheet.
11. In cell A8 of the Documentation worksheet, insert a hyperlink pointing to the **Paris Memo** located in the Tutorial6 ▸ Review folder included with your Data Files. Make sure the text to display is **Click here to read Paris Executive Memo**.

12. Edit the hyperlink to use the ScreenTip **Paris Site Summary for 2016**.

13. Save the Paris IL workbook.

14. Open the **BW** workbook located in the Excel6 ▸ Review folder included with your Data Files. Save the workbook as **BW Totals** in the location specified by your instructor. In the Documentation worksheet enter your name and the date. Open the **Columbia KS**, **Marion IA**, and **Richmond IN** workbooks located in the Excel6 ▸ Review folder included with your Data Files.

15. In each workbook, make the maximum amount of data from the Summary worksheet viewable, make the BW Totals the active worksheet, and then tile the workbooks.

16. In the Summary worksheet, enter external reference formulas to create a set of linked workbooks to summarize the totals for Columbia KS, Marion IA, Paris IL, and Richmond IN, in the BW Totals workbook. Format the Summary worksheet in the BW Totals workbook making sure that the numbers are readable and the range B10:F10 has a bottom border. Save the BW totals workbook. Close the Columbia KS, Marion IA, and Richmond IN workbooks.

17. In the BW Totals workbook, break the links. Select some cells and notice that the formulas have been replaced with the values. Save the workbook as **BW Totals Audited**.

18. Prepare the Summary worksheet for printing. Display the name of the workbook and the name of the worksheet on separate lines in the right section of the header. Display your name and the date on separate lines in the right section of the footer. Save and close the BW Totals Audited workbook.

19. Save the Paris IL workbook as an Excel template with the filename **Paris IL Template** in the location specified by your instructor.

20. Create a new workbook based on the Paris IL Template. Save the workbook as **Paris IL 2017** in the location specified by your instructor. In the Documentation worksheet, enter your name and the date.

21. In the Summary worksheet, enter **2017** in cell A3. In the Quarter 1 worksheet, enter **1000** in each cell in the range B6:D10. In the Quarter 2 worksheet, enter **2000** in each cell in the range B6:D10. Confirm that the values entered in this step are correctly totaled in the Summary worksheet.

22. Save the Paris IL 2017 workbook, and then close it.

Case Problem 1

Data File needed for this Case Problem: Cheese.xlsx

Cheese Plus Pizzeria　Cheese Plus Pizzeria has three locations in Great Bend, Kansas—Downtown, East Side, and West Side. Mitch Samuels manages the three pizzerias. He uses Excel to summarize sales data from each location. He has compiled the year's data for each location in a workbook. He asks you to total the sales by type of service and location for each quarter, and then format each worksheet. Mitch also needs you to calculate sales for all of the locations and types of service. Complete the following:

1. Open the **Cheese** workbook located in the Excel6 ▸ Case1 folder included with your Data Files. Save the document as **Cheese Plus** in the location specified by your instructor.

2. In the Documentation worksheet, enter your name and the date.

3. Group the Downtown, East Side, and West Side worksheets.

4. In the grouped worksheets, calculate the quarterly totals in the range B7:E7 and the types of service totals in the range F4:F7.

5. Improve the look of the quarterly worksheets using the formatting of your choice. Ungroup the worksheets.

6. Place a copy of one of the location worksheets between the Documentation and Downtown worksheets, and then rename the new worksheet as **Summary Sales**.

7. Delete the values in the range B4:E6, and then change the label in cell A2 to **Summary Sales**.

8. In the range B4:E6, enter formulas that add the sales in the corresponding cells of the four quarterly worksheets. Use 3-D references to calculate the totals for each product group and location.

9. Set up the Summary Sales and the three location worksheets for printing. Each worksheet should be centered horizontally, fit on one page, display the name of the worksheet centered in the header, and display your name and the date on separate lines in the right section of the footer.

10. Save the Cheese Plus workbook, and then remove the sales data, but not the formulas, from each of the location worksheets.

11. Go to the Documentation worksheet, and then save the workbook as an Excel template with the name **Cheese Plus Template** in the location specified by your instructor.

12. Create a new workbook based on the Cheese Plus Template file. Save the workbook as **Cheese Plus 2016** in the location specified by your instructor.

13. In all three location worksheets, in the range B4:E6, enter **10**. Verify that the formulas in each worksheet summarize the data accurately.

14. Save and close the workbook.

Case Problem 2

Data Files needed for this Case Problem: Eastern.xlsx, Internet.xlsx, Western.xlsx, Summary.xlsx

Sweet Dreams Bakery Sweet Dreams Bakery opened its first retail location on June 1, 2000 in Jerome, Idaho, on the eastern side of town, with a dream and some great family dessert recipes. It opened a location on the western side of town three years later. In the past year, the bakery has developed a presence on the Internet. Each location tracks its sales by major categories—cupcakes, tarts, cookies, and pies. James Ray, the bakery manager, has asked the three locations to provide sales data for the past year. That data will be used at the next meeting of the senior managers to determine whether the bakery should expand to a fourth location. To analyze sales and service at each division, James wants you to prepare a report showing the sales of bakery items by quarter and location. Complete the following:

1. Open the **Eastern** workbook located in the Excel6 ▶ Case2 folder included with your Data Files, and then save the document as **Sweet Dreams Eastern** in the location specified by your instructor.

2. In the Documentation worksheet, enter your name and the date.

3. In the Eastern Sales worksheet, calculate the totals for each type of product in the range B8:E8, and the total for each quarter in the range F4:F8. Improve the look of the worksheet by using the formatting of your choice including a bottom underline in the range A7:F7.

4. Repeat Steps 1 through 3 for the **Internet** and **Western** workbooks, naming them **Sweet Dreams Internet** and **Sweet Dreams Western**, respectively.

5. Open the **Summary** workbook located in the Excel6 ▶ Case2 folder included with your Data Files, and then save the workbook as **Sweet Dreams Summary** in the location specified by your instructor.

6. In the Documentation worksheet, enter your name and the date.

7. Rename Sheet1 as **Summary**. In cell A2, enter **Summary Sales** as the new label.

🔧 **Troubleshoot** 8. The quarterly totals in the Sweet Dreams Summary worksheet are not displaying the correct results. Make any necessary corrections to the formulas so that they add the correct cells from the Sweet Dreams Eastern, Sweet Dreams Western, and Sweet Dreams Internet workbooks.

9. Insert formulas to calculate the totals for the range B4:E7.

🔧 **Troubleshoot** 10. The Documentation worksheet in the Sweet Dreams Summary workbook includes hyperlinks in the range A10:A12 for each region's corresponding workbook (Sweet Dreams Eastern, Sweet Dreams Internet, and Sweet Dreams Western located in the Excel6 ▶ Case2 folder). The hyperlink descriptions and source files are inconsistent. Check the hyperlinks and correct any links that have different descriptions and source files.

11. Add appropriate text for the ScreenTip to each hyperlink. Test each hyperlink.

12. Prepare each workbook for printing. For all worksheets except the Documentation worksheet, display the name of the workbook and the name of the worksheet on separate lines in the right section of the header and display your name and the date on separate lines in the right section of the footer.

13. Save and close all of the workbooks.

Case Problem 3

APPLY

Data File needed for this Case Problem: Clinic.xlsx

C & M Veterinary Clinic   C & M Veterinary Clinic has been treating small and medium-sized animals in the Marlow, Oklahoma, area for more than 10 years. The staff veterinarians perform all checkups and surgeries, and the staff technician handles all other visits. With the population explosion in the area, the clinic's patient list has increased beyond the current staff's capabilities. Bessie Neal, the manager of the clinic, has been tracking the clinic's activity by month for the past year. Before meeting with the clinic's veterinarians to discuss adding staff or facilities, she wants you to compile the data she has collected and create some preliminary charts. Complete the following:

1. Open the **Clinic** workbook located in the Excel6 ▶ Case3 folder included with your Data Files, and then save the workbook as **Vet Clinic** in the location specified by your instructor.

2. In the Documentation worksheet, enter your name and the date.

3. Group the 12 monthly worksheets to ensure consistency in headings and for ease in entering formulas. Enter the heading **Totals** in cells A11 and E4. For each month (January through December), enter formulas to calculate the total for each type of visit (the range B11:D11) and the total for each type of animal (the range E5:E11).

4. Improve the formatting of the monthly worksheets using the formatting of your choice. Make sure that you have included a lower border in the ranges A4:E4 and A10:E10. Ungroup the worksheets.

5. In the Service Analysis by Month worksheet, enter formulas with worksheet references in the range B5:B16. (=January!B11 through =December!B11) for the total checkup appointments for each month. Copy these formulas to the range C5:C16 (Surgery) and the range D5:D16 (Technician).

6. In cells A17 and E4, enter the label **Total**. Enter formulas to add the total by type of appointment (the range B17:E17) and total appointments each month (the range E5:E17). Bold the ranges A4:A17 and B4:E4. Center the range A4:E4. Place a bottom border in the ranges A4:E4 and A16:E16.

7. Create a bar or column chart to compare the type of service by month (the range A4:D16). Include an appropriate chart title and a legend. Make any formatting changes to the chart that you feel necessary to develop an attractive and effective chart. Position the chart below the data.

8. In the Service Analysis by Animal worksheet, create 3-D cell references to total the appointment type for each animal for each month of the year. Formulas for Small Dog would be Checkup =SUM(January:December!B5), Surgery =SUM(January:December!C5), and Technician =SUM(January:December!D5). These formulas can be copied down through all animal types (the range B5:D10).

9. In cells A11 and E4, enter the label **Total**. Enter formulas to add the total by type of appointment (the range B11:D11) and the total by type of animal (the range E5:E11). Bold the ranges A4:A11 and B4:E4. Center the range A4:E4. Place a bottom border in the ranges A4:E4 and A10:E10.

10. Create a pie chart based on the annual total for each type of animal. Include an appropriate chart title and a legend. Make any formatting changes to the chart that you feel necessary. Position the pie chart below the data in the Service Analysis by Animal worksheet.

11. Group all worksheets except Documentation. Prepare the workbook for printing with the name of the workbook and the name of the worksheet on separate lines in the right section of the header. Display your name and the date on separate lines in the right section of the footer.

12. Save and close the workbook.

Case Problem 4

Data Files needed for this Case Problem: Midwest.xlsx, Northeast.xlsx, Southeast.xlsx, Ice Summary.xlsx, New Midwest.xlsx, Ice Template.xltx

CHALLENGE

Cubed Ice Sales   Cubed Ice Sales manufactures and distributes ice products east of the Mississippi River. Located in Lancaster, Pennsylvania, it claims to make "everything ice," including ice cubes, ice blocks, and dry ice to name a few of its products. The chief financial analyst, Joni Snapp, asks you to prepare the annual sales and bonus summary based on workbooks from the Midwest, Northeast, and Southeast regions. In December, each salesperson establishes his or her monthly target sales and negotiates a bonus percentage for any sales over that amount. Each region submits a workbook that contains a worksheet for each salesperson in that region. The salesperson's worksheet contains his or her sales by month, monthly target sales, and bonus by percentage. Joni wants you to calculate the bonus for each month for each salesperson using the data he or she provided. She also wants you to summarize each workbook, reporting the quarterly gross sales, bonus sales, and bonus amount. After you have added this information to each workbook, Joni wants you to consolidate the information from the three regional workbooks into a single workbook. Complete the following:

1. Open the **Midwest** workbook located in the Excel6 ► Case4 folder included with your Data Files, and then save the workbook as **Cubed Ice Midwest** in the location specified by your instructor.

2. In the Documentation worksheet, enter your name and the date.

3. Repeat Steps 1 and 2, opening the **Northeast** and **Southeast** workbooks, and saving them as **Cubed Ice Northeast** and **Cubed Ice Southeast**, respectively.

4. Complete the salesperson worksheets in each region's workbook by doing the following:

   a. Group the Salesperson worksheets.

   b. Calculate the Bonus Sales for each month using the formula Gross Sales – Target. (A bonus will be paid only on sales over this amount.) If the salesperson did not sell more than the target, he or she receives no bonus. (*Hint*: Use an IF statement and absolute cell references.)

   c. Calculate the Bonus Amount using the formula Bonus Sales * Bonus Rate. (*Hint*: Remember to use absolute cell references.)

   d. Enter **Total** in cell A16. Total the Gross Sales, Bonus Sales, and Bonus Amount.

   e. Bold the ranges A4:A16 and B3:D3. Wrap the text and center the range B3:D3. Display all numbers with a comma and no decimal places. Display the total row values (the range B16:D16) with a dollar sign.

   f. Ungroup the worksheets.

5. In each of the regional workbooks, do the following:

   a. Make a copy of the first salesperson's worksheet. Rename it **Summary**, and then place it after the Documentation worksheet.

   b. Change the subheading (Salesperson name) to **Summary** to indicate this is a summary worksheet. Clear the Gross Sales, Bonus Sales, and Bonus Amounts, leaving the formulas for the totals.

   c. Clear the headings and data in the range A19:B20.

   d. Create 3-D reference formulas to calculate the totals by month for Gross Sales, Bonus Sales, and Bonus Amount.

   e. Group all worksheets except the Documentation worksheet. Prepare the workbook for printing with the name of the workbook and the name of the worksheet on separate lines in the right section of the header. Display your name and the date on separate lines in the right section of the footer. Widen columns as needed so you can see the totals.

   f. Ungroup the worksheets and save the workbook.

6. Open the **Ice Summary** workbook located in the Excel6 ► Case4 folder included with your Data Files, and then save the workbook as **Cubed Ice Summary** in the location specified by your instructor.

7. Make sure all four of the Cubed Ice Workbooks are open and have the Summary worksheet as the active sheet.

7. Click the **Paste List** button. The defined names and their associated cell references are pasted into the range B11:C24.

8. Deselect the range. See Figure 7-7. Only some names in the pasted list of defined names include underscores in place of spaces. The names with underscores were created using the Create from Selection button; you entered the names without underscores in the Name box.

Figure 7-7   **Defined names in the Youth Soccer workbook**

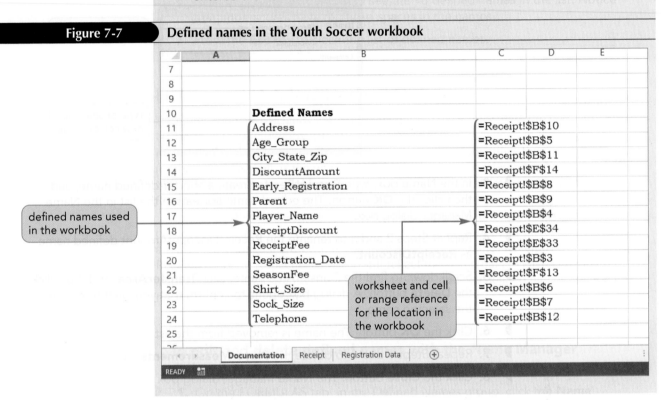

If you edit a defined name or add a new defined name, the list of defined names and their addresses in the Documentation worksheet is not updated. You must paste the list again to update the names and locations. Usually, it is a good idea to wait until the workbook is complete before pasting defined names in the Documentation worksheet.

Using Defined Names in Formulas

You can create more descriptive formulas by using defined names instead of cell or range references in formulas. For example, in the following formulas, the defined name Sales replaces the range reference D1:D100 in a formula to calculate average sales:

Range reference	=AVERAGE(D1:D100)
Defined name	=AVERAGE(Sales)

Keep in mind that range references in formulas are not updated with their defined names. So, if you enter a range reference in a formula, its corresponding defined name does *not* automatically replace the range reference in the formula.

Sharon wants you to enter the formulas required to generate the receipt. You'll start by entering formulas to display the registration date, the parent's name, and the parent's address entered in the Registration Data area in the receipt.

To enter formulas to display the parent's name and address on the receipt:

▶ **1.** Go to the **Receipt** worksheet.

▶ **2.** In cell **B27**, enter **=B9**. James Smith, the parent's name, appears in the cell.

▶ **3.** In cell **B28**, enter **=B10**. 123 Main Street, the parent's street address, appears in the cell.

▶ **4.** In cell **B29**, enter **=B11**. The parent's city, state, and zip code—Oak Hill, WV 25901—appears in the cell.

▶ **5.** Select cell **B29**. The formula =B11 appears in the formula bar. See Figure 7-8.

Figure 7-8 **Formula to display the City, State, and Zip data**

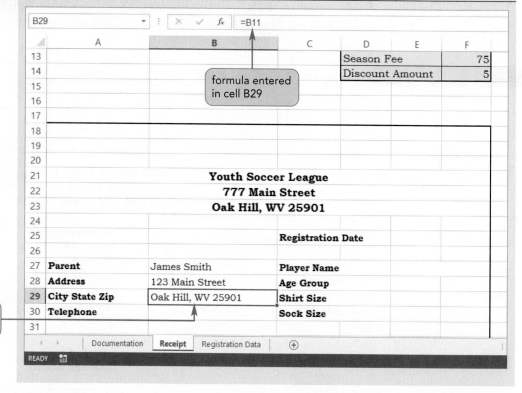

You entered these formulas using cell addresses rather than defined names. Although you defined names for cells B9, B10, and B11, the names do not automatically replace the cell addresses in the formula when you type the cell addresses.

Using Defined Names in Formulas

Defined names make formulas simpler to enter and understand. To use a defined name in a formula, you enter the formula as usual. As you type a defined name in a formula, the Formula AutoComplete box appears, listing functions and defined names that begin with the letters you typed. As you type additional letters, the list narrows. You can double-click the name you want in the Formula AutoComplete box or press the Tab key to enter the selected name. You can also just continue to type the rest of the name.

Sharon wants you to use named cells and ranges in the remaining formulas. You'll enter these now.

To type defined names in formulas:

▶ 1. In cell **B30**, type **=T** to display a list of functions and defined names that begin with the letter *T*.

▶ 2. Type **el** to narrow the list to the defined name =Telephone.

▶ 3. Press the **Tab** key to enter the defined name in the formula, and then press the **Enter** key. The parent's telephone number appears in the cell.

▶ 4. Select cell **B30**. The data from cell B12 appears in the cell, and the formula with the defined name =Telephone appears in the formula bar.

▶ 5. In cell **E25**, enter **=Reg** to list the defined name =Registration_Date, press the **Tab** key to insert the defined name in the formula, and then press the **Enter** key.

▶ 6. Select cell **E25**. The data from cell B3 appears in the cell, and the formula with the defined name =Registration_Date appears in the formula bar. See Figure 7-9.

Figure 7-9   Formula with a defined name

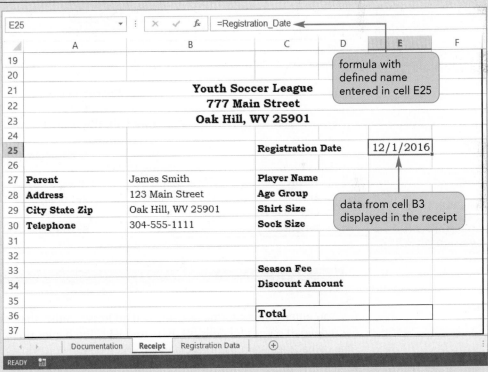

Trouble? If the date is displayed as an integer, you need to reformat the cell as a date. Format cell E25 in the Short Date format (*mm/dd/yyyy*) and then AutoFit column E so that the date is displayed.

You can also use the point-and-click method to create a formula with defined names. When you click a cell or select a range, Excel substitutes the defined name for the cell reference in the formula. You'll use this method to enter formulas that display the Player Name, Age Group, Shirt Size, and Sock Size from the Registration Data area in the Registration Receipt.

To enter formulas with defined names using the point-and-click method:

▶ **1.** Select cell **E27**, type **=**, and then click cell **B4**. The formula uses the defined name Player_Name rather than the cell reference B4.

▶ **2.** Press the **Enter** key. Sandy, which is the name of the player, appears in cell E27.

▶ **3.** In cell **E28**, type **=**, and then click cell **B5**. The formula uses the defined name Age_Group rather than the cell reference B5.

▶ **4.** Press the **Enter** key. The value is U5, indicating the age group U5, appears in cell E28.

▶ **5.** In cell **E29**, type **=**, click cell **B6**, and then press the **Enter** key. The player's shirt size, SM, appears in cell E29, and the formula with the defined name =Shirt_Size appears in the formula bar.

▶ **6.** In cell **E30**, type **=**, click cell **B7**, and then press the **Enter** key. The player's sock size, SH, appears in cell E30, and the formula with the defined name =Sock_Size appears in the formula bar.

▶ **7.** In cell **E33**, type **=**, click cell **F13**, and then click the **Enter** button ✓ on the formula bar. The season fee, 75, appears in cell E33 and the formula with the defined name =SeasonFee appears in the formula bar. See Figure 7-10.

Figure 7-10	SeasonFee formula

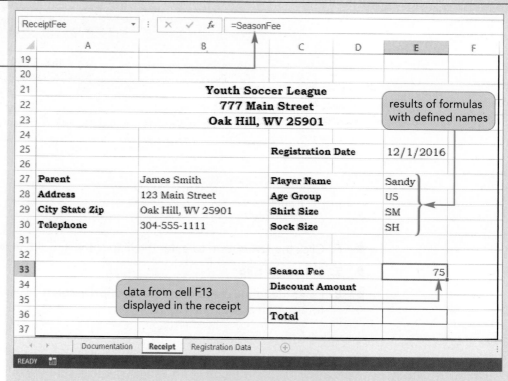

Next, Sharon wants you to enter the formula to calculate the total registration paid based on the data in the Registration Fee/Discount area. All players pay the season fee ($75). Anyone who registers at least four weeks before the season starts receives a $5 discount. Because the formula results are based on the registration date, you need to use an IF function to determine whether the player will receive the $5 discount.

To enter the IF function to calculate the registration total:

▶ **1.** Select cell **E34**. The defined name ReceiptDiscount appears in the Name box.

▶ **2.** On the FORMULAS tab, in the Function Library group, click the **Logical** button, and then click **IF**. The Function Arguments dialog box opens.

TIP

Remember that the IF function uses quotation marks around text.

▶ **3.** In the Logical_test box, type **Early_Registration="Yes"**. This logical test evaluates whether the player qualifies for the early registration discount. If the value in cell B8 equals Yes, then the condition is true. TRUE appears to the right of the Logical_test box, indicating that this player qualifies for the early registration discount of $5.00.

> **Trouble?** If an error value appears to the right of the Logical_test box, you probably mistyped the formula. If the error value is #NAME?, you mistyped the defined name or didn't include quotation marks around the word "Yes." If the error value is Invalid, you used single quotation marks (') around the word "Yes." Edit the content in the Logical_test box as needed.

▶ **4.** In the Value_if_true box, type **DiscountAmount**—the defined name for cell F14, which has the value 5. This discount amount will be added to the receipt if the logical test is true.

▶ **5.** In the Value_if_false box, type **0** to indicate no discount will be applied if the value in cell B8 does not equal Yes. See Figure 7-11.

Figure 7-11	Completed IF Function Arguments dialog box

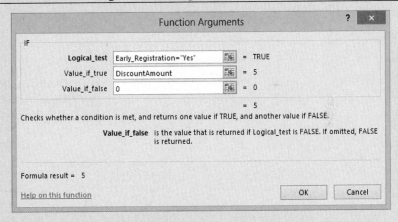

▶ **6.** Click the **OK** button to enter the IF function in cell E34, which displays 5.

▶ **7.** Select cell **E36**.

▶ **8.** Enter the formula **=ReceiptFee-ReceiptDiscount** to calculate the registration total, which is $70. See Figure 7-12.

Figure 7-12   **Receipt with all formulas entered**

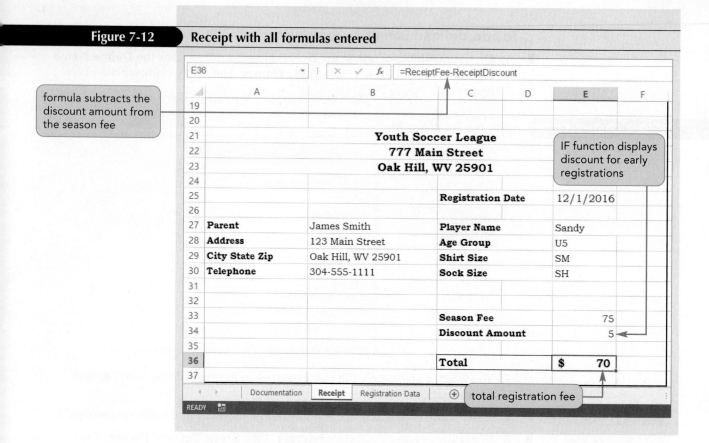

formula subtracts the discount amount from the season fee

IF function displays discount for early registrations

total registration fee

Adding Defined Names to Existing Formulas

Sometimes you might name cells after creating formulas in the worksheet. Other times you might not use the defined names when you create formulas (as with the first three formulas you created in the receipt for the parent; parent address; and city, state, and zip). Because defined names are not automatically substituted for the cell addresses in a formula, you can replace cell addresses in existing formulas in the worksheet with their defined names to make the formulas more understandable.

REFERENCE

Adding Defined Names to Existing Formulas

- On the FORMULAS tab, in the Defined Names group, click the Define Name button arrow, and then click Apply Names (if the cell reference and defined name are in the same worksheet).
- In the Apply Names dialog box, select the names you want to apply.
- Click the OK button.

or

- Edit the formula by selecting the cell reference and typing the defined name or clicking the appropriate cell.

In the two formulas you created to display the parent's name and address in the receipt, Sharon wants you to use defined names instead of cell references. This will make the formulas much clearer to anyone who looks at the worksheet.

To add defined names to existing formulas in the receipt:

▶ **1.** On the FORMULAS tab, in the Defined Names group, click the **Define Name button arrow**, and then click **Apply Names**. The Apply Names dialog box opens. See Figure 7-13.

| Figure 7-13 | Apply Names dialog box |

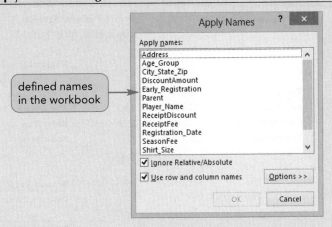

defined names in the workbook

You want to select only the names you need for the existing formulas with cell references.

TIP

You can also select a cell that contains a formula, click the Use in Formula button in the Defined Names group, click the name to replace the cell reference, and then press the Enter key.

▶ **2.** If any name is selected in the Apply names list, click that name to deselect it.

▶ **3.** In the Apply names list, click **Address**, **City_State_Zip**, and **Parent**. The three names you want to apply to the formulas are selected.

▶ **4.** Make sure that the **Use row and column names** check box is unchecked. If you leave this checked, the formula will contain too many characters and return an error.

▶ **5.** Click the **OK** button. The three selected names are applied to the formulas.

▶ **6.** Click cell **B27** and verify that the formula changed to =Parent.

▶ **7.** Click cell **B28** and verify that the formula changed to =Address.

▶ **8.** Click cell **B29** and verify that the formula changed to =City_State_Zip. The formulas now use the defined names in the files.

Sharon wants to store the following items in the Registration Data worksheet—parent, telephone, player name, age group, shirt size, and sock size. Displaying this data in the Transfer Area enables you to copy and paste all of the items to the Registration Data worksheet at once. You'll enter formulas to display the appropriate items in this section of the worksheet.

To enter formulas to display data in the Transfer Area:

▶ **1.** In cell **A40**, enter **=Parent**. The formula displays the parent name (James Smith).

▶ **2.** In cell **B40**, enter **=Telephone**. The formula displays the telephone number (304-555-1111).

> **3.** In cell **C40**, enter **=Player_Name**. The formula displays the name of the player (Sandy).

> **4.** In cell **D40**, enter **=Age_Group**. The formula displays the age group of the player (U5).

> **5.** In cell **E40**, enter **=Shirt_Size**. The formula displays the player shirt size (SM).

> **6.** In cell **F40**, enter **=Sock_Size**. The formula displays the sock size (SH). See Figure 7-14.

Figure 7-14   Formulas entered in the Transfer Area

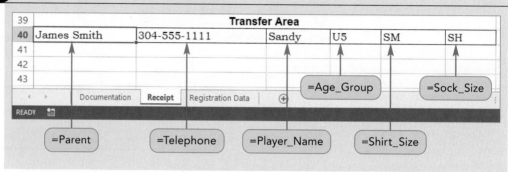

The worksheet contains all of the formulas required to create the receipt based on the registration data. Because Sharon relies on volunteers to enter registration data into the worksheet and print receipts, she wants to be sure the values entered are correct. You will continue to work on Sharon's application by creating validation checks, which are designed to prevent users from inserting incorrect data values. You will also protect cells so that volunteers cannot accidentally overwrite or delete the formulas. You'll complete both of these tasks in the next session.

Session 7.1 Quick Check

REVIEW

1. What is an Excel application?
2. What areas of a worksheet should you consider including in an Excel application?
3. What are two advantages of using defined names in workbooks?
4. What are three ways to create a defined name?
5. Is Annual Sales a valid defined name? Explain why or why not.
6. How do you select a cell or range using its defined name?
7. In the Report workbook, the defined name "Expenses" refers to a list of expenses in the range D2:D100. Currently, the total expenses are calculated by the formula =SUM(D2:D100). Change this formula to use the defined name.
8. How do you add defined names to existing formulas?

Session 7.2 Visual Overview:

A red triangle indicates that the cell contains a comment. Point to the cell to display the comment box.

Cells for data entry must be unlocked before the worksheet is protected so that users can enter and edit data in these cells.

You can use **data validation** to create a set of rules that determine what users can enter in a specific cell or range. For example, Sock Size entries must match the sizes listed in the Player Measurements.

An **input message** appears when the cell becomes active, and can be used to specify the type of data the user should enter in that cell. This input message reminds users to select one of the sock sizes in the list.

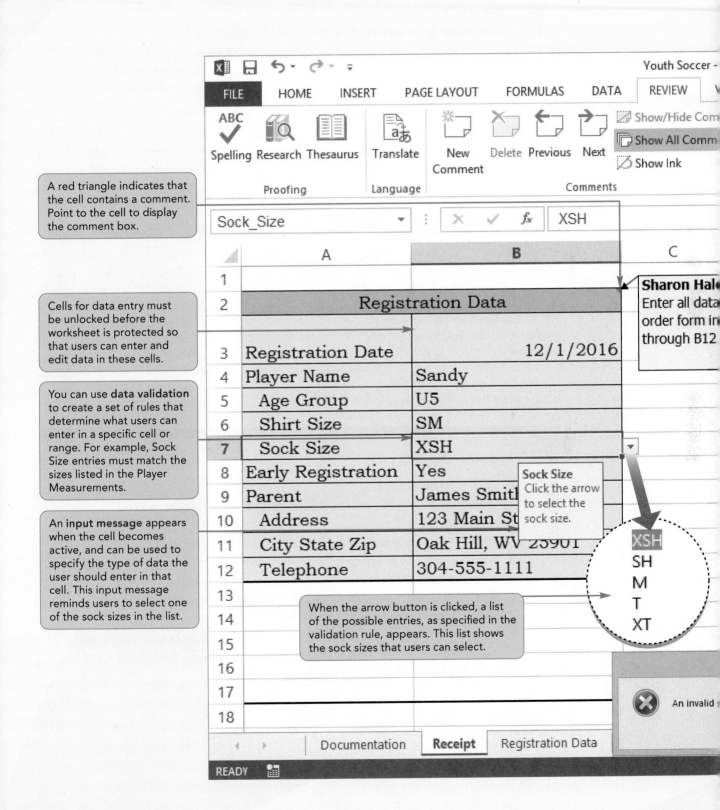

Sock_Size | XSH

	A	B	C
1			**Sharon Hale**
2	Registration Data		Enter all data order form in through B12
3	Registration Date	12/1/2016	
4	Player Name	Sandy	
5	Age Group	U5	
6	Shirt Size	SM	
7	Sock Size	XSH	
8	Early Registration	Yes	
9	Parent	James Smith	
10	Address	123 Main St	
11	City State Zip	Oak Hill, WV 25901	
12	Telephone	304-555-1111	
13			
14			
15			
16			
17			
18			

Sock Size Click the arrow to select the sock size.

XSH
SH
M
T
XT

When the arrow button is clicked, a list of the possible entries, as specified in the validation rule, appears. This list shows the sock sizes that users can select.

An invalid

Documentation | **Receipt** | Registration Data

READY

Data Validation and Protection

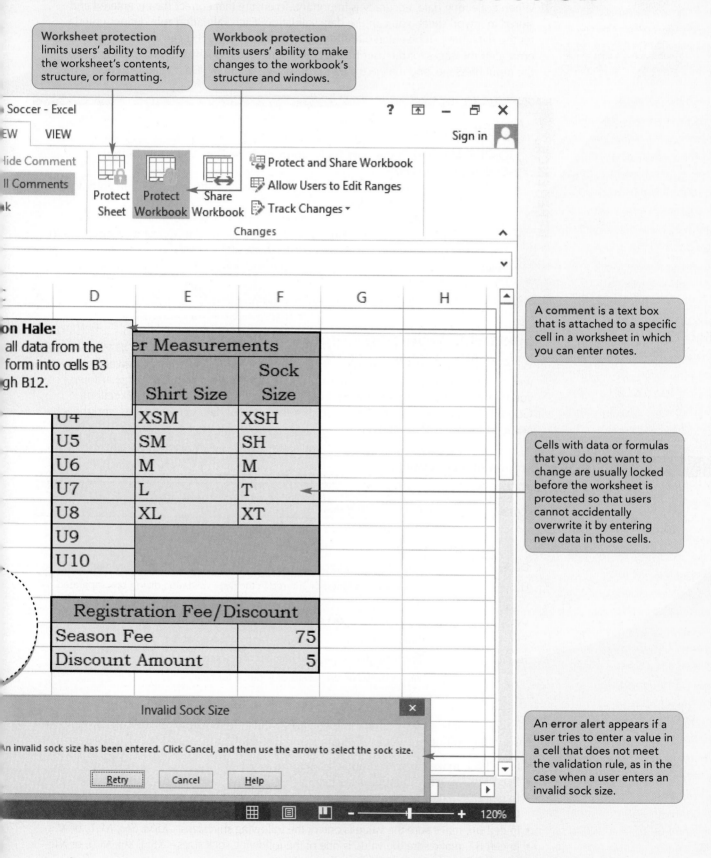

Worksheet protection limits users' ability to modify the worksheet's contents, structure, or formatting.

Workbook protection limits users' ability to make changes to the workbook's structure and windows.

Soccer - Excel

EW   VIEW   Sign in

Hide Comment
ll Comments
k

Protect and Share Workbook
Allow Users to Edit Ranges
Track Changes ▾

Protect Sheet   Protect Workbook   Share Workbook

Changes

A **comment** is a text box that is attached to a specific cell in a worksheet in which you can enter notes.

on Hale:
all data from the form into cells B3 gh B12.

	Shirt Size	Sock Size
U4	XSM	XSH
U5	SM	SH
U6	M	M
U7	L	T
U8	XL	XT
U9		
U10		

r Measurements

Cells with data or formulas that you do not want to change are usually locked before the worksheet is protected so that users cannot accidentally overwrite it by entering new data in those cells.

Registration Fee/Discount	
Season Fee	75
Discount Amount	5

Invalid Sock Size   ✕

An invalid sock size has been entered. Click Cancel, and then use the arrow to select the sock size.

Retry   Cancel   Help

An **error alert** appears if a user tries to enter a value in a cell that does not meet the validation rule, as in the case when a user enters an invalid sock size.

120%

Validating Data Entry

When collecting data, accuracy is important. To ensure that correct data is entered and stored in a worksheet, you can use data validation. Each **validation rule** defines criteria for the data that can be entered and stored in a cell or range. You can also add input and error alert messages for the user to that cell or range. You specify the validation criteria, the input message, and the error alert for the active cell in the Data Validation dialog box.

REFERENCE

Validating Data

- On the DATA tab, in the Data Tools group, click the Data Validation button.
- Click the Settings tab.
- Click the Allow arrow, click the type of data allowed in the cell, and then enter the validation criteria for that data.
- Click the Input Message tab, and then enter a title and text for the input message.
- Click the Error Alert tab, and then, if necessary, click the Show error alert after invalid data is entered check box to insert a checkmark.
- Select an alert style, and then enter the title and text for the error alert message.
- Click the OK button.

Specifying Validation Criteria

When you create a validation rule, you specify the type of data that is allowed as well as a list or range of acceptable values (called **validation criteria**). For example, you might specify integers between 1 and 100, or a list of codes such as Excellent, Good, Fair, and Poor. Figure 7-15 describes the types of data you can allow and the acceptable values for each type.

Figure 7-15 **Allow options for validation**

Type	Acceptable Values
Any value	Any number, text, or date; removes any existing data validation
Whole Number	Integers only; you can specify the range of acceptable integers
Decimal	Any type of number; you can specify the range of acceptable numbers
List	Any value in a range or entered in the Data validation dialog box separated by commas
Date	Dates only; you can specify the range of acceptable dates
Time	Times only; you can specify the range of acceptable times
Text Length	Text limited to a specified number of characters
Custom	Values based on the results of a logical formula

© 2014 Cengage Learning

Sharon wants you to add the following six validation rules to the workbook to help ensure that volunteers enter valid data in the Receipt worksheet:

- In cell B3, make sure a valid date is entered.
- In cell B4, specify an input message.
- In cell B5, make sure the value is one of the following age groups—U4, U5, U6, U7, U8, U9, or U10.
- In cell B6, make sure the value is one of the following shirt sizes—XSM, SM, M, L, or XL.
- In cell B7, make sure the value is one of the following sock sizes—XSH, SH, M, T, or XT.
- In cell B8, make sure the value is Yes or No.

Cell B3, which contains the Registration Date, requires the current date. Sharon wants to be sure everyone enters a valid date in this cell. You will define the validation rule for the Registration Date.

To create the validation rule for the Registration Date cell:

▶ **1.** If you took a break after the previous session, make sure the Youth Soccer workbook is open and the Receipt worksheet is active.

▶ **2.** Select cell **B3**. You will enter a date validation rule to ensure that a valid date is entered in this cell.

▶ **3.** On the ribbon, click the **DATA** tab.

TIP

To apply a validation rule to all cells in an Excel table column, select the column of data, and then create the validation rule.

▶ **4.** In the Data Tools group, click the **Data Validation** button. The Data Validation dialog box opens with the Settings tab displayed. You use the Settings tab to enter the validation rule for the active cell.

▶ **5.** On the Settings tab, click the **Allow** arrow, and then click **Date**. The Data Validation dialog box expands to display the options specific to dates.

▶ **6.** Click the **Ignore blank** check box to deselect it. You want to ensure that cell B3 is not left blank, and require users to enter a date value in the cell.

▶ **7.** If necessary, click the **Data** arrow, and then click **greater than or equal to**. The dialog box reflects the selected criteria.

▶ **8.** Enter **1/1/2010** in the Start date box to provide an example of what to look for when checking the cell. You cannot use data validation to simply check for the presence of data. You must provide an example for checking. See Figure 7-16.

Figure 7-16	**Settings tab in the Data Validation dialog box**

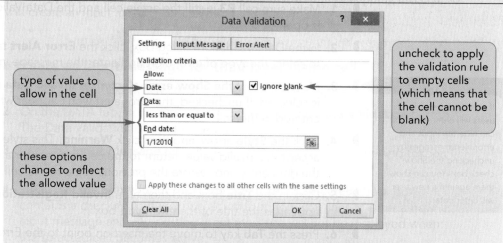

If you wanted to create a validation rule that checks if the date is the current date, you would select "equal to" in the Data list and then enter =TODAY() in the Date box. Then, a user cannot enter any date other than the current date. Sharon wants to check only for the presence of a date because sometimes the registration form is completed on a different day than the data was received.

Figure 7-21 | **Stop error alert for the Age Group cell**

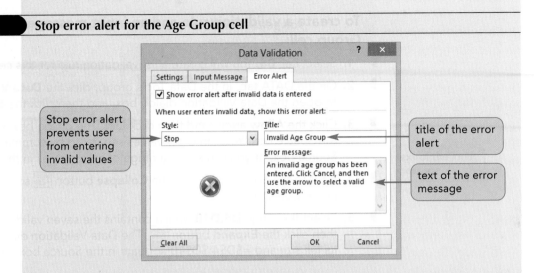

Stop error alert prevents user from entering invalid values

title of the error alert

text of the error message

> **11.** Click the **OK** button. The Data Validation dialog box closes, an arrow appears to the right of cell B5, and the input message appears in a ScreenTip.

> **12.** Click the **arrow** button ▼ to the right of cell B5 to view the list of valid age group entries. See Figure 7-22.

Figure 7-22 | **List of valid age group entries**

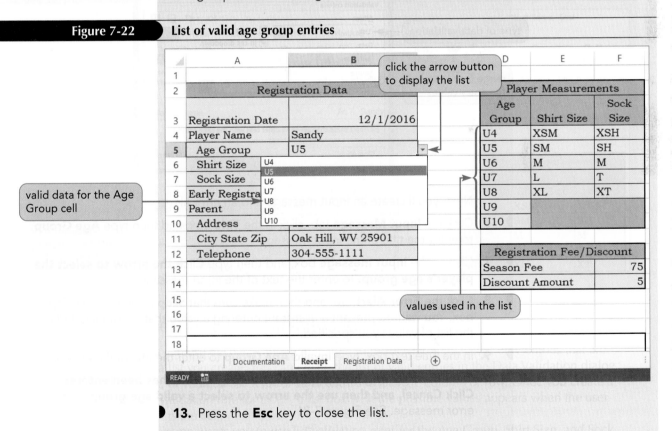

valid data for the Age Group cell

> **13.** Press the **Esc** key to close the list.

Next, Sharon wants you to enter a list validation rule for cells B6 and B7, which specify the player's shirt size (XSM, SM, M, L, or XL) and sock size (XSH, SH, M, T, or XT), respectively. Both rules will include an error alert.

To create list validation rules for the Shirt Size and Sock Size cells:

▶ **1.** Select cell **B6**. You will create a list validation rule for the Shirt Size cell.

▶ **2.** On the DATA tab, in the Data Tools group, click the **Data Validation** button. The Data Validation dialog box opens.

▶ **3.** Click the **Settings** tab, select **List** in the Allow box, click the **Source** box, and then select the range **E4:E8**. This range contains the five values you want to allow users to select for the shirt size.

▶ **4.** Click the **Input Message** tab, type **Shirt Size** in the Title box, and then type **Click the arrow to select the shirt size.** in the Input message box.

▶ **5.** Click the **Error Alert** tab, verify that **Stop** appears in the Style box, type **Invalid Shirt Size** in the Title box, and then type **An invalid shirt size has been entered. Click Cancel, and then use the arrow to select the shirt size.** in the Error message box.

▶ **6.** Click the **OK** button. The dialog box closes, an arrow button appears to the right of cell B6, and the input message appears in a ScreenTip.

▶ **7.** Select cell **B7** so you can create the validation rule for the Sock Size cell.

▶ **8.** In the Data Tools group, click the **Data Validation** button to open the Data Validation dialog box, and then click the **Settings** tab.

▶ **9.** Select **List** in the Allow box, click the **Source** box, and then select the range **F4:F8**. This range contains the five values you want to allow users to select for the sock size.

▶ **10.** Click the **Input Message** tab, type **Sock Size** in the Title box, and then type **Click the arrow to select the sock size.** in the Input message box.

▶ **11.** Click the **Error Alert** tab, make sure that **Stop** appears in the Style box, type **Invalid Sock Size** in the Title box, and then type **An invalid sock size has been entered. Click Cancel, and then use the arrow to select the sock size.** in the Error message box.

▶ **12.** Click the **OK** button. An arrow button appears to the right of cell B7, and the input message appears in a ScreenTip.

Sharon also wants you to enter a validation rule for cell B8 to limit the Early Registration cell to either Yes or No. This rule will also include an input message and an error alert. To specify the entries that the list includes, you will type each entry separated by commas in the Source box on the Settings tab in the Data Validation dialog box.

To create a list validation rule for the Early Registration cell:

▶ **1.** Select cell **B8** so you can create a validation rule for the Early Registration cell.

▶ **2.** On the DATA tab, in the Data Tools group, click the **Data Validation** button. The Data Validation dialog box opens.

▶ **3.** Click the **Settings** tab, select **List** in the Allow box, click the **Source** box, and then type **Yes, No** in the Source box. You typed the items for the list because they are not already contained in any range of the worksheet. See Figure 7-23.

Figure 7-23   Validation rule for the Early Registration cell

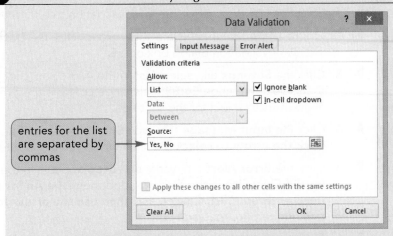

entries for the list are separated by commas

4. Click the **Input Message** tab, type **Early Registration** in the Title box, and then type **Click the arrow to select the correct response.** in the Input message box.

5. Click the **Error Alert** tab, make sure that **Stop** appears in the Style box, type **Invalid Early Registration** in the Title box, and then type **An invalid response for Early Registration has been entered. Click Cancel, and then use the arrow to the right of cell B8 to select the response.** in the Error message box.

6. Click the **OK** button. An arrow button appears to the right of cell B8, and the input message appears in a ScreenTip.

You can edit an existing validation rule, input message, or error alert at any time by selecting the cell with the current validation rule and then opening the Data Validation dialog box. You can also add or remove an input message or error alert to an existing validation rule. Sharon notices that the Registration Date cell does not have an input message. For consistency, she wants you to add one now.

To create an input message for the Registration Date cell:

1. Select cell **B3**.

2. On the DATA tab, in the Data Tools group, click the **Data Validation** button.

3. Click the **Settings** tab. The validation rule you created earlier is displayed.

4. Click the **Input Message** tab, type **Registration Date** in the Title box, and then type **Enter the registration date.** in the Input message box.

5. Click the **OK** button. The input message is added to the Registration Date cell.

Testing Data Validation Rules

After you create validation rules, you should test them. You do this by entering incorrect values that violate the validation rules. Keep in mind that the only way an error occurs in cells that have a list validation is if an incorrect entry is typed or pasted in the cell. Entering invalid data will ensure that validation rules work as expected. Sharon asks you to test the validation rules you just created.

To test the data validation rules:

1. Select cell **B3**, type **01/30/2004**, and then press the **Tab** key. The Invalid Registration Date message box opens, informing you that the value you entered might be incorrect. You'll enter a valid date.

2. Click the **No** button to return to cell B3, type the current date, and then press the **Enter** key. The date is entered in cell B3. Cell B4 is the active cell, and the input message for the Player Name cell appears.

3. In cell **B4**, type your name, and then press the **Enter** key. The value is accepted.

4. Select cell **B5** if necessary to display the list arrow, click the **arrow** to the right of cell B5, and then click **U6**. The value is accepted. The only way an error occurs in cells that have a list validation is if an incorrect entry is typed or copied in the cell. You'll try typing in cell B6.

5. In cell **B6**, enter **LG**. The Invalid Shirt Size message box opens.

6. Click the **Cancel** button to close the message box and return to the original value in the cell.

7. Click the **arrow** button ▼ to the right of cell B6, and then click **SM**.

8. In cell B7, enter **XSH**. An error alert does not appear because this is a valid entry. You could also have selected XSH from the validation list.

9. Select cell **B8**, click the **arrow** button ▼ to the right of cell B8, and then click **Yes** for Early Registration.

TIP

If you click the Retry button in the error alert dialog box, you must press the Esc key to return to the original cell value; otherwise, the error alert reappears when you click the arrow button.

The validation rules that you entered for cells B3 through B8 work as intended.

INSIGHT

Using the Circle Invalid Data Command

Validation rules come into play only during data entry. If you add validation rules to a workbook that already contains data with erroneous values, Excel does not determine if any existing data is invalid.

To ensure the entire workbook contains valid data, you need to also verify any data previously entered in the workbook. You can use the Circle Invalid Data command to find and mark cells that contain invalid data. Red circles appear around any data that does not meet the validation criteria, making it simple to scan a worksheet for errors. After you correct the data in a cell, the circle disappears.

To display circles around invalid data, perform the following steps:

1. Apply validation rules to an existing cell range.
2. On the DATA tab, in the Data Tools group, click the Data Validation button arrow, and then click Circle Invalid Data. Red circles appear around cells that contain invalid data.
3. To remove the circle from a single cell, enter valid data in the cell.
4. To hide all circles, on the DATA tab, in the Data Tools group, click the Data Validation button arrow, and then click Clear Validation Circles.

To ensure an error-free workbook, you should use the Circle Invalid Data command to verify data entered before you set up the validation criteria, or to verify data in a workbook you inherited from someone else, such as a coworker.

Protecting a Worksheet and a Workbook

Another way to minimize data-entry errors is to limit access to certain parts of the workbook. Worksheet protection prevents users from changing cell contents, such as editing formulas in a worksheet. Workbook protection also prevents users from changing the workbook's organization, such as inserting or deleting worksheets in the workbook. You can even keep users from viewing the formulas used in the workbook.

Sharon wants to protect the contents of the Receipt and Registration Data worksheets. She wants volunteers to have access only to the range B3:B12 in the Receipt worksheet, where new receipt data is entered. She also wants to prevent volunteers from editing the contents of any cells in the Registration Data worksheet.

Locking and Unlocking Cells

Every cell in a workbook has a **locked property** that determines whether changes can be made to that cell. The locked property has no impact as long as the worksheet is unprotected. However, after you protect a worksheet, the locked property controls whether the cell can be edited. You unlock a cell by turning off the locked property. By default, the locked property is turned on for each cell, and worksheet protection is turned off.

So, unless you unlock cells in a worksheet *before* protecting the worksheet, all of the cells in the worksheet will be locked, and you won't be able to make any changes in the worksheet. Usually, you will want to protect the worksheet but leave some cells unlocked. For example, you might want to lock cells that contain formulas and formatting so they cannot be changed, but unlock cells in which you want to enter data.

To protect some—but not all—cells in a worksheet, you first turn off the locked property of cells in which data can be entered. Then, you protect the worksheet to activate the locked property for the remaining cells.

In the Receipt worksheet, Sharon wants users to be able to enter data in the range B3:B12, but not in any other cell. To do this, you must unlock the cells in the range B3:B12.

To unlock the cells in the range B3:B12:

1. In the Receipt worksheet, select the range **B3:B12**. You want to unlock the cells in this range before you protect the worksheet.

2. On the ribbon, click the **HOME** tab.

3. In the Cells group, click the **Format** button, and then click **Format Cells** (or press the **Ctrl+1** keys). The Format Cells dialog box opens. The locked property is on the Protection tab.

4. Click the **Protection** tab, and then click the **Locked** check box to remove the checkmark. See Figure 7-24.

Figure 7-24   **Protection tab in the Format Cells dialog box**

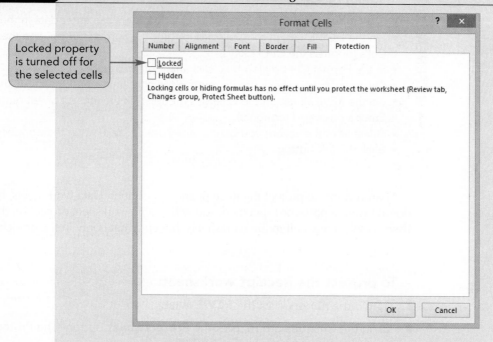

Locked property is turned off for the selected cells

▶ **5.** Click the **OK** button. The cells in the range B3:B12 are unlocked.

▶ **6.** Select cell **A1** to deselect the range.

Protecting a Worksheet

When you set up worksheet protection, you specify which actions are still available to users in the protected worksheet. For example, you can choose to allow users to insert new rows or columns, or to delete rows and columns. You can limit the user to selecting only unlocked cells, or allow the user to select any cell in the worksheet. These choices remain active as long as the worksheet is protected.

A protected worksheet can always be unprotected. You can also add a password to the protected worksheet that users must enter in order to turn off the protection. Passwords are case sensitive, which means the uppercase and lowercase letters are considered different letters. If you are concerned that users will turn off protection and make changes to formulas, you should use a password; otherwise, it is probably best to not specify a password. Keep in mind that if you forget the password, it is very difficult to remove the worksheet protection.

Protecting a Worksheet

- Select the cells and ranges to unlock so that users can enter data in them.
- On the HOME tab, in the Cells group, click the Format button, and then click Format Cells (or press the Ctrl+1 keys).
- In the Format Cells dialog box, click the Protection tab.
- Click the Locked check box to remove the checkmark, and then click the OK button.
- On the REVIEW tab, in the Changes group, click the Protect Sheet button.
- Enter a password (optional).
- Select all of the actions you want to allow users to take when the worksheet is protected.
- Click the OK button.

Sharon wants to protect the Receipt and Registration Data worksheets, but she doesn't want a password specified. You will enable worksheet protection that will allow users to select any cell in the worksheets, but enter data only in the unlocked cells.

To protect the Receipt worksheet:

1. On the ribbon, click the **REVIEW** tab.

2. In the Changes group, click the **Protect Sheet** button. The Protect Sheet dialog box opens. See Figure 7-25.

Figure 7-25   **Protect Sheet dialog box**

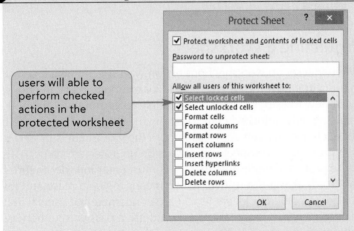

users will able to perform checked actions in the protected worksheet

You will leave the Password to unprotect sheet box blank because you do not want to use a password. By default, users can select both locked and unlocked cells, which constitute all of the cells in the worksheet, but they can enter or edit values only in unlocked cells.

3. Click the **OK** button. The Protect Sheet dialog box closes, and the Protect Sheet button changes to the Unprotect Sheet button.

Any time you modify a worksheet, you should test the worksheet to ensure that changes work as intended. You'll test the protection you added to the Receipt worksheet by trying to edit a locked cell, and then trying to edit an unlocked cell.

To test the Receipt worksheet protection:

▶ **1.** Select cell **F13**, and then type **1**. As soon as you press any key, a dialog box opens, indicating that the cell is protected and cannot be modified. See Figure 7-26.

Figure 7-26   Cell protection error message

▶ **2.** Click the **OK** button.

▶ **3.** Click cell **B8**, type **No**, and then press the **Enter** key. The Early Registration cell is updated because you allowed editing in the range B3:B12. A user can enter and edit values in these cells. Although users can select any cell in the worksheet, they cannot make an entry in any other cell outside of that range.

▶ **4.** On the Quick Access Toolbar, click the **Undo** button to return the Early Registration cell to Yes.

You will repeat this process to protect all of the cells in the Registration Data worksheet. Then you will test to see what would happen if someone tried to edit one of the cells. Because you did not unlock any cells in the Registration Data worksheet, no cells may be edited.

To protect and test the Registration Data worksheet:

▶ **1.** Go to the **Registration Data** worksheet.

▶ **2.** On the REVIEW tab, in the Changes group, click the **Protect Sheet** button. The Protect Sheet dialog box opens.

▶ **3.** Click the **OK** button to accept the default set of user actions.

▶ **4.** Select cell **A2**, and then type **B**. A dialog box opens, indicating that the cell is protected and cannot be modified. All of the cells in this worksheet are protected because no cells have been unlocked.

▶ **5.** Click the **OK** button to close the dialog box.

Protecting a Workbook

Worksheet protection applies only to the contents of a worksheet, not to the worksheet itself. To keep a worksheet from being modified, you need to protect the workbook. You can protect both the structure and the windows of a workbook. Protecting the structure prevents users from renaming, deleting, hiding, or inserting worksheets. Protecting the windows prevents users from moving, resizing, closing, or hiding parts of the Excel window. The default is to protect only the structure of the workbook, not the windows used to display it.

You can also add a password to the workbook protection. However, the same guidelines apply as for protecting worksheets. Add a password only if you are concerned that others might unprotect the workbook and modify it. If you add a password, keep in mind that it is case sensitive and you cannot unprotect the workbook without it.

Protecting a Workbook

• On the REVIEW tab, in the Changes group, click the Protect Workbook button.
• Click the check boxes to indicate whether you want to protect the workbook's structure, windows, or both.
• Enter a password (optional).
• Click the OK button.

The contents of the Receipt and Registration Data worksheets, with the exception of the range B3:B12 in the Receipt worksheet, cannot be changed. However, a volunteer could inadvertently rename or delete the protected worksheet. To keep the worksheets themselves from being modified, you will protect the workbook. Sharon doesn't want users to be able to change the structure of the workbook, so you will set workbook protection for the structure, but not the window.

To protect the Youth Soccer workbook:

▶ **1.** On the REVIEW tab, in the Changes group, click the **Protect Workbook** button. The Protect Structure and Windows dialog box opens. See Figure 7-27.

Figure 7-27	Protect Structure and Windows dialog box

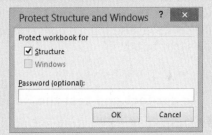

▶ **2.** Make sure the **Structure** check box is checked and the **Password** box is blank. The Windows check box is unavailable and unchecked.

▶ **3.** Click the **OK** button to protect the workbook without specifying a password.

▶ **4.** Right-click the **Registration Data** sheet tab. On the shortcut menu, notice that the Insert, Delete, Rename, Move or Copy, Tab Color, Hide, and Unhide commands are gray. This indicates that the options for modifying the worksheets are no longer available for the Registration Data worksheet.

▶ **5.** Press the **Esc** key to close the shortcut menu.

Unprotecting a Worksheet and a Workbook

You can turn off worksheet protection at any time. This is often referred to as *unprotecting* the worksheet. You must unprotect a worksheet to edit its contents. If you assigned a password when you protected the worksheet, you would need to enter the password to remove worksheet protection. Likewise, you can unprotect the workbook. If you need to insert a new worksheet or rename an existing worksheet, you can unprotect the protected workbook, make the changes to the structure, and then reapply workbook protection.

At this point, Sharon wants you to make additional changes to the Receipt worksheet, so you'll turn off worksheet protection in that worksheet. Later, when you've completed your modifications, Sharon can turn worksheet protection back on.

To turn off worksheet protection for the Receipt worksheet:

▶ **1.** Go to the **Receipt** worksheet.

▶ **2.** On the REVIEW tab, in the Changes group, click the **Unprotect Sheet** button. Worksheet protection is removed from the Receipt worksheet. The button changes back to the Protect Sheet button.

Inserting Comments

Comments are often used in workbooks to: (a) explain the contents of a particular cell, such as a complex formula; (b) provide instructions to users; and (c) share ideas and notes from several users collaborating on a project. The username for your installation of Excel appears in bold at the top of the comments box. If you collaborate on a workbook, the top of the comment boxes would show the name of each user who created that comment. A small red triangle appears in the upper-right corner of a cell with a comment. The comment box appears when you point to a cell with a comment.

REFERENCE

Inserting a Comment

- Select the cell to which you want to attach a comment.
- Right-click the selected cell, and then click Insert Comment on the shortcut menu (or press the Shift+F2 keys; or on the REVIEW tab, in the Comments group, click the New Comment button).
- Type the comment into the box.
- Click a cell to hide the comment.

Sharon wants you to insert a note in cell A2 about entering data from the order form into the input section, and a note in cell E34 explaining how the IF functions are used to determine whether to give the discount for early registration.

To insert comments in cells A2 and E34:

▶ **1.** In the Receipt worksheet, select cell **A2**.

▶ **2.** On the REVIEW tab, in the Comments group, click the **New Comment** button (or press the **Shift**+**F2** keys). A comment box opens to the right of cell A2. The username for your installation of Excel appears in bold at the top of the box. An arrow points from the box to the small red triangle that appears in the upper-right corner of the cell.

▶ **3.** Type **Enter all data from the order form into cells B3 through B11.** in the box. A selection box with sizing handles appears around the comment box. If the box is too small or too large for the comment, you can drag a sizing handle to increase or decrease the size of the box. See Figure 7-28.

Figure 7-28   **Comment added to cell A2**

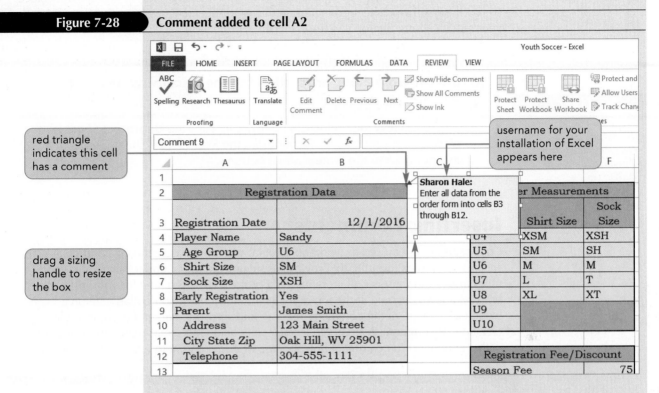

- red triangle indicates this cell has a comment
- username for your installation of Excel appears here
- drag a sizing handle to resize the box

Sharon Hale:
Enter all data from the order form into cells B3 through B12.

4. Click cell **B12** to hide the comment. The comment disappears. A small red triangle remains in the upper-right corner of cell A2 to indicate this cell contains a comment.

   Trouble? If the comment box did not disappear, comments are set to be displayed in the worksheet. On the REVIEW tab, in the Comments group, click the Show All Comments button to deselect it.

5. Move the pointer over cell **A2**. The comment appears.

6. Click cell **A2**.

7. In the Comments group, click the **Edit Comment** button. The comment appears with the insertion point at the end of the comment text, so you can edit the incorrect cell reference.

8. Select **B11** in the comment box, and then type **B12**. The comment in cell A2 now correctly references the range B3:B12.

TIP

To keep an active cell's comment displayed, click the Show/Hide Comment button in the Comments group on the REVIEW tab. Click the button again to hide the active cell's comment.

9. Select any other cell to hide the comment, and then point to cell **A2** to view the edited comment.

10. Click cell **E34**, and then on the REVIEW tab, in the Comments group, click the **New Comment** button. A comment box opens to the right of cell E34.

11. In the comment box, type **This IF function determines whether to allow the early registration discount.**

12. Select cell **E35** to hide the comment. A small red triangle remains in the upper-right corner of cell E34 to indicate it contains a comment.

13. Point to cell **E34** to see the comment.

    Sharon decides that the volunteers don't need to know how the early registration discount is calculated. You'll delete the comment in cell E34.

▶ **14.** Select cell **E34**.

▶ **15.** In the Comments group, click the **Delete** button. The comment is deleted, and the red triangle in the upper-right corner of cell E34 is removed.

The comments provide helpful information for anyone using the Receipt worksheet.

PROSKILLS

Written Communication: Documenting a Spreadsheet

Providing documentation for a spreadsheet is important because it provides instructions on the spreadsheet's use, defines technical terms, explains complex formulas, and identifies assumptions. By documenting a spreadsheet, you help users work more effectively. In addition, documentation helps you recall what is in the spreadsheet that might otherwise be forgotten months or years from now. Furthermore, when someone else becomes responsible for modifying the spreadsheet in the future, the documentation will help that person get up to speed quickly.

You can create a Documentation worksheet to provide an overview, definitions, assumptions, and instructions on how to use various parts of a workbook. Excel also offers a variety of tools to help you document spreadsheets, including:

- Defined names and structured references to make formulas easier to create and understand
- Data validation including input messages specifying what to enter in a cell, and error messages providing instructions on what to do if the data entered is incorrect
- Cell comments to explain complex formulas, give reminders, and so on
- Formula mode to view all formulas in a worksheet at one time

Providing documentation will help users better understand the application, which will save time and minimize frustration.

In this session, you used data validation to help ensure that all values entered in the Receipt worksheet are valid. You created validation rules that included input messages and error alert messages. You learned how to protect and unprotect both the worksheet and the workbook. In addition, you used comments to add notes to specific cells. In the next session, you'll automate some of the steps in the application by recording macros.

REVIEW

Session 7.2 Quick Check

1. Why would you want to validate data?
2. What is the purpose of the input message in the Data Validation command?
3. Describe the three types of error alert messages Excel can display when a user violates a validation rule.
4. What is a locked cell? What are unlocked cells?
5. What is the difference between worksheet protection and workbook protection?
6. Can you rename a protected worksheet? Explain why or why not.
7. Give two reasons for adding a comment to a worksheet cell.

Session 7.3 Visual Overview:

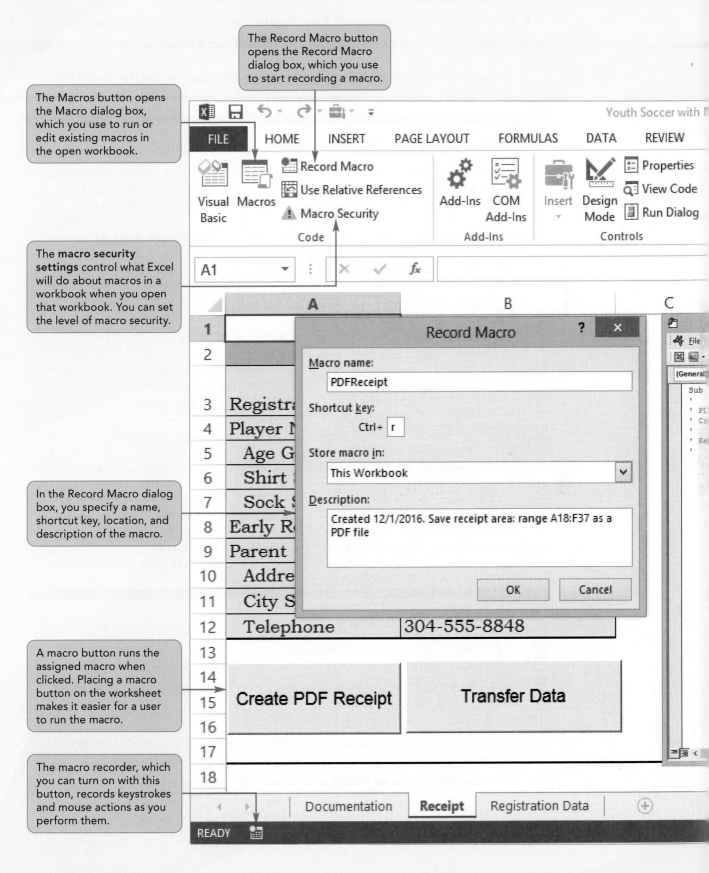

The Record Macro button opens the Record Macro dialog box, which you use to start recording a macro.

The Macros button opens the Macro dialog box, which you use to run or edit existing macros in the open workbook.

The **macro security settings** control what Excel will do about macros in a workbook when you open that workbook. You can set the level of macro security.

In the Record Macro dialog box, you specify a name, shortcut key, location, and description of the macro.

A macro button runs the assigned macro when clicked. Placing a macro button on the worksheet makes it easier for a user to run the macro.

The macro recorder, which you can turn on with this button, records keystrokes and mouse actions as you perform them.

Record Macro

Macro name:
PDFReceipt

Shortcut key:
Ctrl+ r

Store macro in:
This Workbook

Description:
Created 12/1/2016. Save receipt area: range A18:F37 as a PDF file

OK   Cancel

Create PDF Receipt   Transfer Data

Working with Macros

You can customize the ribbon by showing or hiding tabs. You need to show the DEVELOPER tab to create macros.

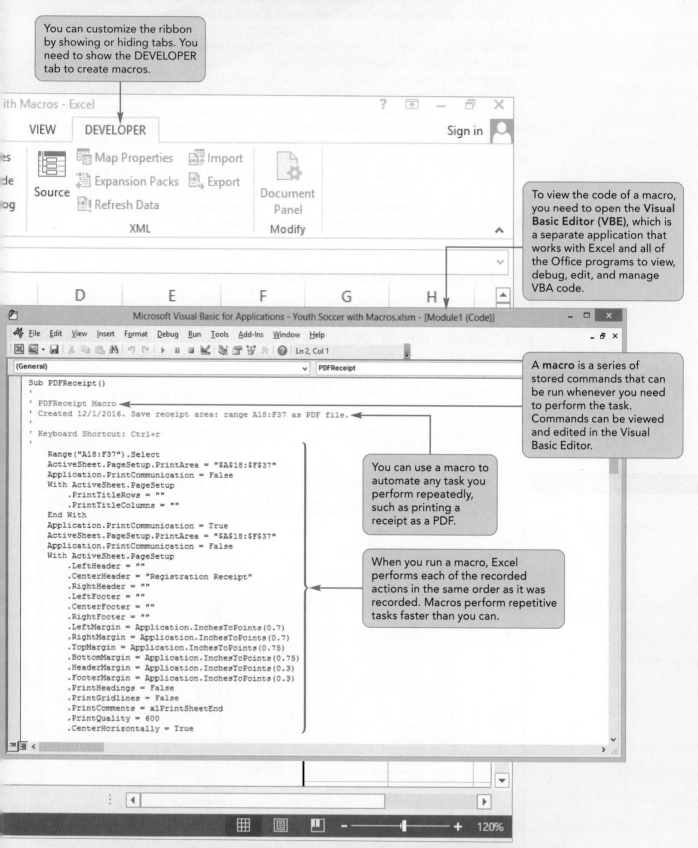

To view the code of a macro, you need to open the **Visual Basic Editor (VBE)**, which is a separate application that works with Excel and all of the Office programs to view, debug, edit, and manage VBA code.

A **macro** is a series of stored commands that can be run whenever you need to perform the task. Commands can be viewed and edited in the Visual Basic Editor.

You can use a macro to automate any task you perform repeatedly, such as printing a receipt as a PDF.

When you run a macro, Excel performs each of the recorded actions in the same order as it was recorded. Macros perform repetitive tasks faster than you can.

```
Sub PDFReceipt()
'
' PDFReceipt Macro
' Created 12/1/2016. Save receipt area: range A18:F37 as PDF file.
'
' Keyboard Shortcut: Ctrl+r
'
    Range("A18:F37").Select
    ActiveSheet.PageSetup.PrintArea = "$A$18:$F$37"
    Application.PrintCommunication = False
    With ActiveSheet.PageSetup
        .PrintTitleRows = ""
        .PrintTitleColumns = ""
    End With
    Application.PrintCommunication = True
    ActiveSheet.PageSetup.PrintArea = "$A$18:$F$37"
    Application.PrintCommunication = False
    With ActiveSheet.PageSetup
        .LeftHeader = ""
        .CenterHeader = "Registration Receipt"
        .RightHeader = ""
        .LeftFooter = ""
        .CenterFooter = ""
        .RightFooter = ""
        .LeftMargin = Application.InchesToPoints(0.7)
        .RightMargin = Application.InchesToPoints(0.7)
        .TopMargin = Application.InchesToPoints(0.75)
        .BottomMargin = Application.InchesToPoints(0.75)
        .HeaderMargin = Application.InchesToPoints(0.3)
        .FooterMargin = Application.InchesToPoints(0.3)
        .PrintHeadings = False
        .PrintGridlines = False
        .PrintComments = xlPrintSheetEnd
        .PrintQuality = 600
        .CenterHorizontally = True
```

Automating Tasks with Macros

Using a macro, you can automate any task you perform repeatedly. For example, you can create a macro to print a worksheet, insert a set of dates and values, or import data from a text file and store it in Excel. Macros perform repetitive tasks consistently and faster than you can. And, after the macro is created and tested, you can be assured the tasks are done exactly the same way each time.

Sharon wants to save the receipt portion of the worksheet as a PDF file that she can send as an attachment to the parent along with an email confirming the registration. In addition, Sharon wants data from the receipt to be transferred to the Registration Data worksheet. Sharon wants to simplify these tasks so volunteers don't need to repeat the same actions for each registration, and also to reduce the possibility of errors being introduced during the repetitive process. You will create a macro for each action.

To create and run macros, you need to use the DEVELOPER tab. The DEVELOPER tab has five groups—one for code, one for add-ins, one for controls, one for XML, and one to modify document controls. You'll use the Code group when working with macros. By default, the DEVELOPER tab is not displayed on the ribbon, so you'll display it.

To display the DEVELOPER tab on the ribbon:

1. If you took a break after the previous session, make sure the Youth Soccer workbook is open and the Receipt worksheet is active.

2. Look for the **DEVELOPER** tab on the ribbon. If you do not see it, continue with Step 3; otherwise continue with Step 7.

3. On the ribbon, click the **FILE** tab to open Backstage view, and then click **Options** in the navigation bar. The Excel Options dialog box opens.

4. In the left pane, click **Customize Ribbon**. The different commands and tabs you can add and remove from the ribbon are displayed. See Figure 7-29.

TIP

You can also right-click the ribbon and click Customize the Ribbon on the shortcut menu to add a ribbon tab.

Figure 7-29   Customize the Ribbon options in the Excel Options dialog box

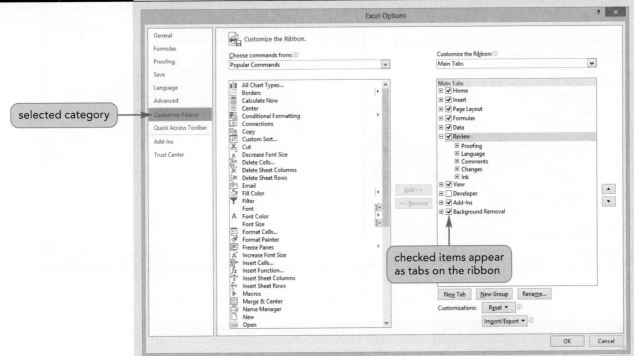

▶ **5.** In the right pane, click the **Developer** check box to insert a checkmark.

▶ **6.** Click the **OK** button. The DEVELOPER tab appears on the ribbon.

▶ **7.** On the ribbon, click the **DEVELOPER** tab. See Figure 7-30.

Figure 7-30 ▶ **DEVELOPER tab on the ribbon**

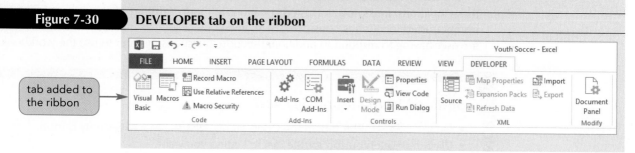

tab added to the ribbon →

Protecting Against Macro Viruses

Viruses can be and have been attached as macros to files created in Excel and other Office programs. A **virus** is a computer program designed to copy itself into other programs with the intention of causing mischief or harm. When unsuspecting users open these infected workbooks, Excel automatically runs the attached virus-infected macro. **Macro viruses** are a type of virus that uses a program's own macro programming language to distribute the virus. Macro viruses can be destructive and can modify or delete files that may not be recoverable. Because it is possible for a macro to contain a virus, Microsoft Office 2013 provides several options from which you can choose to set a security level you feel comfortable with.

Macro Security Settings

The macro security settings control what Excel will do about macros in a workbook when you open that workbook. For example, one user may choose to run macros only if they are "digitally signed" by a developer who is on a list of trusted sources. Another user might want to disable all macros in workbooks and see a notification when a workbook contains macros. The user can then elect to enable the macros. Excel has four macro security settings, which are described in Figure 7-31.

Figure 7-31 ▶ **Macro security settings**

Setting	Description
Disable all macros without notification	All macros in all workbooks are disabled and no security alerts about macros are displayed. Use this setting if you don't want macros to run.
Disable all macros with notification	All macros in all workbooks are disabled, but security alerts appear when the workbook contains a macro. Use this default setting to choose on a case-by-case basis whether to run a macro.
Disable all macros except digitally signed macros	The same as the "Disable all macros with notification" setting except any macro signed by a trusted publisher runs if you have already trusted the publisher. Otherwise, security alerts appear when a workbook contains a macro.
Enable all macros	All macros in all workbooks run. Use this setting temporarily in such cases as when developing an application that contains macros. This setting is not recommended for regular use.

© 2014 Cengage Learning

You set macro security in the Trust Center. The **Trust Center** is a central location for all of the security settings in Office. By default, all potentially dangerous content, such as macros and workbooks with external links, is blocked without warning. If content is blocked, the Message Bar (also called the trust bar) opens below the ribbon, notifying you that some content was disabled. You can click the Message Bar to enable that content.

You can place files you consider trustworthy in locations you specify; the file paths of these locations are stored as Trusted Locations in the Trust Center. Any workbook opened from a trusted location is considered safe, and content such as macros will work without the user having to respond to additional security questions in order to use the workbook.

REFERENCE

Setting Macro Security in Excel

- On the DEVELOPER tab, in the Code group, click the Macro Security button.
- Click the option button for the macro setting you want.
- Click the OK button.

or

- Click the FILE tab, and then click Options in the navigation bar (or right-click the ribbon, and then click Customize the Ribbon on the shortcut menu).
- Click the Trust Center category, and then click the Trust Center Settings button.
- Click the Macro Settings category, and then click the option button for a macro setting.
- Click the OK button.

Sharon wants the workbook to have some protection against macro viruses, so she asks you to set the security level to "Disable all macros with notification." When you open a file with macros, this macro security level disables the macros and displays a security alert, allowing you to enable the macros if you believe the workbook comes from a trusted source. After the macros are enabled, you can run them.

To set the macro security level:

▶ 1. On the DEVELOPER tab, in the Code group, click the **Macro Security** button. The Trust Center dialog box opens with the Macro Settings category displayed.

▶ 2. In the Macro Settings section, click the **Disable all macros with notification** option button if it is not already selected. See Figure 7-32.

Figure 7-32 **Macro Settings in the Trust Center dialog box**

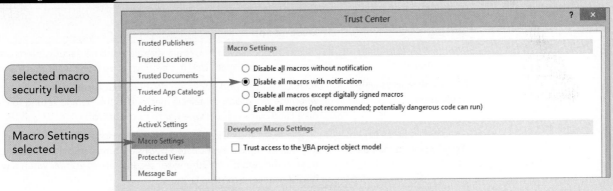

▶ 3. Click the **OK** button.

Each time you open a workbook that contains a macro detected by the Trust Center, the macro is disabled and a Message Bar containing the Security Warning that macros have been disabled appears below the ribbon. If you developed the workbook or trust the person who sent you the workbook, click the Enable Content button to run the macros in the workbook. If you do not click the Enable Content button, you cannot run the macros in the workbook, but you can use the rest of the workbook.

INSIGHT

Using Digital Signatures with Macros

A **digital signature** is like a seal of approval. It is often used to identify the author of a workbook that contains macros. You add a digital signature as the last step before you distribute a file. Before you can add a digital signature to a workbook, you need to obtain a digital ID (also called a digital certificate) that proves your identity. Digital certificates are typically issued by a certificate authority. After you have a digital certificate, do the following to digitally sign a workbook:

- On the ribbon, click the FILE tab, and then, in the navigation bar, click Info.
- On the Info screen, click the Protect Workbook button, and then click Add a Digital Signature.
- If a dialog box opens asking if you would like to get a digital ID from a Microsoft Partner, click the Yes button. Your browser opens to a website with information about digital signature providers and available digital IDs.
- Read the information.
- Select a provider and follow the steps to obtain a digital ID from that provider.

By digitally signing a workbook that contains a macro you intend to publicly distribute, you assure others (1) of the identity of the creator of the macro; and (2) that the macro has not been altered since the digital signature was created. When you open a digitally signed file, you can see who the author is, and decide whether the information in the file is authentic and whether you trust that the macros in the workbook are safe to run.

The digital signature is removed any time a file with a digital signature is saved. This ensures that no one (including the original workbook author) can open a digitally signed file, make changes to the workbook, save the workbook, and then send the file to another user with the digital signature intact.

Recording a Macro

You can create an Excel macro in one of two ways: You can use the macro recorder to record keystrokes and mouse actions as you perform them, or you can enter a series of commands in the **Visual Basic for Applications (VBA)** programming language. The macro recorder can record only those actions you perform with the keyboard or mouse. The macro recorder is a good choice for creating simple macros. For more sophisticated macros, you might need to write VBA code directly in the Visual Basic Editor (VBE).

For Sharon's application, the actions you need to perform can all be done with the keyboard and the mouse, so you will use the macro recorder to record the two macros. One macro will save the receipt as a PDF file, which is a file format created by Adobe Systems for document exchange. The second macro will transfer data from the Receipt worksheet to the Registration Data worksheet.

PROSKILLS

Decision Making: Planning and Recording a Macro

Advance planning and practice help to ensure you create an error-free macro. First, decide what you want to accomplish. Then, consider the best way to achieve those results. Next, practice the keystrokes and mouse actions before you actually record the macro. This may seem like extra work, but it reduces the chance of error when you actually record the macro. As you set up the macro, consider the following:

- Choose a descriptive name that helps you recognize the macro's purpose.
- Weigh the benefits of selecting a shortcut key against its drawbacks. Although a shortcut key is an easy way to run a macro, you are limited to one-letter shortcuts, which can make it difficult to remember the purpose of each shortcut key. In addition, the macro shortcut keys will override the standard Office shortcuts for the workbook.
- Store the macro with the current workbook unless the macro can be used with other workbooks.
- Include a description that provides an overview of the macro and perhaps your name and contact information.

Good decision making includes thinking about what to do and what not to do as you progress to your goals. This is true when developing a macro as well.

Each macro must have a unique name that begins with a letter. The macro name can contain up to 255 characters, including letters, numbers, and the underscore symbol. The macro name cannot include spaces or special characters. It is helpful to use a descriptive name that describes the macro's purpose.

Macro shortcut keys are used to run a macro directly from the keyboard. You can assign a shortcut key to run the macro by selecting the Ctrl key plus a letter or the Ctrl+Shift keys plus a letter. If you use the same set of shortcut keys that are already assigned to a default Excel shortcut, the new shortcut you create overrides the default Excel shortcut for the open workbook. For example, using the Ctrl+p keys to run a macro overrides the default Excel 2013 shortcut for opening the Print screen while the workbook containing the macro is open. Some people find macro shortcut keys a quick way to run a macro; others dislike them because they override the original function of the shortcut key. It's a personal preference.

A macro needs to be stored somewhere. By default, the macro is stored in the current workbook, making the macro available in only that workbook when it is open. Another option is to store the macro in the **Personal Macro workbook**, a hidden workbook named PERSONAL.xlsb that opens whenever you start Excel, making the macro available any time you use Excel. The Personal Macro workbook stores commonly used macros that apply to many workbooks. It is most convenient for users on stand-alone computers. Finally, you can store the macro in a new workbook. Keep in mind that the new workbook must be open in order to use the macro. For example, an accountant might store a set of macros that help with end-of-the-month tasks in a separate workbook.

You can also add a description of the macro to briefly explain what it does. The description can also include the name of the person to contact and the date it was created.

Recording a Macro

- On the DEVELOPER tab, in the Code group, click the Record Macro button.
- Enter a name for the macro.
- Specify a shortcut key (optional).
- Specify the location to store the macro.
- Enter a description of the macro (optional).
- Click the OK button to start the macro recorder.
- Perform the tasks you want to automate.
- Click the Stop Recording button.

Sharon provided you with the following outline of the actions needed for the macro to save the receipt as a PDF file:

1. Set the range A18:F37 as the print area for the Registration Receipt.
2. Create the custom header "Registration Receipt" centered horizontally on the page.
3. Create the PDF file and name it "Receipt."
4. Remove the custom header and horizontal centering from the page.
5. Remove the print area.
6. Make cell A1 the active cell.

You'll record the steps for this macro using a macro named PDFReceipt that is assigned a keyboard shortcut, has a description, and is stored in the Youth Soccer workbook. Practice these steps before recording the macro. Once you feel comfortable with the steps, you can start the macro recorder.

To start the macro recorder:

1. Save the Youth Soccer workbook. If you make a mistake when recording the macro, you can close the workbook without saving, reopen the workbook, and then record the macro again.

> Save the workbook before recording a macro in case you make a mistake and need to restart.

2. On the DEVELOPER tab, in the Code group, click the **Record Macro** button. The Record Macro dialog box opens. The Macro name box displays a default name for the macro that consists of the word "Macro" followed by a number that is one greater than the number of macros already recorded in the workbook during the current Excel session. See Figure 7-33.

Figure 7-33   Record Macro dialog box

enter a descriptive macro name

select the location to store the macro

enter a description of the macro (optional)

enter a shortcut key (optional)

> **3.** In the Macro name box, type **PDFReceipt** to change the selected default name to a more descriptive one, and then press the **Tab** key.

> **4.** In the Shortcut key box, type **r** to set the Ctrl+r keys as the shortcut to run the macro from the keyboard, and then press the **Tab** key.

> **5.** Verify that the Store macro in box is set to **This Workbook** to store the macro in the Youth Soccer workbook, and then press the **Tab** key.

> **6.** In the Description box, type **Created 12/1/2016. Save receipt area, range A18:F37, as PDF file.** to enter notes about the macro.

> **7.** Click the **OK** button. The workbook enters macro record mode. The Record Macro button changes to the Stop Recording button, which also appears on the status bar.

From this point on, *every* mouse click and keystroke you perform will be recorded and stored as part of the PDFReceipt macro. For that reason, it is very important to follow the instructions in the next steps precisely. Take your time as you perform each step, reading the entire step carefully first. After you finish recording the keystrokes, click the Stop Recording button to turn off the macro recorder.

To record the PDFReceipt macro:

> **1.** Select the range **A18:F37**. This range contains the receipt that you want to print.

> **2.** On the ribbon, click the **PAGE LAYOUT** tab.

> **3.** In the Page Setup group, click the **Print Area** button, and then click **Set Print Area**. The receipt is set as the print area. Next, you'll insert a custom header.

> **4.** In the Page Setup group, click the **Dialog Box Launcher** to open the Page Setup dialog box.

> **5.** Click the **Header/Footer** tab, and then click the **Custom Header** button to open the Header dialog box.

> **6.** Click in the **Center section** box, type **Registration Receipt**, and then click the **OK** button to close the Header dialog box.

> **7.** In the Page Setup dialog box, click the **Margins** tab, click the **Horizontally** check box to select it, and then click the **OK** button. The receipt is centered on the page.

> **8.** On the ribbon, click the **FILE** tab to open Backstage view, and then click **Export** in the navigation bar.

> **9.** On the Export screen, make sure **Create PDF/XPS Document** is selected in the left pane, and then click the **Create PDF/XPS** button in the right pane. The Publish as PDF or XPS dialog box opens, which is similar to the Save As dialog box.

> **10.** In the File name box, type **Receipt** to replace the suggested filename.

> **11.** Make sure the folder is set to the location specified by your instructor.

> **12.** Click the **Publish** button. The receipt is saved as a PDF file, and automatically opens in a PDF reader, such as Windows Reader, Adobe Reader, or Adobe Acrobat, depending on which program is installed on your computer.

> **Trouble?** If the receipt doesn't open, you probably don't have a PDF reader installed on your computer. Continue with Step 14.

▶ **13.** Close the PDF file, and then return to the desktop (if necessary). You should now see the Receipt worksheet in the Youth Soccer workbook.

▶ **14.** On the PAGE LAYOUT tab, in the Page Setup group, click the **Print Area** button, and then click **Clear Print Area**.

▶ **15.** In the Page Setup group, click the **Dialog Box Launcher** to open the Page Setup dialog box, click the **Header/Footer** tab, and then click the **Custom Header** button to open the Header dialog box.

▶ **16.** Click in the **Center section** box, delete the custom header, and then click the **OK** button to close the Header dialog box.

▶ **17.** In the Page Setup dialog box, click the **Margins** tab, click the **Horizontally** check box so that the printout is no longer centered on the page, and then click the **OK** button.

▶ **18.** In the Receipt worksheet, click cell **A1**.

You have completed all of the steps in the PDFReceipt macro. You'll turn off the macro recorder.

▶ **19.** Click the **Stop Recording** button ☐ on the status bar. The macro recorder turns off, and the button changes to the Record Macro button.

Trouble? If you made a mistake while recording the macro, close the Youth Soccer workbook without saving. If you got past the creation of the Registration Receipt, you will need to delete the Receipt file that you created.

Reopen the workbook, and then repeat all of the steps beginning with the "To start the macro recorder" steps.

Be aware that the process for saving a workbook that contains a macro is different from saving one that does not contain a macro. If you need to save the workbook before you complete this session, refer to the "Saving a Workbook with Macros" section later in this session.

Running a Macro

After you record a macro, you should run it to test whether it works as intended. Running a macro means Excel performs each of the steps in the same order as when it was recorded. To run the macro you created, you can either use the shortcut key you specified or select the macro in the Macro dialog box. The Macro dialog box lists all of the macros in the open workbooks. From this dialog box, you can select and run a macro, edit the macro with VBA, run the macro one step at a time so you can determine in which step an error occurs, or delete it.

REFERENCE

Running a Macro

• Press the shortcut key assigned to the macro.

or

• On the DEVELOPER tab, in the Code group, click the Macros button.
• Select the macro from the list of macros.
• Click the Run button.

You will test the PDFReceipt macro by running it.

To run the PDFReceipt macro:

▶ **1.** On the ribbon, click the **DEVELOPER** tab.

▶ **2.** In the Code group, click the **Macros** button. The Macro dialog box opens, listing all of the macros in the open workbooks. See Figure 7-34.

Figure 7-34   **Macro dialog box**

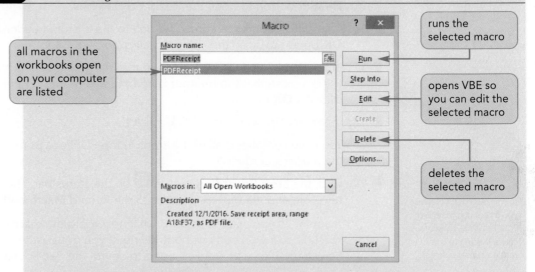

all macros in the workbooks open on your computer are listed

runs the selected macro

opens VBE so you can edit the selected macro

deletes the selected macro

▶ **3.** Verify that **PDFReceipt** is selected in the Macro name box, and then click the **Run** button. The PDFReceipt macro runs. The receipt is saved as a PDF file and the file is opened in Adobe Reader or Adobe Acrobat.

▶ **4.** Close Adobe Reader or Adobe Acrobat. No print area is selected, and cell A1 is the active cell in the Receipt worksheet.

Trouble? If the PDFReceipt macro did not run properly, you might have made a mistake in the steps while recording the macro. On the DEVELOPER tab, in the Code group, click the Macros button. Select the PDFReceipt macro, and then click the Delete button. Click the OK button to confirm the deletion, and then repeat all of the steps beginning with the "To start the macro recorder" steps.

Next, you will test the shortcut keys you used for the PDFReceipt macro.

▶ **5.** Press the **Ctrl+r** keys. The PDFReceipt macro runs. The receipt is saved as a PDF file. No print area is selected, and cell A1 in the Receipt worksheet is the active cell.

▶ **6.** Close Adobe Reader or Adobe Acrobat.

Trouble? If your macro doesn't end on its own, you need to end it. Press the Ctrl+Break keys to stop the macro from running.

The macro works as expected, printing the receipt as a PDF file.

How Edits Can Affect Macros

Be careful when making seemingly small changes to a workbook, as these can have a great impact on macros. If a run-time error (an error that occurs while running a macro) appears when you run a macro that has worked in the past, some part of the macro code no longer makes sense to Excel. For example, simply adding a space to a worksheet name can affect a macro that references the worksheet. If you recorded a macro that referenced a worksheet named RegistrationData (no spaces in the name) that you later changed to Registration Data (space added to the name), the macro no longer works because the RegistrationData worksheet no longer exists. You could record the macro again, or you could edit the macro in VBA by changing RegistrationData to Registration Data.

Creating the TransferData Macro

You need to record one more macro. The data you entered earlier in the input section of the Receipt worksheet was never added to the Registration Data worksheet. Sharon wants to add this data to the next available blank row in the Registration Data worksheet. You'll record another macro to do this. You may want to practice the following steps before recording the macro:

1. Go to the Registration Data worksheet.
2. Turn off worksheet protection in the Registration Data worksheet.
3. Switch to the Receipt worksheet.
4. Select and copy the Transfer Area to the Clipboard.
5. Go to the Registration Data worksheet.
6. Go to cell A1, and then go to the last row in the Registration Data area.
7. Turn on Use Relative References. The Use Relative Reference button controls how Excel records the act of selecting a range in the worksheet. By default, the macro will select the same cells regardless of which cell is first selected because the macro records a selection using absolute cell references. If you want a macro to select cells regardless of the position of the active cell when you run the macro, set the macro recorder to record relative cell references.
8. Move down one row.
9. Turn off Use Relative References.
10. Paste values to the Registration Data worksheet.
11. Go to cell A1.
12. Turn on worksheet protection.
13. Switch to the Receipt worksheet, and then make cell B3 the active cell.

You may want to practice these steps before recording the macro. Sharon wants you to name this new macro "TransferData" and assign the Ctrl+t keys as the shortcut.

To record the TransferData macro:

▶ 1. Click the **Record Macro** button 🔳 on the status bar to open the Record Macro dialog box, type **TransferData** in the Macro name box, type **t** in the Shortcut key box, type **Created 12/1/2016. Copy values in the transfer area in the Receipt worksheet to the Registration Data worksheet.** in the Description box, and then click the **OK** button. The macro recorder is on.

▶ 2. Go to the **Registration Data** worksheet.

▶ 3. Click the **REVIEW** tab on the ribbon, and then click the **Unprotect Sheet** button in the Changes group to turn off protection.

To view the code for the PDFReceipt macro:

▶ **1.** On the ribbon, click the **DEVELOPER** tab.

▶ **2.** In the Code group, click the **Macros** button. The Macro dialog box opens.

▶ **3.** Click **PDFReceipt** in the Macro name list, and then click the **Edit** button. The Visual Basic Editor opens as a separate program, consisting of two windows—the Project Explorer and the Code window.

▶ **4.** If the Code window is not maximized, click the **Maximize** button ☐ on the Code window title bar. The Code window contains the VBA code generated by the macro recorder. You will see the beginning of the PDFReceipt sub. See Figure 7-35 (your window may differ).

Figure 7-35   **Visual Basic for Applications Editor window**

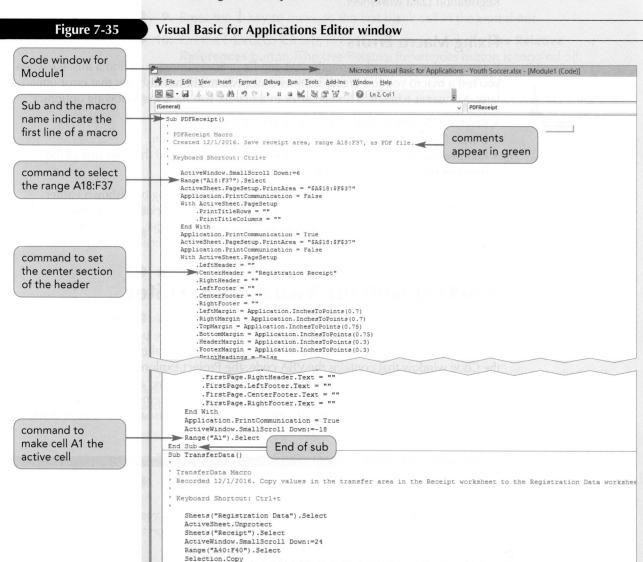

Code window for Module1

Sub and the macro name indicate the first line of a macro

command to select the range A18:F37

command to set the center section of the header

command to make cell A1 the active cell

comments appear in green

End of sub

Trouble? If you see a different number of windows in the Visual Basic Editor, your computer is configured differently. You will be working with the Code window, so you can ignore any other windows.

Understanding the Structure of Macros

The VBA code in the Code window lists all of the actions you performed when recording the PDFReceipt macro. In VBA, macros are called **sub procedures**. Each sub procedure begins with the keyword *Sub* followed by the name of the sub procedure and a set of parentheses. In the example in Figure 7-35, the code begins with

```
Sub PDFReceipt()
```

which provides the name of this sub procedure—PDFReceipt—the name you gave the macro. The parentheses are used to include any arguments in the procedure. These arguments pass information to the sub procedure and have roughly the same purpose as the arguments in an Excel function. If you write your own VBA code, sub procedure arguments are an important part of the programming process. However, they are not used when you create macros with the macro recorder.

Following the `Sub PDFReceipt()` statement are comments about the macro taken from the macro name, shortcut key, and description you entered in the Record Macro dialog box. Each line appears in green and is preceded by an apostrophe ('). The apostrophe indicates that the line is a comment and does not include any actions Excel needs to perform.

After the comments is the body of the macro, a listing of all of the commands performed by the PDFReceipt macro as written in the VBA language. Your list of commands might look slightly different, depending on the exact actions you performed when recording the macro. Even though you might not know VBA, some of the commands are easy to interpret. For example, near the top of the PDFReceipt macro, you should see the command:

```
Range("A18:F37").Select
```

which tells Excel to select the range A18:F37. Several lines below this command you see the following command, which sets the words "Registration Receipt" at the top of the print page in the center of the custom header:

```
.CenterHeader = "Registration Receipt"
```

At the bottom of the macro is the following statement, which indicates the end of the PDFReceipt sub procedure:

```
End Sub
```

A Code window can contain several sub procedures, with each procedure separated from the others by the `SubProcedureName()` statement at the beginning, and the End Sub statement at the end. Sub procedures are organized into **modules**. As was shown in Figure 7-35, all of the macros that have been recorded are stored in the Module1 module (your window may differ).

Editing a Macro Using the Visual Basic Editor

The Visual Basic Editor provides tools to assist you in writing error-free code. As you type a command, the editor will provide pop-up windows and text to help you insert the correct code.

Sharon wants you to edit the following command in the PDFReceipt sub procedure, which sets the active cell to cell A1:

```
Range("A1").Select
```

You'll change the command to

```
Range("B3").Select
```

to change the active cell from cell A1 to cell B3.

To edit a command in the macro:

▶ **1.** Scroll down the Code window to the line immediately before `End Sub` in the PDFReceipt macro.

▶ **2.** In the line with the command `Range("A1")`, select **A1**, and then type **B3**. The command in the macro is edited to select a different cell. See Figure 7-36.

Figure 7-36	Edited Macro

```
            .FirstPage.RightHeader.Text = ""
            .FirstPage.LeftFooter.Text = ""
            .FirstPage.CenterFooter.Text = ""
            .FirstPage.RightFooter.Text = ""
        End With
        Application.PrintCommunication = True
        ActiveWindow.SmallScroll Down:=-18
        Range("B3").Select
    End Sub
    Sub TransferData()
    '
    ' TransferData Macro
    ' Recorded 12/1/2016. Copy values in the transfer area in the Receipt worksheet to the Registration
    '
    ' Keyboard Shortcut: Ctrl+t
    '
        Sheets("Registration Data").Select
        ActiveSheet.Unprotect
        Sheets("Receipt").Select
        ActiveWindow.SmallScroll Down:=24
        Range("A40:F40").Select
        Selection.Copy
```

cell reference changed from A1 to B3

▶ **3.** On the menu bar, click **File**, and then click **Close and Return to Microsoft Excel**. The Visual Basic Editor closes, and the Youth Soccer workbook is displayed.

Sharon wants you to test the macro. You'll check to see whether cell B3 is the active cell once the macro has run.

To test the edited PDFReceipt macro:

▶ **1.** Press the **Ctrl+r** keys. The PDFReceipt macro runs.

Trouble? If a Microsoft Visual Basic message box appears with a run-time error, click the End button, click the Macros button, click PDFReceipt in the Macro name box, and then click the Edit button. In the Code window, find the line you edited (one line above End Sub), and then change it to `Range("B3").Select`. On the menu bar, click File, and then click Close and Return to Microsoft Excel.

▶ **2.** Close Adobe Reader. Cell B3 is the active cell.

Creating Macro Buttons

Another way to run a macro is to assign it to a button placed directly in the worksheet. Macro buttons are often a better way to run macros than shortcut keys. Clicking a button (with a descriptive label) is often more intuitive and simpler for users than trying to remember different combinations of keystrokes.

REFERENCE

Creating a Macro Button

- On the DEVELOPER tab, in the Controls group, click the Insert button.
- In the Form Controls section, click the Button (Form Control) button.
- Click the worksheet where you want the macro button to be located, drag the pointer until the button is the size and shape you want, and then release the mouse button.
- In the Assign Macro dialog box, select the macro you want to assign to the button.
- With the button still selected, type a new label.

Sharon wants you to add two macro buttons to the Receipt worksheet—one for each of the macros you've created. You will create the macro buttons in the blank range A14:B16 so they don't obscure any existing data.

To insert a macro button in the worksheet:

1. Scroll so that the range **A14:B16** of the Receipt worksheet is completely visible.

2. On the DEVELOPER tab, in the Controls group, click the **Insert** button. The Form Controls appear, with a variety of objects that can be placed in the worksheet. You'll insert the Button form control. See Figure 7-37.

| Figure 7-37 | Form Controls |

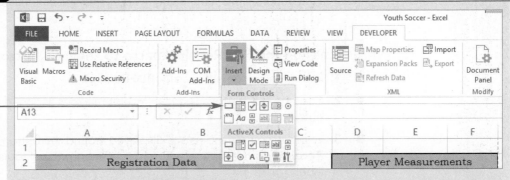

inserts a button on the worksheet

Trouble? If the Insert button is unavailable, the worksheet is protected. Click the REVIEW tab. In the Changes group, click the Unprotect Sheet button to unprotect the Receipt worksheet, and then repeat Step 2.

3. In the Form Controls section, click the **Button (Form Control)** button ⬚, and then point to cell **A14**. The pointer changes to +.

4. Click and drag the pointer over the range **A14:A16**, and then release the mouse button. A button appears on the worksheet. The Assign Macro dialog box opens with the button's default name in the Macro name box. See Figure 7-38.

Figure 7-38   Assign Macro dialog box

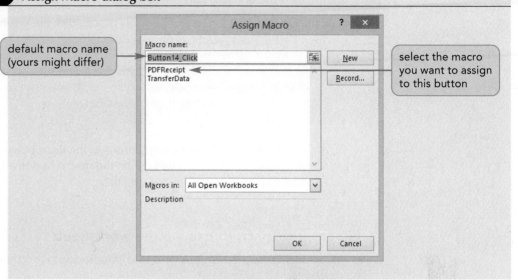

From the Assign Macro dialog box, you can assign a macro to the button. After you assign a macro to the button, the button appears with a default label. You can change the default label to a descriptive one that will indicate which macro will run when the button is clicked.

Sharon wants you to assign the PDFReceipt macro to this new button, and then rename the button with a label that reflects the PDFReceipt macro.

To assign the PDFReceipt macro to the new button:

1. In the Macro name box, click **PDFReceipt**.

2. Click the **OK** button. The PDFReceipt macro is assigned to the selected button.

3. With the sizing handles still displayed around the button, type **Create PDF Receipt** (do not press the Enter key). The new label replaces the default label.

    Trouble? If no sizing handles appear around the button, the button is not selected. Right-click the button, click Edit Text to place the insertion point within the button, and then repeat Step 3.

    Trouble? If a new line appeared in the button, you pressed the Enter key after entering the label. Press the Backspace key to delete the line, and then continue with Step 4.

4. Click any cell in the worksheet to deselect the macro button.

At this point, if you click the Create PDF Receipt button, the PDFReceipt macro will run. Before you test the Create PDF Receipt button, you will add the other button.

To add another macro button to the Receipt worksheet:

1. On the DEVELOPER tab, in the Controls group, click the **Insert** button, and then click the **Button (Form Control)** button ▭.

2. Drag the pointer over the range **B14:B16**.

3. In the Assign Macro dialog box, click **TransferData** in the Macro name box, and then click the **OK** button.

4. Type **Transfer Data** as the button label, and then click any cell in the worksheet to deselect the button. See Figure 7-39.

TIP

To move or resize a macro button, right-click it, press the Esc key, and then drag a sizing handle or the selection box.

Figure 7-39   **Macro buttons on Receipt worksheet**

			Age Group	Shirt Size	Sock Size
3	Registration Date	12/1/2016			
4	Player Name	Jason	U4	XSM	XSH
5	Age Group	U10	U5	SM	SH
6	Shirt Size	XL	U6	M	M
7	Sock Size	XT	U7	L	T
8	Early Registration	No	U8	XL	XT
9	Parent	Sofia Kilmer	U9		
10	Address	294 Hott Street	U10		
11	City State Zip	Moorefield, WV 26836			
12	Telephone	304-555-3444	Registration Fee/Discount		
13			Season Fee		75
14			Discount Amount		5
15	Create PDF Receipt	Transfer Data			
16					
17					
18					

Documentation | **Receipt** | Registration Data | ⊕

READY

macro buttons added to the worksheet

Trouble? If the macro buttons on your screen do not match the size and location of the buttons shown in the figure, right-click a button to select it, press the Esc key to close the shortcut menu, and then resize or reposition the button on the worksheet as needed.

You have completed the application, so you will reset worksheet protection.

5. On the ribbon, click the **REVIEW** tab.

6. In the Changes group, click the **Protect Sheet** button. The Protect Sheet dialog box opens.

7. Click the **OK** button to turn on worksheet protection.

You have completed the Create PDF Receipt and TransferData macro buttons.

Creating a Macro Button with Pictures or Shapes

You are not restricted to using the control buttons on the DEVELOPER tab for macro buttons. A macro can also be assigned to a picture or shape. For example, sometimes you might want to assign to an arrow a macro that takes you to another worksheet.

1. On the INSERT tab, in the Illustrations group, click the button for the picture, online picture, or shape you want to use for a macro button.
2. Drag the pointer over the range where you want to insert the picture or shape on the worksheet.
3. Resize and position the picture or shape as needed.
4. Right-click the picture or shape, and then click Edit Text on the shortcut menu to add a name to the button.
5. Change the style, fill, and outline of the picture or shape as needed.
6. Right-click the picture or shape, and then click Assign Macro on the shortcut menu. The Assign Macro dialog box opens.
7. In the Macro name box, select the macro you want to assign to the button, and then click the OK button.

No matter what picture or shape you use for the macro button, the macro runs when the button is clicked.

Sharon has a new season registration to add to the worksheet. You'll enter this data and then test the Create PDF Receipt and TransferData macro buttons.

To test the macro buttons:

1. In the range **B3:B12**, enter the following subscriber order:

   12/2/2016

   Noah

   U8

   M

   M

   Yes

   Christopher Miller

   1231 Viking Avenue

   Wheeling, WV 26003

   304-555-8848

2. Click the **Create PDF Receipt** button to save the current receipt as a PDF file. See Figure 7-40.

Figure 7-40   PDF file created from the PDFReceipt macro

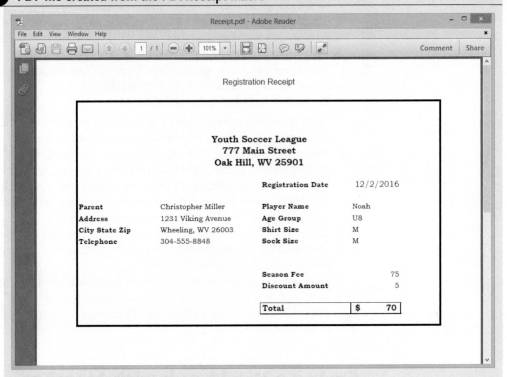

- **3.** Close Adobe Reader to return to the Receipt worksheet.
- **4.** Click the **Transfer Data** button to transfer data to the Registration Data worksheet. Excel inserts the new transaction in the table.
- **5.** Go to the **Registration Data** worksheet and make sure the data was transferred. See Figure 7-41.

Figure 7-41   Data transferred to the Registration Data worksheet with the TransferData macro

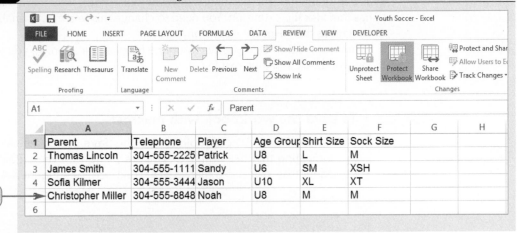

new record inserted

The macro buttons make it simpler to create the receipt and transfer the data from the Receipt worksheet into the Registration Data worksheet.

INSIGHT

Making Data Entry Easier with a Data Form

When a lot of data needs to be entered, consider creating a data form. A data form is a dialog box that lists the labels and entry boxes from an Excel table or structured range of data in a worksheet. Data forms can be helpful when people who are unfamiliar with Excel need to enter the data. They can also be useful when a worksheet is very wide and requires repeated horizontal scrolling.

To create a data form, do the following:

1. Make sure each column in the structured range of data or the Excel table has column headers. These headers become the labels for each field on the form.
2. Add the Form button to the Quick Access Toolbar. Click the Customize Quick Access Toolbar button, and then click More Commands. In the Quick Access Toolbars options, click the Choose commands from arrow, click Commands Not in the Ribbon, click the Form button in the box, click the Add button, and then click the OK button. The Form button appears on the Quick Access Toolbar.
3. Select the range or table for which you want to create the data form.
4. On the Quick Access Toolbar, click the Form button. The data form opens with the selected fields ready for data entry.
5. Enter data in each box, and then click the New button to add the complete record to end of the range or table and create a new record.
6. Click the Close button to close the data form.

Saving a Workbook with Macros

When you save a workbook that contains macros, a dialog box opens indicating that the workbook you are trying to save contains features that cannot be saved in a macro-free workbook. The default Excel workbook does not allow macros to be stored as part of the file. If you want to save the workbook without the macros, click the Yes button. The workbook will be saved as a macro-free workbook, which means the macros you created will be lost. If you want to save the workbook with the macros, click the No button, and then save the workbook as a new file—one that allows macros to be saved as part of the file. The default Excel Workbook format, which is a macro-free workbook, has the .xlsx file extension. You need to change this to a macro-enabled workbook, which has the .xlsm file extension.

You have completed your work on the Excel application, so you will save and close the workbook and then exit Excel.

To save the workbook with macros:

▶ 1. On the Quick Access Toolbar, click the **Save** button 🔒. A dialog box opens indicating that the workbook you are trying to save contains features that cannot be saved in a macro-free workbook. See Figure 7-42.

Figure 7-42	Macro warning dialog box

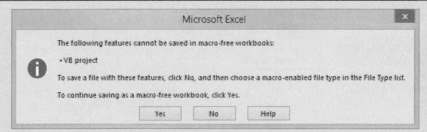

▶ **2.** Click the **No** button. The Save As dialog box opens so you can save the workbook as a macro-enabled workbook.

▶ **3.** In the File name box, type **Youth Soccer with Macros** so you can easily determine which workbook contains macros.

▶ **4.** Click the **Save as type** button, and then click **Excel Macro-Enabled Workbook**.

▶ **5.** Navigate to the location where you saved the files you created in this tutorial.

▶ **6.** Click the **Save** button. The workbook is saved with the macros.

▶ **7.** Close the workbook.

Opening a Workbook with Macros

TIP

After you enable the content, the filename is added to a list of trusted files and the Security Warning will not reappear as long as the workbook name or location is not changed.

When you open a file with macros, Excel checks the opening workbook to see if it contains any macros. The response you see is based on the security level set on the computer. Earlier, you disabled all macros with notification. Therefore, all of the macros will be disabled when the workbook opens. When the workbook opens the first time, a SECURITY WARNING appears in the Message Bar providing the option to enable the macros so they can be run, or to open the workbook with the macros disabled. If you know a workbook contains macros that you or a coworker created, you can enable them, which adds the filename to a list of trusted files so that you won't see the SECURITY WARNING when you open this file again. If you do not click the Enable Content button, the macros remain disabled and unavailable during the current session, but the other features of the workbook are still available.

You'll open the Youth Soccer with Macros workbook and enable the macros.

To open the Youth Soccer with Macros workbook and enable the macros:

▶ **1.** Open the **Youth Soccer with Macros** workbook. The workbook opens, and "SECURITY WARNING Macros have been disabled." appears in the Message Bar below the ribbon. See Figure 7-43.

Figure 7-43   **SECURITY WARNING in the Message Bar**

SECURITY WARNING appears when opening a workbook that contains macros

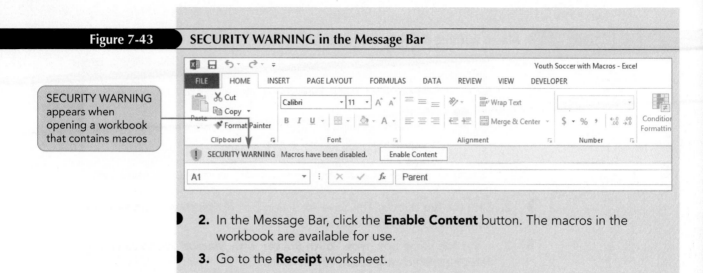

> **2.** In the Message Bar, click the **Enable Content** button. The macros in the workbook are available for use.

> **3.** Go to the **Receipt** worksheet.

Removing a Tab from the Ribbon

If you decide you don't want a tab displayed on the ribbon, you can remove it. Now that the macros are completed, Sharon doesn't need the DEVELOPER tab to appear on the ribbon. You will remove it.

To remove the DEVELOPER tab from the ribbon:

> **1.** Right-click any tab on the ribbon, and then click **Customize the Ribbon** on the shortcut menu. The Excel Options dialog box opens with the Customize Ribbon options displayed.

> **2.** In the right box listing the Main Tabs, click the **Developer** check box to remove the checkmark.

> **3.** Click the **OK** button. The DEVELOPER tab is removed from the ribbon.

> **4.** Save the workbook, and then close it.

Sharon is pleased with your work on the Youth Soccer workbook. The workbook protection and macros will streamline the data entry process for volunteers.

Session 7.3 Quick Check

REVIEW

1. Which tab must be displayed on the ribbon in order to record a macro?
2. What types of actions should you record as a macro?
3. Describe two ways of creating a macro.
4. What are the three places in which you can store a macro?
5. Identify two ways to run a macro.
6. What are the steps to edit a macro?
7. How do you insert a macro button into a worksheet?
8. What happens when you save a workbook with the .xlsx extension and it contains a macro?

Review Assignments

Data File needed for the Review Assignments: TBall.xlsx

You did such a good job helping Sharon with the Youth Soccer application that she recommended you to a friend, Terry Winkel, who has a similar project within the youth sports community. Terry wants to create a receipt system for the Youth T-Ball league. Complete the following:

1. Open the **TBall** workbook located in the Excel7 ▶ Review folder included with your Data Files, and then save the workbook as **Youth TBall** in the location specified by your instructor.
2. In the Documentation worksheet, enter your name and the date.
3. In the Receipt worksheet, do the following:
   a. Create defined names from selection using the range A3:B11 to name all of the input cells.
   b. Change the defined name Address to **Street_Address**.
   c. Use the Name box to create the defined name **Player_Sizes** for the range D2:E8.
   d. Paste the list of defined names in the Documentation worksheet.
4. Create the validation rules shown in Figure 7-44 for the range B5:B7.

| Figure 7-44 | Validation rules for cells B5, B6, and B7 | | |

Cell	Settings	Input Message	Error Alert
B5	List Source (4YO, 5-6YO)	Title: Age Group Message: Click arrow to select the player's age group.	Style: Stop Title: Invalid Age Group Message: Invalid Age Group. Use arrow to select Age Group.
B6	List Source (D4:D8)	Title: Shirt Size Message: Click arrow to select shirt size.	Style: Stop Title: Invalid Shirt Size Message: Invalid Shirt Size. Use arrow to select Shirt Size.
B7	List Source (D4:D7)	Title: Hat Size Message: Click arrow to select hat size.	Style: Stop Title: Invalid Hat Size Message: Invalid Hat Size. Use arrow to select Hat Size.

© 2014 Cengage Learning

5. In the range B3:B11, enter the data shown in Figure 7-45.

Figure 7-45	Registration Data

Registration Date	12/1/2016
Player Name	Nicole
Age Group	5-6YO
Shirt Size	SM
Hat Size	SM
Parent	Jason Headley
Address	1154 Wallenberg Place
City State Zip	Oak Hill, WV 25901
Telephone	304-555-3456

© 2014 Cengage Learning

Figure 7-46   Validation rules for the range B4:B9

Cell	Validation	Input Message	Error Alert
B4	List Source (A2:A10 on Data Tables worksheet)	Title: Major Message: Click arrow to select major.	Type: Stop Title: Invalid Major Message: Invalid Major. Use arrow to select Major.
B5	Whole number greater than or equal to 2012	Title: Year of Study Message: Enter a year of study greater than or equal to 2012 (the starting year of the program).	Type: Stop Title: Invalid Year of Study Message: Invalid Year of Study. Enter a year of study greater than or equal to 2012 (the starting year of the program).
B6	List Source (FA, SP, SU)	Title: Semester of Study Message: Click arrow to select semester of study.	Type: Stop Title: Invalid Semester of Study Message: Invalid Semester of Study. Use arrow to select Semester of Study.
B7	List Source (C2:C11 on Data Tables worksheet)	Title: Country Message: Click arrow to select country.	Type: Stop Title: Invalid Country Message: Invalid Country. Use arrow to select Country.
B8	List Source (Yes, No)	Title: Completed Message: Click arrow to select response.	Type: Stop Title: Invalid Response Message: Invalid response. Use arrow to select response.
B9	Text input. Minimum of 0 characters, maximum of 1500 characters.	Title: Comments Message: Enter your comments. You will be limited to 1500 characters.	Type: Warning Title: Invalid Comments Message: Invalid comments. You have exceeded the limit of characters for comment. Those characters above the limit will be dropped.

© 2014 Cengage Learning

6. In the range B2:B9, enter the following data:

Cell B2: **12/1/2016**
Cell B3: **Otis Davidson**
Cell B4: **International Relations**
Cell B5: **2012**
Cell B6: **SP**
Cell B7: **Switzerland**
Cell B8: **Yes**
Cell B9: **I would LOVE to go back!**

7. Enter the following formulas for the specified cells in the transfer area:

Cell A12: **=B2**
Cell B12: **=B3**
Cell C12: **=B4**
Cell D12: **=B5**
Cell E12: **=B6**
Cell F12: **=B7**
Cell G12: **=B8**
Cell H12: **=B9**

8. Unlock the Input cells in the Input worksheet so that the user can enter data only in the range B2:B9.

9. Protect the Documentation, Data, and Data Tables worksheets so that the user cannot enter data. Do not use a password.

10. Add the DEVELOPER tab to the ribbon.

11. Save the workbook so that you can return to Step 12 and rerecord the macros if you have trouble.

12. Create a macro named **TransferData** with **Ctrl+t** as the shortcut key. Store the macro in the current workbook. Type **Created 12/1/2016. Copy values in the transfer area of the Input worksheet to the Data worksheet.** as the description. Record the following steps to create the TransferData macro:

   a. Go to the Data worksheet and turn off the worksheet protection.

   b. Make the Input worksheet the active worksheet.

   c. Select the transfer area and then copy it to the Clipboard.

   d. Go to the Data worksheet, select cell A1, and then go to the last row with values. (*Hint*: Press the Ctrl+↓ keys.)

   e. On the DEVELOPER tab, turn on Use Relative References.

   f. Move down one row.

   g. Turn off Use Relative References.

   h. Paste the contents of the Clipboard in the Data worksheet using the Values (V) option.

   i. Go to cell A1.

   j. Turn on the worksheet protection.

   k. Go to the Input worksheet, and then make cell B2 the active cell.

13. Create a macro named **ClearInput** with **Ctrl+i** as the shortcut key. Store the macro in the current workbook. Type **Created 12/1/2016. Clear the values in the input area, range B2:B9.** in the macro description. Record the following steps to create the ClearInput macro:

   a. Select the range B2:B9 in the Input worksheet, and then delete the data from those cells.

   b. Make cell B2 the active cell.

14. Test the macros using the shortcut keys you assigned to each of them.

15. Create a macro button for each macro to the right of the Study Abroad Input form. Enter labels that describe the corresponding macro. Protect the Input worksheet. Do not use a password.

16. Remove the DEVELOPER tab from the ribbon.

17. Test the macro buttons. Save your workbook as **Study Abroad with Macros**, a macro-enabled workbook, and then close the workbook.

Case Problem 2

Data File needed for this Case Problem: Cloggers.xlsm

OMG Cloggers   OMG Cloggers is a group of traveling dancers based in Avon, Connecticut. The group goes from event to event demonstrating the techniques of clogging. It has been able to support its travels with a series of fundraisers. The most popular and profitable has been an annual fruit sale. The group sells cartons of various fresh fruits during the winter holidays. Armen Maslov, the director of the group, has started developing a workbook that will allow him to analyze the sales from the fruit fundraiser. He asks you to finish creating the application that would allow volunteers to enter order and sales data for any year and chart the profit. Complete the following:

1. Open the macro-enabled **Cloggers** workbook located in the Excel7 ▸ Case2 folder included with your Data Files, and then save the macro-enabled workbook as **OMG Fundraiser** in the location specified by your instructor.

2. In the Documentation worksheet, enter your name and the date. Review the formulas, defined names, and data validation information in the Fundraiser Data worksheet and the Fundraiser Chart worksheet.

⚙ **Troubleshoot** 3. The profit calculation is not returning the correct results. Identify the error in the calculation and correct it.

16. Create a macro named **AddSong** with the shortcut key **Ctrl+s** that performs the following actions:
    a. Go to the Songs worksheet and remove the cell protection.
    b. Insert a blank line above row 3.
    c. Make the blank cell A3 the active cell.
    d. Make the Music Entry worksheet the active sheet.
    e. Select the Song Transfer Area and copy it to the Clipboard.
    f. Return to the Songs worksheet.
    g. In row 3, paste the values from the Clipboard.
    h. Select cell A1, and then turn on cell protection.
    i. Go to the Music Entry worksheet, and then make cell B2 the active cell.

17. Record a macro named **ClearCDInput** with no shortcut key to clear the range B2:B4 of the New CD input area. The last step should make cell B2 the active cell.

18. Record a macro named **ClearSongInput** with no shortcut key to clear the range B12:B14 of the New Song input area. The last step should make cell B2 the active cell.

19. Test all of the macros by selecting and running the macros on the DEVELOPER tab.

⊕ **Explore** 20. Remove the cell protection on the Music Entry worksheet. Create macro buttons for all four macros using either clip art or shapes. Make sure that you have used descriptive labels for each macro button. Set cell protection again for the Music Entry worksheet.

21. Test all of the macro buttons. Check the CDs and Songs worksheets to see how and where new records were added.

22. Remove the DEVELOPER tab from the ribbon.

23. Save the workbook as **Music Inventory with Macros**, a macro-enabled workbook, and then close the workbook.

Case Problem 4

There are no Data Files needed for this Case Problem.

Trinette's Trilbies & Fedoras   Several years ago, Trinette Jalbert started making trilby hats (commonly called trilbies), which are narrow-brimmed fedora hats, for male family friends. As the requests started pouring in, she turned her hobby into a business. Her customers now include men and women, and she makes fedoras in addition to trilbies. Trinette wants a billing/invoicing system to expedite her work. You will create the finished application for her. Complete the following:

1. Open a new, blank workbook, and then save it as **Hats** in the location specified by your instructor.

2. Rename the sheet as **Documentation**, and then enter the company name, your name, the date, and a purpose statement. Insert two additional sheets, and then rename them as **Invoice** and **Product Information**.

3. In the Product Information worksheet, enter the data for the available colors, fabrics, sizes, hat types, standard hat price, surcharge, and shipping fee shown in Figure 7-47.

Figure 7-47   Input data for Trinette's Trilbies & Fedoras

	A	B	C	D	E	F	G	H
1	Color		Size		Hat Type		Shipping	
2	Dark Brown		XS		Trilby		15	
3	Navy Blue		S		Fedora			
4	Black		M					
5			L		Standard			
6	Fabric		XL		75			
7	Tweed		XXL					
8	Wool		XXXL		Surcharge			
9	Felt				15			
10								
11								

4. In the Invoice worksheet, create the invoice shown in Figure 7-48. Use defined names and structured references to assist in creating formulas. (*Hint*: Review the steps below before you begin to create the invoice.)

a. Enter the labels as shown in Figure 7-48.

b. Change the column widths and format the labels appropriately.

c. Use a function to insert the current date.

d. Insert a comment in the Sold To: cell with a reminder about what data should be entered in cells B10, B11, and B12.

e. Use data validation rules to create lists of the different hat types, fabrics, colors, and sizes you entered on the Product Information worksheet. Use appropriate input messages and error alerts.

f. Create defined names for the data on the invoice.

g. For the unit price, enter a formula to display the standard price listed on the Product Information worksheet.

h. Enter a formula to display for the fabric surcharge listed on the Product Information worksheet only when a customer purchases a hat with felt fabric. (*Hint*: You will need to use an IF function.)

i. In the Subtotal cell, enter a formula that uses defined names to add the unit price and the surcharge.

j. In the Sales Tax cell, enter a formula that uses a defined name to calculate 6.5% of the subtotal.

k. In the Shipping cell, enter a formula to display the shipping fee listed on the Product Information worksheet.

l. In the Total Due cell, enter a formula that sums the Subtotal, Sales Tax, and Shipping cells.

m. Format the cells and add borders and shading where you feel they will make the invoice clearer to read.

Figure 7-48   **Finished invoice for Trinette's Trilbies & Fedoras**

	A	B	C	D	E	F	G	H	I
1									
2				Trinette's Trilbies & Fedoras					
3				56745 North Street					
4				Fredericktown, OH 43019					
5				740-555-6565					
6							Date		
7							7/19/2016		
8									
9		Sold To:							
10		Sam Smith							
11		123 Main Street							
12		Zanesville, OH 43701							
13									
14				Hat Information			Unit Price		
15		Hat Type	Trilby				$ 75.00		
16		Fabric	Tweed			Fabric Surcharge*	$ -		
17		Color	Navy Blue						
18		Size	M						
19									
20						Subtotal	$ 75.00		
21						Sales Tax	$ 4.88		
22						Shipping	$ 15.00		
23						Total Due	$ 94.88		
24		* Fabric Surcharge is on Felt only							
25									
26									

5. Protect the worksheet so a user can enter the Sold To: (cells B10, B11, and B12) and Hat Information (cells C15, C16, C17, and C18) data, but cannot enter data in any other cells. Do not use a password. Protect the entire Documentation and Product Information worksheets. Do not use a password.

6. Save the workbook.

7. Create a macro named **PrintInvoice** that prints the invoice. Assign a shortcut key and type an appropriate macro description as you begin recording this macro. Set the print area to the range A1:H25 and center the worksheet horizontally. The heading has the label **I N V O I C E** in the center of the page heading. Create a macro button on the Invoice worksheet, assign the PrintInvoice macro to the button, and then enter a descriptive label for the button.

8. Create a macro named **ClearInputs** that deletes the values from cells B10, B11, B12, C15, C16, C17, and C18. Assign a shortcut key and type an appropriate macro description as you begin recording this macro. Create a macro button on the Invoice worksheet, assign the ClearInputs macro to the button, and then enter a descriptive label for the button. (*Hint*: Use the Delete key to clear a value from a cell.)

9. Remove the cell protection from the Documentation worksheet. In the Documentation worksheet, paste a list of the defined names with their locations. Below this entry, type a list of the macro names and their shortcut keys. Reapply cell protection to the Documentation worksheet.

10. Test the worksheet by entering the data shown in Figure 7-47.

11. Use the PrintInvoice macro button to print the invoice for the data you entered in Step 10, and then use the ClearInputs macro button to remove the input data.

12. Remove the DEVELOPER tab from the ribbon.

13. Save the workbook as **Hats with Macros**, and then close the workbook.

OBJECTIVES

Session 8.1
- Use the IF function
- Use the AND function
- Use the OR function
- Use structured references in formulas

Session 8.2
- Nest the IF function
- Use the VLOOKUP function
- Use the HLOOKUP function
- Use the IFERROR function

Session 8.3
- Use conditional formatting to highlight duplicate values
- Summarize data using the COUNTIF, SUMIF, and AVERAGEIF functions

Working with Advanced Functions

Calculating Employee Compensation and Benefits

Case | *Educational Video Games*

Educational Video Games (EVG) is a software development company that develops and markets educational games for children in pre-school through second grade. The business has expanded rapidly in the five years since it was founded and now has nearly 100 employees in four locations within the United States.

Patrick Yang, director of compensation and benefits, uses Excel to track basic employee information such as each employee's name, gender, birth date, hire date, medical and dental plans, job status, and current salary. Now he needs to track employee enrollment in and costs related to the compensation and benefit programs offered by the company, such as how much the company contributes to each employee's 401(k) retirement account and medical and dental plans. He also needs to calculate the amount EVG will spend on bonuses and salary increases for the next fiscal year. In addition, the human resources staff wants to send cards to each employee during her/his birthday month.

To provide Patrick with all this information, you'll use a variety of logical and lookup functions. After you calculate those values, you'll summarize information in the Employee Summary worksheet so Patrick can quickly see the impact of the compensation and benefits package on the company.

STARTING DATA FILES

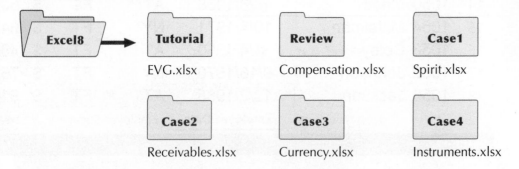

Excel8 → Tutorial
EVG.xlsx

Review
Compensation.xlsx

Case1
Spirit.xlsx

Case2
Receivables.xlsx

Case3
Currency.xlsx

Case4
Instruments.xlsx

Session 8.1 Visual Overview:

When you create a formula that references all or parts of an Excel table, you can replace a specific cell or range address with a **structured reference**, which is the actual table name or column header.

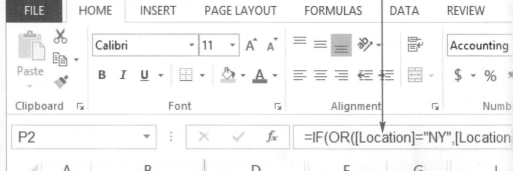

The **IF function** is a logical function that evaluates a condition, and then returns one value if the condition is true and a different value if the condition is false.

A **logical condition** is an expression such as G2="FT" that returns either a TRUE value or a FALSE value.

The **AND function** is a logical function that returns a TRUE value if all of the logical conditions are true, and a FALSE value if any of the logical conditions are false.

The **OR function** is a logical function that returns a TRUE value if any of the logical conditions are true, and a FALSE value if none of the logical conditions are true.

EVG Employees - Excel

FILE   HOME   INSERT   PAGE LAYOUT   FORMULAS   DATA   REVIEW

Calibri   11   A˄ A˅   Accounting

B I U $ ▾ %

Clipboard   Font   Alignment   Numb

P2   =IF(OR([Location]="NY",[Location]

	A	B	D	F	G	I
1	Emp ID	Last Name	Birth Date	Location	Job Status	Curre Salar
2	1002	Lowe	9/6/1966	NY	FT	$ 108,7
3	1006	Forbes	12/15/1985	SF	FT	$ 75,
4	1010	Speulda	9/24/1968	=IF(MONTH(D2)=$A		
5	1014	Hunt	8/9/1959	NY	FT	$ 84,0
6	1018	Hanson	7/15/1950	NY		
7	1022	Philo	5/2/1958	S	=IF(AND(G2="FT"	
8	1026	Stolt	12/7/1977	SF	FT	$ 101,8
9	1030	Akhalaghi	12/4/1961	NY	FT	$ 38,4
10	1034		=IF(OR([Location]="NY",[Location]="SF"),[C			
11	1038	McCorkle				
12	1042	Mattis	8/27/1989	AT	FT	$ 65,1
13	1046	Baker	1/6/1968	DA	FT	$ 71,0
14	1050	Vines	4/28/1958	AT	FT	$ 60,1
15	1054	Mittelman	10/4/1971	NY	FT	$ 64,8
16	1058	Coley	1/4/1960	AT	FT	$ 49,8
17	1062	Johnson	9/16/1970	NY	FT	$ 76,7
18	1066	Jackson	12/2/1985	AT	FT	$ 91,2

Documentation   **Employee Data**   Employee Summary   Looku

READY

Logical Functions

In this formula, the structured reference [Current Salary] references the cells in column I of the Employee table.

When a formula is entered in a cell within an Excel table, the formula is automatically copied to all cells in that column. The column is referred to as a **calculated column**.

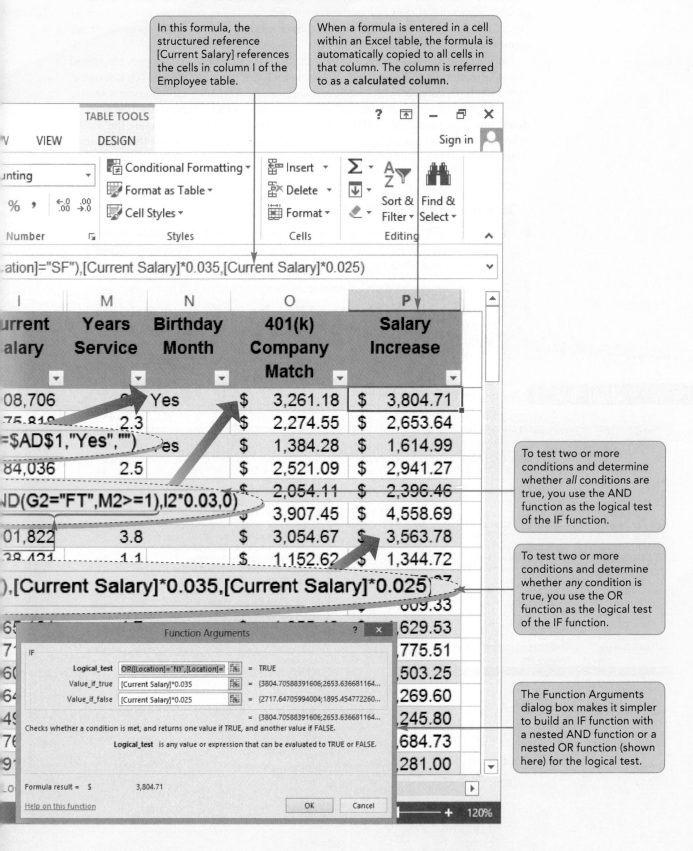

To test two or more conditions and determine whether *all* conditions are true, you use the AND function as the logical test of the IF function.

To test two or more conditions and determine whether *any* condition is true, you use the OR function as the logical test of the IF function.

The Function Arguments dialog box makes it simpler to build an IF function with a nested AND function or a nested OR function (shown here) for the logical test.

Working with Logical Functions

Logical functions such as IF, AND, and OR determine whether a condition is true or false. A condition uses one of the comparison operators <, <=, =, <>, >, or >= to compare two values. You can combine two or more functions in one formula, creating more complex conditions.

Patrick created a workbook that contains data for each EVG employee. He stored this information in an Excel table. The table includes each employee's ID, last name, hire date, birth date, gender, location, job status, performance rating, current salary, medical plan, dental plan, age, and years of service at EVG. Patrick wants you to determine if an employee birthday occurs in a specified month, calculate the 401(k) company cost, and calculate a proposed salary increase. You will use IF, AND, and OR functions to do this after you open Patrick's workbook and review the employee data.

To open and review the EVG workbook:

▶ **1.** Open the **EVG** workbook located in the Excel8 ▸ Tutorial folder included with your Data Files, and then save the workbook as **EVG Employees** in the location specified by your instructor.

▶ **2.** In the Documentation worksheet, enter your name and the date.

▶ **3.** Go to the **Employee Data** worksheet. The worksheet contains an Excel table named Employee, which includes each employee's ID, last name, hire date, birth date, gender, location, job status, performance rating, current salary, medical plan, dental plan, age, and years of service at EVG. See Figure 8-1.

Figure 8-1   **Employee Data worksheet**

Emp ID	Last Name	Hire Date	Birth Date	Gender	Location	Job Status	Perf Rating	Current Salary	Medical Plan	Dental Plan	Age	Years Service
1002	Lowe	5/24/2010	9/6/1966	F	NY	FT	3	$ 108,706	SPOUSE2500	EMP+SPOUSE	49	6.6
1006	Forbes	8/28/2014	12/15/1985	F	SF	FT	2	$ 75,818	NONE	NONE	30	2.3
1010	Speulda	4/24/2015	9/24/1968	M	SF	FT	2	$ 46,143	FAMILY1000	EMP+FAMILY	47	1.7
1014	Hunt	7/18/2014	8/9/1959	M	NY	FT	3	$ 84,036	SPOUSE1000	NONE	56	2.5
1018	Hanson	8/21/2015	7/15/1950	F	NY	FT	1	$ 68,470	FAMILY1000	EMP+FAMILY	65	1.4
1022	Philo	3/5/2015	5/2/1958	F	SF	FT	2	$ 130,248	FAMILY1000	EMP+FAMILY	57	1.8
1026	Stolt	3/1/2013	12/7/1977	M	SF	FT	3	$ 101,822	FAMILY2500	NONE	38	3.8
1030	Akhalaghi	12/8/2015	12/4/1961	F	NY	FT	2	$ 38,421	SPOUSE1000	EMP+SPOUSE	54	1.1
1034	Vankeuren	8/11/2011	1/10/1959	F	NY	PT	3	$ 53,582	FAMILY1000	EMP+FAMILY	56	5.4
1038	Mccorkle	6/12/2009	1/30/1942	F	AT	FT	2	$ 24,373	FAMILY2500	EMP+FAMILY	73	7.6
1042	Mattis	5/4/2012	8/27/1989	M	AT	FT	2	$ 65,181	SINGLE1000	EMP	26	4.7
1046	Baker	12/18/2015	1/6/1968	F	DA	FT	3	$ 71,020	FAMILY2500	EMP+FAMILY	47	1.0
1050	Vines	5/4/2011	4/28/1958	M	AT	FT	2	$ 60,130	SINGLE1000	EMP	57	5.7
1054	Mittelman	11/26/2004	10/4/1971	M	NY	FT	2	$ 64,846	SPOUSE2500	EMP+SPOUSE	44	12.1
1058	Coley	2/22/2008	1/4/1960	F	AT	FT	1	$ 49,832	SINGLE1000	EMP	55	8.9
1062	Johnson	12/4/2015	9/16/1970	F	NY	FT	2	$ 76,707	FAMILY1000	EMP+FAMILY	45	1.1
1066	Jackson	10/12/2015	12/2/1985	F	AT	FT	3	$ 91,240	SINGLE2500	EMP	30	1.2

Documentation   **Employee Data**   Employee Summary   Lookup Tables   ⊕

READY

▶ **4.** Scroll down and to the right. Although the column headers remain visible as you scroll down, the employee ID and name disappear as you scroll to the right.

▶ **5.** Select cell **C2**, and then freeze the panes so columns A and B remain on the screen as you scroll across the screen.

Inserting Calculated Columns in an Excel Table

An Excel table does not have a fixed structure. When you add a column to an Excel table, the table expands and the new column has the same table formatting style as the other columns. If you enter a formula in one cell of a column, the formula is automatically copied to all cells in that column. These calculated columns are helpful as you add formulas to an Excel table.

If you need to modify the formula in a calculated column, you edit the formula in any cell in the column and the formulas in all of the cells in that table column are also modified. If you want to edit only one cell in a calculated column, you need to enter a value or a formula that is different from all the others in that column. A green triangle appears in the upper-left corner of the cell with the custom formula in the calculated column, making the inconsistency easy to find. After a calculated column contains one inconsistent formula or value, any other edits you make to that column are no longer automatically copied to the rest of the cells in that column. Excel does not overwrite custom values.

PROSKILLS

Written Communication: Creating Excel Table Fields

Excel tables should be easy to use as well as understand. This requires labeling and entering data in a way that effectively communicates a table's content or purpose. If a field is entered in a way that is difficult to use and understand, it becomes more difficult to find and present data in a meaningful way.

To effectively communicate a table's function, keep the following guidelines in mind when creating fields in an Excel table:

- **Create fields that require the least maintenance.** For example, hire date and birth date require no maintenance after they are entered, unlike age and years of service, whose values change each year. If you need to know the specific age or years of service, use calculations to determine them based on values in the Hire Date and Birth Date columns.
- **Store the smallest unit of data possible in a field.** For example, use three separate fields for City, State, and Zip code rather than one field. Using separate fields for each unit of data enables you to sort or filter each field. If you want to display data from two or more fields in one column, you can use a formula to reference the City, State, and Zip code columns. For example, you can use the & operator to combine the city, state, and zip code in one cell as follows: =C2&D2&E2
- **Apply a text format to fields with numerical text data.** For example, formatting fields such as zip codes and Social Security numbers as text ensures that leading zeros are stored as part of the data. Otherwise, the zip code 02892 is stored as a number and displayed as 2892.

Using these guidelines means that you and others will spend less time interpreting data and more time analyzing results. This lets you more effectively communicate the data in an Excel table.

Using the IF Function

In many situations, the value you store in a cell depends on certain conditions. Consider the following examples:

- An employee's gross pay depends on whether that employee worked overtime.
- An income tax rate depends on the taxpayer's adjusted taxable income.
- A shipping charge depends on the dollar amount of an order.

To evaluate these types of conditions, you use the IF function. Recall that the IF function is a logical function that evaluates a condition, and then returns one value if the condition is true and another value if the condition is false. The value can be text, numbers, cell references, formulas, or functions. The IF function has the syntax

```
IF(logical_test, value_if_true, value_if_false)
```

where *logical_test* is a condition that is either true or false, *value_if_true* is the value returned by the function if the condition is true, and *value_if_false* is the value returned by the function if the condition is false. The IF function results in only one value—either the *value_if_true* or the *value_if_false*.

You will use an IF function to alert Patrick that an employee has a birthday during a specified month. EVG employees who have an upcoming birthday receive a birthday card. A Yes value in the Birthday Month column will indicate that an employee has a birthday during the specified month, and a blank cell will indicate that an employee does not have a birthday during the specified month.

The flowchart shown in Figure 8-2 illustrates Patrick's logic for determining whether a birthday occurs in a specified month. The flowchart shows that if an employee's birth month occurs in the specified month (*birth month = specified month* is True), "Yes" is entered in the cell. If the employee does not have a birthday in the specified month, the cell is left blank.

| Figure 8-2 | Flowchart with logic to determine if an employee's birthday is in the specified month |

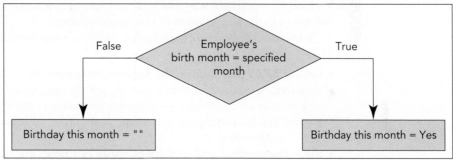

© 2014 Cengage Learning

The Employee table doesn't include a column that lists only the birth month; this information is included as part of the employee's complete birth date, which is stored in column D. To extract the month portion of the employee's birth date, you will use the MONTH function. This function is a Date function that returns the month as a number from 1 (January) to 12 (December). The MONTH function has the syntax

```
MONTH(date)
```

where *date* is a date that includes the month you want to extract. Recall that Excel stores dates as a number equal to the number of days between January 1, 1900 and the specified date so they can be used in calculations. For example, January 1, 2016 is stored as the serial number 42370 because it occurs 42370 days since the start of Excel's calendar. The MONTH function determines the month number from the stored serial number. For example, the birth date of the employee in row 2 of the Employee table is 9/6/1966, which is stored in cell D2. The following MONTH function extracts the month portion of this stored date, which is 9:

```
=MONTH(D2)
```

You'll use the MONTH function in the logical test of the IF function, which will check whether the employee's birth month matches the month number entered in cell AD1 of the Employee Data worksheet. Patrick wants to know which employees have birthdays in September, so he entered 9 as the month number in cell AD1. The following formula includes the complete IF function to determine if an employee has a birthday in September:

```
=IF(MONTH(D2)=$AD$1,"Yes","")
```

The logical test MONTH(D2)=$AD$1 determines if the employee's birth month is equal to the birth month stored in cell AD1. If the condition is TRUE, Yes is displayed in the Birthday Month column; otherwise, the cell is left blank.

You'll add a column to the Employee table to display the results of the IF function that determines if an employee's birthday occurs in the specified month.

To determine which employees have birthdays in the specified month:

▶ 1. In cell **N1**, enter **Birthday Month**. The Excel table expands to include this column and applies the table formatting to all the rows in the new column.

▶ 2. Make sure cell **N2** is the active cell, and then click the **Insert Function** button f_x next to the formula bar. The Insert Function dialog box opens.

▶ 3. Click **Logical** in the Or select a category list, click **IF** in the Select a function box, and then click the **OK** button. The Function Arguments dialog box for the IF function opens.

▶ 4. In the Logical_test box, type **MONTH(D2)=$AD$1** and then press the **Tab** key. This condition tests whether the employee's birth month is equal to the month specified in cell AD1. The function MONTH returns the month number of the date specified in cell D2. TRUE appears to the right of the Logical_test argument box, indicating this employee has a birthday in the specified month.

▶ 5. In the Value_if_true box, type **Yes** and then press the **Tab** key. This argument specifies that if the condition is true (the employee's birth month matches the value in cell AD1), display Yes as the formula result. The value to the right of the Value_if_true argument box is Yes because the condition is true. Notice Excel inserts quotation marks around the text value because you did not include them.

▶ 6. In the Value_if_false box, type **""**. This argument specifies that if the condition is false (the employee's birth month does not match the value in cell AD1), display nothing in cell N2. The value to the right of the Value_if_false argument box is "", which indicates that cell N2 appears blank if the condition is false. See Figure 8-3.

Figure 8-3 **Function Arguments dialog box for the IF function**

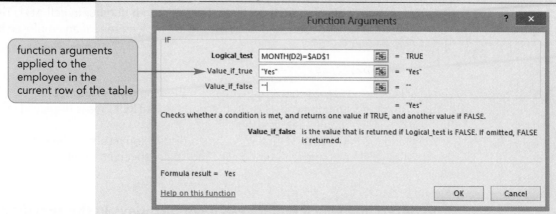

function arguments applied to the employee in the current row of the table

- **7.** Click the **OK** button. The formula =IF(MONTH(D2)=$AD$1,"Yes","") appears in the formula bar, and Yes appears in cell N2 because the condition is true. The formula is automatically copied to all cells in column N of the table. See Figure 8-4.

Figure 8-4 **Birthday Month column added to the Employee table**

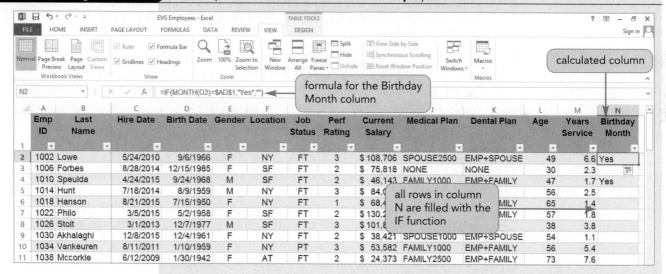

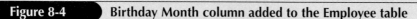

Using the AND Function

The IF function evaluates a single condition. However, you often need to test two or more conditions and determine whether *all* conditions are true. You can do this with the AND function. The AND function is a logical function that returns the value TRUE if all of the logical conditions are true, and returns the value FALSE if any or all of the logical conditions are false. The syntax of the AND function is

```
AND(logical1[,logical2]...)
```

where *logical1* and *logical2* are conditions that can be either true or false. If all of the logical conditions are true, the AND function returns the logical value TRUE; otherwise, the function returns the logical value FALSE. You can include up to 255 logical conditions in an AND function. However, keep in mind that *all* of the logical conditions listed in the AND function must be true for the AND function to return a TRUE value.

Figure 8-5 illustrates how the AND function is used to determine student eligibility for the dean's list. In this scenario, when students have 12 or more credits (stored in cell B1) *and* their GPA is greater than 3.5 (stored in cell B2), they are placed on the dean's list. Both conditions must be true for the AND function to return the logical value TRUE.

| Figure 8-5 | AND function example |

Purpose: To determine dean's list requirements

Logic Scenario: 12 or more semester credits and GPA above 3.5

Formula: AND function with two conditions
                      `=AND(B1>=12,B2>3.5)`

Data: cell B1 stores number of credits
                      cell B2 stores student's GPA

Example:

Data		Condition1	Condition2	Results
Cell B1	**Cell B2**	**B1>=12**	**B2>3.5**	**(Dean's List?)**
15	3.6	True	True	True
12	3.25	True	False	False
6	3.8	False	True	False
10	3.0	False	False	False

© 2014 Cengage Learning

Patrick wants you to use an AND function to determine employee eligibility for the company's 401(k) plan. EVG employees are eligible for the 401(k) benefit if they are full-time employees (FT in Job Status) *and* have worked for the company for one or more years (1 or greater in Years Service). As long as *both* conditions are true, the company contributes an amount equal to 3 percent of the employee's salary to the employee's 401(k). If neither condition is true or if only one condition is true, the employee is not eligible for the 401(k) benefit and the company's contribution is 0. Patrick outlined these eligibility conditions in the flowchart shown in Figure 8-6.

| Figure 8-6 | Flowchart illustrating AND logic for the 401(k) benefit |

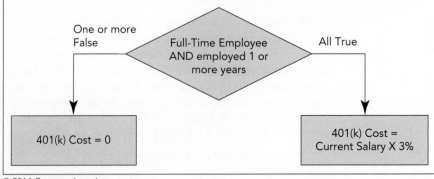

© 2014 Cengage Learning

To calculate the cost of the 401(k) plan for each employee, you need to use the AND function with the IF function. You use the AND function shown in the following formula as the logical test to evaluate whether each employee in the Employee table fulfills the eligibility requirements:

```
=AND(G2="FT",M2>=1)
```

This formula tests whether the value in cell G2 (the job status for the first employee) is equal to FT (an abbreviation for full time), and whether the value in cell M2 (the years of service for the first employee) is greater than or equal to 1 (indicating one or more years of employment at EVG). When an employee is a full-time employee (G2="FT") *and* has worked one or more years at EVG (M2>=1), the AND function returns the value TRUE; otherwise, the AND function returns the value FALSE. Figure 8-7 shows the result returned by the AND function for four different sets of employee values for job status and years of service.

| Figure 8-7 | AND function results for 401(k) plan eligibility |

Purpose: To determine employee eligibility for the company's 401(k) plan

Logic Scenario: An employee is eligible for the 401(k) plan if the employee's status is full time (FT) AND the employee's years of service total one or more years.

Formula: AND function with two conditions
=AND(G2="FT",M2>=1)

Data: cell G2 stores Job Status
cell M2 stores Years Service

Example:

Data		Condition1	Condition2	Results
Cell G2	Cell M2	G2="FT"	M2>=1	(Eligible?)
FT	1	True	True	True
FT	0	True	False	False
PT	5	False	True	False
PT	0	False	False	False

© 2014 Cengage Learning

The AND function shows only whether an employee is eligible for the 401(k) plan. It does not calculate how much EVG will contribute to that employee's 401(k) plan if the employee is eligible. To determine whether an employee is eligible *and* to calculate the amount of the 401(k) contribution, you use this AND function within an IF function. When the results of one function are used as the argument of another function, the functions are *nested*. In the following formula, the AND function (shown in red) is nested within the IF function and is used as the logical test that determines whether the employee is eligible for a 401(k) contribution:

```
=IF(AND(G2="FT",M2>=1),I2*0.03,0)
```

If the employee is eligible, the AND function returns the logical value TRUE and the IF function multiplies the employee's current salary by 3 percent. If the AND function returns the logical value FALSE, the IF function displays the value 0.

You'll insert a new column in the Employee table, and then enter the formula to calculate the 401(k) company match.

To calculate the 401(k) company match using the IF and AND functions:

1. In cell **O1**, enter **401(k) Company Match** as the column header. The Excel table expands to include the new column, and cell O2 is the active cell.

2. Make sure cell **O2** is the active cell, and then click the **Insert Function** button _fx_ next to the formula bar. The Insert Function dialog box opens.

3. Click **IF** in the Select a function box, and then click the **OK** button. The Function Arguments dialog box opens.

4. In the Logical_test box, type **AND(G2="FT",M2>=1)** and then press the **Tab** key. This logical test evaluates whether the employee is full time, indicated by FT in cell G2, *and* has worked at EVG for one year or more. TRUE appears to the right of the Logical_test box, indicating that the condition for the employee in row 2 is true. This employee is eligible for the 401(k) plan.

5. In the Value_if_true box, type **I2*0.03** and then press the **Tab** key. This argument specifies that if the condition is true (the employee is eligible for the 401(k) plan as determined by the AND function), the amount in the employee's salary cell is multiplied by 3 percent. The amount of the employer's 401(k) matching contribution, 3261.18, appears to the right of the Value_if_true box.

6. In the Value_if_false box, type **0**. This argument specifies that if the condition is false (the employee is not eligible for the 401(k) plan as determined by the AND function), the amount displayed in cell O2 is 0, which appears to the right of the Value_if_false box. See Figure 8-8.

Figure 8-8 **Function Arguments dialog box for the IF function with the AND function**

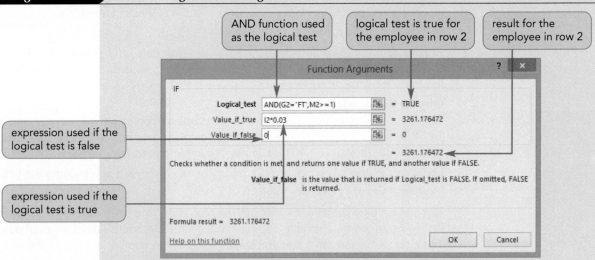

7. Click the **OK** button. The formula with the IF function that you just created is entered in cell O2 and copied to all rows in column O of the table.

8. Position the pointer at the top of cell **O1** until the pointer changes to ↓, click to select the 401(k) data values, format the range using the **Accounting** format, and then widen the column to display all values.

TIP
Double-click above the header row to select the column header and data.

> **9.** Select cell **O2**. The formula =IF(AND(G2="FT",M2>=1),I2*0.03,0) appears in the formula bar and $3,261.18 appears in cell O2 because the condition is true. See Figure 8-9.

Figure 8-9   IF function with the AND function to calculate EVG's 401(k) contribution

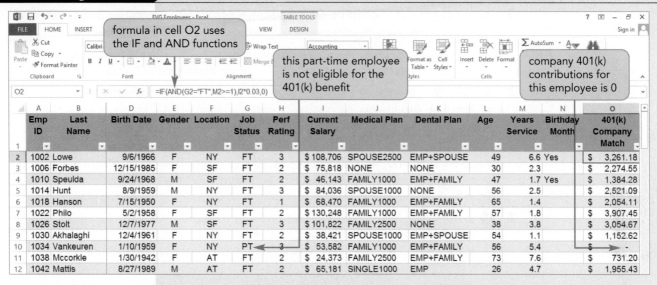

The company match values are calculated for all employees.

Using the DATEDIF Function to Calculate Employee Age

In the Employee table, the Age column was calculated using the DATEDIF function. The **DATEDIF function** calculates the difference between two dates and shows the result in months, days, or years. The syntax for the DATEDIF function is

    DATEDIF(Date1,Date2,Interval)

where *Date1* is the earliest date, *Date2* is the latest date, and *Interval* is the unit of time the DATEDIF function will use in the result. You specify the *Interval* with one of the following interval codes:

Interval Code	Meaning	Description
"m"	Months	The number of complete months between *Date1* and *Date2*
"d"	Days	The number of complete days between *Date1* and *Date2*
"y"	Years	The number of complete years between *Date1* and *Date2*

For example, the following formula calculates an employee's age in complete years:

    =DATEDIF(D2,$AF$1,"y")

The earliest date is located in cell D2, the birth date. The latest date is in cell $AF$1, which shows the date used to compare against the birth date—as of a cut-off date. The interval "y" indicates that you want to display the number of complete years between these two dates.

The DATEDIF function is undocumented in Excel, but it has been available since Excel 97. To learn more about this function, search the web using "DATEDIF function in Excel" as the search text in your favorite search engine.

Using the OR Function

The OR function is a logical function that returns a TRUE value if any of the logical conditions are true, and returns a FALSE value if all of the logical conditions are false. The syntax of the OR function is

OR(*logical1*[,*logical2*]...)

where *logical1* and *logical2* are conditions that can be either true or false. If any of the logical conditions are true, the OR function returns the logical value TRUE; otherwise, the function returns the logical value FALSE. You can include up to 255 logical conditions in the OR function. However, keep in mind that if *any* logical condition listed in the OR function is true, the OR function returns a TRUE value.

Figure 8-10 illustrates how the OR function is used to determine eligibility for a 10 percent discount. In this scenario, anyone who is 65 years or older (stored in cell B1) *or* anyone who is a college student (stored in cell B2) receives a 10 percent discount. At least one condition must be true for the OR function to return the logical value TRUE.

Figure 8-10	Example of the OR function

Purpose:	To determine who is eligible for a discount
Logic Scenario:	Discount is 10 percent for seniors (65 or older) or college students (Status =STU)
Formula:	OR function with two conditions =OR(B1>=65,B2="STU")
Data:	cell B1 stores Age cell B2 stores Status (STU, FAC, STF)

Example:

Data		Condition1	Condition2	Results
Cell B1	**Cell B2**	**B1>=65**	**B2="STU"**	**(Discount?)**
22	STU	False	True	True
67	FAC	True	False	True
65	STU	True	True	True
45	STF	False	False	False

© 2014 Cengage Learning

EVG is considering awarding a 3.5 percent raise to employees working in areas with a high cost of living, and a 2.5 percent raise for all other employees. The criteria for awarding a salary increase are based on location. If the employee is working in either New York (NY) or San Francisco (SF), the employee will receive the 3.5 percent raise. In other words, if either Location equals NY or Location equals SF is True, the condition is true and the employee will receive the 3.5 percent raise. If the condition is false—meaning the employee is located in a city other than New York or San Francisco—the employee receives a 2.5 percent raise. Patrick outlined the salary increase criteria in the flowchart shown in Figure 8-11.

Figure 8-11 Flowchart of the OR function to calculate salary increase

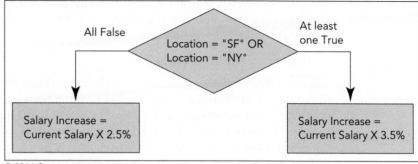

© 2014 Cengage Learning

You need to use the OR function to test whether an employee meets the criteria for the 3.5 percent or 2.5 percent salary increase. The following formula uses the OR function to test whether the value in cell F2 (the work location for the first employee) is equal to NY *or* whether the value in cell F2 is equal to SF:

`=OR(F2="NY",F2="SF")`

If the employee works in New York (NY) *or* the employee works in San Francisco (SF), the OR function returns the value TRUE; otherwise, the OR function returns the value FALSE.

Figure 8-12 shows the results returned using the OR function for four different employee work locations—New York (NY), San Francisco (SF), Dallas (DA), and Atlanta (AT).

Figure 8-12 OR function results for four employee work locations

Purpose: To determine an employee's salary increase percentage

Logic Scenario: Proposed 3.5 percent salary increase to full-time (FT) employees located in NY or SF

Formula: OR function with two conditions
`=OR(F2="NY",F2="SF")`

Data: cell F2 stores Location

Example:

Data	Condition1	Condition1	Results
Cell F2	**F2="NY"**	**F2="NY"**	**(OR function)**
NY	True	True	True
SF	False	False	True
DA	False	False	False
AT	False	False	False

© 2014 Cengage Learning

The OR function only determines which raise an employee is eligible for. It does not calculate the amount of the salary increase. To determine the amount of the salary increase, the OR function must be nested within an IF function. In the formula

```
=IF(OR(F2="NY",F2="SF"),I2*0.035,I2*0.025)
```

the logical test of the IF function uses the OR function (shown in red) to determine whether an employee is either working in New York *or* working in San Francisco. If the OR function returns a TRUE value, the IF function multiplies the Current Salary by 3.5 percent. If the OR function returns a FALSE value, the IF function multiplies the Current Salary by 2.5 percent.

Using Structured References to Create Formulas in Excel Tables

When you create a formula that references all or parts of an Excel table, you can replace the specific cell or range address with a structured reference, the actual table name, or a column header. This makes the formula easier to create and understand. The default Excel table name is Table1, Table2, and so forth unless you entered a more descriptive table name, as Patrick did for the Employee table. Column headers provide a description of the data entered in each column. Structured references make it easier to create formulas that use portions or all of an Excel table because the names or headers are usually simpler to identify than cell addresses. For example, in the Employee table, the table name Employee refers to the range A2:O101, which is the range of data in the table excluding the header row and the Total row. When you want to reference an entire column of data in a table, you create a column qualifier, which has the syntax

```
Tablename[qualifier]
```

where *Tablename* is the name entered in the Table Name box in the Properties group on the TABLE TOOLS DESIGN tab, and *qualifier* is the column header enclosed in square brackets. For example, the following structured reference references the Current Salary data in the range I2:I101 of the Employee table (excluding the column header and total row, if any):

```
Employee[Current Salary]
```

You can use structured references in formulas. The following formula adds the Current Salary data in the range I2:I101 of the Employee table; in this case, [Current Salary] is the column qualifier:

```
=SUM(Employee[Current Salary])
```

When you create a calculated column, as you did to calculate the 401(k) contributions in the Employee table, you can use structured references in the formula. A formula that includes a structured reference can be fully qualified or unqualified. In a fully qualified structured reference, the table name precedes the column qualifier. In an unqualified structured reference, only the column qualifier (column header enclosed in square brackets) appears in the reference. For example, you could have used either of the following formulas with structured references to calculate the 401(k) company match in the calculated column you added to the Employee table:

Fully qualified
```
=IF(AND(Employee[Job Status]="FT",Employee[Years Service]>=1),
[Current Salary]*0.035,0)
```

Unqualified

```
=IF(AND([Job Status]="FT",[Years Service]>=1),
[Current Salary]*0.035,0)
```

If you are creating a calculated column or formula within an Excel table, you can use either the fully qualified structured reference or the unqualified structured reference in the formula. If you use a structured reference outside the table or in another worksheet to reference an Excel table or portion of the table, you must use a fully qualified reference.

You'll use structured references to calculate the salary increases for EVG employees.

To calculate the salary increase using the IF and OR functions:

1. In cell **P1**, enter **Salary Increase** as the column header. The Excel table expands to include the new column, and cell P2 is the active cell.

2. Make sure cell **P2** is the active cell, and then click the **Insert Function** button f_x next to the formula bar. The Insert Function dialog box opens.

3. Click **IF** in the Select a function box, and then click the **OK** button. The Function Arguments dialog box opens.

> Be sure to type square brackets and use the exact spelling and location shown. Otherwise, the formula will return an error.

4. In the Logical_test box, type **OR([Location]="NY",[Location]="SF")** to enter the OR function with structured references. This logical test evaluates whether the employee works in New York or works in San Francisco.

5. Click the **Collapse dialog box** button 🔳 to so you can see the entire function in the Logical_test box. See Figure 8-13.

Figure 8-13   **Logical_test argument for the OR function**

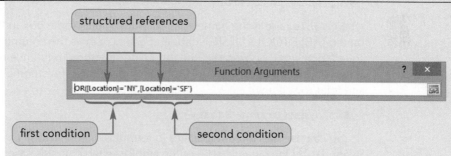

6. Click the **Expand dialog box** button 🔳, and then press the **Tab** key. TRUE appears to the right of the Logical_test box because the employee in the active row, row 2, is eligible for the 3.5 percent salary increase.

Trouble? If Invalid appears instead of TRUE as the logical test results, you probably mistyped the logical test. Compare the function in your Logical_test box to the one shown in Figure 8-13, confirming that you used square brackets around the structured reference [Location] and typed all the text correctly.

7. In the Value_if_true box, type **[Current Salary]*0.035** and then press the **Tab** key. This argument specifies that if the logical test is true (the employee is eligible for the 3.5 percent increase), the amount in the employee's salary cell is multiplied by 3.5 percent. The salary increases for all employees, beginning in row 2, whose logical test is true appear to the right of the Value_if_true box.

8. In the Value_if_false box, type **[Current Salary]*0.025**. This argument specifies that if the logical test is false (the employee is not eligible for the 3.5 percent salary increase), the amount in the employee's salary cell is multiplied by 2.5 percent. The salary increases for all employees, beginning in row 2, whose logical test is false appear to the right of the Value_if_false box. See Figure 8-14.

Figure 8-14	Function Arguments dialog box for the IF function with an OR function

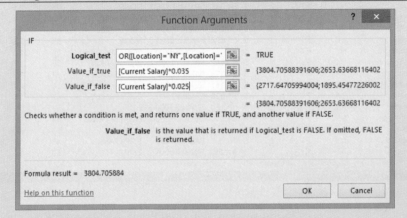

9. Click the **OK** button. The formula =IF(OR([Location]="NY",[Location]="SF"), [Current Salary]*0.035,[Current Salary]*0.025) appears in the formula bar, and the value 3804.705884 appears in cell P2 because the condition is true. The formula is automatically copied to all rows in column P of the table.

10. Position the pointer at the top of cell **P1** until the pointer changes to ⬇, and then click the left mouse button to select the Salary Increase data values.

11. Format the range with the **Accounting** format, and then increase the column width to display all values.

▶ **12.** Select cell **P2** to deselect the column. See Figure 8-15.

Figure 8-15	IF function with the OR function calculates salary increase

formula uses structured references to calculate the salary increases

salary increase for employees

P2   =IF(OR([Location]="NY",[Location]="SF"),[Current Salary]*0.035,[Current Salary]*0.025)

	A	B	F	G	H	I	J	K	L	M	N	O	P		Q
1	Emp ID	Last Name	Location	Job Status	Perf Rating	Current Salary	Medical Plan	Dental Plan	Age	Years Service	Birthday Month	401(k) Company Match	Salary Increase		
2	1002 Lowe		NY	FT	3	$ 108,706	SPOUSE2500	EMP+SPOUSE	49	6.6	Yes	$ 3,261.18	$ 3,804.71		
3	1006 Forbes		SF	FT	2	$ 75,818	NONE	NONE	30	2.3		$ 2,274.55	$ 2,653.64		
4	1010 Speulda		SF	FT	2	$ 46,143	FAMILY1000	EMP+FAMILY	47	1.7	Yes	$ 1,384.28	$ 1,614.99		
5	1014 Hunt		NY	FT	3	$ 84,036	SPOUSE1000	NONE	56	2.5		$ 2,521.09	$ 2,941.27		
6	1018 Hanson		NY	FT	1	$ 68,470	FAMILY1000	EMP+FAMILY	65	1.4		$ 2,054.11	$ 2,396.46		
7	1022 Philo		SF	FT	2	$ 130,248	FAMILY1000	EMP+FAMILY	57	1.8		$ 3,907.45	$ 4,558.69		
8	1026 Stolt		SF	FT	3	$ 101,822	FAMILY2500	NONE	38	3.8		$ 3,054.67	$ 3,563.78		
9	1030 Akhalaghi		NY	FT	2	$ 38,421	SPOUSE1000	EMP+SPOUSE	54	1.1		$ 1,152.62	$ 1,344.72		
10	1034 Vankeuren		NY	PT	3	$ 53,582	FAMILY1000	EMP+FAMILY	56	5.4		$ -	$ 1,875.37		
11	1038 Mccorkle		AT	FT	2	$ 24,373	FAMILY2500	EMP+FAMILY	73	7.6		$ 731.20	$ 609.33		
12	1042 Mattis		AT	FT	2	$ 65,181	SINGLE1000	EMP	26	4.7		$ 1,955.43	$ 1,629.53		
13	1046 Baker		DA	FT	3	$ 71,020	FAMILY2500	EMP+FAMILY	47	1.0		$ 2,130.61	$ 1,775.51		
14	1050 Vines		AT	FT	2	$ 60,130	SINGLE1000	EMP	57	5.7		$ 1,803.90	$ 1,503.25		
15	1054 Mittelman		NY	FT	2	$ 64,846	SPOUSE2500	EMP+SPOUSE	44	12.1		$ 1,945.37	$ 2,269.60		
16	1058 Coley		AT	FT	1	$ 49,832	SINGLE1000	EMP	55	8.9		$ 1,494.96	$ 1,245.80		
17	1062 Johnson		NY	FT	2	$ 76,707	FAMILY1000	EMP+FAMILY	45	1.1	Yes	$ 2,301.20	$ 2,684.73		
18	1066 Jackson		AT	FT	3	$ 91,240	SINGLE2500	EMP	30	1.2		$ 2,737.20	$ 2,281.00		

Documentation | **Employee Data** | Employee Summary | Lookup Tables ⊕

In this session, you used the IF, AND, and OR functions to determine if an employee's birth date occurs in a specified month, calculate 401(k) costs, and calculate next year's salary increases for EVG employees. Patrick still needs to calculate the employee bonuses, medical plan costs, dental plan costs, and the employee service award for each employee. In the next session, you will create formulas with functions to perform these calculations.

REVIEW

Session 8.1 Quick Check

1. What changes occur in the appearance and size of an Excel table after you enter a new column header named "Phone"?

2. Whenever you enter a formula in an empty column of an Excel table, Excel automatically fills the column with the same formula. What is this called?

3. If an Excel worksheet stores the cost per meal in cell Q5, the number of attendees in cell Q6, and the total cost of meals in cell Q7, what IF function would you enter in cell Q7 to calculate the total cost of meals (cost per meal times the number of attendees) with a minimum cost of $10,000?

4. When does the AND function return a TRUE value?

5. Write the formula that displays the label "Outstanding" in cell Y5 if the amount owed (cell X5) is greater than 0 and the transaction date (cell R5) is after 3/1/2016 (stored in cell R1), but otherwise leaves the cell blank.

6. When you create a formula that references all or parts of an Excel table, what can you use to replace the specific cell or range addresses with the actual table or column header names?

7. If the formula =IF(OR(B25="NY",B25="CA",B25="TX"),"Select","Ignore") is entered in cell B26, and "PA" is entered in cell B25, what is displayed in cell B26?

8. Write the OR function that represents the following rule—"A potential enlistee in the Army is not eligible to enlist if younger than 17 or older than 42." The age is stored in cell B25. Display "Eligible" if the potential enlistee can enlist, and display "Not Eligible" if the potential enlistee cannot enlist.

Session 8.2 Visual Overview:

A **nested IF function** is when one IF function is placed inside another IF function to test an additional condition, such as calculating employee bonuses based on three performance levels.

When the lookup value matches the first row of the lookup table, the corresponding value from the second row of the lookup table is returned to the cell with the HLOOKUP function.

This lookup table is organized horizontally and is used in the exact match HLOOKUP function to find the dental plan cost.

The invalid code in the Medical Plan column causes the IFERROR message to appear in the Medical Cost column.

The **IFERROR function** can determine if a cell contains an error value and then display the message you choose rather than the default error value.

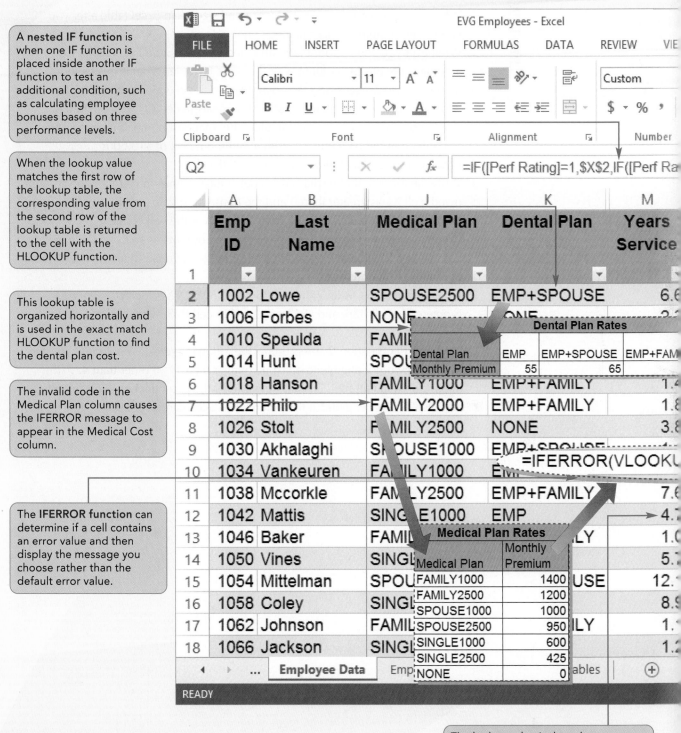

EVG Employees - Excel

FILE   HOME   INSERT   PAGE LAYOUT   FORMULAS   DATA   REVIEW   VIE

Q2   =IF([Perf Rating]=1,$X$2,IF([Perf Ra

	Emp ID	Last Name	Medical Plan	Dental Plan	Years Service
2	1002	Lowe	SPOUSE2500	EMP+SPOUSE	6.6
3	1006	Forbes	NONE	ONE	
4	1010	Speulda	FAMIL		
5	1014	Hunt	SPOU		
6	1018	Hanson	FAMILY1000	EMP+FAMILY	1.4
7	1022	Philo	FAMILY2000	EMP+FAMILY	1.8
8	1026	Stolt	F MILY2500	NONE	3.8
9	1030	Akhalaghi	SPOUSE1000	EMP+SPOUSE	
10	1034	Vankeuren	FA ILY1000	E	
11	1038	Mccorkle	FAM LY2500	EMP+FAMILY	7.6
12	1042	Mattis	SING E1000	EMP	4.
13	1046	Baker	FAMIL	LY	1.0
14	1050	Vines	SINGL		5.
15	1054	Mittelman	SPOU	USE	12.
16	1058	Coley	SINGL		8.9
17	1062	Johnson	FAMIL	ILY	1.
18	1066	Jackson	SINGL		1.2

Dental Plan Rates

Dental Plan	EMP	EMP+SPOUSE	EMP+FAM
Monthly Premium	55	65	

=IFERROR(VLOOKU

Medical Plan Rates

Medical Plan	Monthly Premium
FAMILY1000	1400
FAMILY2500	1200
SPOUSE1000	1000
SPOUSE2500	950
SINGLE1000	600
SINGLE2500	425
NONE	0

Employee Data   Emp   ables

READY

The lookup value is the value you are trying to find. In this case, the lookup value is the employee's years of service in the Years Service column, which is used to find the return value in the Service Award Payout table.

Nested IFs and Lookup Tables

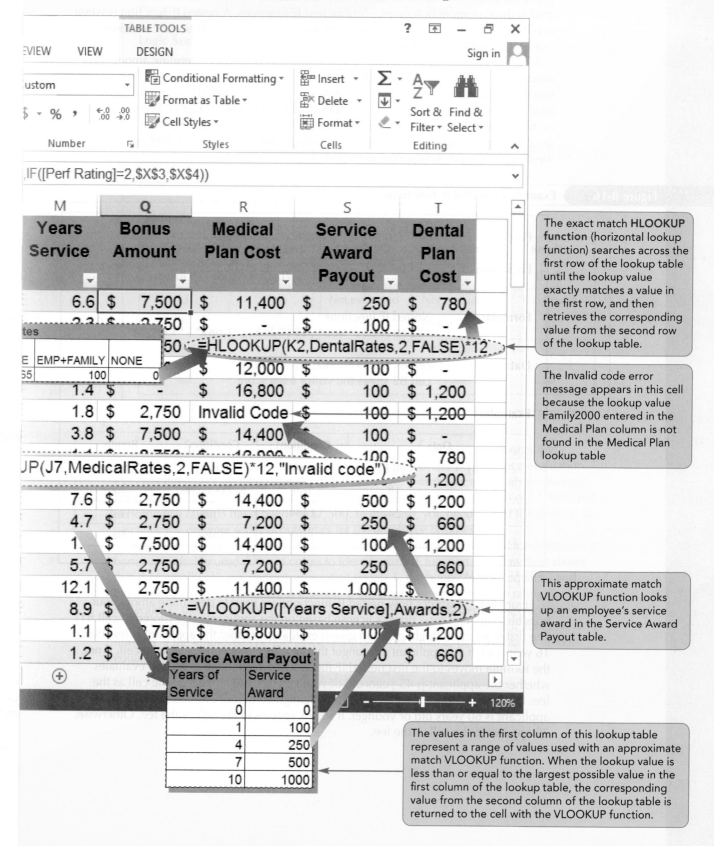

,IF([Perf Rating]=2,$X$3,$X$4))

Years Service	Bonus Amount	Medical Plan Cost	Service Award Payout	Dental Plan Cost
6.6	$ 7,500	$ 11,400	$ 250	$ 780
2.3	$ 2,750	$ -	$ 100	$ -
		50		
		$ 12,000	$ 100	$ -
1.4	$ -	$ 16,800	$ 100	$ 1,200
1.8	$ 2,750	Invalid Code	$ 100	$ 1,200
3.8	$ 7,500	$ 14,400	$ 100	$ -
			$ 100	$ 780
				$ 1,200
7.6	$ 2,750	$ 14,400	$ 500	$ 1,200
4.7	$ 2,750	$ 7,200	$ 250	$ 660
1.	$ 7,500	$ 14,400	$ 100	$ 1,200
5.7	$ 2,750	$ 7,200	$ 250	$ 660
12.1	$ 2,750	$ 11,400	$ 1,000	$ 780
8.9	$ -			
1.1	$ 2,750	$ 16,800	$ 100	$ 1,200
1.2	$ 7,50			$ 660

=HLOOKUP(K2,DentalRates,2,FALSE)*12

UP(J7,MedicalRates,2,FALSE)*12,"Invalid code")

=VLOOKUP([Years Service],Awards,2)

E	EMP+FAMILY	NONE
65	100	0

Service Award Payout

Years of Service	Service Award
0	0
1	100
4	250
7	500
10	1000

The exact match **HLOOKUP** function (horizontal lookup function) searches across the first row of the lookup table until the lookup value exactly matches a value in the first row, and then retrieves the corresponding value from the second row of the lookup table.

The Invalid code error message appears in this cell because the lookup value Family2000 entered in the Medical Plan column is not found in the Medical Plan lookup table

This approximate match VLOOKUP function looks up an employee's service award in the Service Award Payout table.

The values in the first column of this lookup table represent a range of values used with an approximate match VLOOKUP function. When the lookup value is less than or equal to the largest possible value in the first column of the lookup table, the corresponding value from the second column of the lookup table is returned to the cell with the VLOOKUP function.

cost, and EVG pays the entire amount. If an employee provides evidence of health coverage elsewhere, there is no medical plan cost (NONE). You could calculate the medical plan costs for each employee using several nested IF functions. However, a simpler approach is to use a lookup function.

You can use the Medical Plan Rates data shown in Figure 8-21 as an exact match lookup table. The lookup table includes the available plans and their corresponding monthly premiums. The medical plan cost for each eligible employee is based on the plan the employee selected. To retrieve the monthly cost for an employee, Excel moves down the first column in the Medical Plan Rates lookup table until it finds the medical plan code that matches the employee's medical plan. Then it moves to the second column in the lookup table to locate the monthly premium, which is then displayed in the cell where the lookup formula is entered or used as part of a calculation. If the employee's Medical Plan code doesn't match one of the values in the first column of the MedicalRates table (spelling or spaces are different), the #N/A error value is displayed. For example, to find the return value for the SPOUSE2500 lookup value, Excel searches the first column of the lookup table until the SPOUSE2500 entry is found. Then, Excel moves to the second column of the lookup table to locate the corresponding return value, which is 950, in this case.

Figure 8-21   **MedicalRates lookup table used for an exact match lookup**

Lookup Value = "SPOUSE2500"

search down the first column until the lookup value exactly matches the value in the first column

Medical Plan Rates	
Medical Plan	Monthly Premium
FAMILY1000	1400
FAMILY2500	1200
SPOUSE1000	1000
SPOUSE2500	950
SINGLE1000	600
SINGLE2500	425
NONE	0

return the corresponding value from the second column of the lookup table

Return Value = 950

© 2014 Cengage Learning

Lookup tables can also be constructed as approximate match lookups. A discount based on the quantity of items purchased where each discount covers a range of units purchased is an example of an approximate match lookup. Figure 8-22 shows the approximate match lookup table for these quantity discounts. In this example, purchases of fewer than 25 units receive no discount, purchases of between 25 and 99 units receive a 2 percent discount, purchases of between 100 and 499 units receive a 3 percent discount, and purchases of 500 or more units receive a 4 percent discount. For example, to find the quantity discount for a purchase of 55 units, Excel searches the first column of the lookup table until the largest value that is less than or equal to 55 (the lookup value) is found, which is 25 in this example. Then, Excel moves to the second column of the lookup table and returns 2 percent as the quantity discount.

Figure 8-22   Approximate match lookup table

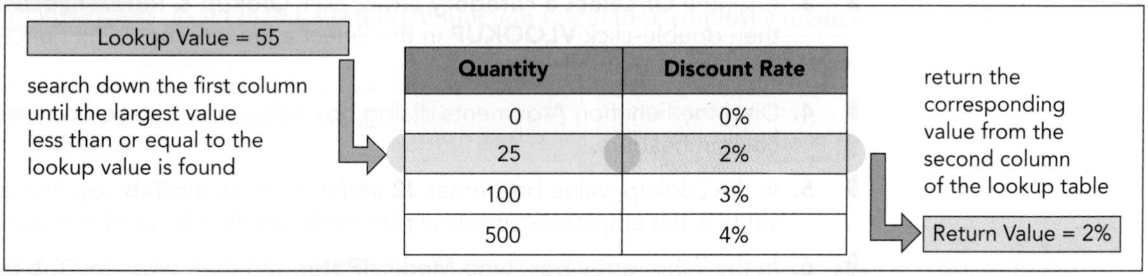

© 2014 Cengage Learning

Using the VLOOKUP Function to Find an Exact Match

To retrieve the correct value from the lookup table, you use the VLOOKUP function. Recall that the VLOOKUP function searches vertically down the first column of the lookup table for the value you entered, and then retrieves the corresponding value from another column of the table. The VLOOKUP function has the syntax

VLOOKUP(*lookup_value,table_array,col_index_num*[,*range_lookup*])

where *lookup_value* is the value, cell reference, a defined name, or a structured reference you want to search for in the first column of the lookup table; *table_array* is a range reference, a defined name, or the name of an Excel table that is the lookup table; *col_index_num* is the number of the column in the lookup table that contains the value you want to return; and *range_lookup* indicates whether the lookup table is an exact match (FALSE) or an approximate match (TRUE). The *range_lookup* argument is optional; if you don't include a *range_lookup* value, the value is considered TRUE (an approximate match).

You'll use the VLOOKUP function to calculate the annual medical plan cost for EVG because you want to search the values in the first column of the lookup table. You can use the range reference (the range A5:B11 on the Lookup Tables worksheet) or the defined name MedicalRates when you reference the lookup table in the VLOOKUP formula to determine the annual medical plan cost for an employee:

Range reference =VLOOKUP(J2,'Lookup Tables'!$A$5:$B$11,2,FALSE)*12

Defined name =VLOOKUP(J2,MedicalRates,2,FALSE)*12

Both of these formulas use the VLOOKUP function to search for the employee's Medical Plan code (column J) in the Employee table, in the first column of the Medical Rates lookup table (the range A5:B11 in the Lookup Tables worksheet), and then return the corresponding value from the second column of the lookup table, which shows the monthly cost. The formulas use FALSE as the *range_lookup* argument because you want the lookup value to exactly match a value in the first column of the lookup table.

Patrick wants you to enter the VLOOKUP function using the defined name to reference the lookup table in the VLOOKUP function so he can easily determine what's included in the function. This is also simpler than entering range references, and you don't need to change the reference to an absolute reference.

To find an exact match in the MedicalRates table using the VLOOKUP function:

1. In cell **R1**, enter **Medical Plan Cost**. The table expands to include the new column.

2. Make sure cell **R2** is the active cell, and then click the **Insert Function** button f_x next to the formula bar. The Insert Function dialog box opens.

| Figure 8-34 | Invalid code message in the Medical Plan Cost column |

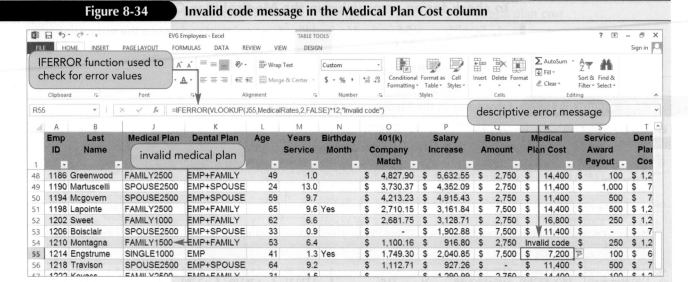

Trouble? If the error #NAME? appears in cell R54, you may have omitted quotation marks around the "Invalid code" error message. Correct the formula, and then continue with Step 5.

5. In cell **J54**, enter **FAMILY2500**. The medical plan code you entered is valid, so the medical cost value $14,400 appears in cell R54.

6. Scroll to the top of the table, select cell **R2**, and then observe in the formula bar that the IFERROR formula was copied to this cell.

In this session, you used nested IF functions to determine employee bonuses, you used the VLOOKUP function to calculate the medical plan cost, and you used the HLOOKUP function to calculate the dental plan cost and service award payouts. You also used the IFERROR function to display a descriptive message if invalid medical plan codes are entered in the Employee table. In the next session, you will use conditional formatting to identify duplicate records, and use the COUNTIF, SUMIF, and AVERAGEIF functions to report on employee salaries.

REVIEW

Session 8.2 Quick Check

1. What is a nested IF function?
2. If cell Y5 displays the value 35, cell Y6 displays the value 42, and cell Y7 contains the following formula, what is displayed in cell Y7?

   `=IF(Y5>Y6,"Older",IF(Y5<Y6,"Younger","Same Age"))`

3. Explain the difference between an exact match and an approximate match lookup.
4. A customer table includes columns for name, street address, city, state abbreviation, and zip code. A second table includes state abbreviations and state names from all 50 states (one state per row). You need to add a new column to the customer table with the state name. What is the most appropriate function to use to display the state name in this new column?
5. Convert the following criteria used to determine a student's level to a table that can be used in a VLOOKUP function to display the level of each student:

Earned Credits	Level
>=0 and <=30	Freshman
>=31 and <=60	Sophomore
>=61 and <=90	Junior
>=91	Senior

6. In cell X5, the error value #DIV/0! appears when you divide by 0. What IFERROR function can you use with the formula =W5/W25 so that instead of the error value #DIV/0! being displayed, the message "Dividing by zero" appears in the cell?
7. In cell X5, the formula =W5/W25 results in the error value #DIV/0! when W25 stores the value 0. Use the IF function to modify the formula =W5/W25 so that instead of the error value #DIV/0! being displayed when W25 stores 0, the message "Dividing by zero" appears in the cell.
8. Which function could be used with the following Sales Tax Rate table to display the sales tax rate for a customer in one of these four states?

State	CO	NM	OK	TX
Sales Tax Rate	10%	7%	9%	9.5%

4. Click the **Format** button. The Format Cells dialog box opens.

5. Click the **Fill** tab, if necessary, and then, in the Background Color palette, click **gold** (the third color in the last row).

6. Click the **OK** button in each dialog box. The duplicate records in the table are formatted with a gold background color. See Figure 8-38.

Figure 8-38   **Edited conditional formatting for duplicate records**

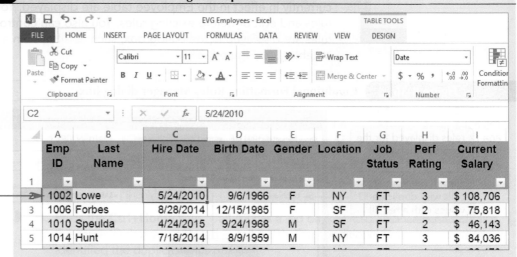

background color of duplicate value is gold

The cell text is easier to read on the gold background. Patrick wants you to correct the duplicate ID in cell A101 by entering the employee's actual ID number. The conditional format will remain active and apply to any new records that Patrick adds to the Employee table.

To correct the duplicate ID:

1. Make cell **A101** the active cell, and then enter **1398**. The employee's ID is updated and the conditional formatting disappears because the value in the ID column is no longer a duplicate.

2. Scroll to the top of the Employee table, and verify that the conditional formatting no longer appears in cell A2.

Keep in mind that the Duplicate Values rule enables you to verify that each entry in the ID column is unique, but it does not ensure that each unique value is accurate.

INSIGHT

Creating a Formula to Conditionally Format Cells

Sometimes the built-in conditional formatting rules do not apply the formatting you need. In these instances, you may be able to create a conditional formatting rule based on a formula that uses a logical expression to describe the condition you want. For example, you can create a formula that uses conditional formatting to compare cells in different columns or to highlight an entire row.

When you create the formula, keep in mind the following guidelines:

- The formula must start with an equal sign.
- The formula must be in the form of a logical test that results in a True or False value.
- In most cases, the formula should use relative references and point to the first row of data in the table. If the formula references a cell or range outside the table, use an absolute reference.
- After you create the formula, enter test values to ensure the conditional formatting works in all situations that you intended.

For example, to use conditional formatting to highlight whether the hire date entered in column C is less than the birth date entered in column D, you need to enter a formula that applies conditional formatting and compares cells in different columns of a table. The following steps describe how to create this formula:

1. Select the range you want to format (in this case, the Hire Date column).
2. On the HOME tab, in the Styles group, click the Conditional Formatting button, and then click New Rule.
3. In the Select a Rule Type box, click the "Use a formula to determine which cells to format" rule.
4. In the "Format values where this formula is true" box, enter the appropriate formula (in this case, =C2<D2).
5. Click the Format button to open the Format Cells dialog box, and then select the formatting you want to apply.
6. Click the OK button in each dialog box.

Another example is to highlight the entire row if an employee has 10 or more years of service. In this case, you would select the range of data, such as A2:T101, and then enter =M$2>=10 in the "Format values where this formula is true" box. The other steps remain the same.

Using Functions to Summarize Data Conditionally

The COUNT function tallies the number of data values in a range, the SUM function adds the values in a range, and the AVERAGE function calculates the average of the values in a range. However, sometimes you need to calculate a conditional count, sum, or average using only those cells that meet a particular condition. In those cases, you need to use the COUNTIF, SUMIF, and AVERAGEIF functions. For example, Patrick wants to create a report that shows the number, total, and average salaries for employees in New York and San Francisco. You will use the COUNTIF, SUMIF, and AVERAGEIF functions to do this.

Using the COUNTIF Function

You can calculate the number of cells in a range that match criteria you specify by using the COUNTIF function, which is sometimes referred to as a **conditional count**. The COUNTIF function has the syntax

COUNTIF(*range*, *criteria*)

where *range* is the range of cells you want to count, and *criteria* is a number, an expression, a cell reference, or text that defines which cells to count.

There are many ways to express the criteria in a COUNTIF function, as shown in Figure 8-39.

Figure 8-39   Examples of COUNTIF function criteria

Formula	Explanation of Formula	Result
=COUNTIF(F2:F101,"DA")	Number of employee in DA (Dallas)	13
=COUNTIF(F2:F101,F2)	Number of employees in cell F2 (NY)	48
=COUNTIF(I2:I101,"<50000")	Number of employees with salary <50000	22
=COUNTIF(I2:I101,">=" &I2)	Number of employees with salary >= value in cell I2 (108706)	24

© 2014 Cengage Learning

TIP

You can use structured references or cell and range addresses to reference cells within an Excel table.

Patrick wants to know how many employees are located in New York. You can use the COUNTIF function to find this answer because you want a conditional count (a count of employees who meet a specified criterion; in this case, employees located in New York). The location information is stored in column F of the Employee table. To count the number of employees in New York, you can use either one of the following formulas:

Range reference   =COUNTIF('Employee Data'!F2:F101,"=NY")

Fully qualified structured reference   =COUNTIF(Employee[Location],"=NY")

With either formula, Excel counts all of the cells in the Location column of the Employee table that contain the text equal to NY. Because NY is text, you must enclose it within quotation marks. It is not necessary to enclose numbers in quotation marks.

You will enter this formula using the COUNTIF function in the Employee Summary worksheet. You will use the Insert Function dialog box to help you build the formula using worksheet and range references to calculate the number of employees who work in New York.

To count employees located in New York using the COUNTIF function:

1. Go to the **Employee Summary** worksheet.

2. Select cell **C4**, and then click the **Insert Function** button f_x next to the formula bar. The Insert Function dialog box opens.

3. Click the **Or select a category** arrow, and then click **Statistical**.

4. In the Select a function box, double-click **COUNTIF**. The Function Arguments dialog box opens.

5. In the Range box, type **'Employee Data'!F2:F101** to enter the range to search, and then press the **Tab** key. The range 'Employee Data'!F2:F101 refers to all data values in the range F2:F101 (Location column) in the Employee Data worksheet.

6. In the Criteria box, type **B4**. Cell B4 contains NY, which is the criterion you want Excel to use to determine which employee records to count. See Figure 8-40. You could also have typed "=NY" or "NY" in the criteria box.

Figure 8-40 **Function Arguments dialog box for the COUNTIF function**

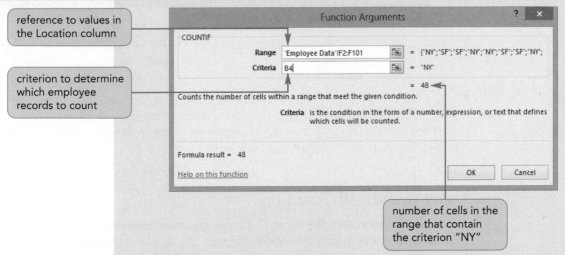

reference to values in the Location column

criterion to determine which employee records to count

number of cells in the range that contain the criterion "NY"

7. Click the **OK** button. Cell C4 remains active. The formula =COUNTIF('Employee Data'!F2:F101,B4) appears in the formula bar, and 48 appears in cell C4, indicating that the company has 48 employees in New York. See Figure 8-41.

Figure 8-41 **Location Summary for NY employees**

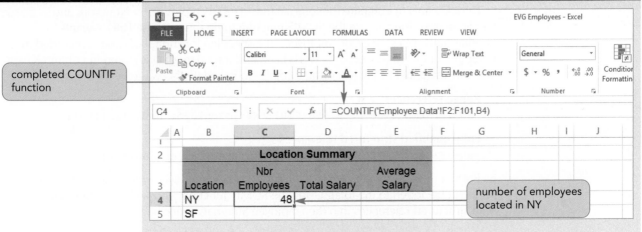

completed COUNTIF function

number of employees located in NY

You will enter a similar formula to calculate the number of employees who work in San Francisco. This time, however, you will use structured references to specify the range to search.

To count the number of employees who work in San Francisco:

1. Select cell **C5**, and then click the **Insert Function** button f_x next to the formula bar. The Insert Function dialog box opens with the Statistical category still selected.

▶ **2.** In the Select a function box, double-click **COUNTIF**. The Function Arguments dialog box opens.

▶ **3.** In the Range box, type **Employee[Location]** to enter the range to search, and then press the **Tab** key. The range Employee[Location] is a structured reference that refers to all data values in the Location column in the Employee table (the range F2:F101). The beginning values in the Location column appear to the right of the Range box.

▶ **4.** In the Criteria box, type **B5**. Cell B5 contains SF (the value shown to the right of the Criteria box), which is the criterion Excel will use to determine which employee records to count.

▶ **5.** Click the **OK** button. Cell C5 remains active. The formula =COUNTIF(Employee[Location],B5) appears in the formula bar and 17 appears in cell C5, indicating 17 employees work in San Francisco.

Using the SUMIF Function

The SUMIF function adds the values in a range that meet criteria you specify. The SUMIF function is also called a **conditional sum**. The syntax of the SUMIF function is

```
SUMIF(range, criteria[, sum_range])
```

where *range* is the range of cells you want to filter before calculating a sum; *criteria* is a number, an expression, a cell reference, or text that defines which cells to count; and *sum_range* is the range of cells to total. The *sum_range* is optional; if you omit it, Excel will total the values specified in the *range* argument. For example, if you want to total the salaries for all employees with salaries greater than $50,000 (">50000"), you do not use the optional third argument.

Patrick wants to compare the total salaries paid to employees in New York and San Francisco. You can use the SUMIF function to do this because Patrick wants to conditionally add salaries of employees at a specified location. Location is recorded in column F of the Employee Data worksheet, and the salary data is stored in column K. You can use either of the following formulas to calculate this value:

Range references
```
=SUMIF('Employee Data'!F2:F101,"NY",'Employee Data'!I2:I101)
```

Fully qualified structured references
```
=SUMIF(Employee[Location],"NY",Employee[Current Salary])
```

Both of these formulas state that the salary of any employee whose location is New York will be added to the total. Using the SUMIF function, you will insert the formula with structured references into the Employee Summary worksheet.

To sum employee salaries in the New York and San Francisco locations using the SUMIF function:

▶ **1.** Select cell **D4**, and then click the **Insert Function** button f_x next to the formula bar. The Insert Function dialog box opens.

▶ **2.** Click the **Or select a category** arrow, and then click **Math & Trig**.

▶ **3.** In the Select a function box, double-click **SUMIF**. The Function Arguments dialog box opens.

4. In the Range box, type **Employee[Location]** to specify the range of data to filter, and then press the **Tab** key. The range Employee[Location] is a structured reference that refers to all data values in the Location column in the Employee table (the range F2:F101).

5. In the Criteria box, type **B4** and then press the **Tab** key. Cell B4 contains "NY" (shown to the right of the Criteria box), which is the criterion Excel will use to determine which employee records to sum.

6. In the Sum_range box, type **Employee[Current Salary]** to indicate that the Current Salary column in the Employee table contains the data to sum in the filtered rows. The values to the right of the Sum_range box are the amounts in the filtered Current Salary column. See Figure 8-42.

Figure 8-42	Function Arguments dialog box for the SUMIF function

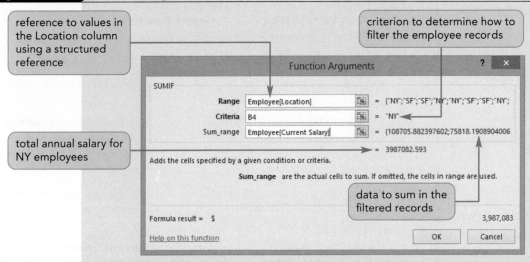

reference to values in the Location column using a structured reference

criterion to determine how to filter the employee records

total annual salary for NY employees

data to sum in the filtered records

7. Click the **OK** button. Cell D4 is active. The formula =SUMIF(Employee[Location],B4,Employee[Current Salary]) appears in the formula bar and $3,987,083 appears in cell D4, indicating the total annual salaries paid to New York employees.

   Trouble? If Invalid appears in the cell or an error message appears, you probably mistyped some part of the formula. Review the SUMIF formula you entered and make sure it matches the formula =SUMIF(Employee[Location],B4, Employee[Current Salary]).

8. Copy the SUMIF formula in cell D4 to **D5**. The total Current Salary for employees working in San Francisco is $1,917,420.

Using the AVERAGEIF Function

The AVERAGEIF function is similar to the SUMIF function. You use the AVERAGEIF function to calculate the average of values in a range that meet criteria you specify. The syntax of the AVERAGEIF function is

AVERAGEIF(*range*, *criteria*[, *average_range*])

where *range* is the range of cells you want to filter before calculating the average, *criteria* is the condition used to filter the range, and *average_range* is the range of cells to average. The *average_range* is optional; if you omit it, Excel will average the values specified in the *range* argument.

Patrick also wants to compare the average salaries paid to employees in New York and San Francisco. Location is recorded in column F of the Employee Data worksheet, and the current salary data is stored in column I. The formulas to calculate this value are:

Range references

```
=AVERAGEIF('Employee Data'!F2:F101,"NY",'Employee Data'!I2:I101)
```

Fully qualified structured references

```
=AVERAGEIF(Employee[Location],"NY",Employee[Current Salary])
```

Both of these formulas state that the current salary of any employee whose location is New York will be included in the average. You will enter the formula into the Employee Summary worksheet using the AVERAGEIF function with structured references.

To average employee salaries in New York and San Francisco using the AVERAGEIF function:

▶ 1. Select cell **E4**, and then click the **Insert Function** button f_x next to the formula bar. The Insert Function dialog box opens.

▶ 2. Click the **Or select a category** arrow, and then click **Statistical**.

▶ 3. In the Select a function box, double-click **AVERAGEIF**. The Function Arguments dialog box opens.

▶ 4. In the Range box, type the structured reference **Employee[Location]** to specify the range of data to filter, and then press the **Tab** key. The range Employee[Location] is a structured reference that refers to all data values in the Location column in the Employee table (the range F2:F101).

▶ 5. In the Criteria box, type **B4** and then press the **Tab** key. Cell B4 contains "NY" (shown to the right of the Criteria box), which is the criterion Excel will use to determine which employee records to average.

▶ 6. In the Average_range box, type **Employee[Current Salary]** to indicate that the Current Salary column in the Employee table contains the data to average in the filtered rows. See Figure 8-43.

| Figure 8-43 | Function Arguments dialog box for the AVERAGEIF function |

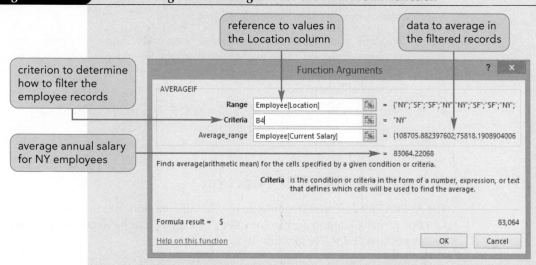

▶ 7. Click the **OK** button. Cell E4 remains active. The formula =AVERAGEIF(Employee[Location],B4,Employee[Current Salary]) appears in the formula bar and $83,064 appears in cell E4, indicating the average salary paid to New York employees.

▶ **8.** Copy the formula in cell E4 to cell **E5**. EVG pays an average of $112,789 to employees working in San Francisco. See Figure 8-44.

Figure 8-44   **Completed Location Analysis report**

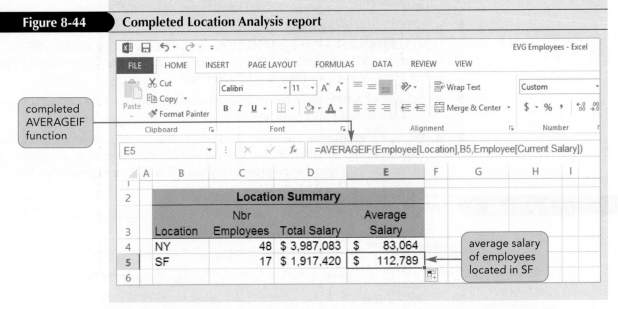

completed AVERAGEIF function

average salary of employees located in SF

As Patrick enters new employees or edits the location or current salary values of current employees, the values in the Employee Summary worksheet will be automatically updated because the formulas reference the Employee table.

Using the TRANSPOSE Function

The **TRANSPOSE function** is used to change the orientation of a range—that is, return a vertical range of cells as a horizontal range, or vice versa. The TRANSPOSE function has the syntax

 TRANSPOSE(array)

where *array* is the range you want to convert from row data to column data (or vice versa). To use the TRANSPOSE function, complete the following steps:

1. Select the range where you want to place the transposed data. Be sure to select the opposite number of rows and columns as the original data. For example, if the range has five rows and three columns you would select a range that has three rows and five columns.
2. In the first cell of the selected range, type =TRANSPOSE(to begin the function.
3. Type the range reference of the original range of data.
4. Type) to complete the function.
5. Press the **Ctrl+Shift+Enter** keys to enter the function. (Note that pressing only the Enter key would create incorrect formula results.) Excel places curly brackets {} around the array formula and enters the formula in every cell of the selected range.

Keep in mind that the TRANSPOSE function only copies the data from the cells in the initial range. Any formatting applied to the original range must be reapplied to the new range. However, any changes made to the data in the original range are automatically made to the data in the transposed range. To delete the transposed range, select the entire range, and then press the Delete key.

Patrick has recently hired a new employee and he asks you to add the new record to the Excel table.

To add a record to the Employee table:

► 1. Go to the **Employee Data** worksheet, and then select cell **A102**. You will enter the new employee record in this row.

► 2. In the range **A102:K102**, enter **1402** for Emp ID, **Joplin** for Last Name, **4/1/2016** for Hire Date, **11/15/1970** for Birth Date, **M** for Gender, **SF** for Location, **PT** for Job Status, **3** for Perf Rating, **23000** for Current Salary, **None** for Medical Plan, and **None** for Dental Plan.

► 3. Select cell **A103**. The new employee record is added to the Employee table, and all values in the calculated columns are automatically updated.

► 4. Go to the **Employee Summary** worksheet. The Location Analysis report has been updated to reflect the new employee. The number of employees in San Francisco is 18 and the average salary is $107,801. See Figure 8-45.

Figure 8-45	Updated Location Analysis report

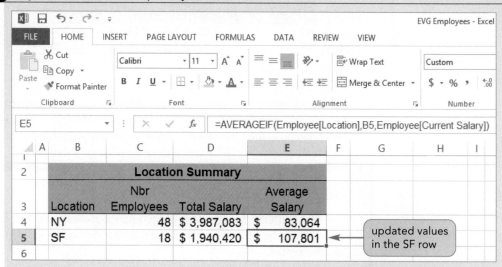

5. Save the workbook, and then close it.

If the employee data had been stored as a range of data instead of an Excel table, the Location Analysis report would not have automatically updated. Instead, you would have had to modify all the formulas in the report to reflect the expanded range of employee data. Patrick is pleased with the formulas you added to the Employee Data and Employee Summary worksheets.

Session 8.3 Quick Check

REVIEW

1. Would you apply the duplicate value conditional formatting rule to a table column of last names? Why or why not?
2. If you receive a worksheet that includes conditional formatting, which dialog box would you use to find out what criteria were used for the formatting?
3. Explain what the following formula calculates:
   =COUNTIF(Employee[Gender],"=F")
4. Explain what the following formula calculates:
   =AVERAGEIF(Employee[Age],">50",Employee[Current Salary]) calculates.
5. Explain what the following formula calculates:
   =SUMIF(Employee[Job Status],"=FT",Employee[Current Salary])
6. Explain what the following formula calculates:
   =COUNTIF(Employee[Current Salary],">100000")
7. To display the number of employees working in Dallas (DA), which function would you use—the VLOOKUP, COUNTIF, IF, or COUNT function?
8. To identify duplicate values in a column of an Excel table, what Excel feature would you use?

Review Assignments

PRACTICE

Data File needed for the Review Assignments: Compensation.xlsx

Patrick wants you to try using some alternative calculations for bonuses and benefits for EVG employees. Complete the following:

1. Open the **Compensation** workbook located in the Excel8 ▶ Review folder included with your Data Files, and then save the workbook as **Bonus and Benefits**.

2. In the Documentation worksheet, enter your name and the date.

3. In the Employee Data worksheet, rename the Excel table as **EmpData**.

4. Employees who are age 50 or older are allowed to contribute up to $22,000 during the year to their 401(k) plan; all employees under age 50 can contribute a maximum of $17,000 during the year. In the 401(k) Max Contrib column, use an IF function to determine the maximum 401(k) contribution for each employee.

5. Only full-time (Job Status) employees over the age of 30 (Age) with more than one year of service are eligible for the 401(k) benefit. In the 401(k) Company Match column, enter the IF and AND functions to calculate the 401(k) company match as a percentage of the employee's current salary; use a reference to cell X1 to obtain the 401(k) matching percent rate (3 percent). If the employee is not eligible, enter **0**.

6. All full-time (FT) employees are eligible for a bonus. Pay Grade A employees receive $3,000 (cell X2), Pay Grade B employees receive $6,000 (cell X3), and Pay Grade C employees receive $8,000 (cell X4). In the Bonus Amount column, enter nested IF functions to calculate the bonus. For employees not eligible for a bonus, display the text **NE**.

7. In the Eligible Salary Increase column, enter IF and OR functions to insert the text **Not Eligible** if the employee's pay grade is C or the employee's job status is a consultant (CN). Leave the cell blank if the individual is eligible for a salary increase.

8. In the Vision Plan Cost column, enter the HLOOKUP function to do an exact match lookup to calculate the annual vision plan cost. Use the VisionRates data (the range $H$3:$K$4 in the Lookup Tables worksheet), which contains the monthly vision rates. (*Hint*: The HLOOKUP function provides the monthly rate, which you will need to multiply by 12 to determine the annual rate.)

9. In the Years Service column, modify the formula to incorporate the IFERROR function and display the message **Invalid hire date** if an error value occurs. Test the modified formula by changing the date in cell C2 from 8/28/2014 to **18/28/2014**. Increase the column width as needed to display the entire message.

10. Edit the Duplicate Values conditional formatting rule applied to the Emp ID column so that the fill color of the duplicate value is formatted as light blue (the seventh color in the bottom row of the Background Color palette). Test this change by typing **1002** in cell A101.

11. In the Employee Summary worksheet, enter the COUNTIF function in cells C3 and C4 to count the number of female and male employees, respectively.

12. In cells D3 and D4, enter the AVERAGEIF function to calculate the average salary of female employees and the average salary of male employees, respectively. Format the average salary column using the Accounting format with two decimal places.

13. Save the workbook, and then close it.

Case Problem 1

Data File needed for this Case Problem: Spirit.xlsx

The Spirit Store   Alice Meachen established The Spirit Store, which sells products to loyal alums of Central State College. Products offered by Alice on her website range from tee shirts and backpacks to mugs and blankets—and all feature the school's logo. Alice has a large, steady base of clients who find these uniquely designed products a great reminder of their college days. To ensure the timely receipt of payments, Alice wants you to use Excel to create an invoice she can use for each customer transaction. Complete the following:

1. Open the **Sprit** workbook located in the Excel8 ▸ Case1 folder included with your Data Files, and then save the workbook as **Spirit Store**.
2. In the Documentation worksheet, enter your name and the date.
3. In the Product Pricing and Shipping worksheet, assign the defined name **ShippingCost** to the data stored in the range D2:E7, which can be used for an approximate match lookup. (*Hint*: The lookup table includes only the values, not the descriptive labels.)
4. In the Invoice worksheet, use data validation to make it easier to enter ordered items in the range C16:C36 by creating a list of the different items in the Product Pricing table in the Product Pricing and Shipping worksheet. (*Hint*: Select the entire range before setting the validation rule.)
5. In the Per Unit column (the range G16:G36), use a VLOOKUP function to retrieve the per-unit price of each ordered product from the Product Pricing data in the range A3:B28 in the Product and Shipping worksheet. (*Hint*: Use the defined name ProductPrice that was assigned to the Product Pricing data.)
6. Modify the formula in the Per Unit column by combining the IFERROR function with the VLOOKUP function to display either the per-unit price or a blank cell if an error value occurs.
7. In the Total column (the range H16:H36), enter a formula to calculate the total charge for that row (Qty × Per Unit). Use the IFERROR function to display either the total charge or a blank cell if an error value occurs. Format the column appropriately.
8. In the Subtotal cell (cell H37), add a formula to sum the Total column. Use the IFERROR function to display either the subtotal or a blank cell if an error value occurs. Format this cell appropriately.
9. In the Sales Tax cell (cell H38), enter a formula with nested IF functions to calculate 8.25 percent of the subtotal (cell H37) if the customer's state (cell D12) is OH, or 8.75 percent if the state is MI; otherwise, use 0 percent for the sales tax. Format this cell appropriately. (*Hint*: The defined name Subtotl is assigned to cell H37. Note that the defined name "Subtotl" is intentionally not spelled as "Subtotal," which is the name of an Excel function. The defined name State is assigned to cell D12.)
10. In the Shipping cell (cell H39), enter a formula that looks up the shipping cost from the Shipping Cost table in the Product Pricing and Shipping worksheet based on the subtotal in cell H37. If the subtotal is 0, the shipping cost should display 0. Format this cell appropriately. (*Hint*: Use the defined name you created for the Shipping Cost table data.)
11. In the Total Due cell (cell H40), calculate the invoice total by entering a formula that adds the values in the Subtotal, Sales Tax, and Shipping cells. Format this cell appropriately.
12. Test the worksheet using the following data:

   Sold to: **Ellen Farmer**
   　　　　　　　　222 Central Avenue
   　　　　　　　　Arlington, MI 60005
   Date: **6/15/2016**
   Items ordered: **Blanket**, **2**
   　　　　　　　　Duffle Bag - Large, **1**
   　　　　　　　　Scarf, **2**

13. Save the workbook, and then close it.

TROUBLESHOOT

Case Problem 2

Data File needed for this Case Problem: Receivables.xlsx

Ward Consulting   Doug Gold is an accountant for Ward Consulting, a firm that provides research services for various corporate and government agencies. Each month, Doug provides the controller with an analysis of the outstanding accounts. Doug uses Excel to track these accounts. He asks you to enter formulas to allow him to analyze the data. Complete the following:

1. Open the **Receivables** workbook located in the Excel8 ► Case2 folder included with your Data Files, and then save the workbook as **Receivables Overdue**.
2. In the Documentation worksheet, enter your name and the date.
3. In the Invoices worksheet, in cell B1, enter **7/1/2016** as the current date. Note the defined name CurrentDate has been assigned to cell B1.

⚙ **Troubleshoot** 4. The sales rep commission rate varies for each sales rep. In column D, Doug used a VLOOKUP function to look up the commission rate for each sales rep, and then multiplied the commission rate by the invoice amount to calculate the commission. Although the first two rows in column D of the Excel table named Aging display the correct commission, all the other cells display #N/A. Find the problem with the formulas in the Commission column and fix it.

5. In column G, calculate the days past due. If the number of days since the invoice was sent (CurrentDate – Invoice Date) is greater than 30, calculate the days past due (Current Date – Invoice Date – 30); otherwise, enter 0.

6. Create the following formulas to assign the value in the Invoice Amount column to one of five columns—Current, 1–30 days, 31–60 days, 61–90 days, and Over 90 days:
   a. In the Current column, create a formula to display the invoice amount (column F) in the Current column if the number of days past due is 0.
   b. In the 1–30 days column, create a formula to display the invoice amount if the number of days past due is greater than or equal to 1 and less than or equal to 30.
   c. In the 31–60 days column, create a formula to display the invoice amount if the number of days past due is greater than or equal to 31 and less than or equal to 60.
   d. In the 61–90 days column, create a formula to display the invoice amount if the number of days past due is greater than or equal to 61 and less than or equal to 90.
   e. In the Over 90 days column, create a formula to display the invoice amount if the number of days past due is greater than or equal to 91 days.
   f. Format columns H through L in the Accounting format with two decimal places.

7. The invoice amount (column F) for each invoice can only appear once in columns H through L. In column N, do the following to create a formula to verify this rule.
   a. In cell N3, enter the label **Error Check**.
   b. In the range N4:N105, enter a formula using the IF and COUNT functions. The logical test of the IF function counts the number of cells that have an entry in columns H through L for each invoice. If the count is greater than one, the formula displays **Error**; otherwise, it leaves the cell blank.

8. Copy the Invoices worksheet to a new sheet and name it **Overdue Accts**. In the Overdue Accts worksheet, do the following:
   a. Filter the records so only invoices whose balance is past due are displayed.
   b. Sort the filtered data by invoice date (oldest first).
   c. Include a Total row in this table and display sums for columns I through L.
   d. Hide columns C, D, F, H, and N.
   e. Remove the filter buttons and gridlines from the table. (*Hint*: Use options on VIEW tab and the TABLE TOOLS DESIGN tab.)

⚙ **Troubleshoot** 9. In the Invoice Reports worksheet, Doug used the COUNTIF function to count the number of invoices for each sales rep. The formulas he created display only zeros. Fix the formulas in the range B3:B7 so that they display the number of invoices processed by each sales rep.

10. In the Invoice Reports worksheet, complete the Sales Rep Analysis report. In the Commission and Total Amount columns (columns C and D), use the SUMIF function to summarize commissions (column D in the Aging table in the Invoice worksheet) and the invoice amount (column F in the Aging table) for each sales rep. In row 7 of the report, calculate the totals. Format these columns appropriately.

11. In the Invoice Reports worksheet, complete the Accounts Receivable Aging report in the range F1:H8 by creating formulas that count the number of invoices for each group in the Invoices worksheet and sum the total amounts for those invoices.

12. In the Invoice Reports worksheet, in the range A12:B17, use the COUNTIF, SUMIF, and AVERAGEIF functions to complete the report. (*Hint*: The formulas will reference the Invoice Amount (column F) in the Invoices worksheet. Review Figure 8-39 to see various ways to enter criteria in the COUNTIF, SUMIF and AVERAGEIF functions.)

   a. In cell B15, use the COUNTIF function to count the number of invoices greater than the amount in cell B13.

   b. In cell B16, use the SUMIF function to add the total value of invoices greater than the amount in cell B13.

   c. In cell B17, use the AVERAGEIF function to calculate the average value of these invoices.

13. In cell B13, enter **1000** as the invoice amount above which invoices are included in the report.

14. Save the workbook, and then close it.

Case Problem 3

CREATE

Data File needed for this Case Problem: Currency.xlsx

Convenient Currency Exchange   Tourists about to travel from the United States to another country often need to obtain funds in the local currency of the country to which they are traveling. To satisfy this need, the Convenient Currency Exchange (CCE) set up kiosks at international airports around the country to provide currency exchange for a small fee. CCE's owner has asked you to complete the Excel workbook to simplify the calculation process. Complete the following:

1. Open the **Currency** workbook located in the Excel8 ▸ Case3 folder included with your Data Files, and then save the workbook as **Currency Calculator** in the location specified by your instructor.

2. In the Documentation worksheet, enter your name and the date.

3. In the Currency Calculator worksheet, in the range A3:D14, complete the Currency Conversion Table. Search the web to find the name of each country's currency (column B), its three-character currency code (column D), and what $1 (U.S.) equals in each country's currency (column C). As an example, the first row in the table has been completed for Australia. Be sure to update the $1 U.S. Equals cell for Australia to the current exchange rate.

4. In cell H4, create a data validation to create a list of countries in column A that users can select from to avoid data entry errors when entering the country name. (*Hint*: Use the defined name CountryList to reference countries.) Select Australia from the list.

5. In cell H5, enter **1000** as the U.S. dollars received.

6. In cell H6, enter a formula to calculate the conversion fee. If cell H5 is blank, cell H6 should also be blank. Otherwise, CCE charges a conversion fee of 3 percent (cell B17) of the total U.S. dollars received with a minimum charge of $5 (cell B18).

7. In cell H7, subtract the conversion fee (entered in cell H6) from the dollars received (in cell H5) to obtain the amount to be converted to the foreign currency.

8. In cell H9, use a VLOOKUP function to calculate the amount of foreign currency the traveler will receive. Multiply the amount being converted (in cell H7) by the correct exchange rate.

9. In cell G10, display the appropriate currency name of the country being visited. (*Hint*: Use a VLOOKUP function to retrieve the currency name. If cell H4 is blank, cell G10 should also be blank.)

10. In cell G12, look up and display the exchange rate for this transaction from the Currency Conversion Table.

11. In cell H12, lookup and display the currency code for this transaction from the Currency conversion table. If cell H4 is blank, cell G12 should also be blank.

12. In cell I12, enter the function that displays today's date.

13. Test the Currency Converter by deleting the country visiting (cell H4) and amount (cell H5) entries, and then modifying the formulas in any cell that displays an error value so that a blank cell is displayed instead of the error value.

14. Protect all cells except the cells into which you enter data (cells H4 and H5). Do not use a password.

15. Test the calculator by converting **500** U.S. dollars to Japanese yen.

16. Save the workbook, and then close it.

Case Problem 4

Data File needed for this Case Problem: Instruments.xlsx

Anthony's Music Store   Anthony Malone sells and rents musical instruments. One part of his business involves renting instruments to K–12 students who participate in school bands and orchestras. Instruments available for rent include flutes, clarinets, trombones, oboes, piccolos, saxophones, accordions, bassoons, and French horns. Anthony maintains an Excel worksheet to track instrument rentals that includes the following information:

- **Renter**—the name of the renter
- **Instrument**—the type of instrument rented
- **Rental Date**—the date the instrument was rented
- **Rental Period**—either 3 or 9 months, as shown in the Rental Period column; no other rental periods are allowed
- **Ins Cov**—indicates whether renters elected to purchase instrument insurance; if elected, Yes appears in the Ins Cov column; otherwise, No is entered
- **Shipping Code**—indicates whether the renter wants the instrument delivered directly to the school (either Ground or Rush), or the renter will pick up the instrument at the store (Pickup).

Anthony wants you to expand the information that is tracked. Complete the following:

1. Open the **Instruments** workbook located in the Excel8 ▸ Case4 folder included with your Data Files, and then save the workbook as **Instrument Rentals** in the location specified by your instructor.

2. In the Documentation worksheet, enter your name and the date.

3. In the Rental Data worksheet, in column G, create a formula that uses the HLOOKUP function to assign a group code (A, B, C, D, or E) from the InstrumentGroups range in the Rental Information worksheet to the instrument listed in column B.

⊕ **Explore** 4. In column H, create a formula to determine the return date. Add the 3 or 9 month rental period (column D) to the rental date (column C) to calculate the return date. For example, if the rental date is 9/10/2016 and the rental period is 3 months, the return date is 12/10/2016. If the rental period is 9 months, then the return date is 6/10/2017. (*Hint*: Use the DATE function to calculate the return date. Use MONTH([Rental Date]), DAY([Rental Date]), and YEAR([Rental Date]) functions as arguments of the DATE function. Finally, add the rental period to the month argument.)

5. In column I, create a formula using the IF and VLOOKUP functions to calculate the rental charges for each instrument based on the instrument's group code, the rental period, and the Instrument Rental Charges table. (*Hint*: For the IF function arguments, use one VLOOKUP function for 3 months and another for 9 months. The defined name RentalCharges has been assigned to the Instrument Rental Charges table.)

6. In column J, enter a formula to calculate the insurance cost if the renter has elected insurance coverage (Yes in column E). Use the instrument's group code and the Monthly Insurance column in the RentalCharges table to look up the insurance cost. Remember to multiply the monthly insurance charge by the rental period. If the renter has not elected insurance, the cost is 0.

7. In column K, create a nested IF function to determine the shipping cost for each instrument. Use the shipping code (column F) and the shipping charge options Pickup (0), Ground ($25), and Rush ($50) to assign shipping costs to each rental instrument.

8. In column L, calculate the total cost, which is the sum of the rental charges, the insurance cost, and the shipping cost.

9. Format columns I through L with the Accounting format with no decimal places.

10. In the Rental Report worksheet, complete the Rental Summary report by creating formulas in the range C4:D5 using the COUNTIF and SUMIF functions.

11. In the Rental Data worksheet, enter the following new record:

Renter: **Allen**
Instrument: **Flute**
Rental Date: **9/15/2016**
Rental Period: **9**
Ins Cov: **Yes**
Shipping Code: **Rush**

⊕ **Explore** 12. Create the PivotTable shown in Figure 8-46 to display the number of rentals and rental $ by rental month. Rename the worksheet as **Monthly Rentals**. (*Hint*: Select any Rental Date in the PivotTable, and then on the PIVOTTABLE TOOLS ANALYZE tab, in the Group group, click the Group Field button to open the Grouping dialog box. Use Months as the grouping field.)

Figure 8-46	Monthly Rental Summary PivotTable

	# of Renters	Total Rental $
Jul	14	$ 2,262
Aug	16	$ 1,322
Sep	11	$ 1,494
Grand Total	**41**	**$ 5,078**

⊕ **Explore** 13. In the PivotTable, drill down to display the renters (all fields) in the source data that represent the 11 rentals in September. Rename the worksheet that is created as **SeptDetail**. (*Hint*: Double-click the appropriate cell in PivotTable to open a new worksheet with the supporting data.)

14. Save the workbook, and then close it.

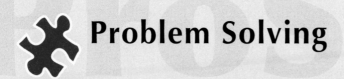

Problem Solving

Solving a Problem Using an Excel Table

Problem solving is the ability to identify a gap between an existing state and a desired state of being. A problem can be a one-time issue such as which car to purchase, or a process-oriented dilemma such as how to track orders. The process of solving a problem follows a logical progression that consists of (1) recognizing and defining the problem; (2) determining feasible courses of action; (3) collecting information about those actions; and (4) evaluating the merits and drawbacks of each one in order to make a choice. Problem solving leads to decision making, and enables you to evaluate different courses of action and make an informed decision or select a good solution.

Recognize and Define the Problem

A problem is the gap between a desired state and reality. In order to recognize and define a problem, ask questions to determine the real issue and identify your ultimate goal. For example, ask such questions as: Why do I think there is a problem? Where is it occurring? When and how frequently is it occurring? What is causing the problem? Who is involved? Why is it occurring? The answers to these questions help you define the problem and determine what information you need in order to solve the problem. For instance, a company might want to make sure that employee benefits and overtime payments don't exceed a certain amount; therefore, it needs to track the cost of each employee's benefit package, salary, and overtime as well as determine that the total costs fall within the intended levels.

Determine Feasible Alternatives

With the problem defined, you can brainstorm possible solutions by collecting as many ideas as possible about how to correct the problem or achieve your goal. Write them all down. Don't discount any ideas as too radical, expensive, or impossible to achieve. Think creatively. Ask what-if questions, such as the following: What if we had unlimited resources? What if we had new skills? What if our competitors, suppliers, or customers acted in a certain way? What if I do nothing? For instance, a company might want to create a consistent way to track employee data—collecting the same data each time, categorizing the data by department or employee type, and then ensuring that paid benefits and overtime don't exceed a certain amount.

Collect Information Needed to Evaluate the Alternatives

Data is crucial to problem solving. Collect data and information related to each possible solution or alternative. This information can include data expressed as currency or numbers, as well as data that cannot be measured numerically. All collected data should be organized in a way that provides information for effective decision making and follow-up. For example, a business needs to collect data that enables it to write checks to employees, prepare reports about overtime, report payroll taxes to government agencies, provide premiums to health insurance companies, track Social Security payments, and so on. This requires an organized system to capture the appropriate data such as employee IDs, employee names, hours worked each day, salary or hourly rate, and insurance premium. You'll likely start to see relationships between the collected information that can provide insights into the feasibility of the possible solutions.

Evaluate and Choose an Alternative

Document both the benefits and costs of all alternatives, whether numerical (cost savings) or other (employee morale). Spreadsheet software often helps problem solvers track and quantify merits and drawbacks. Consider the resources required—financial, human, equipment, and so on. Are they affordable? Is there enough time to implement the different solutions? What risks are associated with an alternative? What consequences would result if the solution didn't work? The best choice is to go with the solution that offers the greatest reward for the least amount of risk. In some cases, the solution may require developing

a "Plan B" to fall back on in case the chosen solution fails to solve the problem. For instance, when collecting payroll data, it may become apparent that insurance premiums constitute a higher percentage of payroll than previously thought, which requires further investigation and an alternative solution.

Don't try to select a solution that addresses every aspect of a problem, especially if it is complex. Solutions are rarely perfect. Instead, consider the overall effect each alternative may have. Will the resulting change generate positive results while solving the problem? Will the chosen alternative resolve the problem in the long term? Given the merits and drawbacks identified, what is realistic?

PROSKILLS

Develop an Excel Table

In daily life, you solve all sorts of problems, such as which car purchase makes the most economic sense when comparing purchase price, mileage, and maintenance, or which software package will help your biking club manage its funds, plan road trips, and keep memberships up to date. To solve these and other problems, you need to collect data that tracks the current situation, determine your ultimate goal, and then follow a logical progression to the best solution. Developing an Excel table can help you track the data you need to solve such problems.

In this exercise, you need to select an activity in which you participate or an organization to which you belong, and identify a one-time or process-oriented problem that needs to be solved. Then, create a worksheet and develop an Excel table to track relevant data and create a solution to the problem, using the Excel skills and features presented in Tutorials 5 through 8.

Note: Please be sure *not* to include any personal information of a sensitive nature in any worksheets you create to submit to your instructor. Later, you can update the worksheets with such information for your own personal use.

1. Identify a problem to solve. This can be a one-time problem, such as a car purchase, or a process-oriented problem, such as tracking membership data for a club to which you belong. Determine feasible alternatives to solve the problem, and then collect the data you need to evaluate these alternatives.

2. Plan the organization of your workbook and the Excel table you will develop based on how you will use the data. Consider the outputs you want to create, and the fields needed to produce those outputs. Decide what each record represents (such as data on a participant), and then identify the fields and field names (such as last name, first name, birth date, and so on) within each record. What calculations will you need to perform? How do you want to format the information?

3. Create a Documentation worksheet that includes your name, the date, and the purpose of your workbook. Include a data definition table to document the fields in each record. Format the worksheet appropriately.

4. Create an Excel table to track the data needed to solve the problem you identified. Enter an appropriate table name and column headers. Add one or more calculated columns to the table to perform calculations on the data that you will use to solve the problem.

5. Improve the appearance of the table by using appropriate formatting.

6. Apply validity checks to improve the accuracy of data entry.

7. Add records to the table.

8. Apply conditional formatting to at least one column in the table to visually highlight some aspect of the data that will help you evaluate and solve the problem.

9. Add a comment to the column with the conditional formatting to explain what the conditional formatting shows, and how it will help you to evaluate and solve the problem.

10. Insert a Total row in the table, and then make appropriate summary calculations that you can use to evaluate and solve the problem.

11. Divide the table into two horizontal panes—one for the data, and one for the Total row.

12. Sort the data in a logical way.

13. Use a filter to answer a question about the data to help you evaluate and solve the problem.

14. Create a PivotTable and a PivotChart to analyze the data. Format, filter, and sort the PivotTable appropriately.

15. In a Word document, explain the problem you solved, identify the alternatives you considered, document the data you collected to evaluate the alternatives, and then describe the results of your analysis. Include the PivotChart in the Word document.

16. In an appropriate worksheet, insert a hyperlink that links to the Word document you created.

17. Create at least one macro to automate a repetitive task you need to perform in the workbook, such as printing or saving a worksheet as a PDF file.

18. Prepare your workbook for printing. Include headers and footers that indicate the filename of your workbook, the workbook's author, and the date on which the report is printed. If a printed worksheet will extend across several pages, repeat appropriate print titles across all of the pages, and include page numbers and the total number of pages on each printed page.

19. Save the workbook.

EXCEL

OBJECTIVES

- Open a workbook in Compatibility Mode
- Use the LEN function
- Use the LEFT function
- Apply the Paste Values command
- Use the PROPER function
- Use the CONCATENATE function
- Apply the Text to Columns command
- Use the UPPER function
- Use the SUBSTITUTE function
- Apply a special format to phone numbers
- Create custom formats for numbers and dates
- Use the Compatibility Checker

Working with Text Functions and Creating Custom Formats

Cleaning Data in a Spreadsheet

Case | *Sharp Blades Hockey Club*

The town of Drumright, Oklahoma, started the Sharp Blades Hockey Club in 2010. The adult division of the club has members from the towns in the area, and the average age of the members is 42. They have elected officers for president, secretary, and treasurer. James Perez has been elected secretary, and part of his job is to keep the records for the club. The officers of the club would like to know more about the players and the prospects for the growth of the club.

The club has a spreadsheet containing data about the current players, but the data was compiled by volunteers and is not organized for any kind of analysis. Before James begins his analysis, he needs to "clean" the data, and he has asked for your help.

STARTING DATA FILES

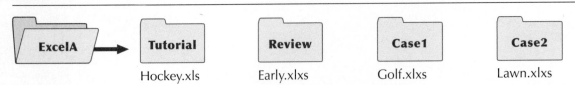

ExcelA	Tutorial	Review	Case1	Case2
	Hockey.xls	Early.xlxs	Golf.xlxs	Lawn.xlxs

Opening and Saving Workbooks Created in Earlier Versions of Excel

When you open a workbook that was created in Excel 2003 or earlier, it opens in Compatibility Mode. **Compatibility Mode** keeps the workbook in the older file format with the .xls file extension, making the workbook accessible for users who do not have the current version of Excel installed. The words "[Compatibility Mode]" appear in the title bar, indicating the file is not in the latest Excel format. You can work in Compatibility Mode. However, to have access to all the latest features and tools in Excel 2013, you must convert the workbook to the current file format, which has the .xlsx file extension. This is the file format you have used to save workbooks in the tutorials.

The workbook James received from the previous secretary was created in Excel 2003. James wants you to convert the workbook to the current format.

To save the workbook in the current Excel file format:

▶ **1.** Open the **Hockey** workbook located in the ExcelA ▶ Tutorial folder included with your Data Files. The workbook opens in Compatibility Mode because the workbook was created in an earlier version of Excel. See Figure A-1.

Figure A-1   Workbook in Compatibility Mode

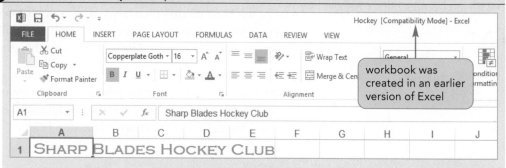

▶ **2.** On the ribbon, click the **FILE** tab to open Backstage view, and then click the **Save As** command in the navigation bar.

▶ **3.** Click the **Browse** button to open the Save As dialog box.

▶ **4.** In the File name box, type **Sharp Blades**. The Save as type box shows that the current file format is Excel 97-2003 Workbook, which is the earlier file format. You'll change this to the latest file format.

▶ **5.** Click the **Save as type** button, and then click **Excel Workbook**. This is the file format for Excel 2007, 2010, and 2013.

▶ **6.** Click the **Save** button. The workbook is saved with the new name and file type.

As you can see from the title bar, the workbook remains in Compatibility Mode. You can continue to work in Compatibility Mode, or you can close the workbook and then reopen it in the new file format. You will open the workbook in the current file format.

To open the Sharp Blades workbook in the current file format:

▶ **1.** Close the Sharp Blades workbook.

▶ **2.** Open the **Sharp Blades** workbook. The text "[Compatibility Mode]" no longer appears in the title bar, indicating that the workbook is in the current version file format of Excel.

▶ **3.** In the Documentation worksheet, enter your name and the date.

The Players worksheet contains data about the club members. Before working with this data, James wants you to convert it to an Excel table.

To create an Excel table from the list of player information:

▶ **1.** Go to the **Players** worksheet.

▶ **2.** On the ribbon, click the **INSERT** tab.

▶ **3.** In the Tables group, click the **Table** button. The Create Table dialog box opens with the range $A$1:$G$45 selected, and the My table has headers box is checked.

▶ **4.** Click the **OK** button to create the Excel table. Note that filter arrows appear in the column heading cells.

▶ **5.** On the TABLE TOOLS DESIGN tab, in the Properties group, enter **Player** in the Table Name box to rename the table.

▶ **6.** On the ribbon, click the **DATA** tab.

▶ **7.** Select any cell in the Excel table.

Using Text Functions

If you receive a workbook from a coworker or obtain data from other software packages, you often have to edit (sometimes referred to as *clean* or *scrub*) and manipulate the data before it is ready to use. To help users edit and correct the text values in their workbooks, Excel provides Text functions. Text, also referred to as a *text string* or *string*, contains one or more characters and can include spaces, symbols, and numbers as well as uppercase and lowercase letters. You can use Text functions to return the number of characters in a string, remove extra spaces, and change the case of text strings. Figure A-2 reviews some of the common Text functions available in Excel.

Figure A-4	Table column with five-digit zip codes

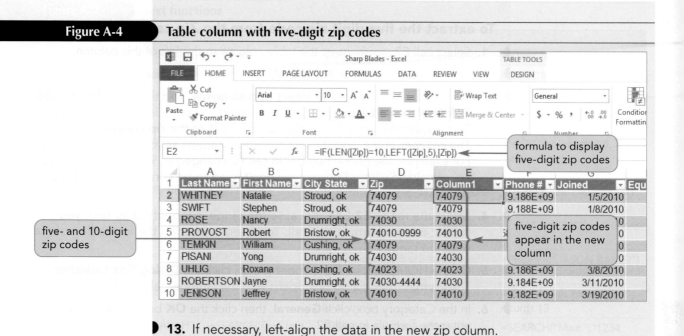

five- and 10-digit zip codes

formula to display five-digit zip codes

five-digit zip codes appear in the new column

13. If necessary, left-align the data in the new zip column.

Using the Paste Values Command

You now have two columns with zip codes (columns D and E). You need to keep only the column that displays the five-digit zip code. However, the data in column E is dependent on column D. If you delete column D, column E will display the #REF! error value. Therefore, before you delete column D, you need to convert the data in column E, which is based on a formula, to values. The easiest way to do that is to copy and paste the formula results, but not the actual formula, in the same column using the Paste Values command. Then, you can delete column D.

To convert the five-digit zip code formula results to values:

1. Select the range **E2:E45**, which contains the formula results you want to convert to values.

2. On the HOME tab, in the Clipboard group, click the **Copy** button 📋, and then select cell **E2**.

3. In the Clipboard group, click the **Paste button arrow**, and then click the **Values** button 📋. The values are pasted over the original formulas, replacing them.

4. Select the range **E2:E45**. You need to format these values as text, in case any zip codes start with zeros.

5. In the Number group, click the **Number Format box arrow**, and then click **Text**.

6. Select column **D**, right-click the selected column, and then click **Delete** on the shortcut menu. The column is removed.

▶ **7.** In cell **D1**, enter **Zip**. Column D, which stores the five-digit zip code values, now has a descriptive column header.

▶ **8.** Autofit the Zip column to fit the five-digit zip codes.

Using the PROPER Function and the CONCATENATE Function

The **PROPER function** converts the first letter of each word to uppercase, capitalizes any letter that does not follow another letter, and changes all other letters to lowercase. The formula =PROPER("WHITNEY") changes the word "WHITNEY" to "Whitney." You will first use the PROPER function to convert the last name so that the first letter is capitalized.

The **CONCATENATE function** joins, or concatenates, two or more text values. The syntax of the CONCATENATE function is

=CONCATENATE(*text1,text2,...*)

where *text1*, *text2*, etc., are constants or cells storing text or numbers. The CONCATENATE function joins these values to produce a single string. For example, if the last name "WHITNEY" is in cell A2 and the first name "Natalie" is in cell B2, you can use the formula =CONCATENATE(A2,B2) to join the contents of the two cells (last name and first name) to display the full name in cell C2. However, this formula returns "WHITNEYNatalie" in cell C2. To include a comma and a space between the two names, you must change the formula to =CONCATENATE(PROPER(A2),", ",B2), which uses a function, two values, and a string constant (a comma and a space enclosed in quotation marks) to display "Whitney, Natalie" in the cell.

James wants to combine the Last Name and First Name columns into one column and use standard capitalization for the names. You will use a formula that includes the PROPER function and the CONCATENATION function to do this.

To combine the names in one column with standard capitalization:

▶ **1.** Select cell **C2**, and then insert a table column to the left. A new column named Column1 is inserted to the left of the City State column.

▶ **2.** In cell **C2**, type **=CONCATENATE(PROPER([Last Name]),", ",[First Name])** and then press the **Enter** key. The formula is entered for every record in column C, and displays the player's last name and first name with standard capitalization separated by a comma.

▶ **3.** AutoFit column C to accommodate the longest entry. Each cell in column C displays the player's name in the form *Last name, First name* with the first letter of each name capitalized. Notice that the Joined column is no longer wide enough to display some of the entries; you will resize the column later. See Figure A-5.

Figure A-7	City and State displayed in separate columns

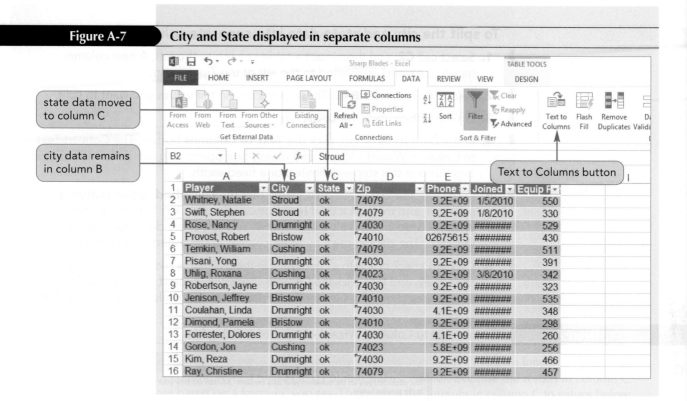

state data moved to column C

city data remains in column B

Text to Columns button

B2   Stroud

	A	B	C	D	E			
1	Player	City	State	Zip	Phone	Joined	Equip F	
2	Whitney, Natalie	Stroud	ok	74079	9.2E+09	1/5/2010	550	
3	Swift, Stephen	Stroud	ok	'74079	9.2E+09	1/8/2010	330	
4	Rose, Nancy	Drumright	ok	74030	9.2E+09	######	529	
5	Provost, Robert	Bristow	ok	'74010	02675615	######	430	
6	Temkin, William	Cushing	ok	74079	9.2E+09	######	511	
7	Pisani, Yong	Drumright	ok	'74030	9.2E+09	######	391	
8	Uhlig, Roxana	Cushing	ok	'74023	9.2E+09	3/8/2010	342	
9	Robertson, Jayne	Drumright	ok	'74030	9.2E+09	######	323	
10	Jenison, Jeffrey	Bristow	ok	'74010	9.2E+09	######	535	
11	Coulahan, Linda	Drumright	ok	'74030	4.1E+09	######	348	
12	Dimond, Pamela	Bristow	ok	'74010	9.2E+09	######	298	
13	Forrester, Dolores	Drumright	ok	74030	4.1E+09	######	260	
14	Gordon, Jon	Cushing	ok	74023	5.8E+09	######	256	
15	Kim, Reza	Drumright	ok	'74030	9.2E+09	######	466	
16	Ray, Christine	Drumright	ok	74079	9.2E+09	######	457	

Using the UPPER Function to Convert Case

The **UPPER function** converts all letters of each word in a text string to uppercase. For example, the formula =UPPER("ri") returns RI. James wants you to change state abbreviations in column D from lowercase to uppercase. You'll use the UPPER function to do this.

To use the UPPER function to capitalize the state abbreviations:

1. Select cell **D2**, and then insert a table column to the left. A new column named Column1 is inserted to the left of the Zip column.

2. In cell **D2**, type **=U** and then double-click the **UPPER** function in the list. The beginning of the formula =UPPER(is in the cell and the formula bar.

3. Type **[** to begin the column specifier, double-click **State** in the list of column qualifiers, type **]** to end the column specifier, and then type **)**. The formula =UPPER([State]) appears in the formula bar.

4. Press the **Enter** key. The state abbreviation appears in all uppercase letters in column E. See Figure A-8.

| Figure A-8 | UPPER function converted state abbreviations to uppercase |

UPPER function formula converts cell contents to uppercase

state abbreviations are capitalized

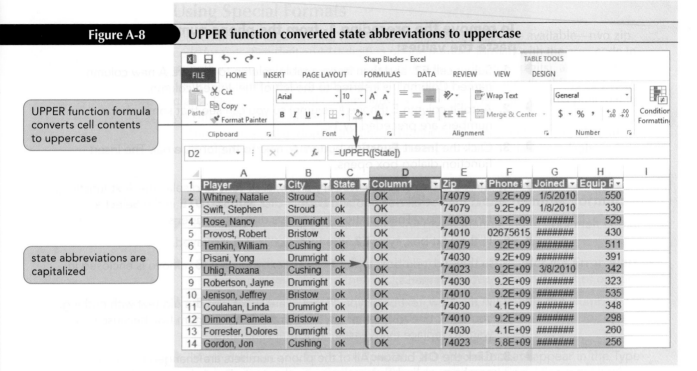

You want to keep only the data in column D. Because the results of column D are based on a formula, you again will convert the formula in column D to values before you delete column C.

To paste the state abbreviations as values:

▶ **1.** Select the range **D2:D45**, and then copy the range to the Clipboard.

▶ **2.** Select cell **D2**, and then paste the values from the Clipboard. Verify that the formula bar displays a value and not a formula.

▶ **3.** Press the **Esc** key.

▶ **4.** Delete column **C**.

▶ **5.** In cell **C1**, enter **State**. The column is renamed with a more descriptive header.

Using the SUBSTITUTE Function

The **SUBSTITUTE function** replaces existing text with new text. The SUBSTITUTE function has the syntax

    SUBSTITUTE(text,old_text,new_text,instance_num)

where *text* is a string constant or reference to a cell containing text you want to replace, *old_text* is the existing text you want to replace, *new_text* is the text you want to replace *old_text* with, and *instance_num* specifies which occurrence of *old_text* you want to replace. If you omit *instance_num*, every instance of *old_text* is replaced. The formula

    =SUBSTITUTE("164-45-890","-","")

returns 16445890.

The entries for the phone numbers in column E are inconsistent. Sometimes they are an eight-digit value, and other times they are preceded with 1- (which James wants you to remove from the Phone # column). You'll enter a formula with the SUBSTITUTE function to remove the preceding 1- from this data.

Figure A-17   **Compatibility Checker with error message**

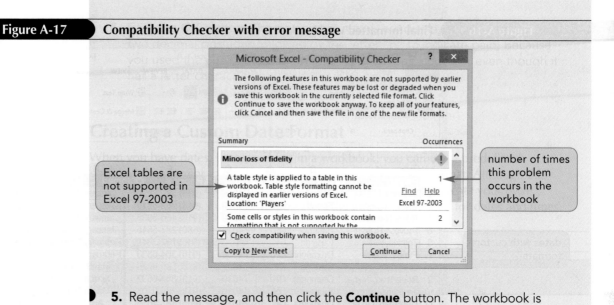

Excel tables are not supported in Excel 97-2003

number of times this problem occurs in the workbook

5. Read the message, and then click the **Continue** button. The workbook is saved in the earlier file format with the .xls file extension. Close the workbook.

The workbook data is clean and the workbook is formatted as James requested. He'll be able to analyze this data for the club.

Review Assignments

Data File needed for the Review Assignments: Early.xlsx

The Sharp Blades Hockey Club also has a youth division for players from 6 to 18 years of age. James has a second workbook to store the information that has been collected for these players. James asks you to clean and format the data. Complete the following:

1. Open the **Early** workbook located in the ExcelA ▶ Review folder included with your Data Files, and then save the workbook in Excel Workbook format as **Sharp Youth** in the location specified by your instructor.
2. In the Documentation worksheet, enter your name and the date.
3. In the Youth Players worksheet, create an Excel table for the data in the range A1:F40. Name the table **Youth**. (*Hint*: Remember to remove the filter arrows.)
4. Insert a blank column to the left of column B to store the first name, and leave the last name in column A.
5. Use the Text to Columns command to split the Player column into two columns named **Last Name** and **First Name**.
6. In cell H1, enter **Status** as the column header. In cell H2, use the IF and LEFT functions to display the word **Discard** if the address begins with PO; otherwise, leave the cell blank.
7. In cell I1, enter **Addr** as the column header. In cell I2, enter a formula to trim the extra spaces from the address.
8. In cell J1, enter **Twn** as the column header. In cell J2, enter a formula to convert the data in the Town column to proper case.
9. In cell K1, enter **St** as the column header. In column K, enter a formula to convert the data in the State column to uppercase.
10. In cell L1, enter **Town State** as the column header. In column L, combine the town and state data from columns J and K into one column using the format *town, state*.
11. Format the data in the Phone column (column F) with the Phone Number format.
12. Save the workbook, and then close it.

Case Problem 1

Data File needed for this Case Problem: Golf.xlsx

Early Bird Golf Group Camilla Cortez, organizer of the Early Bird Golf Group, has begun compiling a list of the group's members. She has asked you to clean and format the data in the worksheet before she continues working on the project. Complete the following:

1. Open the **Golf** workbook located in the ExcelA ▶ Case1 folder and save the workbook in the Excel Workbook format as **Early Bird** in the location specified by your instructor.
2. In the Documentation worksheet, enter your name and the date.
3. In the Members worksheet, create an Excel table for the data. Name the table **Golf**.
4. Apply the Phone Number format to the data in the Telephone column.
5. Split the data in the Name column into two columns. Store the first names in column B and the last names in column C. Change the column headers to **First Name** and **Last Name**, respectively.
6. In the Member Since column, apply a custom format that displays only the year.
7. Split the City, State Zip column into three columns named **City**, **State**, and **Zip**, respectively. (*Hint*: Repeat the split twice. The second split is a fixed width.)
8. The locker numbers were entered from an old system. The only characters that are important are the three numbers after the letter. Use the MID function in column I (name it **L Number**) to separate those numbers.

Using Advanced Filters

Advanced filtering displays a subset of the rows in an Excel table or a range of data that match the criteria you specify. With advanced filtering, you specify the filter criteria in a separate range. Advanced filtering enables you to perform Or conditions across multiple fields, such as the criteria Patricia wants you to use to find eligible equipment for replacement within E-Quip Tools. You can also use advanced filtering to create complex criteria using functions and formulas. For example, Patricia could use advanced filtering to find all equipment with no service agreement at the end of life.

Patricia created a workbook that contains an Excel table named Equipment to store the data for all of the equipment. For each piece of equipment, Patricia has listed the Date Acquired, Life (Years), and End of Life, which is calculated using the Date Acquired and Life data. You will open Patricia's workbook and filter the inventory data to identify equipment eligible for replacement.

To open and review Patricia's workbook:

1. Open the **Tools** workbook located in the ExcelB ▶ Tutorial folder included with your Data Files, and then save the workbook as **E-Quip** in the location specified by your instructor.

2. In the Documentation worksheet, enter your name and the date.

3. Go to the **Equipment Inventory** worksheet, and then review the Equipment table. See Figure B-1.

Figure B-1   Equipment table in the Equipment Inventory worksheet

	A	B	C	D	E	F	G	H	I
4									
5									
6	ID	Description	Date Acquired	Life	End of Life	Location	Status	Service	Value
7	1064	Tower	1/8/2014	5	1/7/2019	Tundra	R	Y	$ 350
8	1025	Server	5/24/2009	8	5/22/2017	Hoffman	A	Y	$12,000
9	1026	Keyboard	11/26/2014	2	11/25/2016	Hoffman	A	N	$ 60
10	1024	Tower	11/26/2014	5	11/25/2019	Tundra	A	Y	$ 475
11	1027	Tower	11/26/2014	5	11/25/2019	Tundra	A	Y	$ 475
12	1029	Keyboard	11/26/2014	2	11/25/2016	Hoffman	A	N	$ 60
13	1028	Tower	11/26/2014	5	11/25/2019	Tundra	A	Y	$ 475
14	1030	Tower	11/26/2014	5	11/25/2019	Hoffman	A	Y	$ 500
15	1032	Keyboard	8/28/2016	2	8/28/2018	Hoffman	R	N	$ 55
16	1033	Monitor	11/26/2014	5	11/25/2019	Hoffman	A	N	$ 150
17	1034	Monitor	11/26/2014	5	11/25/2019	Tundra	A	N	$ 120
18	1031	Tower	11/26/2014	5	11/25/2019	Hoffman	A	Y	$ 500
19	1036	Monitor	5/4/2016	5	5/3/2021	Tundra	R	N	$ 495
20	1042	Tower	11/26/2014	5	11/25/2019	Tundra	A	Y	$ 475
21	1038	Monitor	11/26/2016	5	11/25/2021	Hoffman	A	N	$ 150
22	1043	Tower	11/26/2014	5	11/25/2019	Hoffman	A	Y	$ 500
23	1040	Keyboard	11/26/2014	2	11/25/2016	Tundra	A	N	$ 90

Documentation | **Equipment Inventory** | Inventory Summary | (+)

READY

Understanding the Criteria Range

The **criteria range** is an area in a worksheet, separate from a range of data or an Excel table, used to specify the criteria for the data to be displayed after the filter is applied to the range or Excel table. The criteria range consists of a header row that lists field names from the table's header row, and at least one row with the specific filtering criteria for each field. The criteria range specifies which records from the data range will be included in the filtered data.

Criteria placed on the same row are considered to be connected with the logical operator And. That means all criteria in the same row must be met before a record is included in the filtered data. Figure B-2 shows an And criteria range filter to retrieve all equipment not under service agreements at end of life on or before December 31, 2016.

Figure B-2	And filter specified in a criteria range

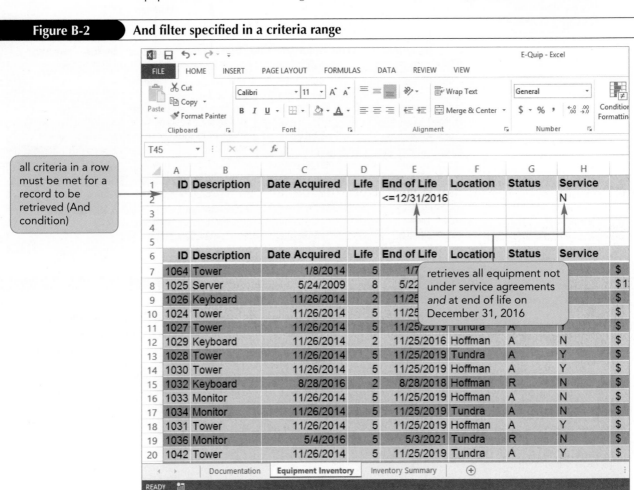

all criteria in a row must be met for a record to be retrieved (And condition)

retrieves all equipment not under service agreements *and* at end of life on December 31, 2016

Criteria placed on separate rows of the criteria range are treated as being connected by the logical operator Or. That means records that meet all the criteria on either row in the criteria range will be displayed. Figure B-3 shows an example of the Or filter to retrieve all equipment not under service agreements at end of life on December 31, 2016 or equipment in the Hoffman location.

Figure B-3   **Or filter specified in a criteria range**

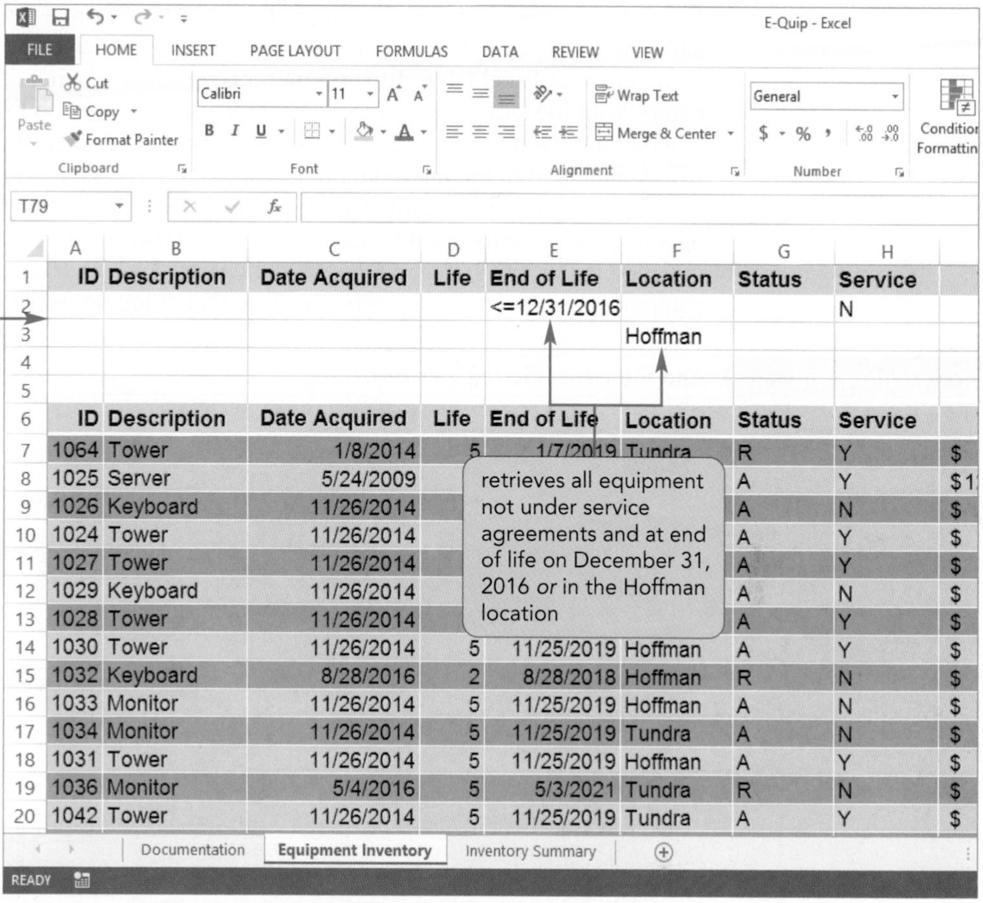

criteria for the Or condition are entered on different rows

	A	B	C	D	E	F	G	H	
1	**ID**	**Description**	**Date Acquired**	**Life**	**End of Life**	**Location**	**Status**	**Service**	
2					<=12/31/2016			N	
3						Hoffman			
4									
5									
6	**ID**	**Description**	**Date Acquired**	**Life**	**End of Life**	**Location**	**Status**	**Service**	
7	1064	Tower	1/8/2014	5	1/7/2019	Tundra	R	Y	$
8	1025	Server	5/24/2009				A	Y	$1
9	1026	Keyboard	11/26/2014				A	N	$
10	1024	Tower	11/26/2014				A	Y	$
11	1027	Tower	11/26/2014				A	Y	$
12	1029	Keyboard	11/26/2014				A	N	$
13	1028	Tower	11/26/2014				A	Y	$
14	1030	Tower	11/26/2014	5	11/25/2019	Hoffman	A	Y	$
15	1032	Keyboard	8/28/2016	2	8/28/2018	Hoffman	R	N	$
16	1033	Monitor	11/26/2014	5	11/25/2019	Hoffman	A	N	$
17	1034	Monitor	11/26/2014	5	11/25/2019	Tundra	A	N	$
18	1031	Tower	11/26/2014	5	11/25/2019	Hoffman	A	Y	$
19	1036	Monitor	5/4/2016	5	5/3/2021	Tundra	R	N	$
20	1042	Tower	11/26/2014	5	11/25/2019	Tundra	A	Y	$

retrieves all equipment not under service agreements and at end of life on December 31, 2016 or in the Hoffman location

To specify criteria between a range of values in the same field, you use the same field name repeated in separate cells within the same row to match a range of values (Between criteria). Figure B-4 shows a criteria range to retrieve all equipment at end of life between January 1, 2016 and December 31, 2016.

| Figure B-4 | Between filter specified in a criteria range |

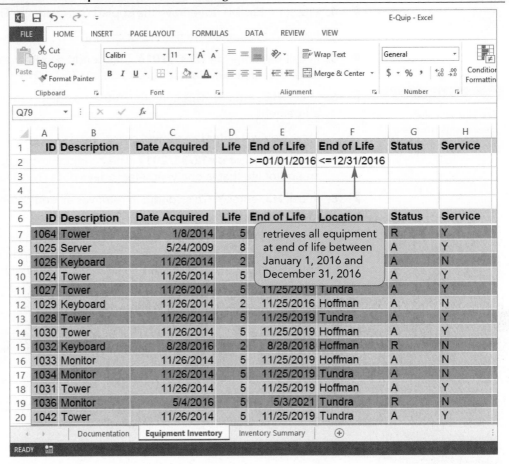

Creating a Criteria Range

Typically, you place a criteria range above the data range to keep it separate from the data. If you place a criteria range next to the data range, the criteria might be hidden when the advanced filtering causes rows to be hidden. You can also place a criteria range in a separate worksheet, particularly if you need to use several criteria ranges in different cells to perform calculations based on various sets of filtered records.

You will place the criteria range in rows 1 through 4 of the Equipment Inventory worksheet to make it easier to locate. Because the field names in the criteria range must exactly match the field names in the Excel table or range except for capitalization, you should copy and paste the field names instead of retyping them. In row 2, you will enter an And criteria range with the criteria for equipment with no service agreement at end of life. In row 3, you will enter the criteria for equipment under service agreement with a value of less than $600 and an end of life one year before today's date.

To create the criteria range to find equipment with or without service agreements:

▶ **1.** Point to the left side of cell **A6** until the pointer changes to ➡, and then click the mouse button. The column headers in row 6 are selected.

▶ **2.** Copy the field names to the Clipboard.

▶ **3.** Select cell **A1**, and then paste the field names. The field names for the criteria range appear in row 1.

4. Press the **Esc** key to remove the copied data from the Clipboard.

Now, you will enter the first set of criteria.

5. In cell **E2**, enter **<=12/31/2016**. This condition retrieves all equipment with an end of life equivalent to today's date (12/31/2016).

6. In cell **H2**, enter **N**. This condition retrieves equipment with no service agreement.

Next, you will enter the second set of criteria.

7. In cell **E3**, enter **<=12/31/2017**. The condition retrieves all equipment with an end of life that is one year after today's date (12/31/2016).

8. In cell **H3**, enter **Y**. This condition retrieves all equipment with a service agreement.

9. In cell **I3**, enter **<600**. This condition retrieves all equipment with a value of less than $600. The criteria in row 3 retrieve equipment with a service agreement that has a value of less than $600 and is within a year of its end of life. See Figure B-5.

| Figure B-5 | Criteria range to filter records |

all criteria in a row must be met for a record to be retrieved (And condition)

Or condition represented by two rows

	A	B	C	D	E	F	G	H
1	ID	Description	Date Acquired	Life	End of Life	Location	Status	Service
2					<=12/31/2016			N
3					<=12/31/2017			Y
4								
5								
6	ID	Description	Date Acquired	Life	End of Life	Location	Status	Service
7	1064	Tower	1/8/2014			undra	R	Y
8	1025	Server	5/24/2009			offman	A	Y
9	1026	Keyboard	11/26/2014			offman	A	N
10	1024	Tower	11/26/2014	5	11/25/2019	Tundra	A	Y
11	1027	Tower	11/26/2014	5	11/25/2019	Tundra	A	Y
12	1029	Keyboard	11/26/2014	2	11/25/2016	Hoffman	A	N
13	1028	Tower	11/26/2014	5	11/25/2019	Tundra	A	Y
14	1030	Tower	11/26/2014	5	11/25/2019	Hoffman	A	Y
15	1032	Keyboard	8/28/2016	2	8/28/2018	Hoffman	R	N
16	1033	Monitor	11/26/2014	5	11/25/2019	Hoffman	A	N
17	1034	Monitor	11/26/2014	5	11/25/2019	Tundra	A	N
18	1031	Tower	11/26/2014	5	11/25/2019	Hoffman	A	Y
19	1036	Monitor	5/4/2016	5	5/3/2021	Tundra	R	N
20	1042	Tower	11/26/2014	5	11/25/2019	Tundra	A	Y

Now that the criteria range is established, you can use the Advanced Filter command to filter the Equipment table. You can filter the records in their current location by hiding rows that don't match your criteria, as you have done with the Filter command. Or, you can copy the records that match your criteria to another location in the worksheet. Patricia wants you to filter the records in their current location.

To filter the Equipment table in its current location:

▶ **1.** Select any cell in the Equipment table to make the table active.

▶ **2.** On the ribbon, click the **DATA** tab.

▶ **3.** In the Sort & Filter group, click the **Advanced** button. The Advanced Filter dialog box opens.

▶ **4.** Make sure the **Filter the list, in-place** option button is selected and the range **$A$6:$I$79** appears in the List range box. The range $A$6:$I$79 is the current location of the Equipment table, which is the table you want to filter.

▶ **5.** Make sure the Criteria range box displays **$A$1:$I$3**. This range references the criteria range, which includes the field names.

▶ **6.** Make sure the **Unique records only** option box is unchecked. Every record in the Equipment table is unique. You would check this option if the table contained duplicate records that you did not want to display. See Figure B-6.

| Figure B-6 | Advanced Filter dialog box |

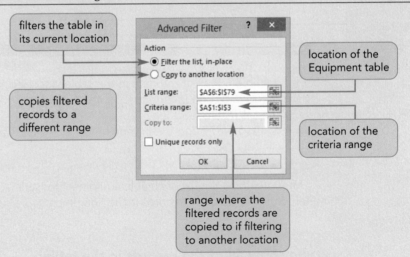

filters the table in its current location

location of the Equipment table

copies filtered records to a different range

location of the criteria range

range where the filtered records are copied to if filtering to another location

▶ **7.** Click the **OK** button, and then scroll through the worksheet. The list is filtered in its current location, and 15 equipment records (as shown in the status bar) match the criteria. See Figure B-7.

| Figure B-7 | Filtered equipment inventory data |

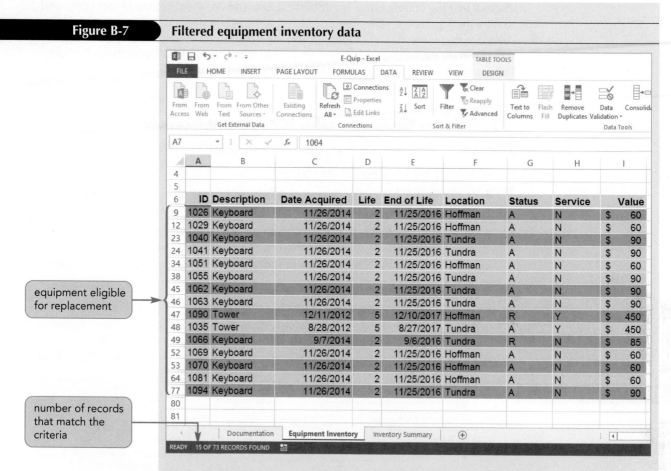

equipment eligible
for replacement

number of records
that match the
criteria

Trouble? If all of the data in the table is filtered, the list range or criteria range might be incorrect. Click the Clear button in the Sort & Filter group on the DATA tab, and then repeat Steps 1 through 6, making sure the list range is $A$6:$I$79 and the criteria range is $A$1:$I$3 in the Advanced Filter dialog box.

After providing the list of eligible equipment to Patricia, she asks you to remove the filter to display all of the records in the Equipment table.

To show all of the records in the table:

▶ 1. On the DATA tab, in the Sort & Filter group, click the **Clear** button. All of the records in the Equipment table are redisplayed.

Using Database Functions to Summarize Data

Database functions (or **Dfunctions**) perform summary data analysis, such as sum, average, and count, on an Excel table or data range based on criteria specified in a criteria range. Figure B-8 lists the Database functions. Although you can often use the SUMIF, AVERAGEIF, and COUNTIF functions; the Total row of an Excel table; and PivotTables to achieve the same results as Database functions, some situations require Database functions. For example, the type of summary analysis, the placement of the summary results, or the complexity of the criteria might require using Database functions.

Figure B-8	Database functions

Function	Description
DAVERAGE	Returns the average of the values that meet specified criteria
DCOUNT	Returns the number of cells containing numbers that meet specified criteria
DCOUNTA	Returns the number of nonblank cells that meet specified criteria
DMAX	Returns the maximum value in the search column that meets specified criteria
DMIN	Returns the minimum value in the search column that meets specified criteria
DSTDEV	Returns the estimate of standard deviation based on a sample of entries that meet the specified criteria
DSUM	Returns the sum of the values in the summary column that meet specified criteria

© 2014 Cengage Learning

Patricia needs to know the average value of the equipment by location and by status. The status of the equipment indicates whether or not it is in use (active), or whether it is not in use but available if needed (reserve). To generate this information, you must set up a criteria range to retrieve the appropriate records for each calculation. Consequently, a Database function is a good approach.

Database functions use a criteria range to specify the records to summarize. In a Database function, the criteria range is used as one of the arguments of the function. The general syntax for any Database function is

```
DatabaseFunctionName(table range, column to summarize,
criteria range)
```

where *table range* refers to the cells where the data to summarize is located, including the column header; *column to summarize* is the column name of the field to summarize entered within quotation marks; and *criteria range* is the range where the criteria that determine which records are used in the calculation are specified.

You will use Database functions to summarize the average inventory for each location by status. First, you will set up a criteria range. Although the criteria range often includes all fields from the table, even those not needed to select records, you do not have to include all field names from the table when setting up a criteria range. In this case, you will use only the fields needed to specify the criteria.

You will create two criteria ranges to complete the Average Inventory section in the Inventory Summary sheet.

▶ **8.** Select cell **C6**, and then click the **Insert Function** button f_x next to the formula bar.

▶ **9.** Repeat Step 3 to open the DAVERAGE Function Arguments dialog box, and then repeat Steps 4 and 5 to enter the first two arguments for the DAVERAGE function, specifying all data values in the Equipment table and the field name.

▶ **10.** In the Criteria box, type **G9:H10** to specify the active equipment in the Hoffman location.

▶ **11.** Click the **OK** button. The formula =DAVERAGE ('Equipment Inventory' !$A$6:$I$79,"Value",G9:H10) appears in the formula bar, and $827 appears in cell C6, indicating the average value of the active equipment in the Hoffman location.

To calculate the average inventory value for the reserve equipment in the Tundra and Hoffman locations, you will copy the formulas in the range C5:C6 to cells D5 and D6, and then edit the third argument.

To find the average inventory value for reserve equipment for the Tundra and Hoffman locations:

▶ **1.** Copy the formula in cell **C5** to cell **D5**.

▶ **2.** Select cell **D5**, and then change the criteria range (the third argument) from H5:I6 to **J5:K6**. The formula =DAVERAGE('Equipment Inventory'!$A$6:$I$79,"Value",J5:K6) appears in the formula bar, and $2,816 appears in cell D5, indicating the average value of the reserve equipment in the Tundra location.

▶ **3.** Copy the formula from cell **C6** to cell **D6**.

▶ **4.** Select cell **D6**, and then change the criteria range (the third argument) from K5:L6 to **J9:K10**. The formula =DAVERAGE('Equipment Inventory'!$A$6:$I$79, "Value",J9:K10) appears in the formula bar, and $2,151 appears in cell D6, indicating the average value of the reserve equipment in the Hoffman location. See Figure B-12.

Figure B-12   **Average inventory values**

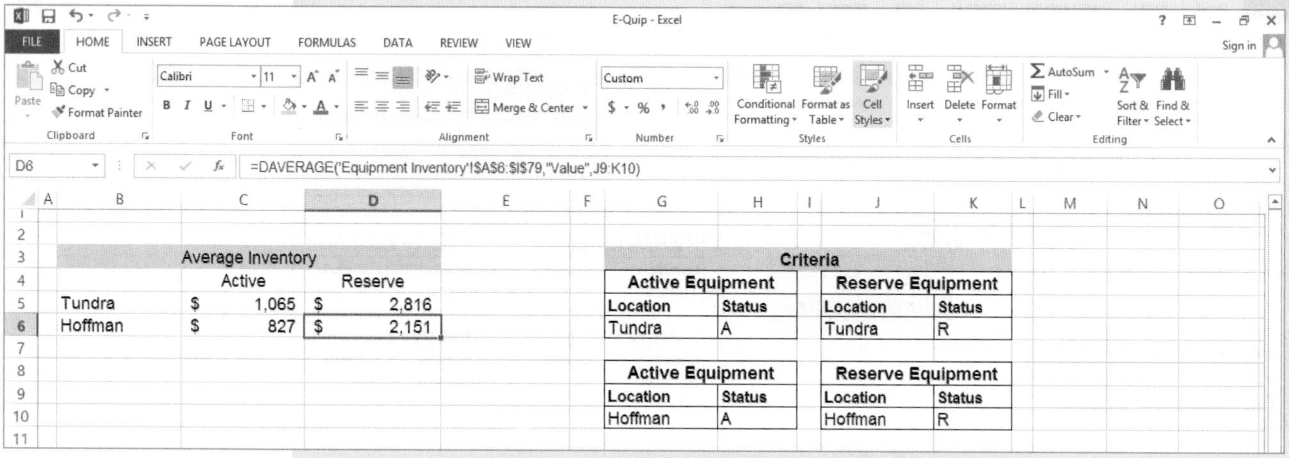

Summarizing Data Using the COUNTIFS, SUMIFS, and AVERAGEIFS Functions

Patricia wants you to summarize the years of service for the company's inventory. She needs to know the total and average values of the active equipment based on the life of the equipment.

The COUNTIFS, SUMIFS, and AVERAGEIFS functions are similar to the COUNTIF, SUMIF, and AVERAGEIF functions except the latter functions enable you to specify only one condition to summarize the data, whereas the former functions enable you to summarize the data using several conditions.

The **COUNTIFS function** counts the number of cells within a range that meet multiple criteria. Its syntax is

```
COUNTIFS(criteria_range1,criteria1[,criteria_range2,criteria2,…])
```

where *criteria_range1, criteria_range2*, and so on represent up to 127 ranges (columns of data) in which to evaluate the associated criteria; and *criteria1, criteria2*, and so on represent up to 127 criteria in the form of a number, an expression, a cell reference, or text that define which cells will be counted. Criteria can be expressed as a number such as 50 to find a number equal to 50; an expression such as ">10000" to find an amount greater than 10,000; text such as "A" to find a text value equal to A; or a cell reference such as B4 to find the value equal to the value stored in cell B4. Each cell in a range is counted only if all of the corresponding criteria specified in the COUNTIFS function are true.

To count the number of pieces of Active (A) equipment in the Tundra location (Tundra) and with a value more than $500, you can use the COUNTIFS function.

```
=COUNTIFS(Equipment[Status],"A",Equipment[Location],"Tundra",
Equipment[Value],">500")
```

The criteria are treated as if they are connected by an AND function, so all conditions must be true for a record to be counted.

The SUMIFS and AVERAGEIFS functions have a slightly different syntax. The **SUMIFS function** adds values in a range that meet multiple criteria using the syntax

```
SUMIFS(sum_range,criteria_range1,criteria1[,criteria_range2,
criteria2,…])
```

where *sum_range* is the range you want to add; *criteria_range1, criteria_range2*, and so on represent up to 127 ranges (columns of data) in which to evaluate the associated criteria; and *criteria1, criteria2*, and so on represent up to 127 criteria in the form of a number, an expression, a cell reference, or text that define which cells will be added.

To calculate the total value of active equipment acquired after 2016 in the Tundra location, you can use the following SUMIFS function to add the values (Equipment[Value]) of the equipment located in Tundra (Equipment[Location],"Tundra") that was acquired on or later than 1/1/2016 (Equipment[Date Acquired],">=1/1/2016") and has an active status (Equipment[Status],"A"):

```
=SUMIFS(Equipment[Value],Equipment[Location],"Tundra",
Equipment[Date Acquired],">=1/1/2016",Equipment[Status],"A")
```

The **AVERAGEIFS function** calculates the average of values within a range of cells that meet multiple conditions. Its syntax is

```
AVERAGEIFS(average_range,criteria_range1,criteria1
[,criteria_range2, criteria2,…])
```

where *average_range* is the range to average; *criteria_range1, criteria_range2*, and so on represent up to 127 ranges in which to evaluate the associated criteria; and *criteria1, criteria2*, and so on represent up to 127 criteria in the form of a number, an expression, a cell reference, or text that define which cells will be averaged.

To calculate the value of active equipment that has a two-year lifetime, you can use the following AVERAGEIFS function to average the values (Equipment[Value]) of active equipment (Equipment[Status],"A") having two years of life (Equipment[Life],"2"):

```
=AVERAGEIFS(Equipment[Value],Equipment[Status],"A",
Equipment[Life],"2")
```

One of the first items you need for the Years' Service Summary report is a count of equipment with a two-year lifetime. You will use the COUNTIFS function to compute statistical information for the active equipment in both locations.

To calculate the total amount of active equipment with lifetimes of two, five, and greater than five years:

1. Select cell **C16**, and then click the **Insert Function** button f_x next to the formula bar. The Insert Function dialog box opens.

2. Click the **Or select a category** arrow, and then click **Statistical**.

3. In the Select a function box, click **COUNTIFS**, and then click the **OK** button. The Function Arguments dialog box opens.

TIP

You could also use the worksheet reference 'Equipment Inventory'!G7:G79 to reference all of the equipment.

4. In the Criteria_range1 box, enter **Equipment[Status]** and then press the **Tab** key. This criterion selects all of the equipment in the Equipment table that is in active use.

5. In the Criteria1 box, type **"A"** to specify active equipment, and then press the **Tab** key. The first condition is complete, and 60 appears as the total count in the middle of the Function Arguments dialog box.

6. In the Criteria_range2 box, enter **Equipment[Life]** and then press the **Tab** key. This criterion selects equipment that will have a lifetime of two years.

7. In the Criteria2 box, type **"2"** to select equipment with a lifetime of two years, and then press the **Tab** key. The second condition is complete, and 17 appears as the total count. See Figure B-13.

Figure B-13 | **COUNTIFS Function Arguments box**

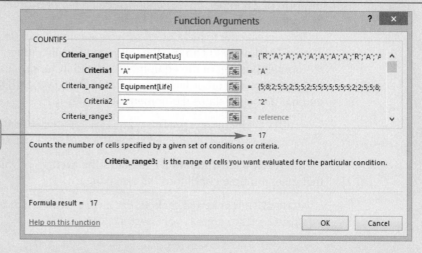

value updates as each criterion is entered

8. Click the **OK** button. The formula =COUNTIFS(Equipment[Status],"A",
    Equipment[Life],"2") appears in the formula bar, and the value 17 appears in
    cell C16. See Figure B-14.

| Figure B-14 | Summary of the equipment with a two-year lifetime |

COUNTIFS
function calculates
the number of
items that have a
life of two years

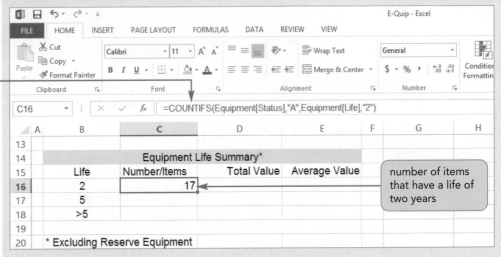

number of items
that have a life of
two years

9. Copy the formula from cell **C16** to the range **C17:C18**.

10. In cell **C17**, change the second criteria argument from "2" to **"5"**. The criteria
    specify a lifetime of five years. The formula =COUNTIFS(Equipment[Status],
    "A",Equipment[Life],"5") appears in the formula bar, and 40 appears in cell C17.

11. In cell **C18**, change the second criteria argument from 2 to **">5"**. The
    criteria specify a lifetime of greater than five years. The formula
    =COUNTIFS(Equipment[Status],"A",Equipment[Life],">5") appears in
    the formula bar, and 3 appears in cell C18.

Next, you will calculate the total value of the active equipment based on the life of
the equipment. To do this, you will use the SUMIFS function.

To calculate the total value of active equipment based on the life of the equipment:

1. Select cell **D16**, and then click the **Insert Function** button f_x next to the
    formula bar. The Insert Function dialog box opens.

2. Click the **Or select a category** arrow, and then click **Math & Trig**.

3. In the Select a function box, click **SUMIFS**, and then click the **OK** button. The
    Function Arguments dialog box opens.

4. In the Sum_range box, type **Equipment[Value]** to enter the range of data to
    sum, and then press the **Tab** key.

5. In the Criteria_range1 box, enter **Equipment[Status]** and then press the
    Tab key.

▶ **6.** In the Criteria1 box, type **"A"** to specify active equipment, and then press the **Tab** key. The first condition is complete. See Figure B-15.

Figure B-15 ▶ **SUMIFS Function Arguments dialog box**

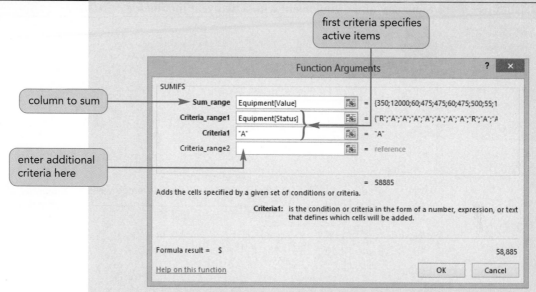

first criteria specifies active items

column to sum

enter additional criteria here

Function Arguments

SUMIFS
Sum_range   Equipment[Value]   = {350;12000;60;475;475;60;475;500;55;1
Criteria_range1   Equipment[Status]   = {"R";"A";"A";"A";"A";"A";"A";"R";"A";"A
Criteria1   "A"   = "A"
Criteria_range2   = reference

= 58885

Adds the cells specified by a given set of conditions or criteria.

Criteria1: is the condition or criteria in the form of a number, expression, or text that defines which cells will be added.

Formula result = $ 58,885

Help on this function   OK   Cancel

▶ **7.** In the Criteria_range2 box, enter **Equipment[Life]** for the range referencing the life of the equipment, and then press the **Tab** key.

▶ **8.** In the Criteria2 box, type **"2"** to specify the lifetime of the equipment, and then press the **Tab** key.

▶ **9.** Click the **OK** button. The formula =SUMIFS(Equipment[Value], Equipment[Status],"A",Equipment[Life],"2") appears in the formula bar, and $1,325 appears in cell D16.

▶ **10.** Copy the formula from cell **D16** to the range **D17:D18**.

▶ **11.** In cell **D17**, change the second criteria argument from "2" to **"5"**. The formula =SUMIFS(Equipment[Value],Equipment[Status],"A", Equipment[Life],"5") appears in the formula bar, and $25,560 appears in cell D17.

▶ **12.** In cell **D18**, change the second criteria argument to **">5"**. The formula =SUMIFS(Equipment[Value],Equipment[Status],"A",Equipment[Life],">5") appears in the formula bar, and $32,000 appears in cell D18.

Next, you will calculate the average value of active equipment based on the life of the equipment. You will use the AVERAGEIFS function to do this.

To calculate the average value of active equipment based on the life of the equipment:

▶ 1. Select cell **E16**, and then click the **Insert Function** button f_x next to the formula bar. The Insert Function dialog box opens.

▶ 2. Click the **Or select a category** arrow, and then click **Statistical**.

▶ 3. In the Select a function box, click **AVERAGEIFS**, and then click the **OK** button. The Function Arguments dialog box opens.

▶ 4. In the Average_range box, type **Equipment[Value]** to enter the range to be averaged, and then press the **Tab** key.

▶ 5. In the Criteria_range1 box, enter **Equipment[Status]** and then press the **Tab** key.

▶ 6. In the Criteria1 box, type **"A"** to specify active equipment, and then press the **Tab** key. The first condition is complete.

▶ 7. In the Criteria_range2 box, enter **Equipment[Life]** for the range referencing the life of the equipment, and then press the **Tab** key.

▶ 8. In the Criteria2 box, type **"2"** to specify a lifetime of two years for the equipment, and then press the **Tab** key.

▶ 9. Click the **OK** button. The formula =AVERAGEIFS(Equipment[Value], Equipment[Status],"A",Equipment[Life],"2") appears in the formula bar, and $78 appears in cell E16.

▶ 10. Copy the formula from cell E16 to the range **E17:E18**.

▶ 11. In cell **E17**, change the second criteria argument from "2" to **"5"**. The formula =AVERAGEIFS(Equipment[Value],Equipment[Status],"A", Equipment[Life],"5") appears in the formula bar, and $639 appears in cell E17.

▶ 12. In cell **E18**, change the second criteria argument to **">5"**. The formula =AVERAGEIFS(Equipment[Value],Equipment[Status],"A", Equipment[Life],">5" appears in the formula bar, and $10,667 appears in cell E18.

▶ 13. Select cell **E18**. See Figure B-16.

Figure B-16   **Equipment Life Summary report**

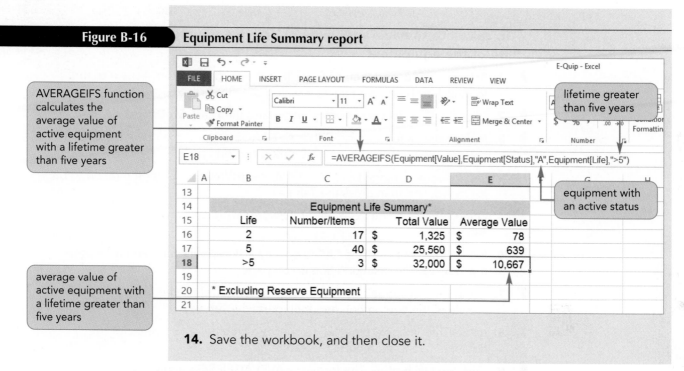

AVERAGEIFS function calculates the average value of active equipment with a lifetime greater than five years

lifetime greater than five years

equipment with an active status

average value of active equipment with a lifetime greater than five years

14. Save the workbook, and then close it.

The Inventory Summary worksheet is complete. In this appendix, you used advanced filtering techniques to evaluate the equipment inventory. You also used the DAVERAGE and AVERAGEIFS functions to calculate the average value of inventory broken down by location and status.

Review Assignments

Data File needed for the Review Assignments: Tools Review.xlsx

Patricia wants you to perform advanced filtering tasks that focus on items with service contracts in the Hoffman location. Complete the following:

1. Open the **Tools Review** workbook located in the ExcelB ▸ Review folder included in your Data Files, and then save the workbook as **Tools Update** in the location specified by your instructor.
2. In the Documentation worksheet, enter your name and the date.
3. Place the criteria range in rows 1 to 4 of the Equipment Inventory worksheet. Enter the And criteria to select items at the Hoffman location with a service contract (Y in column H). Then, enter the Or criteria to select items with a value of >1000. Filter the data. (*Hint*: Watch the criteria range to make sure that the proper range is selected.)
4. Use the DAVERAGE function on the Inventory Summary worksheet to calculate the average value of equipment with and without service agreements at the Tundra and Hoffman locations:
   a. Enter criteria in the criteria ranges G5:H6, G9:H10, J5:K6, and J9:K10.
   b. Enter the DAVERAGE formulas in the range C5:D6 using the criteria you entered in the criteria ranges.
5. Complete the Equipment Summary for each type of item (Description). The summary should only include active items. Complete the summary using the following:
   a. Use COUNTIFS for the range C16:C18.
   b. Use SUMIFS for the range D16:D18.
   c. Use AVERAGEIFS for the range E16:E18.
6. Save the workbook, and then close it.

Case Problem 1

Data File needed for this Case Problem: Donations.xlsx

Personal Donations   Bradley Cassidy wants to analyze the donations and monetary gifts he has made over the past few years. Complete the following:

1. Open the **Donations** workbook located in the ExcelB ▸ Case1 folder included with your Data Files, and then save the workbook as **Bradley Gifts** in the location specified by your instructor.
2. In the Documentation worksheet, enter your name and the date.
3. Make a copy of the Gifts worksheet and rename the copied sheet as **Q4**. Format the data on each sheet as a table; name the table on the Gifts worksheet **Gifts** and name the table on the Q4 sheet **Gifts4**.
4. In the Q4 worksheet, use advanced filtering to display donations in 2016 that were greater than $25. Sort the filtered data in the Amount column from highest to lowest, and format the Amount column appropriately.
5. In the Summary worksheet, complete the following gift analysis:
   a. Total tax deductions and non-tax deductions by year
   b. Total count by gift type by year
6. Save the workbook, and then close it.

APPLY

Case Problem 2

Data File needed for this Case Problem: House.xlsx

Tea House   Linda Hill is analyzing sales orders from salespeople in several European countries. Complete the following:

1. Open the **House** workbook located in the ExcelB ▸ Case2 folder included with your Data Files, and then save the workbook as **Tea House** in the location specified by your instructor.
2. In the Documentation worksheet, enter your name and the date.
3. Make a copy of the Orders worksheet, and then rename the copied worksheet as **March**. In the March worksheet, use advanced filtering to display all sales in Sweden and all sales for Janet Leverling.
4. Make a copy of the Orders worksheet, and then rename the copied worksheet as **Sept**. In the Sept worksheet, use advanced filtering to display all records for Laura Callahan with sales greater than $1,500 in September.
5. In the Summary worksheet, complete the summary analysis for France. Use the DAVERAGE and DSUM functions to enter formulas in row 11 to average and sum the orders in March for France. Format the range B11:C11 with the Accounting format and no decimal places. Set up an appropriate criteria range in rows 1 and 2.
6. In the Summary worksheet, complete the summary analysis for the United Kingdom (UK). Use the AVERAGEIFS and SUMIFS functions to enter formulas in row 12 to average and sum the orders in March in the U.K. Format the range B12:C12 with the Accounting format and no decimal places.
7. Save the workbook, and then close it.

OBJECTIVES

Session 5.1
- Review object naming standards
- Use the Like, In, Not, and & operators in queries
- Filter data using an AutoFilter
- Use the IIf function to assign a conditional value to a calculated field in a query
- Create a parameter query

Session 5.2
- Use query wizards to create a crosstab query, a find duplicates query, and a find unmatched query
- Create a top values query

Session 5.3
- Modify table designs using lookup fields, input masks, and data validation rules
- Identify object dependencies
- Review a Long Text field's properties
- Designate a trusted folder

ACCESS

Creating Advanced Queries and Enhancing Table Design

Making the Clinic Database Easier to Use

Case | *Chatham Community Health Services*

Chatham Community Health Services is a nonprofit health clinic located in Hartford, Connecticut. It provides a range of medical services to patients of all ages. The clinic specializes in the areas of pulmonology, cardiac care, and chronic disease management. Cindi Rodriguez, the office manager for Chatham Community Health Services, oversees a small staff and is responsible for maintaining the medical records of the clinic's patients.

Cindi and her staff rely on Microsoft Access 2013 to manage electronic medical records for patient information, billing, inventory control, purchasing, and accounts payable. The Chatham staff developed the Clinic database, which contains tables, queries, forms, and reports that Cindi and other staff members use to track patient, visit, and billing information.

Cindi is interested in taking better advantage of the power of Access to make the database easier to use and to create more sophisticated queries. For example, Cindi wants to obtain lists of patients in certain cities. She also needs a summarized list of invoice amounts by city. In this tutorial, you'll modify and customize the Clinic database to satisfy these and other requirements.

STARTING DATA FILES

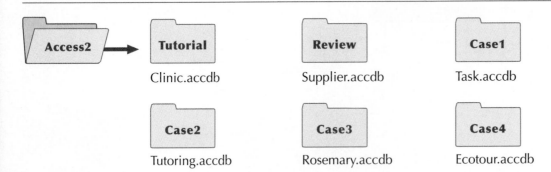

Access2 →	Tutorial	Review	Case1
	Clinic.accdb	Supplier.accdb	Task.accdb
	Case2	Case3	Case4
	Tutoring.accdb	Rosemary.accdb	Ecotour.accdb

Session 5.1 Visual Overview:

A Select query selects the records in the fields that satisfy the criteria.

The tbl prefix tag identifies a table object.

The qry prefix tag identifies a query object.

The frm prefix tag identifies a form object.

The rpt prefix tag identifies a report object.

A calculated field contains an expression that calculates the values of the data in the field.

The design grid contains the fields and criteria that will be used in the query.

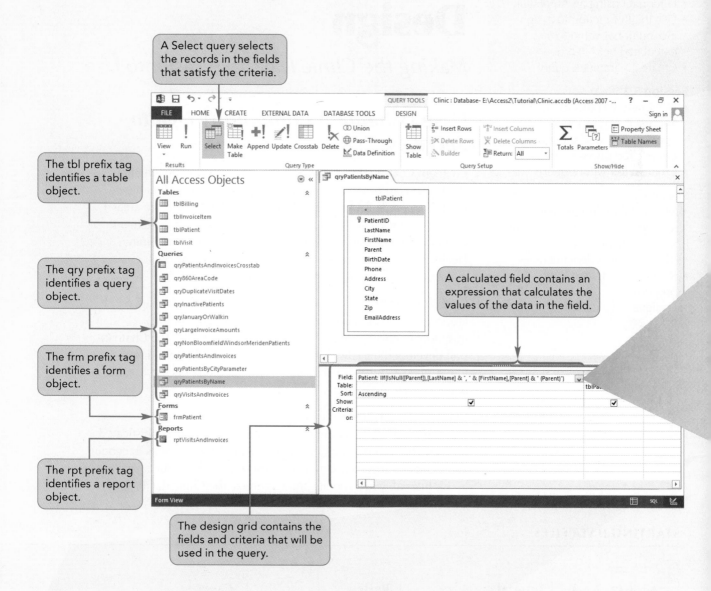

Calculated Field

The name of the new calculated field is placed to the left of the expression, separated with a colon.

The IIf function tests a condition and returns one of two values. The function returns the first value if the condition is true, and the second value if the condition is false.

The Expression Builder can be used to create an expression for a calculated field.

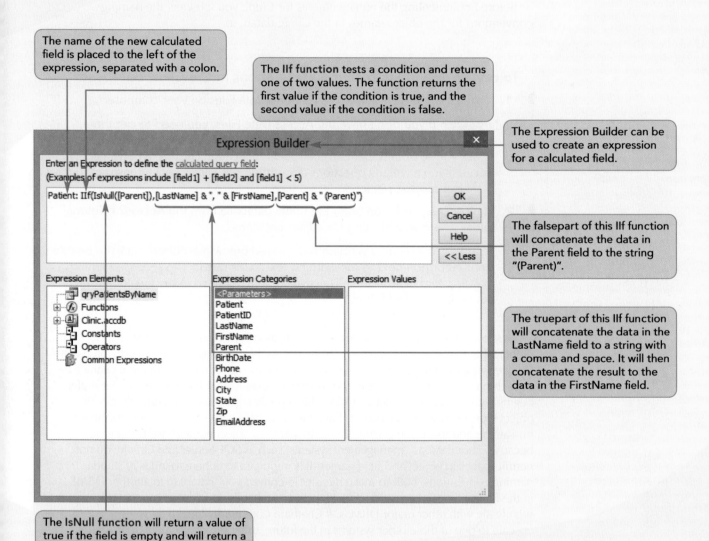

Expression Builder ⬅   ✕

Enter an Expression to define the calculated query field:
(Examples of expressions include [field1] + [field2] and [field1] < 5)

Patient: IIf(IsNull([Parent]),[LastName] & ", " & [FirstName],[Parent] & " (Parent)")

OK
Cancel
Help
<< Less

Expression Elements   Expression Categories   Expression Values
    qryPatientsByName   <Parameters>
  ⊞ Functions   Patient
  ⊞ Clinic.accdb   PatientID
    Constants   LastName
    Operators   FirstName
    Common Expressions   Parent
                                 BirthDate
                                 Phone
                                 Address
                                 City
                                 State
                                 Zip
                                 EmailAddress

The falsepart of this IIf function will concatenate the data in the Parent field to the string "(Parent)".

The truepart of this IIf function will concatenate the data in the LastName field to a string with a comma and space. It will then concatenate the result to the data in the FirstName field.

The IsNull function will return a value of true if the field is empty and will return a value of false if the field is not empty.

Reviewing the Clinic Database

TIP

Read the Microsoft Access Naming Conventions section in the appendix titled "Relational Databases and Database Design" for more information about naming conventions.

Cindi and her staff had no previous database experience when they created the Clinic database; they simply used the wizards and other easy-to-use Access tools. As business continued to grow at Chatham Community Health Services, Cindi realized she needed a database expert to further enhance the Clinic database. She hired Raj Gupta, who has a business information systems degree and nine years of experience developing database systems. Raj spent a few days reviewing the Clinic database, making sure the database adhered to simple naming standards for the objects and field names to make his future work easier.

Before implementing the enhancements for Cindi, you'll review the naming conventions for the object names in the Clinic database.

To review the object naming conventions in the Clinic database:

▶ **1.** Make sure you have the Access starting Data Files on your computer.

   Trouble? If you don't have the Access Data Files, you need to get them before you can proceed. Your instructor will either give you the Data Files or ask you to obtain them from a specified location (such as a network drive). If you have any questions about the Data Files, see your instructor or technical support person for assistance.

▶ **2.** Start Access, and then open the **Clinic** database from the Access2 ▶ Tutorial folder where your starting Data Files are stored.

   Trouble? If a security warning is displayed below the ribbon, click the Enable Content button next to the warning text to dismiss it. The security warning may appear because there is active content (a query) in the file and it may not be in a trusted folder.

As shown in Visual Overview 5.1, the Navigation Pane displays the objects grouped by object type. Each object name has a prefix tag—a tbl prefix tag for tables, a qry prefix tag for queries, a frm prefix tag for forms, and a rpt prefix tag for reports. All three characters in each prefix tag are lower case. The word immediately after the three-character prefix begins with an upper case letter. Using object prefix tags, you can readily identify the object type, even when the objects have the same base name—for instance, tblPatient, frmPatient, and rptCustomersAndBilling. In addition, object names have no spaces, because other database management systems, such as SQL Server and Oracle, do not permit spaces in object and field names. It is important to adhere to industry standard naming conventions, both to make it easier to convert your database to another DBMS in the future, if necessary, and to develop personal habits that enable you to work seamlessly with other major DBMSs. If Chatham Community Health Services needs to upscale to one of these other systems in the future, using standard naming conventions means that Raj will have to do less work to make the transition.

Teamwork: Following Naming Conventions

Most Access databases have hundreds of fields, objects, and controls. You'll find it easier to identify the type and purpose of these database items when you use a naming convention or standard. Most companies adopt a standard naming convention, such as the one used for the Clinic database, so that multiple people can develop a database, troubleshoot database problems, and enhance and improve existing databases. When working on a database, a team's tasks are difficult, if not impossible, to perform if a standard naming convention isn't used. In addition, most databases and database samples on Web sites and in training books use standard naming conventions that are similar to the ones used for the Clinic database. By following the standard naming convention established by your company or organization, you'll help to ensure smooth collaboration among all team members.

Now you'll create the queries that Cindi needs.

Using a Pattern Match in a Query

You are already familiar with queries that use an exact match or a range of values (for example, queries that use the > or < comparison operators) to select records. Access provides many other operators for creating select queries. These operators let you build more complicated queries that are difficult or impossible to create with exact-match or range-of-values selection criteria.

Cindi created a list of questions she wants to answer using the Clinic database:

- Which patients have the 860 area code?
- What is the patient information for patients located in Bloomfield, Windsor, or Meriden?
- What is the patient information for all patients except those located in Bloomfield, Windsor, or Meriden?
- What is the patient and visit information for patients in Hartford or West Hartford who have invoice amounts for less than $100 or who visited during the winter?
- What are the first and last names of Chatham Community Health Services' patients, or the parent name if it is listed? Children should not be contacted directly.
- What is the patient information for patients in a particular city? This query needs to be flexible to allow the user to specify the city.

Next, you will create the queries necessary to answer these questions. Cindi wants to view the records for all patients located in the 860 area code. These patients are located nearby and Cindi would like to start planning to arrange transportation for any of these patients who have difficulty travelling to the clinic. To answer Cindi's question, you can create a query that uses a pattern match. A **pattern match** selects records with a value for the designated field that matches the pattern of a simple condition value—in this case, patients with the 860 area code. You do this using the Like comparison operator.

The **Like comparison operator** selects records by matching field values to a specific pattern that includes one or more of these wildcard characters: asterisk (*), question mark (?), and number symbol (#). The asterisk represents any string of characters, the question mark represents any single character, and the number symbol represents any single digit. Using a pattern match is similar to using an exact match, except that a pattern match includes wildcard characters.

To create the new query, you must first place the tblPatient table field list in the Query window in Design view.

To create the new query in Design view:

1. If necessary, click the **Shutter Bar Open/Close Button** « at the top of the Navigation Pane to close it.

2. On the ribbon, click the **CREATE** tab.

3. In the Queries group, click the **Query Design** button. Access opens the Show Table dialog box in front of the Query window in Design view.

TIP

You can also double-click a table name to add the table's field list to the Query window.

4. Click **tblPatient** in the Tables box, click the **Add** button, and then click the **Close** button. Access places the tblPatient table field list in the Query window and closes the Show Table dialog box.

5. Drag the bottom border of the tblPatient window down until you can see the full list of fields.

6. Double-click the **title bar** of the tblPatient field list to highlight all the fields, and then drag the highlighted fields to the first column's Field box in the design grid. Access places each field in a separate column in the design grid, in the same order that the fields appear in the table. See Figure 5-1.

Figure 5-1	Adding the fields for the pattern match query

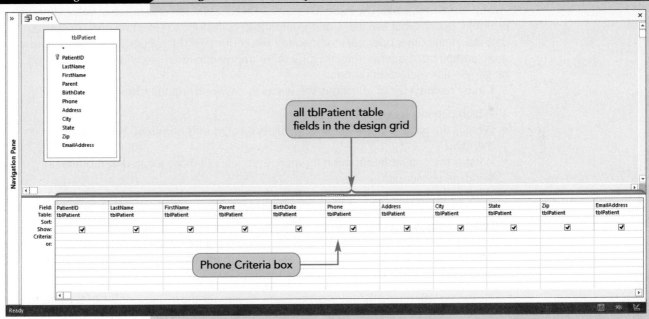

Trouble? If tblPatient.* appears in the first column's Field box, you dragged the * from the field list instead of the highlighted fields. Press the Delete key, and then repeat Step 6.

Now you will enter the pattern match condition Like "860*" for the Phone field. Access will select records with a Phone field value of 860 in positions one through three. The asterisk wildcard character specifies that any characters can appear in the remaining positions of the field value.

To specify records that match the indicated pattern:

TIP

If you omit the Like operator, Access automatically adds it when you run the query.

1. Click the **Phone Criteria** box, and then type **L**. The Formula AutoComplete menu displays a list of functions beginning with the letter L, but the Like operator is not one of the choices in the list. You'll finish typing the condition.

2. Type **ike "860*"**. See Figure 5-2.

Figure 5-2	Record selection based on matching a specific pattern

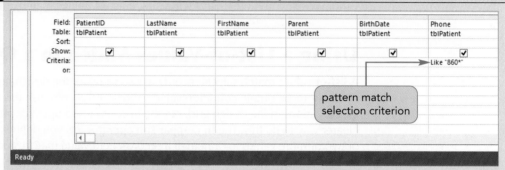

pattern match selection criterion

Ready

3. Click the **Save** button 🖫 on the Quick Access Toolbar to open the Save As dialog box.

4. Type **qry860AreaCode** in the Query Name box, and then press the **Enter** key. Access saves the query and displays the name on the object tab.

5. On the DESIGN tab, in the Results group, click the **Run** button. The query results are displayed in the query window. Access finds 46 records with the area code 860 in the Phone field. Not all records fit in the window, and you can scroll down to see more records. See Figure 5-3.

Figure 5-3	tblPatient table records for area code 860

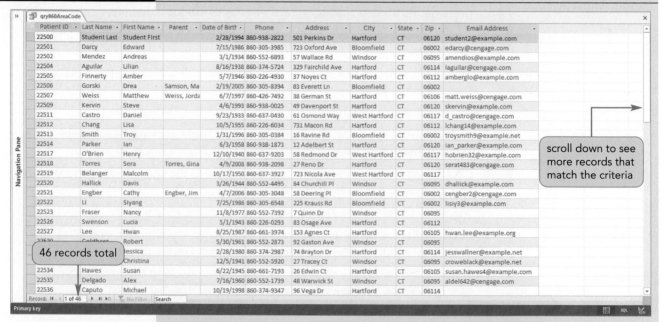

scroll down to see more records that match the criteria

46 records total

Note that Raj removed the hyphens from the Phone field values; for example, 8609382822 in the first record used to be 860-938-2822. You'll modify the Phone field later in this tutorial to format its values with hyphens.

▶ **6.** Change the first record in the table, with Patient ID 22500, so the Last Name and First Name columns contain your last and first names, respectively.

▶ **7.** Close the qry860AreaCode query.

Next, Cindi asks you to create a query that displays information about patients who live in Bloomfield, Windsor, or Meriden. She wants a printout of the patient data for her administrative assistant, who will contact these patients. To produce the results Cindi wants, you'll create a query using a list-of-values match.

Using a List-of-Values Match in a Query

A **list-of-values match** selects records whose value for the designated field matches one of two or more simple condition values. You could accomplish this by including several Or conditions in the design grid, but the In comparison operator provides an easier and clearer way to do this. The **In comparison operator** lets you define a condition with a list of two or more values for a field. If a record's field value matches one value from the list of defined values, then Access selects and includes that record in the query results.

To display the information Cindi requested, you want to select records if their City field value equals Bloomfield, Windsor, or Meriden. These are the values you will use with the In comparison operator. Cindi wants the query to contain the same fields as the qry860AreaCode query, so you'll make a copy of that query and modify it.

To create the query using a list-of-values match:

▶ **1.** Open the Navigation Pane.

▶ **2.** In the Queries group on the Navigation Pane, right-click **qry860AreaCode** and then click **Copy** on the shortcut menu.

Trouble? If you don't see the qry860AreaCode query in the Queries group, press the F5 function key to refresh the object listings in the Navigation pane.

▶ **3.** Right-click in the empty area in the Navigation Pane below the report and click **Paste**.

▶ **4.** In the Query Name box, type **qryBloomfieldWindsorMeridenPatients** and then press the **Enter** key.

To modify the copied query, you need to open it in Design view.

▶ **5.** In the Queries group on the Navigation Pane, right-click **qryBloomfield WindsorMeridenPatients** to select it and display the shortcut menu.

▶ **6.** Click **Design View** on the shortcut menu to open the query in Design view, and then close the Navigation Pane.

You need to delete the existing condition from the Phone field.

▶ **7.** Click the **Phone Criteria** box, press the **F2** key to highlight the entire condition, and then press the **Delete** key to remove the condition.

Now you can enter the criterion for the new query using the In comparison operator. When you use this operator, you must enclose the list of values you want to match within parentheses and separate the values with commas. In addition, for fields defined using the Text data type, you enclose each value in quotation marks, although Access adds the quotation marks if you omit them. For fields defined using the Number or Currency data type, you don't enclose the values in quotation marks.

8. Right-click the **City Criteria** box to open the shortcut menu, click **Zoom** to open the Zoom dialog box, and then type **In ("Bloomfield","Windsor", "Meriden")**, as shown in Figure 5-4.

Figure 5-4   **Record selection based on matching field values to a list of values**

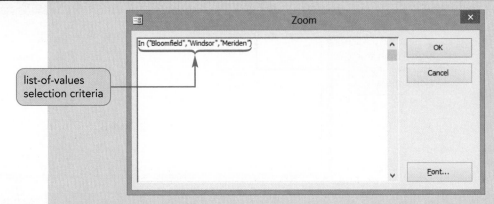

list-of-values
selection criteria

TIP

After clicking in a box, you can also open its Zoom dialog box by holding down the Shift key and pressing the F2 key.

9. Click the **OK** button to close the Zoom dialog box, and then save and run the query. Access displays the recordset, which shows the 20 records with Bloomfield, Windsor, or Meriden in the City field.

10. Close the query.

Cindi also asks her assistant to contact Chatham Community Health Services patients who don't live in Bloomfield, Windsor, or Meriden. You can provide Cindi with this information by creating a query with the Not logical operator.

Using the Not Logical Operator in a Query

The **Not logical operator** negates a criterion or selects records for which the designated field does not match the criterion. For example, if you enter *Not "Windsor"* in the Criteria box for the City field, the query results show records that do not have the City field value Windsor—that is, records of all patients not located in Windsor.

To create Cindi's query, you will combine the Not logical operator with the In comparison operator to select patients whose City field value is not in the list *("Bloomfield", "Windsor","Meriden")*. The qryBloomfieldWindsorMeridenPatients query has the fields that Cindi needs to see in the query results. Cindi doesn't need to keep the qryBloomfieldWindsorMeridenPatients query, so you'll rename and then modify the query.

TIP

You can rename any type of object, including a table, in the Navigation Pane using the Rename command on the shortcut menu.

To create the query using the Not logical operator:

1. Open the Navigation Pane.

2. In the Queries group, right-click **qryBloomfieldWindsorMeridenPatients**, and then on the shortcut menu click **Rename**.

3. Position the insertion point after "qry," type **Non**, and then press the **Enter** key. The query name is now qryNonBloomfieldWindsorMeridenPatients.

4. Open the **qryNonBloomfieldWindsorMeridenPatients** query in Design view, and then close the Navigation Pane.

You need to change the existing condition in the City field to add the Not logical operator.

5. Click the **City Criteria** box, open the Zoom dialog box, click at the beginning of the expression, type **Not**, and then press the **spacebar**. See Figure 5-5.

Figure 5-5 **Record selection based on not matching a list of values**

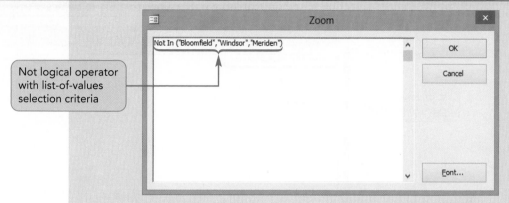

Not logical operator with list-of-values selection criteria

6. Click the **OK** button, and then save and run the query. The recordset displays only those records with a City field value that is not Bloomfield, Windsor, or Meriden. The recordset includes a total of 31 patient records.

7. Scroll down the datasheet to make sure that no Bloomfield or Windsor or Meriden patients appear in your results.

Now you can close and delete the query, because Cindi does not need to run this query again.

8. Close the query, and then open the Navigation Pane.

TIP

You can delete any type of object, including a table, in the Navigation Pane using the Delete command on the shortcut menu.

9. Right-click **qryNonBloomfieldWindsorMeridenPatients**, click **Delete** on the shortcut menu, and then click **Yes** in the dialog box warning that deleting this object will remove it from all groups.

You now are ready to answer Cindi's question about patients in Hartford or West Hartford that have invoice amounts for less than $100 or that visited during the winter.

Using an AutoFilter to Filter Data

Cindi wants to view the patient last and first names, cities, visit dates, walk-in statuses, and visit reasons for patients in Hartford or West Hartford who either walked in without an appointment or visited during the first week in January. The qryJanuaryOrWalkin query contains the same fields Cindi wants to view. This query also uses the Or logical operator to select records if the Walkin field has a value of true or if the VisitDate field value is between 1/1/2016 and 1/7/2016. These are two of the conditions needed to answer Cindi's question. You could modify the qryJanuaryOrWalkin query in Design view to further restrict the records selected to patients located only in Hartford or West Hartford. However, you can use the AutoFilter feature to choose the city restrictions faster and with more flexibility. You previously used the AutoFilter feature to sort records, and you previously used Filter By Selection to filter records. Now you'll use the AutoFilter feature to filter records.

To filter the records using an AutoFilter:

1. Open the **qryJanuaryOrWalkin** query in Design view, and then close the Navigation Pane.

The true condition for the Walkin field selects records for patients who walked in without an appointment, and the Between #1/1/2016# And #1/7/2016# condition for the VisitDate field selects records for patients whose visit date was in the first week of January 2016. Although the Walkin field is a yes/no field, these values are represented by true (yes) and false (no). Because the conditions are in two different rows, the query uses the Or logical operator. If you wanted to answer Cindi's question in Design view, you would add a condition for the City field, using either the Or logical operator—"Hartford" Or "West Hartford"—or the In comparison operator—In ("Hartford","West Hartford"). If you were to use Like *Hartford instead of the In function, the asterisk wildcard (*) would include East Hartford as well as Hartford and West Hartford. You'd place the condition for the City field in both the Criteria row and in the Or row. The query recordset would include a record only if both conditions in either row are satisfied. Instead of changing the conditions in Design view, though, you'll choose the information Cindi wants using an AutoFilter.

2. Run the query, and then click the **arrow** on the City column heading to display the AutoFilter menu. See Figure 5-6.

| Figure 5-6 | Using an AutoFilter to filter records in the query recordset |

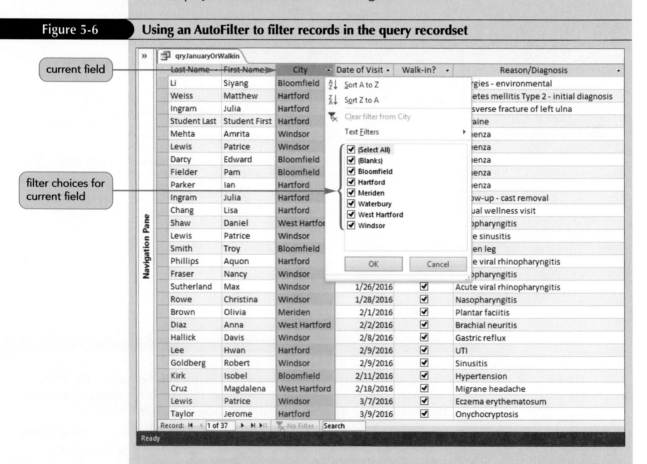

current field

filter choices for current field

The AutoFilter menu lists all City field values that appear in the recordset. A check mark next to an entry indicates that records with that City field value appear in the recordset. To filter for selected City field values, you uncheck the cities you don't want selected and leave checked the cities you do want selected. You can click the "(Select All)" check box to select or deselect all field values. The "(Blanks)" option includes null values when checked and excludes null values when unchecked. (Recall that a null field value is the absence of a value for the field.)

3. Click the **(Select All)** check box to deselect all check boxes, click the **Hartford** check box, and then click the **West Hartford** check box.

The two check boxes indicate that the AutoFilter will include only Hartford and West Hartford City field values.

4. Click the **OK** button. Access displays the 18 records for patients in Hartford and West Hartford who walked in without an appointment, or who had a visit in the first week in January. See Figure 5-7.

| Figure 5-7 | **Using an AutoFilter to filter records in the query recordset** |

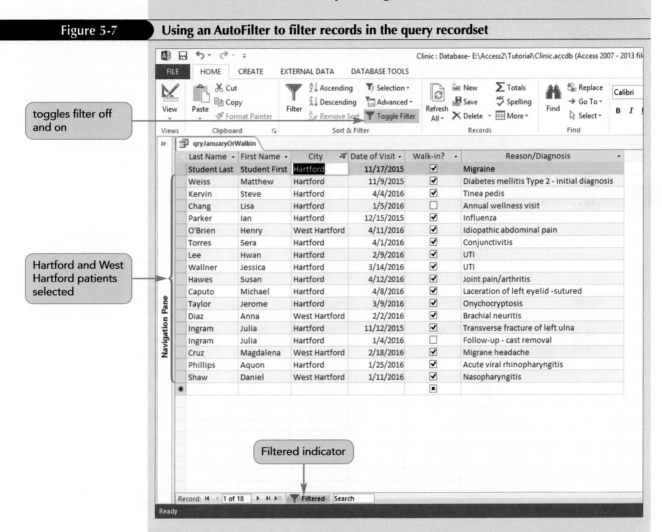

You click the Toggle Filter button in the Sort & Filter group on the HOME tab to remove the current filter and display all records in the query. If you click the Toggle Filter button a second time, you reapply the filter.

5. On the HOME tab, in the Sort & Filter group, click the **Toggle Filter** button. Access removes the filter, and all 37 records appear in the recordset.

6. Click the **Toggle Filter** button. Access applies the City filter, displaying the 18 records for patients in Hartford and West Hartford.

7. Save the query and close it.

Next, Cindi wants to view all fields from the tblPatient table, along with the patient name or the parent name if the patient is a child.

Assigning a Conditional Value to a Calculated Field

If a field in a record does not contain any information at all, it has a null value. Such a field is also referred to as a null field. A field in a record that contains any data at all—even a single space—is nonnull. Records for patients who are adults have nonnull FirstName and LastName field values and null Parent field values in the tblPatient table, while records for children have nonnull values for all three fields. Cindi wants to view records from the tblPatient table in order by the Parent value, if it's nonnull, and at the same time in order by the LastName and then FirstName field values, if the Parent field value is null. To produce this information for Cindi, you need to create a query that includes all fields from the tblPatient table and then add a calculated field that will display the patient name—either the Parent field value, which is input using the form LastName, FirstName, or the LastName and FirstName field values, separated by a comma and a space.

To combine the LastName and FirstName fields, you'll use the expression *LastName & ", " & FirstName*. The **& (ampersand) operator** is a concatenation operator that joins text expressions. **Concatenation** refers to joining two or more text fields or characters encapsulated in quotes. When you join the LastName field value to the string that contains the comma and space, you are concatenating these two strings. If the LastName field value is Fernandez and the FirstName field value is Sabrina, for example, the result of the expression *LastName & ", " & FirstName* is *Fernandez & ", " & Sabrina* which results in *Fernandez, Sabrina*.

INSIGHT

Using Concatenation

IT professionals generally refer to a piece of text data as a string. Most programming languages include the ability to join two or more strings using concatenation.

Imagine you're working with a database table that contains Title, FirstName, and LastName values for people who have made donations, and you've been asked to add their names to a report. You could add each individual field separately, but the data would look awkward, with each field in a separate column. Alternatively, you could create a calculated field with an expression that combines the fields with spaces into a more readable format, such as "Mr. Jim Sullivan". To do this, you would concatenate the fields with a space separator. The expression to perform this task might look like *=Title & " " & FirstName & " " & LastName*.

To display the correct patient value, you'll use the IIf function. The **IIf (Immediate If) function** assigns one value to a calculated field or control if a condition is true, and a second value if the condition is false. The IIf function has three parts: a condition that is true or false, the result when the condition is true, and the result when the condition is false. Each part of the IIf function is separated by a comma. The condition you'll use is *IsNull(Parent)*. The **IsNull function** tests a field value or an expression for a null value; if the field value or expression is null, the result is true; otherwise, the result is false. The expression *IsNull(Parent)* is true when the Parent field value is null, and is false when the Parent field value is not null.

For the calculated field, you'll enter *IIf(IsNull(Parent),LastName & ", " & FirstName, Parent & " (Parent)")*. You interpret this expression as follows: If the Parent field value is null, then set the calculated field value to the concatenation of the LastName field value and the text string ", " and the FirstName field value. If the Parent field value is not null, then set the calculated field value to the Parent field value and the text string "(Parent)" to indicate the patient name is the parent of a child patient.

Now you're ready to create Cindi's query to display the patient name.

To create the query to display the patient name:

▶ **1.** Click the **CREATE** tab, and then in the Queries group, click the **Query Design** button. The Show Table dialog box opens on top of the Query window in Design View.

▶ **2.** Click **tblPatient** in the Tables box, click the **Add** button, and then click the **Close** button. The tblPatient table field list is placed in the Query window and the Show Table dialog box closes.

Cindi wants all fields from the tblPatient table to appear in the query recordset, with the new calculated field in the first column.

▶ **3.** Drag the bottom border of the tblPatient field list down until all fields are visible, double-click the **title bar** of the tblPatient field list to highlight all the fields, and then drag the highlighted fields to the second column's Field box in the design grid. Access places each field in a separate column in the design grid starting with the second column, in the same order that the fields appear in the table.

Trouble? If you accidentally drag the highlighted fields to the first column in the design grid, click the PatientID Field box, and then in the Query Setup group, click the Insert Columns button. Continue with Step 4.

TIP

After clicking in a box, you can also open its Expression Builder dialog box by holding down the Ctrl key and pressing the F2 key.

▶ **4.** Right-click the blank Field box to the left of the PatientID field, and then click **Build** on the shortcut menu. The Expression Builder dialog box opens.

Cindi wants to use "Patient" as the name of the calculated field, so you'll type that name, followed by a colon, and then you'll choose the IIf function.

▶ **5.** Type **Patient:** and then press the **spacebar**.

▶ **6.** Double-click **Functions** in the Expression Elements (left) column, and then click **Built-In Functions**.

Make sure you double-click instead of single-click the IIf function.

▶ **7.** Scroll down the Expression Categories (middle) column, click **Program Flow**, and then in the Expression Values (right) column, double-click **IIf**. Access adds the IIf function with four placeholders to the right of the calculated field name in the expression box. See Figure 5-8.

Figure 5-8 **IIf function inserted for the calculated field**

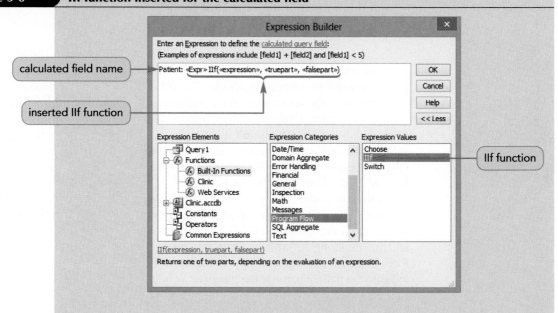

The expression you will create does not need the leftmost placeholder (<<Expr>>), so you'll delete it. You'll replace the second placeholder (<<expression>>) with the condition using the IsNull function, the third placeholder (<<truepart>>) with the expression using the & operator, and the fourth placeholder (<<falsepart>>) with the Parent field name and expression to include the " (Parent)" text.

▶ 8. Click **<<Expr>>** in the expression box, and then press the **Delete** key. The first placeholder is deleted.

▶ 9. Click **<<expression>>** in the expression box, and then click **Inspection** in the Expression Categories (middle) column.

▶ 10. Double-click **IsNull** in the Expression Values (right) column, click **<<expression>>** in the expression box, and then type **Parent**. You've completed the entry of the condition in the IIf function. See Figure 5-9.

Figure 5-9   **After entering the condition for the calculated field's IIf function**

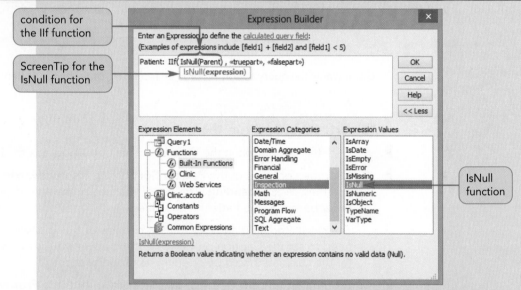

condition for the IIf function

ScreenTip for the IsNull function

IsNull function

After you typed the first letter of "Parent," the Formula AutoComplete box displayed a list of functions beginning with the letter P, and a ScreenTip for the IsNull function was displayed above the box. The box closed after you typed the third letter, but the ScreenTip remains on the screen.

Instead of typing the field name of Parent in the previous step, you could have double-clicked Clinic.accdb in the Expression Elements column, double-clicked Tables in the Expression Elements column, clicked tblPatient in the Expression Elements column, and then double-clicked Parent in the Expression Categories column.

Now you'll replace the third placeholder and then the fourth placeholder.

▶ 11. Click **<<truepart>>**, and then type **LastName & ", " & FirstName** to finish creating the calculated field. Be sure you type a space after the comma within the quotation marks.

▶ 12. Click **<<falsepart>>**, and then type **Parent & " (Parent)"**. Be sure you type a space after the first quotation mark. See Figure 5-10.

TIP

The expression "[tblPatient]![Parent]", meaning the Parent field in the tblPatient table, is the same as "Parent".

Figure 5-10   Completed calculated field

truepart expression

Expression Builder

Enter an Expression to define the calculated query field:
(Examples of expressions include [field1] + [field2] and [field1] < 5)

Patient: IIf(IsNull(Parent) , LastName & ", " & FirstName, Parent & " (Parent)")

OK
Cancel
Help
<< Less

falsepart expression

Expression Elements
- Query1
  - Functions
    - Built-In Functions
    - Clinic
    - Web Services
  - Clinic.accdb
  - Constants
  - Operators
  - Common Expressions

Expression Categories
Date/Time
Domain Aggregate
Error Handling
Financial
General
Inspection
Math
Messages
Program Flow
SQL Aggregate
Text

Expression Values
IsArray
IsDate
IsEmpty
IsError
IsMissing
IsNull
IsNumeric
IsObject
TypeName
VarType

IsNull(expression)
Returns a Boolean value indicating whether an expression contains no valid data (Null).

Cindi wants the query to sort records in ascending order by the Patient calculated field.

To sort, save, and run the query:

1. Click the **OK** button in the Expression Builder dialog box to close it.

2. Click the right side of the **Patient Sort** box to display the sort order options, and then click **Ascending**. The query will display the records in alphabetical order based on the Patient field values.

   The calculated field name of Patient consists of a single word, so you do not need to set the Caption property for it. However, you'll review the properties for the calculated field by opening its property sheet.

3. On the DESIGN tab, in the Show/Hide group, click the **Property Sheet** button. The property sheet opens and displays the properties for the Patient calculated field. See Figure 5-11.

Figure 5-11   Property sheet for the Patient calculated field

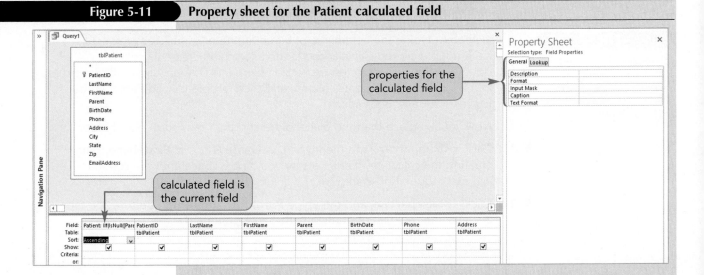

Among the properties for the calculated field, which is the current field, is the Caption property. Leaving the Caption property set to null means that the column name for the calculated field in the query recordset will be Patient, which is the calculated field name. The Property Sheet button is a toggle, so you'll click it again to close the property sheet.

▶ 4. Click the **Property Sheet** button again to close the property sheet.

▶ 5. Save the query as **qryPatientsByName**, run the query, and then resize the Patient column to its best fit. Access displays all records from the tblPatient table in alphabetical order by the Patient field. See Figure 5-12.

| Figure 5-12 | Completed query displaying the Patient calculated field |

patient names are the concatenation of LastName, FirstName for null Parent values

patient names are the same as nonnull Parent values with the additional "(Parent)" text

Patient	Patient ID	Last Name	First Name	Parent	Date of Birth
Aguilar, Lilian	22504	Aguilar	Lilian		8/16/1938
Belanger, Malcolm	22519	Belanger	Malcolm		10/17/1950
Billings, Claire	22541	Billings	Claire		11/16/1990
Booker, Thomas	22510	Booker	Thomas		8/25/1966
Boucher, Sam	22543	Boucher	Sam		3/11/1975
Brown, Olivia	22530	Brown	Olivia		11/24/1943
Caputo, Michael	22536	Caputo	Michael		10/19/1998
Castro, Daniel	22511	Castro	Daniel		9/23/1933
Chang, Lisa	22512	Chang	Lisa		10/5/1955
Cruz, Magdalena	22550	Cruz	Magdalena		7/24/1984
Darcy, Edward	22501	Darcy	Edward		7/15/1986
Delgado, Alex	22535	Delgado	Alex		7/16/1960
Diaz, Anna	22542	Diaz	Anna		9/25/1987
Engber, Jim (Parent)	22521	Engber	Cathy	Engber, Jim	4/7/2006
Fielder, Pam	22549	Fielder	Pam		12/6/1978
Finnerty, Amber	22505	Finnerty	Amber		5/7/1946
Franklin, Chaney	22551	Franklin	Chaney		1/18/1954
Fraser, Nancy	22523	Fraser	Nancy		11/8/1977
Garrett, Ashley	22552	Garrett	Ashley		3/24/1989

▶ 6. Save and close the query.

You're now ready to create the query to satisfy Cindi's request for information about patients in a particular city.

Creating a Parameter Query

Cindi's next request is for records in the qryPatientsByName query for patients in a particular city. For this query, she wants to specify a city, such as Windsor or Hartford, each time she runs the query.

To create this query, you will copy, rename, and modify the qryPatientsByName query. You could create a simple condition using an exact match for the City field, but you would need to change it in Design view every time you run the query. Alternatively, Cindi or a member of her staff could filter the qryPatientsByName query for the city records they want to view. Instead, you will create a parameter query. A **parameter query** displays a dialog box that prompts the user to enter one or more criteria values when the query is run. In this case, you want to create a query that prompts for the city and selects only those patient records with that City field value from the table. You will enter the prompt in

the Like operator to the original criterion and concatenate the criterion to a wildcard character. When you run the parameter query with this new entry, Access will display one of the following recordsets:

- If you enter a specific City field value in the dialog box, such as *Windsor*, the entry is the same as *Like "Windsor" & "*"*, which becomes *Like "Windsor*"* after the concatenation operation. That is, Access selects all records whose City field values have Windsor in the first nine positions and any characters in the remaining positions. If the table on which the query is based contains records with City field values of Windsor, Access displays only those records. However, if the table on which the query is based also contains records with City field values of Windsor City, then Access would display both the Windsor and the Windsor City records.
- If you enter a letter in the dialog box, such as *W*, the entry is the same as *Like "W*"*, and the recordset displays all records with City field values that begin with the letter W, which would include Waterbury, West Hartford, Windsor, and Windsor City.
- If you enter no value in the dialog box, the entry is the same as *Like Null & "*"*, which becomes *Like "*"* after the concatenation operation, and the recordset displays all records.

Now you'll modify the parameter query to satisfy Cindi's request and you'll test the new version of the query.

To modify and test the parameter query:

▶ **1.** Switch to Design view.

▶ **2.** Click the **City Criteria** box, and then open the Zoom dialog box.

You'll use the Zoom dialog box to modify the value in the City Criteria box.

▶ **3.** Click to the left of the expression in the Zoom dialog box, type **Like**, press the **spacebar**, and then press the **End** key.

Be sure you type "*" at the end of the expression.

▶ **4.** Press the **spacebar**, type **&**, press the **spacebar**, and then type **"*"** as shown in Figure 5-16.

Figure 5-16   **Modified City Criteria value in the Zoom dialog box**

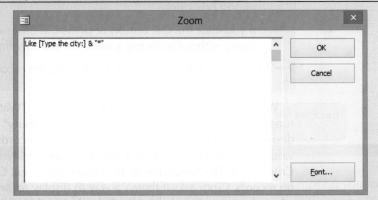

Now you can test the modified parameter query.

▶ **5.** Click the **OK** button to close the Zoom dialog box, save your query design changes, and then run the query.

First, you'll test the query to display patients in Windsor.

▶ **6.** Type **Windsor**, and then press the **Enter** key. The recordset displays the data for the 10 patients in Windsor.

Now you'll test the query without entering a value when prompted.

7. Switch to Design view, run the query, and then click the **OK** button. The recordset displays all 51 original records from the tblPatient table.

Finally, you'll test how the query performs when you enter W in the dialog box.

8. On the HOME tab, in the Records group, click the **Refresh All** button to open the Enter Parameter Value dialog box.

9. Type **W**, press the **Enter** key, and then scroll to the right, if necessary, to display the City field values. The recordset displays the 19 records for patients in Windsor, West Hartford, and Waterbury.

10. Close the query.

11. If you are not continuing on to the next session, close the Clinic database and click the **Yes** button if necessary to empty the Clipboard.

The queries you created will make the Clinic database easier to use. In the next session, you'll create a top values query and use query wizards to create three additional queries.

Session 5.1 Quick Check

REVIEW

1. According to the naming conventions used in this session, you use the _____ prefix tag to identify queries.

2. Which comparison operator selects records based on a specific pattern?

3. What is the purpose of the asterisk (*) in a pattern match query?

4. When do you use the In comparison operator?

5. How do you negate a selection criterion?

6. The _____ function returns one of two values based on whether the condition being tested is true or false.

7. When do you use a parameter query?

Session 5.2 Visual Overview:

A crosstab query uses aggregate functions such as Sum and Count to perform arithmetic operations on selected records.

A simple query selects records from one of more tables that satisfy criteria.

A find duplicates query is a select query that finds duplicate records in a table or query.

A find unmatched query is a select query that finds all records in a table or query that have no related records in a second table or query.

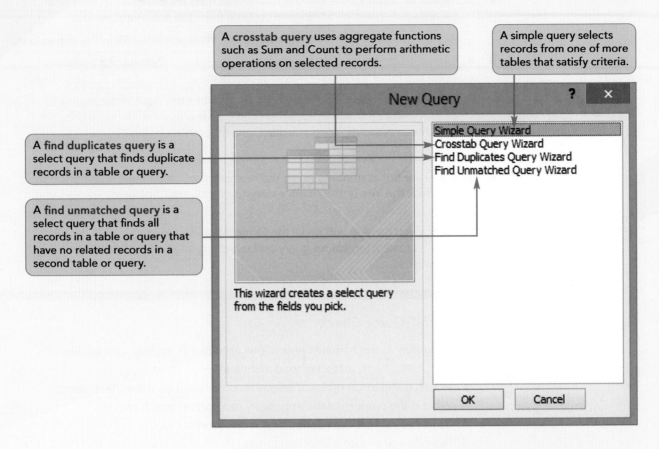

New Query

Simple Query Wizard
Crosstab Query Wizard
Find Duplicates Query Wizard
Find Unmatched Query Wizard

This wizard creates a select query from the fields you pick.

OK   Cancel

Each column and row intersection will display the sum of the InvoiceAmt values.

The selected field (InvoiceAmt) is used in the calculations for each column and row intersection.

This option determines whether to display an overall totals column in the crosstab query.

The crosstab query will display one column for the paid invoices and a second column for the unpaid invoices.

The crosstab query will display one row for each unique City field value.

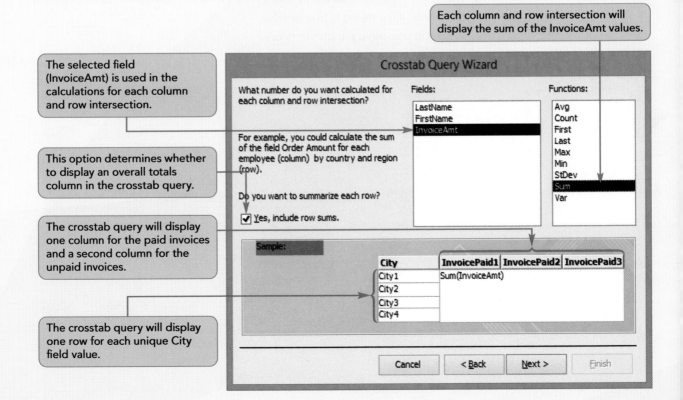

Crosstab Query Wizard

What number do you want calculated for each column and row intersection?

For example, you could calculate the sum of the field Order Amount for each employee (column) by country and region (row).

Do you want to summarize each row?

☑ Yes, include row sums.

Fields:
LastName
FirstName
InvoiceAmt

Functions:
Avg
Count
First
Last
Max
Min
StDev
Sum
Var

Sample:

City	InvoicePaid1	InvoicePaid2	InvoicePaid3
City1	Sum(InvoiceAmt)		
City2			
City3			
City4			

Cancel   < Back   Next >   Finish

Advanced Query Wizards

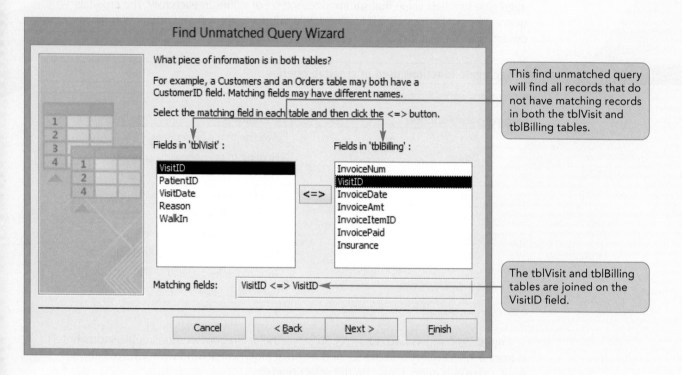

Find Unmatched Query Wizard

What piece of information is in both tables?

For example, a Customers and an Orders table may both have a CustomerID field. Matching fields may have different names.

Select the matching field in each table and then click the <=> button.

Fields in 'tblVisit' :

- VisitID
- PatientID
- VisitDate
- Reason
- WalkIn

Fields in 'tblBilling' :

- InvoiceNum
- VisitID
- InvoiceDate
- InvoiceAmt
- InvoiceItemID
- InvoicePaid
- Insurance

<=>

This find unmatched query will find all records that do not have matching records in both the tblVisit and tblBilling tables.

Matching fields: VisitID <=> VisitID

The tblVisit and tblBilling tables are joined on the VisitID field.

Cancel   < Back   Next >   Finish

This list contains the remaining fields in the tblVisit table that will not be considered for duplicate values.

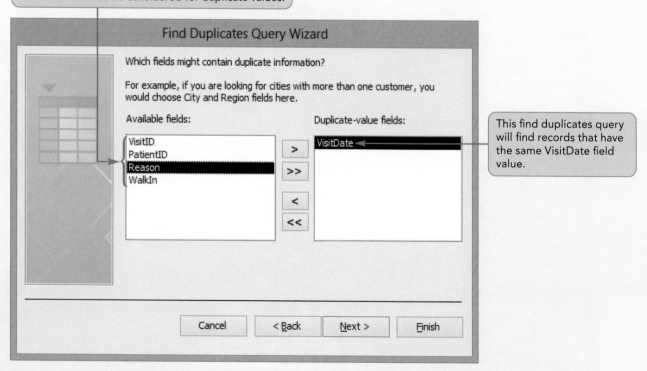

Find Duplicates Query Wizard

Which fields might contain duplicate information?

For example, if you are looking for cities with more than one customer, you would choose City and Region fields here.

Available fields:

- VisitID
- PatientID
- Reason
- WalkIn

Duplicate-value fields:

- VisitDate

>
>>
<
<<

This find duplicates query will find records that have the same VisitDate field value.

Cancel   < Back   Next >   Finish

Creating a Crosstab Query

Cindi wants to analyze the Chatham Community Health Services invoices by city, so she can view the paid and unpaid invoice amounts for all patients located in each city. Crosstab queries use the aggregate functions shown in Figure 5-17 to perform arithmetic operations on selected records. A crosstab query can also display one additional aggregate function value that summarizes the set of values in each row. The crosstab query uses one or more fields for the row headings on the left and one field for the column headings at the top.

Figure 5-17   Aggregate functions used in crosstab queries

Aggregate Function	Definition
Avg	Average of the field values
Count	Number of the nonnull field values
First	First field value
Last	Last field value
Max	Highest field value
Min	Lowest field value
StDev	Standard deviation of the field values
Sum	Total of the field values
Var	Variance of the field values

© 2014 Cengage Learning

Figure 5-18 shows two query recordsets—the first recordset (qryPatientsAndInvoices) is from a select query and the second recordset (qryPatientsAndInvoicesCrosstab) is from a crosstab query based on the select query.

Figure 5-18   Comparing a select query to a crosstab query

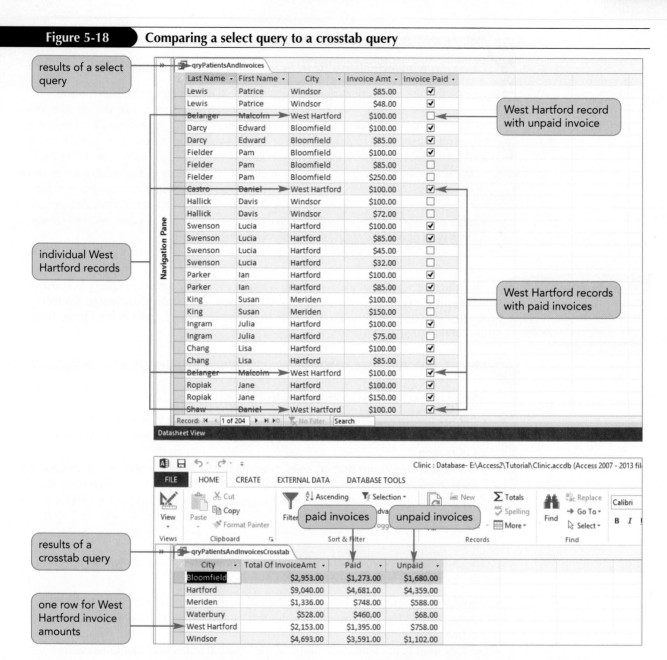

The qryPatientsAndInvoices query, a select query, joins the tblPatient, tblVisit, and tblBilling tables to display selected data from those tables for all invoices. The qryPatientsAndInvoicesCrosstab query, a crosstab query, uses the qryPatientsAndInvoices query as its source query and displays one row for each unique City field value. The City column in the crosstab query identifies each row. The crosstab query uses the Sum aggregate function on the InvoiceAmt field to produce the displayed values in the Paid and Unpaid columns for each City row. An entry in the Total Of InvoiceAmt column represents the sum of the Paid and Unpaid values for the City field value in that row.

PROSKILLS

Decision Making: Using Both Select Queries and Crosstab Queries

Companies use both select queries and crosstab queries in their decision making. A select query displays several records—one for each row selected by the select query— while a crosstab query displays only one summarized record for each unique field value. When managers want to analyze data at a high level to see the big picture, they might start with a crosstab query, identify which field values to analyze further, and then look in detail at specific field values using select queries. Both select and crosstab queries serve as valuable tools in tracking and analyzing a company's business, and companies use both types of queries in the appropriate situations. By understanding how managers and other employees use the information in a database to make decisions, you can create the correct type of query to provide the information they need.

TIP

Microsoft Access Help provides more information on creating a crosstab query without using a wizard.

The quickest way to create a crosstab query is to use the **Crosstab Query Wizard**, which guides you through the steps for creating one. You could also change a select query to a crosstab query in Design view using the Crosstab button in the Query Type group on the DESIGN tab.

REFERENCE

Using the Crosstab Query Wizard

- In the Queries group on the CREATE tab, click the Query Wizard button.
- In the New Query dialog box, click Crosstab Query Wizard, and then click the OK button.
- Complete the Wizard dialog boxes to select the table or query on which to base the crosstab query, select the row heading field (or fields), select the column heading field, select the calculation field and its aggregate function, and enter a name for the crosstab query.

The crosstab query you will create, which is similar to the one shown in Figure 5-18, has the following characteristics:

- The qryPatientsAndInvoices query in the Clinic database is the basis for the new crosstab query. The base query includes the LastName, FirstName, City, InvoiceAmt, and InvoicePaid fields.
- The City field is the leftmost column in the crosstab query and identifies each crosstab query row.
- The values from the InvoicePaid field, which is a Yes/No field, identify the rightmost columns of the crosstab query.
- The crosstab query applies the Sum aggregate function to the InvoiceAmt field values and displays the resulting total values in the Paid and Unpaid columns of the query results.
- The grand total of the InvoiceAmt field values appears for each row in a column with the heading Total Of InvoiceAmt.

Next you will create the crosstab query based on the qryPatientsAndInvoices query.

To start the Crosstab Query Wizard:

▶ 1. If you took a break after the previous session, make sure that the Clinic database is open and the Navigation Pane is closed.

Trouble? If the security warning is displayed below the ribbon, click the Enable Content button next to the security warning.

2. Click the **CREATE** tab on the ribbon.

3. In the Queries group, click the **Query Wizard** button. The New Query dialog box opens.

4. Click **Crosstab Query Wizard**, and then click the **OK** button. The first Crosstab Query Wizard dialog box opens.

You'll now use the Crosstab Query Wizard to create the crosstab query for Cindi.

To finish the Crosstab Query Wizard:

1. Click the **Queries** option button in the View section to display the list of queries in the Clinic database, and then click **Query: qryPatientsAndInvoices**. See Figure 5-19.

| Figure 5-19 | Choosing the query for the crosstab query |

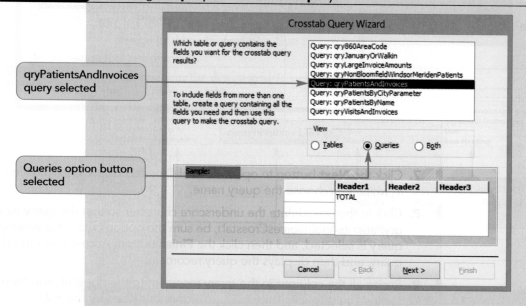

qryPatientsAndInvoices query selected

Queries option button selected

2. Click the **Next** button to open the next Crosstab Query Wizard dialog box. This is the dialog box where you choose the field (or fields) for the *row* headings. Because Cindi wants the crosstab query to display one row for each unique City field value, you will select that field for the row headings.

TIP

When you select a field, Access changes the sample crosstab query in the dialog box to illustrate your choice.

3. In the Available Fields box, click **City**, and then click the ▷ button to move the City field to the Selected Fields box.

4. Click the **Next** button to open the next Crosstab Query Wizard dialog box, in which you select the field values that will serve as *column* headings. Cindi wants to see the paid and unpaid total invoice amounts, so you need to select the InvoicePaid field for the column headings.

5. Click **InvoicePaid** in the box, and then click the **Next** button.

In the next Crosstab Query Wizard dialog box, you choose the field that will be calculated for each row and column intersection and the function to use for the calculation. The results of the calculation will appear in the row and column intersections in the query results. Cindi needs to calculate the sum of the InvoiceAmt field value for each row and column intersection.

Figure 5-24	Query recordset for duplicate visit dates

Date of Visit ▾	Visit ID ▾	Patient ID ▾	Reason/Diagnosis ▾	Walk-in? ▾
11/9/2015	1528	22507	Diabetes mellitus Type 2 - initial diagnosis	✔
11/9/2015	1527	22522	Allergies - environmental	✔
11/17/2015	1536	22526	Gastroenteritis	☐
11/17/2015	1538	22500	Migraine	✔
11/24/2015	1541	22526	Gastroenteritis - follow up	☐
11/24/2015	1542	22537	Influenza	✔
11/30/2015	1548	22519	Hypertension	☐
11/30/2015	1549	22501	Influenza	✔
1/11/2016	1569	22558	COPD management visit	☐
1/11/2016	1570	22561	Nasopharyngitis	✔
1/13/2016	1573	22511	Cardiac monitoring	☐
1/13/2016	1575	22513	Broken leg	✔
1/13/2016	1572	22560	Acute sinusitis	✔
1/25/2016	1586	22523	Nasopharyngitis	✔
1/25/2016	1588	22535	Hypertension	☐
1/25/2016	1585	22555	Acute viral rhinopharyngitis	✔
1/26/2016	1590	22505	Annual wellness visit	☐
1/26/2016	1591	22544	Acute viral rhinopharyngitis	✔
2/1/2016	1597	22517	Annual wellness visit	☐
2/1/2016	1598	22530	Plantar faciitis	✔
2/8/2016	1605	22535	Hypertension monitoring	☐
2/8/2016	1606	22520	Gastric reflux	✔
2/9/2016	1610	22529	Sinusitis	✔
2/9/2016	1608	22527	UTI	✔
2/9/2016	1607	22507	Diabetes mellitus Type 2 - serum glucose che	☐
2/24/2016	1626	22513	Follow-up - cast removal	☐
2/24/2016	1625	22551	Elevated blood lipids-monitoring meds	☐

Record: ◄ ◄ 1 of 50 ► ►I ►☐   No Filter   Search

Date of Visit

7. Close the query.

Cindi now asks you to find the records for patients with no visits. These are patients who have been referred to Chatham Community Health Services but have not had a first visit. Cindi wants to contact these patients to see if they would like to book initial appointments. To provide Cindi with this information, you need to create a find unmatched query.

Creating a Find Unmatched Query

A find unmatched query is a select query that finds all records in a table or query that have no related records in a second table or query. For example, you could display all patients who have had an appointment but have never been invoiced, or all students who are not currently enrolled in classes. Such a query provides information for a medical office to ensure all patients who have received services have also been billed for those services, and for a school administrator to contact the students to find out their future educational plans. You can use the **Find Unmatched Query Wizard** to create this type of query.

Using the Find Unmatched Query Wizard

- In the Queries group on the CREATE tab, click the Query Wizard button.
- In the New Query dialog box, click Find Unmatched Query Wizard, and then click the OK button.
- Complete the Wizard dialog boxes to select the table or query on which to base the new query, select the table or query that contains the related records, specify the common field in each table or query, select the additional fields to include in the query results, enter a name for the query, and then click the Finish button.

Cindi wants to know which patients have no visits. She will contact these patients to determine if they will be visiting Chatham Community Health Services Clinic or whether they are receiving their medical services elsewhere. To create a list of patients who have not had a visit to the clinic, you'll use the Find Unmatched Query Wizard to display only those records from the tblPatient table with no matching PatientID field value in the related tblVisit table.

To create the query using the Find Unmatched Query Wizard:

1. On the CREATE tab, in the Queries group, click the **Query Wizard** button to open the New Query dialog box.

2. Click **Find Unmatched Query Wizard**, and then click the **OK** button. The first Find Unmatched Query Wizard dialog box opens. In this dialog box, you select the table or query on which to base the new query. You'll use the qryPatientsByName query.

3. In the View section, click the **Queries** option button to display the list of queries, click **Query: qryPatientsByName** in the box to select this query, and then click the **Next** button. The next Find Unmatched Query Wizard dialog box opens, in which you choose the table that contains the related records. You'll select the tblVisit table.

4. Click **Table: tblVisit** in the box (if necessary), and then click the **Next** button. The next dialog box opens, in which you choose the common field for both tables. See Figure 5-25.

Figure 5-25   **Selecting the common field**

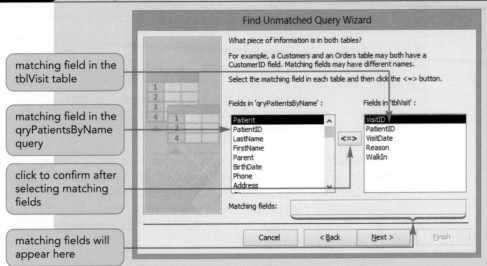

matching field in the tblVisit table

matching field in the qryPatientsByName query

click to confirm after selecting matching fields

matching fields will appear here

The common field between the query and the table is the PatientID field. You need to click the common field in each box, and then click the $\boxed{\texttt{<=>}}$ button between the two boxes to join the two objects. The Matching fields box then will display PatientID <=> PatientID to indicate the joining of the two matching fields. If the two selected objects already have a one-to-many relationship defined in the Relationships window, the Matching fields box will join the correct fields automatically.

Be sure you click the Patient ID field in both boxes.

▶ **5.** In the Fields in 'qryPatientsByName' box click **PatientID**, in the Fields in 'tblVisit' box click **PatientID**, click the $\boxed{\texttt{<=>}}$ button to connect the two selected fields, and then click the **Next** button. The next Find Unmatched Query Wizard dialog box opens, in which you choose the fields you want to see in the query recordset. Cindi wants the query recordset to display all available fields.

▶ **6.** Click the $\boxed{\texttt{>>}}$ button to move all fields from the Available fields box to the Selected fields box, and then click the **Next** button. The final dialog box opens, in which you enter the query name.

▶ **7.** Type **qryInactivePatients**, be sure the option button for viewing the results is selected, and then click the **Finish** button. Access saves the query and then displays four records in the query recordset. See Figure 5-26.

Figure 5-26   **Query recordset displaying four patients without visits**

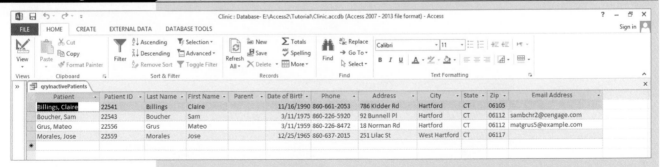

▶ **8.** Close the query.

Next, Cindi wants to contact those patients who have the highest invoice amounts to make sure that Chatham Community Health Services is providing satisfactory service. To display the information Cindi needs, you will create a top values query.

Creating a Top Values Query

Whenever a query displays a large group of records, you might want to limit the number to a more manageable size by displaying, for example, just the first 10 records. The **Top Values property** for a query lets you limit the number of records in the query results. To find a limited number of records using the Top Values property, you can click one of the preset values from a list, or enter either an integer (such as 15, to display the first 15 records) or a percentage (such as 20%, to display the first fifth of the records).

For instance, suppose you have a select query that displays 45 records. If you want the query recordset to show only the first five records, you can change the query by entering a Top Values property value of either 5 or 10%. If the query contains a sort and the last record that Access can display is one of two or more records with the same value for the primary sort field, Access displays all records with that matching key value.

Cindi wants to view the same data that appears in the qryLargeInvoiceAmounts query for patients with the highest 25 percent contract amounts. Based on the number or percentage you enter, a top values query selects that number or percentage of records starting from the top of the recordset. Thus, you usually include a sort in a top values query to display the records with the highest or lowest values for the sorted field. You will modify the query and then use the Top Values property to produce this information for Cindi.

To set the Top Values property for the query:

▶ **1.** Open the Navigation Pane, open the **qryLargeInvoiceAmounts** query in Datasheet view, and then close the Navigation Pane. Access displays 14 records, all with InvoiceAmt field values greater than $200, in descending order by InvoiceAmt.

▶ **2.** Switch to Design view.

▶ **3.** In the Query Setup group on the DESIGN tab, click the **Return** arrow (with the ScreenTip "Top Values"), and then click **25%**. See Figure 5-27.

Figure 5-27 | Creating the top values query

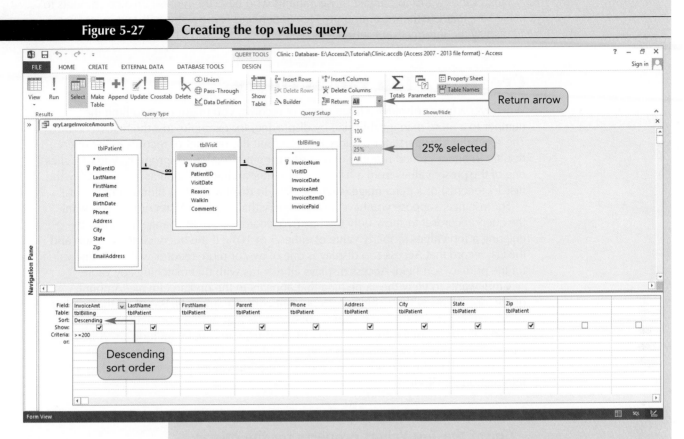

If the number or percentage of records you want to select, such as 15 or 20%, doesn't appear in the Top Values list, you can type the number or percentage in the Return box.

4. Run the query. Access displays four records in the query recordset; these records represent the patients with the highest 25 percent of the invoice amounts (25 percent of the original 14 records). See Figure 5-28.

Figure 5-28   **Top values query recordset**

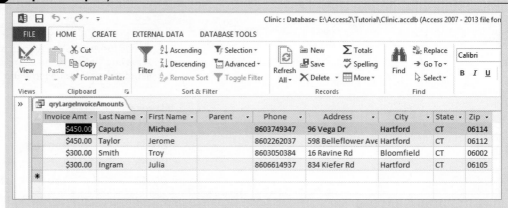

> **5.** Save and close the query.

> **6.** If you are not continuing on to the next session, close the Clinic database.

Cindi will use the information provided by the queries you created to analyze the Chatham Community Health Services business and to contact patients. In the next session, you will enhance the tblPatient and tblVisit tables.

Session 5.2 Quick Check

REVIEW

1. What is the purpose of a crosstab query?
2. What are the four query wizards you can use to create a new query?
3. What is a find duplicates query?
4. What does a find unmatched query do?
5. What happens when you set a query's Top Values property?
6. What happens if you set a query's Top Values property to 2 and the first five records have the same value for the primary sort field?

Session 5.3 Visual Overview:

The tblInvoiceItem query supplies the field values for the lookup field in the tblBilling table. A **lookup field** lets the user select a value from a list of possible values to enter data into the field.

tblInvoiceItem

Invoice Item ID	Invoice Item
⊞ DG111	Lab work
⊞ DG115	Lab work - culture
⊞ DG118	Lab work - glycated hemoglobin (A1C)
⊞ DG119	Lab work - urine glucose
⊞ DG225	Lab - culture
⊞ DG287	Lab - serum glucose
⊞ DG424	EKG with interpretation
⊞ DG532	Radiograph
⊞ OST145	Bone setting and cast
⊞ OST150	Cast of fracture

The tblBilling table contains the lookup field.

The InvoiceItemID and InvoiceItem fields from the tblInvoiceItem table are used to look up InvoiceItemID values in the tblBilling table.

tblBilling

Invoice Num	Visit ID	Invoice Date	Invoice Amt	Invoice Item	Invoice Paid	Insurance
35801	1527	11/10/2015	$100.00	Office visit	☑	$50.00
35802	1528	11/10/2015	$100.00	Lab - culture DG225		$0.00
35803	1528	11/10/2015	$45.00	Lab - serum glucose DG287		$0.00
35804	1528	11/13/2015	$238.00	EKG with interpretation DG424		$0.00
35805	1528	11/13/2015	$48.00	Radiograph DG532		$0.00
35808	1530	11/12/2015	$100.00	Bone setting and cast OST145		$0.00
35809	1530	11/12/2015	$85.00	Cast of fracture OST150		$0.00
35810	1530	11/12/2015	$65.00	Cast removal OST158		$0.00
35811	1530	11/13/2015	$48.00	Pharmacy PRM712		$0.00
35813	1535	11/13/2015	$100.00	Office visit REP001		$0.00
35814	1535	11/13/2015	$45.00	IM injection REP139		$0.00
35815	1535	11/16/2015	$300.00	Physical therapy REP187		$0.00
35816	1535	11/16/2015	$250.00	Phlebotomy REP298		$0.00
35818	1536	11/18/2015	$100.00	Influenza vaccine REP725		$100.00
35819	1536	11/18/2015	$65.00	Respiratory therapy REP752		$0.00
35821	1538	11/18/2015	$100.00	Surgery SUR001		$0.00
35822	1538	11/18/2015	$125.00	Suture removal SUR145		$0.00
35825	1539	11/19/2015	$100.00	Office visit	☑	$0.00

Values in the lookup field appear in alphabetical order, sorted by Invoice Item.

Only the InvoiceItemID values are stored in the InvoiceItemID field in the tblBilling table even though the user also sees the InvoiceItem values in the datasheet.

Lookup Fields and Input Masks

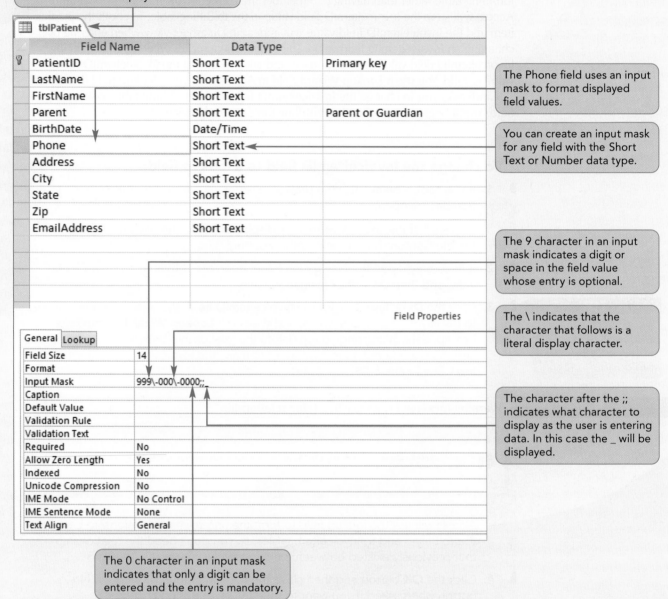

The tblPatient table contains the field that displays values with an input mask. An **input mask** is a predefined format that is used to enter and display data in a field.

The Phone field uses an input mask to format displayed field values.

You can create an input mask for any field with the Short Text or Number data type.

The 9 character in an input mask indicates a digit or space in the field value whose entry is optional.

The \ indicates that the character that follows is a literal display character.

The character after the ;; indicates what character to display as the user is entering data. In this case the _ will be displayed.

The 0 character in an input mask indicates that only a digit can be entered and the entry is mandatory.

tblPatient

Field Name	Data Type	
PatientID	Short Text	Primary key
LastName	Short Text	
FirstName	Short Text	
Parent	Short Text	Parent or Guardian
BirthDate	Date/Time	
Phone	Short Text	
Address	Short Text	
City	Short Text	
State	Short Text	
Zip	Short Text	
EmailAddress	Short Text	

Field Properties

General | Lookup

Field Size	14
Format	
Input Mask	999\-000\-0000;;
Caption	
Default Value	
Validation Rule	
Validation Text	
Required	No
Allow Zero Length	Yes
Indexed	No
Unicode Compression	No
IME Mode	No Control
IME Sentence Mode	None
Text Align	General

Creating a Lookup Field

The tblBilling table in the Clinic database contains information about patient invoices. Cindi wants to make entering data in the table easier for her staff. In particular, data entry is easier if they do not need to remember the correct InvoiceItemID field value for each treatment. Because the tblInvoiceItem and tblBIlling tables have a one-to-many relationship, Cindi asks you to change the tblBilling table's InvoiceItemID field, which is a foreign key to the tblInvoiceItem table, to a lookup field. A lookup field lets the user select a value from a list of possible values. For the InvoiceItemID field, a user will be able to select an invoice item's ID number from the list of invoice item names in the tblBilling table rather than having to remember the correct InvoiceItemID field value. Access will store the InvoiceItemID field value in the tblBilling table, but both the invoice item and the InvoiceItemID field value will appear in Datasheet view when entering or changing an InvoiceItemID field value. This arrangement makes entering and changing InvoiceItemID field values easier for users and guarantees that the InvoiceItemID field value is valid. You use a **Lookup Wizard field** in Access to create a lookup field in a table.

Cindi asks you to change the InvoiceItemID field in the tblBilling table to a lookup field. You'll begin by opening the tblBilling table in Design view.

To change the InvoiceItemID field to a lookup field:

1. If you took a break after the previous session, make sure that the Clinic database is open.

    Trouble? If the security warning is displayed below the ribbon, click the Enable Content button next to the warning.

2. If necessary, open the Navigation Pane, open the **tblBilling** table in Design view, and then close the Navigation Pane.

    > **TIP**
    >
    > You can display the arrow and the menu simultaneously if you click the box near its right side.

3. Click the **Data Type** box for the InvoiceItemID field, click the drop-down arrow to display the list of data types, and then click **Lookup Wizard**. A message box appears, instructing you to delete the relationship between the tblBilling and tblInvoiceItem tables if you want to make the InvoiceItemID field a lookup field. See Figure 5-29.

Figure 5-29   **Warning message for an existing table relationship**

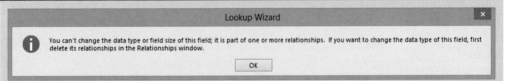

Access will use the lookup field to form the one-to-many relationship between the tblBilling and tblInvoiceItem tables, so you don't need the relationship that previously existed between the two tables.

4. Click the **OK** button and then close the tblBilling table, clicking the **No** button when asked if you want to save the table design changes.

5. Click the **DATABASE TOOLS** tab on the ribbon, and then in the Relationships group, click the **Relationships** button to open the Relationships window.

6. Right-click the join line between the tblBilling and tblInvoiceItem tables, click **Delete**, and then click the **Yes** button to confirm the deletion.

Trouble? If the Delete command does not appear on the shortcut menu, click a blank area in the Relationships window to close the shortcut menu, and then repeat Step 6, ensuring you right-click on the relationship line.

▶ **7.** Close the Relationships window.

Now you can resume changing the InvoiceItemID field to a lookup field.

To finish changing the InvoiceItemID field to a lookup field:

▶ **1.** Open the **tblBilling** table in Design view, and then close the Navigation Pane.

▶ **2.** Click the right side of the **Data Type** box for the InvoiceItemID field, if necessary click the drop-down arrow, and then click **Lookup Wizard**. The first Lookup Wizard dialog box opens.

This dialog box lets you specify a list of allowed values for the InvoiceItemID field in a record in the tblBilling table. You can specify a table or query from which users select the value, or you can enter a new list of values. You want the InvoiceItemID values to come from the tblInvoiceItem table.

▶ **3.** Make sure the option for "I want the lookup field to get the values from another table or query" is selected, and then click the **Next** button to display the next Lookup Wizard dialog box.

▶ **4.** Click the **Tables** option button in the View section to display the list of tables, if it is not already displayed, click **Table: tblInvoiceItem**, and then click the **Next** button to display the next Lookup Wizard dialog box. See Figure 5-30.

Figure 5-30 **Selecting the lookup fields**

This dialog box lets you select the lookup fields from the tblInvoiceItem table. You need to select the InvoiceItemID field because it's the common field that links the tblInvoiceItem table and the tblBilling table. You also must select the InvoiceItem field because Cindi wants the user to be able to select from a list of invoice item names when entering a new contract record or changing an existing InvoiceItemID field value.

▶ **5.** Click the 〉〉 button to move the InvoiceItemID and InvoiceItem fields to the Selected Fields box, and then click the **Next** button to display the next Lookup Wizard dialog box. This dialog box lets you choose a sort order for the box entries. Cindi wants the entries to appear in ascending Invoice Item order. Note that ascending is the default sort order.

▶ **6.** Click the **arrow** for the first box, click **InvoiceItem**, and then click the **Next** button to open the next dialog box.

   In this dialog box, you can adjust the widths of the lookup columns. Note that when you resize a column to its best fit, Access resizes the column so that the widest column heading and the visible field values fit the column width. However, some field values that aren't visible in this dialog box might be wider than the column width, so you must scroll down the column to make sure you don't have to repeat the column resizing.

▶ **7.** Click the Hide key column check box to remove the checkmark and display the InvoiceItemID field.

▶ **8.** Click the InvoiceItemID column heading to select it. With the mouse pointer on the InvoiceItemID heading, drag it to the right of the InvoiceItem field to move the InvoiceItemID field to the right.

▶ **9.** Place the pointer on the right edge of the InvoiceItem field column heading, and then when the pointer changes to ╂╂, double-click to resize the column to its best fit.

▶ **10.** Scroll down the columns and repeat Step 9 as necessary until the InvoiceItem column accommodates all contents, and then press **Ctrl + Home** to scroll back to the top of the InvoiceItem column. See Figure 5-31.

Figure 5-31	Adjusting the width of the lookup column

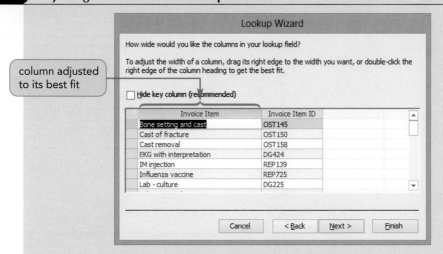

▶ **11.** Click the **Next** button.

   In the next dialog box, you select the field you want to store in the table. You'll store the InvoiceItemID field in the tblBilling table because it's the foreign key to the tblInvoiceItem table.

▶ **12.** Click **InvoiceItemID** in the Available Fields box if it's not already selected, and then click the **Next** button.

In the next dialog box, you specify the field name for the lookup field. Because you'll be storing the InvoiceItemID field in the table, you'll accept the default field name, InvoiceItemID.

▶ **13.** Click the **Finish** button, and then click Yes to save the table.

The Data Type value for the InvoiceItemID field is still Short Text because this field contains text data. However, when you update the field, Access uses the InvoiceItemID field value to look up and display in the tblBilling table datasheet both the InvoiceItem and InvoiceItemID field values from the tblInvoiceItem table.

In reviewing patient visits recently, Cindi noticed that the InvoiceItemID field value stored in the tblBilling table for visit number 1552 is incorrect. She asks you to test the new lookup field to select the correct field value. To do so, you need to switch to Datasheet view.

To change the InvoiceItemID field value:

▶ **1.** Switch to Datasheet view, and then resize the **Invoice Item** column to its best fit.

Notice that the Invoice Item column displays InvoiceItem field values, even though the InvoiceItemID field values are stored in the table.

▶ **2.** For Visit Num 1552, click **Office visit** in the Invoice Item column, and then click the **arrow** to display the list of InvoiceItem and InvoiceItemID field values from the tblInvoiceItems table. See Figure 5-32.

Figure 5-32	List of InvoiceItem and InvoiceItemID field values

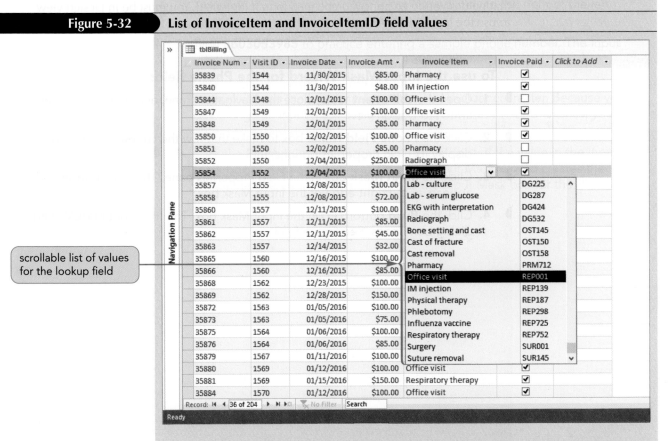

scrollable list of values for the lookup field

The invoice item for visit 1552 is Pharmacy, so you need to select this entry in the list to change the InvoiceItemID field value.

and slashes, so it's best to always type the backslashes. Since all of the existing data includes the area code, it will not make a difference whether the input mask applied to the data fills the data from left to right or from right to left, so you'll omit the ! symbol.

3. In the Input Mask box for the Phone field, change the input mask to **999\-000\-0000;;_** and then press the **Tab** key.

Because you've modified a field property, the Property Update Options button appears to the left of the Input Mask property.

4. Click the **Property Update Options** button. A menu opens below the button, as shown in Figure 5-36.

Figure 5-36   **Property Update Options button menu**

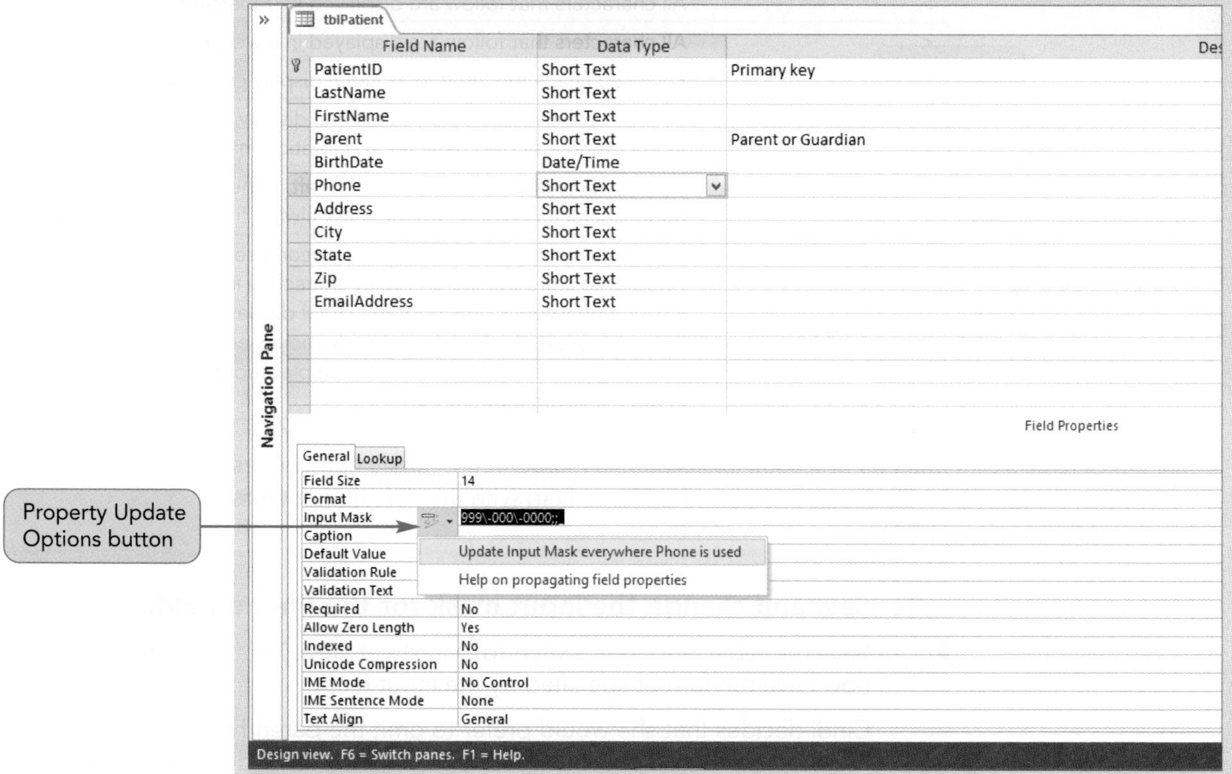

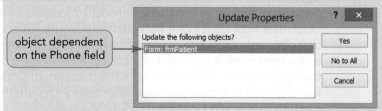

Property Update Options button

5. Click **Update Input Mask everywhere Phone is used**. The Update Properties dialog box opens. See Figure 5-37.

Figure 5-37   **Update Properties dialog box**

object dependent on the Phone field

Because the frmPatient form displays the Phone field values from the tblPatient table, Access will automatically change the Phone field's Input Mask property in this object to your new input mask. If other form objects

included the Phone field from the tblPatient table, they would be included in this dialog box as well. This capability to update field properties in objects automatically when you modify a table field property is called **property propagation**. Although the Update Properties dialog box displays no queries, property propagation also does occur with queries automatically. Property propagation is limited to field properties such as the Decimal Places, Description, Format, and Input Mask properties.

▶ **6.** Click the **Yes** button, save the table, switch to Datasheet view, and then resize the Phone column to its best fit. The Phone field values now have the format Cindi requested. See Figure 5-38.

| Figure 5-38 | After changing the Phone field input mask |

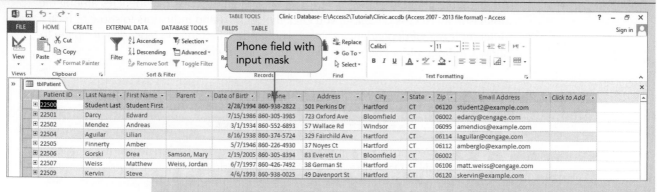

Because Cindi wants her staff to store only standard 10-digit U.S. phone numbers for patients, the input mask you've created will enforce the standard entry and display format that Cindi desires.

Understanding When to Use Input Masks

INSIGHT

An input mask is appropriate for a field only if all field values have a consistent format. For example, you can use an input mask with hyphens as literal display characters to store U.S. phone numbers in a consistent format of 987-654-3210. However, a multinational company would not be able to use an input mask to store phone numbers from all countries because international phone numbers do not have a consistent format. In the same way, U.S. zip codes have a consistent format, and you could use an input mask of 00000#9999 to enter and display U.S. zip codes such as 98765 and 98765-4321, but you could not use an input mask if you need to store and display foreign postal codes in the same field. If you need to store and display phone numbers, zip/postal codes, and other fields in a variety of formats, it's best to define them as Short Text fields without an input mask so users can enter the correct literal display characters.

After the change to the Phone field's input mask, Access gave you the option to update, selectively and automatically, the Phone field's Input Mask property in other objects in the database. Cindi is thinking about making significant changes to the way data is stored in the tblPatient table, and wants to understand which other elements those changes might impact. To determine the dependencies among objects in an Access database, you'll open the Object Dependencies pane.

Identifying Object Dependencies

An **object dependency** exists between two objects when a change to the properties of data in one object affects the properties of data in the other object. Dependencies between Access objects, such as tables, queries, and forms, can occur in various ways. For example, the tblVisit and tblBilling tables are dependent on each other because they have a one-to-many relationship. In the same way, the tblVisit table uses the qryPatientsByName query to obtain the Patient field to display along with the PatientID field, and this creates a dependency between these two objects. Any query, form, or other object that uses fields from a given table is dependent on that table. Any form or report that uses fields from a query is directly dependent on the query and is indirectly dependent on the tables that provide the data to the query. Large databases contain hundreds of objects, so it is useful to have a way to easily view the dependencies among objects before you attempt to delete or modify an object. The **Object Dependencies pane** displays a collapsible list of the dependencies among the objects in an Access database; you click the list's expand indicators to show or hide different levels of dependencies. Next, you'll open the Object Dependencies pane to show Cindi the object dependencies in the Clinic database.

To open and use the Object Dependencies pane:

1. Click the **DATABASE TOOLS** tab on the ribbon.

2. In the Relationships group, click the **Object Dependencies** button to open the Object Dependencies pane, and then drag the left edge of the pane to the left until the horizontal scroll bar at the bottom of the pane disappears. See Figure 5-39.

Figure 5-39   After opening the Object Dependencies pane

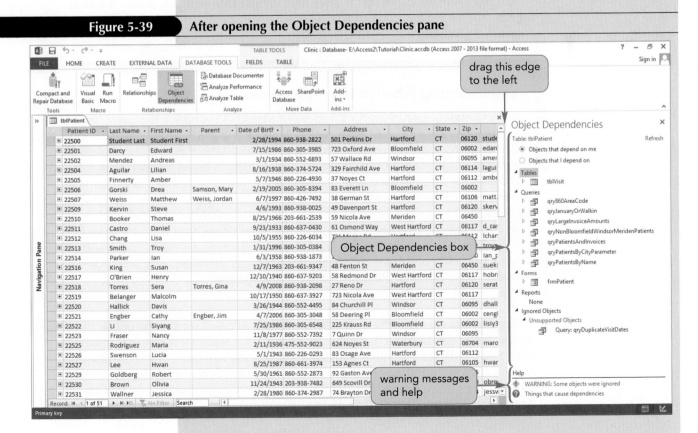

Trouble? If the "Objects that depend on me" option button is not selected, click the option button to select it.

The Object Dependencies pane displays the objects that depend on the tblPatient table, the object name that appears at the top of the pane. If you change the design of the tblPatient table, the change might affect objects in the pane. Changing a property for a field in the tblPatient table that's also used by a listed object affects that listed object. If a listed object does not use the field you are changing, that listed object is not affected.

Objects listed in the Ignored Objects section of the box might have an object dependency with the tblPatient table, and you'd have to review them individually to determine if a dependency exists. The Help section at the bottom of the pane displays links for further information about object dependencies.

▶ 3. Click the **frmPatient** link in the Object Dependencies pane. The frmPatient form opens in Design view. All the fields in the form are fields from the tblPatient table, which is why the form has an object dependency with the table.

▶ 4. Switch to Form view for the frmPatient form. Note that the Phone field value is displayed using the input mask you applied to the field in the tblPatient table. Access propagated this change from the table to the form.

▶ 5. Close the frmPatient form, open the Navigation Pane, open the **tblVisit** table in Datasheet view, and then click the **Refresh** link near the top of the Object Dependencies pane. The Object Dependencies box now displays the objects that depend on the tblVisit table.

▶ 6. Click the **Objects that I depend on** option button near the top of the pane to view the objects that affect the tblVisit table.

▶ 7. Click the **Objects that depend on me** option button and then click the **expand indicator** ▷ for the qryVisitsAndInvoices query in the Object Dependencies pane. The list expands to display the rptVisitsAndInvoices report, which is a report that the query depends upon.

▶ 8. Close the tblVisit table, close the Object Dependencies pane, and then save and close the tblPatient table.

Cindi now better understands object dependencies and how to identify them by using the Object Dependencies pane. She's decided to leave the tblPatient table the way it is for the moment to avoid making changes to forms and/or queries.

Defining Data Validation Rules

Cindi wants to minimize the amount of incorrect data in the database caused by typing errors. To do so, she wants to limit the entry of InvoiceAmt field values in the tblBilling table to values greater than $10 because Chatham Community Health Services does not invoice patients for balances of $10 or less. In addition, she wants to make sure that the Insurance field value entered in each tblBilling table record is either the same or less than the InvoiceAmt field value. The InvoiceAmt value represents the total price for the visit or procedure, and the Insurance value is the amount covered by the patient's insurance. The Insurance value may be equal to or less than the InvoiceAmt value, but it will never be more, so comparing these numbers is an additional test to ensure the data entered in a record makes sense. To provide these checks on entered data, you'll set field validation properties for the InvoiceAmt field in the tblBilling table and set table validation properties in the tblBilling table.

Defining Field Validation Rules

To prevent a user from entering an unacceptable value in the InvoiceAmt field, you can create a **field validation rule** that verifies a field value by comparing it to a constant or to a set of constants. You create a field validation rule by setting the Validation Rule and the Validation Text field properties. The **Validation Rule property** value specifies the valid values that users can enter in a field. The **Validation Text property** value will be displayed in a dialog box if a user enters an invalid value (in this case, an InvoiceAmt field value of $10 or less). After you set these two InvoiceAmt field properties in the tblBilling table, Access will prevent users from entering an invalid InvoiceAmt field value in the tblBilling table and in all current and future queries and future forms that include the InvoiceAmt field.

You'll now set the Validation Rule and Validation Text properties for the InvoiceAmt field in the tblBilling table.

To create and test a field validation rule for the InvoiceAmt field:

1. Open the **tblBilling** table in Design view, close the Navigation Pane, and then click the **InvoiceAmt Field Name** box to make that row the current row.

   To make sure that all values entered in the InvoiceAmt field are greater than 10, you'll use the > comparison operator in the Validation Rule box.

2. In the Field Properties pane, click the **Validation Rule** box, type **>10**, and then press the **Tab** key.

   You can set the Validation Text property to a value that appears in a dialog box that opens if a user enters a value not listed in the Validation Rule box.

3. In the Validation Text box, type **Invoice amounts must be greater than 10**. See Figure 5-40.

Figure 5-40	Validation properties for the InvoiceAmt field

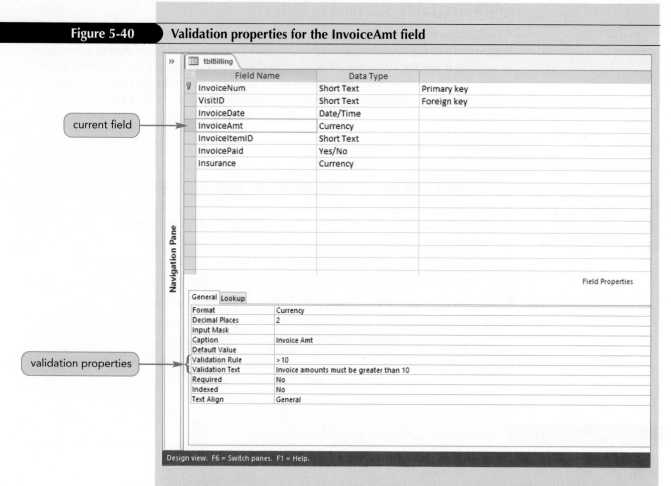

current field

validation properties

You can now save the table design changes and then test the validation properties.

4. Save the table, and then click the **Yes** button when asked if you want to test the existing InvoiceAmt field values in the tblBilling table against the new validation rule.

Access tests the existing records in the tblBilling table against the validation rule. If any existing record violated the rule, you would be prompted to continue testing or to revert to the previous Validation Rule property setting. Next, you'll test the validation rule.

5. Switch to Datasheet view, select **$100.00** in the first row's InvoiceAmt field box, type **5**, and then press the **Tab** key. A dialog box opens containing the message "Invoice amounts must be greater than 10," which is the Validation Text property setting you created in Step 3.

6. Click the **OK** button, and then press the **Esc** key. The first row's InvoiceAmt field reverts to its original value, $100.00.

7. Close the tblBilling table.

Now that you've finished entering the field validation rule for the InvoiceAmt field in the tblBilling table, you'll enter the table validation rule for the date fields in the tblVisit table.

Defining Table Validation Rules

To make sure that the Insurance field value that a user enters in the tblBilling table is not larger than the InvoiceAmt field value, you can create a **table validation rule**. Once again, you'll use the Validation Rule and Validation Text properties, but this time you'll set these properties for the table instead of for an individual field. You'll use a table validation rule because this validation involves multiple fields. A field validation rule is used when the validation involves a restriction for only the selected field, and does not depend on other fields.

To create and test a table validation rule in the tblBilling table:

Be sure "Table Properties" is listed as the selection type in the property sheet.

▶ 1. Open the tblBilling table in Design view and then on the DESIGN tab, in the Show/Hide group, click the **Property Sheet** button to open the property sheet for the table.

To make sure that each Insurance field value is less than or equal to the InvoiceAmt field value, you use the Validation Rule box for the table.

▶ 2. In the property sheet, click the **Validation Rule** box.

▶ 3. Type **Insur**, press the **Tab** key to select Insurance in the AutoComplete box, type **<= InvoiceAm**, and then press the **Tab** key.

▶ 4. In the Validation Text box, type **Insurance coverage cannot be larger than the invoice amount**, and then if necessary widen the Property Sheet so the Validation Rule text is visible. See Figure 5-41.

| Figure 5-41 | Setting table validation properties |

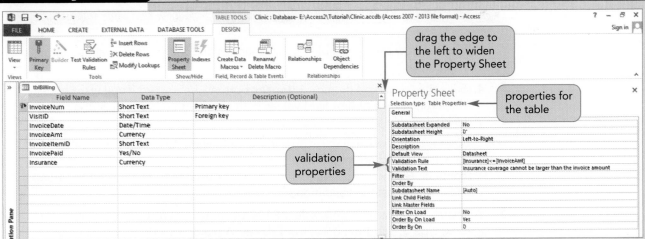

You can now test the validation properties.

▶ 5. Close the property sheet, save the table, and then click the **Yes** button when asked if you want to test the existing dates in the tblBilling table against the new validation rule.

▶ 6. Close the Navigation Pane, switch to Datasheet view, and then click the Insurance column value in the first record. Edit the Insurance value to change it to $150.00, and then press the **Tab** key to complete your changes to the record. A dialog box opens containing the message "**Insurance coverage cannot be larger than the invoice amount**," which is the Validation Text property setting you entered in Step 4.

Unlike field validation rule violations, which Access detects immediately after you finish a field entry and advance to another field, Access detects table validation rule violations only when you finish all changes to the current record and advance to another record.

▶ **7.** Click the **OK** button, and then press the **Esc** key to undo your change to the Insurance column value.

▶ **8.** Close the tblBilling table.

PROSKILLS

Problem Solving: Perfecting Data Quality

It's important that you design useful queries, forms, and reports and that you test them thoroughly. But the key to any database is the accuracy of the data stored in its tables. It's critical that the data be as error-free as possible. Most companies employ people who spend many hours tracking down and correcting errors and discrepancies in their data, and you can greatly assist and minimize their problem solving by using as many database features as possible to ensure the data is correct from the start. Among these features for fields are selecting the proper data type, setting default values whenever possible, restricting the permitted values by using field and table validation rules, enforcing referential integrity, and forcing users to select values from lists instead of typing the values. Likewise, having an arsenal of queries—such as find duplicates and top values queries—available to users will expedite the work they do to find and correct data errors.

Based on a request from Cindi, Raj added a Long Text field to the tblVisit table, and now you'll review Raj's work.

Working with Long Text Fields

You use a Long Text field to store long comments and explanations. Short Text fields are limited to 255 characters, but Long Text fields can hold up to 65,535 characters. In addition, Short Text fields limit you to plain text with no special formatting, but you can define Long Text fields to store plain text similar to Short Text fields or to store rich text, which you can selectively format with options such as bold, italic, and different fonts and colors.

You'll review the Long Text field, named Comments, that Raj added to the tblVisit table.

To review the Long Text field in the tblVisit table:

▶ **1.** Open the Navigation Pane, open the **tblVisit** table in Datasheet view, and then close the Navigation Pane.

▶ **2.** Increase the width of the **Comments** field so most of the comments fit in the column.

Although everything fits on the screen size and resolution shown in the figure, on some computer systems freezing panes is necessary to be able to view everything at once. On a smaller screen, if you scroll to the right to view the Comments field, you'll no longer be able to identify which patient applies to a row because the Patient ID column will be hidden. You'll also see this effect if you shrink the size of the Access window. You'll freeze the Visit ID, Patient ID, and Date of Visit columns so they remain visible in the datasheet as you scroll to the right.

3. Click the **Visit ID** column selector, press and hold down the **Shift** key, click the **Date of Visit** column selector, and then release the **Shift** key. The Visit ID, Patient ID, and Date of Visit columns should be selected.

4. On the HOME tab, in the Records group, click the **More** button, and then click **Freeze Fields**.

5. Scroll to the right until you see the Comments column. If all columns fit in the Access window, size the Access window smaller until the horizontal scroll bar is visible and not all columns are visible. Notice that the Visit ID, Patient ID, and Date of Visit columns, the three leftmost columns, remain visible. See Figure 5-42.

Figure 5-42 | **Freezing three datasheet columns**

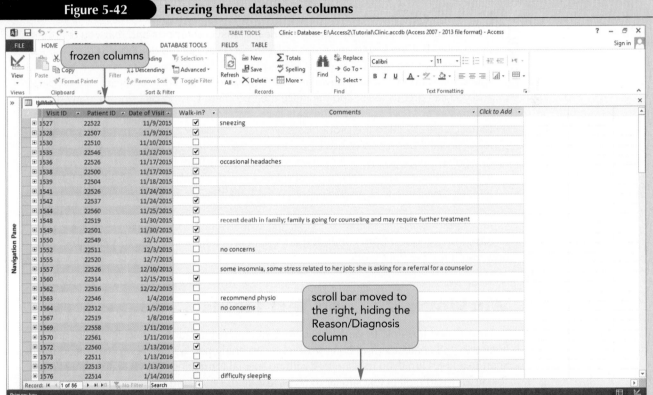

The Comments column is a Long Text field that Chatham Community Health Services clinicians use to store observations and other commentary about each patient. Note that the Comment for Visit ID 1548 displays rich text using a bold and blue font. Comments field values are partially hidden because the datasheet column is not wide enough. You'll view a record's Comments field value in the Zoom dialog box.

6. Click the **Comments** box for the record for Visit ID 1548, hold down the **Shift** key, press the **F2** key, and then release the **Shift** key. The Zoom dialog box displays the entire Comments field value.

7. Click the **OK** button to close the Zoom dialog box.

INSIGHT

Viewing Long Text Fields with Large Contents in Datasheet View

For a Long Text field that contains many characters, you can widen the field's column to view more of its contents by dragging the right edge of the field's column selector to the right or by using the Field Width command when you click the More button in the Records group on the HOME tab. However, increasing the column width reduces the number of other columns you can view at the same time. Further, for Long Text fields containing thousands of characters, you can't widen the column enough to be able to view the entire contents of the field at one time across the width of the screen. Therefore, increasing the column width of a Long Text field isn't necessarily the best strategy for viewing table contents.

Alternatively, you can increase the row height of a datasheet by dragging the bottom edge of a row selector down or by using the Row Height command when you click the More button in the Records group on the HOME tab. Increasing the row height causes the text in a Long Text field to wrap to the next line, so that you can view multiple lines at one time. Once again, however, for a Long Text field containing thousands of characters, you can't increase the row height enough to ensure that you can view the entire contents of the field at one time on screen. Additionally, you'd view fewer records at one time, and the row height setting for a table propagates to all queries that have an object dependency with the table. Thus, you generally shouldn't increase the row height of a table datasheet to accommodate a Long Text field.

What is the best way to view the contents of a Long Text field that contains a large number of characters? It is best to use the Zoom dialog box in a datasheet, or to use a large scrollable box on a form. It's really a matter of your own preference.

Now you'll review the property settings for the Comments field Raj added to the tblPatient table.

To review the property settings of the Long Text field:

1. Save the table, switch to Design view, click the **Comments Field Name** box to make that row the current row, and then, if necessary, scroll to the bottom of the list of properties in the Field Properties pane.

2. Click the **Text Format** box in the Field Properties pane, and then click its **arrow**. The list of available text formats appears in the box. See Figure 5-43.

Figure 5-43   **Viewing the properties for a Long Text field**

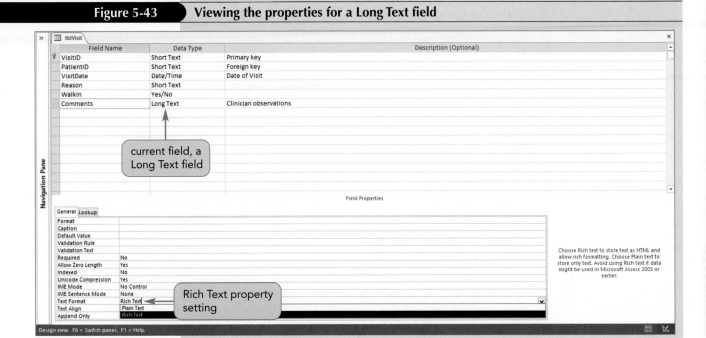

Raj set the **Text Format property** for the Comments field to Rich Text, which lets you format the field contents using the options in the Font group on the HOME tab. The default Text Format property setting for a Long Text field is Plain Text, which doesn't allow text formatting.

3. Click the **arrow** on the Text Format box to close the list, and then click the **Append Only** box.

The **Append Only property,** which appears at the bottom of the list of properties, enables you to track the changes that you make to a Long Text field. Setting this property to Yes causes Access to keep a historical record of all versions of the Long Text field value. You can view each version of the field value, along with a date and time stamp of when each version change occurred.

You've finished your review of the Long Text field, so you can close the table.

4. Close the tblVisit table.

When employees at Chatham Community Health Services open the Clinic database, a security warning might appear below the ribbon, and they must enable the content of the database before beginning their work. Cindi asks if you can eliminate this extra step when employees open the database.

Designating a Trusted Folder

A database is a file, and files can contain malicious instructions that can damage other files on your computer or files on other computers on your network. Unless you take special steps, Access treats every database as a potential threat to your computer. One special step that you can take is to designate a folder as a trusted folder. A **trusted folder** is a folder on a drive or network that you designate as trusted and where you place databases you know are safe. When you open a database located in a trusted folder, Access treats it as a safe file and no longer displays a security warning. You can also place files used with other Microsoft Office programs, such as Word documents and Excel workbooks, in a trusted folder to eliminate warnings when you open them.

Because the Clinic database is from a trusted source, you'll specify its location as a trusted folder to eliminate the security warning when a user opens the database.

To designate a trusted folder:

1. Click the **FILE** tab, and then click **Options** in the navigation bar. The Access Options dialog box opens.

2. In the left section of the dialog box, click **Trust Center**. The Trust Center options are displayed in the dialog box.

3. In the right section of the dialog box, click the **Trust Center Settings** button to open the Trust Center dialog box.

4. In the left section of the Trust Center dialog box, click **Trusted Locations**. The trusted locations for your installation of Access and other trust options are displayed on the right. See Figure 5-44.

Figure 5-44   Designating a trusted folder

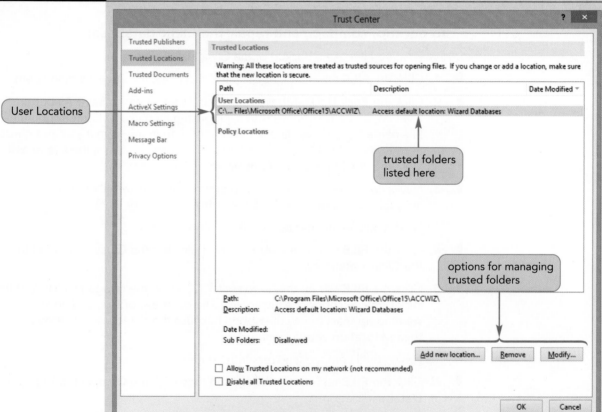

Existing trusted locations appear in the list at the top, and options to add, remove, and modify trusted locations appear at the bottom.

Trouble? Check with your instructor before adding a new trusted location. If your instructor tells you not to create a new trusted location, skip to Step 8.

5. Click the **Add new location** button to open the Microsoft Office Trusted Location dialog box.

6. In the Microsoft Office Trusted Location dialog box, click the **Browse** button, navigate to the Access2 ▸ Tutorial folder where your Data Files are stored, and then click the **OK** button.

You can also choose to designate subfolders of the selected location as trusted locations, but you won't select this option. By default, files in subfolders are not trusted.

▶ **7.** Click the **OK** button. Access adds the Access2 ▶ Tutorial folder to the list of trusted locations.

▶ **8.** Click the **OK** button to close the Trust Center dialog box, and then click the **OK** button to close the Access Options dialog box.

You've created several queries and completed several table design changes, so you should compact and repair the Clinic database. Raj doesn't use the Compact on Close option with the Clinic database because it's possible to lose the database if there's a computer malfunction when the Compact on Close operation runs. As a precaution, you'll make a backup copy of the database before you compact and repair it. Making frequent backup copies of your critical files safeguards your data from hardware and software malfunctions, which can occur at any time.

To backup, compact, and repair the Clinic database:

First, you'll make a backup of the Clinic database.

▶ **1.** Click the **FILE** tab on the ribbon, and then click the **Save As** menu item.

▶ **2.** Click the **Back Up Database** option, and then click the **Save As** button. The Save As dialog box opens with a suggested filename of Clinic_date in the File name box, where date is the current date in the format year-month-day. For instance, if you made a backup on February 15, 2016, the suggested filename would be Clinic_2016-02-15.

▶ **3.** Navigate to the location of a USB drive or other external medium, if available, and then click the **Save** button to save the backup file.

Next, you'll verify that the trusted location is working.

▶ **4.** Click the **FILE** tab on the ribbon, and then click the **Close** command to close the Clinic database.

▶ **5.** Click the **FILE** tab on the ribbon, click **Open** on the navigation bar, and then click **Clinic.accdb** in the Recent list. The database opens, and no security warning appears below the ribbon because the database is located in the trusted location you designated.

Next, you'll compact and repair the database.

▶ **6.** Click the **FILE** tab on the ribbon, and then click the **Compact & Repair Database** button.

▶ **7.** Close the Clinic database.

You've completed the table design changes to the Clinic database, which will make working with it easier and more accurate.

REVIEW

Session 5.3 Quick Check

1. What is a lookup field?
2. A(n) _____ is a predefined format you use to enter and display data in a field.
3. What is property propagation?
4. Define the Validation Rule property, and give an example of when you would use it.
5. Define the Validation Text property, and give an example of when you would use it.
6. Setting a Long Text field's Text Format property to _____ lets you format its contents.
7. A(n) _____ folder is a location where you can place databases that you know are safe.

ASSESS

SAM Projects

Put your skills into practice with SAM Projects! SAM Projects for this tutorial can be found online. If you have a SAM account, go to www.cengage.com/sam2013 to download the most recent Project Instructions and Start Files.

PRACTICE

Review Assignments

Data File needed for the Review Assignments: Supplier.accdb

Cindi asks you to create several new queries and enhance the table design for the Supplier database. This database contains information about the vendors that Chatham Community Health Services works with to obtain medical supplies and equipment for the clinic, as well as the vendors who service and maintain the equipment. Complete the following steps:

1. Open the **Supplier** database located in the Access2 ▸ Review folder provided with your Data Files.

2. Modify the first record in the **tblSupplier** table datasheet by changing the Contact First Name and Contact Last Name field values to your first and last names. Close the table.

3. Create a query to find all records in the tblSupplier table in which the City field value starts with the letter T. Display all fields in the query recordset, and sort in ascending order by CompanyName. Save the query as **qryTSelectedCities**, run the query, and then close it.

4. Make a copy of the qryTSelectedCities query using the new name **qryOtherSelectedCities**. Modify the new query to find all records in the tblSupplier table in which the City field values are not Dayton, Madison, or Edison. Save and run the query, and then close it.

5. Create a query to find all records from the tblSupplier table in which the State value is CT, NJ, or NY. Use a list-of-values match for the selection criteria. Display all fields in the query recordset, and sort in descending order by CompanyName. Save the query as **qrySelectedStates**, run the query, and then close it.

6. Create a query to display all records from the tblSupplier table, selecting the CompanyName, City, and ContactPhone fields, and sorting in ascending order by CompanyName. Add a calculated field named **ContactName** as the first column that concatenates the ContactFirstName, a space, and the ContactLastName. Set the Caption property for the ContactName field to **Contact Name**. Save the query as **qryCompanyContacts**, run the query, resize the Contact Name column to its best fit, and then save and close the query.

7. Create a parameter query to select the tblSupplier table records for a State field value that the user specifies. If the user doesn't enter a State field value, select all records from the table. Display the CompanyName, Category, City, State, ContactFirstName, ContactLastName, and ContactPhone fields in the query recordset, sorting in ascending order by City. Save the query as **qryStateParameter**. Run the query and enter no value as the State field value, and then run the query again and enter **CT** as the State field value. Close the query.

8. Create a find duplicates query based on the tblProduct table. Select ProductName as the field that might contain duplicates, and select the ProductID, SupplierID, Price, and Units fields as additional fields in the query recordset. Save the query as **qryDuplicateProductTypes**, run the query, and then close it. Because the tblProduct table does not have any duplicate ProductName values, running this query should show that no duplicate records are found.

9. Create a find unmatched query that finds all records in the tblSupplier table for which there is no matching record in the tblProduct table. Display the SupplierID, CompanyName, City, State, ContactPhone, ContactFirstName, and ContactLastName fields from the tblSupplier table in the query recordset. Save the query as **qrySuppliersWithoutMatchingProducts**, run the query, and then close it. Because the tblSupplier and tblProduct tables do not have unmatched records, running this query should show that no unmatched records are found.

10. Create a query to display all records from the tblProduct table, selecting the ProductID, SupplierID, ProductName, and Price fields, and sorting in descending order by Price. Use the Top Values property to select the top 25 percent of records. Save the query as **qryTop25Price** run the query, and then close it.

11. In the **tblProduct** table, change the SupplierID field to a lookup field. Select the CompanyName field and then the SupplierID field from the tblSupplier table. Sort in ascending order by the CompanyName field, do not hide the key column, make sure the Company Name column is the leftmost column, resize the lookup columns to their best fit, select SupplierID as the field to store in the table, and accept the default label for the lookup column. View the tblProduct table datasheet, resize the Supplier ID column to its best fit, test the lookup field without changing a value permanently, and then save and close the table.

12. Use the Input Mask Wizard to add an input mask to the ContactPhone field in the **tblSupplier** table. The ending input mask should use periods as separators, as in 987.654.3210 with only the last seven digits required; do not store the literal display characters, if you are asked to do so. Update the Input Mask property everywhere the ContactPhone field is used. Resize all columns in the datasheet to their best fit, and then test the input mask by typing over an existing Phone field value, being sure not to change the value by pressing the Esc key after you type the last digit in the Phone field.

13. Designate the Access2 ▶ Review folder as a trusted folder. (*Note:* Check with your instructor before adding a new trusted location.)

14. Make a backup copy of the database, compact and repair the database, and then close it.

Case Problem 1

APPLY

Data File needed for this Case Problem: Task.accdb

GoGopher! Amol Mehta, a recent college graduate living in Boulder, Colorado, spent months earning money by running errands and completing basic chores for family members and acquaintances, while looking for full-time employment. As his list of customers needing such services continued to grow, Amol decided to start his own business called GoGopher! The business, which Amol operates completely online from his home, offers customers a variety of services—from grocery shopping and household chores to yard work and pet care—on a subscription basis. Clients become members of GoGopher! by choosing the plan that best suits their needs. Each plan provides a certain number of tasks per month to members for a specified period of time. Amol created an Access database named Task to store data about members, plans, and contracts. He wants to create several new queries and make design changes to the tables. Complete the following steps:

1. Open the **Task** database located in the Access2 ▶ Case1 folder provided with your Data Files.

2. Modify the first record in the **tblMember** table datasheet by changing the First Name and Last Name column values to your first and last names. Close the table.

3. Create a query to find all records in the tblPlan table in which the PlanCost field is 600, 900, or 1500. Use a list-of-values match for the selection criterion, and include all fields from the table in the query recordset. Sort the query in descending order by the PlanID field. Save the query as **qryLowVolumePlans**, run the query, and then close it.

4. Make a copy of the qryLowVolumePlans query using the new name **qryHighVolumePlans**. Modify the new query to find all records in the tblPlan table in which the PlanCost field is not 600, 900, or 1500. Save and run the query, and then close it.

5. Create a query to display all records from the tblMember table, selecting the LastName, FirstName, Street, and Phone fields, and sorting in ascending order by LastName and then in ascending order by FirstName. Add a calculated field named **MemberName** as the first column that concatenates FirstName, a space, and LastName. Set the Caption property for the MemberName field to **Member Name**. Do not display the LastName and FirstName fields in the query recordset. Create a second calculated field named **CityLine**, inserting it between the

Street and Phone fields. The CityLine field concatenates City, a space, State, two spaces, and Zip. Set the Caption property for the CityLine field to **City Line**. Save the query as **qryMemberNames**, run the query, resize all columns to their best fit, and then save and close the query.

6. Create a query to display all matching records from the tblPlan and tblMember tables, selecting the LastName and FirstName fields from the tblMember table and the PlanDescription and PlanCost fields from the tblPlan table. Add a calculated field named **FeeStatus** as the last column that equals *Fee Waived* if the FeeWaived field is equal *to yes*, and that equals *Fee Not Waived* otherwise. Set the Caption property for the calculated field to **Fee Status**. Sort the list in ascending order on the LastName field. Save the query as **qryFeeStatus**, run the query, resize all columns to their best fit, and then save and close the query.

7. Create a query based on the tblPlan and tblMember tables, selecting the LastName, FirstName, and City fields from the tblMember table and the FeeWaived, PlanDescription, and PlanCost fields from the tblPlan table. The query should find the records in which the City field value is Boulder or Erie and the FeeWaived field value is *Yes*. Save the query as **qryBoulderAndErieFeeWaived**. Save and run the query, and then close the query.

8. Create a parameter query to select the tblMember table records for a City field value that the user specifies. If the user doesn't enter a City field value, select all records from the table. Display all fields from the tblMember table in the query recordset. Save the query as **qryMemberCityParameter**. Run the query and enter no value as the City field value, and then run the query again and enter **Boulder** as the City field value. Close the query.

9. Create a find duplicates query based on the tblMember table. Select Expiration as the field that might contain duplicates, and select all other fields in the table as additional fields in the query recordset. Save the query as **qryDuplicateMemberExpirationDates**, run the query, and then close it.

10. Create a find unmatched query that finds all records in the tblMember table for which there is no matching record in the tblPlan table. Select FirstName, LastName, and Phone fields from the tblMembers table. Save the query as **qryMembersWithoutPlans**, run the query, and then close it.

11. Create a new query based on the tblMember table. Display the FirstName, LastName, Phone, Expiration, and PlanID fields, in this order, in the query recordset. Sort in ascending order by the Expiration field, and then use the Top Values property to select the top 25 percent of records. Save the query as **qryUpcomingExpirations**, run the query, and then close it.

12. Use the Input Mask Wizard to add an input mask to the Phone field in the **tblMember** table. Create the input mask such that the phone number is displayed with a dot separating each part of the phone number. For instance, if the phone number is (303) 123-4567 it should be displayed as 303.123.4567 for new entries. Test the input mask by typing over an existing Phone column value, being certain not to change the value by pressing the Esc key after you type the last digit in the Phone column, and then save and close the table.

13. Define a field validation rule for the PlanCost field in the **tblPlan** table. Acceptable field values for the PlanCost field are values greater than 500. Enter the message **Value must be greater than 500** so it appears if a user enters an invalid PlanCost field value. Save your table changes, and then test the field validation rule for the PlanCost field; be certain the field values are the same as they were before your testing, and then close the table.

14. Define a table validation rule for the **tblMember** table to verify that DateJoined field values precede Expiration field values in time. Use an appropriate validation message. Save your table changes, and then test the table validation rule, making sure any tested field values are the same as they were before your testing.

15. Add a Long Text field named **MemberComments** as the last field in the tblMember table. Set the Caption property to **Member Comments** and the Text Format property to Rich Text. In the table datasheet, resize the new column to its best fit, and then add a comment in the Member Comments column in the first record about a job you would do for someone else, formatting the text with blue, italic font. Save your table changes, and then close the table.

16. Designate the Access2 ▶ Case1 folder as a trusted folder. (*Note:* Check with your instructor before adding a new trusted location.)

17. Make a backup copy of the database, compact and repair the database, and then close it.

Case Problem 2

Data File needed for this Case Problem: Tutoring.accdb

APPLY

O'Brien Educational Services   After teaching English in a public high school for 15 years, Karen O'Brien decided to channel her experience in education in a new direction and founded O'Brien Educational Services, a small educational consulting company located in South Bend, Indiana. The company offers tutoring services to high school students to help prepare them for standardized tests, such as the SAT and the ACT. The company provides group, private, and semiprivate tutoring sessions to best meet the needs of its students. To make the database easier to use, Karen wants you to create several queries and modify its table design. Complete the following steps:

1. Open the **Tutoring** database located in the Access2 ▸ Case2 folder provided with your Data Files.

2. Change the record in the **tblTutor** table datasheet that contains Student First and Student Last so the First Name and Last Name field values contain your first and last names. Close the table.

3. Create a query to find all records in the tblStudent table in which the LastName field value begins with M. Display the FirstName, LastName, City, and HomePhone fields in the query recordset, and sort in ascending order by LastName. Save the query as **qryLastNameM**, run the query, and then close it.

4. Create a query that finds all records in the tblTutor table in which the Degree field value is either BA or MA. Use a list-of-values criterion and include the fields First Name, Last Name, and Degree in the recordset, sorted in ascending order on the LastName field. Save the query using the name **qrySelectedDegrees**. Run the query, and then close it.

5. Create a query to find all records in the tblStudent table in which the City field value is not equal to South Bend. Display the FirstName, LastName, City, and HomePhone fields in the query recordset, and sort in ascending order by City. Save the query as **qryNonSouthBend**, run the query, and then close it.

6. Create a query to display all records from the tblTutor table, selecting all fields, and sorting in ascending order by LastName and then in ascending order by FirstName. Add a calculated field named **TutorName** as the second column that concatenates FirstName, a space, and LastName for each teacher. Set the Caption property for the TutorName field to **Tutor Name**. Do not display the FirstName and LastName fields in the query recordset. Save the query as **qryTutorNames**, run the query, resize the Tutor Name column to its best fit, and then save and close the query.

7. Create a parameter query to select the tblContract table records for a SessionType field value that the user specifies. If the user doesn't enter a SessionType field value, select all records from the table. Include all fields from the tblContract table in the query recordset. Save the query as **qrySessionTypeParameter**. Run the query and enter no value as the SessionType field value, and then run the query again and enter **Private** as the SessionType field value. Close the query.

8. Create a crosstab query based on the tblContract table. Use the SessionType field values for the row headings, the Length field values for the column headings, and the count of the ContractID field values as the summarized value, and include row sums. Save the query as **qrySessionTypeCrosstab**. Change the column heading for the row sum column to **Total Number of Sessions.** Resize the columns in the query recordset to their best fit, and then save and close the query.

9. Create a find duplicates query based on the tblContract table. Select StudentID and SessionType as the fields that might contain duplicates, and select all other fields in the table as additional fields in the query recordset. Save the query as **qryMultipleSessionsForStudents**, run the query, and then close it.

10. Create a find unmatched query that finds all records in the tblStudent table for which there is no matching record in the tblContract table. Display all fields from the tblStudent table in the query recordset. Save the query as **qryStudentsWithoutContracts**, run the query, and then close it.

11. In the **tblContract** table, change the TutorID field data type to Lookup Wizard. Select the FirstName, LastName, and TutorID fields from the tblTutor table, sort in ascending order by LastName, resize the lookup columns to their best fit, select TutorID as the field to store in the table, and accept the default label for the lookup column. View the tblContract table datasheet, resize the Tutor ID column to its best fit, and then save and close the table.

12. Use the Input Mask Wizard to add an input mask to the HomePhone field in the **tblStudent** table. The ending input mask should use periods as separators, as in 987.654.3210, with only the last seven digits required; do not store the literal display characters, if you are asked to do so. Resize the Home Phone column to its best fit, and then test the input mask by typing over an existing Phone field value, being sure not to change the value permanently by pressing the Esc key after you type the last digit in the Phone field.

13. Define a field validation rule for the Gender field in the tblStudent table. Acceptable field values for the Gender field are F or M. Use the message "Gender value must be F or M" to notify a user who enters an invalid Gender field value. Save your table changes, test the field validation rule for the Gender field, making sure any tested field values are the same as they were before your testing, and then close the table.

14. Designate the Access2 ▸ Case2 folder as a trusted folder. (*Note:* Check with your instructor before adding a new trusted location.)

15. Make a backup copy of the database, compact and repair the database, and then close it.

Case Problem 3

CHALLENGE

Data File needed for this Case Problem: Rosemary.accdb

Rosemary Animal Shelter Ryan Lang is the director of the Rosemary Animal Shelter in Cobb County, Georgia. The main goals of the shelter, which has several locations in the county, are to rescue dogs and cats and to find people who will adopt them. The shelter was established by Rosemary Hanson, who dedicated her life to rescuing pets and finding good homes for them. Residents of Cobb County generously donate money, food, and equipment in support of the shelter. Some of these patrons also adopt animals from the shelter. Ryan has created an Access database to manage information about the animals, patrons, and donations. Ryan now wants to create several queries and to make changes to the table design of the database. You'll help Ryan by completing the following steps:

1. Open the **Rosemary** database located in the Access2 ▸ Case3 folder provided with your Data Files.

2. Modify the first record in the **tblPatron** table datasheet by changing the Title, FirstName, and LastName column values to your title and name. Close the table.

3. Create a query to find all records in the tblAnimal table for dogs that have been adopted. Display the AnimalName, AnimalGender, AnimalType, AdoptionDate, and Adopted fields in the query recordset. Sort by ascending order by AnimalName. Save the query as **qryDogsAdopted**, run the query, and then close it.

4. Create a query to find all records in the tblDonation table in which the DonationDesc field value is not equal to Cash Donation. Display the Title, FirstName, and LastName, from the tblPatron table, and DonationDesc from the tblDonation table. Sort in ascending order by LastName. Save the query as **qryNonCashDonations**, run the query, and then close it.

5. Create a query called **qryNetDonationsAprilOrLater** that will contain all fields from the tblDonation and tblPatron tables except for PatronID and DonationID, for all donations that are on or after April 1, 2016. Sort this query by DonationValue in descending order. Save and run the query, and then close it.

6. Create a query to display all records from the tblPatron table, selecting the Title and Phone fields. Add a calculated field named **PatronName** that concatenates FirstName, a space, and LastName. Position this column as the second column, and sort the recordset in ascending order by LastName. Set the Caption property for the PatronName field to **Patron Name**. Save the query as **qryPatronNames**, run the query, resize the new column to its best fit, and then save and close the query.

7. Create a parameter query to select the tblAnimal table records for an AnimalType field value that the user specifies. If the user doesn't enter an AnimalType field value, select all records from the table. Display all fields from the tblAnimal table in the query recordset, and sort in ascending order by AnimalName. Save the query as **qryAnimalTypeParameter**. Run the query and enter no value as the AnimalType field value, and then run the query again and enter **Cat** as the AnimalType field value. Close the query.

8. Create a crosstab query based on the qryNetDonationsAprilOrLater query. Use the DonationDate field values for the row headings, the DonationTypeID field values for the column headings, and the sum of the DonationValue field values as the summarized value, and include row sums. Save the query as **qryNetDonationsAprilOrLaterCrosstab**. Change the format of the displayed values (DonationValue and Total Of DonationValue columns in Design view) to Fixed. Resize the columns in the query recordset to their best fit, and then save and close the query.

9. Create a find duplicates query based on the qryNetDonationsAprilOrLater query. Select FirstName and LastName as the fields that might contain duplicates, and select the DonationTypeID and DonationValue fields in the query as additional fields in the query recordset. Save the query as **qryMultipleDonorDonations**, run the query, and then close it.

10. Create a find unmatched query that finds all records in the tblPatron table for which there is no matching record in the tblDonation table. Include all fields from the tblPatron table, except for PatronID, in the query recordset. Save the query as **qryPatronsWithoutDonations**, run the query, and then close it.

11. Make a copy of the qryNetDonationsAprilOrLater query using the new name **qryTopNetDonations**. Modify the new query by using the Top Values property to select the top 40 percent of the records. Save and run the query, and then close the query.

12. Use the Input Mask Wizard to add an input mask to the Phone field in the **tblPatron** table. The ending input mask should use hyphens as separators, as in 987-654-3210, with only the last seven digits required; do not store the literal display characters, if you are asked to do so. Update the Input Mask property everywhere the Phone field is used. Test the input mask by typing over an existing Phone field value, being sure not to change the value permanently by pressing the Esc key after you type the last digit in the Phone field. Close the table.

13. Designate the Access2 ► Case3 folder as a trusted folder. (*Note:* Check with your instructor before adding a new trusted location.)

14. Make a backup copy of the database, compact and repair the database, and then close it.

Case Problem 4

CHALLENGE

Data File needed for this Case Problem: Ecotour.accdb

Stanley EcoTours   Janice and Bill Stanley live in Pocatello, Idaho, and are the proud owners and operators of Stanley EcoTours. Their passion is to encourage people to visit natural areas around the world in a responsible manner that does not harm the environment. Their advertising has drawn clients from Idaho, Wyoming, Montana, and Canada. As the interest in ecotourism grows, Janice and Bill's business is also expanding to include more tours in Africa and South America. Janice and Bill have created an Access database for their business and now want you to create several queries and modify the table design. To do so, you'll complete the following steps:

1. Open the **Ecotour** database located in the Access2 ► Case4 folder provided with your Data Files.

2. Modify the first record in the **tblGuest** table datasheet by changing the Guest First Name and Guest Last Name column values to your first and last names, and then close the table.

3. Create a query to find all records in the tblGuest table in which the GuestLast field value starts with the letter G, sorted in ascending order by GuestLast. Display all fields except the GuestID field in the query recordset. Save the query as **qryGuestLastNameG**, run the query, and then close it.

4. Create a query to find all records in the tblTour table where the country is not Brazil or Peru. Name this query **qryNonBrazilOrPeruTours**. Display all fields, sorting by Country and then by Location. Save and run the query, and then close it.

Session 6.1 Visual Overview:

A tabular layout arranges text box controls in a datasheet format with a label above each column.

A stacked layout arranges text box controls vertically with a label control to the left of each text box control.

This form was created using the **Split Form Tool**, which creates a customizable form that simultaneously displays the data in both Form view and Datasheet view.

These controls are anchored to the top left.

These controls have been removed from the stacked layout.

This form is displayed in Layout view.

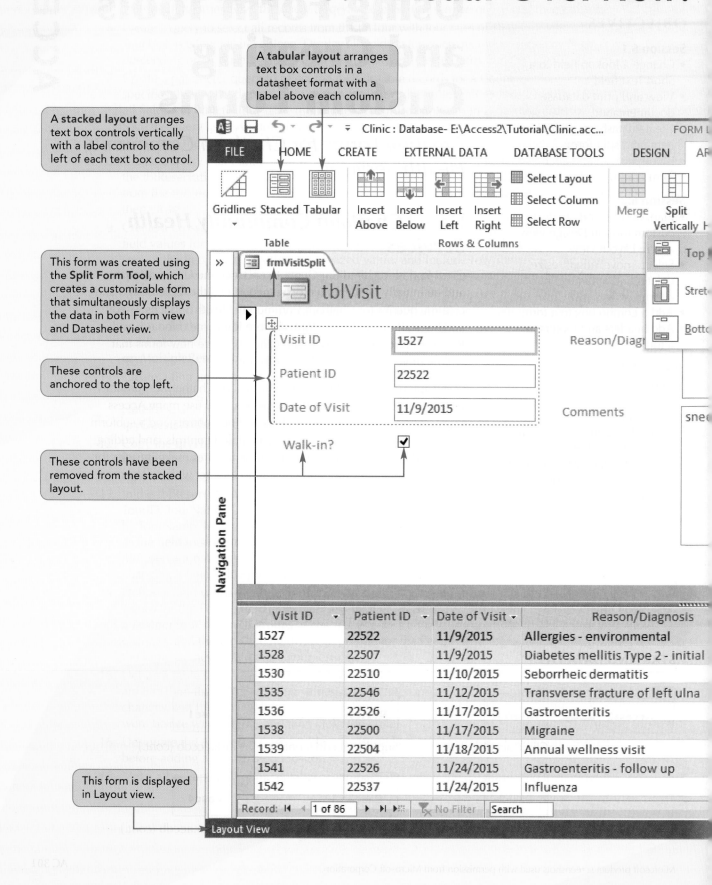

Clinic : Database- E:\Access2\Tutorial\Clinic.acc...   FORM L

FILE   HOME   CREATE   EXTERNAL DATA   DATABASE TOOLS   DESIGN   AR

Gridlines   Stacked   Tabular   Insert Above   Insert Below   Insert Left   Insert Right   Select Layout   Select Column   Select Row   Merge   Split Vertically H

Table   Rows & Columns

Top

Stret

Botto

frmVisitSplit

tblVisit

Visit ID	1527	Reason/Diagr
Patient ID	22522	
Date of Visit	11/9/2015	Comments snee

Walk-in?   ☑

Visit ID	Patient ID	Date of Visit	Reason/Diagnosis
1527	22522	11/9/2015	Allergies - environmental
1528	22507	11/9/2015	Diabetes mellitis Type 2 - initial
1530	22510	11/10/2015	Seborrheic dermatitis
1535	22546	11/12/2015	Transverse fracture of left ulna
1536	22526	11/17/2015	Gastroenteritis
1538	22500	11/17/2015	Migraine
1539	22504	11/18/2015	Annual wellness visit
1541	22526	11/24/2015	Gastroenteritis - follow up
1542	22537	11/24/2015	Influenza

Record: I◄ ◄ 1 of 86 ► ►I ►▮◄   No Filter   Search

Layout View

Anchoring Controls

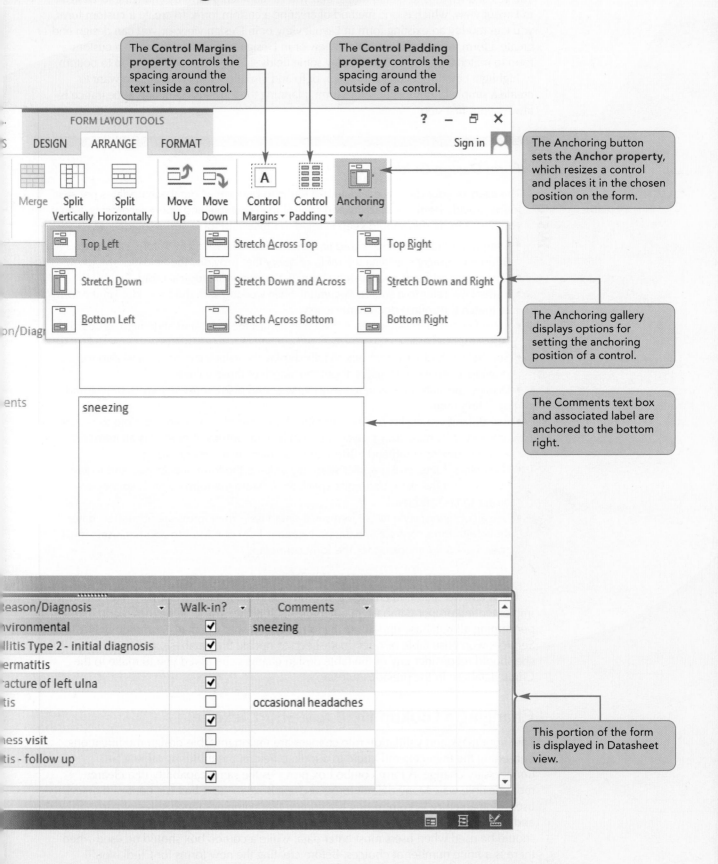

The **Control Margins** property controls the spacing around the text inside a control.

The **Control Padding** property controls the spacing around the outside of a control.

The Anchoring button sets the **Anchor property**, which resizes a control and places it in the chosen position on the form.

The Anchoring gallery displays options for setting the anchoring position of a control.

The Comments text box and associated label are anchored to the bottom right.

This portion of the form is displayed in Datasheet view.

Designing Forms

You've used wizards to create forms, and you've modified a form by changing its design in Layout view, which is one method of creating a custom form. To create a **custom form**, you can modify an existing form in Layout view or in Design view, or you can design and create a form from scratch in Layout view or in Design view. You can design a custom form to match a paper form, to display some fields side by side and others top to bottom, to highlight certain sections with color, or to add visual effects. Whether you want to create a simple or complex custom form, planning the form's content and appearance is always your first step.

INSIGHT

Form Design Guidelines

The users of your database should use forms to perform all database updates because forms provide better readability and control than do table and query recordsets. When you plan a form, you should keep in mind the following form design guidelines:

- Determine the fields and record source needed for each form. A form's **Record Source property** specifies the table or query that provides the fields for the form.
- Group related fields and position them in a meaningful, logical order.
- If users will refer to a source document while working with the form, design the form to match the source document closely.
- Identify each field value with a label that names the field, and align field values and labels for readability.
- Set the width of each text box to fully display the values it contains and also to provide a visual cue to users about the length of those values.
- Display calculated fields in a distinctive way, and prevent users from changing and updating them.
- Use default values, list boxes, and other form controls whenever possible to reduce user errors by minimizing keystrokes and limiting entries. A control is an item, such as a text box or command button, that you place in a form or report.
- Use colors, fonts, and graphics sparingly to keep the form uncluttered and to keep the focus on the data. Use white space to separate the form controls so they are easier to find and read.
- Use a consistent style for all forms in a database. When forms are formatted differently, with form controls in different locations from one form to another, users must spend extra time looking for the form controls.

Cindi and her staff had created a few forms and made table design changes before implementing proper database maintenance guidelines. These guidelines recommend performing all database updates using forms. As a result, Chatham Community Health Services won't use table or query datasheets to update the database, and Cindi asks if she should reconsider any of the table design changes she asked you to make to the Clinic database in the previous tutorial.

Changing a Lookup Field to a Short Text field

The input mask and validation rule changes are important table design modifications, but setting the InvoiceItemID field to a lookup field in the tblBilling table is an unnecessary change. A form combo box provides the same capability in a clearer, more flexible way. Many default forms use text boxes. A **text box** is a control that lets users type an entry. A **combo box** is a control that combines the features of a text box and a list box; it lets users either choose a value from a list or type an entry. A text box should be used when users must enter data, while a combo box should be used when there is a finite number of choices. Before creating the new forms for Cindi, you'll

change the data type of the InvoiceItemID field in the tblBilling table from a Lookup Wizard field to a Short Text field, so you can create the relationship with referential integrity between the tblBilling and tblInvoiceItems tables.

To change the data type of the InvoiceItemID field:

▶ **1.** Start Access, and then open the **Clinic** database you worked with in Tutorial 5.

Trouble? If the security warning is displayed below the Ribbon, either the Clinic database is not located in the Access2 ▶ Tutorial folder or you did not designate that folder as a trusted folder. Make sure you opened the database in the Access2 ▶ Tutorial folder, and make sure that it's designated as a trusted folder.

TIP

You can press the F11 key to open or close the Navigation Pane.

▶ **2.** Open the Navigation Pane, open the **tblBilling** table in Design view, and then close the Navigation Pane.

▶ **3.** Click the **InvoiceItemID** Field Name box, and then click the **Lookup** tab in the Field Properties pane. The Field Properties pane now displays the lookup properties for the InvoiceItemID field. See Figure 6-1.

Figure 6-1	Lookup properties for the InvoiceItemID field

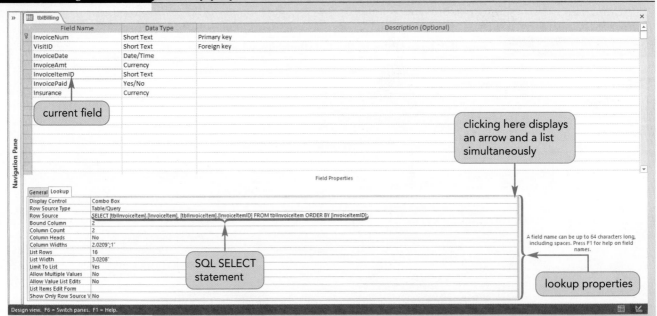

Notice the **Row Source property**, which specifies the data source for a control in a form or report or for a field in a table or query. The Row Source property is usually set to a table name, a query name, or an SQL statement. For the InvoiceItemID field, the Row Source property is set to an SQL SELECT statement. You'll learn more about SQL later in this text.

To remove the lookup feature for the InvoiceItemID field, you need to change the **Display Control property**, which specifies the default control used to display a field, from Combo Box to Text Box.

▶ **4.** Click the right side of the **Display Control** box, and then click **Text Box**. All the lookup properties in the Field Properties pane disappear, and the InvoiceItemID field changes back to a standard Short Text field without lookup properties.

▶ **5.** Click the **General** tab in the Field Properties pane and notice that the properties for a Short Text field still apply to the InvoiceItemID field.

▶ **6.** Save the table, switch to Datasheet view, resize the Invoice Item column to its best fit, and then click one of the Invoice Item boxes. An arrow does not appear in the Invoice Item box because the InvoiceItemID field is no longer a lookup field.

▶ **7.** Save the table, and then close the tblBilling table.

Before you could change the InvoiceItemID field in the tblBilling table to a lookup field in the previous tutorial, you had to delete the one-to-many relationship between the tblInvoiceItem and tblBilling tables. Now that you've changed the data type of the InvoiceItemID field back to a Short Text field, you'll view the table relationships to make sure that the tables in the Clinic database are related correctly.

To view the table relationships in the Relationships window:

▶ **1.** On the Ribbon, click the **DATABASE TOOLS** tab, and then in the Relationships group, click the **Relationships** button to open the Relationships window. See Figure 6-2.

| Figure 6-2 | Clinic database tables in the Relationships window |

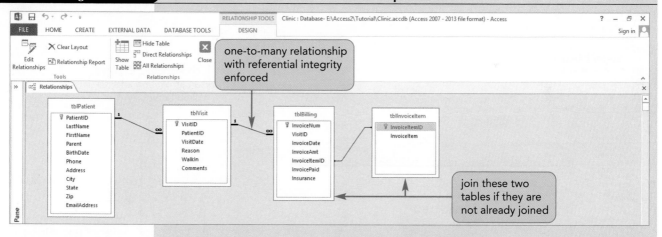

The tblVisit table and the related tblBilling table have a one-to-many relationship with referential integrity enforced. You need to establish a similar one-to-many relationship between the tblInvoiceItem and tblBilling tables.

▶ **2.** Double-click the **relationship line** between the tblInvoiceItem and tblBilling tables to open the Edit Relationships dialog box.

▶ **3.** Click the **Enforce Referential Integrity** check box, click the **Cascade Update Related Fields** check box, and then click the **OK** button to define the one-to-many relationship between the two tables and to close the dialog box. The join line connecting the tblInvoiceItem and tblBilling tables indicates the type of relationship (one-to-many) with referential integrity enforced.

Cindi asks you to print a copy of the database relationships to use as a reference, and she asks if other Access documentation is available.

Printing Database Relationships and Using the Documenter

You can print the Relationships window to document the fields, tables, and relationships in a database. You can also use the **Documenter**, another Access tool, to create detailed documentation of all, or selected, objects in a database. For each selected object, the Documenter lets you print documentation, such as the object's properties and relationships, and the names and properties of fields used by the object. You can use the documentation to help you understand an object and to help you plan changes to that object.

REFERENCE

Using the Documenter

- Start Access and open the database you want to document.
- In the Analyze group on the DATABASE TOOLS tab, click the Database Documenter button.
- Select the object(s) you want to document.
- If necessary, click the Options button to select specific documentation options for the selected object(s), and then click the OK button.
- Click the OK button, print the documentation, and then close the Object Definition window.

Next, you'll print the Relationships window and use the Documenter to create documentation for the tblVisit table.

PROSKILLS

Written Communication: Satisfying User Documentation Requirements

The Documenter produces object documentation that is useful to the technical designers, analysts, and programmers who develop and maintain Access databases and who need to understand the minutiae of a database's design. However, users who interact with databases generally have little interest in the documentation produced by the Documenter. Users need to know how to enter and maintain data using forms and how to obtain information using forms and reports, so they require special documentation that matches these needs; this documentation isn't produced by the Documenter, though. Many companies assign one or more users the task of creating the documentation needed by users based on the idea that users themselves are the most familiar with their company's procedures and understand most clearly the specific documentation that they and other users require. Databases with dozens of tables and with hundreds of other objects are complicated structures, so be sure you provide documentation that satisfies the needs of users separate from the documentation for database developers.

Cindi will show her staff the tblVisit table documentation as a sample of the information that the Documenter provides.

To view the Relationships report and use the Documenter:

▶ **1.** On the DESIGN tab, in the Tools group, click the **Relationship Report** button to open the Relationships for Clinic report in Print Preview. See Figure 6-3.

Figure 6-3 Relationships for Clinic report

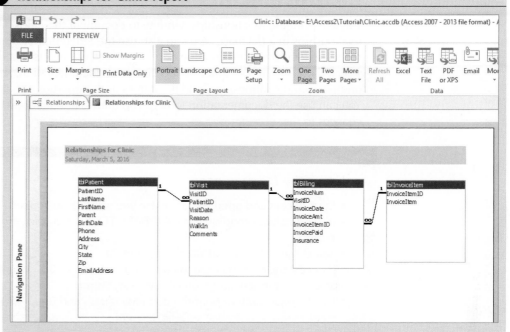

2. Right-click the **Relationships for Clinic** tab and click **Close** to close the tab. A dialog box opens and asks if you want to save the report.

3. Click the **Yes** button to save the report, click the OK button to save using the default name Relationships for Clinic, and then close the Relationships window.

Now you'll use the Documenter to create detailed documentation for the tblVisit table as a sample to show Cindi.

4. On the Ribbon, click the **DATABASE TOOLS** tab. In the Analyze group, click the **Database Documenter** button, and then click the **Tables** tab (if necessary) in the Documenter dialog box. See Figure 6-4.

Figure 6-4 Documenter dialog box

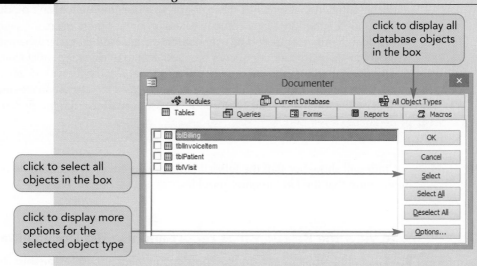

5. Click the **tblVisit** check box, and then click the **Options** button. The Print Table Definition dialog box opens on top of the Documenter dialog box.

You select which documentation you want the Documenter to include for the selected table, its fields, and its indexes. Cindi asks you to include all table documentation and the second options for fields and for indexes.

6. Make sure all check boxes are checked in the Include for Table section, click the **Names, Data Types, and Sizes** option button in the Include for Fields section (if necessary), then click the **Names and Fields** option button in the Include for Indexes section (if necessary). See Figure 6-5.

Figure 6-5   **Print Table Definition dialog box**

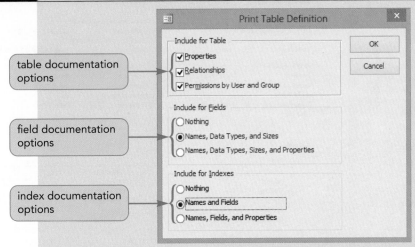

table documentation options

field documentation options

index documentation options

7. Click the **OK** button, and then click the **OK** button. The Documenter dialog box closes and the Object Definition report opens in Print Preview.

8. On the PRINT PREVIEW tab, in the Zoom group, click the **Zoom button arrow**, and then click **Zoom 100%**.

When you need to view more of the horizontal contents of an open object, you can close the Navigation Pane. You can also collapse the Ribbon when you want to view more of the vertical contents of an open object. To collapse the Ribbon, double-click any tab on the Ribbon, or right-click a tab and then click Collapse the Ribbon on the shortcut menu. To restore the Ribbon, double-click any tab on the Ribbon, or right-click a tab and then click Collapse the Ribbon (it's a toggle option) on the shortcut menu.

TIP

If you click, instead of double-click, any tab on the collapsed Ribbon, the full Ribbon appears until you click anywhere outside the Ribbon.

9. Double-click the **PRINT PREVIEW** tab on the Ribbon to minimize the Ribbon, and then scroll down the report and examine its contents. See Figure 6-6.

Figure 6-6	Object Definition report for the tblVisit table

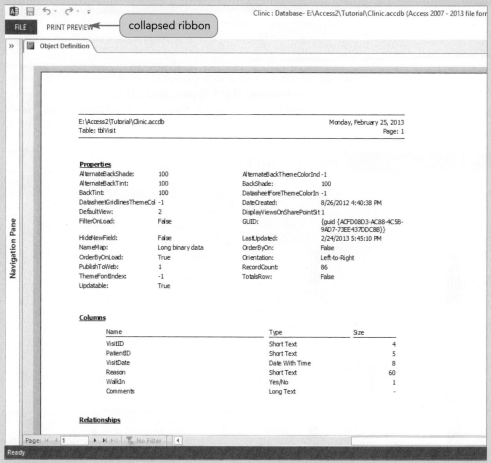

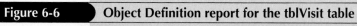

The Object Definition report displays table, field, and relationship documentation for the tblVisit table. Next, you'll save the report as a PDF document.

▶ **10.** Click the **PRINT PREVIEW** tab, in the Data group, click the **PDF or XPS** button, change the filename to **ClinicDocumenter.pdf**, click the **Publish** button to save the file, and then click the **Close** button to close without saving the steps.

Trouble? If the PDF you created opens automatically during Step 10, close the PDF viewer and then complete the step.

▶ **11.** Print the documentation if your instructor asks you to do so, and then close the Object Definition report. Notice that the Navigation Pane is closed and the Ribbon is minimized.

Cindi and her staff will review the Relationships report and the documentation about the tblVisit table and decide if they need to view additional documentation.

Next Cindi would like you to create a form that allows her and her staff to see and modify the relevant data for patient visits. You'll create a selection of form designs for Cindi to choose from. You'll create two simple forms that show the contents of the tblVisit in a layout that looks like a table, and you'll create a custom form that Cindi's staff may find a bit more user-friendly. First, you'll create the simple forms for Cindi and her staff.

Creating Forms Using Form Tools

The Clinic database currently contains the frmPatient form. The frmPatient form was created using the Form Wizard with some design changes that were made in Layout view including changing the theme, changing the form title color and line type, adding a picture, and moving a field.

PROSKILLS

Decision Making: Creating Multiple Forms and Reports

When developing a larger database application for a client, it's not uncommon for the client not to know exactly what they want with respect to forms and reports. You may obtain some sample data and sample reports during the requirements gathering phase that give you some ideas, but in the end, the client must approve the final versions.

While you are actively developing the application, you may design different versions of forms and reports that you think will meet the client's needs; later in the process, you might narrow the selection to a few forms and reports. Ultimately, you bring the selections to the client, who makes the final choices of which forms and reports to incorporate into the database. By basing your forms and reports on both a planning phase, performed in conjunction with the client, and a final selection made by the client, the project is much more likely to meet the client's needs.

You can create a simple form using the Datasheet Tool. This form can display all of the fields from a table or query, using a datasheet layout. The datasheet layout for a table provides the same view as the datasheet view for a table. Cindi may prefer this if she and her staff are very comfortable entering data in an Access table using the datasheet.

Creating a Form Using the Datasheet Tool

The **Datasheet tool** creates a form in a datasheet format that contains all the fields in the source table or query. You'll use the Datasheet tool to create a form based on the tblVisit table.

To create the form using the Datasheet tool:

▶ 1. Open the Navigation Pane, and then click **tblVisit** (if necessary).

   When you use the Datasheet tool, the record source (either a table or query) for the form must either be open or selected in the Navigation Pane.

▶ 2. Double-click the **CREATE** tab on the Ribbon to restore the Ribbon and to display the CREATE tab.

▶ 3. In the Forms group, click the **More Forms** button, click **Datasheet**, and then, if necessary, close the Property Sheet. The Datasheet tool creates a form showing every field in the tblVisit table in a datasheet format. It looks like the Datasheet view for the table but it does not have the expand buttons at the beginning of each row. See Figure 6-7.

Figure 6-7 Form created by the Datasheet tool

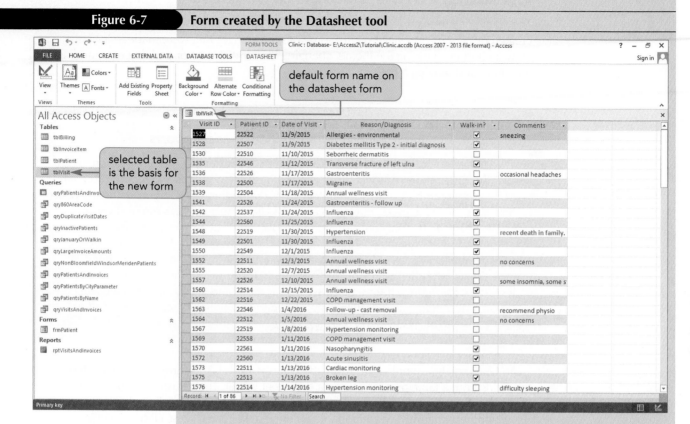

On the right side of the status bar, two view icons appear, one for Datasheet view (selected) and the other for Design view. The form name, tblVisit, is the same name as the table used as the basis for the form. Each table and query in a database must have a unique name. Although you could give a form or report the same name as a table or query, doing so would likely cause confusion. Fortunately, using object name prefixes prevents this confusing practice, and you would change the name when you save the form.

When working with forms, you view and update data in Form view, you view and make simple design changes in Layout view, and you make simple and complex design changes in Design view. Not all of these views are available for every form. For the form created with the Datasheet tool, you'll check the available view options.

4. In the Views group on the DATASHEET tab, click the **View button arrow**. See Figure 6-8.

Figure 6-8 View options for a form created by the Datasheet tool

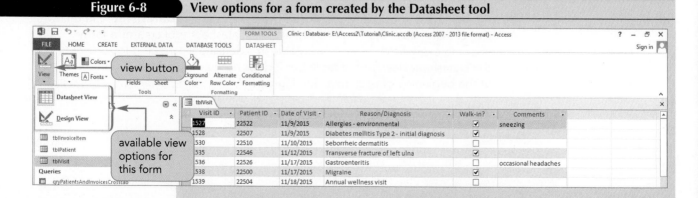

Form view and Layout view are not options in the list, which means that they are unavailable for this form type. Datasheet view allows you to view and update data, and Design view is the only other view option for this form.

You'll save this form to show Cindi as one of the options for the forms for patient visits.

▶ **5.** Save the form as **frmVisitDatasheet** and close the form.

Cindi might not like the datasheet view since the Comments field is not fully displayed. She might like the form created using the Multiple Items tool better since it will provide larger text boxes for the data. Next, you'll create a form for Cindi using the Multiple Items tool.

Creating a Form Using the Multiple Items Tool

The **Multiple Items tool** creates a customizable form that displays multiple records from a source table or query in a datasheet format. You'll use the Multiple Items tool to create a form based on the tblVisit table.

To create the form using the Multiple Items tool:

▶ **1.** Make sure that the tblVisit table is selected in the Navigation Pane, and then click the **CREATE** tab on the Ribbon.

▶ **2.** In the Forms group, click the **More Forms** button and then click **Multiple Items**. The Multiple Items tool creates a form showing every field in the tblVisit table and opens the form in Layout view. See Figure 6-9.

Figure 6-9	Form created by the Multiple Items tool

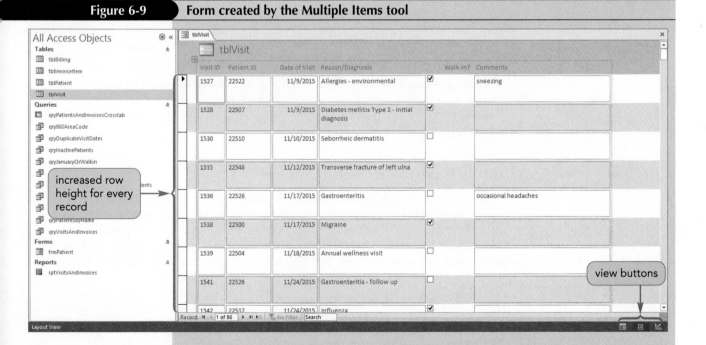

The new form displays all the records and fields from the tblVisit table in a format similar to a datasheet, but the row height for every record is increased compared to a standard datasheet. Unlike a form created by the Datasheet tool, which has only Datasheet view and Design view available, a Multiple Items form is a standard form that can be displayed in Form view, Layout view, and Design view, as indicated by the buttons on the right side of the status bar.

For the form created with the Multiple Items tool, you'll check the available view options.

TIP

You can click one of the view buttons on the right side of the status bar to switch to another view.

▶ **3.** On the DESIGN tab, in the Views group, click the **View button arrow**. Form view, Layout view, and Design view are the available views for this form. See Figure 6-10.

Figure 6-10 | **View options for a form created by the Multiple Items tool**

available view options for this form

You'll want to show this form to Cindi as one of the options, so you'll save it.

▶ **4.** Save the form as **frmVisitMultipleItems**, and then close the form.

The final form you'll create to show Cindi will include the standard form inputs and the datasheet view. She might like this to satisfy both the staff that are more technical and the staff that would like a more user-friendly form. The tool you'll use to create this is the Split Form tool.

Creating a Form Using the Split Form Tool

The Split Form tool creates a customizable form that displays the data in a form in both Form view and Datasheet view at the same time. The two views are synchronized with each other at all times. Selecting a record in one view selects the same record in the other view. You can add, change, or delete data from either view. Typically, you'd use Datasheet view to locate a record, and then use Form view to update the record. You'll use the Split Form tool to create a form based on the tblVisit table.

To create the form using the Split Form tool:

▶ **1.** Make sure that the tblVisit table is selected in the Navigation Pane, and then click the **CREATE** tab on the Ribbon.

> **2.** In the Forms group, click the **More Forms** button, click **Split Form** on the menu, and then close the Navigation Pane. The Split Form tool creates a split form that opens in Layout view and displays a form with the contents of the first record in the tblVisit table on the top and a datasheet of the first several records in the tblVisit table on the bottom. The position of the form in Layout view will be either a single column or two columns, depending on the height of the Access window when the form was created. If you have a two-column layout, that won't affect your ability to complete the steps that follow. Figure 6-11 shows the single column layout.

Figure 6-11	Form created by the Split Form tool

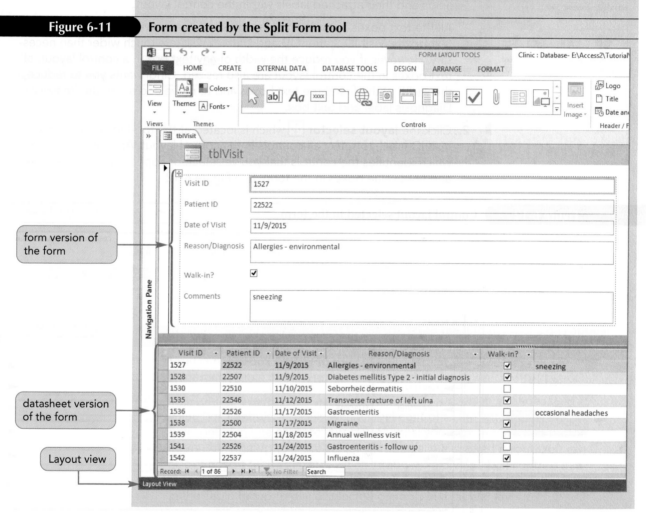

In Layout view, you can make layout and design changes to the form and layout changes to the datasheet. Cindi thinks the split form will be a useful addition to the Clinic database, and she wants you to show her the types of design modifications that are possible with a split form.

Modifying a Split Form in Layout View

You use the options on the DESIGN tab on the Ribbon to add controls and make other modifications to the form but not to the datasheet. In previous tutorials, you've modified forms using options on the FORMAT tab. Other powerful options are available on the ARRANGE tab. For a split form, options on the ARRANGE tab apply only to the form and do not apply to the datasheet.

Figure 6-19 Adding field value boxes and attached labels as bound controls to a form

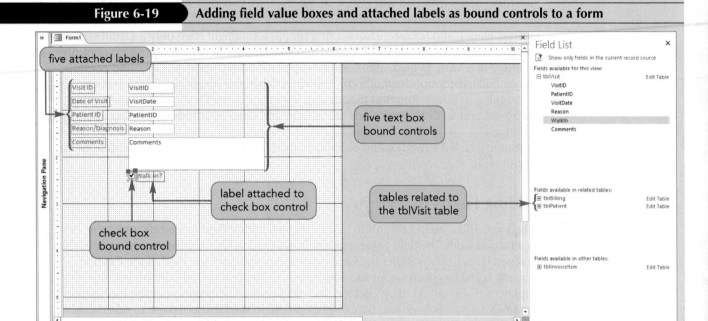

You should periodically save your work as you create a form, so you'll save the form now.

3. Click the **Save** button 💾 on the Quick Access Toolbar. The Save As dialog box opens.

4. With the default name Form1 (your name might be different) selected in the Form Name box, type **frmVisitsAndInvoices**, and then press the **Enter** key. The tab for the form now displays the form name, and the form design is saved in the Clinic database.

You've added the fields you need to the grid, so you can close the Field List pane.

5. Click the DESIGN tab and then, in the Tools group, click the **Add Existing Fields** button to close the Field List pane.

Suggestions for Building Forms

To help prevent common problems and more easily recover from errors while building forms, you should keep in mind the following suggestions:

- You can click the Undo button one or more times immediately after you make one or more errors or make form adjustments you don't wish to keep.
- You should back up your database frequently, especially before you create new objects or customize existing objects. If you run into difficulty, you can revert to your most recent backup copy of the database.
- You should save your form after you've completed a portion of your work successfully and before you need to perform steps you've never done before. If you're not satisfied with subsequent steps, close the form without saving the changes you made since your last save, and then open the form and perform the steps again.
- You can always close the form, make a copy of the form in the Navigation Pane, and practice with the copy.
- Adding controls, setting properties, and performing other tasks correctly in Access should work all the time with consistent results, but in rare instances, you might find a feature doesn't work properly. If a feature you've previously used successfully suddenly doesn't work, you should save your work, close the database, make a backup copy of the database, open the database, and then compact and repair the database. Performing a compact and repair resolves most of these types of problems.

To make your form's Detail section match Raj's design (Figure 6-17), you need to move the WalkIn bound control up and to the right. To do so, you must start by selecting the bound control.

Selecting, Moving, and Aligning Controls

Six field value boxes now appear in the form's Detail section, one below the other. Each field value box is a bound control connected to a field in the underlying table, with an attached label to its left. Each field value box and each label is a control in the form; in addition, each pairing of a field value box and its associated label is itself a control. When you select a control, the control becomes outlined in orange, and eight squares, called handles, appear on its four corners and at the midpoints of its four edges. The larger handle in a control's upper-left corner is its move handle, which you use to move the control. You use the other seven handles, called sizing handles, to resize the control. When you work in Design view, controls you place in the form do not become part of a control layout, so you can individually select, move, resize, and otherwise manipulate one control without also changing the other controls. However, at any time you can select a group of controls and place them in a control layout—either a stacked layout or a tabular layout.

REFERENCE

Selecting and Moving Controls

- Click a control to select it. To select several controls at once, press and hold down the Shift key while clicking each control. Handles appear around all selected controls.
- To move a single selected control, drag the control's move handle, which is the handle in the upper-left corner, to its new position.
- To move a group of selected controls, point to any selected control until the pointer changes to a move pointer, and then drag the group of selected controls to its new position.
- To move selected controls in a small increment, press the appropriate arrow key.
- To move selected controls to the next nearest grid dot, hold down the Ctrl key and press the appropriate arrow key.

Based on Raj's design for the custom form, shown in Figure 6-17, you must select the WalkIn bound control and move it up and to the right in the Detail section. The WalkIn bound control consists of a check box and an attached label, displaying the text "Walk-in?" to its right.

To select the WalkIn bound control:

1. If necessary, click the **Walk-in?** label box to select it. Move handles, which are the larger handles, appear on the upper-left corners of the selected label box and its associated bound control. Sizing handles also appear, but only on the label box. See Figure 6-20.

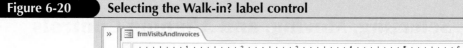

Figure 6-20   Selecting the Walk-in? label control

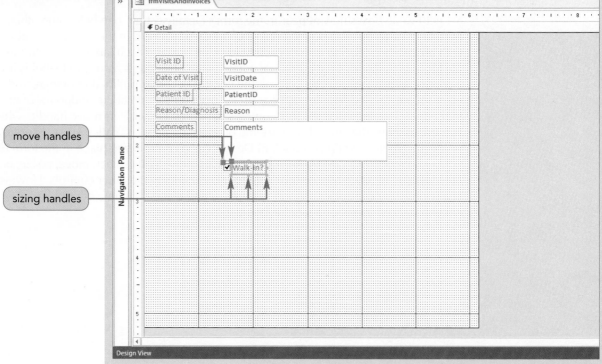

You can move a field value box and its attached label together. To move them, you place the pointer anywhere on the border of the field value box, but not on a move handle or a sizing handle. When the pointer changes to a ⬉ shape, you can drag the field value box and its attached label to the new location. As you move a control, an outline of the control moves on the rulers to indicate the current position of the control as you drag it. To move a group of selected controls, point to any selected control until the pointer changes to a ⬉ shape, and then drag the group of selected controls to its new position. You can move controls with more precision when you use the arrow keys instead of the mouse. To move selected controls in a small increment, press the appropriate arrow key on the keyboard. To move selected controls to the next nearest grid dot, hold down the Ctrl key and press the appropriate arrow key on the keyboard.

You can also move either a field value box or its label individually. If you want to move the field value box but not its label, for example, place the pointer on the field value box's move handle. When the pointer changes to a ⬉ shape, drag the field value box to the new location. You use the label's move handle in a similar way to move only the label.

You'll now arrange the controls to match Raj's design.

To move the WalkIn bound control:

> **1.** Position the pointer on one of the edges of the Walk-in? label, but not on a move handle or a sizing handle. When the pointer changes to a ⬉ shape, drag the control to the upper-right area and then release the mouse button. See Figure 6-21.

Be sure to position the pointer on one of the edges, but not on a move handle or sizing handle.

Figure 6-21 ▶ **After moving the Walk-in? label and associated bound control**

selected label and associated bound control moved here

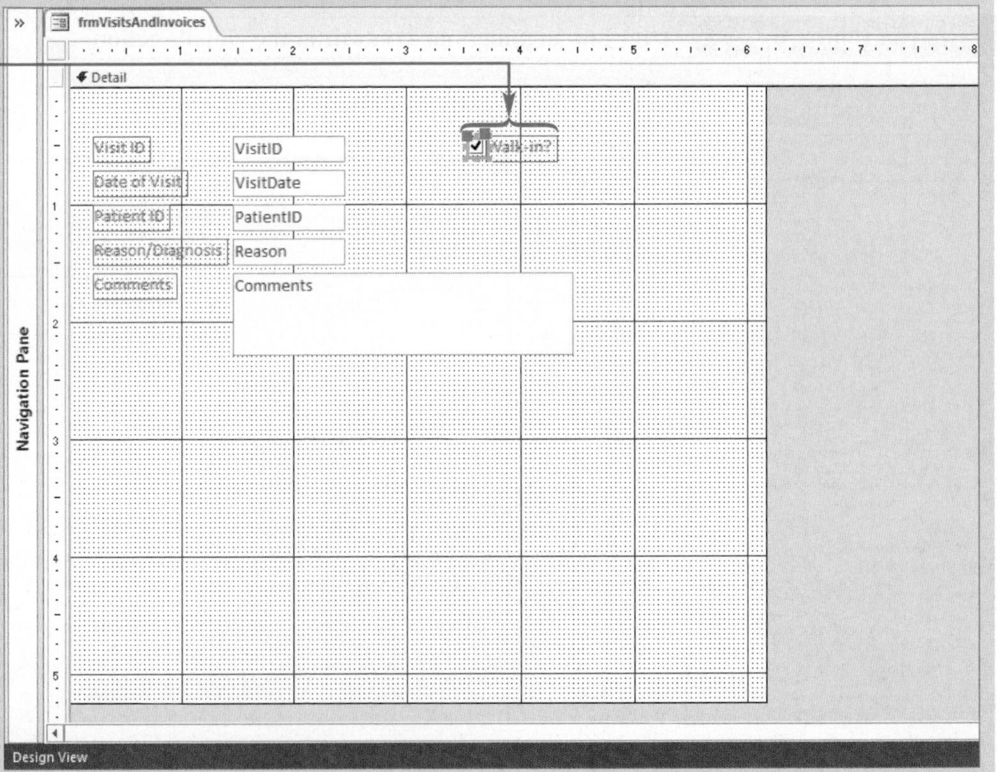

Trouble? If you need to make major adjustments to the placement of the WalkIn bound control, click the Undo button ↺ on the Quick Access Toolbar one or more times until the bound control is back to its starting position, and then repeat Step 1. If you need to make minor adjustments to the placement of the WalkIn bound control, use the arrow keys on the keyboard.

Now you need to align the WalkIn and VisitID bound controls on their top edges. When you select a column of controls, you can align the left edges or the right edges of the controls. When you select a row of controls, you can align the top edges or the bottom edges of the controls. A fifth alignment option, To Grid, aligns selected controls with the dots in the grid. You can find the five alignment options on the ARRANGE tab on the ribbon or on the shortcut menu for the selected controls.

You'll use the shortcut menu to align the two bound controls. Then you'll save the modified form and review your work in Form view.

To align the WalkIn and VisitID bound controls:

1. Make sure the Walk-in? label box is selected, hold down the **Shift** key, click the **WalkIn check box**, click the **VisitID** text box, click the **Visit ID** label, and then release the **Shift** key. This action selects the four controls; each selected control has an orange border.

2. Right-click one of the selected controls, point to **Align** on the shortcut menu, and then click **Top**. The four selected controls are aligned on their top edges. See Figure 6-22.

Figure 6-22 After top-aligning four controls in the Detail section

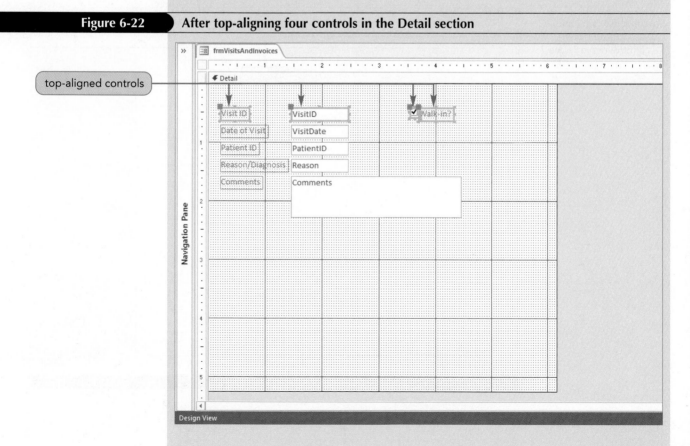

top-aligned controls

As you create a form, you should periodically save your modifications to the form and review your progress in Form view.

▶ **3.** Save your form design changes, and then switch to Form view. See Figure 6-23.

Figure 6-23   Form displayed in Form view

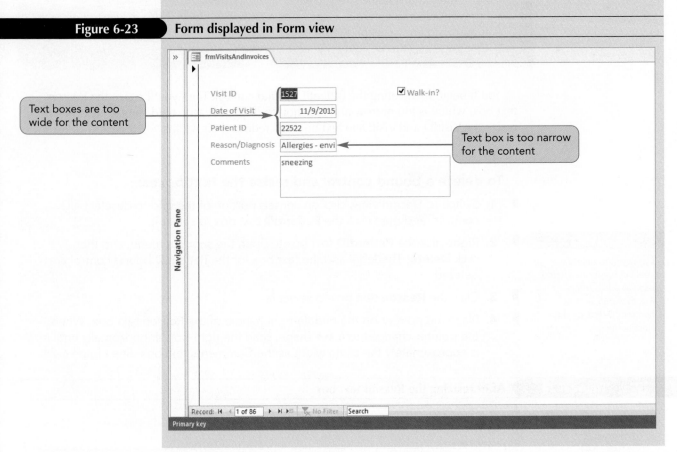

Text boxes are too wide for the content

Text box is too narrow for the content

The value in the Reason text box is not fully displayed, so you need to increase the width of the text box. The widths of the VisitID and VisitDate text boxes are wider than necessary, so you'll reduce their widths. Also, the PatientID bound control consists of a label and a text box, but the plan for the form shows a combo box for the PatientID positioned below the WalkIn bound control. You'll delete the PatientID bound control in preparation for adding it to the form as a combo box.

Resizing and Deleting Controls

A selected control displays seven sizing handles: four at the midpoints on each edge of the control and one at each corner except the upper-left corner. Recall that the upper-left corner displays the move handle. Positioning the pointer over a sizing handle changes the pointer to a two-headed arrow; the directions in which the arrows point indicate in which direction you can resize the selected control. When you drag a sizing handle, you resize the control. As you resize the control, a thin line appears inside the sizing handle to guide you in completing the task accurately, along with outlines that appear on the horizontal and vertical rulers.

Resizing a Control in Design View

- Click the control to select it and display the sizing handles.
- Place the pointer over the sizing handle you want to use, and then drag the edge of the control until it is the size you want.
- To resize selected controls in small increments, hold down the Shift key and press the appropriate arrow key on the keyboard. This technique applies the resizing to the right edge and the bottom edge of the control.

You'll begin by deleting the PatientID bound control. Then you'll resize the Reason text box, which is too narrow and too short to display Reason field values. Next you'll resize the VisitID and VisitDate text boxes to reduce their widths.

To delete a bound control and resize the text boxes:

1. Switch to Design view, click an unused portion of the grid to deselect all controls, and then click the **PatientID** text box to select it.

2. Right-click the **PatientID** text box to open the shortcut menu, and then click **Delete**. The label and the text box for the PatientID bound control are deleted.

3. Click the **Reason** text box to select it.

4. Place the pointer on the middle-right handle of the Reason text box. When the pointer changes to a ↔ shape, drag the right border horizontally until it is approximately the same width as the Comments text box. See Figure 6-24.

Figure 6-24 After resizing the Reason text box

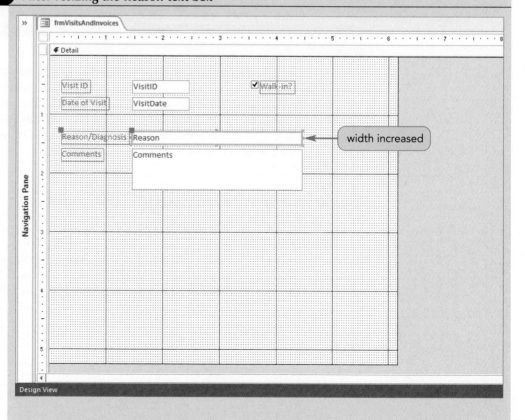

Resizing controls in Design view is a trial-and-error process, in which you resize a control in Design view, switch to Form view to observe the effect of the resizing, switch back to Design view to make further refinements to the control's size, and continue until the control is sized correctly. It's easier to resize controls in Layout view because you can see actual field values while you resize the controls. You'll resize the other two text boxes in Layout view. The sizes of the VisitID and VisitDate text boxes will look fine if you reduce them to have the same widths, so you'll select both text boxes and resize them as a group.

5. Switch to Layout view, and then click the **VisitID** text box (if necessary) to select it. Hold the **Shift** key down and click the **VisitDate** text box (next to the label "Date of Visit") to select it.

6. Position the pointer on the right edge of the **VistDate** text box. When the pointer changes to a ↔ shape, drag the right border horizontally to the left until the text box is slightly wider than the field value it contains, and the date in the VisitID field is also visible. See Figure 6-25.

Figure 6-25   After resizing field value boxes in Layout view

width of field value boxes decreased in Layout view

Trouble? If you resized the text boxes too far to the left, number signs will be displayed inside the VisitDate text box. Drag the right edge of the text boxes slightly to the right and repeat the process until the date value is visible inside the text box.

TIP

If you select a control by mistake, hold down the Shift key, and then click the selected control to deselect it.

7. Navigate through the first several records to make sure the three text boxes are sized properly and display the full field values. If any text box is too small, select the text box and increase its width the appropriate amount.

8. Save your form design changes, switch to Design view, and then deselect all controls by clicking in an unused portion of the grid.

Making Form Design Modifications

When you design forms and other objects, you'll find it helpful to switch frequently between Design view and Layout view. Some form modifications are easier to make in Layout view, other form modifications are easier to make in Design view, and still other form modifications can be made only in Design view. You should check your progress frequently in either Layout view or Form view, and you should save your modifications after completing a set of changes successfully.

Recall that you removed the lookup feature from the PatientID field because a combo box provides the same lookup capability in a form. Next, you'll add a combo box for the PatientID field to the custom form.

Adding a Combo Box to a Form

The tblPatient and tblVisit tables are related in a one-to-many relationship. The PatientID field in the tblVisit table is a foreign key to the tblPatient table, and you can use a combo box in the custom form to view and maintain PatientID field values more easily and accurately than using a text box. Recall that a combo box is a control that provides the features of a text box and a list box; you can choose a value from the list or type an entry.

Problem Solving: Using Combo Boxes for Foreign Keys

When you design forms, combo boxes are a natural choice for foreign keys because foreign key values must match one of the primary key values in the related primary table. If you do not use a combo box for a foreign key, you force users to type values in the text box. When they make typing mistakes, Access rejects the values and displays frustrating nonmatching error messages. Combo boxes allow users to select only from a list of valid foreign key values, so nonmatching situations are eliminated. At the same time, combo boxes allow users who are skilled at data entry to more rapidly type the values, instead of using the more time-consuming technique of choosing a value from the combo box list. Whenever you use an Access feature such as combo boxes for foreign keys, it takes extra time during development to add the feature, but you save users time and improve their accuracy for the many months or years they use the database.

You use the **Combo Box tool** in Design view to add a combo box to a form. If you want help when adding the combo box, you can select one of the Control Wizards. A **Control Wizard** asks a series of questions and then uses your answers to create a control in a form or report. Access offers Control Wizards for the Combo Box, List Box, Option Group, Command Button, Subform/Subreport, and other control tools.

You will use the Combo Box Wizard to add a combo box to the form for the PatientID field.

To add a combo box to the form:

▶ 1. Click the DESIGN tab, and then in the Controls group, click the **More** button to open the Controls gallery. See Figure 6-26.

Figure 6-26 Controls gallery

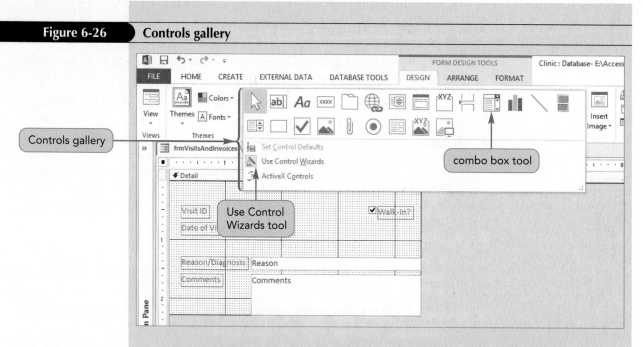

The Controls gallery contains tools that allow you to add controls (such as text boxes, lines, charts, and labels) to a form. You drag a control from the Controls gallery and place it in position in the grid.

2. In the gallery, make sure the Use Control Wizards tool ⬡ is selected (with an orange background) in the Controls gallery. If the tool is not selected, click the **Use Control Wizards** tool ⬡ to select it, and then click the **More** button to open the Controls gallery again.

3. In the Controls gallery, click the **Combo Box** tool ⬡. The Controls gallery closes. After you click the Combo Box tool or most other tools in the Controls gallery, nothing happens until you move the pointer over the form. When you move the pointer over the form, the pointer changes to a shape that is unique for the control with a plus symbol in its upper-left corner. You position the plus symbol in the location where you want to place the upper-left corner of the control.

You'll place the combo box near the top of the form, below the WalkIn bound control, and then position it more precisely after you've finished the wizard.

4. Position the + portion of the pointer below the WalkIn bound control and at the 4-inch mark on the horizontal ruler, and then click the mouse button. Access places a combo box control in the form and opens the first Combo Box Wizard dialog box.

You can use an existing table or query as the source for a new combo box or type the values for the combo box. In this case, you'll use the qryPatientsByName query as the basis for the new combo box. This query includes the Patient calculated field, whose value equals the concatenation of the LastName and FirstName field values.

5. Click the **I want the combo box to get the values from another table or query** option button (if necessary), click the **Next** button to open the next Combo Box Wizard dialog box, click the **Queries** option button in the View group, click **Query: qryPatientsByName**, and then click the **Next** button. Access opens the third Combo Box Wizard dialog box. This dialog box lets you select the fields from the query to appear as columns in the combo box. You'll select the first two fields.

▶ **6.** Double-click **Patient** to move this field to the Selected Fields box, double-click **PatientID**, and then click the **Next** button. This dialog box lets you choose a sort order for the combo box entries. Raj wants the entries to appear in ascending order on the Patient field.

▶ **7.** Click the **arrow** for the first box, click **Patient**, and then click the **Next** button to open the next Combo Box Wizard dialog box.

▶ **8.** Resize the columns a bit wider than the widest data because the form font is a bit larger than the wizard font, scrolling down the columns to make sure all values are visible and resizing again if they're not, and then click the **Next** button.

In this dialog box, you select the foreign key, which is the PatientID field.

▶ **9.** Click **PatientID** and then click the **Next** button.

In this dialog box, you specify the field in the tblVisit table where you will store the selected PatientID value from the combo box. You'll store the value in the PatientID field in the tblVisit table.

▶ **10.** Click the **Store that value in this field** option button, click its **arrow**, click **PatientID**, and then click the **Next** button.

Trouble? If PatientID doesn't appear in the list, click the Cancel button, press the Delete key to delete the combo box, click the Add Existing Fields button in the Tools group on the DESIGN tab, double-click PatientID in the Field List pane, press the Delete key to delete PatientID, close the Field List pane, and then repeat Steps 1–10.

In this dialog box, you specify the name for the combo box control. You'll use the field name of PatientID.

▶ **11.** Type **PatientID** and then click the **Finish** button. The completed PatientID combo box appears in the form.

You need to position and resize the combo box control, but first you'll change the text for the attached label from PatientID to Patient ID to match the format used for other label controls in the form. To change the text for a label control, you set the control's Caption property value.

REFERENCE

Changing a Label's Caption

• Right-click the label to select it and to display the shortcut menu, and then click Properties to display the Property Sheet.
• If necessary, click the All tab to display the All page in the Property Sheet.
• Edit the existing text in the Caption box; or click the Caption box, press the F2 key to select the current value, and then type a new caption.
• On the DESIGN tab, in the Tools group, click the Property Sheet button to close the Property Sheet.

Next, you'll change the text that displays in the combo box label.

To set the Caption property value for the PatientID label:

TIP

After selecting a control, you can press the F4 key to open and close the Property Sheet for the control.

1. Right-click the **PatientID** label, which is the control to the left of the PatientID text box, to select it and to display the shortcut menu, and then click **Properties** on the shortcut menu. The Property Sheet for the PatientID label opens.

2. If necessary, click the **All** tab to display all properties for the selected PatientID label.

   Trouble? If the Selection type entry below the Property Sheet title bar is not "Label," then you selected the wrong control in Step 1. Click the PatientID label to change to the Property Sheet for this control.

3. Click before the "ID" in the Caption box, press the **spacebar**, and then press the **Tab** key to move to the next property in the Property Sheet. The Caption property value should now be Patient ID and the label for the PatientID bound control should now display Patient ID. See Figure 6-27.

Figure 6-27   **PatientID combo box and updated label added to the form**

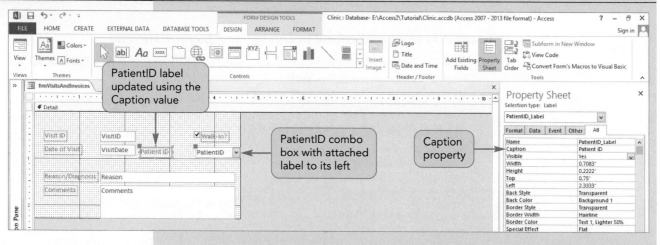

Trouble? Some property values in your Property Sheet, such as the Width and Top property values, might differ if your label's position slightly differs from the label position used as the basis for Figure 6-27. These differences cause no problems.

Trouble? You won't see the effects of the new property setting until you select another property, select another control, or close the Property Sheet.

The Selection type entry, which appears below the Property Sheet title bar, displays the control type (Label in this case) for the selected control. Below the Selection type entry in the Property Sheet is the Control box, which you can use to select another control in the form and then change its properties in the Property Sheet. Alternately, you can simply click a control in the form to change its properties in the Property Sheet. The first property in the Property Sheet, the **Name property**, specifies the name of a control, section, or object (PatientID_Label in this case). The Name property value is the same as the value displayed in the Control box, unless the Caption property has been set. For bound controls, the Name property value matches the field name. For unbound controls, Access adds an underscore and a suffix of the control type (for example, Label) to the Name property setting. For unbound controls, you can set the Name property to another, more meaningful value at any time.

▶ **4.** Close the Property Sheet, and then save your design changes.

Now that you've added the combo box to the form, you can position the combo box and its attached label and resize the combo box. You'll need to view the form in Form view to determine any fine tuning necessary for the width of the combo box.

To modify the combo box in Design and Layout views:

▶ **1.** Click the **PatientID** combo box, hold down the **Shift** key, click the **Patient ID** label, and then release the **Shift** key to select both controls.

First, you'll move the selected controls above the VisitID controls. Then you'll align the PatientID, VisitID, VisitDate, Reason, and Comments labels on their left edges, align the PatientID combo box with the VisitID, VisitDate, Reason, and Comments text box controls on their left edges, and then align the WalkIn label and check box with the right edges of the Reason and Comments text boxes.

▶ **2.** Drag the selected controls to a position above the VisitID controls. Do not try to align them.

▶ **3.** Click in an unused area of the grid to deselect the selected controls, press and hold the **Shift** key while you click the **Patient ID** label, the **Visit ID** label, **Date of Visit** label, **Reason/Diagnosis** label, and the **Comments** label, and then release the **Shift** key.

▶ **4.** Click the **ARRANGE** tab on the Ribbon, in the Sizing & Ordering group click the **Align** button, and then click **Left**. The selected controls are aligned on their left edges.

▶ **5.** Repeat Steps 3 and 4 to align the **PatientID** combo box, **VisitID** text box, **VisitDate** text box, **Reason** text box, and the **Comments** text box on their left edges.

▶ **6.** Select the **Walk-in?** label, **Walkin?** check box, **Reason** text box, and **Comments** text box, and in the Sizing & Ordering group on the ARRANGE tab, click the **Align** button, and then click **Right**. The selected controls are aligned on their right edges.

▶ **7.** Switch to Form view, and then click the **PatientID** arrow to open the control's list box. Note that the column is not wide enough to show the full data values. See Figure 6-28.

Figure 6-28   PatientID combo box in Form view

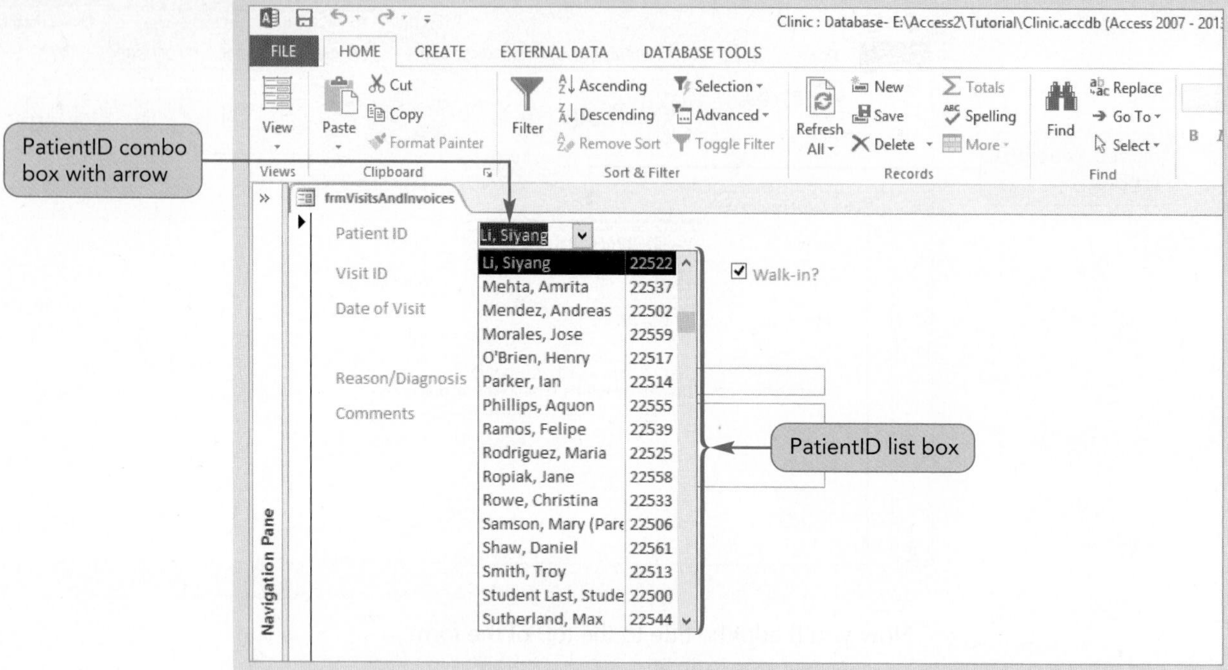

PatientID combo box with arrow

PatientID list box

You need to widen the PatientID combo box, so that the widest customer value in the list is displayed in the combo box. You can widen the combo box in Layout view or in Design view. Because Form view and Layout view display actual data from the table rather than placeholder text in each bound control, these views let you immediately see the effects of your layout changes. You'll use Layout view instead of Design view to make this change because you can determine the proper width more accurately in Layout view.

8. Switch to Layout view, and then navigate to record 2. Weiss, Jordan (Parent), which is the patient value for this record, is one of the widest values that is displayed in the combo box. You want to widen the combo box so that the value in record 2 is completely visible, with a little bit more room.

9. Make sure that only the combo box is selected, and then pointing to the right edge, widen the combo box until the entire patient value is visible. See Figure 6-29.

Figure 6-29   **After resizing the PatientID combo box in Layout view**

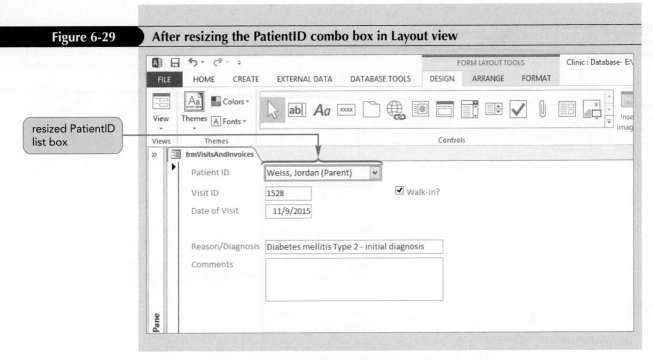

Now you'll add the title to the top of the form.

Using Form Headers and Form Footers

The **Form Header** and **Form Footer sections** let you add titles, instructions, command buttons, and other controls to the top and bottom of your form, respectively. Controls placed in the Form Header or Form Footer sections remain on the screen whenever the form is displayed in Form view or Layout view; they do not change when the contents of the Detail section change as you navigate from one record to another record.

To add either a form header or footer to your form, you must first add both the Form Header and Form Footer sections as a pair to the form. If your form needs one of these sections but not the other, you can remove a section by setting its height to zero, which is the same method you would use to remove any form section. You can also prevent a section from appearing in Form view or in Print Preview by setting its Visible property to No. The **Visible property** determines if Access displays a control or section. You set the Visible property to Yes to display the control or section, and set the Visible property to No to hide it.

If you've set the Form Footer section's height to zero or set its Visible property to No and a future form design change makes adding controls to the Form Footer section necessary, you can restore the section by using the pointer to drag its bottom edge back down or by setting its Visible property to Yes.

You can add the Form Header and Form Footer sections as a pair to a form either directly or indirectly. The direct way to add these sections is to right-click the Detail section selector, and then click Form Header/Footer. This direct method is available only in Design view. The indirect way to add the Form Header and Form Footer sections in Layout view or Design view is to use one of three buttons on the DESIGN tab in the Header/Footer group: the Logo button, the Title button, or the Date and Time button. Clicking any of these three buttons causes Access to add the Form Header and Form Footer sections to the form and to place an appropriate control in the Form Header section. If you use the indirect method in Layout view, Access sets the Form Footer section's height to zero. In Design view, the indirect method creates a Form Footer section with the Height property set to one-quarter inch.

Adding and Removing Form Header and Form Footer Sections

- In Design view, right-click the Detail section selector, and then click Form Header/Footer on the shortcut menu; or in Layout view or Design view, click a button on the DESIGN tab in the Header/Footer group to add a logo, title, or date and time to the form.
- To remove a Form Header or Form Footer section, drag its bottom edge up until the section area disappears or set the section's Visible property to No.

Raj's design includes a title at the top of the form. Because the title will not change as you navigate through the form records, you will add the title to the Form Header section in the form.

Adding a Title to a Form

You'll add the title to Raj's form in Layout view. When you add a title to a form in Layout view, Access adds the Form Header section to the form and places the title in the Form Header section. At the same time, Access adds the Page Footer section to the form and sets its height to zero.

To add a title to the form:

▶ **1.** On the DESIGN tab, in the Header/Footer group, click the **Title** button. Access adds the title to the form, displaying it in the upper-left of the form and using the form name as the title.

You need to change the title. Because the title is already selected, you can type over or edit the selected title.

▶ **2.** Type **Visits and Invoices** to replace the default title text. See Figure 6-30.

Figure 6-30	Title placed in the Form Header section

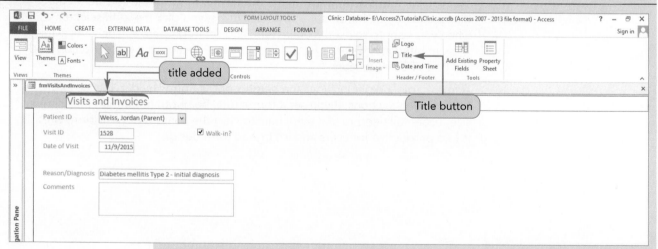

Raj wants the title to be prominent in the form. The title is already a larger font size than the font used for the form's labels and field value boxes, so you'll change the title's font weight to bold to increase its prominence.

3. Select the title control, click the **FORMAT** tab, and then in the Font group, click the **Bold** button B. The title is displayed in 18-point, bold text.

It is not obvious in Layout view that the title is displayed in the Form Header section, so you'll view the form design in Design view.

4. Switch to Design view, click outside the grid to deselect all controls, and then save your design changes. The title is displayed in the Form Header section. See Figure 6-31.

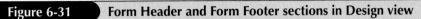

Figure 6-31   **Form Header and Form Footer sections in Design view**

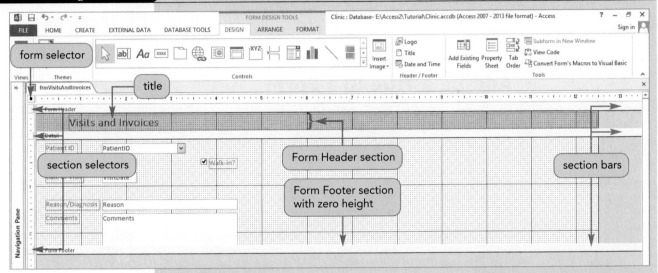

The form now contains a Form Header section that displays the title, a Detail section that displays the bound controls and labels, and a Form Footer section that is set to a height of zero. Each section consists of a **section selector** and a section bar, either of which you can click to select and set properties for the entire section, and a grid or background, which is where you place controls that you want to display in the form. The **form selector** is the selector at the intersection of the horizontal and vertical rulers; you click the form selector when you want to select the entire form and set its properties. The vertical ruler is segmented into sections for the Form Header section, the Detail section, and the Form Footer section.

A form's total height includes the heights of the Form Header, Detail, and Form Footer sections. If you set a form's total height to more than the screen size, users will need to use scroll bars to view the content of your form, which is less productive for users and isn't good form design.

So far, you've added controls to the form and modified the controls by selecting, moving, aligning, resizing, and deleting them. You've added and modified a combo box and added a title in the Form Header section. In the next session, you will continue your work with the custom form by adding a combo box to find records, adding a subform, adding calculated controls, changing form and section properties, and changing control properties.

REVIEW

Session 6.2 Quick Check

1. What is a bound form, and when do you use bound forms?
2. What is the difference between a bound control and an unbound control?
3. The _____ consists of the dotted and solid lines that appear in the Header, Detail, and Footer sections to help you position controls precisely in a form.
4. The handle in a selected object's upper-left corner is the _____ handle.
5. How do you move a selected field value box and its label at the same time?
6. How do you resize a control?
7. A(n) _____ control provides the features of a text box and a list box.
8. How do you change a label's caption?
9. What is the Form Header section?

Session 6.3 Visual Overview:

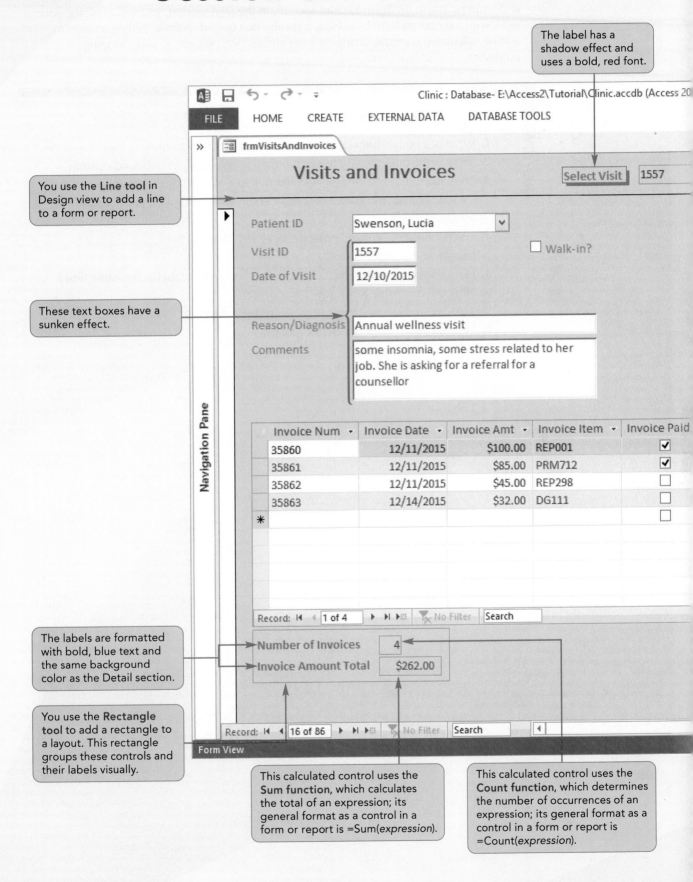

The label has a shadow effect and uses a bold, red font.

You use the **Line tool** in Design view to add a line to a form or report.

These text boxes have a sunken effect.

The labels are formatted with bold, blue text and the same background color as the Detail section.

You use the **Rectangle tool** to add a rectangle to a layout. This rectangle groups these controls and their labels visually.

This calculated control uses the **Sum function**, which calculates the total of an expression; its general format as a control in a form or report is =Sum(expression).

This calculated control uses the **Count function**, which determines the number of occurrences of an expression; its general format as a control in a form or report is =Count(expression).

Custom Form in Form View

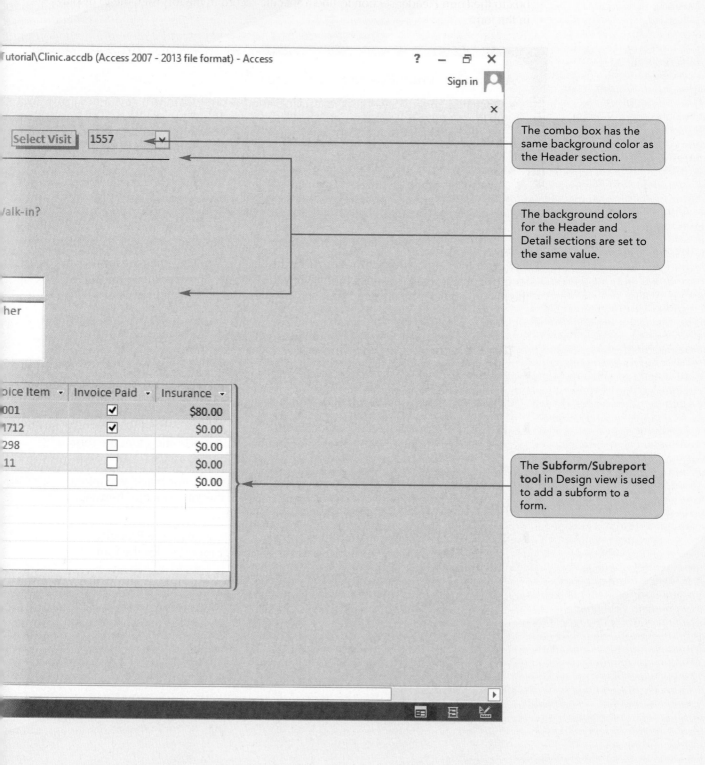

The combo box has the same background color as the Header section.

The background colors for the Header and Detail sections are set to the same value.

The **Subform/Subreport tool** in Design view is used to add a subform to a form.

Adding a Combo Box to Find Records

Most combo boxes are used to display and update data. You can also use combo boxes to find records. To continue creating the form that Raj sketched, you will add a combo box to the Form Header section to find a specific record in the tblVisit table to display in the form.

REFERENCE

Adding a Combo Box to Find Records

- Open the Property Sheet for the form in Design view, make sure the record source is a table or query, and then close the Property Sheet.
- On the DESIGN tab, in the Controls group, click the More button, click the Combo Box tool, and then click the position in the form where you want to place the control.
- Click the third option button ("Find a record on my form based on the value I selected in my combo box") in the first Combo Box Wizard dialog box, and then complete the remaining Combo Box Wizard dialog boxes.

You can use the Combo Box Wizard to add a combo box to find records in a form. However, the Combo Box Wizard provides this find option only when the form's record source is a table or query. You'll view the Property Sheet for the form to view the Record Source property, and you'll change the property setting, if necessary.

To add a combo box to find records to the form:

▶ **1.** If you took a break after the previous session, make sure that the Clinic database is open, the frmVisitsAndInvoices form is open in Design view, and the Navigation Pane is closed.

▶ **2.** Click the **form selector** ☐ (located to the left of the horizontal ruler) to select the form. The form selector changes to ■, indicating that the form is selected.

Trouble? If the Form Header section head instead turns black, you might have clicked the header selector button. Click the form selector button, which is just above the header selector button.

▶ **3.** Click the DESIGN tab, and then in the Tools group, click the Property Sheet button. The Property Sheet displays the properties for the form. See Figure 6-32.

Figure 6-32   Property sheet for the form

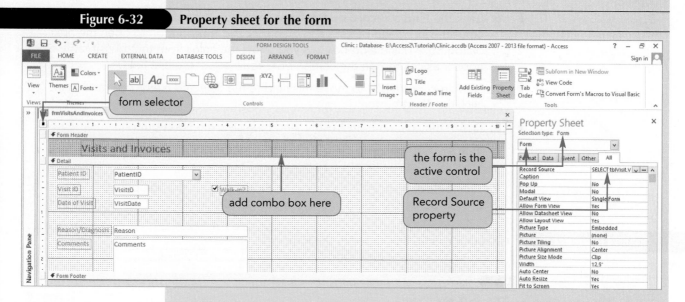

The Record Source property is set to an SQL SELECT statement, which is code that references a table. You need to change the Record Source property to a table or query, or the Combo Box Wizard will not present you with the option to find records in a form. You'll change the Record Source property to the tblVisit table because this table is the record source for all the bound controls you added to the Detail section.

4. Click the **All** tab if necessary, and click the **Record Source** box. Click the arrow, select **tblVisit**, and then close the Property Sheet.

You'll now use the Combo Box Wizard to add a combo box to the form's Form Header section, which will enable a user to find a record in the tblVisit table to display in the form.

5. On the DESIGN tab, in the Controls group, click the **More** button to open the Controls gallery, make sure the Use Control Wizards tool is selected in the Controls gallery, click the **Combo Box** tool, position the + portion of the pointer at the top of the Form Header section and at the 5-inch mark on the horizontal ruler (see Figure 6-32), and then click the mouse button. Access places a combo box control in the form and opens the first Combo Box Wizard dialog box.

Trouble? If the Combo Box Wizard dialog box does not open, delete the new controls and try again, ensuring the + pointer is very near the top of the Form Header grid.

The dialog box now displays a third option to "Find a record on my form based on the value I selected in my combo box," which you'll use for this combo box. You would choose the first option, which you used for the PatientID combo box, if you wanted to select a value from a list of foreign key values from an existing table or query. You would choose the second option if you wanted users to select a value from a short fixed list of values that don't change. For example, if Chatham Community Health Services wanted to include a field in the tblPatient table to identify the state in which the patient resides, you could use a combo box with this second option to display a list of states.

> **6.** Click the **Find a record on my form based on the value I selected in my combo box** option button, and then click the **Next** button to open the next dialog box. This dialog box lets you select the fields from the tblVisit table to appear as columns in the combo box. You'll select the first field.

> **7.** Double-click **VisitID** to move this field to the Selected Fields box, and then click the **Next** button.

> **8.** Resize the column to its best fit, and then click the **Next** button.

In this dialog box, you specify the name for the combo box's label. You'll use Select Visit as the label.

> **9.** Type **Select Visit**, and then click the **Finish** button. The completed unbound combo box is displayed in the form. See Figure 6-33.

Figure 6-33	Unbound combo box added to the form

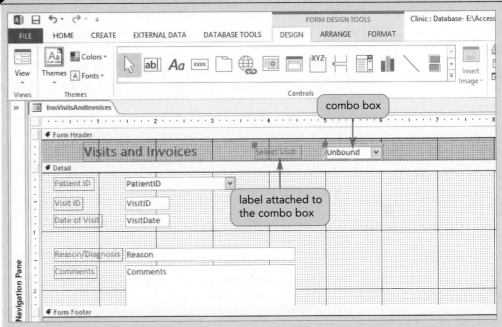

You'll move the attached label closer to the combo box, and then you'll align the bottoms of the combo box and its attached label with the bottom of the title in the Form Header section.

> **10.** Click the **Select Visit** label, point to the label's move handle (upper left corner), and then drag the label to the right until its right edge is two grid dots to the left of the combo box.

> **11.** Select the combo box in the Form Header section, the **Select Visit** label, and the title, right-click one of the selected controls, point to **Align**, and then click **Bottom**. The three selected controls are aligned on their bottom edges. See Figure 6-34.

Figure 6-34 | After aligning the combo box control and the title

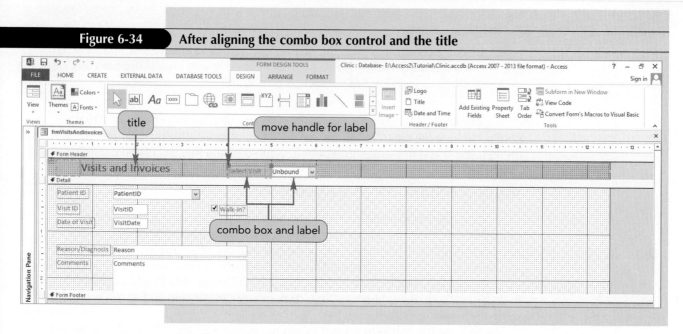

You'll save your form changes and view the new combo box in Form view.

To find contract records using the combo box:

▶ **1.** Save the form design changes, and then switch to Form view.

▶ **2.** Click the **Select Visit** combo box arrow to open the list box. See Figure 6-35.

Figure 6-35 | Displaying the combo box's list of visit IDs

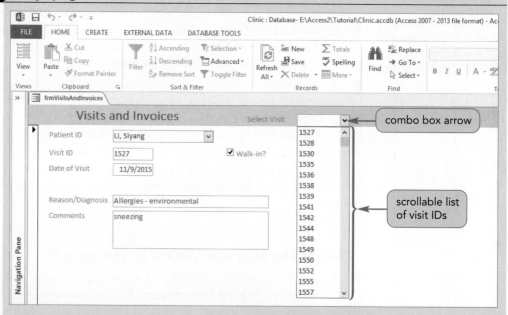

▶ **3.** Scroll down the list, and then click **1557**. The current record changes from record 1 to record 16, which is the record for visit ID 1557.

Trouble? If you see the data for record 1, the navigation combo box is not working correctly. Delete the combo box, check to ensure that you have set the Record Source for the form object correctly, and repeat the previous set of steps to recreate the navigation combo box.

The form design currently is very plain, with no color, special effects, or visual contrast among the controls. Before making the form more attractive and useful, though, you'll add the remaining controls: a subform and two calculated controls.

Adding a Subform to a Form

Raj's plan for the form includes a subform that displays the related invoices for the displayed visit. The form you've been creating is the main form for records from the primary tblVisit table (the "one" side of the one-to-many relationship), and the subform will display records from the related tblBilling table (the "many" side of the one-to-many relationship). You use the Subform/Subreport tool in Design view to add a subform to a form. You can add the subform on your own, or you can get help adding the subform by using the SubForm Wizard.

You will use the SubForm Wizard to add the subform for the tblBilling table records to the bottom of the form. First, you'll increase the height of the Detail section to make room for the subform.

To add the subform to the form:

1. Switch to Design view.

2. Place the pointer on the bottom edge of the Detail section. When the pointer changes to a ↕ shape, drag the section's edge down until it is at the 5-inch mark on the vertical ruler.

TIP

Drag slightly beyond the desired ending position to expose the vertical ruler measurement, and then decrease the height back to the correct position.

3. On the DESIGN tab, in the Controls group, click the **More** button to open the Controls gallery, make sure the Use Control Wizards tool ▨ is selected, and then click the **Subform/Subreport** tool ▣.

4. Position the + portion of the pointer in the Detail section at the 2.5-inch mark on the vertical ruler and at the 1-inch mark on the horizontal ruler, and then click the mouse button. Access places a subform control in the form's Detail section and opens the first SubForm Wizard dialog box.

You can use a table, a query, or an existing form as the record source for a subform. In this case, you'll use the related tblInvoice table as the record source for the new subform.

To use the SubForm Wizard to configure the subform:

1. Make sure the Use existing Tables and Queries option button is selected, and then click the **Next** button. Access opens the next SubForm Wizard dialog box, which lets you select a table or query as the record source for the subform and pick which fields to use from the selected table or query.

2. Click the **Tables/Queries arrow** to display the list of tables and queries in the Clinic database, scroll to the top of the list, and then click **Table: tblBilling**. The Available Fields box shows the fields in the tblBilling table.

Raj's form design includes all fields from the tblBilling table in the subform, except for the VisitID field, which you already placed in the Detail section of the form from the tblVisit table.

3. Click the >> button to move all available fields to the Selected Fields box, click **VisitID** in the Selected Fields box, click the < button, and then click the **Next** button to open the next SubForm Wizard dialog box. See Figure 6-36.

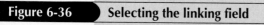

Figure 6-36   Selecting the linking field

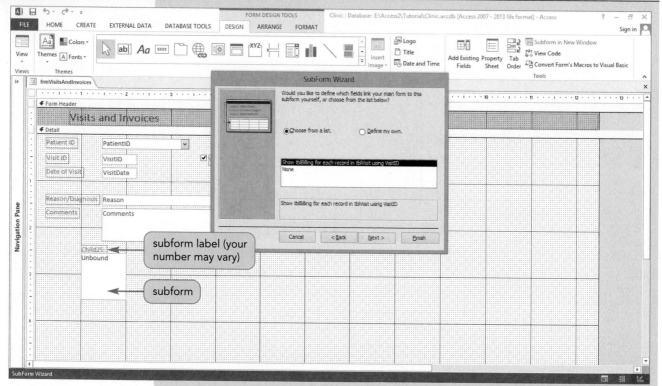

In this dialog box, you select the link between the primary tblVisit table and the related tblBilling table. The common field in the two tables, VisitID, links the tables. Access uses the VisitID field to display a record in the main form, which displays data from the primary tblVisit table, and to select and display the related records for that contract in the subform, which displays data from the related tblBilling table.

4. Make sure the "Choose from a list" option button is selected, make sure "Show tblBilling for each record in tblVisit using VisitID" is highlighted in the list, and then click the **Next** button. The next SubForm Wizard dialog box lets you specify a name for the subform.

5. Type **frmBillingSubform** and then click the **Finish** button. Access increases the height and width of the subform in the form. The subform will display the related tblBilling records; its label appears above the subform and displays the subform name.

6. Deselect all controls, save your form changes, switch to Form view, and then click the **VisitID** text box to deselect the value. If the record for VisitID 1557 is not selected, then click the drop-down arrow for the Select Visit combo box and scroll down the list to select VisitID 1557. See Figure 6-37.

Figure 6-37	Viewing the subform in Form view

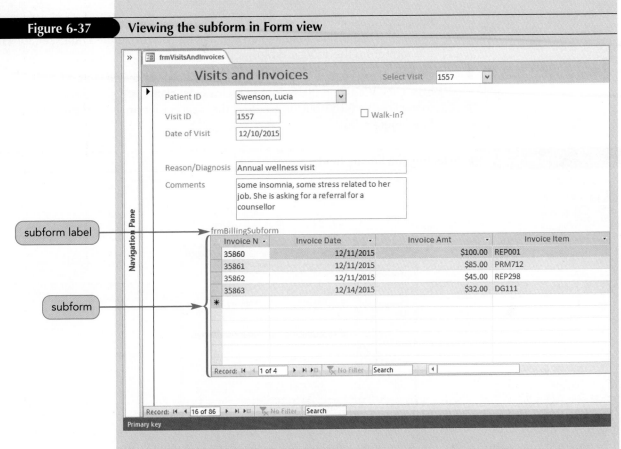

subform label

subform

The subform displays the four invoices related to visit ID 1557.

Trouble? If the widths of the columns in your datasheet differ or the position of your subform is different, don't worry. You'll resize all columns to their best fit and move the subform later.

After viewing the form, Raj identifies some modifications he wants you to make. The subform is not properly sized and the columns in the subform are not sized to their best fit. He wants you to resize the subform and its columns, so that all columns in the subform are entirely visible. Also, he asks you to delete the subform label, because the label is unnecessary for identifying the subform contents. You'll use Design view and Layout view to make these changes.

To modify the subform's design:

1. Switch to Design view. Notice that in Design view, the subform data does not appear in a datasheet format as it does in Form view. That difference causes no problem; you can ignore it.

   First, you'll delete the subform label.

2. Deselect all controls (if necessary), right-click the **frmBillingSubform** subform label to open the shortcut menu (make sure no other controls have handles), and then click **Cut**.

   Next, you'll move the subform by aligning it with the Comments label.

3. Click the edge of the subform to select it (an orange border and handles appear on the subform's border when the subform is selected), hold down the **Shift** key, click the **Comments** label, and then release the **Shift** key. The subform and the Comments label are selected. Next you'll align the two controls on their left edges.

4. Right-click the **Comments** label, point to **Align** on the shortcut menu, and then click **Left**. The two controls are aligned on their left edges. You'll resize the subform in Layout view, so you can see your changes as you make them.

5. Switch to Layout view, click the edge of the subform to select it, and then drag the right edge of the subform to the right until all six datasheet columns are fully visible.

   Before resizing the columns in the subform, you'll display record 16 in the main form. The subform for this record contains the related records in the tblBilling table with one of the longest field values.

6. Use the record navigation bar for the main form (at the bottom left of the form window) to display record 16, for visit number 1557, and then resize each column in the subform to its best fit.

   Next, you'll resize the subform again so its width matches the width of the five resized columns.

7. Resize the subform's right edge, so it is aligned with the right edge of the Insurance column. See Figure 6-38.

Figure 6-38   After moving and resizing the subform

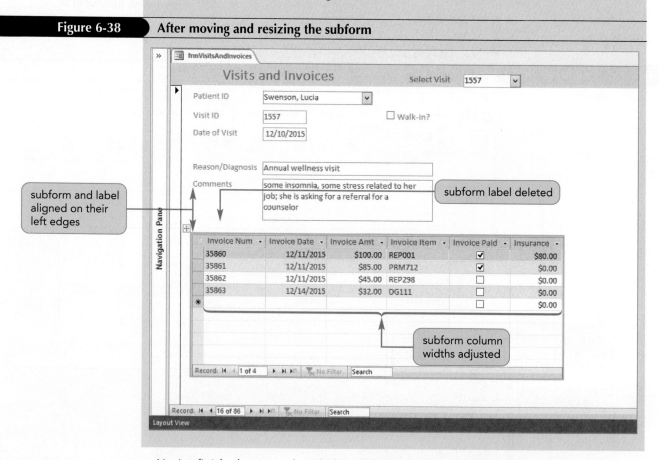

You've finished your work with the subform. Now you need to add two calculated controls to the main form.

Displaying a Subform's Calculated Controls in the Main Form

Raj's form design includes the display of calculated controls in the main form that tally the number of invoices and the total of the invoice amounts for the related records displayed in the subform. To display these calculated controls in a form or report, you use the Count and Sum functions. The Count function determines the number of occurrences of an expression; its general format as a control in a form or report is =Count(*expression*). The Sum function calculates the total of an expression, and its general format as a control in a form or report is =Sum(*expression*). The number of invoices and total of invoice amounts are displayed in the subform's Detail section, so you'll need to place the calculated controls in the subform's Form Footer section.

Adding Calculated Controls to a Subform's Form Footer Section

First, you'll open the subform in Design view in another window and add the calculated controls to the subform's Form Footer section.

To add calculated controls to the subform's Form Footer section:

1. Save your form design changes, switch to Design view, click an unused area of the grid to deselect any selected controls, click the subform border to select the subform, right-click the border, and then click **Subform in New Window** on the shortcut menu. The subform opens in Design view. See Figure 6-39.

Figure 6-39   Subform in Design view

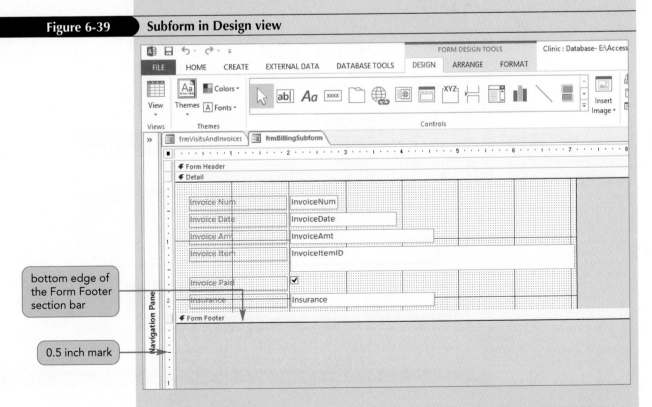

bottom edge of the Form Footer section bar

0.5 inch mark

The subform's Detail section contains the tblBilling table fields. As a subform in the main form, the fields appear in a datasheet even though the fields do not appear that way in Design view. The heights of the subform's Form

Header and Form Footer sections are zero, meaning that these sections have been removed from the subform. You'll increase the height of the Form Footer section so that you can add the two calculated controls to the section.

2. Place the pointer at the bottom edge of the Form Footer section bar. When the pointer changes to a ↕ shape, drag the bottom edge of the section down to the 0.5-inch mark on the vertical ruler.

Now you'll add the first calculated control to the Form Footer section. To create the text box for the calculated control, you use the **Text Box tool** in the Controls group on the DESIGN tab. Because the Form Footer section is not displayed in a datasheet, you do not need to position the control precisely.

3. On the DESIGN tab, in the Controls group, click the **Text Box** tool ab .

4. Position the + portion of the pointer near the top of the Form Footer section and at the 1-inch mark on the horizontal ruler, and then click the mouse button. Access places a text box control and an attached label control to its left in the Form Footer section.

Next, you'll set the Name and Control Source properties for the text box. Recall that the Name property specifies the name of an object or control. Later, when you add the calculated control in the main form, you'll reference the subform's calculated control value by using its Name property value. The **Control Source property** specifies the source of the data that appears in the control; the Control Source property setting can be either a field name or an expression.

TIP

Read the Naming Conventions section in the appendix titled "Relational Databases and Database Design" for more information about naming conventions.

5. Open the Property Sheet for the text box in the Form Footer section (the word "Unbound" is displayed inside the text box), click the **All** tab (if necessary), select the value in the Name box, type **txtInvoiceAmtSum** in the Name box, press the **Tab** key, type **=Sum(Inv** in the Control Source box, press the **Tab** key to accept the rest of the field name of InvoiceAmt suggested by Formula AutoComplete, type **)** (a right parenthesis), and then press the **Tab** key. InvoiceAmt is enclosed in brackets in the expression because it's a field name. See Figure 6-40.

Figure 6-40   **Setting properties for the subform calculated control**

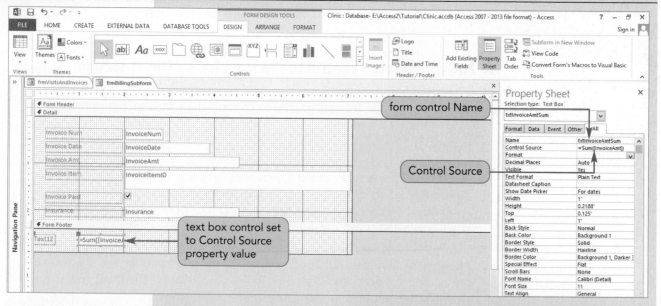

You've finished creating the first calculated control; now you'll create the other calculated control.

TIP

In txtInvoiceNum-Count, txt identifies the control type (a text box), InvoiceNum is the related field name, and Count identifies the control as a count control.

6. Repeat Steps 3 through 5, positioning the + portion of the pointer near the top of the Form Footer section and at the 4-inch mark on the horizontal ruler, setting the Name property value to **txtInvoiceNumCount**, and setting the Control Source property value to **=Count([InvoiceNum])**.

When you use the Count function, you are counting the number of displayed records—in this case, the number of records displayed in the subform. Instead of using InvoiceNum as the expression for the Count function, you could use any of the other fields displayed in the subform.

You've finished creating the subform's calculated controls, so you can close the Property Sheet, save your subform design changes, and return to the main form.

7. Close the Property Sheet, save your subform changes, and then close the subform. The active object is now the main form in Design view.

Trouble? The subform in the frmContractsAndInvoices form might appear to be blank after you close the frmInvoiceSubform form. This is a temporary effect; the subform's controls do still exist. Switch to Form view and then back to Design view to display the subform's controls.

8. Switch to Form view. The calculated controls you added in the subform's Form Footer section are *not* displayed in the subform.

9. Switch to Design view.

Next, you'll add two calculated controls in the main form to display the two calculated controls from the subform.

Adding Calculated Controls to a Main Form

The subform's calculated controls now contain a count of the number of invoices and a total of the invoice amounts. Raj's design has the two calculated controls displayed in the main form, not in the subform. You need to add two calculated controls in the main form that reference the values in the subform's calculated controls. Because it's easy to make a typing mistake with these references, you'll use Expression Builder to set the Control Source property for the two main form calculated controls.

To add a calculated control to the main form's Detail section:

1. Adjust the length of the Detail section if necessary so there is approximately 0.5 inch below the frmBillingSubform control. The Detail section should be approximately 5.5 inches.

2. On the DESIGN tab, in the Controls group, click the **Text Box** tool |ab|, and then add the text box and its attached label in the Detail section, clicking the + portion of the pointer at the 1-inch mark on the horizontal ruler and below the frmBillingSubform control, approximately the 5-inch mark on the vertical ruler. Don't be concerned about positioning the control precisely because you'll resize and move the label and text box later.

3. Select the label and open the Property Sheet, set its Caption property to **Number of Invoices**, right-click an edge of the label to open the shortcut menu, point to **Size**, and then click **To Fit**. Don't worry if the label now overlaps the text box.

You'll use Expression Builder to set Control Source property for the text box.

4. Click the text box (the word "Unbound" is displayed inside the text box) to select it, click the **Control Source** box in the Property Sheet, and then click the property's **Build** button ... to open Expression Builder.

5. In the Expression Elements box, click the **expand indicator** ▷ next to frmVisitsAndInvoices, click **frmBillingSubform** in the Expression Elements box, scroll down the Expression Categories box, and then double-click **txtInvoiceNumCount** in the Expression Categories box. See Figure 6-41.

Figure 6-41   Text box control's expression in the Expression Builder dialog box

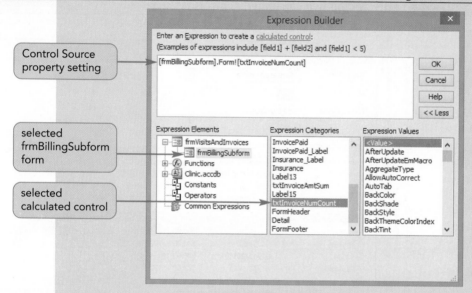

Control Source property setting

selected frmBillingSubform form

selected calculated control

Instead of adding txtInvoiceNumCount to the expression box at the top, Access changed it to Form![frmBillingSubform]![txtInvoiceNumCount]. This expression asks Access to display the value of the txtInvoiceNumCount control that is located in the frmBillingSubform form, which is a form object.

You need to add an equal sign to the beginning of the expression.

6. Press the **Home** key, type = (an equal sign), and then click the **OK** button. Access closes the Expression Builder dialog box and sets the Control Source property.

Next, you'll add a second text box to the main form, set the Caption property for the label, and use Expression Builder to set the text box's Control Source property.

Be sure you resize the label to its best fit.

7. Repeat Steps 2 and 3 to add a text box to the main form, clicking the + portion of the pointer at the 4-inch mark on the horizontal ruler and approximately the 5-inch mark on the vertical ruler, and setting the label's Caption property to **Invoice Amount Total**.

8. Click the new text box (containing the word "Unbound") to select it, click the **Control Source** box in the Property Sheet, and then click the property's **Build** button ... to open Expression Builder.

9. With the Expression Builder dialog box open for the new text box, type = (an equal sign), click the **expand indicator** next to frmVisitsAndInvoices in the Expression Elements box, click **frmBillingSubform** in the Expression Elements box, scroll down the Expression Categories box, and then

double-click **txtInvoiceAmtSum** in the Expression Categories box. Access changes the txtInvoiceAmtSum calculated field to the expression = [frmBillingSubform].Form![txtInvoiceAmtSum].

Next, you'll save your form changes and view the form in Layout view.

10. Click the **OK** button to accept the expression and close the Expression Builder dialog box, close the Property Sheet, save your form changes, and then switch to Form view. If the record for VisitID 1557 is not selected, then click the drop-down arrow for the Select Visit combo box and scroll down the list to select VisitID 1557. See Figure 6-42.

Figure 6-42	After adding two calculated controls

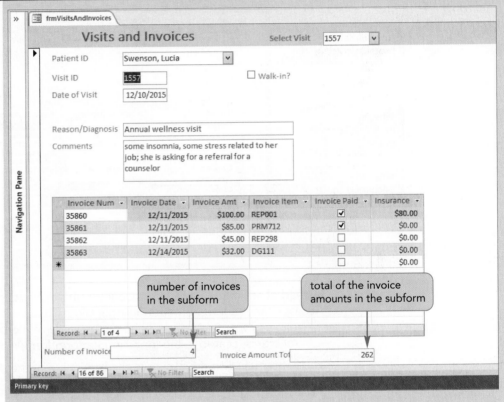

Next, you need to resize, move, and format the two calculated controls and their attached labels.

Resizing, Moving, and Formatting Calculated Controls

In addition to resizing and repositioning the two calculated controls and their attached labels, you need to change the format of the rightmost calculated control to Currency and to set the following properties for both calculated controls:

- Set the Tab Stop property to a value of No. The **Tab Stop property** specifies whether users can use the Tab key to move to a control on a form. If the Tab Stop property is set to No, users can't tab to the control.
- Set the ControlTip Text property to a value of "Calculated total number of invoices for this patient visit" for the calculated control on the left and "Calculated invoice total for this patient visit" for the calculated control on the right. The **ControlTip Text property** specifies the text that appears in a ScreenTip when users hold the mouse pointer over a control in a form.

Setting Properties in the Property Sheet

You can set many properties in the Property Sheet by typing a value in the property's box, by clicking the arrow on the property and then selecting a value from the menu, or by double-clicking the property name. If you need to set a property by typing a long text entry, you can open the Zoom dialog box and type the entry in the dialog box. You can also use Expression Builder to help you enter expressions.

Now you'll resize, move, and format the calculated controls and their attached labels, and you'll set other properties for the calculated controls.

To modify the calculated controls and their attached labels:

▶ **1.** Switch to Layout view, right-click the calculated control on the right, click **Properties** on the shortcut menu to open the Property Sheet, click the **All** tab in the Property Sheet (if necessary), set the Format property to **Currency**, and then close the Property Sheet. The value displayed in the calculated control changes from 262 to $262.00.

Now you'll resize the calculated controls, adjust the positions of each paired label and field value box with respect to each other, and then move the controls into their final positions in the form.

▶ **2.** Individually, reduce the widths of the two calculated controls by dragging the left or right border to shrink the text box width.

▶ **3.** Click the **Number of Invoices** label, use the → key on the keyboard to move the text box and label into the position shown in Figure 6-43, repeat the process for the **Invoice Amount Total** label and its related calculated control, and then deselect all controls. See Figure 6-43.

To add a line to the form:

▶ **1.** Switch to Design view, and then drag down the bottom of the Form Header section to the 1-inch mark on the vertical ruler to make room to draw a horizontal line at the bottom of the Form Header section.

▶ **2.** On the DESIGN tab, in the Controls group, click the **More** button to open the Controls gallery, and then click the **Line** tool ◻.

▶ **3.** Position the pointer's plus symbol (+) at the left edge of the Form Header section just below the title.

▶ **4.** Hold down the **Shift** key, drag a horizontal line from left to right so the end of the line ends at the 6-inch mark on the vertical ruler, release the mouse button, and then release the **Shift** key. See Figure 6-48.

Figure 6-48	Adding a line to the form

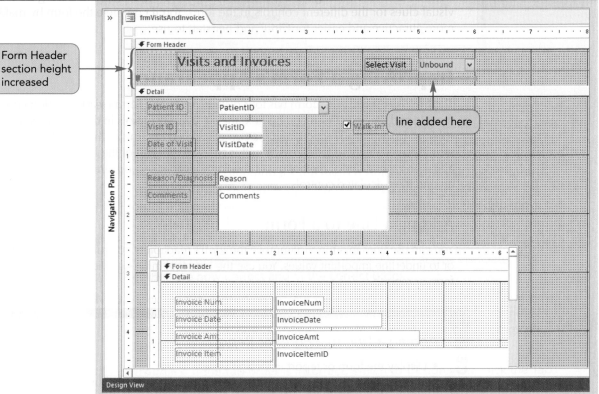

Trouble? If the line is not straight or not positioned correctly, click the Undo button on the Quick Access Toolbar, and then repeat Steps 2 through 4. If the line is not the correct length, be sure the line is selected, hold down the Shift key, and press the left or right arrow key until the line's length is the same as that of the line shown in Figure 6-48.

▶ **5.** Drag up the bottom of the Form Header section to just below the line.

▶ **6.** Save your form design changes.

Next, you'll add a rectangle around the calculated controls in the Detail section.

Adding a Rectangle to a Form

You can use a rectangle in a form to group related controls and to separate the group from other controls. You use the **Rectangle tool** in Design view to add a rectangle to a form or report.

Adding a Rectangle to a Form or Report

- Display the form or report in Design view.
- On the DESIGN tab, in the Controls group, click the More button, and then click the Rectangle tool.
- Click in the form or report to create a default-sized rectangle, or drag a rectangle in the position and size you want.

You will add a rectangle around the calculated controls and their labels to separate them from the subform and from the other controls in the Detail section.

To add a rectangle to the form:

1. On the DESIGN tab, in the Controls group, click the **More** button to open the Controls gallery, and then click the **Rectangle** tool ▢.

2. Position the pointer's plus symbol (+) approximately two grid dots above and two grid dots to the left of the Number of Invoices label.

3. Drag a rectangle down and to the right until all four sides are approximately two grid dots from the two calculated controls and their labels. See Figure 6-49.

Figure 6-49   Adding a rectangle to the form

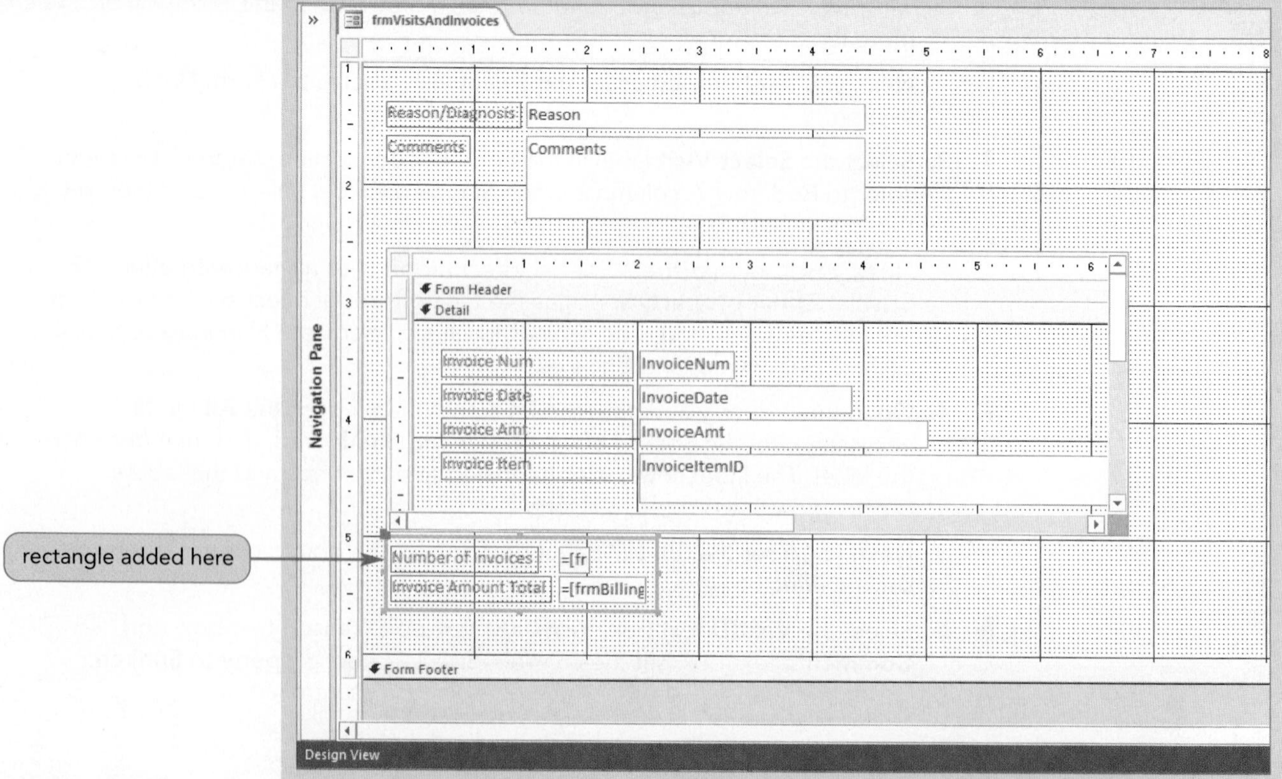

rectangle added here

Trouble? If the rectangle is not sized or positioned correctly, use the sizing handles to adjust its size and the move handle to adjust its position.

Next, you'll set the thickness of the rectangle's lines.

▶ **4.** Click the **FORMAT** tab.

▶ **5.** In the Control Formatting group, click the **Shape Outline arrow**, point to **Line Thickness** at the bottom of the gallery, and then click the line with the ScreenTip **1 pt** in the list (2nd line from the top).

▶ **6.** Deselect the control.

Next, you'll add color and visual effects to the form's controls.

Modifying the Visual Effects of the Controls in a Form

Distinguishing one group of controls in a form from other groups is an important visual cue to the users of the form. For example, users should be able to distinguish the bound controls in the form from the calculated controls and from the Select Visit control in the Form Header section. You'll now modify the controls in the form to provide these visual cues. You'll start by setting font properties for the calculated control's labels.

To modify the controls in the form:

▶ **1.** Select the **Number of Invoices** label and the **Invoice Amount Total** label, using the Shift key to select multiple controls.

▶ **2.** On the FORMAT tab, in the Font group, click the **Font Color button arrow** 🅰️ ⏷ , click the **Blue** color (row 7, column 8 in the Standard Colors palette), and then on the FORMAT tab in the Font group, click the **Bold** button 🅱️ . The labels' captions now use a bold, blue font. In the Form view, the controls will have a white background rather than a gray one, so this color will be more legible.

Next, you'll set properties for the Select Visit label in the Form Header section.

▶ **3.** Select the **Select Visit** label in the Form Header section, set the label's font color to **Red** (row 7, column 2 in the Standard Colors palette), and then set the font style to bold.

Next, you'll set the label's Special Effect property to a shadowed effect. The **Special Effect property** specifies the type of special effect applied to a control in a form or report. The choices for this property are Flat, Raised, Sunken, Etched, Shadowed, and Chiseled.

▶ **4.** Open the Property Sheet for the Select Visit label, click the **All** tab (if necessary), set the Special Effect property to **Shadowed**, and then deselect the label. The label now has a shadowed special effect, and the label's caption now uses a bold, red font.

Next, you'll set the Special Effect property for the bound control labels to a sunken effect.

▶ **5.** Select the **VisitID** text box, **VisitDate** text box, **Reason** text box, and **Comments** text box, set the controls' Special Effect property to **Sunken**, close the Property Sheet, and then deselect the controls.

Finally, you'll set the background color of the Form Header section, the Detail section, the combo box, and the two calculated controls. You can use the **Background Color button** in the Font group on the DESIGN tab to change the background color of a control, section, or object (form or report).

6. Click the Form Header section bar.

7. On the FORMAT tab, in the Font group, click the **Background Color button arrow** , and then click the **Light Blue 2** color (row 3, column 5 in the Standard Colors palette). The Form Header's background color changes to the Light Blue 2 color.

8. Click the Detail section bar, and then on the FORMAT tab, in the Font Group, click the **Background Color** button to change the Detail section's background color to the **Light Blue 2** color.

9. Select the **Select Visit** combo box, **Number of Invoices** text box, and the **Invoice Amount Total** text box, set the selected controls' background color to the **Light Blue 2** color, and then deselect all controls by clicking to the right of the Detail section's grid. See Figure 6-50.

Figure 6-50   Completed custom form in Design view

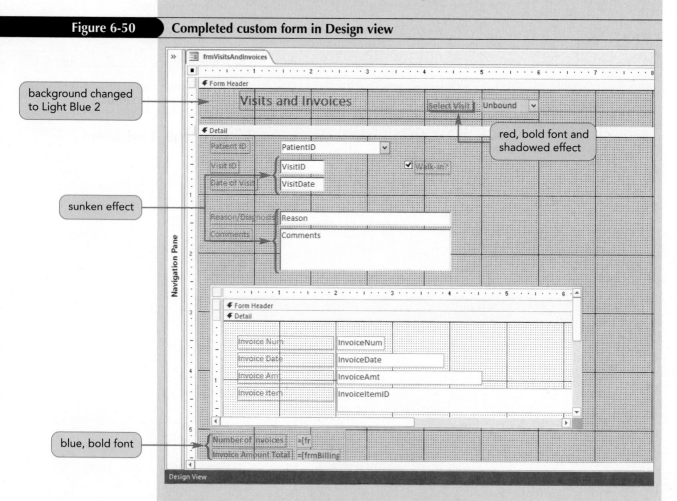

10. Switch to Form view, and then click the **VisitID** text box to select the first value in the list, 1527. The Session 6.3 Visual Overview shows the completed form.

▶ **11.** Test the form by tabbing between fields, navigating between records, and using the Select Visit combo box to find records, making sure you don't change any field values and observing that the calculated controls display the correct values.

▶ **12.** Save your form design changes, close the form, make a backup copy of the database, compact and repair the database, and then close the database.

Cindi looked at the datasheet form, the multiple items form, and the custom form. She is really pleased with the choices you provided for her and she'll discuss the choices with her staff.

REVIEW

Session 6.3 Quick Check

1. To create a combo box to find records in a form with the Combo Box Wizard, the form's record source must be a(n) _____.

2. You use the _____ tool to add a subform to a form.

3. To calculate subtotals and overall totals in a form or report, you use the _____ function.

4. The Control Source property setting can be either a(n) _____ or a(n) _____.

5. Explain the difference between the Tab Stop property and tab order.

6. What is focus?

7. The _____ property has settings such as Raised and Sunken.

ASSESS

SAM Projects

PRACTICE

Review Assignments

Data File needed for the Review Assignments: Supplier.accdb (*cont. from Tutorial 5*)

Cindi wants you to create several forms, including a custom form that displays and updates companies and the products they offer. Complete the following steps:

1. Open the **Supplier** database you worked with in Tutorial 5.
2. In the **tblProduct** table, remove the lookup feature from the SupplierID field, and then resize the Supplier ID column in the datasheet to its best fit. Save and close the table.
3. Edit the relationship between the primary tblSupplier and related tblProduct tables to enforce referential integrity and to cascade update related fields. Create the relationship report, save the report as **rptRelationshipsForProducts**, and then close it.
4. Use the Documenter to document the qryCompanyContacts query. Select all query options; use the Names, Data Types, and Sizes option for fields; and use the Names and Fields option for indexes. Print the report produced by the Documenter and then close it.
5. Use the Datasheet tool to create a form based on the tblProduct table, save the form as **frmProductDatasheet**, and then close it.
6. Use the Multiple Items tool to create a form based on the qryDuplicateProductTypes query, save the form as **frmProductTypeMultipleItems**, and then close it.
7. Use the Split Form tool to create a split form based on the tblProduct table, and then make the following changes to the form in Layout view:
   a. Remove the two Units controls from the stacked layout, reduce the width of the Units text box by about half, and then anchor the two Units controls to the bottom left. Depending on the size of your window, the two Units controls may be positioned at the bottom left of the right column.
   b. Remove the five control pairs in the right column from the stacked layout, and then anchor the group to the bottom right. You may see a dotted border outlining the location of the previously removed controls. This may be automatically selected as well.
   c. Remove the ProductName control pair from the stacked layout, move them to the top right, and then anchor them to the top right.
   d. Reduce the widths of the ProductID and SupplierID text boxes to a reasonable size.
   e. Change the title to **Product**, save the modified form as **frmProductSplitForm**, and then close it.
8. Use Figure 6-51 and the following steps to create a custom form named **frmSuppliersWithProducts** based on the tblSupplier and tblProduct tables.

| Figure 6-51 | Vendor database custom form design |

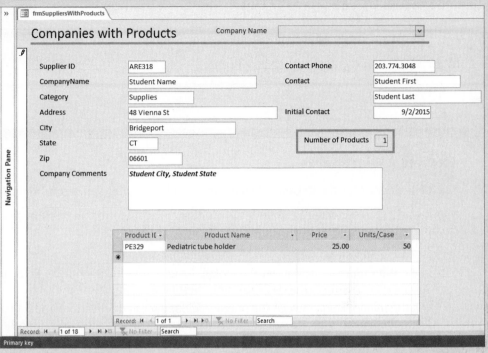

a. Place the fields from the tblSupplier table at the top of the Detail section. Delete the Contact Last Name label and change the caption for the Contact First Name label to Contact.

b. Move the fields into two columns in the Detail section, as shown in Figure 6-51, resizing and aligning controls, as necessary, and increasing the width of the form.

c. Add the title in the Form Header section.

d. Make sure the form's Record Source property is set to tblSupplier, and then add a combo box in the Form Header section to find CompanyName field values. In the wizard steps, select the CompanyName and SupplierID fields, and hide the key column. Resize and move the control. Ensure the label displays the text Company Name.

e. Add a subform based on the tblProduct table, include only the fields shown in Figure 6-51, link with SupplierID, name the subform **frmPartialProductSubform**, delete the subform label, resize the columns in the subform to their best fit, and resize and position the subform.

f. Add a calculated control that displays the number of products displayed in the subform. Set the calculated control's Tab Stop property to No, and the ControlTip Text property to **Calculated number of products**.

g. Add a line in the Form Header section, and add a rectangle around the calculated control and its label, setting the line thickness of both controls to the line style with the ScreenTip 3 pt. Set the rectangle's color the same as the line's color.

h. In the main form, use the Black, Text 1 font color (row 1, column 2 in the Theme Colors palette) for all text boxes and for the title text in the Header section, and use the White, Background 1, Darker 5% fill color (row 2, column 1 in the Theme Colors palette) for the sections, the calculated control, and the Company Name combo box.

i. Make sure the tab order is top-to-bottom, left-to-right for the main form text boxes.

9. Make a backup copy of the database, compact and repair the database, and then close the database.

Case Problem 1

APPLY

Data File needed for this Case Problem: Task.accdb (*cont. from Tutorial 5*)

GoGopher!   Amol Mehta wants you to create several forms, including two custom forms that display and update data in the database. Complete the following steps:

1. Open the **Task** database you worked with in Tutorial 5.

2. Use the Documenter to document the qryMemberNames query. Select all query options; use the Names, Data Types, and Sizes option for fields; and use the Names and Fields option for indexes. Print the first page of the report produced by the Documenter.

3. Use the Datasheet tool to create a form based on the tblPlan table, and then save the form as **frmPlanDatasheet**.

4. Create a custom form based on the qryUpcomingExpirations query. Display all fields from the query in the form. Create your own design for the form. Add a label to the bottom of the Detail section that contains your first and last names. Change the label's font so that your name appears in bold, blue text. Change the ExpirationDate text box format so that the field value displays in bold, red text. Save the form as **frmUpcomingExpirations**.

5. Use Figure 6-52 and the following steps to create a custom form named **frmPlansWithMembers** based on the tblPlan and tblMember tables.

Figure 6-52   **Plans custom form design**

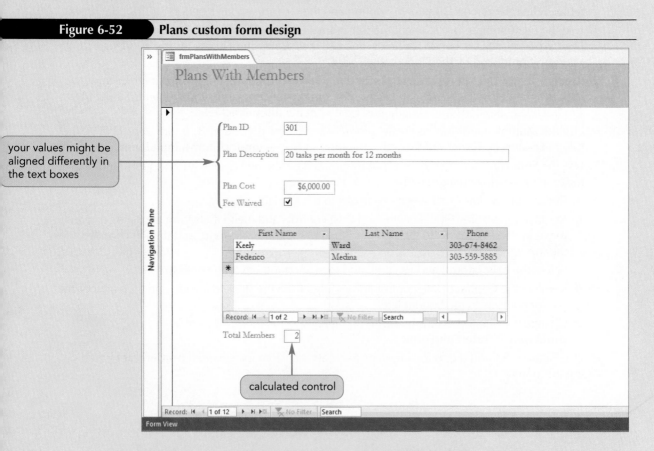

a. Place the fields from the tblPlan table at the top of the Detail section and edit the captions in the associated label controls as shown.

b. Selected fields from the tblMember table appear in a subform named **frmPlanMemberSubform**.

    c. The calculated control displays the total number of records that appear in the subform. Set the calculated control's ControlTip Text property to **Total number of members in this plan**. Set the calculated control's Tab Stop property to No.

    d. Apply the Organic theme to the form.

    e. Save and view the form, and then print the first record.

6. Make a backup copy of the database, compact and repair the database, and then close the database.

Case Problem 2

Data File needed for this Case Problem: Tutoring.accdb (*cont. from Tutorial 5*)

O'Brien Educational Services   Karen O'Brien wants you to create several forms, including a custom form that displays and updates the tutoring service's contracts with students. Complete the following steps:

1. Open the **Tutoring** database you worked with in Tutorial 5.

2. Remove the lookup feature from the TutorID field in the tblContract table, and then resize the Tutor ID column to its best fit. Save and close the table.

3. Define a one-to-many relationship between the primary tblTutor table and the related tblContract table. Select the referential integrity option and the cascade updates option for this relationship.

4. Use the Documenter to document the tblContract table. Select all table options; use the Names, Data Types, and Sizes option for fields; and use the Names and Fields option for indexes. Print the report produced by the Documenter.

5. Create a query called **qryLessonsByTutor** that uses the tblTutor and tblContract tables and includes the fields FirstName and LastName from the tblTutor table, and the fields StudentID, ContractDate, SessionType, Length, and Cost from the tblContract table.

6. Use the Multiple Items tool to create a form based on the qryLessonsByTutor query, change the title to **Lessons by Tutor**, and then save the form as **frmLessonsByTutorMultipleItems**.

7. Use the Split Form tool to create a split form based on the qryLessonsByTutor query, and then make the following changes to the form in Layout view.

    a. Reduce the widths of all seven text boxes to a reasonable size.

    b. Remove the SessionType, Length, and Cost controls and their labels from the stacked layout, move these six controls to the right and then to the top of the form, and then anchor them to the top right.

    c. Select the Cost control and its label, and then anchor them to the bottom right.

    d. Remove the Contract Date control and its label from the stacked layout, and then anchor the pair of controls to the bottom left.

    e. Change the title to **Lessons by Tutor**, and then save the modified form as **frmLessonsByTutorSplitForm**.

8. Use Figure 6-53 and the following steps to create a custom form named **frmContract** based on the tblContract table.

Figure 6-53   Tutoring database custom form design

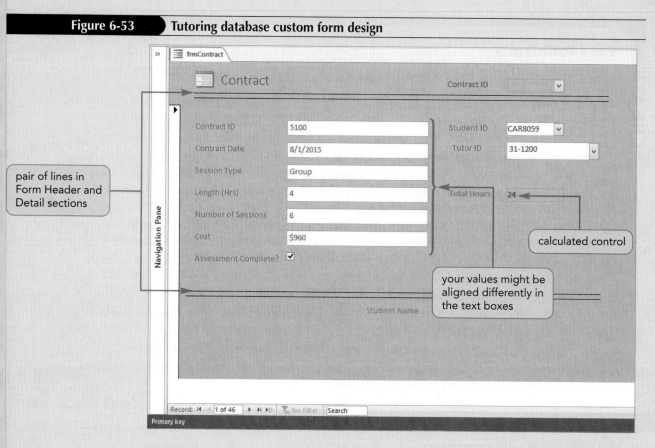

a. For the StudentID combo box, select the LastName, FirstName, and StudentID fields from the tblStudent table, in order, and sort in ascending order by the LastName field and then by the FirstName field.

b. For the TutorID combo box, select the LastName, FirstName, and TutorID fields from the tblTutor table, in order, and sort in ascending order by the LastName field and then by the FirstName field.

c. Make sure the form's Record Source property is set to tblContract, and then add a combo box in the Form Header section to find ContractID field values.

d. Add a calculated control that displays the total number of hours (length multiplied by sessions). *Hint*: Use the * symbol for multiplication. Set the calculated control's Tab Stop property to No and format the values with one decimal place.

e. Add a line in the Form Header section, add a second line below it, and then add a second pair of lines near the bottom of the Detail section. Set the line thickness of all lines to the line setting with the ScreenTip 1 pt.

f. Use the Label tool to add your name below the pair of lines at the bottom of the Detail section.

g. For the labels in the Detail section, except for the Total Hours label and the label displaying your name, use the Red font color (row 7, column 2 in the Standard Colors palette).

h. For the title and Contract ID label, use the Dark Red font color (row 7, column 1 in the Standard Colors palette).

i. For the calculated control and its label, bold the font.

j. For the background fill color of the sections, the calculated control, and the Contract ID combo box, use the Medium Gray color (row 1, column 3 in the Standard Colors palette).

k. Make sure the tab order is top-to-bottom, left-to-right for the main form field value boxes.

9. Make a backup copy of the database, compact and repair the database, and then close the database.

Figure 6-55   **Ecotour database custom form design**

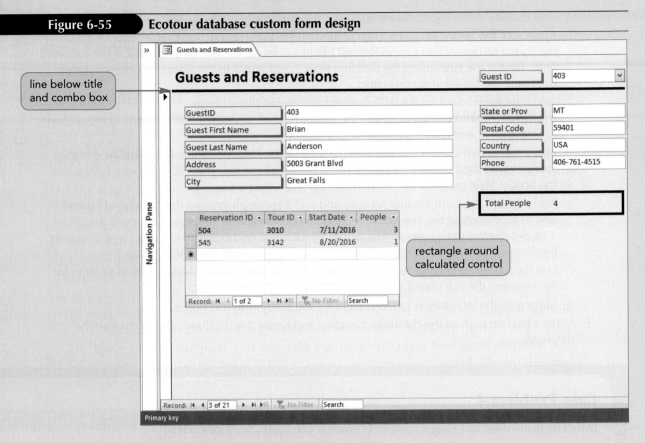

a. Add the title in the Form Header section and apply bold formatting.

b. Add the fields from the tblGuest table. Size the associated labels so they're all the same length. Size the text boxes in variable lengths to fit a reasonable amount of data, as shown in Figure 6-55.

c. Make sure the form's Record Source property is set to tblGuest, and then add a combo box in the Form Header section to find GuestID field values.

d. Add a subform based on the tblReservation table, name the subform **frmGuestsWithReservationsSubform**, delete the subform label, resize the columns in the subform to their best fit, and then resize and position the subform.

e. Add a calculated control that displays the total of the People field displayed in the subform. Set the calculated control's Tab Stop property to No, and set the calculated control's Border Style property to Transparent.

f. Add a line in the Form Header section, and add a rectangle around the calculated control and its label, setting the line thickness of both controls to the line style with the ScreenTip 3 pt. Set the rectangle color to Black (row 1, column 2 in the Standard Colors section) using the Shape Outline button in the Control Formatting group on the Format tab.

g. Use black font color for all controls, including the controls in the subform.

h. Use the "Green 1" fill color (row 2, column 7 in the Standard Colors palette) for the sections and the calculated control.

i. Use the Shadowed special effect for the labels in the Detail section, except for the calculated control label, and the Form Header section, except for the title.

j. Make sure the tab order is top-to-bottom and left-to-right for the main form text boxes.

8. Make a backup copy of the database, compact and repair the database, and then close the database.

ACCESS

TUTORIAL **7**

OBJECTIVES

Session 7.1
- View, filter, and copy report information in Report view
- Modify a report in Layout view
- Modify a report in Design view

Session 7.2
- Design and create a custom report
- Sort and group data in a report
- Add, move, resize, and align controls in a report
- Add lines to a report
- Hide duplicate values in a report

Session 7.3
- Add the date, page numbers, and title to a report
- Create and modify mailing labels

Creating Custom Reports

Creating Custom Reports for Chatham Community Health Services

Case | *Chatham Community Health Services*

At a recent staff meeting, Kelly Schwarz, the office manager, indicated that she would like to make some changes to an existing report in the database. She also requested a new report that she can use to produce a printed list of all invoices for all visits.

In this tutorial, you will modify an existing report and create the new report for Kelly. In modifying and building these reports, you will use many Access report customization features, including grouping data, calculating totals, and adding lines to separate report sections. These features will enhance Kelly's reports and make them easier to read and use.

STARTING DATA FILES

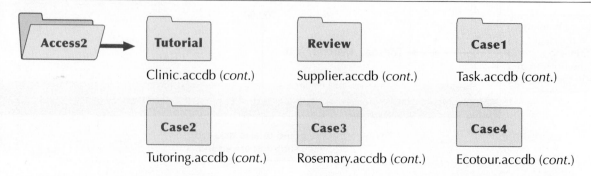

Access2 → Tutorial
Clinic.accdb (*cont.*)

Review
Supplier.accdb (*cont.*)

Case1
Task.accdb (*cont.*)

Case2
Tutoring.accdb (*cont.*)

Case3
Rosemary.accdb (*cont.*)

Case4
Ecotour.accdb (*cont.*)

Session 7.1 Visual Overview:

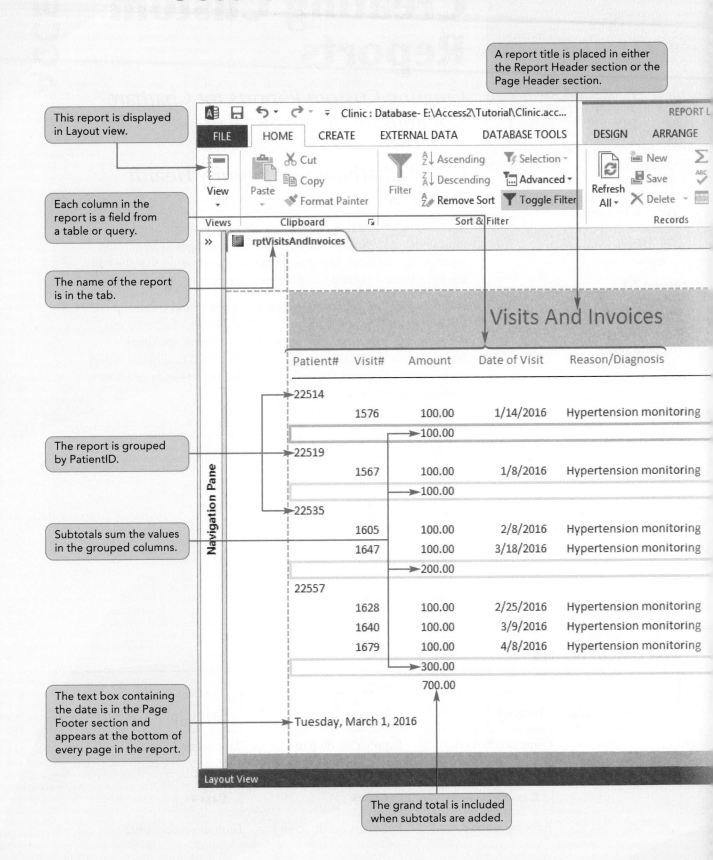

A report title is placed in either the Report Header section or the Page Header section.

This report is displayed in Layout view.

Each column in the report is a field from a table or query.

The name of the report is in the tab.

The report is grouped by PatientID.

Subtotals sum the values in the grouped columns.

The text box containing the date is in the Page Footer section and appears at the bottom of every page in the report.

The grand total is included when subtotals are added.

Clinic : Database- E:\Access2\Tutorial\Clinic.acc...

FILE   HOME   CREATE   EXTERNAL DATA   DATABASE TOOLS   DESIGN   ARRANGE

Cut
Copy
Format Painter

Paste   View

Filter

Ascending
Descending
Remove Sort

Selection
Advanced
Toggle Filter

Refresh All

New
Save
Delete

Views   Clipboard   Sort & Filter   Records

rptVisitsAndInvoices

Visits And Invoices

Patient#	Visit#	Amount	Date of Visit	Reason/Diagnosis
22514				
	1576	100.00	1/14/2016	Hypertension monitoring
		100.00		
22519				
	1567	100.00	1/8/2016	Hypertension monitoring
		100.00		
22535				
	1605	100.00	2/8/2016	Hypertension monitoring
	1647	100.00	3/18/2016	Hypertension monitoring
		200.00		
22557				
	1628	100.00	2/25/2016	Hypertension monitoring
	1640	100.00	3/9/2016	Hypertension monitoring
	1679	100.00	4/8/2016	Hypertension monitoring
		300.00		
		700.00		

Tuesday, March 1, 2016

Layout View

Report Sections

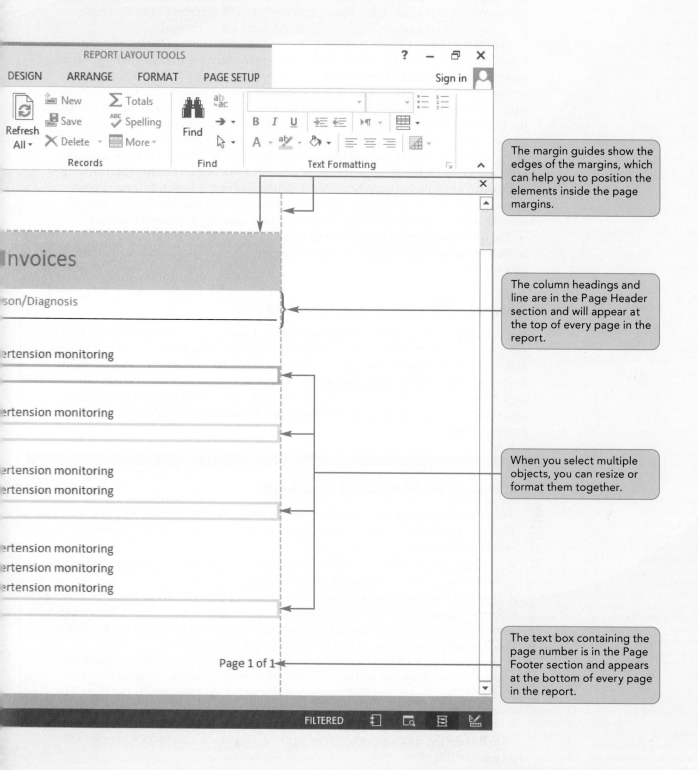

The margin guides show the edges of the margins, which can help you to position the elements inside the page margins.

The column headings and line are in the Page Header section and will appear at the top of every page in the report.

When you select multiple objects, you can resize or format them together.

The text box containing the page number is in the Page Footer section and appears at the bottom of every page in the report.

Customizing Existing Reports

A report is a formatted output (screen display or printout) of the contents of one or more tables in a database. Although you can format and print data using datasheets, queries, and forms, reports offer greater flexibility and provide a more professional, readable appearance. For example, a billing statement created using a datasheet would not look professional, but the staff at Chatham Community Health Services can easily create professional-looking billing statements from the database using reports.

Before Raj Gupta joined Chatham Community Health Services to enhance the Clinic database, Kelly Schwarz and her staff created two reports. Kelly used the Report tool to create the rptVisitsAndInvoices report and the Report Wizard to create the rptPatientsAndVisits report. One of Kelly's staff members changed the rptPatientsAnd-Visits report in Layout view by modifying the title, moving and resizing fields, changing the font color of field names, and inserting a picture. The rptPatientsAndVisits report is an example of a custom report. When you modify a report created by the Report tool or the Report Wizard in Layout view or in Design view, or when you create a report from scratch in Layout view or in Design view, you produce a **custom report**. You need to produce a custom report whenever the Report tool or the Report Wizard cannot automatically create the specific report you need, or when you need to fine-tune an existing report to fix formatting problems or to add controls and special features.

The rptVisitsAndInvoices report is included in the Clinic database. Kelly asks Raj to review the rptVisitsAndInvoices report and make improvements to it so it's more user friendly.

Viewing a Report in Report View

You can view reports on screen in Print Preview, Layout view, Design view, and Report view. You've already viewed and worked with reports in Print Preview and Layout view. Making modifications to reports in Design view is similar to making changes to forms in Design view. **Report view** provides an interactive view of a report. You can use Report view to view the contents of a report and to apply a filter to its data. You can also copy selected portions of the report to the Clipboard and use the selected data in another program.

INSIGHT

Choosing the View to Use for a Report

You can view a report on screen using Report view, Print Preview, Layout view, or Design view. Which view you choose depends on what you intend to do with the report and its data.

- Use Report view when you want to filter the report data before printing a report, or when you want to copy a selected portion of a report.
- Use Print Preview when you want to see what a report will look like when it is printed. Print Preview is the only view in which you can navigate the pages of a report, zoom in or out, or view a **multiple-column report**, which is a report that prints the same collection of field values in two or more sets across the page.
- Use Layout view when you want to modify a report while seeing actual report data.
- Use Design view when you want to fine-tune a report's design, or when you want to add lines, rectangles, and other controls that are available only in Design view.

You'll open the rptVisitsAndInvoices report in Report view and you'll interact with the report in this view.

To interact with the rptVisitsAndInvoices report in Report view:

1. Start Access, and then open the **Clinic** database you worked with in Tutorials 5 and 6.

   Trouble? If the Security Warning is displayed below the Ribbon, either the Clinic database is not located in the Access2 ▸ Tutorial folder or you did not designate that folder as a trusted folder. Make sure you opened the database in the Access2 ▸ Tutorial folder, and make sure that it's designated as a trusted folder.

2. Open the Navigation Pane, scroll down the Navigation Pane (if necessary), double-click **rptVisitsAndInvoices**, and then close the Navigation Pane. The rptVisitsAndInvoices report opens in Report view.

   In Report view, you can view the live version of the report prior to printing it, just as you can do in Print Preview. Unlike Print Preview, Report view lets you apply filters to the report before printing it. You'll apply a text filter to the rptVisitsAndInvoices report.

3. Scroll down to Patient ID 22514: Visit ID 1576, right-click **Hypertension monitoring** in the Reason column to open the shortcut menu, and then point to **Text Filters**. A submenu of filter options for the Text field opens. See Figure 7-1.

Figure 7-1	Filter options for a Text field in Report view

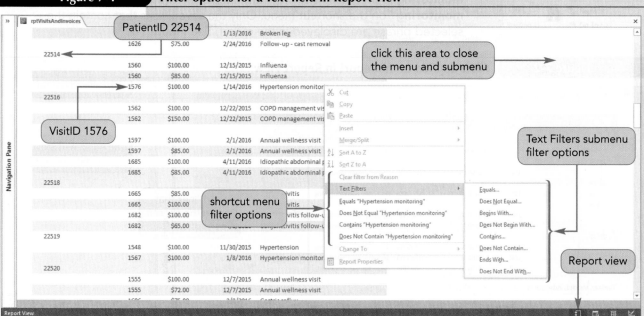

Trouble? Your Text Filters submenu may open to the left of the shortcut menu when you click the right side of the text in the Reason column. This will not cause a problem.

The filter options that appear on the shortcut menu depend on the selected field's data type and the selected value. Because you clicked the Reason field value without selecting a portion of the value, the shortcut menu displays filter options—various conditions using the value "Hypertension monitoring"—for the entire Reason field value. You'll close the menus and select a portion of the Reason column value to explore a different way of filtering the report.

Figure 7-6	After resizing columns in Layout view

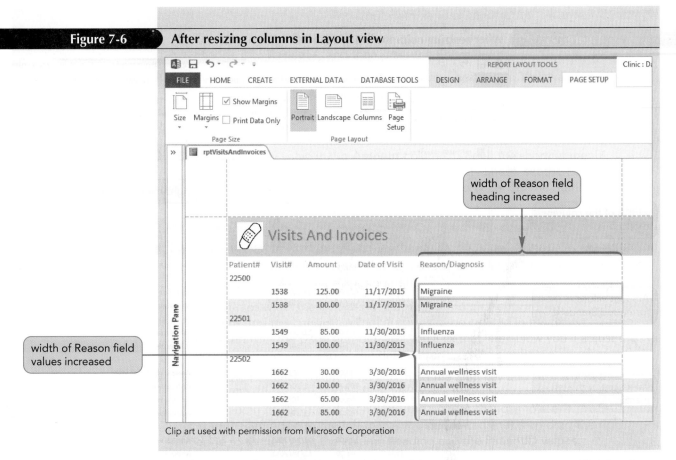

Clip art used with permission from Microsoft Corporation

Kelly doesn't think the picture at the top of the report is necessary, so you'll delete it and center the report heading. You'll also adjust the width of the page and remove the alternate row color.

To modify the appearance of the report:

1. Scroll to the top of the report, right-click the picture at the top of the report to open the shortcut menu, and then click **Delete** to remove the picture.

2. Click the **Visits And Invoices** title to select it, and then move it to the left-margin guide.

3. Drag the right edge of the title to the right-margin guide to increase the size of the title box to the full width of the page.

4. Click the **FORMAT** tab, and then in the Font group, click the **Center** button to center the title in the title box.

   Kelly finds the alternate row color setting in the group header and detail lines distracting, and asks you to remove this feature.

5. Click to the left of the left-margin guide to the left of the first PatientID value to select the group headers, in the Background group click the **Alternate Row Color** arrow to display the gallery of available colors, and then at the bottom of the gallery, click **No Color**. The alternate row color is removed from the PatientID rows.

You've removed the alternate row color from the PatientID values in the report, and next you'll remove the alternate row color from the detail lines. Because the Alternate Row Color button is now set to "No Color," you can just click the button to remove the color.

6. Click to the left of the left-margin guide next to the first VisitID in the first Patient record detail lines, and then in the Background group click the **Alternate Row Color** button to remove the alternate row color from the group header lines.

Kelly's last change to the report is to add a grand total of the Amount field values. First, you must select the Amount column or one of the values in the column.

To add a grand total to the report in Layout view:

1. In the detail line for VisitID 1538, click **125.00** in the Amount column, click the **DESIGN tab**, and then in the Grouping & Totals group, click the **Totals** button to display the Totals menu. See Figure 7-7.

Figure 7-7	Displaying options on the Totals menu

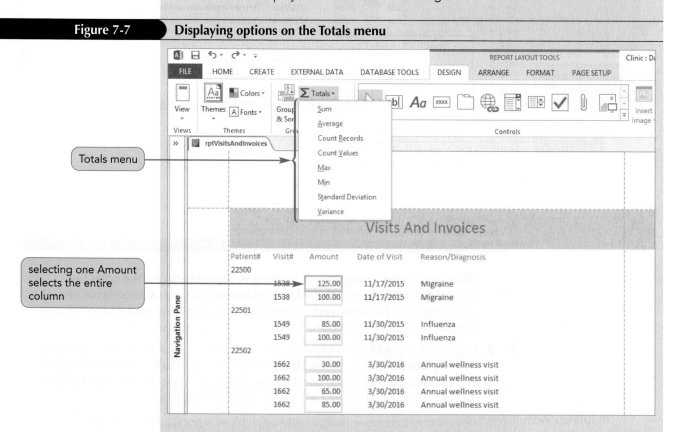

Totals menu

selecting one Amount selects the entire column

You select one of the eight aggregate functions on the Totals menu to summarize values in the selected column. To calculate and display the grand total visit amount, you'll select the Sum aggregate function.

TIP
A text box displays pound signs when the text box is too narrow to display the full field value.

2. Click **Sum** in the Totals menu, scroll to the bottom of the report, and then if the last text box contains ###### instead of numbers, click the text box to select it, then drag its left edge to the left to increase its width. In addition to the grand total of 20,703.00, subtotals for each group of visits are displayed for each PatientID field value (423.00 for the last patient). See Figure 7-8.

A report in Design view is divided into seven sections:

- **Report Header section**—appears once at the beginning of a report and is used for report titles, company logos, report introductions, dates, visual elements such as lines, and cover pages.
- **Page Header section**—appears at the top of each page of a report and is used for page numbers, column headings, report titles, and report dates.
- **Group Header section**—appears before each group of records that share the same sort field value, and usually displays the group name and the sort field value for the group.
- **Detail section**—contains the bound controls to display the field values for each record in the record source.
- **Group Footer section**—appears after each group of records that share the same sort field value, and usually displays subtotals or counts for the records in that group.
- **Page Footer section**—appears at the bottom of each page of a report and is used for page numbers, brief explanations of symbols or abbreviations, or other information such as a company name.
- **Report Footer section**—appears once at the end of a report and is used for report totals and other summary information.

To view and modify the report in Design view:

▶ **1.** Switch to Design view. See Figure 7-10.

Figure 7-10	**rptVisitsAndInvoices report in Design view**

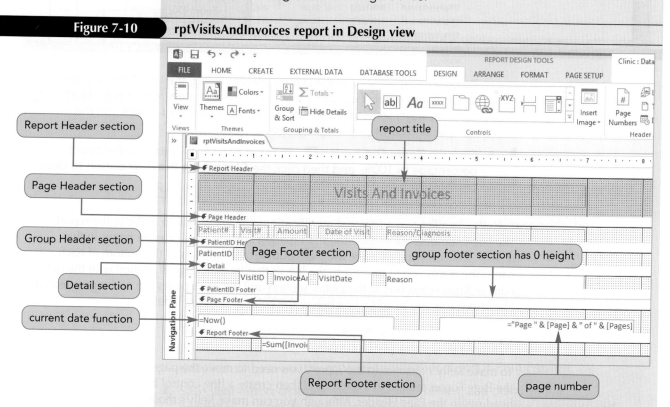

Notice that Design view for a report has most of the same components as Design view for a form. For example, Design view for forms and reports includes horizontal and vertical rulers, grids in each section, and similar buttons in the groups on the DESIGN tab.

Design view for the rptVisitsAndInvoices report displays seven sections: the Report Header section contains the report title; the Page Header section contains the column heading labels; the Group Header section (PatientID Header) contains the PatientID grouping field; the Detail section contains the bound controls to display the field values for each record in the record source (tblVisit); the Group Footer section (PatientID Footer) isn't displayed in the report; the Page Footer section contains the current date and the page number; and the Report Footer section contains the Sum function, which calculates the grand total of the InvoiceAmt field values.

You'll begin on Kelly's changes by moving the page number control in the Page Footer section.

2. Click the **Page Number** text box (the control on the right side of the Page Footer section), and then press the ← key to move the text box to the left until the right edge of the text box is roughly aligned with the right edge of the Reason text box in the Detail section.

   Trouble? If the page number text box overlaps the date text box, don't worry about it. The contents of both will still be displayed.

3. With the Page Number text box still selected, hold down the **Shift** key, click the **Reason** text box, and then release the **Shift** key. Both controls are now selected.

4. Right-click one of the selected controls, point to **Align** on the shortcut menu, and then click **Right**. Both controls are now aligned on their right edges.

   Finally, you'll create the line in the Page Header section.

5. Drag the lower edge of the Page Header section down to increase the height approximately half an inch more. You'll resize this again after the line is created.

   You'll hold the Shift key down while dragging the mouse pointer to create a horizontal line easily.

6. On the DESIGN tab, in the Controls group, click the **More** button and then click the **Line** button ⬜.

7. Under the headings in the Page Header section, position the mouse pointer approximately two grid dots below the page header text boxes, press and hold the **Shift** key, drag to the right to create a horizontal line that will stretch the width of the page and align with the right edge of the Reason text boxes, and then release the Shift key. Holding the Shift key while drawing or extending a line snaps the line to either horizontal or vertical—whichever is nearest to the angle at which the line is drawn.

8. Drag the lower edge of the Page header section up so it is approximately two grid dots below the line. See Figure 7-11.

Figure 7-11   **After modifying the rptVisitsAndInvoices report in Design view**

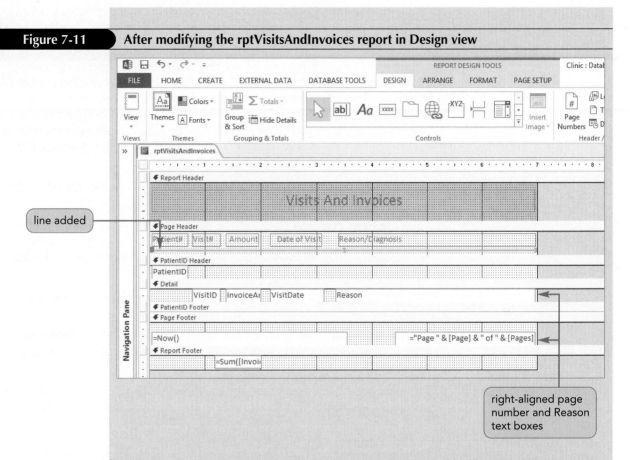

line added

right-aligned page number and Reason text boxes

> **9.** Save your report changes, switch to Print Preview, and then scroll and use the navigation buttons to page through the report, paying particular attention to the placement of the line in the Page Header section and the page number in the Page Footer section. The page number data is right-aligned in the text box, so the text appears flush with the right margin. The data in the Reason field value text boxes are left-aligned, so this data does not appear flush with the right margin.
>
> **Trouble?** If you resize a field to position it outside the current margin, the report may widen to accommodate it, triggering a dialog box about the section width being greater than the page width. If this dialog box opens, click OK, manually move form elements as necessary so that no elements extend past 7.5 inches, and then adjust the report width to 7.5 inches.

> **10.** Save and close the report.

> **11.** If you are not continuing on to the next session, close the Clinic database.

Kelly is happy with the changes you've made to the rptVisitsAndInvoices report. In the next session, you create a new custom report for her based on queries instead of tables.

REVIEW

Session 7.1 Quick Check

1. What is a custom report?
2. You can view a report in Report view. What other actions can you perform in Report view?
3. What is a grouping field?
4. List and describe the seven sections of an Access report.

Session 7.2 Visual Overview:

The InvoiceItem Group Header section contains the text box for the InvoiceItem value. Records with a common InvoiceItem value will be grouped together in the report.

The expression used to calculate the subtotal for the InvoiceItem group is placed in the InvoiceItem Group Footer section.

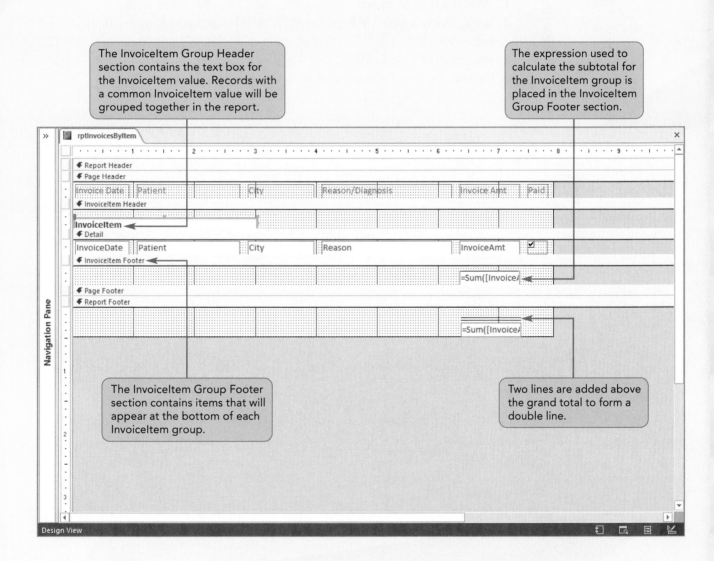

The InvoiceItem Group Footer section contains items that will appear at the bottom of each InvoiceItem group.

Two lines are added above the grand total to form a double line.

Report Design view and Print Preview

The detail items are sorted in ascending order beneath each group item.

The group band field is a field that is used to group the detail items.

A yes/no or true/false field is represented with check boxes in a report.

The field heading labels are in the Page Header section and appear at the top of each page.

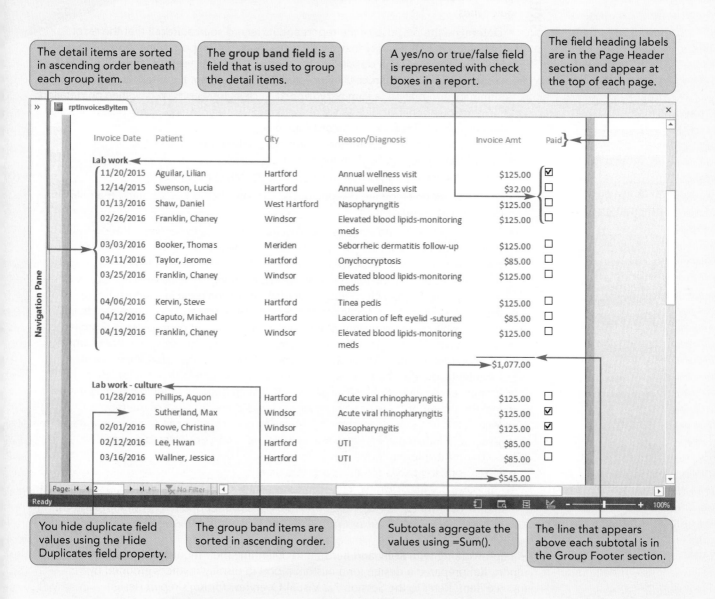

Invoice Date	Patient	City	Reason/Diagnosis	Invoice Amt	Paid
Lab work					
11/20/2015	Aguilar, Lilian	Hartford	Annual wellness visit	$125.00	☑
12/14/2015	Swenson, Lucia	Hartford	Annual wellness visit	$32.00	☐
01/13/2016	Shaw, Daniel	West Hartford	Nasopharyngitis	$125.00	☐
02/26/2016	Franklin, Chaney	Windsor	Elevated blood lipids-monitoring meds	$125.00	☐
03/03/2016	Booker, Thomas	Meriden	Seborrheic dermatitis follow-up	$125.00	☐
03/11/2016	Taylor, Jerome	Hartford	Onychocryptosis	$85.00	☐
03/25/2016	Franklin, Chaney	Windsor	Elevated blood lipids-monitoring meds	$125.00	☐
04/06/2016	Kervin, Steve	Hartford	Tinea pedis	$125.00	☐
04/12/2016	Caputo, Michael	Hartford	Laceration of left eyelid -sutured	$85.00	☐
04/19/2016	Franklin, Chaney	Windsor	Elevated blood lipids-monitoring meds	$125.00	☐
				$1,077.00	
Lab work - culture					
01/28/2016	Phillips, Aquon	Hartford	Acute viral rhinopharyngitis	$125.00	☐
	Sutherland, Max	Windsor	Acute viral rhinopharyngitis	$125.00	☑
02/01/2016	Rowe, Christina	Windsor	Nasopharyngitis	$125.00	☑
02/12/2016	Lee, Hwan	Hartford	UTI	$85.00	☐
03/16/2016	Wallner, Jessica	Hartford	UTI	$85.00	☐
				$545.00	

Page: ◄ ◄ 2 ► ►► No Filter ◄
Ready   100%

You hide duplicate field values using the Hide Duplicates field property.

The group band items are sorted in ascending order.

Subtotals aggregate the values using =Sum().

The line that appears above each subtotal is in the Group Footer section.

Designing a Custom Report

Before you create a custom report, you should first plan the report's contents and appearance.

PROSKILLS

Decision Making: Guidelines for Designing and Formatting a Report

When you plan a report, you should keep in mind the following report design guidelines:

- Determine the purpose of the report and its record source. Recall that the record source is a table or query that provides the fields for a report. If the report displays detailed information (a **detail report**), such as a list of all visits, then the report will display fields from the record source in the Detail section. If the report displays only summary information (a **summary report**), such as total visits by city, then no detailed information appears; only grand totals and possibly subtotals appear based on calculations using fields from the record source.
- Determine the sort order for the information in the report.
- Identify any grouping fields in the report.
- Consider creating a sketch of the report design using pen and paper.

At the same time you are designing a report, you should keep in mind the following report formatting guidelines:

- Balance the report's attractiveness against its readability and economy. Keep in mind that an attractive, readable, two-page report is more economical than a report of three pages or more. Unlike forms, which usually display one record at a time in the main form, reports display multiple records. Instead of arranging fields vertically as you do in a form, you usually position fields horizontally across the page in a report. Typically, you set the detail lines to be single space in a report. At the same time, make sure to include enough white space between columns so the values do not overlap or run together.
- Group related fields and position them in a meaningful, logical order. For example, position identifying fields, such as names and codes, on the left. Group together all location fields, such as street and city, and position them in their customary order.
- Identify each column of field values with a column heading label that names the field.
- Include the report title, page number, and date on every page of the report.
- Identify the end of a report either by displaying grand totals or an end-of-report message.
- Use few colors, fonts, and graphics to keep the report uncluttered and to keep the focus on the information.
- Use a consistent style for all reports in a database.

By following these report design and formatting guidelines, you'll create reports that make it easier for users to conduct their daily business and to make better decisions.

After working with Kelly and her staff to determine their requirements for a new report, Raj prepared a design for a custom report to display invoices grouped by invoice item. Refer to the Session 7.2 Visual Overview for Raj's report design.

The custom report will list the records for all invoices and will contain five sections:

- The Page Header section will contain the report title ("Invoices by Item") centered between the current date on the left and the page number on the right. A horizontal line will separate the column heading labels from the rest of the report page. From your work with the Report tool and the Report Wizard, you know that, by default, Access places the report title in the Report Header section and the date and page number in the Page Footer section. Sarah prefers that the date, report title, and page number appear at the top of each page, so you need to place this information in the custom report's Page Header section.

- The InvoiceItem field value from the tblBilling table will be displayed in a Group Header section.
- The Detail section will contain the InvoiceDate, InvoiceAmt, and InvoicePaid field values from the tblBilling table; the Reason field value from the tblVisit table; the City field value from the tblPatient table; and the Patient calculated field value from the qryPatientsByName query. The detail records will be sorted in ascending value by the InvoiceDate field.
- A subtotal of the InvoiceAmt field values will be displayed below a line in the Group Footer section.
- The grand total of the InvoiceAmt field values will be displayed below a double line in the Report Footer section.

Before you start creating the custom report, you need to create a query that will serve as the record source for the report.

Creating a Query for a Custom Report

The data for a report can come from a single table, from a single query based on one or more tables, or from multiple tables and/or queries. Raj's report will contain data from the tblBilling, tblVisit, and tblPatient tables, and from the qryPatientsByName query. You'll use the Simple Query Wizard to create a query to retrieve all the data required for the custom report and to serve as the report's record source. A query filters data from one or more tables using criteria that can be quite complex. Creating a report based on a query allows you to display and distribute the results of the query in a readable, professional format, rather than only in a datasheet view.

To create the query to serve as the report's record source:

1. If you took a break after the previous session, make sure that the Clinic database is open and the Navigation Pane is closed.

2. Click the **CREATE tab**, in the Queries group click the **Query Wizard** button, make sure **Simple Query Wizard** is selected, and then click the **OK** button. The first Simple Query Wizard dialog box opens.

   You need to select fields from the tblBilling, tblVisit, and tblPatient tables, and from the qryPatientsByName query, in that order.

3. In the Tables/Queries box, select **Table:tblInvoiceItem**, and then move the **InvoiceItem** field to the Selected Fields box.

4. In the Tables/Queries box, select **Table: tblBilling**, and then move the **InvoiceItemID**, **InvoiceDate**, **InvoiceAmt**, and **InvoicePaid** fields, in that order, to the Selected Fields box.

5. In the Tables/Queries box, select **Table: tblVisit**, and then move the **Reason** field to the Selected Fields box.

6. In the Tables/Queries box, select **Table: tblPatient**, and then move the **City** field to the Selected Fields box.

7. In the Tables/Queries box, select **Query: qryPatientsByName**, move the **Patient** calculated field to the Selected Fields box, and then click the **Next** button.

8. Make sure the **Detail (shows every field of every record)** option button is selected, and then click the **Next** button to open the final Simple Query Wizard dialog box.

Referring to Raj's report design, you'll add six of the eight fields to the report in a tabular layout, which is the default control layout when you add fields to a report in Layout view.

▶ **5.** Double-click **InvoiceDate** in the Field List pane, and then, in order, double-click **Patient**, **City**, **Reason**, **InvoiceAmt**, and **InvoicePaid** in the Field List pane. The six bound controls are displayed in a tabular layout in the report. See Figure 7-14.

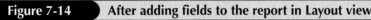

Figure 7-14	After adding fields to the report in Layout view

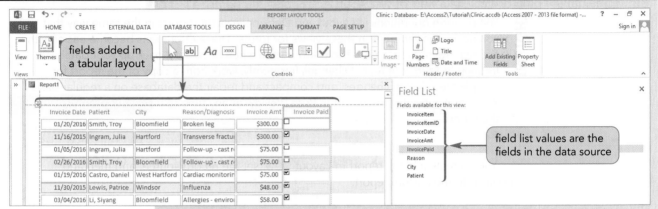

Trouble? If you add the wrong field to the report, click the field's column heading, press and hold the Shift key, click one of the field values in the column to select the column, release the Shift key, click the HOME tab on the Ribbon, and then in the Records group, click the Delete button to delete the field. If you add a field in the wrong order, click the column heading in the tabular layout, press and hold the Shift key, click one of the field values in the column, release the Shift key, and then drag the column to its correct columnar position.

You'll add the sixth field, the InvoiceItem field, as a grouping field, so you are done working with the Field List pane.

▶ **6.** Close the Field List pane, and then save the report as **rptInvoicesByItem**.

Next, you'll adjust the column widths in Layout view. Also, because the Invoice Amt and Invoice Paid columns are adjacent, you'll change the rightmost column heading to Paid to save space.

To resize and rename columns in Layout view:

▶ **1.** Double-click **Invoice Paid** in the rightmost column, delete **Invoice** and the following space, and then press the **Enter** key.

▶ **2.** Drag the right edge of the **Paid** control to the left to decrease the column's width so it just fits the column heading.

▶ **3.** Click **Patient** to select the column, and then drag the right edge of the control to the right to increase its width, until it accommodates the contents of all data in the column.

▶ **4.** Repeat Step 3 to resize the **City** and **Reason** columns, as shown in Figure 7-15.

The full text will not be displayed in the Reason text boxes, which is okay for now. You'll fine-tune the adjustments and the spacing between columns later in Design view.

Figure 7-15   **After resizing and renaming columns in Layout view**

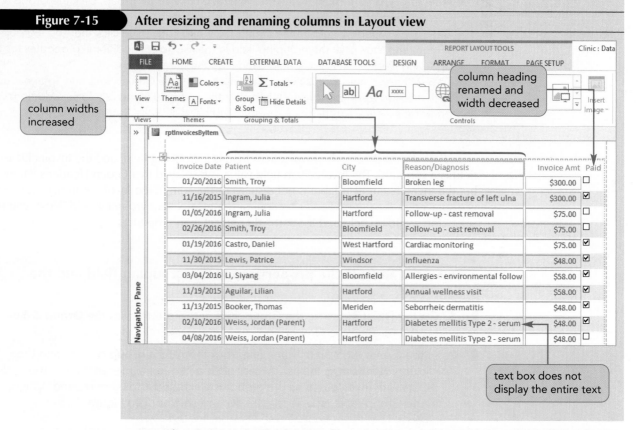

According to Raj's plan for the report (see the Session 7.2 Visual Overview), the InvoiceItem field is a grouping field that is displayed in a Group Header section. Subtotals for the InvoiceAmt field are displayed in a Group Footer section for each InvoiceItem field value. Next you need to add the sorting and grouping data to the report.

Sorting and Grouping Data in a Report

Access lets you organize records in a report by sorting them using one or more sort fields. Each sort field can also be a grouping field. If you specify a sort field as a grouping field, you can include a Group Header section and a Group Footer section for the group. A Group Header section typically includes the name of the group, and a Group Footer section typically includes a count or subtotal for records in that group. Some reports have a Group Header section but not a Group Footer section, some reports have a Group Footer section but not a Group Header section, and some reports have both sections or have neither section.

You use the Group, Sort, and Total pane to select sort fields and grouping fields for a report. Each report can have up to 10 sort fields, and any of its sort fields can also be grouping fields.

Sorting and Grouping Data in a Report

- Display the report in Layout view or Design view.
- If necessary, on the DESIGN tab, in the Grouping & Totals group, click the Group & Sort button to display the Group, Sort, and Total pane.
- To select a grouping field, in the Group, Sort, and Total pane click the Add a group button, and then click the grouping field in the list. To set additional properties for the grouping field, on the group field band click the More button.
- To select a sort field that is not a grouping field, in the Group, Sort, and Total pane click the Add a sort button, and then click the sort field in the list. To set additional properties for the sort field, on the sort field band click the More button.

In Raj's report design, the InvoiceItem field is a grouping field, and the InvoiceDate field is a sort field. The InvoiceItem field value is displayed in a Group Header section, but the InvoiceItem field label is not displayed. The sum of the InvoiceAmt field values is displayed in the Group Footer section for the InvoiceItem grouping field. Next, you'll select the grouping field and the sort field and set their properties.

To select and set the properties for the grouping field and the sort field:

1. On the DESIGN tab, in the Grouping & Totals group, click the **Group & Sort** button to open the Group, Sort, and Total pane.

2. In the Group, Sort, and Total pane, click the **Add a group** button, and then click **InvoiceItem** in the list. Access adds a Group Header section to the report with InvoiceItem as the grouping field, and adds group band options in the Group, Sort, and Total pane for this section. See Figure 7-16.

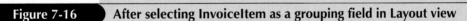

Figure 7-16   **After selecting InvoiceItem as a grouping field in Layout view**

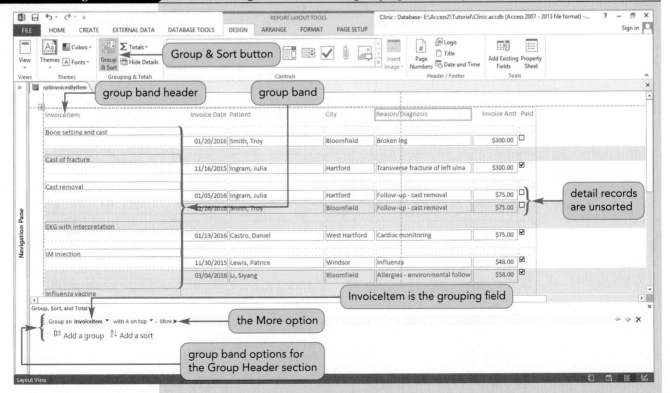

InvoiceItem is now a bound control in the report in a Group Header section that displays a field value text box. The group band options in the Group, Sort, and Total pane contains the name of the grouping field (InvoiceItem), the sort order ("with A on top" to indicate ascending), and the More option, which you click to display more options for the grouping field. You can click the "with A on top" arrow to change to descending sort order ("with Z on top").

Notice that the addition of the grouping field has moved the detail records to the right; you'll move them back to the left later in this tutorial. Also, notice that the detail records are unsorted, and Raj's design specifies an ascending sort on the InvoiceDate field. Next, you'll select this field as a secondary sort field; the InvoiceItem grouping field is the primary sort field.

3. In the Group, Sort, and Total pane, click the **Add a sort** button, and then click **InvoiceDate** in the list. Access displays the detail records in ascending order by InvoiceDate and adds a sort band for the InvoiceDate field in the Group, Sort, and Total pane.

   Next, you'll display all the options for the InvoiceItem group band field, and set group band options as shown in Raj's report design.

4. Click ⁝ to the left of the group band options to select them, and then click **More** to display all group band options. See Figure 7-17. Next, you need to delete the Invoice Item label.

Figure 7-17	After expanding the group band

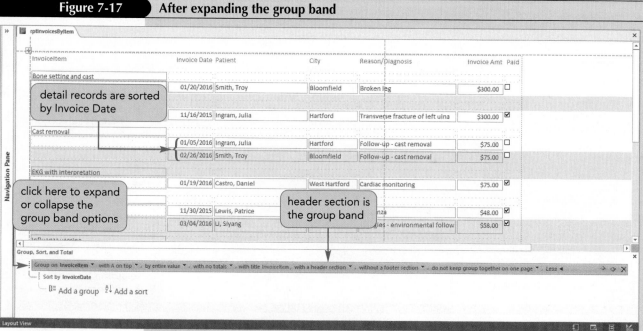

5. In the "with title Invoice Item" option, click the **Invoice Item** link to open the Zoom dialog box, press the **Delete** key to delete the expression, and then click the **OK** button. The Invoice Item label is deleted from the report, and the option in the group band options changes to "with title click to add."

   Next you'll set the Keep Together property. The **Keep Together property** prints a group header on a page only if there is enough room on the page to print the first detail record for the group; otherwise, the group header prints at the top of the next page.

▶ **6.** In the group band options, click the **do not keep group together on one page** arrow, and then click **keep header and first record together on one page**.

▶ **7.** In the group band options, click **More** to expand the options (if necessary), click the **without a footer section** arrow, and then click **with a footer section**. Access adds a Group Footer section for the InvoiceItem grouping band field, but the report doesn't display this new section until you add controls to it.

▶ **8.** In the group band options, click **More** to expand the options (if necessary), click the **with no totals** arrow to open the Totals menu, click the **Total On** arrow, click **InvoiceAmt**, make sure **Sum** is selected in the Type box, and then click the **Show Grand Total** check box. The group band options collapse.

▶ **9.** In the group band options, click **More** to expand the options (if necessary), click the **with InvoiceAmt totaled** arrow, click the **Total On** arrow, click **InvoiceAmt**, and then click the **Show subtotal in group footer** check box. This adds subtotals in the Amount column, at the bottom of each group.

▶ **10.** In the group band options, click **More** to expand the options (if necessary). The group band options shows the InvoiceAmt subtotals and a grand total added to the report. See Figure 7-18.

Figure 7-18	After setting properties in the group band

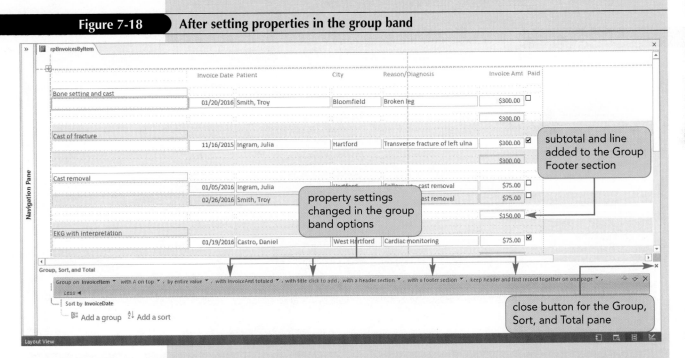

▶ **11.** Save your report changes, switch to Print Preview, and then use the navigation buttons to review every page until you reach the end of the report—noticing in particular the details of the report format and the effects of the Keep Together property. Also, notice that because the grouping field forces the detail values to the right, the current report design prints the detail values across two pages.

Before you can move the detail values to the left onto one page, you need to remove all controls from the control layout.

To remove controls from a control layout in Layout view:

1. Switch to Layout view.

2. Click the **layout selector** ⊞, which is located at the top-left corner of the column heading line, to select the entire control layout. An orange outline, which identifies the controls that you've selected, appears around the labels and text boxes in the report, and a yellow outline appears around the other controls in the report.

3. Right-click one of the selected controls to open the shortcut menu, point to **Layout**, and then click **Remove Layout**. This removes the selected controls from the layout so they can be moved without affecting the other controls.

   Next you'll move all the controls to the left except for the InvoiceItem text box. You have to be careful when you move the remaining controls to the left. If you try to select all the column headings and the text boxes, you're likely to miss the subtotal and grand total controls. The safest technique is to select all controls in the report, and then remove the InvoiceItem text box from the selection. This latter step, removing individual controls from a selection, must be done in Design view because it doesn't work in Layout view.

4. Switch to Design view, click the **Format** tab, and then in the Selection group, click the **Select All** button. All controls in the report are now selected.

5. Hold down the **Shift** key, click the **InvoiceItem** text box in the InvoiceItem Header section to remove this control from the selection, and then release the **Shift** key.

6. Hold down the ← key to move the selected controls rapidly to the left edge of the report, and then release the ← key. See Figure 7-19.

Figure 7-19   After moving all controls to the left in the report

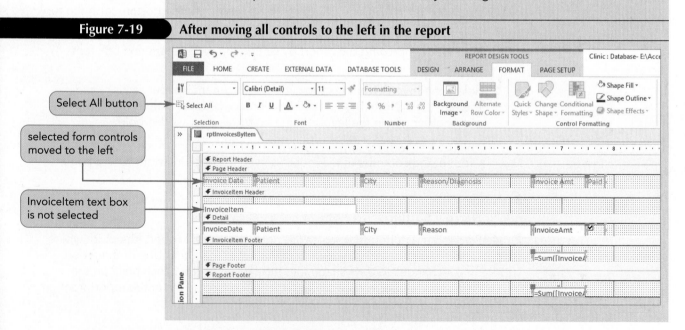

The grand total of the InvoiceAmt field values is displayed at the end of the report, and subtotals are displayed for each unique InvoiceItem field value in the Group Footer section. It's possible for subtotals to appear in an orphaned footer section. An **orphaned footer section** appears by itself at the top of a page, and the detail lines for the section appear on the previous page. When you set the Keep Together property for the grouping field, you set it to keep the group and the first detail record together on one page to

prevent an **orphaned header section**, which is a section that appears by itself at the bottom of a page. To prevent both types of orphaned sections, you'll set the Keep Together property to keep the whole group together on one page.

In addition, you need to fine-tune the sizes of the text boxes in the Detail section, adjust the spacing between columns, and make other adjustments to the current content of the report design before adding a report title, the date, and page number to the Page Header section. You'll make most of these report design changes in Design view.

Working with Controls in Design View

Compared to Layout view, Design view gives you greater control over the placement and sizing of controls, and lets you add and manipulate many more controls; however, this power comes at the expense of not being able to see live data in the controls to guide you as you make changes.

The rptInvoicesByItem report has five sections that contain controls: the Page Header section contains the six column heading labels; the InvoiceItem Header section (a Group Header section) contains the InvoiceItem text box; the Detail section contains the six bound controls; the InvoiceItem Footer section (a Group Footer section) contains a line and the subtotal text box; and the Report Footer section contains a line and the grand total text box.

You'll move and resize controls in the report in Design view. The Group, Sort, and Total pane is still open, so first you'll change the Keep Together property setting.

To change the report size:

▶ 1. In the Group, Sort, and Total pane, click ⁝ to the left of the group band options to select it, click **More** to display all group options, click the **keep header and first record together on one page** arrow, click **keep whole group together on one page**, and then click the Close button ⊠ in the top right corner of the Group, Sort, and Total pane to close it.

   You'll start improving the report by setting the InvoiceItem text box font to bold.

▶ 2. Select the **InvoiceItem** text box in the InvoiceItem Header section, and then on the FORMAT tab, in the Font group, click the **Bold** button. The placeholder text in the InvoiceItem text box is displayed in bold.

   The report's width is approximately 16 inches, which is much wider than the width of the contents of the report, so you'll reduce its width to fit a page that is 8.5 inches wide with narrow margins.

▶ 3. Click the PAGE SETUP tab, click the **Margins button**, and then click the **Narrow button**.

▶ 4. Scroll to the right until you see the right edge of the report (the point where the dotted grid ends), move the pointer over the right edge of the report until it changes to a ↔ shape, drag to the left to the 8-inch mark on the horizontal ruler, and then scroll to the left to display the entire report from the left (if necessary). See Figure 7-20.

Figure 7-20   After reducing the width of the report

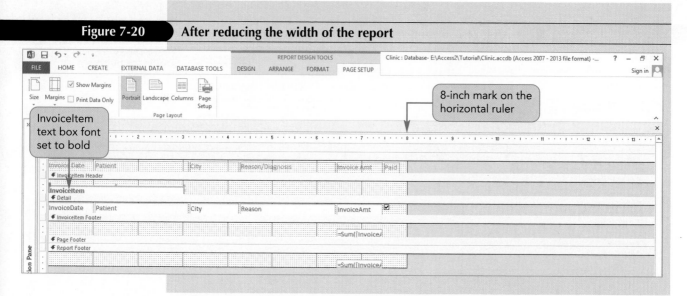

The text boxes in the Detail section are crowded together with little space between them, and the form controls are too wide for a page with normal margins. Your reports shouldn't have too much space between columns, but reports are easier to read when the columns are separated more than they are in the rptInvoicesByItem report. Sometimes the amount of spacing is dictated by the users of the report, but you also need to work with the minimum size of the form controls as well. To design this report to fit on a page with narrow margins, the report width will have to be 8.5 inches minus the left and right margins of 0.25 inches each, which results in a maximum report width of 8 inches (8.5"–0.25"–0.25"). This is the size you already used to reduce the report grid in Design view. Next, you'll add some space between the columns while ensuring they still fit in the 8-inch report width. First, you'll resize the Invoice Date and Patient form controls in Layout view, and then you'll arrange the columns in Design view. You'll size the corresponding heading and field value text boxes for each column to be the same width.

To move and resize controls in the report:

1. Switch to Layout view, click the **Invoice Date** heading, press and hold the **Shift** key, and then click on one of the Invoice Date field values to select all of the Invoice Date text boxes.

2. Drag the right side of the controls to the left to reduce the size of the text boxes to fit the data better.

3. Repeat Steps 1 and 2 for the Patient heading and field values to reduce their widths to fit the data better.

   Next you'll adjust the spacing between the controls to distribute them evenly across the page.

4. Switch to Design view, click the **FORMAT** tab, and then in the Selection group click the **Select All button** to select all controls.

5. Press and hold the **Shift** key and click the **Invoice Item** control to deselect it.

6. Click the **ARRANGE** tab, in the Size & Ordering group click the **Size/Space button**, and then click **Equal Horizontal**. The form controls are shifted horizontally so the spacing between them is equal. See Figure 7-21.

Figure 7-21   After resizing and spacing controls in Design view

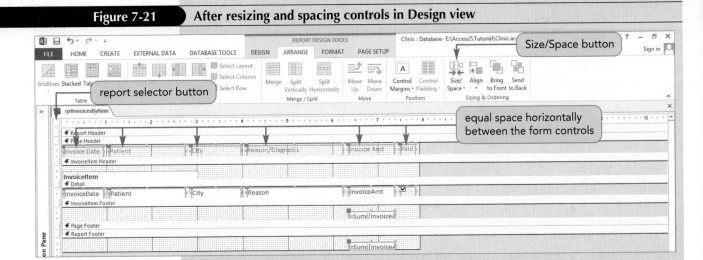

The Patient and Reason text boxes may not be wide enough to display the entire field value in all cases. For the Patient and Reason text boxes, you'll set their Can Grow property to Yes. The **Can Grow property**, when set to Yes, expands a text box vertically to fit the field value when the report is printed, previewed, or viewed in Layout and Report views.

7. Click the **DESIGN** tab, click the **Report Selector** button to deselect all controls, select the **Patient** and **Reason** text boxes in the Detail section, right-click one of the selected controls, and then on the contextual menu click **Properties**.

8. On the Property Sheet, click the **Format** tab, scroll down the Property Sheet to the Can Grow property, and then if the Can Grow property is set to Yes, set it to **No**. The default setting for this feature may not work properly, so to ensure the setting is applied correctly, you must make sure it is first set to No.

   Trouble? If you don't see the CanGrow property on the Format tab, double-check to ensure you've selected the Patient and Reason controls in the Detail section, not in the Page Header section.

9. Change the Can Grow property value to **Yes**, close the Property Sheet, and then save your report changes.

10. Switch to Print Preview, and then review every page of the report, ending on the last page. See Figure 7-22.

| Figure 7-22 | Reviewing the report changes in Print Preview |

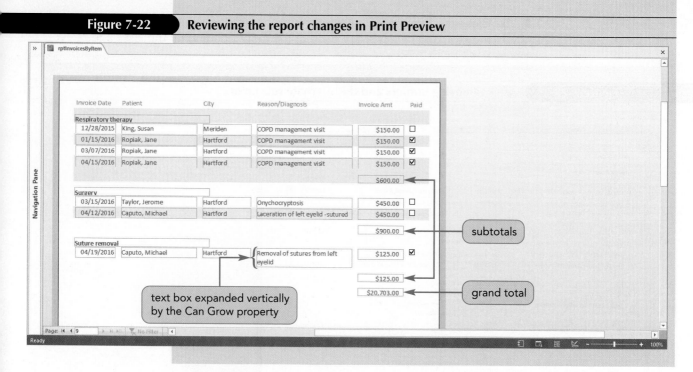

The groups stay together on one page, except for the groups that have too many detail lines to fit on one page. The Can Grow property correctly expands the height of the Patient and Reason text boxes.

Also, the lines that were displayed above the subtotals and grand total are no longer displayed, and the commas in the values are not fully visible. You'll add those lines back in the report and resize the text boxes. First, Raj thinks the borders around the text boxes and the alternate row color are too distracting, so you'll remove them from the report.

To remove the borders and alternate row color:

1. Close the Print Preview and switch to Design view.

2. Click the **FORMAT** tab, and then in the Selection group, click the **Select All** button.

3. Right-click one of the selected controls, and then click **Properties** on the shortcut menu to open the Property Sheet.

4. Click the **Format** tab (if necessary) in the Property Sheet, click the right side of the **Border Style** box, and then click **Transparent**. The transparent setting will remove the boxes from the report by making them transparent.

TIP

You can also control the Alternate Back Color property using the Alternate Row Color button because the two options set the same property.

5. Click the **InvoiceItem Header** section bar, click the right side of the **Alternate Back Color** box in the Property Sheet, and then click **No Color** at the bottom of the gallery. This setting removes the alternate row color from the InvoiceItem Header section.

6. Click the **Detail** section bar, and then on the **FORMAT** tab, in the Background group, click the **Alternate Row Color** button, and then click **No Color** at the bottom of the gallery. The Alternate Back Color property setting in the Property Sheet is now set to No Color.

7. Repeat Step 6 for the **InvoiceItem Footer** section.

> **8.** Close the Property Sheet, save your report changes, switch to Print Preview, and review every page of the report, ending on the last page. See Figure 7-23.

Figure 7-23 | **After removing borders and the alternate row color**

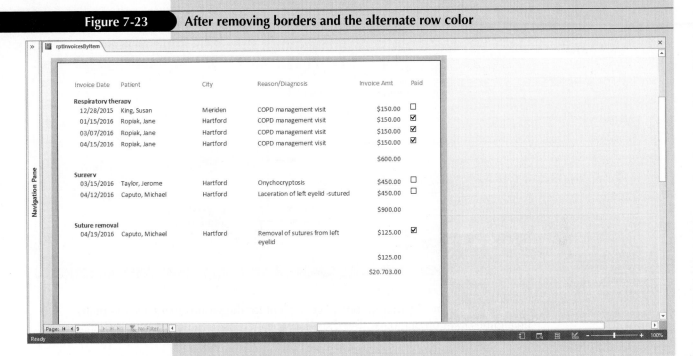

Next, you'll add lines to the report.

Adding Lines to a Report

You've used the Line tool to add lines to a form. You can also use the Line tool to add lines to a report. Previously, you added a line to separate the header content from the rest of the report. Now you'll add lines to separate the values from the subtotals and grand total. You'll switch to Design view and use the Line tool to add a single line above the subtotal control and a double line above the grand total control. First, you'll resize the subtotal and grand total text boxes.

To add lines to the report:

> **1.** Close the Print Preview and switch to Design view.

> **2.** In the InvoiceItem Footer section, click the text box control to select it, and then resize the control from the top so its height increases by one row of grid dots.

> **3.** Repeat Step 2 to resize the text box control in the Report Footer section.

> **4.** On the DESIGN tab, in the Controls group, click the **More** button to open the Controls gallery.

> **5.** Click the **Line** tool, position the pointer's plus symbol (+) in the InvoiceItem Footer section at the upper-left corner of the text box, hold down the **Shift** key, drag a horizontal line from left to right so the end of the line aligns with the upper-right corner of the text box, release the mouse button, and then release the **Shift** key.

▶ **6.** In the Report Footer section, click the text box, press the ↓ key four times to move the control down slightly in the section, and then deselect all controls.

▶ **7.** On the DESIGN tab, in the Controls group, click the **More** button, click the **Line** tool ◻, position the pointer's plus symbol (+) in the Report Footer section at the grid dot just above the upper-left corner of the text box, hold down the **Shift** key, drag a horizontal line from left to right so the end of the line aligns with the right edge of the text box, release the mouse button, and then release the **Shift** key.

Next, you'll copy and paste the line in the Report Footer section, and then align the copied line into position.

▶ **8.** Right-click the selected line in the Report Footer section, and then click **Copy** on the shortcut menu.

▶ **9.** Right-click the **Report Footer** section bar, and then click **Paste** on the shortcut menu. A copy of the line is pasted in the upper-left corner of the Report Footer section.

▶ **10.** Press the ↓ key four times to move the copied line down in the section, hold down the **Shift** key, click the original line in the Report Footer section to select both lines, release the **Shift** key, right-click the copied line to open the shortcut menu, point to **Align**, and then click **Right**. A double line is now positioned above the grand total text box.

▶ **11.** Save your report changes, switch to Print Preview, and then navigate to the last page of the report. See Figure 7-24.

| Figure 7-24 | After adding lines to the report |

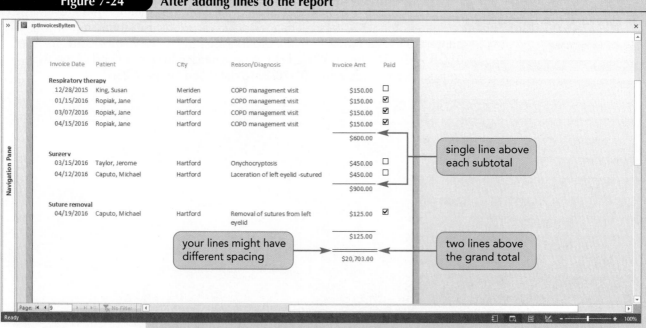

For the rptInvoicesByItem report, the InvoiceDate field is a sort field. Two or more consecutive detail report lines can have the same InvoiceDate field value. In these cases, Raj wants the InvoiceDate field value printed for the first detail line but not for subsequent detail lines because he believes it makes the printed information easier to read.

Hiding Duplicate Values in a Report

You use the **Hide Duplicates property** to hide a control in a report when the control's value is the same as that of the preceding record in the group.

REFERENCE

Hiding Duplicate Values in a Report

- Display the report in Layout or Design view.
- Open the Property Sheet for the field whose duplicate values you want to hide.
- Set the Hide Duplicates property to Yes, and then close the Property Sheet.

TIP

Use Hide Duplicates only on fields that are sorted. Otherwise it may look as if data is missing.

Your next design change to the report is to hide duplicate InvoiceDate field values in the Detail section. This change will make the report easier to read.

To hide the duplicate InvoiceDate field values:

1. Close Print Preview, switch to Design view, and then click below the grid to deselect all controls.

2. Open the Property Sheet for the **InvoiceDate** text box in the Detail section.

TIP

For properties offering a list of choices, you can double-click the property name repeatedly to cycle through the options in the list.

3. Click the **Format** tab (if necessary), scroll down the Property Sheet (if necessary), click the right side of the **Hide Duplicates** box, and then click **Yes**.

4. Close the Property Sheet, save your report changes, switch to Print Preview, navigate to page 2 (the actual page you view might vary depending on your printer) to the Lab work - Culture group to see the two invoice records for 01/28/2016. The InvoiceDate field value is hidden for the second of the two consecutive records with a 01/28/2016 date. See Figure 7-25.

| Figure 7-25 | Report in Print Preview with hidden duplicate values |

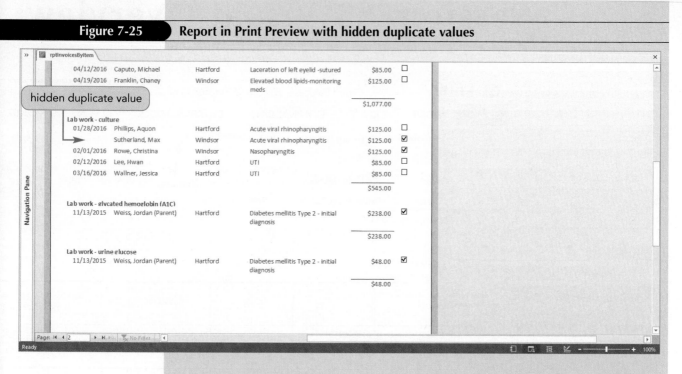

5. If you are not continuing on to the next session, close the Clinic database.

You have completed the Detail section, the Group Header section, and the Group Footer section of the custom report. In the next session, you will complete the custom report according to Raj's design by adding controls to the Page Header section.

Session 7.2 Quick Check

REVIEW

1. What is a detail report? A summary report?
2. The _____ property prints a group header on a page only if there is enough room on the page to print the first detail record for the group; otherwise, the group header prints at the top of the next page.
3. A(n) _____ section appears by itself at the top of a page, and the detail lines for the section appear on the previous page.
4. The _____ property, when set to Yes, expands a text box vertically to fit the field value when a report is printed, previewed, or viewed in Layout and Report views.
5. Why might you want to hide duplicate values in a report?

Session 7.3 Visual Overview:

The contents in the Report Header section appear at the top of the first page of the report. This Report Header section has a height of 0 and no contents.

The **Date function** will display the current date.

The Group Footer section contents appear at the bottom of each group.

The Page Footer section contents appear at the bottom of every page. This Page Footer section has 0 height and no contents.

The Report Footer section contents appear at the bottom of the last page of the report.

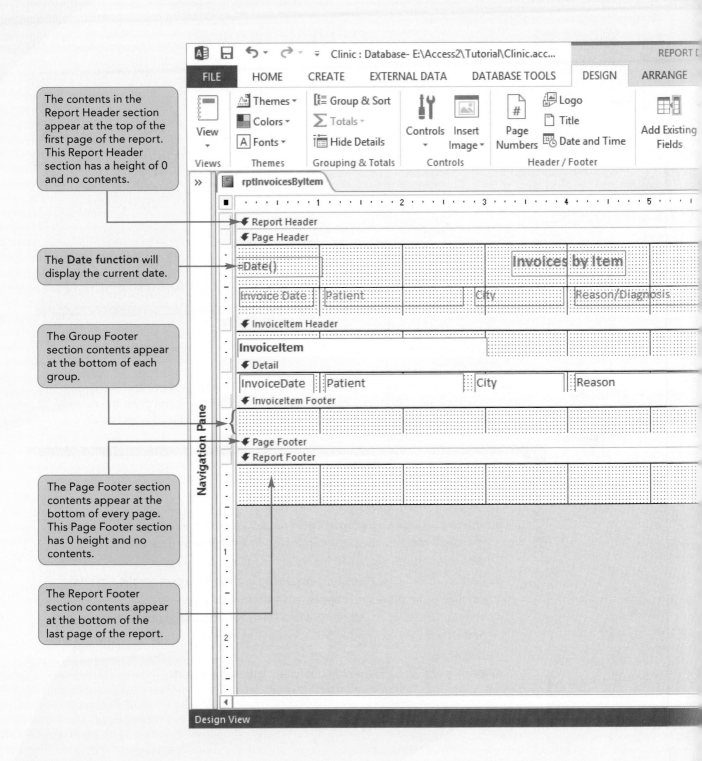

Custom report in Design view

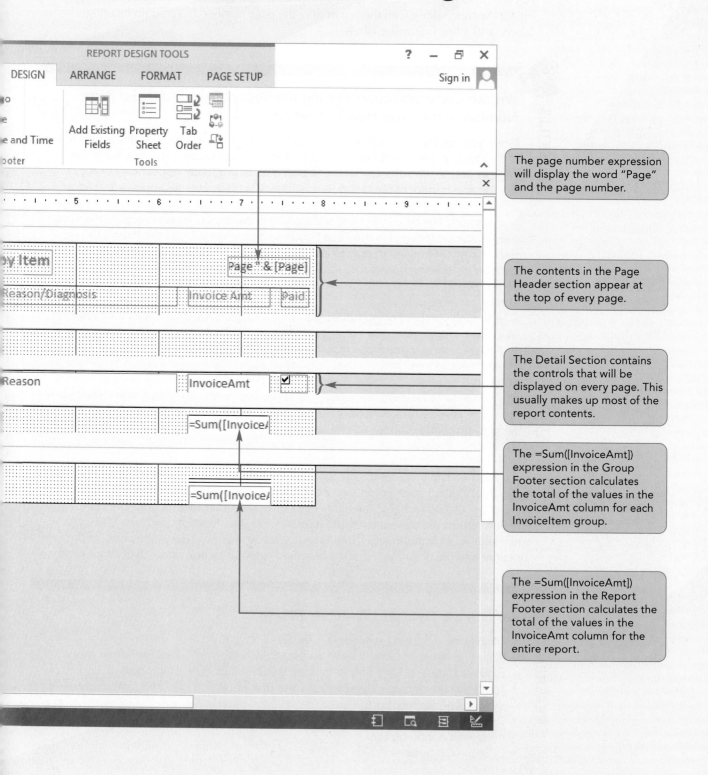

The page number expression will display the word "Page" and the page number.

The contents in the Page Header section appear at the top of every page.

The Detail Section contains the controls that will be displayed on every page. This usually makes up most of the report contents.

The =Sum([InvoiceAmt]) expression in the Group Footer section calculates the total of the values in the InvoiceAmt column for each InvoiceItem group.

The =Sum([InvoiceAmt]) expression in the Report Footer section calculates the total of the values in the InvoiceAmt column for the entire report.

Adding the Date to a Report

According to Raj's design, the rptInvoicesByItem report includes the date in the Page Header section, along with the report title, the page number, the column heading labels, and a line below the labels.

PROSKILLS

Written Communication: Placing the Report Title, Date, and Page Number in the Page Header Section

When you use the Report tool or the Report Wizard to create a report, the report title is displayed in the Report Header section and the page number is displayed in the Page Footer section. Recall that the Report header and footer appear only once, at the top and bottom of the report, respectively. The Page Header appears at the top of every page in the report and the Page Footer appears at the bottom of every page in the report. The date (and time) is displayed in the Report Header section when you use the Report tool and in the Page Footer section when you use the Report Wizard. Because report formatting guidelines require that all the reports in a database display controls in consistent positions, you have to move the date control for reports created by the Report tool or by the Report Wizard so the date is displayed in the same section for all reports.

Although company standards vary, a common report standard places the report title, date, and page number on the same line in the Page Header section. Using one line saves vertical space in the report compared to placing some controls in the Page Header section and others in the Page Footer section. Placing the report title in the Page Header section, instead of in the Report Header section, allows users to identify the report name on any page without having to turn to the first page. When you develop reports with a consistent format, the report users become more productive and more confident working with the information in the reports.

To add the date to a report, you can click the Date and Time button on the DESIGN tab in the Header/Footer group, and Access will insert the Date function in a text box without an attached label at the right edge of the Report Header section. The Date function returns the current date. The format of the Date function is *=Date()*. The equal sign (=) indicates that what follows it is an expression; *Date* is the name of the function; and the empty set of parentheses indicates a function rather than simple text.

REFERENCE

Adding the Date and Time to a Report

- Display the report in Layout or Design view.
- In Design view or in Layout view, on the DESIGN tab, in the Header/Footer group, click the Date and Time button to open the Date and Time dialog box.
- To display the date, click the Include Date check box, and then click one of the three date option buttons.
- To display the time, click the Include Time check box, and then click one of the three time option buttons.
- Click the OK button.

In Raj's design for the report, the date appears at the left edge of the Page Header section. You'll add the date to the report, and then cut the date from its default location in the Report Header section and paste it into the Page Header section.

To add the date to the Page Header section:

1. If you took a break after the previous session, make sure that the Clinic database is open, that the rptInvoicesByItem report is open, and that the Navigation Pane is closed.

   You can add the current date in Layout view or Design view. However, because you can't cut and paste controls between sections in Layout view, you'll add the date in Design view. First, you'll move the column heading labels down in the Page Header section to make room for the controls you'll be adding above them.

2. Switch to Design view, increase the height of the Page Header section by dragging down the bottom of the Page Header border until the 1-inch mark on the vertical ruler appears, select all six labels in the Page Header section, and then move the labels down until the tops of the labels are at the 0.5-inch mark on the vertical ruler. You may find it easier to use the arrow keys to position the labels, rather than the mouse.

   Raj's report design has a horizontal line below the labels. You'll add this line next.

3. On the DESIGN tab, in the Controls group, click the **More** button, click the **Line** tool , position the pointer's plus symbol (+) one grid dot below the lower-left corner of the Invoice Date label in the Page Header section, hold down the **Shift** key, drag a horizontal line from left to right so the end of the line aligns with the right edge of the Paid label, release the mouse button, and then release the **Shift** key.

4. Reduce the height of the Page Header section by dragging the bottom of the section up until it touches the bottom of the line you just added.

5. On the DESIGN tab, in the Header/Footer group, click the **Date and Time** button to open the Date and Time dialog box, make sure the **Include Date** check box is checked and the **Include Time** check box is unchecked, and then click the third date option button. See Figure 7-26.

Figure 7-26   **Completed Date and Time dialog box**

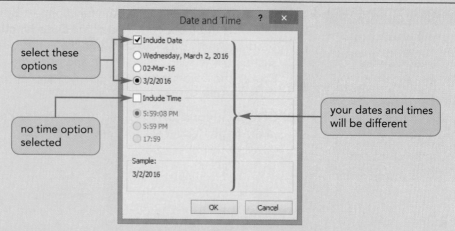

6. Click the **OK** button. The Date function is added to the Report Header section.

7. Click the **Date function** text box, and then click the **layout selector** ⊞ in the upper-left corner of the Report Header section. The Date function text box is part of a control layout with three additional boxes, which are empty cells. See Figure 7-27.

| Figure 7-27 | Date function added to the Report Header section |

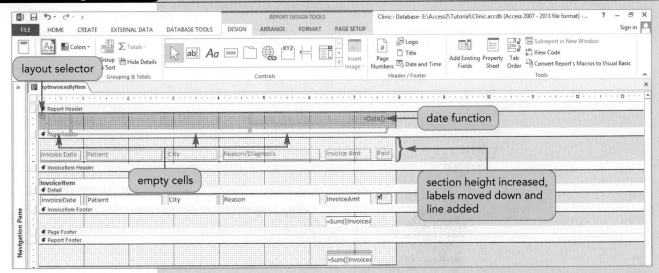

You need to remove these controls from the control layout before you work further with the Date function text box.

8. Right-click one of the selected controls, point to **Layout** on the shortcut menu, and then click **Remove Layout**. The three empty cells are deleted, and the Date function text box remains selected.

The default size for the Date function text box accommodates long dates and long times, so the text box is much wider than needed for the date that will appear in the custom report. You'll decrease its width and move it to the Page Header section.

9. Decrease the width of the Date function text box from the left until it is one inch wide, right-click an edge of the **Date function** text box to open the shortcut menu, click **Cut** to delete the control, right-click the **Page Header** section bar to select that section and open the shortcut menu, and then click **Paste**. The Date function text box is pasted in the upper-left corner of the Page Header section.

10. Save your report changes, and then switch to Print Preview to view the date in the Page Header section. See Figure 7-28.

TIP

If a report includes a control with the Date function, the current date will be displayed each time the report is run. If you instead want a specific date to appear each time the report is run, use a label control that contains the date, rather than the Date function.

Figure 7-28	Viewing the date in Print Preview

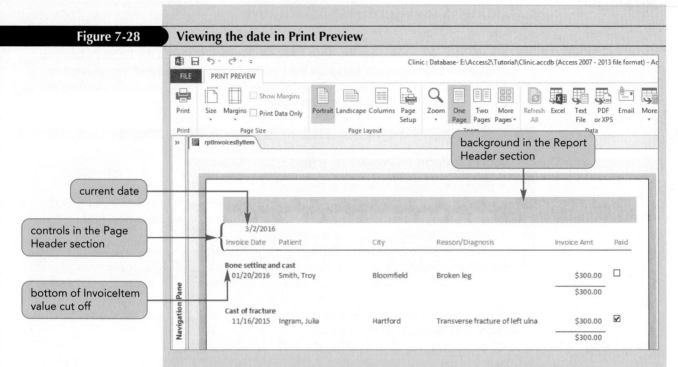

current date

controls in the Page
Header section

bottom of InvoiceItem
value cut off

background in the Report
Header section

3/2/2016

Invoice Date	Patient	City	Reason/Diagnosis	Invoice Amt	Paid
Bone setting and cast					
01/20/2016	Smith, Troy	Bloomfield	Broken leg	$300.00	☐
				$300.00	
Cast of fracture					
11/16/2015	Ingram, Julia	Hartford	Transverse fracture of left ulna	$300.00	☑
				$300.00	

Trouble? Your year might appear with two digits instead of four digits as shown in Figure 7-28. Your date format might also differ, depending on your computer's date settings. These differences do not cause any problems.

Next you'll left-align the date in the text box in Design view.

▶ **11.** Switch to Design view, make sure the Date function text box is selected, click the **FORMAT** tab, and then in the Font group, click the **Align Left** button ☰.

Finally, notice that when you bolded the font in the InvoiceItem text box, you increased the size of the characters. You need to increase the height of the text boxes to fully display all characters in the text box.

▶ **12.** Click the **InvoiceItem** text box, and then increase the height of the text box from the top by one row of grid dots.

INSIGHT

Choosing a Theme for a Database

Access has nine themes that you can use to set the font type and size and the color and other effects for the objects in a database. The default theme is the Office theme, which uses Calibri 11 font. You should either use the default theme or choose a theme immediately after creating the first table in the database. If you wait to choose a theme until after you've created a large number of objects in the database, the theme you choose will probably have a font different from Calibri 11, and you'll have to go back and resize the table and query datasheets and the form and report text boxes and labels.

You are now ready to add page numbers to the Page Header section. You'll also delete the empty Report Header section by decreasing its height to zero.

Adding Page Numbers to a Report

You can display page numbers in a report by including an expression in the Page Header or Page Footer section. In Layout view or Design view, on the DESIGN tab, you can click the Page Numbers button in the Header/Footer group to add a page number expression to a report. The inserted page number expression automatically displays the correct page number on each page of a report.

REFERENCE

Adding Page Numbers to a Report

- Display the report in Layout or Design view.
- In Design view or in Layout view, on the DESIGN tab, in the Header/Footer group, click the Page Numbers button to open the Page Numbers dialog box.
- Select the format, position, and alignment options you want.
- Select whether you want to display the page number on the first page.
- Click the OK button to place the page number expression in the report.

Raj's design shows the page number displayed on the right side of the Page Header section, bottom-aligned with the date.

To add page numbers to the Page Header section:

1. In the Report Header section, drag the bottom border up to the top of the section so the section's height is reduced to zero.

2. Click the **DESIGN tab**, and then in the Header/Footer group, click the **Page Numbers** button. The Page Numbers dialog box opens.

   You use the Format options to specify the format of the page number. Raj wants page numbers to appear as Page 1, Page 2, and so on. This is the "Page N" format option. You use the Position options to place the page numbers at the top of the page in the Page Header section or at the bottom of the page in the Page Footer section. Raj's design shows page numbers at the top of the page.

3. In the Format section, make sure that the **Page N** option button is selected, and then in the Position section, make sure that the **Top of Page [Header]** option button is selected.

   The report design shows page numbers at the right side of the page. You can specify this placement in the Alignment box.

4. Click the **Alignment** arrow, and then click **Right**.

5. Make sure the **Show Number on First Page** check box is checked, so the page number prints on the first page and all other pages as well. See Figure 7-29.

Figure 7-29   **Completed Page Numbers dialog box**

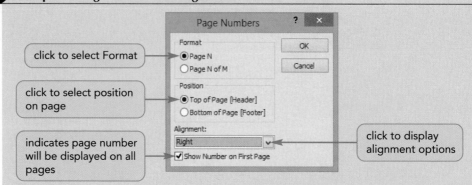

click to select Format

click to select position on page

indicates page number will be displayed on all pages

click to display alignment options

6. Click the **OK** button. A text box containing the expression =*"Page " & [Page]* appears in the upper-right corner of the Page Header section. See Figure 7-30. The expression =*"Page " & [Page]* in the text box means that the printed report will show the word "Page" followed by a space and the page number.

Figure 7-30   **Page number expression added to the Page Header section**

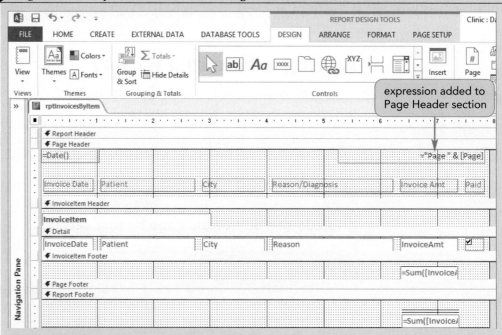

The page number text box is much wider than needed for the page number expression that will appear in the custom report. You'll decrease its width.

7. Click the **Page Number** text box, decrease its width from the left until it is one inch wide, and then move it to the left so its right edge aligns with the right edge of the Paid text box.

8. Save your report changes, and then switch to Print Preview. See Figure 7-31.

| Figure 7-31 | Date and page number in the Page Header section |

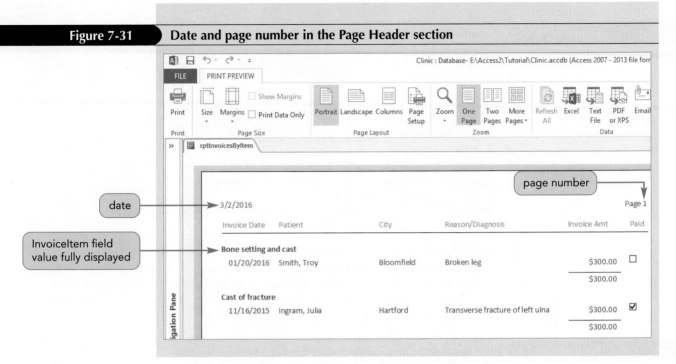

Now you are ready to add the title to the Page Header section.

Adding a Title to a Report

Raj's report design includes the title "Invoices by Item," which you'll add to the Page Header section centered between the date and the page number. You could use the Title button on the DESIGN tab in the Header/Footer group to add the report title, but Access adds the title to the Report Header section, and Raj's design positions the title in the Page Header section. It will be easier to use the Label tool to add the title directly in the Page Header section.

To add the title to the Page Header section:

1. Close Print Preview and switch to Design view.

2. On the DESIGN tab, in the Controls group, click the **Label** tool Aa, position the pointer's plus symbol (+) at the top of the Page Header section at the 3-inch mark on the horizontal ruler, and then click the mouse button. The insertion point flashes inside a narrow box, which will expand as you type the report title.

   To match Raj's design, you need to type the title as "Invoices by Item," and then change its font size to 14 points and its style to bold.

3. Type **Invoices by Item**, and then press the **Enter** key.

4. Click the **FORMAT** tab, in the Font group click the **Font Size** arrow, click **14**, and then click the **Bold** button B. Increase the width of the label to fit the title, increase the height by two grid dots and move the label to the right so it is centered at the 4-inch mark. See Figure 7-32.

Figure 7-32	Report title in the Page Header section

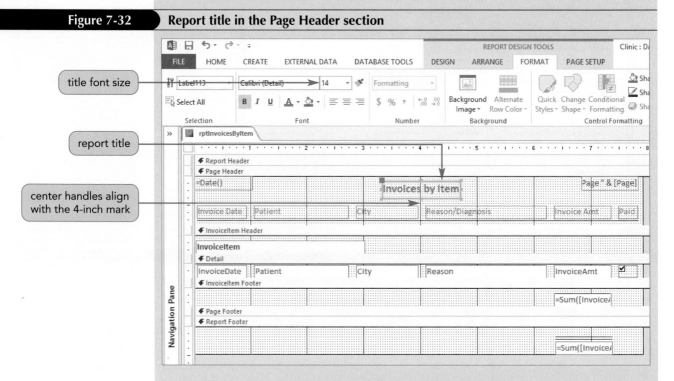

title font size

report title

center handles align
with the 4-inch mark

Finally, you'll align the date, report title, and page number controls on their bottom edges. Yours may be aligned already, but if not, this step will align the controls.

5. Select the date, report title, and page number controls in the Page Header section, right-click one of the selected controls, point to **Align**, and then click **Bottom**.

6. Save your report changes. You have completed the design of the custom report as shown in the Session 7.3 Visual Overview.

7. Switch to Print Preview to review the completed report, and then navigate to the top of the last page of the report to view your changes. See Figure 7-33.

Figure 7-33	Completed rptInvoicesByItem report in Print Preview

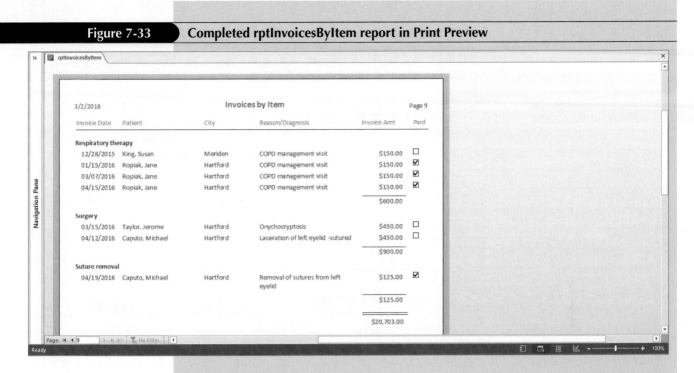

> **8.** Close the report.

Next, Sarah wants you to create mailing labels that she can use to address materials to Chatham Community Health Services patients.

Creating Mailing Labels

Sarah needs a set of mailing labels printed for all Patients so she can mail a marketing brochure and other materials to them. The tblPatient table contains the name and address information that will serve as the record source for the labels. Each mailing label will have the same format: first name and last name on the first line; address on the second line; and city, state, and zip code on the third line.

You could create a custom report to produce the mailing labels, but using the Label Wizard is an easier and faster way to produce them. The **Label Wizard** provides templates for hundreds of standard label formats, each of which is uniquely identified by a label manufacturer's name and number. These templates specify the dimensions and arrangement of labels on each page. Standard label formats can have between one and five labels across a page; the number of labels printed on a single page also varies. Sarah's mailing labels are manufactured by Avery and their product number is C2163. Each sheet contains twelve labels; each label is 1.5 inches by 3.9 inches, and the labels are arranged in two columns and six rows on the page.

Creating Mailing Labels and Other Labels

- In the Navigation Pane, click the table or query that will serve as the record source for the labels.
- In the Reports group on the CREATE tab, click the Labels button to start the Label Wizard and open its first dialog box.
- Select the label manufacturer and product number, and then click the Next button.
- Select the label font, color, and style, and then click the Next button.
- Construct the label content by selecting the fields from the record source and specifying their placement and spacing on the label, and then click the Next button.
- Select one or more optional sort fields, click the Next button, specify the report name, and then click the Finish button.

You'll use the Label Wizard to create a report to produce mailing labels for all patients.

To use the Label Wizard to create the mailing label report:

1. Open the Navigation Pane, click **tblPatient** to make it the current object that will serve as the record source for the labels, close the Navigation Pane, and then click the **CREATE tab**.

2. In the Reports group, click the **Labels** button. The first Label Wizard dialog box opens and asks you to select the standard or custom label you'll use.

3. In the Unit of Measure section make sure that the **English** option button is selected, in the Label Type section make sure that the **Sheet feed** option button is selected, in the Filter by manufacturer box make sure that **Avery** is selected, and then in the Product number box click **C2163**. See Figure 7-34.

| Figure 7-34 | Selecting a standard label |

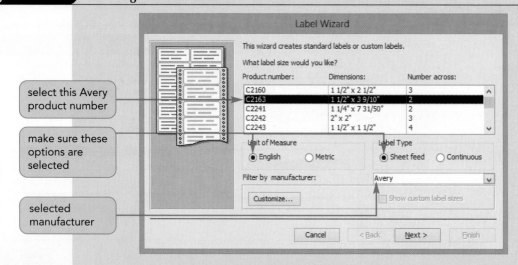

select this Avery product number

make sure these options are selected

selected manufacturer

Because the labels are already filtered for products manufactured by Avery, the top box shows the Avery product number, dimensions, and number of labels across the page for each of its standard label formats. You can display the dimensions in the list in either inches or millimeters by choosing the appropriate option in the Unit of Measure section. You can also specify in the Label Type section whether the labels are on individual sheets or are continuous forms.

▶ **4.** Click the **Next** button to open the second Label Wizard dialog box, in which you choose font specifications for the labels.

Kelly wants the labels to use 10-point Arial with a medium font weight and without italics or underlines. The font weight determines how light or dark the characters will print; you can choose from nine values ranging from thin to heavy.

▶ **5.** If necessary, select **Arial** for the font name, **10** for the font size, and **Medium** for the font weight, make sure the Italic and the Underline check boxes are not checked and that black is the text color, and then click the **Next** button. The third Label Wizard dialog box opens, from which you select the data to appear on the labels.

Kelly wants the mailing labels to print the FirstName and LastName fields on the first line, the Address field on the second line, and the City, State, and Zip fields on the third line. A single space will separate the FirstName and LastName fields, the City and State fields, and the State and Zip fields.

TIP

As you select fields from the Available fields box or type text for the label, the Prototype label box shows the format for the label.

▶ **6.** In the Available fields box click **FirstName**, click the ⎣ > ⎦ button to move the field to the Prototype label box, press the **spacebar**, in the Available fields box click **LastName** (if necessary), and then click the ⎣ > ⎦ button. The braces around the field names in the Prototype label box indicate that the name represents a field rather than text that you entered.

Trouble? If you select the wrong field or type the wrong text, click the incorrect item in the Prototype label box, press the Delete key to remove the item, and then select the correct field or type the correct text.

▶ **7.** Press the **Enter** key to move to the next line in the Prototype label box, and then use Figure 7-35 to complete the entries in the Prototype label box. Make sure you press the spacebar after selecting the City field and the State field.

Figure 7-35 **Completed label prototype**

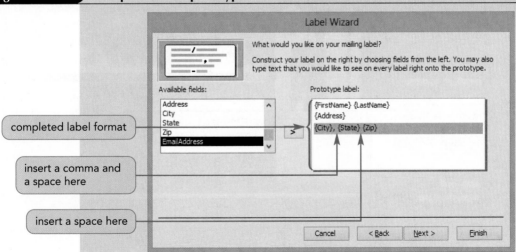

completed label format

insert a comma and a space here

insert a space here

▶ **8.** Click the **Next** button to open the fourth Label Wizard dialog box, in which you choose the sort fields for the labels.

Kelly wants Zip to be the primary sort field and LastName to be the secondary sort field.

9. Scroll down the list and click the **Zip** field, click the > button to select Zip as the primary sort field, click the **LastName** field, click the > button to select LastName as the secondary sort field, and then click the **Next** button to open the last Label Wizard dialog box, in which you enter a name for the report.

10. Change the report name to **rptPatientMailingLabels**, and then click the **Finish** button. Access saves the report as rptPatientMailingLabels and then opens the first page of the report in Print Preview. Note that two columns of labels appear across the page. See Figure 7-36.

Figure 7-36   Previewing the label content and sequence

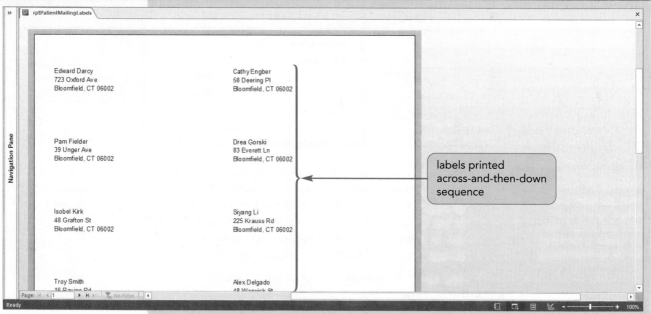

The rptPatientMailingLabels report is a multiple-column report. The labels will be printed in ascending order by zip code and, within each zip code, in ascending order by last name. The first label will be printed in the upper-left corner on the first page, the second label will be printed to its right, the third label will be printed below the first label, and so on. This style of multiple-column report is the "across, then down" layout. Instead, Kelly wants the labels to print with the "down, then across" layout because she prefers to pull the labels from the sheet in this manner. In this layout, the first label is printed, the second label is printed below the first, and so on. After the bottom label in the first column is printed, the next label is printed at the top of the second column. The "down, then across" layout is also called **newspaper-style columns**, or **snaking columns**.

To change the layout of the mailing label report:

1. Close Print Preview and switch to Design view. The Detail section, the only section in the report, is sized for a single label.

   First, you'll change the layout to snaking columns.

2. Click the **PAGE SETUP** tab, in the Page Layout group click the **Page Setup** button, and then click the **Columns** tab. The Page Setup dialog box displays the column options for the report. See Figure 7-37.

Figure 7-37   **Column options in the Page Setup dialog box**

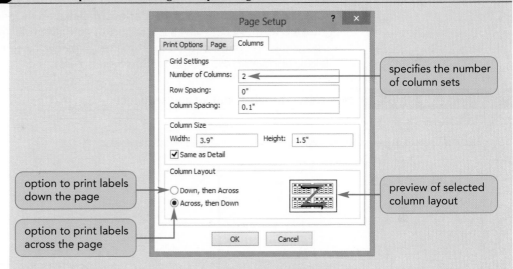

specifies the number of column sets

option to print labels down the page

preview of selected column layout

option to print labels across the page

The options in the Page Setup dialog box let you change the properties of a multiple-column report. In the Grid Settings section, you specify the number of column sets and the row and column spacing between the column sets. In the Column Size section, you specify the width and height of each column set. In the Column Layout section, you select between the "down, then across" and the "across, then down" layouts.

You can now change the layout for the labels.

3. Click the **Down, then Across** option button, and then click the **OK** button.

You've finished the report changes, so you can now save and preview the report.

4. Save your report design changes, and then switch to Print Preview. The labels appear in the snaking columns layout.

You've finished all work on Kelly's reports.

5. Close the report, make a backup copy of the database, compact and repair the database, and then close it.

Kelly is very pleased with the modified report and the two new reports, which will provide her with improved information and help expedite her written communications with patients.

Session 7.3 Quick Check

REVIEW

1. What is the function and syntax to print the current date in a report?
2. How do you insert a page number in the Page Header section?
3. Clicking the Title button in the Header/Footer group on the DESIGN tab adds a report title to the _____ section.
4. What is a multiple-column report?

SAM Projects

ASSESS

Review Assignments

PRACTICE

Data File needed for the Review Assignments: Supplier.accdb (*cont. from Tutorial 6*)

Kelly wants you to create a custom report for the Supplier database that prints all companies and the products they offer. She also wants you to customize an existing report. Complete the following steps:

1. Open the **Supplier** database you worked with in Tutorials 5 and 6.
2. Modify the **rptSupplierDetails** report by completing the following steps:
   a. Change the report title to **Chatham Suppliers**.
   b. Remove the alternate row color from the detail lines in the report.
   c. Change the fourth column heading to First Name and the fifth column heading to Last Name.
   d. In the Report Footer section, add a grand total count of the number of suppliers that appear in the report, make sure the text box control has a transparent border, and left-align the count with the left edge of the CompanyName text box. Left-align the count value in the text box.
   e. Add a label that contains the text **Suppliers:** to the left of the count of the total number of suppliers, aligned to the left margin, and aligned with the bottom of the count text box.
   f. Set the Margins to Normal, and adjust the width of the grid to 7.8 inches. Extend the width of the controls in the Report Header to one grid point to the left of the width of the right margin. Increase the width of the Company header label and CompanyName detail text box to approximately double, until the Contact Last Name controls are one grid dot to the left of the right margin.
   g. Move the page number text box control to the right until it is one grid dot to the left of the right margin. Right-align the page number value in the text box control.
3. After you've completed and saved your modifications to the rptSupplierDetails report, filter the report in Report view, selecting all records that contain the word "surgical" in the Company field. Copy the entire filtered report and paste it into a new Word document. Save the document as **surgical** in the Access2 ▸ Review folder. Close Word, save your changes to the Access report, and then close it.
4. Create a query that displays the CompanyName and Category fields from the tblSupplier table, and the ProductName, Price, and Units fields from the tblProduct table. Sort in ascending order by the first three fields in the query, and then save the query as **qrySupplierProducts**.
5. Create a custom report based on the qrySupplierProducts query. Figure 7-38 shows a sample of the completed report. Refer to the figure as you create the report. Distribute the fields horizontally to produce a visually balanced report.

Figure 7-38   Products database custom report

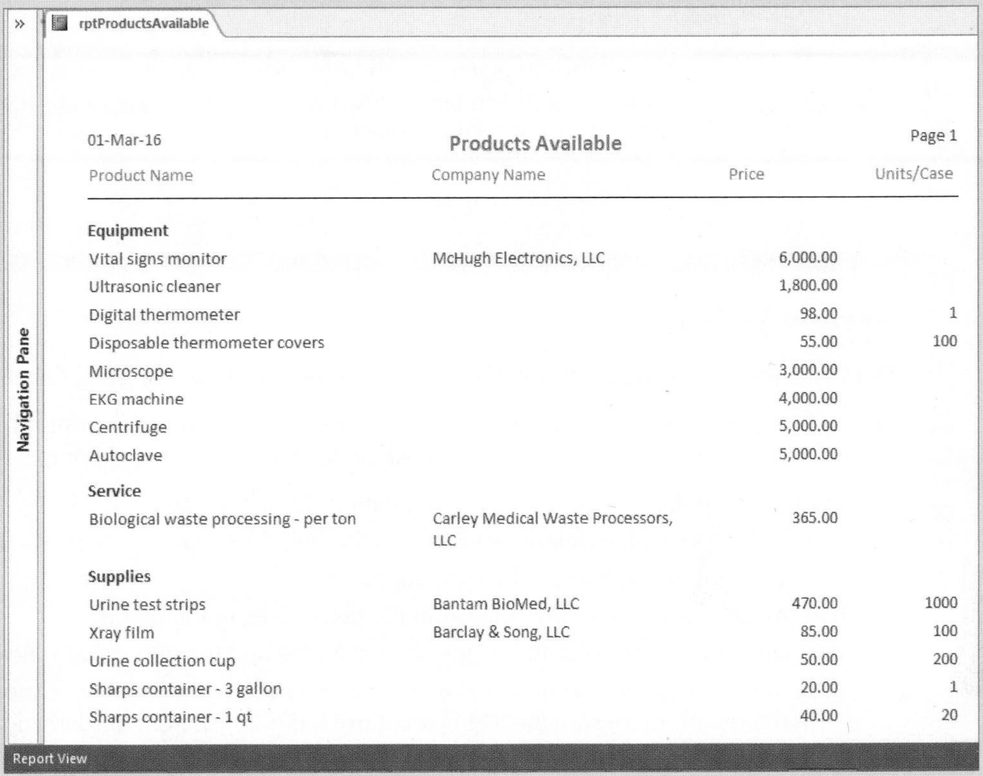

a. Save the report as **rptProductsAvailable**.

b. Use the Category field (from the tblSupplier table) as a grouping field, and use the CompanyName field (from the tblSupplier table) as a sort field.

c. Hide duplicate values for the CompanyName field.

d. Keep the whole group together on one page.

e. Remove the text box borders.

f. Remove the alternate row color from the group header and detail line.

g. Add a Page title **Products Available** using 14-point font, centered horizontally.

h. Apply a text filter for companies that contain "LLC" in the Company Name.

6. Create a mailing label report according to the following instructions:

a. Use the tblSupplier table as the record source.

b. Use Avery C2160 labels, and use the default font, size, weight, and color.

c. For the prototype label, add the ContactFirstName, a space, and ContactLastName on the first line; the CompanyName on the second line; the Address on the third line; and the City, a comma and a space, State, a space, and Zip on the fourth line.

d. Sort by Zip and then by CompanyName, and then enter the report name **rptCompanyMailingLabels**.

7. Make a backup copy of the database, compact and repair, and then close the Supplier database.

Case Problem 1

Data File needed for this Case Problem: Task.accdb (*cont. from Tutorial 6*)

GoGopher!   Amol Mehta wants you to create a custom report and mailing labels for the Gopher database. The custom report will be based on the results of a query you will create. Complete the following steps:

1. Open the **Task** database you worked with in Tutorials 5 and 6.
2. Create a query that displays the PlanID, FeeWaived, PlanDescription, and PlanCost fields from the tblPlan table, and the FirstName, and LastName fields from the tblMember table. Sort in ascending order by the PlanID, FeeWaived, and LastName fields, and then save the query as **qryPlanMembership**.
3. Create a custom report based on the qryPlanMembership query. Figure 7-39 shows a sample of the first page of the completed report. Refer to the figure as you create the report.

Figure 7-39   Task database custom report

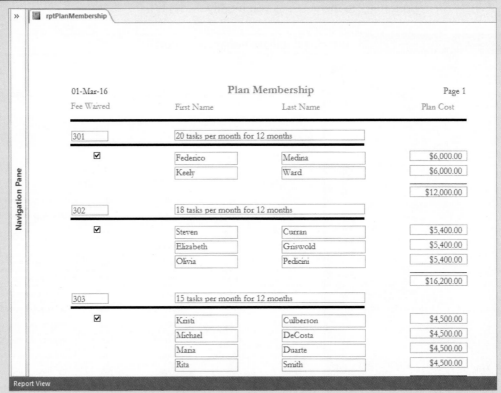

a. Save the report as **rptPlanMembership**.
b. Use the PlanID field as a grouping field.
c. Select the FeeWaived field as a sort field, and the LastName field as a secondary sort field.
d. Hide duplicate values for the FeeWaived field.
e. Add the PlanDescription field to the Group Header section, and then delete its attached label.
f. Keep the whole group together on one page.
g. Use Wide margins and spacing to distribute the columns evenly across the page.
h. Remove the alternate row color for all sections.
i. Use black font for all the controls, and set the lines' thickness to 3 pt.
4. Use the following instructions to create the mailing labels:
a. Use the tblMember table as the record source for the mailing labels.
b. Use Avery C2160 labels, and use the default font, size, weight, and color.
c. For the prototype label, place FirstName, a space, and LastName on the first line; Street on the second line; and City, a comma and space, State, a space, and Zip on the third line.
d. Sort by Zip and then by LastName, and then type the report name **rptMemberLabels**.
5. Make a backup copy of the database, compact and repair it, and then close the Task database.

APPLY

Case Problem 2

Data File needed for this Case Problem: Tutoring.accdb (*cont. from Tutorial 6*)

O'Brien Educational Services   Karen O'Brien wants you to modify an existing report and to create a custom report and mailing labels for the Tutoring database. Complete the following steps:

1. Open the **Tutoring** database you worked with in Tutorials 5 and 6.
2. Modify the **rptTutorList** report. Figure 7-40 shows a sample of the last page of the completed report. Refer to the figure as you modify the report.

Figure 7-40   **Tutoring database enhanced report**

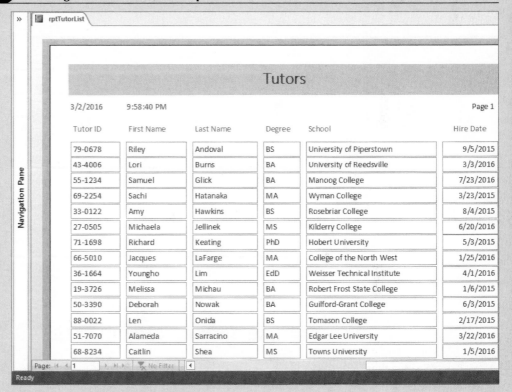

a. Delete the picture at the top of the report.
b. Set Normal margins, and a grid width of 7.8 inches.
c. Center the report title and ensure the text is "Tutors", bold and 22 pt.
d. Move the Hire Date column to the right margin, and center the Hire Date label value. Use horizontal spacing to evenly distribute the columns.
e. Remove the alternate row color from the detail lines in the report.
f. Change the page number format from "Page n of m" to "Page n" and align the text to the right.
g. Move the date, time, and page number to the Page Header section.
h. Change the date format to short date and align the text to the left.
i. Add a grand total control that calculates the total number of tutors and add a label with the text "Total Tutors".
j. Sort the tutors by Last Name.

3. Create a query that displays, in order, the LastName and FirstName fields from the tblTutor table, the SessionType field from the tblContract table, the FirstName and LastName fields from the tblStudent table, and the NumSessions and Cost fields from the tblContract table. Sort in ascending order by the first three fields in the query, and then save the query as **qryTutorSessions**.

4. Create a custom report based on the qryTutorSessions query. Figure 7-41 shows a sample of the first page of the completed report. Refer to the figure as you create the report.

Figure 7-41   **Contract database custom report**

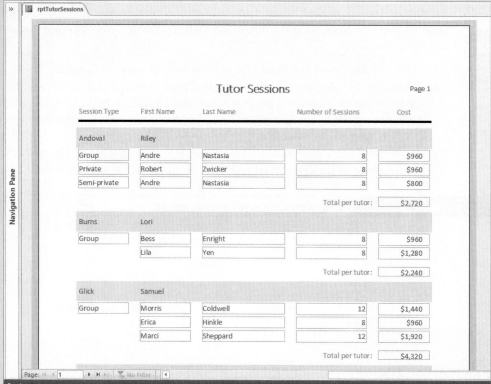

a. Save the report as **rptTutorSessions**.

b. The LastName field (from the tblTutor table) is a grouping field, and the FirstName field also appears in the Group Header section.

c. The SessionType field is a sort field, and the LastName field (from the tblStudent table) is a sort field.

d. Hide duplicate values for the SessionType field.

e. Use Wide margins and set the grid width to 7 inches. Size fields as shown and distribute horizontally using spacing to create a balanced look.

f. Set the background color for the grouped header and its controls to Background 2 in the Theme colors.

g. Use black font for all the controls, setting the lines' thickness to 3 pt.

5. Create a mailing label report according to the following instructions:

a. Use the tblStudent table as the record source.

b. Use Avery C2160 labels, use a 12-point font size and use the other default font and color options.

c. For the prototype label, place FirstName, a space, and LastName on the first line; Address on the second line; and City, a comma and a space, State, a space, and Zip on the third line.

d. Sort by Zip and then by LastName, and then enter the report name **rptStudentMailingLabels**.

e. Change the mailing label layout to snaking columns.

6. Make a backup copy of the database, compact and repair it, and then close the Tutoring database.

CREATE

Case Problem 3

Data File needed for this Case Problem: Rosemary.accdb (*cont. from Tutorial 6*)

Rosemary Animal Shelter Ryan Lang asks you to create a custom report for the Rosemary database so that he can better track donations made by donors and to create mailing labels. Complete the following steps:

1. Open the **Rosemary** database you worked with in Tutorials 5 and 6.
2. Create a query that displays the DonationDesc, DonationDate, and DonationValue fields from the tblDonation table, and the FirstName and LastName fields from the tblPatron table. Sort in ascending order by the DonationDesc, DonationDate, and LastName fields, and then save the query as **qryPatronDonations**.
3. Create a custom report based on the qryPatronDonations query. Figure 7-42 shows a sample of the first page of the completed report. Refer to the figure as you create the report.

Figure 7-42 **Rosemary database custom report**

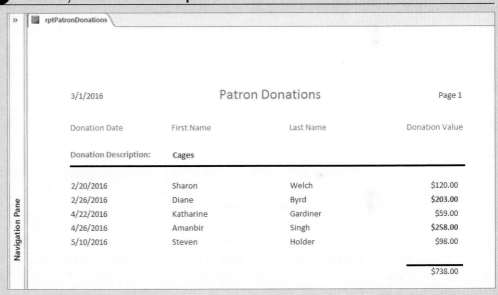

a. Save the report as **rptPatronDonations**.
b. Ryan would like you to use the DonationDesc field as a grouping field; however, it is currently a Long Text field, and you can't group on a Long Text field. Ryan realized that the donation description will always be a short description. In the tblDonation table, change the data type of the DonationDesc field to Short Text.
c. Use the DonationDesc field as a grouping field.
d. Select the DonationDate field as a sort field, and the LastName field as a secondary sort field.
e. Hide duplicate values for the DonationDate field.
f. Use black font for all the controls, and set the lines' thickness to 2 pt.
g. Keep the whole group together on one page.
h. Use Wide margins and set the grid width to 7 inches. Size fields as shown and distribute horizontally, using spacing to create a balanced look.
i. Create a conditional formatting rule for the DonationValue field to display the value in blue, bold font when the amount is more than $200.
j. Make any additional changes to the layout and formatting of the report that are necessary for it to match Figure 7-42.

4. After you've created and saved the rptPatronDonations report, filter the report in Report view, selecting all records that contain the name "Lew" in the LastName field. Copy the entire filtered report and paste it into a new Word document. Save the document as **PatronLew** in the Access2 ▸ Case3 folder. Close Word, and then save and close the Access report.

5. The Rosemary Animal Shelter is having a fundraiser dinner and Ryan would like name tags for the patrons. Use the following instructions to create mailing labels that will be used as name tags:

a. Use the tblPatron table as the record source for the mailing labels.

b. Use Avery C2160 labels, and use a font size of 16, with Normal weight, and black color.

c. For the prototype label, place FirstName, a space, and LastName on the first line.

d. Sort by LastName, and then type the report name **rptPatronNameTags**.

e. Change the mailing label layout to snaking columns.

6. Make a backup copy of the database, compact and repair it, and then close it.

Case Problem 4

CREATE

Data File needed for this Case Problem: Ecotour.accdb (*cont. from Tutorial 6*)

Stanley EcoTours Janice and Bill Stanley want you to create a custom report and mailing labels for the Ecotour database. Complete the following steps:

1. Open the **Ecotour** database you worked with in Tutorials 5 and 6.

2. Create a query that displays the TourName and Country fields from the tblTour table; the GuestFirst, GuestLast, and StateProv field from the tblGuest table; and the StartDate and People fields from the tblReservation table. Sort in ascending order by the TourName, StateProv, and StartDate fields, and then save the query as **qryTourReservations**.

3. Create a custom report based on the qryTourReservations query. Figure 7-43 shows a sample of the last page of the completed report. Refer to the figure as you create the report.

Figure 7-43   **Ecotour database custom report**

a. Save the report as **rptTourReservations**.

b. Use the TourName field as a grouping field.

c. Select the StartDate field as a sort field, and the StateProv field as a secondary sort field.

d. Hide duplicate values for the StartDate field.

e. Use black font for all the controls, and set the lines' thickness to 2 pt.

f. Keep the whole group together on one page.

g. Add the Country field to the Group Header section.

h. Use Wide margins and set the grid width to 7 inches. Size fields as shown and distribute horizontally, using spacing to create a balanced look.

i. Remove the color for alternate rows, and then make any other layout and formatting changes necessary to match the report shown in Figure 7-43.

4. Use the following instructions to create the mailing labels:

a. Use the tblGuest table as the record source for the mailing labels.

b. Use Avery C2163 labels, with 12 point font size, Medium weight, and black color settings.

c. For the prototype label, place GuestFirst, a space, and GuestLast on the first line; Address on the second line; City, a comma and a space, StateProv, a space, and PostalCode on the third line; and Country on the fourth line.

d. Sort by PostalCode, then by GuestLastName, and then enter the report name **rptGuestLabels**.

e. Change the mailing label layout to snaking columns.

5. Make a copy of the rptTourReservations report using the name **rptTourReservationsSummary**, and then customize it according to the following instructions. Figure 7-44 shows a sample of the first page of the completed report.

Figure 7-44	Ecotour database custom summary report

a. Delete the column heading labels and line in the Page Header section, and then reduce the height of the section.

b. Add subtotals for the number of reservations and number of people.

6. Make a backup copy of the database, compact and repair it, and then close the Ecotour database.

ACCESS

OBJECTIVES

Session 8.1
- Export an Access query to an HTML document and view the document
- Import a CSV file as an Access table
- Use the Table Analyzer
- Import a table from another Access database
- Import and export XML files
- Save and run import and export specifications

Session 8.2
- Create a tabbed form using a tab control
- Understand the difference between importing, embedding, and linking external objects
- Embed a chart in a form
- Create and use an application part
- Export a PDF file
- Link data from an Excel workbook

Sharing, Integrating, and Analyzing Data

Importing, Exporting, Linking, and Analyzing Data in the Clinic Database

Case | *Chatham Community Health Services*

Cindi Rodriguez, Kelly Schwarz, and Ethan Ward are pleased with the design and contents of the Clinic database. Cindi feels that other employees would benefit from gaining access to the Clinic database and from sharing data among the different programs employees use. Cindi and Kelly would also like to be able to analyze the data in the database.

In this tutorial, you will import, export, link, and embed data, and you will create application parts. You will also explore the charting features of Access.

STARTING DATA FILES

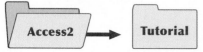

Access2 → **Tutorial**

Clinic.accdb (*cont.*)
NewPatientReferrals.accdb
peoplecalled.csv
Referral.xml
Volunteer.xlsx

Review

Ads.xlsx
Partners.accdb
Payables.csv
Payments.xml
Vendor.accdb (*cont.*)

Case1

CreditCard.xml
Schedule.xlsx
Task.accdb (*cont.*)

Case2

AddSubject.xml
NewStudentReferrals.accdb
Room.xlsx
Subject.csv
Tutoring.accdb (*cont.*)

Case3

Facility.csv
Rosemary.accdb (*cont.*)
Volunteer.accdb

Case4

Ecotour.accdb (*cont.*)
Personnel.xlsx
PotentialTours1.xml
PotentialTours2.xml

Session 8.1 Visual Overview:

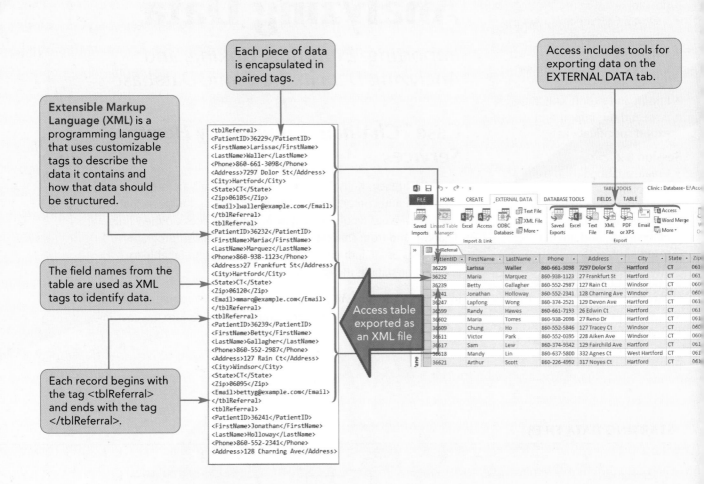

Each piece of data is encapsulated in paired tags.

Access includes tools for exporting data on the EXTERNAL DATA tab.

Extensible Markup Language (XML) is a programming language that uses customizable tags to describe the data it contains and how that data should be structured.

The field names from the table are used as XML tags to identify data.

Each record begins with the tag <tblReferral> and ends with the tag </tblReferral>.

Access table exported as an XML file

Exporting data to XML and HTML

The table field names are used as column headings in the table on the web page.

The Export to HTML tool generates an HTML document, embedding the Access content in the document. An **HTML document** contains tags and other instructions that a web browser processes and displays as a web page.

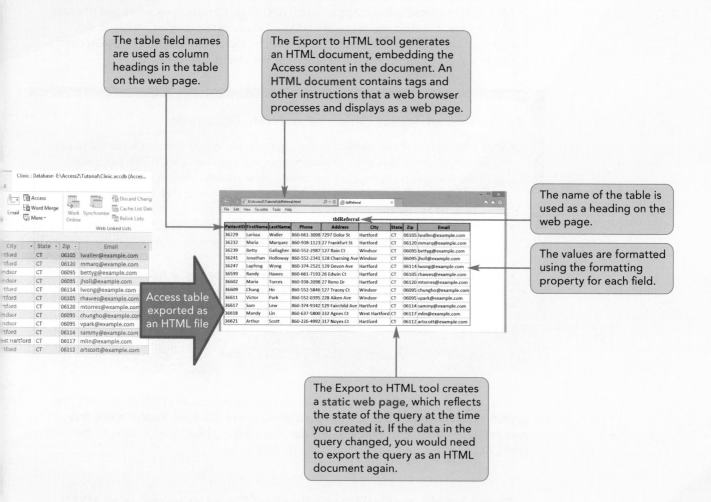

Access table exported as an HTML file

The name of the table is used as a heading on the web page.

The values are formatted using the formatting property for each field.

The Export to HTML tool creates a **static web page**, which reflects the state of the query at the time you created it. If the data in the query changed, you would need to export the query as an HTML document again.

Exporting an Access Query to an HTML Document

Cindi wants to display the summary data in the qryPatientsAndInvoicesCrosstab query on the company's intranet so that all employees working in the office are able to view it. To store the data on the company's intranet, you'll create a web page version of the qryPatientsAndInvoicesCrosstab query.

An HTML document contains tags and other instructions that a Web browser, such as Microsoft Internet Explorer, Apple Safari, or Google Chrome, processes and displays as a Web page. Creating the necessary HTML document to provide Cindi with the information she wants is not as difficult as it might appear at first. You can use Access to export the query and convert it to an HTML document automatically.

REFERENCE

Exporting an Access Object to an HTML Document

- In the Navigation Pane, right-click the object (table, query, form, or report) you want to export, point to Export on the shortcut menu, and then click HTML Document; or in the Navigation Pane, click the object (table, query, form, or report) you want to export, click the EXTERNAL DATA tab, in the Export group click the More button, and then click HTML Document.
- In the Export – HTML Document dialog box, click the Browse button, select the location where you want to save the file, enter the filename in the File name box, and then click the Save button.
- Click the Export data with formatting and layout check box to retain most formatting and layout information, and then click the OK button.
- In the HTML Output Options dialog box, if using a template click the Select a HTML Template check box, click the Browse button, select the location for the template, click the template filename, and then click the OK button.
- Click the OK button, and then click the Close button.

You'll export the qryPatientsAndInvoicesCrosstab query as an HTML document. The qryPatientsAndInvoicesCrosstab query is a select query that joins the tblPatient, tblVisit, and tblBilling tables to display selected data from those tables for all invoices. The query displays one row for each unique City field value.

To export the qryPatientsAndInvoicesCrosstab query as an HTML document:

1. Start Access, and then open the **Clinic** database you worked with in Tutorials 5–7.

2. Open the Navigation Pane (if necessary), right-click **qryPatientsAndInvoicesCrosstab** to display the shortcut menu, point to **Export**, and then click **HTML Document**. The Export - HTML Document dialog box opens.

3. Click the **Browse** button to open the File Save dialog box, navigate to the **Access2 ▸ Tutorial** folder in the location where your data files are stored, select the text in the File name box, type **Crosstab.html**, and then click the **Save** button. The File Save dialog box closes, and you return to the Export – HTML Document dialog box.

TIP

Always select the "Export data with formatting and layout" option, or the HTML document you create will be poorly formatted and difficult to read.

Figure 8-1   **Export - HTML Document dialog box**

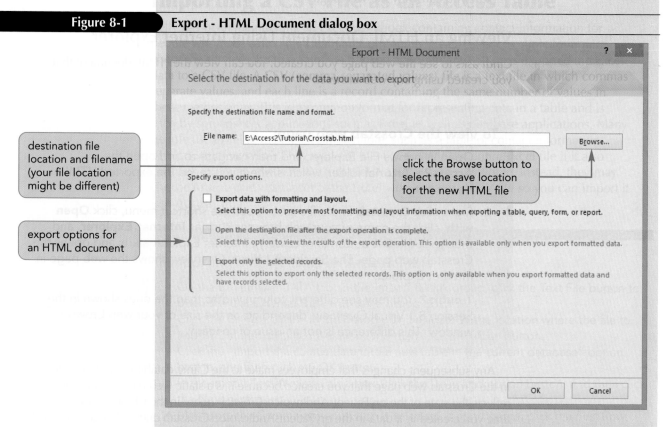

destination file
location and filename
(your file location
might be different)

click the Browse button to
select the save location
for the new HTML file

export options for
an HTML document

The dialog box provides options for exporting the data with formatting and layout, opening the exported file after the export operation is complete, and exporting selected records from the source object (available only when you select records in an object instead of selecting an object in the Navigation Pane). You need to select the option for exporting the data with formatting and layout.

▶ **4.** Click the **Export data with formatting and layout** check box to select it, and then click the **OK** button. The Export - HTML Document dialog box closes and the HTML Output Options dialog box opens. See Figure 8-2.

Figure 8-2   **HTML Output Options dialog box**

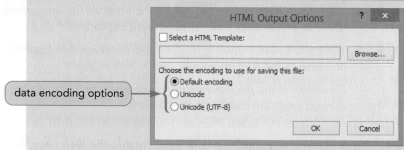

data encoding options

▶ **5.** Click the **OK** button. The HTML Output Options dialog box closes, the HTML document named Crosstab is saved in the Access2 ▶ Tutorial folder, and the Export - HTML Document dialog box is displayed with an option to save the export steps. You won't save these export steps.

▶ **6.** Click the **Close** button in the dialog box to close it without saving the steps and to close the Navigation Pane.

4. In Access, click the **EXTERNAL DATA** tab, and then in the Import & Link group, click the **Text File** button (with the ScreenTip "Import text file") to open the Get External Data - Text File dialog box.

> **Trouble?** If the Export - Text File dialog box opens, you clicked the Text File button in the Export group. Click the Cancel button and then repeat Step 4, being sure to select the Text File button from the Import & Link group.

5. Click the **Browse** button, navigate to the **Access2 ▸ Tutorial** folder, click **peoplecalled.csv**, click the **Open** button, and then click the **Import the source data into a new table in the current database** option button (if necessary). The selected path and filename appear in the File name box. See Figure 8-3.

Figure 8-3	Get External Data - Text File dialog box

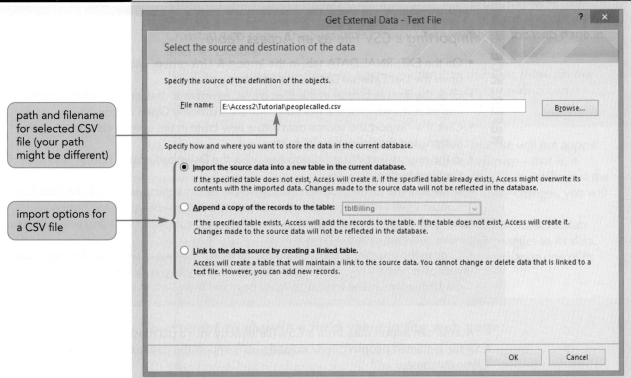

path and filename for selected CSV file (your path might be different)

import options for a CSV file

The dialog box provides options for importing the data into a new table in the database, appending a copy of the data to an existing table in the database, and linking to the source data. In the future, Kelly wants to maintain the potential new patient data in the Clinic database, instead of using her Excel workbook, so you'll import the data into a new table.

6. Click the **OK** button to open the first Import Text Wizard dialog box, in which you designate how to identify the separation between field values in each line in the source data. The choices are the use of commas, tabs, or another character to separate, or delimit, the values, or the use of fixed-width columns with spaces between each column. The wizard has correctly identified that values are delimited by commas.

7. Click the **Next** button to open the second Import Text Wizard dialog box, in which you verify the delimiter for values in each line. See Figure 8-4.

Figure 8-4　　Verifying the delimiter for values in the CSV file

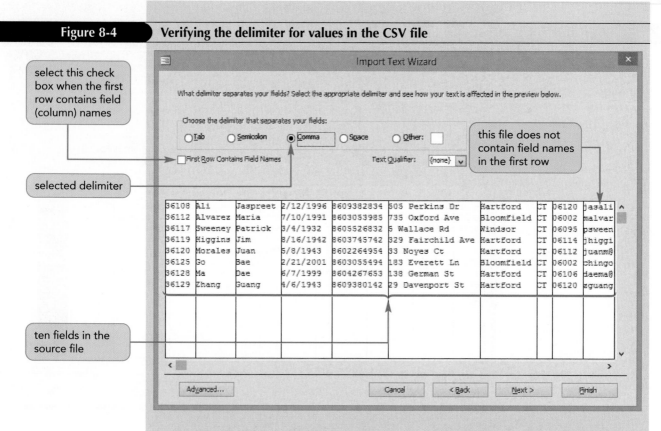

select this check box when the first row contains field (column) names

selected delimiter

ten fields in the source file

this file does not contain field names in the first row

The CSV source file contains eight records with ten fields in each record. A comma serves as the delimiter for values in each line, so the Comma option button is selected. The first row in the source file contains the first record, not field names, so the "First Row Contains Field Names" check box is not checked. If the source file used either single or double quotation marks to enclose values, you would click the Text Qualifier arrow to choose the appropriate option.

8. Click the **Next** button to open the third Import Text Wizard dialog box, in which you enter the field name and set other properties for the imported fields. You will import all fields from the source file and use the default data type and indexed settings for each field, except for the first field's data type.

9. Type **PatientID** in the Field Name box, click the **Data Type** arrow, click **Short Text** in the list, and then click **Field2** in the table list. The heading for the first column changes to PatientID (partially hidden) in the table list, and the second column is selected.

Be sure the data type for DOB is Date With Time, and the data type for Phone and Zip is Short Text.

10. Repeat Step 9 for the remaining nine columns, making sure Short Text is the data type for all fields, except for DOB, which should be Date With Time, typing **LastName**, **FirstName**, **DOB**, **Phone**, **Address**, **City**, **State**, **Zip**, and **Email** in the Field Name box. See Figure 8-5.

Figure 8-5 **After setting field names for the ten fields in the source file**

field name for selected column

leave this option unchecked for all fields

field names for the ten columns

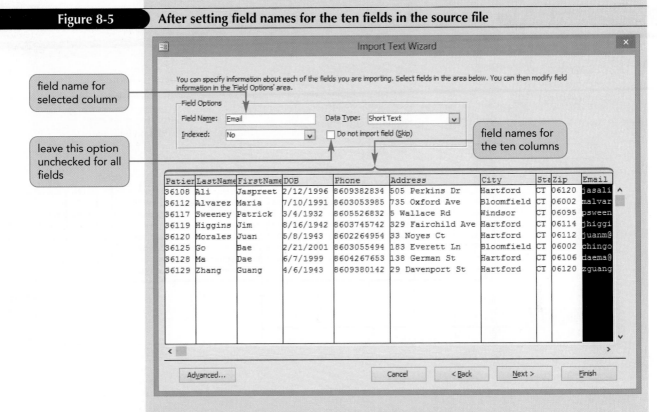

11. Click the **Next** button to open the fourth Import Text Wizard dialog box, in which you select the primary key for the imported table. PatientID, the first column, will be the primary key. When you select this column as the table's primary key, Access will delete the ID column it created.

12. Click the **Choose my own primary key** option button, make sure **PatientID** appears in the box for the option, click the **Next** button, type **tblPeopleCalled** as the table name in the Import to Table box, click the **I would like a wizard to analyze my table after importing the data** check box to select it, and then click the **Finish** button. An Import Text Wizard dialog box opens asking if you want to analyze the table; you'll continue working with this dialog box in the next set of steps.

After importing data and creating a new table, you can use the Import Text Wizard to analyze the imported table. When you choose this option, you start the Table Analyzer.

Analyzing a Table with the Table Analyzer

TIP

Read the Normalization section in the appendix titled "Relational Databases and Database Design" for more information about normalization and third normal form.

The **Table Analyzer** analyzes a single table and, if necessary, splits it into two or more tables that are in third normal form. The Table Analyzer looks for redundant data in the table. When the Table Analyzer encounters redundant data, it removes redundant fields from the table and then places them in new tables. The analyzer results must always be reviewed carefully by the database designer to determine if the suggestions are appropriate.

To use the Table Analyzer to analyze the imported table:

TIP

You can start the Table Analyzer directly by clicking the DATABASE TOOLS tab, and then in the Analyze group clicking the Analyze Table button.

▶ **1.** Click the **Yes** button to close the dialog box and to open the first Table Analyzer Wizard dialog box. The wizard identifies duplicate data in your table and displays a diagram and explanation in the dialog box describing the potential problem.

▶ **2.** Click the first **Show me an example** button ⟩⟩, read the explanation, close the example box, click the second **Show me an example** button ⟩⟩, read the explanation, close the example box, and then click the Next button to open the second Table Analyzer Wizard dialog box. The diagram and explanation in this dialog box describe how the Table Analyzer solves the duplicate data problem.

▶ **3.** Again, click the first **Show me an example** button ⟩⟩, read the explanation, close the example box, click the second **Show me an example** button ⟩⟩, read the explanation, close the example box, and then click the **Next** button to open the third Table Analyzer Wizard dialog box. In this dialog box, you choose whether to let the wizard decide the appropriate table placement for the fields, if the table is not already normalized. Normalizing is the process of identifying and eliminating anomalies from a collection of tables. You'll let the wizard decide.

▶ **4.** Make sure the **Yes, let the wizard decide** option button is selected, and then click the **Next** button. The wizard indicates that the City and State fields should be split into a separate table. Although this data is redundant, it is an industry practice to keep the city, state, and zip information with the address information in a table, so you'll cancel the wizard rather than split the table.

▶ **5.** Click the **Cancel** button to close the message box and exit the wizard. Access returns you to the Get External Data - Text File dialog box, in which you are asked if you want to save the import steps. You don't need to save these steps because you're importing the data only this one time.

▶ **6.** Click the **Close** button to close the dialog box.

The tblPeopleCalled table is now listed in the Tables section in the Navigation Pane. You'll open the table to verify the import results.

To open the imported tblPeopleCalled table:

▶ **1.** Open the Navigation Pane and double-click **tblPeopleCalled** to open the table datasheet, resize all columns to their best fit, and then click **36108** in the first row in the PatientID column to deselect all values. Close the Navigation Pane. See Figure 8-6.

Figure 8-6 **Imported tblPeopleCalled table datasheet**

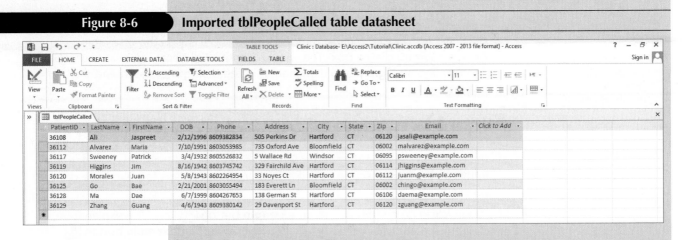

PatientID	LastName	FirstName	DOB	Phone	Address	City	State	Zip	Email	Click to Add
36108	Ali	Jaspreet	2/12/1996	8609382834	505 Perkins Dr	Hartford	CT	06120	jasali@example.com	
36112	Alvarez	Maria	7/10/1991	8603053985	735 Oxford Ave	Bloomfield	CT	06002	malvarez@example.com	
36117	Sweeney	Patrick	3/4/1932	8605526832	5 Wallace Rd	Windsor	CT	06095	psweeney@example.com	
36119	Higgins	Jim	8/16/1942	8603745742	329 Fairchild Ave	Hartford	CT	06114	jhiggins@example.com	
36120	Morales	Juan	5/8/1943	8602264954	33 Noyes Ct	Hartford	CT	06112	juanm@example.com	
36125	Go	Bae	2/21/2001	8603055494	183 Everett Ln	Bloomfield	CT	06002	chingo@example.com	
36128	Ma	Dae	6/7/1999	8604267653	138 German St	Hartford	CT	06106	daema@example.com	
36129	Zhang	Guang	4/6/1943	8609380142	29 Davenport St	Hartford	CT	06120	zguang@example.com	

2. Save and close the table.

Kelly has received a file from another clinic that contains a table of referral patients in an Access database. She'd like you to import this table into the Clinic database, creating a new table called tblReferral.

Importing a table from an Access Database

You can import tables, queries, reports, and other Access database objects. While you can import only a table's structure to create a blank new table, Kelly wants the data in the referral file imported into the Clinic database as well. You'll import the structure and data of the table into the Clinic database as a new table.

To import an Access table:

1. Click the **EXTERNAL DATA** tab (if necessary), and then in the Import & Link group, click the **Access** button. The Get External Data-Access Database dialog box opens.

> **Trouble?** If the Export - Access File dialog box opens, you clicked the Access File button in the Export group. Click the Cancel button and then repeat Step 1, being sure to select the Access File button from the Import & Link group.

2. Click the **Browse** button. The File Open dialog box opens. The Access database file from which you need to import the table structure is named NewPatientReferrals and is located in the Access2 ▸ Tutorial folder provided with your Data Files.

3. Navigate to the **Access2 ▸ Tutorial** folder where your starting Data Files are stored, click the **NewPatientReferrals** database file to select it, and then click the **Open** button.

4. Make sure the **Import tables, queries, forms, reports, macros, and modules into the current database** option button is selected, and then click the **OK** button. The Import Objects dialog box opens.

5. Click the **Options** button in the dialog box to see all the options for importing tables.

There is only one table in the NewPatientReferrals database. You'll import the tblReferral table and all of its data.

▶ **6.** On the Tables tab, click **tblReferral** to select this table. See Figure 8-7.

Figure 8-7   **Import Objects dialog box showing tblReferral**

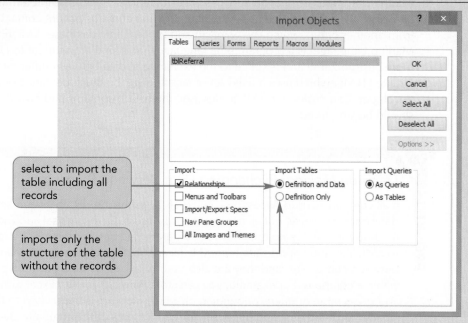

▶ **7.** In the Import Tables section of the dialog box, click the **Definition and Data** option button if necessary, and then click the **OK** button. Access creates the tblReferral table in the Clinic database using the structure and contents of the tblReferral table in the NewPatientReferrals database, and opens a dialog box asking if you want to save the import steps.

▶ **8.** Click the **Close** button to close the dialog box without saving the import steps.

▶ **9.** Open the Navigation Pane (if necessary) and note that the tblReferral table is listed in the Tables section.

▶ **10.** Double-click **tblReferral** to open the table. The tblReferral table opens in Datasheet view. See Figure 8-8.

Figure 8-8   **Imported tblReferral table datasheet**

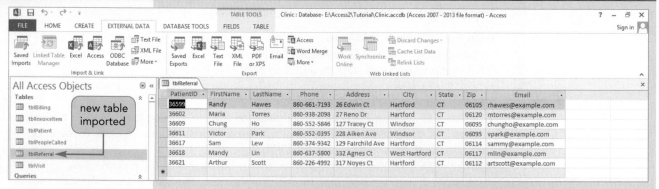

▶ **11.** Close the tblReferral table.

Next, Kelly would like you to import data from another file containing new patient referrals from another clinic. However, this data is not in an Access table; instead, it's stored in XML format.

Using XML

Chatham Community Health Services occasionally receives patient referrals from other clinics. Kelly was provided an XML document that contains patient contact information from another clinic, which she wants to add to the Clinic database. XML (Extensible Markup Language) is a programming language that is similar in format to HTML, but is more customizable and is suited to the exchange of data between different programs. Unlike HTML, which uses a fixed set of tags to describe the appearance of a web page, developers can customize XML to describe the data it contains and how that data should be structured.

PROSKILLS

Decision Making: Exchanging Data Between Programs

If all companies used Access, you could easily exchange data between any two databases. However, not all companies use Access. One universal and widely used method for transferring data between different database systems is to export data to XML files and import data from XML files. XML files are used to exchange data between companies, and they are also used to exchange data between programs within a company. For example, you can store data either in an Excel workbook or in an Access table or query, depending on which program is best suited to the personnel working with the data and the business requirements of the company. Because the XML file format is a common format for both Excel and Access—as well as many other programs—whenever the data is needed in another program, you can export the data from one program as an XML file and then import the file into the other program. You should consider the needs of the users and the characteristics of the programs they use when deciding the best means for exchanging data between programs.

Importing Data from an XML File

Access can import data from an XML file directly into a database table. Kelly's XML file is named Referral.xml, and you'll import it into the tblReferral table in the Clinic database, adding the XML records to the end of the table.

REFERENCE

Importing an XML File as an Access Table

- On the EXTERNAL DATA tab, in the Import & Link group, click the XML File button to open the Get External Data - XML File dialog box; or right-click the table name in the Navigation pane, click Import, and then click XML File.
- Click the Browse button, navigate to the location of the XML file, click the XML file-name, and then click the Open button.
- Click the OK button in the Get External Data - XML File dialog box, click the table name in the Import XML dialog box, click the appropriate option button in the Import Options section, and then click the OK button.
- Click the Close button; or if you need to save the import steps, click the Save import steps check box, enter a name for the saved steps in the Save as box, and then click the Save Import button.

Now you will import the Referral XML document as an Access database table.

To import the contents of the XML document:

▶ **1.** In the Navigation Pane, right-click the **tblReferral** table name in the Tables objects listing, point to **Import**, then click **XML File**. The Get External Data - XML File dialog box opens.

▶ **2.** Click the **Browse** button, navigate to the **Access2 ▸ Tutorial** folder, click **Referral**, and then click the **Open** button. The selected path and filename now appear in the File name box.

▶ **3.** Click the **OK** button. The Import XML dialog box opens. See Figure 8-9.

| Figure 8-9 | Import XML dialog box |

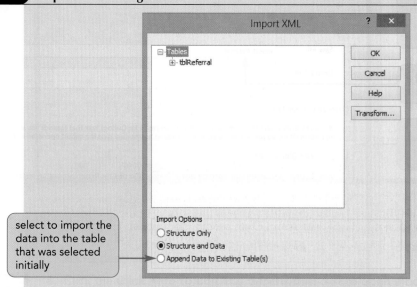

select to import the data into the table that was selected initially

From the XML file, you can import only the table structure to a new table, import the table structure and data to a new table, or append the data in the XML file to an existing table. You'll import the data to the tblReferral table, which you selected to begin this import process.

TIP

To add records from an XML file to an existing table, in the Import XML dialog box click the Append Data to Existing Table(s) option button.

▶ **4.** Make sure the **Append Data to Existing Table(s)** option button is selected, click **tblReferral** in the box, and then click the **OK** button. The Import XML dialog box closes, and the last Get External Data - XML File dialog box is displayed. You'll continue to work with this dialog box in the next set of steps.

Saving and Running Import Specifications

If you need to repeat the same import procedure many times, you can save the steps for the procedure and expedite future imports by running the saved import steps without using a wizard. Because the other clinic will send Kelly additional lists of patient referrals in the future, you'll save the import steps for Kelly so she can reuse them whenever she receives a new list.

Figure 8-16   **Saving the export steps**

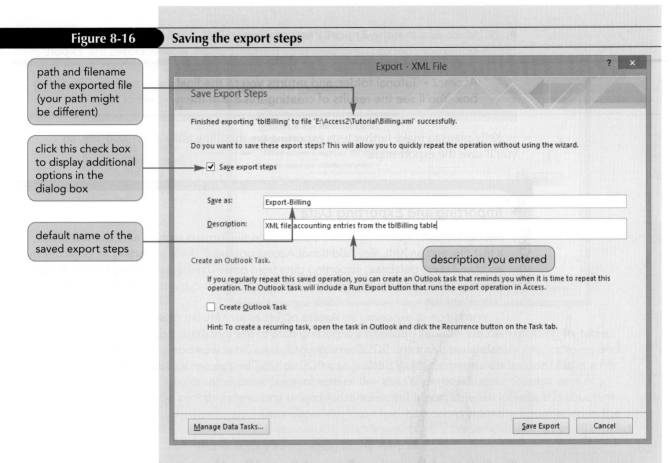

path and filename of the exported file (your path might be different)

click this check box to display additional options in the dialog box

default name of the saved export steps

Export - XML File

Save Export Steps

Finished exporting 'tblBilling' to file 'E:\Access2\Tutorial\Billing.xml' successfully.

Do you want to save these export steps? This will allow you to quickly repeat the operation without using the wizard.

☑ Save export steps

Save as: Export-Billing

Description: XML file accounting entries from the tblBilling table

description you entered

Create an Outlook Task.

If you regularly repeat this saved operation, you can create an Outlook task that reminds you when it is time to repeat this operation. The Outlook task will include a Run Export button that runs the export operation in Access.

☐ Create Outlook Task

Hint: To create a recurring task, open the task in Outlook and click the Recurrence button on the Task tab.

Manage Data Tasks...   Save Export   Cancel

3. Click the **Save Export** button. The export steps are saved as Export-Billing and the Export - XML File dialog box closes.

Now you'll run the saved steps.

4. Click the **EXTERNAL DATA** tab (if necessary), and then in the Export group, click the **Saved Exports** button. The Manage Data Tasks dialog box opens with the Saved Exports tab selected. See Figure 8-17.

Trouble? If the Saved Imports tab is visible, then you selected the Saved Imports button instead of the Saved Exports button. Click the Close button and repeat Step 4.

Figure 8-17	Manage Data Tasks dialog box

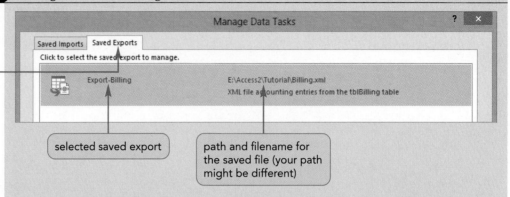

Saved Exports tab selected

selected saved export

path and filename for the saved file (your path might be different)

▶ **5.** Verify that the Export-Billing procedure you created in Step 3 is selected, and then click the **Run** button. The saved procedure runs and a message box opens, asking if you want to replace the existing XML file you created earlier.

▶ **6.** Click the **Yes** button to replace the existing XML file. A message box informs you that the export was completed successfully.

▶ **7.** Click the **OK** button to close the message box, and then click the **Close** button to close the Manage Data Tasks dialog box.

▶ **8.** Open Windows File Explorer, navigate to the **Access2 ▸ Tutorial** folder, right-click **Billing.xml** in the file list to open the shortcut menu, click **Open with**, and then click **Notepad**.

The Billing.xml file contains the data itself, along with code that describes the data, as shown in Visual Overview 8.1.

▶ **9.** Close the Notepad window.

▶ **10.** If you are not continuing on to the next session, close the Clinic database.

You've imported and exported data, analyzed a table's design, and saved and run import and export specifications. In the next session, you will analyze data by working with a chart, create and use an application part, link external data, and add a tab control to a form.

REVIEW

Session 8.1 Quick Check

1. What is HTML?
2. What is an HTML template?
3. What is a static web page?
4. What is a CSV file?
5. What is the Table Analyzer?
6. _____ is a programming language that describes data and its structure.

Session 8.2 Visual Overview:

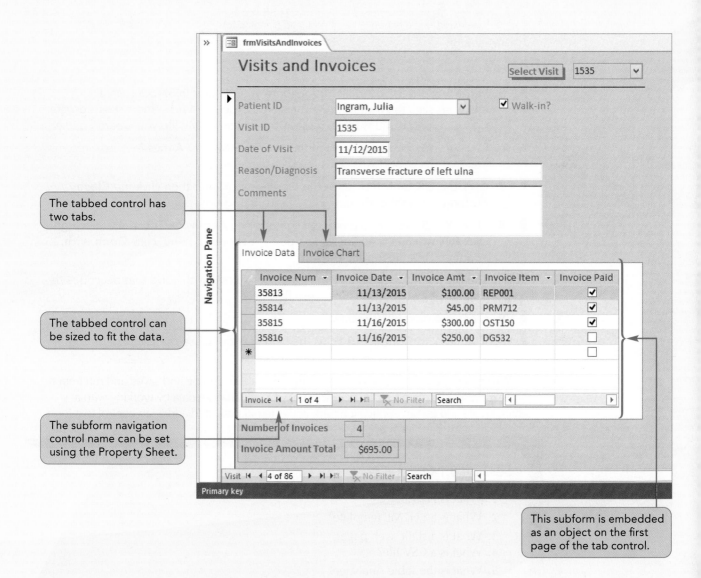

The tabbed control has two tabs.

The tabbed control can be sized to fit the data.

The subform navigation control name can be set using the Property Sheet.

This subform is embedded as an object on the first page of the tab control.

Navigation Pane

frmVisitsAndInvoices

Visits and Invoices

Select Visit | 1535

Patient ID	Ingram, Julia	☑ Walk-in?
Visit ID	1535
Date of Visit	11/12/2015
Reason/Diagnosis	Transverse fracture of left ulna
Comments	

Invoice Data | Invoice Chart

Invoice Num	Invoice Date	Invoice Amt	Invoice Item	Invoice Paid
35813	11/13/2015	$100.00	REP001	☑
35814	11/13/2015	$45.00	PRM712	☑
35815	11/16/2015	$300.00	OST150	☑
35816	11/16/2015	$250.00	DG532	☐
*				☐

Invoice ◄ 1 of 4 ► ►► No Filter Search ◄ ►

Number of Invoices	4
Invoice Amount Total	$695.00

Visit ◄ 4 of 86 ► ►► No Filter Search ◄

Primary key

Tabbed Control with a Chart

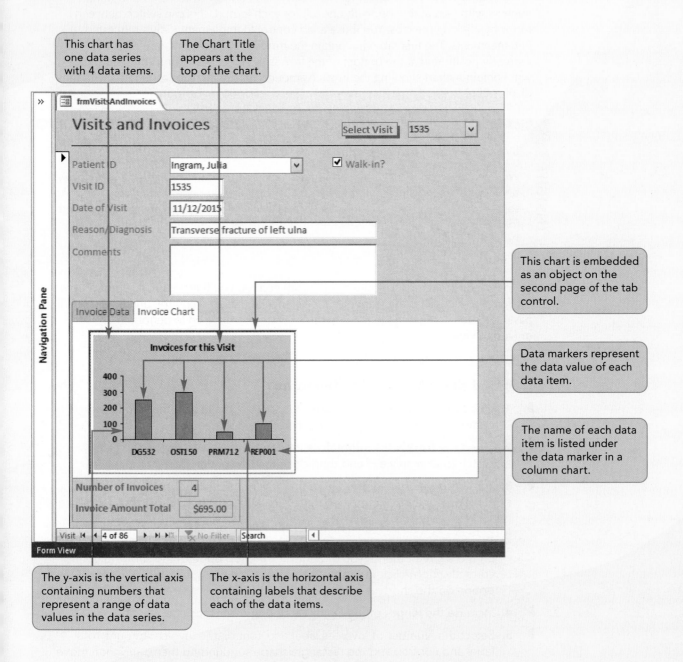

This chart has one data series with 4 data items.

The Chart Title appears at the top of the chart.

This chart is embedded as an object on the second page of the tab control.

Data markers represent the data value of each data item.

The name of each data item is listed under the data marker in a column chart.

The y-axis is the vertical axis containing numbers that represent a range of data values in the data series.

The x-axis is the horizontal axis containing labels that describe each of the data items.

Creating a Tabbed Form Using a Tab Control

Kelly wants you to enhance the frmVisitsAndInvoices form to enable users to switch between different content. Specifically, she wants users to be able to choose between viewing the frmBillingSubform subform or viewing a chart showing the invoices associated with the displayed visit.

You can use the **Tab Control tool** to insert a tab control, which is a control that appears with tabs at the top, with one tab for each form. Users can switch between forms by clicking the tabs. You'll use a tab control to implement Kelly's requested enhancements. The first tab will contain the frmBillingSubform subform that is currently positioned at the bottom of the frmVisitsAndInvoices form. The second tab will contain a chart showing the invoice amounts for the invoices associated with the displayed visit.

INSIGHT

Working with Large Forms

When you want to work with a form that is too large to display in the Access window, one way to help you navigate the form is to manually add page breaks, where it makes sense to do so. You can use the **Page Break tool** to insert a page break control in the form, which lets users move between the form pages by pressing the Page Up and Page Down keys.

To expedite placing the subform in the tab control, you'll first cut the subform from the form, placing it on the Clipboard. You'll then add the tab control, and finally you'll paste the subform into the left tab on the tab control. You need to perform these steps in Design view.

To add the tab control to the form:

▶ 1. If you took a break after the previous session, make sure that the Clinic database is open with the Navigation Pane displayed.

▶ 2. Open the **frmVisitsAndInvoices** form in Form view to review the form, switch to Design view, and then close the Navigation Pane.

▶ 3. Scroll down to the subform (if necessary), right-click the top edge of the subform control to open the shortcut menu, and then click **Cut** to delete the subform control and place it on the Clipboard.

Trouble? If you do not see Subform in New Window as one of the options on the shortcut menu, you did not click the top edge of the subform control correctly. Right-click the top edge of the subform control until you see this option on the shortcut menu, and then click Cut.

▶ 4. Increase the length of the Detail section to 6.5 inches.

▶ 5. Select the Number of Invoices label and control, the Invoice Amount Total label and control, and the rectangle shape surrounding them, and then move them below the 6-inch horizontal line in the grid.

▶ 6. On the DESIGN tab, in the Controls group, click the **Tab Control** tool 🗋.

▶ 7. Position the + portion of the pointer in the Detail section at the 2.75-inch mark on the vertical ruler and three grid dots from the left edge of the grid, and then click the mouse button. Access places a tab control with two pages in the form.

8. Right-click in the middle of the tab control, and then when an orange outline appears inside the tab control, click **Paste** on the shortcut menu. The subform is pasted in the tab control. See Figure 8-18.

Figure 8-18   Subform on the tab control in the Detail section

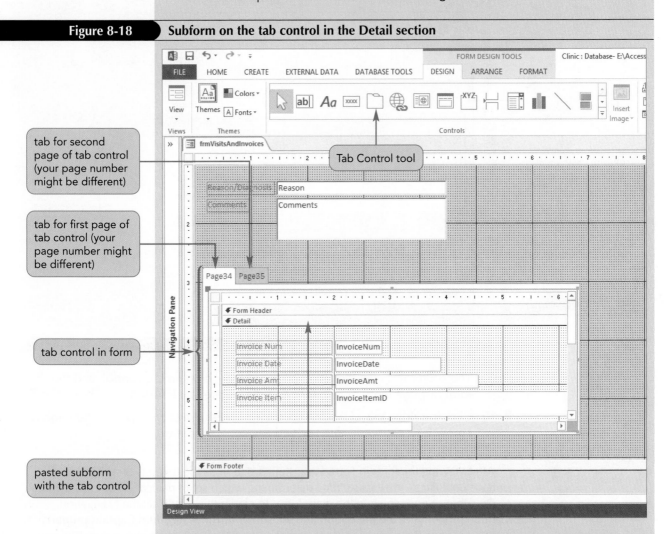

tab for second page of tab control (your page number might be different)

tab for first page of tab control (your page number might be different)

tab control in form

pasted subform with the tab control

9. Switch to Form view, and then click **1527** in the VisitID text box to deselect all controls. The left tab, which represents the first page in the tab control, is the active tab. See Figure 8-19.

Figure 8-19   **Subform on the tab control in Form view**

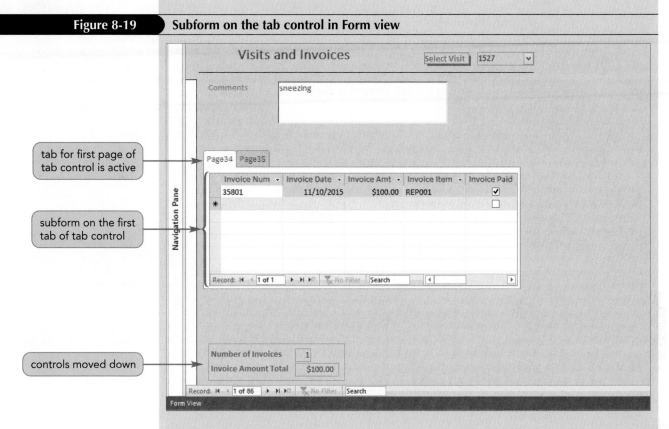

tab for first page of
tab control is active

subform on the first
tab of tab control

controls moved down

The subform is now displayed on the first page of the tab control, and the
form displays the same content as it did before you inserted the tab control.

▶ **10.** Click the **right tab** of the tab control to display the second page. The page is
empty because you haven't added any controls to it yet.

After viewing the form in Form view, Kelly's staff finds the two sets of navigation
buttons confusing—they waste time determining which set of navigation buttons applies
to the subform and which to the main form. To clarify this, you'll set the Navigation
Caption property for the main form and the subform. The **Navigation Caption property**
lets you change the navigation label from the word "Record" to another value. Because
the main form displays data about visits and the subform displays data about invoices,
you'll change the Navigation Caption property for the main form to "Visit" and for the
subform to "Invoice."

You'll also edit the labels for the tabs in the tab control, so they indicate the contents
of each page.

To change the captions for the navigation buttons and the tabs:

▶ **1.** Switch to Design view.

▶ **2.** Click the **form selector** for the main form to select the form control in the
main form, open the property sheet to display the properties for the selected
form control, click the **All** tab (if necessary), click the **Navigation Caption**
box, and then type **Visit**. See Figure 8-20.

Figure 8-20   Setting the Navigation Caption property for the main form

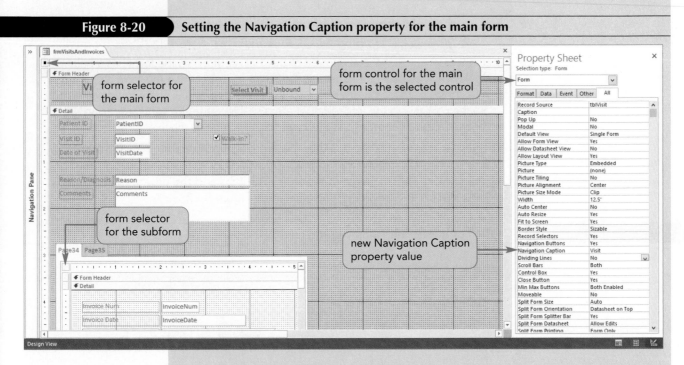

3. Click the **form selector** for the subform to select the subform, click the **form selector** for the subform again to select the form control in the subform and to display the properties for the selected form control, on the Property Sheet click the **Navigation Caption** box, and then type **Invoice**. Navigation buttons don't appear in Design view, so you won't see the effects of the Navigation Caption property settings until you switch to Form view.

4. Click the **left tab** in the subform, click the **left tab** in the subform again to select it, on the Property Sheet in the Caption box type **Invoice Data**, and then press the **Tab** key. The Caption property value now appears in the left tab. See Figure 8-21.

Figure 8-21   Setting the Caption property for the left tab

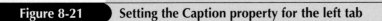

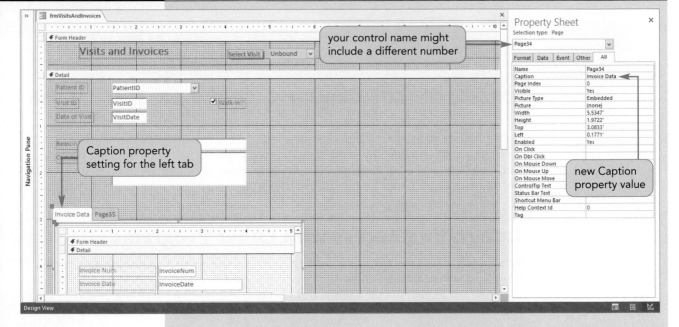

▶ **5.** Click the **right tab** in the subform to select it, on the Property Sheet in the Caption box, type **Invoice Chart**, and then close the property sheet.

▶ **6.** If necessary, adjust the alignment of the form controls so the form has a balanced look. You may need to adjust the vertical spacing between the form controls so the controls are evenly spaced, and adjust the placement of the heading controls so they align with the left and right margins. Decrease the vertical spacing between form controls to fit the form on the screen as much as possible.

▶ **7.** Save your form design changes, switch to Form view, select VisitID 1527 in the combo box, click **1527** in the VisitID text box to deselect all controls, and then scroll to the bottom of the form. The tabs and the navigation buttons now display the new caption values. See Figure 8-22.

Figure 8-22	Caption properties and aligned form controls

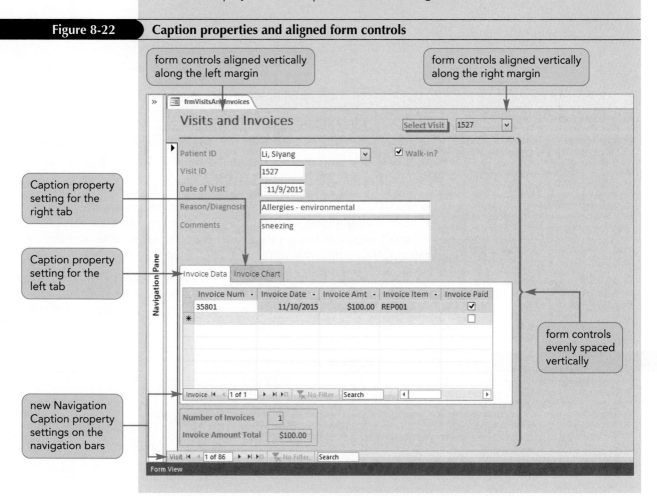

Next, Kelly wants you to add a simple chart to the second page of the tab control. This chart will be created by another program that's part of Microsoft Office, called Microsoft Graph. Before creating and adding the chart, it's important to understand the different ways of integrating external data with Access.

Integrating Access with Other Programs

When you create a form or report in Access, you include more than just the data from the record source table or query. You've added controls such as lines, rectangles, tab controls, and graphics in your forms and reports to improve their appearance and usability. You can also add charts, drawings, and other objects to your forms and

reports, but Access doesn't have the capability to create them. Instead, you create these objects using other programs and then place them in a form or report using the appropriate integration method.

When you integrate information between programs, the program containing the original information, or object, is called the **source program**, and the program in which you place the information created by the source program is called the **destination program**. Access offers three ways for you to integrate objects created by other programs.

- **Importing**. When you import an object, you include the contents of a file in a new table or append it to an existing table, or you include the contents of the file in a form, report, or field. For example, when you add a picture to a form, you import it into the form; likewise, in this tutorial you imported CSV and XML files as new tables in the Clinic database. An imported picture is a file with a .bmp extension that was created by a graphics program, and the CSV and XML files you imported were also created by other programs. After importing an object, it no longer has a connection to the program that created it. Any subsequent changes you make to the object using the source program are not reflected in the imported object.

- **Embedding**. When you embed an object in a form, report, or field, you preserve its connection to the source program, which enables you to edit the object, if necessary, using the features of the source program. However, any changes you make to the object are reflected only in the form, report, or field in which it is embedded; the changes do not affect the original object in the file from which it was embedded. Likewise, if you start the source program outside Access and make any changes to the original object, these changes are not reflected in the embedded object. The features of the source program determine which features are available for the embedded object.

- **Linking**. When you link an object to a form, report, or field, you include a connection in the destination program to the original file maintained by the source program; you do not store data from the file in the destination program. Any changes you make to the original file using the source program are reflected in the linked file version in the destination program.

Decision Making: Importing, Embedding, and Linking Data

How do you decide which method to use when you need to include in an Access database data that is stored in another file or format? When you intend to use Access to maintain the data and no longer need an updated version of the data in the source program, you can import a file as a new table or append the records in the file to an existing table. You link to the data when the source program will continue to maintain the data in the file, and you need to use an updated version of the file at all times in the destination program. When linking to the data, you can also maintain the data using the destination program, and the source program will always use the updated version of the file.

- For objects in forms or reports, you import an object (such as a picture) when you want a copy of the object in your form or report and you don't intend to make any changes to the object. You embed or link an object when you want a copy of the object in your form or report and you intend to edit the object using the source program in the future. You embed the object when you do not want your edits to the object in the destination program to affect any other copies of the object used by other programs. You link the object when you want your edits to the object in the destination program to affect the object used by other programs.

- The decision to import, embed, or link to data depends on how you will use the data in your database, and what connection is required to the original data. You should carefully consider the effect of changes to the original data and to the copied data before choosing which method to use.

To add the chart that Kelly wants on the second page of the tab control, you'll embed data from another program.

Embedding a Chart in a Form

The Chart Wizard in Access helps you to embed a chart in a form or report. The chart is actually created by another program, Microsoft Graph, but the Chart Wizard does the work of embedding the chart. After embedding the chart in a form or report, you can edit it using the Microsoft Graph program.

REFERENCE

Embedding a Chart in a Form or Report

- In Design view, on the DESIGN tab, in the Controls group, click the More button, and then click the Chart tool 📊.
- Position the + portion of the pointer where you want to position the upper-left corner of the chart, and then click the mouse button to start the Chart Wizard.
- Select the record source, fields, and chart type.
- Edit the chart contents, and select the fields that link the object and chart, if necessary.
- Enter a chart title, select whether to include a legend, and then click the Finish button.

The tblBilling table contains the information needed for the chart Kelly wants you to include in the form's right tab in the tab control.

To add a chart in the tab control and start the Chart Wizard:

1. Switch to Design view, then on the Invoice Chart tab on the tab control click the **subform**, and then click the **subform** again to ensure the tab content is selected.

2. On the DESIGN tab, in the Controls group, click the **Chart** tool 📊, and then move the pointer to the tab control. When the pointer is inside the tab control, the rectangular portion of the tab control you can use to place controls is filled in black.

3. Position the + portion of the pointer in the upper-left corner of the black portion of the tab control, and then click the mouse button. Access places a chart control in the form and opens the first Chart Wizard dialog box, in which you select the source record for the chart.

Kelly wants the chart to provide her staff with a simple visual display of the relative proportions of the invoice amounts for the invoice items for the currently displayed patient visit. You'll use the tblBilling table as the record source for the chart and select the InvoiceAmt and InvoiceItem fields as the fields to use in the chart.

The order of the items is important. Be sure to add InvoiceItemID first, then InvoiceAmt. If you make a mistake, move both back to the Available Fields and start again.

To create the chart with the Chart Wizard:

1. Click **Table: tblBilling** in the box, and then click the **Next** button to display the second Chart Wizard dialog box.

2. Add the InvoiceItemID and InvoiceAmt fields to the Fields for Chart box, in that order, and then click the **Next** button to display the third Chart Wizard dialog box, in which you choose the chart type.

3. Click the **Pie Chart** button (row 4, column 1) to select the pie chart as the chart type to use for Kelly's chart. The box on the right displays a brief description of the selected chart type. See Figure 8-23.

Figure 8-23   **Selecting the chart type**

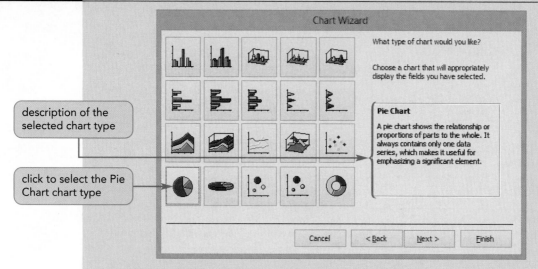

description of the selected chart type

click to select the Pie Chart chart type

4. Click the **Next** button to display the next Chart Wizard dialog box, which displays a preview of the chart and options to modify the data and its placement in the chart. You'll use the default layout based on the two selected fields. You can easily modify the chart after you create it.

5. Click the **Next** button to display the next Chart Wizard dialog box, which lets you choose the fields that link records in the main form (which uses the tblVisit table as its record source) to records in the chart (which uses the tblBilling table as its record source). You don't need to make any changes in this dialog box, as the wizard has already identified VisitID as the common field linking these two tables. You can use the VisitID field as the linking field even though you didn't select it as a field for the chart.

6. Click the **Next** button to display the final dialog box, which allows you to enter the title that will appear at the top of the chart and choose whether to include a legend in the chart.

7. Type **Invoices for this Visit**, make sure the **Yes, display a legend** option button is selected, and then click the **Finish** button. The completed chart appears in the tab control.

You'll view the form in Form view, where it's easier to assess the chart's appearance.

8. Save your form design changes, switch to Form view, in the combo box select Visit ID **1535**, click the **Invoice Chart** tab to display the chart, and then scroll down to the bottom of the form (if necessary). See Figure 8-24.

Figure 8-24   **Embedded chart in Form view**

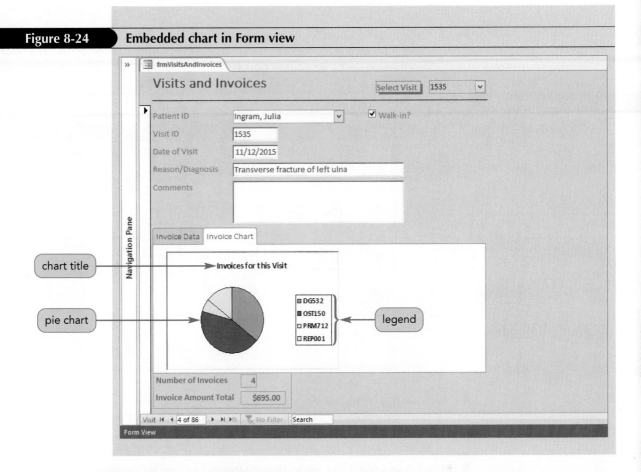

Linking Record Sources

The record source for a primary main form must have a one-to-many relationship to the record source for a related subform or chart. The subform or chart object has its Link Master Fields property set to the primary key in the record source for the main form and its Link Child Fields property set to the foreign key in the record source for the subform or chart.

After viewing the chart, Kelly decides it needs some modifications. She wants you to change the chart type from a pie chart to a bar chart, remove the legend, and modify the chart's background color. To make these changes, you'll switch to Design view and then you'll start Microsoft Graph.

To edit the chart using Microsoft Graph:

▶ **1.** Switch to Design view, right-click an edge of the chart object to open the shortcut menu, point to **Chart Object**, and then click **Open**. Microsoft Graph starts and displays the chart. See Figure 8-25.

   Trouble? If Chart Object doesn't appear on the shortcut menu, right-click the edge until it does.

| Figure 8-25 | Editing the chart with Microsoft Graph |

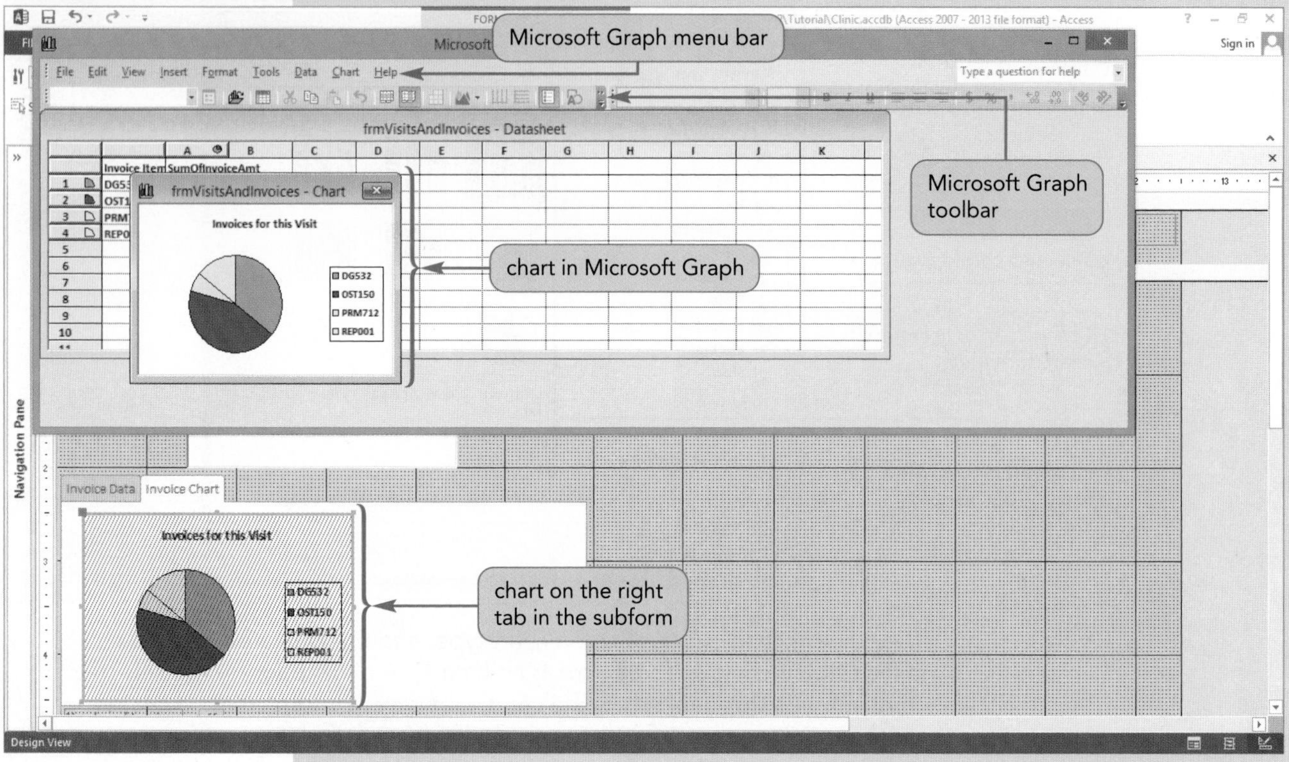

Microsoft Graph is the source program that the Chart Wizard used to create the chart. Because the chart was embedded in the form, editing the chart object starts Graph and allows you to edit the chart using the Graph menu bar and toolbar. In addition to displaying the selected chart, the Graph window displays a datasheet containing the data on which the chart is based. You'll now make Kelly's chart changes using Graph.

2. On the Graph menu bar, click **Chart**, click **Chart Type** to open the Chart Type dialog box, and then click **Column** in the Chart type box to display the types of column charts. See Figure 8-26.

Figure 8-26   **Chart Type dialog box**

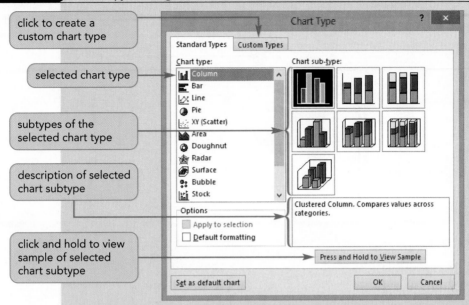

click to create a custom chart type

selected chart type

subtypes of the selected chart type

description of selected chart subtype

click and hold to view sample of selected chart subtype

The column chart is the selected chart type, and the clustered column chart is the default chart subtype (row 1, column 1). A description of the selected chart subtype appears below the chart subtypes. You can create a custom chart by clicking the Custom Types tab. If you click and hold on the Press and Hold to View Sample button, you'll see a sample of the selected subtype.

3. Click the **Press and Hold to View Sample** button to view a sample of the chart, release the mouse button, and then click the **OK** button to close the dialog box and change the chart to a column chart in the Graph window and in the form.

4. On the Graph menu bar, click **Chart**, click **Chart Options** to open the Chart Options dialog box, click the **Legend** tab to display the chart's legend options, click the **Show legend** check box to clear it, and then click the **OK** button. The legend is removed from the chart object in the Graph window and in the form.

To change the color or other properties of a chart control—the chart background (or chart area), axes, labels to the left of the y-axis, labels below the x-axis, or data markers (columnar bars for a column chart)—you need to double-click the control.

5. In the Chart window, double-click one of the blue data markers inside the chart to open the Format Data Series dialog box, and then in the Area section, in the color palette, click the orange box (row 2, column 2). The sample color in the dialog box changes to orange to match the selected color in the color palette. See Figure 8-27.

Trouble? If you click off the chart in MS Graph, and the chart disappears, just click View on the menu bar, and then click Datasheet to bring the chart back.

TIP

A data marker is a bar, dot, segment, or other symbol that represents a single data value.

Figure 8-27   **Format Data Series dialog box**

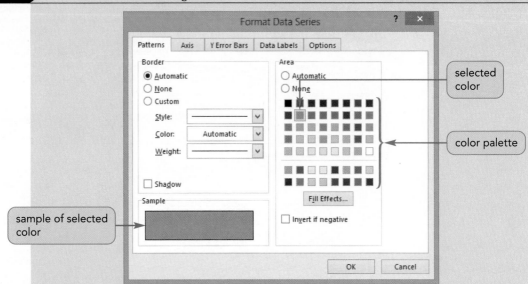

6. Click the **OK** button to close the dialog box. The color of the data markers in the chart in the Graph window and in the form changes to orange.

   Trouble? If only one of the bars changed color, you selected one bar instead of the entire series. Click Edit, click Undo, and then repeat Steps 5 and 6.

7. In the Chart window, double-click the white chart background to the left of the title to open the Format Chart Area dialog box, in the Area section in the color palette click the light orange box (row 5, column 2), and then click the **OK** button. The chart's background color changes from white to light orange in the chart in the Graph window and in the form.

8. Click **File** on the Graph menu bar, and then click **Exit & Return to frmVisitsAndInvoices** to exit Graph and return to the form.

9. Save your form design changes, switch to Form view, in the combo box select Visit ID **1535** and then click the **Invoice Chart** tab to display the chart. See Figure 8-28.

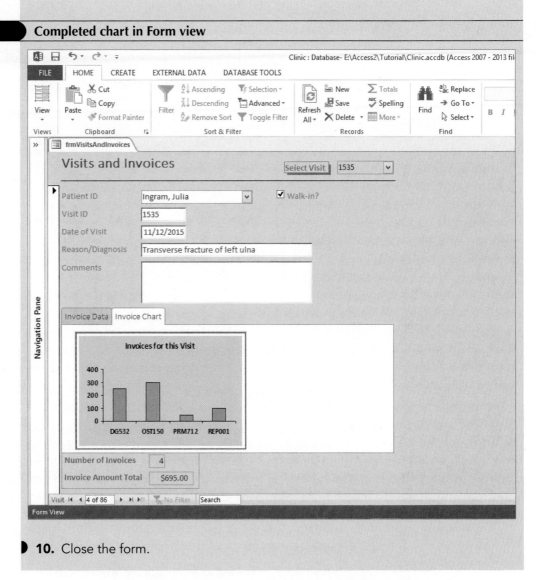

| Figure 8-28 | Completed chart in Form view |

10. Close the form.

Kelly has found the tblReferral table so useful that she'd like to be able to use the same table structure in other databases. One option would be to import the table structure from the NewPatientReferrals.accdb database file into each database. Another option is to create an application part from the NewPatientReferrals database, which could then easily be included in any Access database file on Kelly's computer.

Using Templates and Application Parts

A template is a predefined database that can include tables, relationships, queries, forms, reports, and other database objects. When you create a new database using Backstage view, Access displays a list of predefined templates. You can also create your own template from an existing database file. In addition to creating a standard template, you can also create an **application part**, which is a specialized template that can be imported into an existing database. A standard template would be used to create a new database file. An application part is used when you already have a database file that you're working with, and would like to include the content from an application part in your existing database. Like a template, an application part can contain tables, relationships, queries, forms, reports, and other database objects.

Kelly would like to reuse the tblReferral table structure to store a table of referrals from local pharmacists. You'll use the NewPatientReferrals.accdb database file to create an Application Part for the tblReferral table structure, then you'll import the new application part into the Clinic database to use for referrals from local pharmacists.

To create an application part from a database file:

► **1.** Click the **CREATE tab**, and then in the Templates group, click the **Application Parts** button to open the gallery of predefined application parts. See Figure 8-29.

Figure 8-29   **Predefined Application Parts**

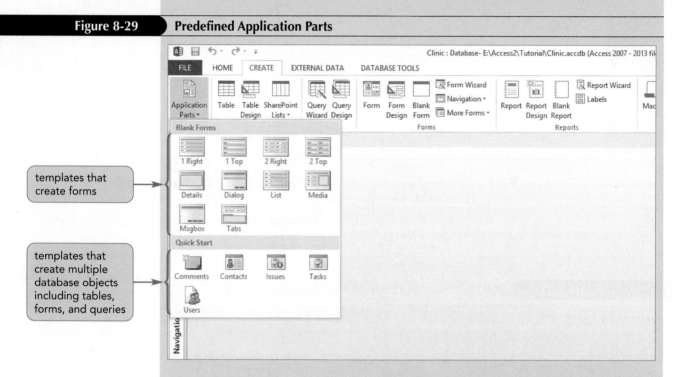

templates that create forms

templates that create multiple database objects including tables, forms, and queries

Note that there are Blank Forms and Quick Start Application Parts, but there are no user-defined application parts.

Trouble? If you see user-application parts listed in the Application Parts gallery it could be that these application parts were created by other users. Access will store Application Parts created from any Access database file and they will be available in all Access database files on the computer. You can disregard any user-defined application parts that you may see on your local computer.

► **2.** Close the Clinic database file.

► **3.** Open the NewPatientReferrals database file from the Access2 ► Tutorial folder included with your Data Files.

When you save this file as a template, all database objects that are in the file will be included in the template file. This file contains only the tblReferral table.

► **4.** Click the **FILE** tab to display Backstage view, and then click **Save As**.

► **5.** Click **Save Database As** (if necessary) and then in the Save Database As box in the Database File Types list click **Template**. See Figure 8-30.

Figure 8-30   Saving a database as a template

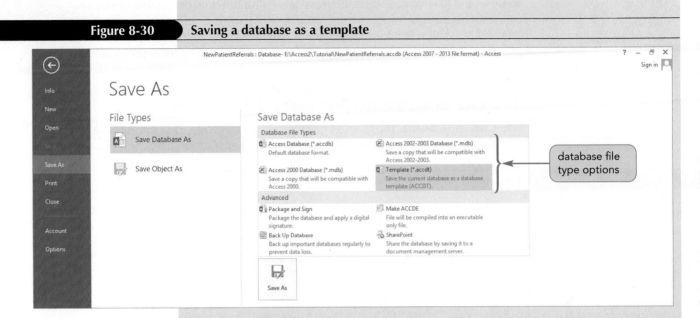

6. Click the **Save As** button. Access displays the **Create New Template from This Database** dialog box .

7. In the Name text box, type **Referral**. In the Description text box, type **New patient referral**, and then click the Application Part check box to select it. See Figure 8-31.

Figure 8-31   Create New Template from This Database dialog box

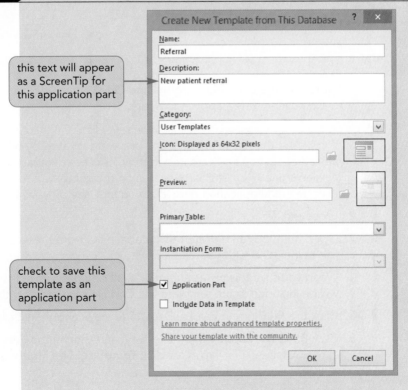

8. Click the **OK** button to close the dialog box. An alert box opens indicating that the template has been saved.

9. Click the **OK** button to close the message box, and then close the NewPatientReferrals database.

Now that you've created the application part, you'll use it in the Clinic database to create the referral table for patients who have been referred to the clinic by a pharmacist.

To use the application part to create the referral table:

1. Open the **Clinic** database, click the **CREATE** tab, and then click the **Application Parts** button. The Referral template is displayed in the User Templates section in the Application Parts list. See Figure 8-32.

| Figure 8-32 | Application Parts showing Referral template |

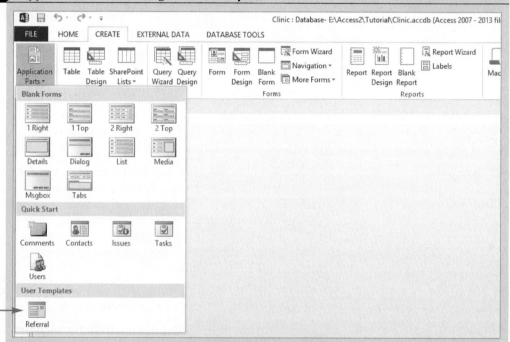

user-defined template added as an Application Part

2. Click **Referral**. The Create Relationship dialog box opens because the application part includes a table.

3. Click the **There is no relationship** option button. This indicates that the new table is not related to other tables in the current database. See figure 8-33.

Figure 8-33	Create Relationship dialog box

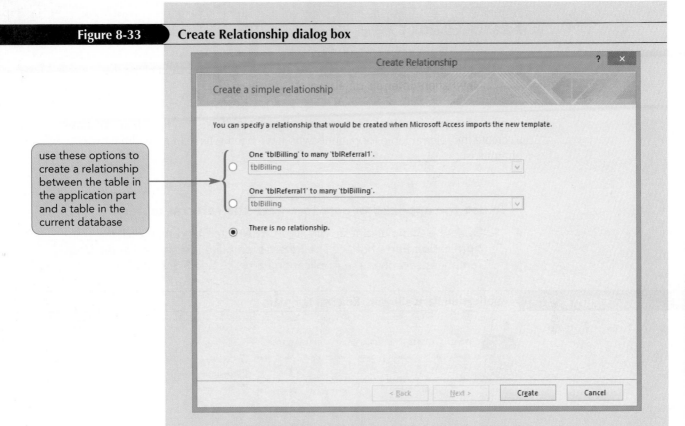

use these options to create a relationship between the table in the application part and a table in the current database

4. Click the **Create** button to insert the Referral database object into the current database, and then open the Navigation Pane.

    Only the tblReferral table will be inserted into the current database since the Referral template contains only one database object, which is the tblReferral table. Because the Clinic database already contains a table called tblReferral, the newly inserted table is named tblReferral1, to avoid overwriting the table that already exists. The newly inserted tblReferral1 will be used to store the patient information for patients referred by pharmacists. You'll rename this table as tblReferralPharm.

5. In the Navigation Pane, right-click the **tblReferral1** table, click **Rename**, change the name to **tblReferralPharm**, and then press **Enter**.

6. In the Navigation Pane, double-click **tblReferralPharm** to open it in Datasheet view.

    Note that the tblReferralPharm table contains the same fields as the tblReferral table but does not contain any records.

7. Close the tblReferralPharm table.

Kelly would like to be able to send an electronic copy of the rptVisitDetails report that other people can read on their computers, rather than distributing printed reports. You can export tables, queries, reports, and other database objects as files that can be opened in other programs such as Excel and PDF readers. Kelly would like to distribute rptVisitDetails as a PDF and asks you to export the report in this format.

Exporting a Report to a PDF File

PDF (portable document format) is a file format that preserves the original formatting and pagination of its contents no matter where it's viewed. Current versions of all major operating systems for desktop computers and handheld devices include software that opens PDF files. Most web browsers allow you to view PDF files as well. You'll create a PDF document from the rptVisitDetails report so Kelly can send this report to colleagues.

To export the rptVisitDetails report to a PDF file:

1. In the Navigation Pane, right-click **rptVisitDetails**, point to **Export** on the shortcut menu, and then click **PDF or XPS**. The Publish as PDF or XPS dialog box opens.

2. Navigate to the **Access2 ▸ Tutorial** folder included with your Data Files, and then change the name in the File name box to **Visit Details Report.pdf**. See Figure 8-34.

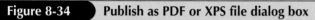

Figure 8-34   Publish as PDF or XPS file dialog box

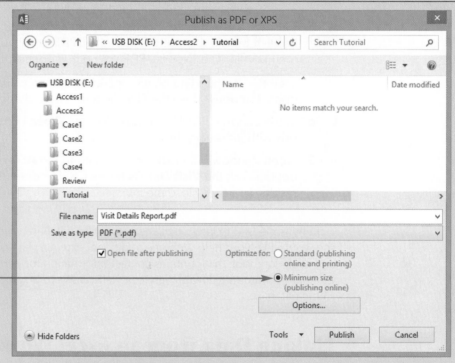

file size is reduced to minimize downloading time

Kelly would like people who are visually impaired to be able to use the PDF document with their screen readers. When a PDF file is saved using the minimum size option, there is no additional functionality for screen readers. You can include document structure tags that allow people using screen readers to navigate the document easily. Screen reader software voices the structure tags, such as a tag that provides a description of an image. Structure tags also reflow text so that screen readers understand the flow of information and can read it in a logical order. For instance, a page with a sidebar shouldn't be read as two columns; the main column needs to be read as a continuation of the previous page.

In order to add this functionality, you'll specify that document structure tags should be included.

> **3.** Click the **Options** button. The Options dialog box opens.

> **4.** Click the **Document structure tags for accessibility** check box to select it. See Figure 8-35.

Figure 8-35   **Options dialog box for PDF file export**

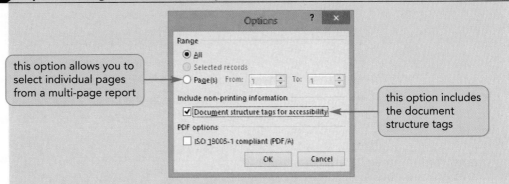

this option allows you to select individual pages from a multi-page report

this option includes the document structure tags

> **5.** Click the **OK** button to close the Options dialog box, and then click the **Publish** button to close the Publish as PDF or XPS dialog box and to create the PDF file. The Export – PDF dialog box opens.
>
> **Trouble?** Depending on the operating system you're using, the PDF file may open. If it does, close the PDF file and return to Access.

> **6.** In the Export – PDF dialog box, click the **Close** button to close the dialog box without saving the export steps.

> **7.** Open Windows File Explorer, navigate to the **Access2 ▸ Tutorial** folder, double-click the **Visit Details Report.pdf** to open the PDF file, examine the results, and then close the PDF file.

Kelly is pleased to know that she can export database objects as PDF files. Now she would like your help with one additional external data issue. Her staff maintains an Excel workbook that contains contact information for people who volunteer at Chatham Community Health Services. Kelly wants to be able to use this data in the Clinic database.

Linking Data from an Excel Worksheet

Kelly's staff has extensive experience working with Excel, and one of her staff members prefers to maintain the data for people who volunteer in the Volunteer workbook using Excel. However, Kelly needs to reference the volunteer data in the Clinic database on occasion, and the data she's referencing must always be the current version of the worksheet data. Importing the Excel workbook data as an Access table would provide Kelly with data that's quickly out of date unless she repeats the import steps each time the data in the Excel workbook changes. Because Kelly doesn't personally need to update the volunteer data in the Clinic database, you'll link to the workbook from the database. When the staff changes the Volunteer workbook, the changes will be reflected automatically in the linked version of the database table. At the same time, Kelly won't be able to update the volunteer data from the Clinic database, which ensures that only the staff members responsible for maintaining the volunteer workbook can update the data.

To link to the data in the Excel workbook:

▶ **1.** Click the **EXTERNAL DATA** tab, and then in the Import & Link group, click the **Excel** button (with the ScreenTip "Import Excel spreadsheet"). The Get External Data - Excel Spreadsheet dialog box opens.

   Trouble? If the Export - Excel File dialog box opens, you clicked the Excel File button in the Export group. Click the Cancel button and then repeat Step 1, being sure to select the Excel File button from the Import & Link group.

▶ **2.** Click the **Browse** button, navigate to the **Access2 ▸ Tutorial** folder included with your Data Files, click **Volunteer**, click the **Open** button, and then click the **Link to the data source by creating a linked table** option button. This option links to the data instead of importing or appending it. The selected path and filename are displayed in the File name box. See Figure 8-36.

| Figure 8-36 | Linking to data in an Excel workbook |

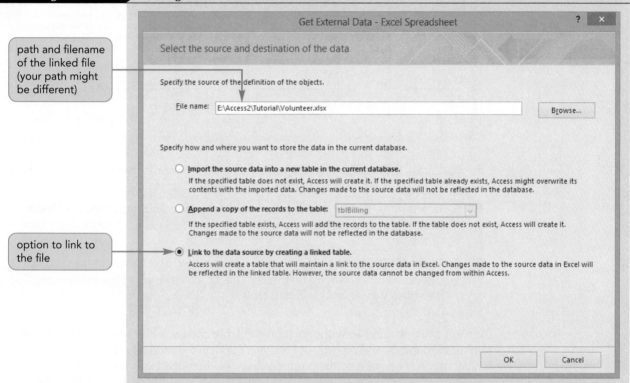

path and filename of the linked file (your path might be different)

File name: E:\Access2\Tutorial\Volunteer.xlsx

option to link to the file

▶ **3.** Click the **OK** button. The first Link Spreadsheet Wizard dialog box opens.

   The first row in the worksheet contains column heading names, and each row in the worksheet represents the data about a single product.

▶ **4.** Click the **First Row Contains Column Headings** check box to select it. See Figure 8-37.

Figure 8-37 **Link Spreadsheet Wizard dialog box**

option to use the first
row in the worksheet
as column heading
names

data in the worksheet
to be linked

5. Click the **Next** button to open the final Link Spreadsheet Wizard dialog box, in which you choose a name for the linked table.

6. Change the default table name to **tblVolunteer** and then click the **Finish** button. A message box informs you that you've created a table that's linked to the workbook.

7. Click the **OK** button to close the message box. The tblVolunteer table is displayed in the Navigation Pane. The icon to the left of the table name identifies the table as a linked table.

You can open and view the tblVolunteer table and use fields from the linked table in queries, forms, and reports, but you can't update the products data using the Clinic database. You can update the products data only from the Excel workbook.

Next, you'll make a change to data in the workbook and see the update in the linked table. Kelly tells you that the volunteer Crawford had not been able to volunteer for a while, so her Active status was **no**. She's now able to volunteer, and Kelly would like to change her Active status to **yes**.

To update the Excel workbook and view the data in the linked table:

1. Open Windows File Explorer, navigate to the **Access2 ▸ Tutorial** folder, right-click **Volunteer.xlsx**, and then open the file using **Microsoft Excel**. The Volunteer workbook opens and displays the Volunteer worksheet.

   Trouble? If you attempt to open the table in Access before you open the workbook, you'll get an error message and won't be able to open the workbook. Make sure you always open the workbook or other source file before you open a linked table.

▶ **2.** Switch to the Clinic database, and then open the **tblVolunteer** datasheet. The fields and records in the tblVolunteer table display the same data as the Volunteer worksheet.

▶ **3.** Switch to the Volunteer workbook, select the value **no** in the Active column for Maria Crawford (row 7), type **yes** to replace the value, and then press the **Enter** key.

▶ **4.** Switch to the Clinic database. Maria Crawford's Active status is now **yes**.

   You've completed your work for Kelly and her staff.

▶ **5.** Close the tblVolunteer table in Access.

▶ **6.** Switch to the Volunteer workbook, save your worksheet change, and then exit Excel.

▶ **7.** Make a backup copy of the database, compact and repair the database, and then close it.

Knowing how to create tabbed form controls and Application Parts, export data to PDF documents, and link to data maintained by other programs will make it easier for Kelly and her staff to work efficiently and manage their data.

REVIEW

Session 8.2 Quick Check

1. The _____ property lets you change the default navigation label from the word "Record" to another value.
2. What is the Microsoft Graph program?
3. What is a PDF file?
4. What is an application part?
5. What is the difference between an application part and a template?
6. How can you edit data in a table that has been linked to an Excel file?

ASSESS

SAM Projects

Put your skills into practice with SAM Projects! SAM Projects for this tutorial can be found online. If you have a SAM account, go to www.cengage.com/sam2013 to download the most recent Project Instructions and Start Files.

PRACTICE

Review Assignments

Data Files needed for the Review Assignments: Ads.xlsx, Partners.accdb, Payables.csv, Payments.xml, and Supplier.accdb *(cont. from Tutorial 7)*

Kelly wants you to integrate the data in the Supplier database with other programs, and she wants to be able to analyze the data in the database. Complete the following steps:

1. Open the **Supplier** database you worked with in Tutorials 5–7.
2. Export the qrySupplierProducts query as an HTML document to the Access2 ▸ Review folder provided with your Data Files, saving the file as **qrySupplierProducts.html**. Do not save the export steps.
3. Import the CSV file named Payables, which is located in the Access2 ▸ Review folder, as a new table in the database. Use the names in the first row as field names, use Currency as the data type for the numeric fields, choose your own primary key, name the table **tblPayable**, run the Table Analyzer, record the Table Analyzer's recommendation, and then cancel out of the Table Analyzer Wizard without making the recommended changes. Do not save the import steps.
4. Import the data and structure from the XML file named Payments, which is located in the Access2 ▸ Review folder, as a new table named **tblPayments** in the database. Save the import steps, and then rename the table **tblPayment**.
5. Export the tblSupplier table as an XML file named **Supplier.xml** to the Access2 ▸ Review folder; do not create a separate XSD file. Save the export steps.
6. The Chatham Community Health Services clinic also pays for advertisements. Link to the Ads.xlsx workbook, which is located in the Access2 ▸ Review folder, using **tblAd** as the table name. Change the cost of the flyer for Ad Num 5 to $300 and save the workbook.
7. Modify the **frmSuppliersWithProducts** form in the following ways:
   a. Size the text box controls for SupplierID, Company Name, Category, City, State, and Zip so that they are all the same width as the Address text box.
   b. Size the text box controls for ContactPhone, ContactFirstName, and ContactLastName so that they are all the same width as the InitialContact text box.
   c. Move the Number of Products label, text box, and rectangle so the right edge of the rectangle is aligned with the right edge of the InitialContact text box.
   d. Add a tab control to the bottom of the Detail section, so the left edge is aligned with the left edge of the Company Comments label, and then place the existing subform on the first page of the tab control.
   e. Change the caption for the left tab to **Product Data** and for the right tab to **Product Chart**.
   f. Change the caption for the main form's navigation buttons to **Supplier**.
   g. Add a chart to the second page of the tab control. Use the tblProduct table as the record source, select the ProductName and Price, use the 3-D Column Chart type (row 1, column 2), do not include a legend, and use **Products Offered** as the chart title.
   h. Change the chart to a 3-D Bar chart, and change the blue colored data markers to pink.
8. Export the **tblPayment** table as a PDF file called Payments.pdf, using document structure tags for accessibility. Do not save the export steps.

9. Open the **Partners** database from the Access2 ▶ Review folder, and then create and implement an application part as follows:

   a. Create an application part called **vendor** with the description **New vendor**, and do not include the data.

   b. Close the **Partners** database.

   c. Open the **Supplier** database and import the **vendor** application part, which has no relationship to any of the other tables. Open the tblNewVendor table to verify the data has been imported.

10. Make a backup copy of the database, compact and repair the database, and then close it.

Case Problem 1

APPLY

Data Files needed for this Case Problem: CreditCard.xml, Task.accdb (*cont. from Tutorial 7*), and Schedule.xlsx.

GoGopher!   Amol Mehta wants you to integrate the data in the Task database with other programs, and he wants to be able to analyze the data in the database. Complete the following steps:

1. Open the **Task** database you worked with in Tutorials 5–7.

2. Export the qryMemberNames query as an HTML document to the Access2 ▶ Case1 folder using a filename of **MemberNames.html**. Save the export steps.

3. Export the rptPlanMembership report as a PDF document with a filename of **Plan.pdf** to the Access2 ▶ Case1 folder. Include the document structure tags for accessibility, and do not save the export steps.

4. Import the data and structure from the XML file named CreditCard, which is located in the Access2 ▶ Case1 folder, as a new table. Save the import steps. Rename the table as **tblCreditCard**.

5. Export the tblPlan table as an XML file named **Plan** to the Access2 ▶ Case1 folder; do not create a separate XSD file. Save the export steps.

6. Link to the Schedule workbook, which is located in the Access2 ▶ Case1 folder, using **tblSchedule** as the table name. For TaskID 301, change the Day value to **F**.

7. Modify the **frmPlansWithMembers** form in the following ways:

   a. Add a tab control to the bottom of the Detail section, and place the existing subform on the first page of the tab control.

   b. Change the caption for the left tab to **Member Data** and for the right tab to **Member Chart**.

   c. Change the caption for the main form's navigation buttons to **Plan** and for the subform's navigation buttons to **Member**.

   d. Add a chart to the second page of the tab control. Use the tblPlan table as the record source, select the PlanID and PlanCost fields, use the Column Chart chart type, do not include a legend, and use **Plan Cost** as the chart title.

   e. Change the color of the data marker to red (row 3, column 1).

8. Make a backup copy of the database, compact and repair the database, and then close it.

Case Problem 2

CHALLENGE

Data Files needed for this Case Problem: AddSubject.xml, NewStudentReferrals.accdb, Tutoring.accdb (*cont. from Tutorial 7*), Room.xlsx and Subject.csv.

O'Brien Educational Services   Karen O'Brien wants you to integrate the data in the Tutoring database with other programs, and she wants to be able to analyze the data in the database. Complete the following steps:

1. Open the **Tutoring** database you worked with in Tutorials 5–7.

2. Export the rptTutorSessions report as a PDF document with a filename of **TutorSessions.pdf** to the Access2 ▸ Case2 folder. Include the document structure tags for accessibility, and do not save the export steps.

3. Import the CSV file named Subject.csv, which is located in the Access2 ▸ Case2 folder, as a new table in the database. Use the names in the first row as field names, set the third column's data type to Currency and the other fields' data types to Short Text, choose your own primary key, name the table **tblSubject**, run the Table Analyzer, and record the Table Analyzer's recommendation, but do not accept the recommendation. Do not save the import steps.

4. Export the tblTutor table as an XML file named **Tutor** to the Access2 ▸ Case2 folder; do not create a separate XSD file. Save the export steps.

5. Link to the Room workbook, which is located in the Access2 ▸ Case2 folder, using **tblRoom** as the table name. Add the following new record to the Room workbook: Room Num 5, Rental Cost **$25**, and Type **Private**.

✦ **Explore** 6. Import the **AddSubject.xml** file, which is located in the Access2 ▸ Case2 folder, appending the records to the tblSubject table. Do not save the import steps. Open the tblSubject table in Datasheet view and then verify that the record with SubjectID 50 and Subject Math4 has been appended, along with other records. Close the tblSubject table and then close the Tutoring database.

✦ **Explore** 7. Open the **NewStudentReferrals** database from the Access2 ▸ Case2 folder, and then create and work with an application part as follows:

   a. Create an application part called **NewStudentContact** with the description **New student referrals** and include the data.

   b. Close the **NewStudentReferrals** database.

   c. Open the **Tutoring** database and import the **NewStudentContact** Application Part, which has no relationship to any of the other tables. Open the tblContact table to verify the data has been imported.

   d. Karen would like to import an empty tblContact table in the future. Delete the **NewStudentContact** Application Part by clicking on the Application Parts button, right-clicking on the **NewStudentContact** template, selecting **Delete Template Part from Gallery**, and then clicking **Yes** in the dialog box that opens.

   e. Save and close the Tutoring database.

   f. Open the **NewStudentReferrals** database, then create an Application Part called **Contact** with the description **Contact information** and do not include the data.

   g. Close the NewStudentReferrals database.

   h. Open the Tutoring database and then add the Contact Application Part. Open the tblContact1 table to verify that it does not contain records.

8. Make a backup copy of the database, compact and repair the database, and then close it.

Case Problem 3

Data Files needed for this Case Problem: Facility.csv, Rosemary.accdb (*cont. from Tutorial 7*), and Volunteer.accdb.

Rosemary Animal Shelter Ryan Lang wants you to integrate the data in the Rosemary database with other programs, and he wants to be able to analyze the data in the database. Complete the following steps:

1. Open the **Rosemary** database you worked with in Tutorials 5–7.

2. Export the qryNetDonationsAprilOrLaterCrosstab query as an HTML document named **Crosstab** to the Access2 ▸ Case3 folder. Save the export steps.

CHALLENGE

3. Export the rptPatronDonations report as a PDF document with a filename of **PatronDonations.pdf** to the Access2 ▸ Case3 folder. Include the document structure tags for accessibility, and do not save the export steps.

🔁 **Explore** 4. Import the CSV file named Facility, which is located in the Access2 ▸ Case3 folder, as a new table in the database. Use the Short Text data type for all fields, choose your own primary key, name the table **tblTemporary**, and run the Table Analyzer. Accept the Table Analyzer's recommendations, which will be to create two tables. Rename the tables as **tblStorage** and **tblFacility**. (*Hint*: Use the Rename Table button to the right of "What name do you want for each table?") Make sure each table has the correct primary key. (*Hint*: Use the Set Unique Identifier button to set a primary key if necessary.) Let the Table Analzyer create a query. Do not save the import steps. Review the tblTemporary query, review the tblTemporary table (it might be named tblTemporary_OLD), and then review the tblStorage and tblFacility tables. Close all tables.

5. Export the tblDonation table as an XML file named **Donation.xml** to the Access2 ▸ Case3 folder; do not create a separate XSD file. Save the export steps.

6. Modify the **frmPatronDonations** form in the following ways:

   a. Add a tab control to the bottom of the Detail section, and place the existing subform on the first page of the tab control.

   b. Change the caption for the left tab to **Donation Data** and for the right tab to **Donation Chart**.

   c. Change the caption for the main form's navigation buttons to **Donor** and for the subform's navigation buttons to **Donation**.

   d. Add a chart to the second page of the tab control. Use the tblDonation table as the record source, select the PatronID, DonationValue, and DonationDate fields, use the 3-D Column Chart type, include a legend, and use **Donations by Patron** as the chart title.

   e. Change the chart to a Clustered Bar chart.

7. Close the Rosemary database.

8. Open the **Volunteer** database, which is located in the Access2 ▸ Case3 folder. Create an application part called **Volunteer** with the description **Volunteer information**, and do not include the data. Close the Volunteer database.

9. Open the **Rosemary** database. Create a table called **tblPotentialVolunteer** from the Volunteer application part.

10. Make a backup copy of the database, compact and repair the database, and then close it.

Case Problem 4

Data Files needed for this Case Problem: Personnel.xlsx, PotentialTours1.xml, PotentialTours2.xml, and Ecotour.accdb (*cont. from Tutorial 7*)

Stanley EcoTours   Janice and Bill Stanley want you to integrate the data in the Stanley database with other programs, and they want to be able to analyze the data in the database. Complete the following steps:

1. Open the **Ecotour** database you worked with in Tutorials 5–7.

2. Export the qryGuestsWithoutReservations query as an HTML document named **GuestsWithoutReservations.html** to the Access2 ▸ Case4 folder. Do not save the export steps.

3. Import the data and structure from the XML file named **PotentialTours1.xml**, which is located in the Access2 ▸ Case4 folder, as a new table in the database. Do not save the import steps. Open the PotentialTours table to verify the records were imported. Close the PotentialTours table.

🔁 **Explore** 4. Import the data from the XML file named **PotentialTours2.xml**, which is located in the Access2 ▸ Case4 folder, appending the data to the **PotentialTours** table. Rename the table as **tblPotentialTours**. Open the tblPotentialTours table to verify the records were appended. Close the tblPotentialTours table.

5. Export the qryTourReservations query as an XML file named **TourReservations** to the Access2 ► Case4 folder; do not create a separate XSD file. Do not save the export steps.

6. Link to the Personnel Excel workbook, which is located in the Access2 ► Case4 folder, using **tblPersonnel** as the table name. Change the Job Title in the last record from Staff Manager to **HR Staff Manager**.

7. Modify the **frmGuestsWithReservations** form in the following ways:

   a. Add a tab control to the bottom of the Detail section, and place the existing subform on the first page of the tab control.

   b. Change the caption for the left tab to **Reservation Data** and for the right tab to **Reservation Chart**.

   c. Change the caption for the main form's navigation buttons to **Guest** and for the subform's navigation buttons to **Reservation**.

   d. Add a chart to the second page of the tab control. Use the tblReservation table as the record source, select the StartDate, TourID, and People fields, use the Column Chart chart type, do not include a legend, and use **Reservations** as the chart title.

8. Export the rptTourReservations report as a PDF document with a filename of **TourReservations.pdf** to the Access2 ► Case4 folder. Include the document structure tags for accessibility, and do not save the export steps.

9. Make a backup copy of the database, compact and repair the database, and then close it.

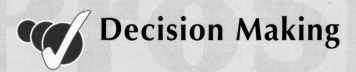 Decision Making

Deciding When to Create a Personal Database

Decision making is a process of choosing between alternative courses of action. When you make decisions, you normally follow these steps:

1. Gather information relevant to the decision
2. Consider viable alternatives
3. Select the best alternative
4. Prepare an implementation action plan
5. Take action and monitor results
6. Verify the accuracy of the decision

For some decisions, you might combine some steps, and you might even skip steps for the simplest decisions.

Gathering Information, Considering Alternatives, and Selecting the Best Alternative

Suppose you were charged with tracking volunteers and their jobs for a service organization or other entity that requires coordination of a large group of people. The first step in decision making—gathering relevant information—starts with the choice of how to organize the people and their jobs. For example, if your information shows that each person completes only one job, few people are involved in the process, and volunteers all report to the same coordinator, then you could use a Word document or an Excel workbook to manage the volunteers and their jobs.

However, what if your information shows a very large number of volunteers, and many volunteers work in multiple jobs and report to more than one coordinator? When the relevant information changes so that one volunteer is no longer completing only one job and no longer reporting to a single coordinator, managing the data in a Word document or Excel workbook becomes problematic.

When making the decision to use a database to manage your data, at first you might find that some data exists in another format, such as in an Excel workbook. After considering the data that you have already collected (such as in a workbook) or data that you will collect in the future, consider the types of decisions you need to make. These decisions might include determining whether a database will effectively and efficiently manage your data, deciding which DBMS you will use, and evaluating the ability of users to manage and use the database to get the information they need.

Preparing an Implementation Action Plan

Once you have made the choice to use a DBMS, determine the steps needed to design and create the database. The first step is to analyze the data you have collected or will collect and start compiling it into tables. Then, you can begin identifying the primary and foreign keys in the tables to create the relationships between those tables. Finally, you can determine the field properties in anticipation of making data entry easier and reducing the likelihood of errors. For example, you might use the Default Value property to enter a city or state field value if all of your volunteers reside in the same area.

Taking Action and Monitoring Results

The next step in decision making involves implementation, which includes creating the database, defining the tables, and entering the data. After designing and installing the database, you need to make decisions about the types of queries, forms, and reports to create to produce the data in the format that users need. After implementation, you should make decisions about how the database will be updated so it remains current and ready for any future decisions you need to make.

Verifying the Accuracy of the Decision

At the end of your decision-making process, review your steps and evaluate how well they worked. Did you discover data you wish you had originally collected and stored in the database, but didn't have available? How did that limitation affect your ability to make a good decision? What changes do you need to make to your database so that it will provide better information for future decisions?

PROSKILLS

Create a Personal Database

Most businesses use databases for decision making, and you can also use databases to track data in your personal life. Examples of personal database use include tracking personal collections, such as music or books; hobby data, such as crafts or antiques; or items related to sports teams, theater clubs, or other organizations to which you might belong. In this exercise, you'll use Access to create a database that will contain information of your choice, using the Access skills and features you've learned in these tutorials.

Note: Please be sure *not* to include any personal information of a sensitive nature in the database you create to be submitted to your instructor for this exercise. Later on, you can update the data in your database with such information for your own personal use.

1. Consider your personal interests and activities, school-related functions, and work-related duties, and select from them one set of requirements that includes data that is best tracked using a DBMS. (If you completed Tutorials 1–4 of this book and the ProSkills Exercise at the end of Tutorial 4, you can use and enhance the database you've already created, and you can skip this step and the next step.) Make sure the data is sufficiently complex that a Word document or Excel workbook would not be viable alternatives to store and manage the data.

2. Create a new Access database to contain the data you want to track. The database must include two or more tables that you can join through one-to-many relationships. Define the properties for each field in each table. Make sure you include a mix of data types for the fields (for example, do not include only Text fields in each table). Specify a primary key for each table, define the table relationships with referential integrity enforced, and enter records in each table.

3. Create queries that include at least one of each of the following: pattern query match, list-of-values match, parameter, crosstab, find duplicates, find unmatched, and the use of a conditional value in a calculated field.

4. For one or more fields, apply an input mask and specify field validation rules.

5. Create a split form and modify the form.

6. Create a custom form that uses at least one of each of the following: combo box for a lookup, combo box to find records, subform, lines and rectangles, and tab control. Add one or more calculated controls to the main form based on the subform's calculated control(s), and add a chart, if appropriate. Check the main form's tab order, and improve the form's appearance.

7. Create a custom report that uses at least one of each of the following: grouping field, sort field(s), lines, and rectangles. Hide duplicates, and add the date, page numbers, and a report title.

8. Export two or more objects in different formats, and save the step specifications.

9. Designate a trusted folder, make a backup copy of the database, and compact and repair it.

10. Submit your completed database to your instructor as requested. Include printouts of any database objects, if required. Also, prepare a document that addresses the specific data you selected to store and track and why a DBMS was the best choice.

OBJECTIVES

- Learn the characteristics of a table
- Learn about primary, candidate, alternate, composite, and foreign keys
- Study one-to-one, one-to-many, and many-to-many relationships
- Learn to describe tables and relationships with entity-relationship diagrams and with a shorthand method
- Study database integrity constraints for primary keys, referential integrity, and domains
- Learn about determinants, functional dependencies, anomalies, and normalization
- Understand the differences among natural, artificial, and surrogate keys
- Learn about naming conventions

Relational Databases and Database Design

This appendix introduces you to the basics of database design. Before trying to master this material, be sure you understand the following concepts: data, information, field, field value, record, table, relational database, common field, database management system (DBMS), and relational database management system (RDBMS).

STARTING DATA FILES

There are no starting Data Files needed for this appendix.

Tables

A relational database stores its data in tables. A **table** is a two-dimensional structure made up of rows and columns. The terms table, **record** (row), and **field** (column) are the popular names for the more formal terms **relation** (table), **tuple** (row), and **attribute** (column), as shown in Figure A-1.

Figure A-1	A table (relation) consisting of records and fields

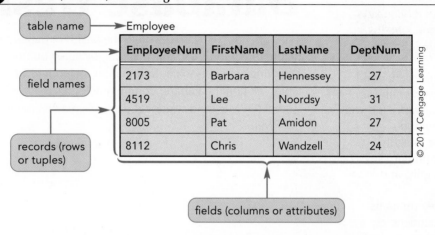

The Employee table shown in Figure A-1 is an example of a relational database table, a two-dimensional structure with the following characteristics:

- Each row is unique. Because no two rows are the same, you can easily locate and update specific data. For example, you can locate the row for EmployeeNum 8005 and change the FirstName value, Pat, the LastName value, Amidon, or the DeptNum value, 27.
- The order of the rows is unimportant. You can add or view rows in any order. For example, you can view the rows in LastName order instead of EmployeeNum order.
- Each table entry contains a single value. At the intersection of each row and column, you cannot have more than one value. For example, each row in Figure A-1 contains one EmployeeNum value, one FirstName value, one LastName value, and one DeptNum value.
- The order of the columns is unimportant. You can add or view columns in any order.
- Each column has a unique name called the **field name**. The field name allows you to access a specific column without needing to know its position within the table.
- Each row in a table describes, or shows the characteristics of, an entity. An **entity** is a person, place, object, event, or idea for which you want to store and process data. For example, EmployeeNum, FirstName, LastName, and DeptNum are characteristics of the employees of a company. The Employee table represents all the employee entities and their characteristics. That is, each row of the Employee table describes a different employee of the company using the characteristics of EmployeeNum, FirstName, LastName, and DeptNum. The Employee table includes only characteristics of employees. Other tables would exist for the company's other entities. For example, a Department table would describe the company's departments and a Position table would describe the company's job positions.

Knowing the characteristics of a table leads directly to a definition of a relational database. A **relational database** is a collection of tables (relations).

Note that this book uses singular table names, such as Employee and Department, but some people use plural table names, such as Employees and Departments. You can use either singular table names or plural table names, as long as you consistently use the style you choose.

Keys

Primary keys ensure that each row in a table is unique. A **primary key** is a column, or a collection of columns, whose values uniquely identify each row in a table. In addition to being *unique*, a primary key must be *minimal* (that is, contain no unnecessary extra columns) and must not change in value. For example, in Figure A-2 the State table contains one record per state and uses the StateAbbrev column as its primary key.

State

StateAbbrev	StateName	EnteredUnionOrder	StateBird	StatePopulation
CT	Connecticut	5	American robin	3,590,347
MI	Michigan	26	robin	9,883,360
SD	South Dakota	40	pheasant	833,354
TN	Tennessee	16	mockingbird	6,456,243
TX	Texas	28	mockingbird	26,059,203

© 2014 Cengage Learning

Could any other column, or collection of columns, be the primary key of the State table?

- Could the StateBird column serve as the primary key? No, because the StateBird column does not have unique values (for example, the mockingbird is the state bird of more than one state).
- Could the StatePopulation column serve as the primary key? No, because the StatePopulation column values change periodically and are not guaranteed to be unique.
- Could the StateAbbrev and StateName columns together serve as the primary key? No, because the combination of these two columns is not minimal. Something less, such as the StateAbbrev column by itself, can serve as the primary key.
- Could the StateName column serve as the primary key? Yes, because the StateName column has unique values. In a similar way, you could select the EnteredUnionOrder column as the primary key for the State table. One column, or a collection of columns, that can serve as a primary key is called a **candidate key**. The candidate keys for the State table are the StateAbbrev column, the StateName column, and the EnteredUnionOrder column. You choose one of the candidate keys to be the primary key, and each remaining candidate key is called an **alternate key**. The StateAbbrev column is the State table's primary key in Figure A-2, so the StateName and EnteredUnionOrder columns become alternate keys in the table.

Figure A-3 shows a City table containing the fields StateAbbrev, CityName, and CityPopulation.

Figure A-3	A table with a composite key

composite primary key

City

StateAbbrev	CityName	CityPopulation
CT	Hartford	124,062
CT	Madison	18,803
CT	Portland	9,551
MI	Lansing	119,128
SD	Madison	6,482
SD	Pierre	13,899
TN	Nashville	569,462
TX	Austin	757,688
TX	Portland	16,490

© 2014 Cengage Learning

What is the primary key for the City table? The values for the CityPopulation column periodically change and are not guaranteed to be unique, so the CityPopulation column cannot be the primary key. Because the values for each of the other two columns are not unique, the StateAbbrev column alone cannot be the primary key and neither can the CityName column (for example, there are two cities named Madison and two cities named Portland). The primary key is the combination of the StateAbbrev and CityName columns. Both columns together are needed to identify—uniquely and minimally—each row in the City table. A multiple-column key is called a **composite key** or a **concatenated key**. A multiple-column primary key is called a **composite primary key**.

The StateAbbrev column in the City table is also a foreign key. A **foreign key** is a column, or a collection of columns, in one table in which each column value must match the value of the primary key of some table or must be null. A **null** is the absence of a value in a particular table entry. A null value is not blank, nor zero, nor any other value. You give a null value to a column value when you do not know its value or when a value does not apply. As shown in Figure A-4, the values in the City table's StateAbbrev column match the values in the State table's StateAbbrev column. Thus, the StateAbbrev column, the primary key of the State table, is a foreign key in the City table. Although the field name StateAbbrev is the same in both tables, the names could be different. As a rule, experts use the same name for a field stored in two or more tables to broadcast clearly that they store similar values; however, some exceptions exist.

| Figure A-4 | StateAbbrev as a primary key (State table) and a foreign key (City table) |

primary key (State table)

State

StateAbbrev	StateName	EnteredUnionOrder	StateBird	StatePopulation
CT	Connecticut	5	American robin	3,518,288
MI	Michigan	26	robin	9,969,727
SD	South Dakota	40	pheasant	812,383
TN	Tennessee	16	mockingbird	6,296,254
TX	Texas	28	mockingbird	24,782,302

composite primary key (City table)

City

foreign key

StateAbbrev	CityName	CityPopulation
CT	Hartford	124,062
CT	Madison	18,803
CT	Portland	9,551
MI	Lansing	119,128
SD	Madison	6,482
SD	Pierre	13,899
TN	Nashville	596,462
TX	Austin	757,688
TX	Portland	16,490

© 2014 Cengage Learning

A **nonkey field** is a field that is not part of the primary key. In the two tables shown in Figure A-4, all fields are nonkey fields except the StateAbbrev field in the State and City tables and the CityName field in the City table. "Key" is an ambiguous word because it can refer to a primary, candidate, alternate, or foreign key. When the word key appears alone, however, it means primary key and the definition for a nonkey field consequently makes sense.

Relationships

In a database, a table can be associated with another table in one of three ways: a one-to-many relationship, a many-to-many relationship, or a one-to-one relationship.

One-to-Many Relationship

The Department and Employee tables, shown in Figure A-5, have a one-to-many relationship. A **one-to-many relationship** (abbreviated **1:M** or **1:N**) exists between two tables when each row in the first table (sometimes called the **primary table**) matches many rows in the second table and each row in the second table (sometimes called the **related table**) matches at most one row in the first table. "Many" can mean zero

rows, one row, or two or more rows. As Figure A-5 shows, the DeptNum field, which is a foreign key in the Employee table and the primary key in the Department table, is the common field that ties together the rows of the two tables. Each department has many employees; and each employee works in exactly one department or hasn't been assigned to a department, if the DeptNum field value for that employee is null.

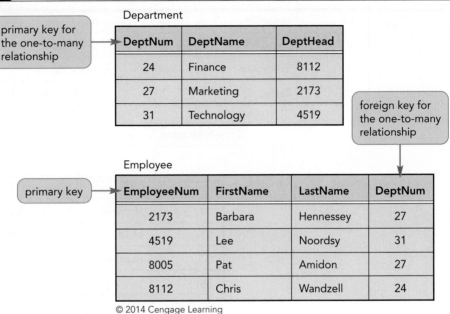

© 2014 Cengage Learning

Many-to-Many Relationship

In Figure A-6, the Employee table (with the EmployeeNum field as its primary key) and the Position table (with the PositionID field as its primary key) have a many-to-many relationship. A **many-to-many relationship** (abbreviated as **M:N**) exists between two tables when each row in the first table matches many rows in the second table and each row in the second table matches many rows in the first table. In a relational database, you must use a third table (often called an **intersection table, junction table**, or **link table**) to serve as a bridge between the two many-to-many tables; the third table has the primary keys of the two many-to-many tables as its primary key. The original tables now each have a one-to-many relationship with the new table. The EmployeeNum and PositionID fields represent the primary key of the Employment table that is shown in Figure A-6. The EmployeeNum field, which is a foreign key in the Employment table and the primary key in the Employee table, is the common field that ties together the rows of the Employee and Employment tables. Likewise, the PositionID field is the common field for the Position and Employment tables. Each employee may serve in many different positions within the company over time, and each position in the company will be filled by different employees over time.

Figure A-6	A many-to-many relationship

primary key (Position table)

Employee

primary key (Employee table)

EmployeeNum	FirstName	LastName	DeptNum
2173	Barbara	Hennessey	27
4519	Lee	Noordsy	31
8005	Pat	Amidon	27
8112	Chris	Wandzell	24

Position

PositionID	PositionDesc	PayGrade
1	Director	45
2	Manager	40
3	Analyst	30
4	Clerk	20

composite primary key of the intersection table

Employment

foreign keys related to the Employee and Position tables

EmployeeNum	PositionID	StartDate	EndDate
2173	2	12/14/2011	
4519	1	04/23/2013	
4519	3	11/11/2007	04/22/2013
8005	3	06/05/2012	08/25/2013
8005	4	07/02/2010	06/04/2012
8112	1	12/15/2012	
8112	2	10/04/2011	12/14/2012

© 2014 Cengage Learning

One-to-One Relationship

In Figure A-5, recall that there's a one-to-many relationship between the Department table (the primary table) and the Employee table (the related table). Each department has many employees, and each employee works in one department. The DeptNum field in the Employee table serves as a foreign key to connect records in that table to records with matching DeptNum field values in the Department table.

Furthermore, each department has a single employee who serves as the head of the department, and each employee either serves as the head of a department or simply works in a department without being the department head. Therefore, the Department and Employee tables not only have a one-to-many relationship, but these two tables also have a second relationship, a one-to-one relationship. A **one-to-one relationship** (abbreviated **1:1**) exists between two tables when each row in each table has at most one matching row in the other table. As shown in Figure A-7, each DeptHead field value in the Department table represents the employee number in the Employee table of the employee who heads the department. In other words, each DeptHead field value in the Department table matches exactly one EmployeeNum field value in the Employee table. At the same time, each EmployeeNum field value in the Employee table matches at most one DeptHead field value in the Department table—matching one DeptHead field value if the employee is a department head, or matching zero DeptHead field values if the employee is not a department head. For this one-to-one relationship, the EmployeeNum field in the Employee table and the DeptHead field in the Department table are the fields that link the two tables, with the DeptHead field serving as a foreign key in the Department table and the EmployeeNum field serving as a primary key in the Employee table.

Some database designers might use EmployeeNum instead of DeptHead as the field name for the foreign key in the Department table because they both represent the employee number for the employees of the company. However, DeptHead better identifies the purpose of the field and would more commonly be used as the field name.

| Figure A-7 | A one-to-one relationship |

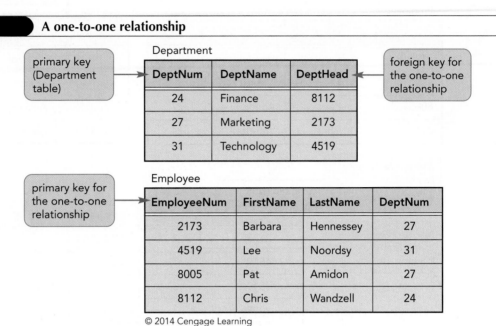

© 2014 Cengage Learning

Entity Subtype

Suppose the company awards annual bonuses to a small number of employees who fill director positions in selected departments. As shown in Figure A-8, you could store the Bonus field in the Employee table because a bonus is an attribute associated with employees. The Bonus field would contain either the amount of the employee's bonus (record 4 in the Employee table) or a null value for employees without bonuses (records 1 through 3 in the Employee table).

| Figure A-8 | Bonus field added to the Employee table |

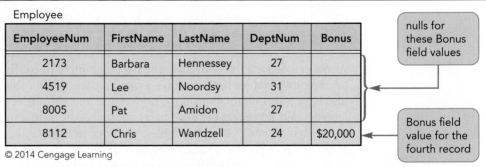

© 2014 Cengage Learning

Figure A-9 shows an alternative approach, in which the Bonus field is placed in a separate table, the EmployeeBonus table. The EmployeeBonus table's primary key is the EmployeeNum field, and the table contains one row for each employee earning a bonus. Because some employees do not earn a bonus, the EmployeeBonus table has fewer rows than the Employee table. However, each row in the EmployeeBonus table has a matching row in the Employee table, with the EmployeeNum field serving as the common field; the EmployeeNum field is the primary key in the Employee table and is a foreign key in the EmployeeBonus table.

Figure A-9	Storing Bonus values in a separate table, an entity subtype

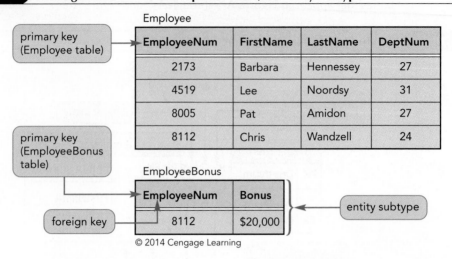

© 2014 Cengage Learning

The EmployeeBonus table, in this situation, is called an **entity subtype**, a table whose primary key is a foreign key to a second table and whose fields are additional fields for the second table. Database designers create an entity subtype in two situations. In the first situation, some users might need access to all employee fields, including employee bonuses, while other employees might need access to all employee fields except bonuses. Because most DBMSs allow you to control which tables a user can access, you can specify that some users can access both tables and that other users can access the Employee table but not the EmployeeBonus table, keeping the employee bonus information hidden from the latter group. In the second situation, you can create an entity subtype when a table has fields that could have nulls, as was the case for the Bonus field stored in the Employee table in Figure A-8. You should be aware that database experts are currently debating the validity of the use of nulls in relational databases, and many experts insist that you should never use nulls. This warning against nulls is partly based on the inconsistent way different RDBMSs treat nulls and partly due to the lack of a firm theoretical foundation for how to use nulls. In any case, entity subtypes are an alternative to the use of nulls.

Entity-Relationship Diagrams

A common shorthand method for describing tables is to write the table name followed by its fields in parentheses, underlining the fields that represent the primary key and identifying the foreign keys for a table immediately after the table. Using this method, the tables that appear in Figures A-5 through A-7 and Figure A-9 are described in the following way:

Department (<u>DeptNum</u>, DeptName, DeptHead)
    Foreign key: DeptHead to Employee table
Employee (<u>EmployeeNum</u>, FirstName, LastName, DeptNum)
    Foreign key: DeptNum to Department table
Position (<u>PositionID</u>, PositionDesc, PayGrade)
Employment (<u>EmployeeNum</u>, <u>PositionID</u>, StartDate, EndDate)
    Foreign key: EmployeeNum to Employee table
    Foreign key: PositionID to Position table
EmployeeBonus (<u>EmployeeNum</u>, Bonus)
    Foreign key: EmployeeNum to Employee table

Another popular way to describe tables *and their relationships* is with entity-relationship diagrams. An **entity-relationship diagram (ERD)** shows a database's entities and the relationships among the entities in a symbolic, visual way. In an ERD, an entity

and a table are equivalent. Figure A-10 shows an entity-relationship diagram for the tables that appear in Figures A-5 through A-7 and Figure A-9.

| Figure A-10 | An entity-relationship diagram (ERD) |

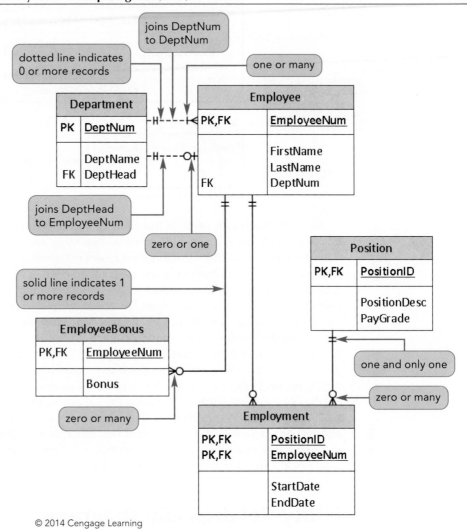

© 2014 Cengage Learning

ERDs have the following characteristics:

- A table is represented by a rectangle that contains the table name and lists the field names. Within each rectangle, the primary key is identified with the abbreviation PK, and any foreign keys are designated with FK. Required fields are formatted in bold.
- Relationships are identified by lines joining the tables. A solid relationship line between two tables indicates there could be 1 or more related records. A dotted relationship line between two tables indicates there could be 0 or more related records.

- At the ends of each relationship line, symbols identify the minimum and maximum possible number of related records from each entity in the relationship. A single perpendicular line represents 1 record, a circle represents 0 records, and a group of three branching lines—known as a crow's foot—represents many records. A one-to-many relationship is represented by a 1 at one end of the relationship line and a crow's foot at the opposite end of the relationship line. For example, the Department and Employee tables have a one-to-many relationship from the DeptNum field in the Department table to the DeptNum field in the Employee table. In a similar manner, a one-to-many relationship exists between the Employee and EmployeeBonus tables and a one-to-one relationship exists between the Department and Employee tables from the DeptHead field in the Department table to the EmployeeNum field in the Employee table. The relationships in Figure A-10 illustrate all the possible designations for the ends of lines.

Integrity Constraints

A database has **integrity** if its data follows certain rules; each rule is called an **integrity constraint**. The ideal is to have the DBMS enforce all integrity constraints. If a DBMS can enforce some integrity constraints but not others, the other integrity constraints must be enforced by other programs or by the people who use the DBMS. Integrity constraints can be divided into three groups: primary key constraints, foreign key constraints, and domain integrity constraints.

- One primary key constraint is inherent in the definition of a primary key, which says that the primary key must be unique. The **entity integrity constraint** says that the primary key cannot be null. For a composite key, none of the individual fields can be null. The uniqueness and nonnull properties of a primary key ensure that you can reference any data value in a database by supplying its table name, field name, and primary key value.
- Foreign keys provide the mechanism for forming a relationship between two tables, and referential integrity ensures that only valid relationships exist. **Referential integrity** is the constraint specifying that each nonnull foreign key value must match a primary key value in the primary table. Specifically, referential integrity means that you cannot add a row containing an unmatched foreign key value. Referential integrity also means that you cannot change or delete the related primary key value and leave the foreign key orphaned. In some RDBMSs, when you create a relationship, you can specify one of these options: restricted, cascades, or nullifies. If you specify **restricted** and then change or delete a primary key, the DBMS updates or deletes the value only if there are no matching foreign key values. If you choose **cascades** and then change a primary key value, the DBMS changes the matching foreign key values to the new primary key value, or, if you delete a primary key value, the DBMS also deletes the matching foreign key rows. If you choose **nullifies** and then change or delete a primary key value, the DBMS sets all matching foreign key values to null.
- A **domain** is a set of values from which one or more fields draw their actual values. A **domain integrity constraint** is a rule you specify for a field. By choosing a data type for a field, you impose a constraint on the set of values allowed for the field. You can create specific validation rules for a field to limit its domain further. As you make a field's domain definition more precise, you exclude more and more unacceptable values for the field. For example, in the State table, shown in Figures A-2 and A-4, you could define the domain for the EnteredUnionOrder field to be a unique integer between 1 and 50 and the domain for the StateBird field to be any text string containing 25 or fewer characters.

Dependencies and Determinants

Just as tables are related to other tables, fields are also related to other fields. Consider the modified Employee table shown in Figure A-11. Its description is:

Employee (EmployeeNum, PositionID, LastName, PositionDesc, StartDate, HealthPlan, PlanDesc)

Figure A-11	A table combining fields from three tables

composite primary key

Employee

EmployeeNum	PositionID	LastName	PositionDesc	StartDate	HealthPlan	PlanDesc
2173	2	Hennessey	Manager	12/14/2011	B	Managed HMO
4519	1	Noordsy	Director	04/23/2013	A	Managed PPO
4519	3	Noordsy	Analyst	11/11/2007	A	Managed PPO
8005	3	Amidon	Analyst	06/05/2012	C	Health Savings
8005	4	Amidon	Clerk	07/02/2010	C	Health Savings
8112	1	Wandzell	Director	12/15/2012	A	Managed PPO
8112	2	Wandzell	Manager	10/04/2011	A	Managed PPO

© 2014 Cengage Learning

The modified Employee table combines several fields from the Employee, Position, and Employment tables that appeared in Figure A-6. The EmployeeNum and LastName fields are from the Employee table. The PositionID and PositionDesc fields are from the Position table. The EmployeeNum, PositionID, and StartDate fields are from the Employment table. The HealthPlan and PlanDesc fields are new fields for the Employee table, whose primary key is now the combination of the EmployeeNum and PositionID fields.

In the Employee table, each field is related to other fields. To determine field relationships, you ask "Does a value for a particular field give me a single value for another field?" If the answer is Yes, then the two fields are **functionally** related. For example, a value for the EmployeeNum field determines a single value for the LastName field, and a value for the LastName field depends on the value of the EmployeeNum field. In other words, EmployeeNum functionally determines LastName, and LastName is functionally dependent on EmployeeNum. In this case, EmployeeNum is called a determinant. A **determinant** is a field, or a collection of fields, whose values determine the values of another field. A field is functionally dependent on another field (or a collection of fields) if that other field is a determinant for it.

You can graphically show a table's functional dependencies and determinants in a **bubble diagram**; a bubble diagram is also called a **data model diagram** or a **functional dependency diagram**. Figure A-12 shows the bubble diagram for the Employee table shown in Figure A-11.

Figure A-12	A bubble diagram for the modified Employee table

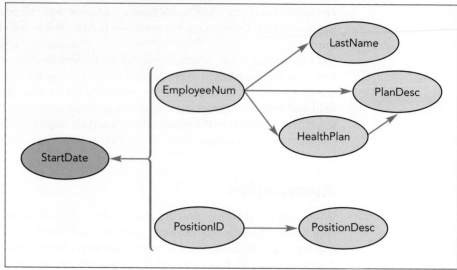

© 2014 Cengage Learning

You can read the bubble diagram in Figure A-12 as follows:

- The EmployeeNum field is a determinant for the LastName, HealthPlan, and PlanDesc fields.
- The PositionID field is a determinant for the PositionDesc field.
- The StartDate field is functionally dependent on the EmployeeNum and PositionID fields together.
- The HealthPlan field is a determinant for the PlanDesc field.

Note that EmployeeNum and PositionID together serve as a determinant for the StartDate field and for all fields that depend on the EmployeeNum field alone and the PositionID field alone. Some experts include these additional fields and some don't. The previous list of determinants does not include these additional fields.

An alternative way to show determinants is to list the determinant, a right arrow, and then the dependent fields, separated by commas. Using this alternative, the determinants shown in Figure A-12 are:

EmployeeNum → LastName, HealthPlan, PlanDesc
PositionID → PositionDesc
EmployeeNum, PositionID → StartDate
HealthPlan → PlanDesc

Only the StartDate field is functionally dependent on the table's full primary key, the EmployeeNum and PositionID fields. The LastName, HealthPlan, and PlanDesc fields have partial dependencies because they are functionally dependent on the EmployeeNum field, which is part of the primary key. A **partial dependency** is a functional dependency on part of the primary key, instead of the entire primary key. Does another partial dependency exist in the Employee table? Yes, the PositionDesc field has a partial dependency on the PositionID field.

Because the EmployeeNum field is a determinant of both the HealthPlan and PlanDesc fields, and the HealthPlan field is a determinant of the PlanDesc field, the HealthPlan and PlanDesc fields have a transitive dependency. A **transitive dependency** is a functional dependency between two nonkey fields, which are both dependent on a third field.

How do you know which functional dependencies exist among a collection of fields, and how do you recognize partial and transitive dependencies? The answers lie with the questions you ask as you gather the requirements for a database application. For each field and entity, you must gain an accurate understanding of its meaning and relationships in the context of the application. **Semantic object modeling** is an entire area of study within the database field devoted to the meanings and relationships of data.

Anomalies

When you use a DBMS, you are more likely to get results you can trust if you create your tables carefully. For example, problems might occur with tables that have partial and transitive dependencies, whereas you won't have as much trouble if you ensure that your tables include only fields that are directly related to each other. Also, when you remove data redundancy from a table, you improve that table. **Data redundancy** occurs when you store the same data in more than one place.

The problems caused by data redundancy and by partial and transitive dependencies are called **anomalies** because they are undesirable irregularities of tables. Anomalies are of three types: insertion, deletion, and update.

To examine the effects of these anomalies, consider the modified Employee table that is shown again in Figure A-13.

| Figure A-13 | A table with insertion, deletion, and update anomalies |

composite primary key

Employee

EmployeeNum	PositionID	LastName	PositionDesc	StartDate	HealthPlan	PlanDesc
2173	2	Hennessey	Manager	12/14/2011	B	Managed HMO
4519	1	Noordsy	Director	04/23/2013	A	Managed PPO
4519	3	Noordsy	Analyst	11/11/2007	A	Managed PPO
8005	3	Amidon	Analyst	06/05/2012	C	Health Savings
8005	4	Amidon	Clerk	07/02/2010	C	Health Savings
8112	1	Wandzell	Director	12/15/2012	A	Managed PPO
8112	2	Wandzell	Manager	10/04/2011	A	Managed PPO

© 2014 Cengage Learning

- An **insertion anomaly** occurs when you cannot add a record to a table because you do not know the entire primary key value. For example, you cannot add the new employee Cathy Corbett with an EmployeeNum of 3322 to the Employee table if you do not know her position in the company. Entity integrity prevents you from leaving any part of a primary key null. Because the PositionID field is part of the primary key, you cannot leave it null. To add the new employee, your only option is to make up a PositionID field value, until you determine the correct position. This solution misrepresents the facts and is unacceptable, if a better approach is available.

- A **deletion anomaly** occurs when you delete data from a table and unintentionally lose other critical data. For example, if you delete EmployeeNum 2173 because Hennessey is no longer an employee, you also lose the only instance of HealthPlan B in the database. Thus, you no longer know that HealthPlan B is the "Managed HMO" plan.
- An **update anomaly** occurs when a change to one field value requires the DBMS to make more than one change to the database, and a failure by the database to make all the changes results in inconsistent data. For example, if you change a LastName, HealthPlan, or PlanDesc field value for EmployeeNum 8005, the DBMS must change multiple rows of the Employee table. If the DBMS fails to change all the rows, the LastName, HealthPlan, or PlanDesc field now has different values in the database and is inconsistent.

Normalization

Database design is the process of determining the content and structure of data in a database in order to support some activity on behalf of a user or group of users. After you have determined the collection of fields users need to support an activity, you need to determine the precise tables needed for the collection of fields and then place those fields into the correct tables. Understanding the functional dependencies of all fields; recognizing the anomalies caused by data redundancy, partial dependencies, and transitive dependencies when they exist; and knowing how to eliminate the anomalies are all crucial to good database design. Failure to eliminate anomalies leads to data redundancy and can cause data integrity and other problems as your database grows in size.

The process of identifying and eliminating anomalies is called **normalization**. Using normalization, you start with a collection of tables, apply sets of rules to eliminate anomalies, and produce a new collection of problem-free tables. The sets of rules are called **normal forms**. Of special interest for our purposes are the first three normal forms: first normal form, second normal form, and third normal form. First normal form improves the design of your tables, second normal form improves the first normal form design, and third normal form applies even more stringent rules to produce an even better design. Note that normal forms beyond third normal form exist; these higher normal forms can improve a database design in some situations but won't be covered in this section.

First Normal Form

Consider the Employee table shown in Figure A-14. For each employee, the table contains EmployeeNum, which is the primary key; the employee's first name, last name, health plan code and description; and the ID, description, pay grade, and start date of each position held by the employee. For example, Barbara Hennessey has held one position, while the other three employees have held two positions. Because each entry in a table must contain a single value, the structure shown in Figure A-14 does not meet the requirements for a table, or relation; therefore, it is called an **unnormalized relation**. The set of fields that includes the PositionID, PositionDesc, PayGrade, and StartDate fields, which can have more than one value, is called a **repeating group**.

Figure A-14   Repeating groups of data in an unnormalized Employee table

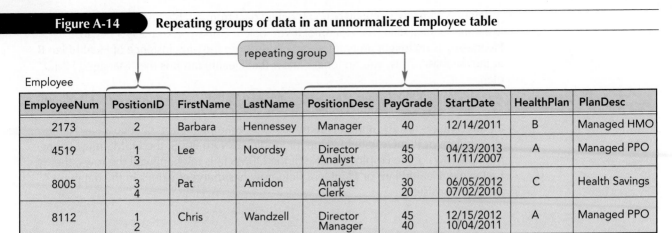

© 2014 Cengage Learning

First normal form addresses this repeating-group situation. A table is in **first normal form (1NF)** if it does not contain repeating groups. To remove a repeating group and convert to first normal form, you expand the primary key to include the primary key of the repeating group, forming a composite key. Performing the conversion step produces the 1NF table shown in Figure A-15.

Figure A-15   After conversion to 1NF

Employee

composite primary key

EmployeeNum	PositionID	FirstName	LastName	PositionDesc	PayGrade	StartDate	HealthPlan	PlanDesc
2173	2	Barbara	Hennessey	Manager	40	12/14/2011	B	Managed HMO
4519	1	Lee	Noordsy	Director	45	04/23/2013	A	Managed PPO
4519	3	Lee	Noordsy	Analyst	30	11/11/2007	A	Managed PPO
8005	3	Pat	Amidon	Analyst	30	06/05/2012	C	Health Savings
8005	4	Pat	Amidon	Clerk	20	07/02/2010	C	Health Savings
8112	1	Chris	Wandzell	Director	45	12/15/2012	A	Managed PPO
8112	2	Chris	Wandzell	Manager	40	10/04/2011	A	Managed PPO

© 2014 Cengage Learning

The alternative way to describe the 1NF table is:

Employee (<u>EmployeeNum</u>, <u>PositionID</u>, FirstName, LastName, PositionDesc, PayGrade, StartDate, HealthPlan, PlanDesc)

The Employee table is now a true table and has a composite key. The table, however, suffers from insertion, deletion, and update anomalies. (As an exercise, find examples of the three anomalies in the table.) The EmployeeNum field is a determinant for the FirstName, LastName, HealthPlan, and PlanDesc fields, so partial dependencies exist in the Employee table. It is these partial dependencies that cause the anomalies in the Employee table, and second normal form addresses the partial-dependency problem.

Second Normal Form

A table in 1NF is in **second normal form (2NF)** if it does not contain any partial dependencies. To remove partial dependencies from a table and convert it to second normal form, you perform two steps. First, identify the functional dependencies for every field in the table. Second, if necessary, create new tables and place each field in a table such that the field is functionally dependent on the entire primary key, not part of the primary key. If you need to create new tables, restrict them to tables with a primary key that is a subset of the original composite key. Note that partial dependencies occur only when you have a composite key; a table in first normal form with a single-field primary key is automatically in second normal form.

First, identifying the functional dependencies leads to the following determinants for the Employee table:

EmployeeNum → FirstName, LastName, HealthPlan, PlanDesc
PositionID → PositionDesc, PayGrade
EmployeeNum, PositionID → StartDate
HealthPlan → PlanDesc

The EmployeeNum field is a determinant for the FirstName, LastName, HealthPlan, and PlanDesc fields. The PositionID field is a determinant for the PositionDesc and PayGrade fields. The composite key EmployeeNum and PositionID is a determinant for the StartDate field. The HealthPlan field is a determinant for the PlanDesc field. Performing the second step in the conversion from first normal form to second form produces the three 2NF tables shown in Figure A-16.

Figure A-16   **After conversion to 2NF**

Employee

primary key →	**EmployeeNum**	**FirstName**	**LastName**	**HealthPlan**	**PlanDesc**
	2173	Barbara	Hennessey	B	Managed HMO
	4519	Lee	Noordsy	A	Managed PPO
	8005	Pat	Amidon	C	Health Savings
	8112	Chris	Wandzell	A	Managed PPO

Position

primary key →	**PositionID**	**PositionDesc**	**PayGrade**
	1	Director	45
	2	Manager	40
	3	Analyst	30
	4	Clerk	20

composite primary key

Employment

EmployeeNum	**PositionID**	**StartDate**
2173	2	12/14/2011
4519	1	04/23/2013
4519	3	11/11/2007
8005	3	06/05/2012
8005	4	07/02/2010
8112	1	12/15/2012
8112	2	10/04/2011

© 2014 Cengage Learning

The alternative way to describe the 2NF tables is:

Employee (EmployeeNum, FirstName, LastName, HealthPlan, PlanDesc)
Position (PositionID, PositionDesc, PayGrade)
Employment (EmployeeNum, PositionID, StartDate)
    Foreign key: EmployeeNum to Employee table
    Foreign key: PositionID to Position table

All three tables are in second normal form. Do anomalies still exist? The Position and Employment tables show no anomalies, but the Employee table suffers from anomalies caused by the transitive dependency between the HealthPlan and PlanDesc fields. (As an exercise, find examples of the three anomalies caused by the transitive dependency.) That is, the HealthPlan field is a determinant for the PlanDesc field, and the EmployeeNum field is a determinant for the HealthPlan and PlanDesc fields. Third normal form addresses the transitive-dependency problem.

Third Normal Form

A table in 2NF is in **third normal form (3NF)** if every determinant is a candidate key. This definition for 3NF is referred to as **Boyce-Codd normal form (BCNF)** and is an improvement over the original version of 3NF. What are the determinants in the Employee table? The EmployeeNum and HealthPlan fields are the determinants; however, the EmployeeNum field is a candidate key because it's the table's primary key, and the HealthPlan field is not a candidate key. Therefore, the Employee table is in second normal form, but it is not in third normal form.

To convert a table to third normal form, remove the fields that depend on the non-candidate-key determinant and place them into a new table with the determinant as the primary key. For the Employee table, the PlanDesc field depends on the HealthPlan field, which is a non-candidate-key determinant. Thus, you remove the PlanDesc field from the table, create a new HealthBenefits table, place the PlanDesc field in the HealthBenefits table, and then make the HealthPlan field the primary key of the HealthBenefits table. Note that only the PlanDesc field is removed from the Employee table; the HealthPlan field remains as a foreign key in the Employee table. Figure A-17 shows the database design for the four 3NF tables.

Figure A-17   **After conversion to 3NF**

Employee

EmployeeNum	FirstName	LastName	HealthPlan
2173	Barbara	Hennessey	B
4519	Lee	Noordsy	A
8005	Pat	Amidon	C
8112	Chris	Wandzell	A

primary key

HealthBenefits

primary key

HealthPlan	PlanDesc
A	Managed PPO
B	Managed HMO
C	Health Savings

Position

primary key

PositionID	PositionDesc	PayGrade
1	Director	45
2	Manager	40
3	Analyst	30
4	Clerk	20

composite primary key

Employment

EmployeeNum	PositionID	StartDate
2173	2	12/14/2011
4519	1	04/23/2013
4519	3	11/11/2007
8005	3	06/05/2012
8005	4	07/02/2010
8112	1	12/15/2012
8112	2	10/04/2011

© 2014 Cengage Learning

The alternative way to describe the 3NF relations is:

Employee (EmployeeNum, FirstName, LastName, HealthPlan)
   Foreign key: HealthPlan to HealthBenefits table
HealthBenefits (HealthPlan, PlanDesc)
Position (PositionID, PositionDesc, PayGrade)
Employment (EmployeeNum, PositionID, StartDate)
   Foreign key: EmployeeNum to Employee table
   Foreign key: PositionID to Position table

The four tables have no anomalies because you have eliminated all the data redundancy, partial dependencies, and transitive dependencies. Normalization provides the framework for eliminating anomalies and delivering an optimal database design, which you should always strive to achieve. You should be aware, however, that experts sometimes denormalize tables to improve database performance—specifically, to decrease the time it takes the database to respond to a user's commands and requests. Typically, when you denormalize tables, you combine separate tables into one table to reduce the need for the DBMS to join the separate tables to process queries and other informational requests. When you denormalize a table, you reintroduce redundancy to the table. At the same time, you reintroduce anomalies. Thus, improving performance exposes a database to potential integrity problems. Only database experts should denormalize tables, but even experts first complete the normalization of their tables.

Natural, Artificial, and Surrogate Keys

When you complete the design of a database, your tables should be in third normal form, free of anomalies and redundancy. Some tables, such as the State table (see Figure A-2), have obvious third normal form designs with obvious primary keys. The State table's description is:

State (<u>StateAbbrev</u>, StateName, EnteredUnionOrder, StateBird, StatePopulation)

Recall that the candidate keys for the State table are StateAbbrev, StateName, and EnteredUnionOrder. Choosing the StateAbbrev field as the State table's primary key makes the StateName and EnteredUnionOrder fields alternate keys. Primary keys such as the StateAbbrev field are sometimes called natural keys. A **natural key** (also called a **logical key** or an **intelligent key**) is a primary key that consists of a field, or a collection of fields, that is an inherent characteristic of the entity described by the table and that is visible to users. Other examples of natural keys are the ISBN (International Standard Book Number) for a book, the SSN (Social Security number) for a U.S. individual, the UPC (Universal Product Code) for a product, and the VIN (vehicle identification number) for a vehicle.

Is the PositionID field, which is the primary key for the Position table (see Figure A-17), a natural key? No, the PositionID field is not an inherent characteristic of a position. Instead, the PositionID field has been added to the Position table only as a way to identify each position uniquely. The PositionID field is an **artificial key**, which is a field that you add to a table to serve solely as the primary key and that is visible to users.

Another reason for using an artificial key arises in tables that allow duplicate records. Although relational database theory and most experts do not allow duplicate records in a table, consider a database that tracks donors and their donations. Figure A-18 shows a Donor table with an artificial key of DonorID and with the DonorFirstName and DonorLastName fields. Some cash donations are anonymous, which accounts for the fourth record in the Donor table. Figure A-18 also shows the Donation table with the DonorID field, a foreign key to the Donor table, and the DonationDate and DonationAmt fields.

Donor

DonorID	DonorFirstName	DonorLastName
1	Christina	Chang
2	Franco	Diaz
3	Angie	Diaz
4		Anonymous
5	Tracy	Burns

primary key →

Donation

DonorID	DonationDate	DonationAmt
1	10/12/2013	$50.00
1	09/30/2014	$50.00
2	10/03/2014	$75.00
4	10/10/2014	$50.00
4	10/10/2014	$50.00
4	10/11/2014	$25.00
5	10/13/2014	$50.00

duplicate records ←

© 2014 Cengage Learning

What is the primary key of the Donation table? No single field is unique, and neither is any combination of fields. For example, on 10/10/2014, two anonymous donors (DonorID value of 4) donated $50 each. You need to add an artificial key, DonationID for example, to the Donation table. The addition of the artificial key makes every record in the Donation table unique, as shown in Figure A-19.

| Figure A-19 | Donation table after adding DonationID, an artificial key |

Donation

DonationID	DonorID	DonationDate	DonationAmt
1	1	10/12/2013	$50.00
2	1	09/30/2014	$50.00
3	2	10/03/2014	$75.00
4	4	10/10/2014	$50.00
5	4	10/10/2014	$50.00
6	4	10/11/2014	$25.00
7	5	10/13/2014	$50.00

artificial key →

© 2014 Cengage Learning

The descriptions of the Donor and Donation tables now are:

Donor (DonorID, DonorFirstName, DonorLastName)
Donation (DonationID, DonorID, DonationDate, DonationAmt)
    Foreign key: DonorID to Donor table

For another common situation, consider the 3NF tables you reviewed in the previous section (see Figure A-17) that have the following descriptions:

Employee (EmployeeNum, FirstName, LastName, HealthPlan)
    Foreign key: HealthPlan to HealthBenefits table
HealthBenefits (HealthPlan, PlanDesc)
Position (PositionID, PositionDesc, PayGrade)
Employment (EmployeeNum, PositionID, StartDate)
    Foreign key: EmployeeNum to Employee table
    Foreign key: PositionID to Position table

Recall that a primary key must be unique, must be minimal, and must not change in value. In theory, primary keys don't change in value. However, in practice, you might have to change EmployeeNum field values that you incorrectly entered in the Employment table. Further, if you need to change an EmployeeNum field value in the Employee table, the change must cascade to the EmployeeNum field values in the Employment table. Also, changes to a PositionID field value in the Position table must cascade to the Employment table. For these and other reasons, many experts add surrogate keys to their tables. A **surrogate key** (also called a **synthetic key**) is a system-generated primary key that is hidden from users. Usually you can use an automatic numbering data type, such as the Access AutoNumber data type, for a surrogate key. Figure A-20 shows the four tables with surrogate keys added to each table.

Figure A-20   Using surrogate keys

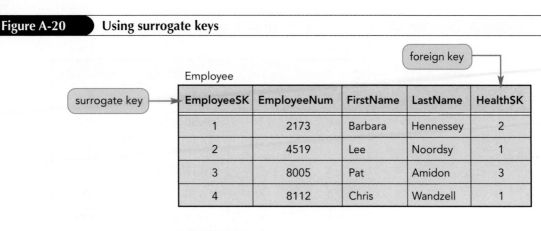

Employee

surrogate key →	**EmployeeSK**	**EmployeeNum**	**FirstName**	**LastName**	**HealthSK**
	1	2173	Barbara	Hennessey	2
	2	4519	Lee	Noordsy	1
	3	8005	Pat	Amidon	3
	4	8112	Chris	Wandzell	1

HealthBenefits

surrogate key →	**HealthSK**	**HealthPlan**	**PlanDesc**
	1	A	Managed PPO
	2	B	Managed HMO
	3	C	Health Savings

Position

artificial key →	**PositionID**	**PositionDesc**	**PayGrade**
	1	Director	45
	2	Manager	40
	3	Analyst	30
	4	Clerk	20

Employment

surrogate key →	**EmploymentSK**	**EmployeeSK**	**PositionID**	**StartDate**
	1	1	2	12/14/2011
	2	2	1	04/23/2013
	3	2	3	11/11/2007
	4	3	3	06/05/2012
	5	3	4	07/02/2010
	6	4	1	12/15/2012
	7	4	2	10/04/2011

© 2014 Cengage Learning

The HealthSK field replaces the HealthPlan field as a foreign key in the Employee table, and the EmployeeSK field replaces the EmployeeNum field in the Employment table. Now when you change an incorrectly entered EmployeeNum field value in the Employee table, you don't need to cascade the change to the Employment table. Likewise, when you change an incorrectly entered HealthPlan field value in the HealthBenefits table, you don't need to cascade the change to the Employee table.

As you design a database, you should *not* consider the use of surrogate keys, and you should use an artificial key only for the rare table that has duplicate records. At the point when you implement a database, you might choose to use artificial and surrogate keys, but be aware that database experts debate their use and effectiveness. You need to consider the following tradeoffs between natural and surrogate keys:

- You use surrogate keys to avoid cascading updates to foreign key values. Surrogate keys can also replace lengthier foreign keys when those foreign keys reference composite fields.
- You don't need a surrogate key for a table whose primary key is not used as a foreign key in another table because cascading updates is not an issue.
- Tables with surrogate keys require more joins than do tables with natural keys. For example, if you need to know all employees with a HealthPlan field value of A, the surrogate key in Figure A-20 requires that you join the Employee and HealthBenefits tables to answer the question. Using natural keys as shown in Figure A-17, the HealthPlan field appears in the Employee table, so no join is necessary.
- Although surrogate keys are meant to be hidden from users, they cannot be hidden from users who create SQL statements and use other ad hoc tools.
- Because you need a unique index for the natural key and a unique index for the surrogate key, your database size is larger and index maintenance takes more time when you use a surrogate key. On the other hand, a foreign key using a surrogate key is usually smaller than a foreign key using a natural key, especially when the natural key is a composite key, so those indexes are smaller and faster to access for lookups and joins.

Microsoft Access Naming Conventions

In the early 1980s, Microsoft's Charles Simonyi introduced an identifier naming convention that became known as Hungarian notation. Microsoft and other companies use this naming convention for variable, control, and other object naming in Basic, Visual Basic, and other programming languages. When Access was introduced in the early 1990s, Stan Leszynski and Greg Reddick adapted Hungarian notation for Microsoft Access databases; their guidelines became known as the Leszynski/Reddick naming conventions. In recent years, the Leszynski naming conventions, the Reddick naming conventions, and other naming conventions have been published. Individuals and companies have created their own Access naming conventions, but many are based on the Leszynski/Reddick naming conventions, as are the naming conventions covered in this section.

An Access database can contain thousands of objects, fields, controls, and other items, and keeping track of their names and what they represent is a difficult task. Consequently, you should use naming conventions that identify the type and purpose of each item in an Access database. You can use naming conventions that identify items generally or very specifically.

For an object, include a prefix tag to identify the type of object, as shown in Figure A-21. In each example in Figure A-21, the final object name consists of a three-character tag prefixed to the base object name. For example, the form name of frmEmployeesAndPositions consists of the frm tag and the EmployeesAndPositions base form name.

Figure A-21   **Object naming tags**

Object type	Tag	Example
Form	frm	frmEmployeesAndPositions
Macro	mcr	mcrSwitchboard
Module	bas	basCalculations
Query	qry	qryEmployee
Report	rpt	rptEmployeesAndPositions
Table	tbl	tblEmployee

© 2014 Cengage Learning

The tags in Figure A-21 identify each object type in general. If you want to identify object types more specifically, you could expand Figure A-21 to include tags such as fsub for a subform, qxtb for a crosstab query, tlkp for a lookup table, rsub for a subreport, and so on.

For controls in forms and reports, a general naming convention uses lbl as a prefix tag for labels and ctl as a prefix tag for other types of controls. For more specific naming conventions for controls, you'd use a specific prefix tag for each type of control. Figure A-22 shows the prefix tags for some common controls in forms and reports.

Figure A-22   **Control naming tags**

Control type	Tag
Check box	chk
Combo box	cbo
Command button	cmd
Image	img
Label	lbl
Line	lin
List box	lst
Option button	opt
Rectangle	shp
Subform/Subreport	sub
Text box	txt

© 2014 Cengage Learning

Some database developers use a prefix tag for each field name to identify the field's data type (for example, dtm for Date/Time, num for Number, and chr for Text or Character), others use a prefix tag for each field name to identify in which table the field is located (for example, emp for the Employee table and pos for the Position table), and still others don't use a prefix tag for field names.

You might use suffix tags for controls that might otherwise have identical names. For example, if you have two text boxes in a form for calculated controls that display the average and the sum of the OrderAmt field, both could legitimately be named txtOrderAmt unless you used suffix tags to name them txtOrderAmtAvg and txtOrderAmtSum.

You should ensure that any name you use does not duplicate a property name or any keyword Access reserves for special purposes. In general, you can avoid property and keyword name conflicts by using two-word field, control, and object names. For example, use StudentName instead of Name, and use OrderDate instead of Date to avoid name conflicts.

All database developers avoid spaces in names, mainly because spaces are not allowed in server DBMSs, such as SQL Server, Oracle, and DB2. If you are prototyping a Microsoft Access database that you'll migrate to one of these server DBMSs, or if future requirements might force a migration, you should restrict your Access identifier names so that they conform to the rules common to them all. Figure A-23 shows the identifier naming rules for Access, SQL Server, Oracle, and DB2.

Figure A-23	Identifier naming rules for common database management systems

Identifier naming rule	Access	SQL Server	Oracle	DB2
Maximum character length	64	30	30	30
Allowable characters	Letters, digits, space, and special characters, except for period (.), exclamation point (!), grave accent ('), and square brackets ([ ])	Letters, digits, dollar sign ($), underscore (_), number symbol (#), and at symbol (@)	Letters, digits, dollar sign ($), underscore (_), and number symbol (#)	Letters, digits, at symbol (@), dollar sign ($), underscore (_), and number symbol (#)
Special rules		No spaces; first character must be a letter or at symbol (@)	No spaces; first character must be a letter; stored in the database in uppercase	No spaces; first character must be a letter, at symbol (@), dollar sign ($), or number symbol (#); stored in the database in uppercase

© 2014 Cengage Learning

Review Assignments

1. What are the formal names for a table, for a row, and for a column? What are the popular names for a row and for a column?

2. What is a domain?

3. What is an entity?

4. What is the relationship between a primary key and a candidate key?

5. What is a composite key?

6. What is a foreign key?

7. Look for an example of a one-to-one relationship, an example of a one-to-many relationship, and an example of a many-to-many relationship in a newspaper, magazine, book, or everyday situation you encounter.

8. When do you use an entity subtype?

9. What is the entity integrity constraint?

10. What is referential integrity?

11. What does the cascades option, which is used with referential integrity, accomplish?

12. What are partial and transitive dependencies?

13. What three types of anomalies can be exhibited by a table, and what problems do they cause?

14. Figure A-24 shows the Employee, Position, and Employment tables with primary keys EmployeeNum, PositionID, and both EmployeeNum and PositionID, respectively. Which two integrity constraints do these tables violate and why?

Figure A-24   **Integrity constraint violations**

Employee

EmployeeNum	FirstName	LastName	HealthPlan
2173	Barbara	Hennessey	B
4519	Lee	Noordsy	A
8005	Pat	Amidon	C
8112	Chris	Wandzell	A

Position

PositionID	PositionDesc	PayGrade
1	Director	45
2	Manager	40
3	Analyst	30
4	Clerk	20

Employment

EmployeeNum	PositionID	StartDate
2173	2	12/14/2011
4519	1	04/23/2013
4519		11/11/2007
8005	3	06/05/2012
8005	4	07/02/2010
8112	1	12/15/2012
9876	2	10/04/2011

© 2014 Cengage Learning

15. The State and City tables, shown in Figure A-4, are described as follows:
    State (StateAbbrev, StateName, EnteredUnionOrder, StateBird, StatePopulation)
    City (StateAbbrev, CityName, CityPopulation)
    Foreign key: StateAbbrev to State table
    Add the field named CountyName for the county or counties in a state containing the city to this database, justify where you placed it (that is, in an existing table or in a new one), and draw the entity-relationship diagram for all the entities. Counties for some of the cities shown in Figure A-4 are Travis and Williamson counties for Austin TX; Hartford county for Hartford CT; Clinton, Eaton, and Ingham counties for Lansing MI; Davidson county for Nashville TN; Hughes county for Pierre SD; and Nueces and San Patricio counties for Portland TX.
16. Suppose you have a table for a dance studio. The fields are dancer's identification number, dancer's name, dancer's address, dancer's telephone number, class identification number, day that the class meets, time that the class meets, instructor name, and instructor identification number. Assume that each dancer takes one class, each class meets only once a week and has

one instructor, and each instructor can teach more than one class. In what normal form is the table currently, given the following alternative description?

Dancer (<u>DancerID</u>, DancerName, DancerAddr, DancerPhone, ClassID, ClassDay, ClassTime, InstrName, InstrID)

Convert this relation to 3NF and represent the design using the alternative description method.

17. Store the following fields for a library database: AuthorCode, AuthorName, BookTitle, BorrowerAddress, BorrowerName, BorrowerCardNumber, CopiesOfBook, ISBN (International Standard Book Number), LoanDate, PublisherCode, PublisherName, and PublisherAddress. A one-to-many relationship exists between publishers and books. Many-to-many relationships exist between authors and books and between borrowers and books.

   a. Name the entities for the library database.

   b. Create the tables for the library database and describe them using the alternative method. Be sure the tables are in third normal form.

   c. Draw an entity-relationship diagram for the library database.

18. In the database shown in Figure A-25, which consists of the Department and Employee tables, add one record to the end of the Employee table that violates both the entity integrity constraint and the referential integrity constraint.

Figure A-25   Creating integrity constraint violations

Department

DeptID	DeptName	Location
M	Marketing	New York
R	Research	Houston
S	Sales	Chicago

Employee

EmployeeID	EmployeeName	DeptID
1111	Sue	R
2222	Pam	M
3333	Bob	S
4444	Chris	S
5555	Pat	R
6666	Meg	R

© 2014 Cengage Learning

19. Consider the following table:

Patient (PatientID, PatientName, BalanceOwed, DoctorID, DoctorName, ServiceCode, Service-Desc, ServiceFee, ServiceDate)

This is a table concerning data about patients of doctors at a clinic and the services the doctors perform for their patients. The following dependencies exist in the Patient table:

PatientID → PatientName, BalanceOwed

DoctorID → DoctorName

ServiceCode → ServiceDesc, ServiceFee

PatientID, DoctorID, ServiceCode → PatientName, BalanceOwed, DoctorName, ServiceDesc, ServiceFee, ServiceDate

   a. Based on the dependencies, convert the Patient table to first normal form.

   b. Next, convert the Patient table to third normal form.

20. Suppose you need to track data for mountain climbing expeditions. Each member of an expedition is called a climber, and one of the climbers is named to lead an expedition. Climbers can be members of many expeditions over time. The climbers in each expedition attempt to ascend one or more peaks by scaling one of the many faces of the peaks. The data you need to track includes the name of the expedition, the leader of the expedition, and comments about the expedition; the first name, last name, nationality, birth date, death date, and comments about each climber; the name, location, height, and comments about each peak; the name and comments about each face of a peak; comments about each climber for each expedition; and the highest height reached and the date for each ascent attempt by a climber on a face with commentary.

   a. Create the tables for the expedition database and describe them using the alternative method. Be sure the tables are in third normal form.

   b. Draw an entity-relationship diagram for the expedition database.

21. What is the difference among natural, artificial, and surrogate keys?

22. Why should you use naming conventions for the identifiers in a database?

OBJECTIVES

Session 3.1
- Create a SmartArt diagram
- Modify a SmartArt diagram
- Add an audio clip to a slide
- Create a chart
- Modify a chart
- Insert and format text boxes
- Apply a WordArt style to text

Session 3.2
- Correct photos using photo editing tools
- Remove the background from a photo
- Apply an artistic effect to a photo
- Create a custom shape
- Adjust and align shapes
- Fill a shape with a texture and a custom gradient
- Add alt text to graphics

Applying Advanced Formatting to Objects

Formatting Objects in a Presentation for a Seminar Management Company

Case | *Spring Lake Seminar Management, Inc.*

Rashad Menche is a senior coordinator for Spring Lake Seminar Management, an international seminar management company with headquarters in Champaign, Illinois. The company provides assistance in planning and implementing seminars for companies and facilitating follow-up activities. As a senior coordinator, Rashad is responsible for everything from identifying and inviting appropriate speakers, to organizing the activities for the event, and finally sending out thank you letters and surveys to obtain feedback. He is preparing a presentation to potential clients about the services offered by the company, and he asks for your help in enhancing the presentation with some more advanced formatting of the presentation's content.

In this tutorial, you will add interest to the presentation by creating a SmartArt graphic and a chart and by inserting an audio clip. You will also create a text box and use WordArt styles. You will improve the photos in the presentation using PowerPoint's photo editing tools. In addition, you will create a custom shape, and apply advanced formatting to the shape. Finally, you will add text to describe some of the graphics to make the presentation more accessible for people who use screen readers.

STARTING DATA FILES

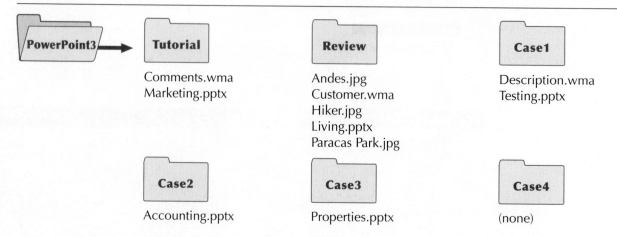

PowerPoint3 →

Tutorial
Comments.wma
Marketing.pptx

Review
Andes.jpg
Customer.wma
Hiker.jpg
Living.pptx
Paracas Park.jpg

Case1
Description.wma
Testing.pptx

Case2
Accounting.pptx

Case3
Properties.pptx

Case4
(none)

Session 3.1 Visual Overview:

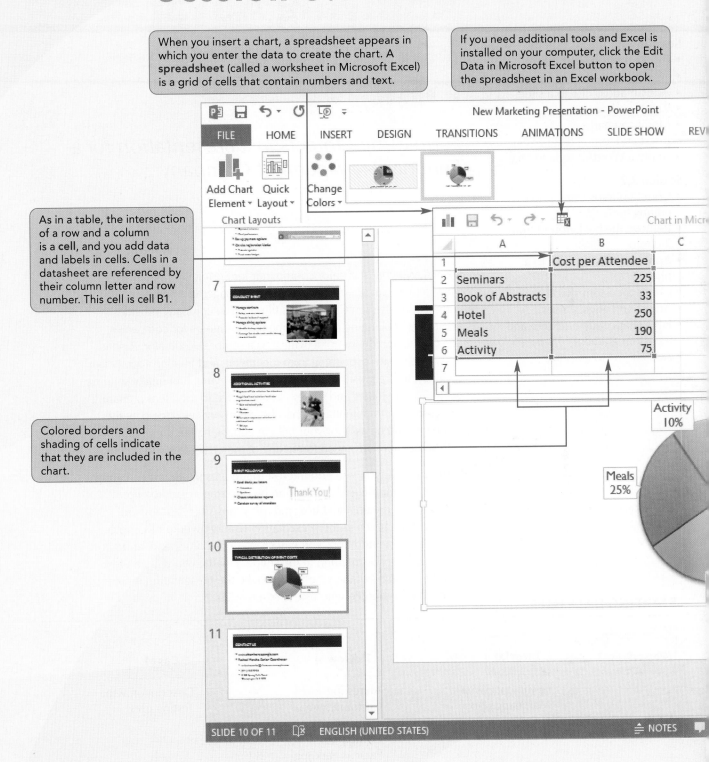

When you insert a chart, a spreadsheet appears in which you enter the data to create the chart. A **spreadsheet** (called a worksheet in Microsoft Excel) is a grid of cells that contain numbers and text.

If you need additional tools and Excel is installed on your computer, click the Edit Data in Microsoft Excel button to open the spreadsheet in an Excel workbook.

As in a table, the intersection of a row and a column is a **cell**, and you add data and labels in cells. Cells in a datasheet are referenced by their column letter and row number. This cell is cell B1.

Colored borders and shading of cells indicate that they are included in the chart.

New Marketing Presentation - PowerPoint

FILE   HOME   INSERT   DESIGN   TRANSITIONS   ANIMATIONS   SLIDE SHOW   REVI

Add Chart Element ▾   Quick Layout ▾   Change Colors ▾

Chart Layouts

Chart in Micro

	A	B	C
1		Cost per Attendee	
2	Seminars	225	
3	Book of Abstracts	33	
4	Hotel	250	
5	Meals	190	
6	Activity	75	
7			

Activity 10%

Meals 25%

SLIDE 10 OF 11   ENGLISH (UNITED STATES)   ≜ NOTES

Creating a Chart on a Slide

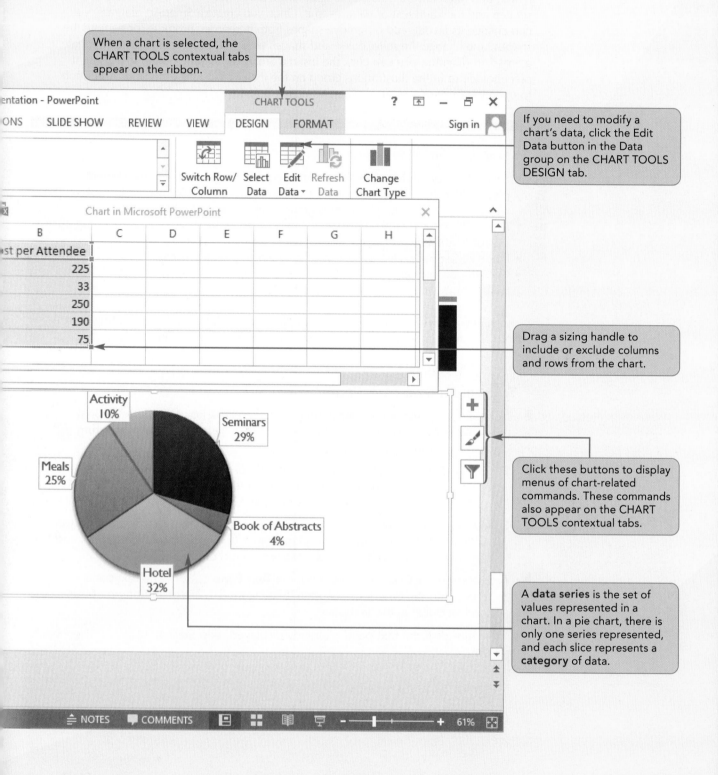

When a chart is selected, the CHART TOOLS contextual tabs appear on the ribbon.

If you need to modify a chart's data, click the Edit Data button in the Data group on the CHART TOOLS DESIGN tab.

Drag a sizing handle to include or exclude columns and rows from the chart.

Click these buttons to display menus of chart-related commands. These commands also appear on the CHART TOOLS contextual tabs.

A **data series** is the set of values represented in a chart. In a pie chart, there is only one series represented, and each slice represents a **category** of data.

Creating SmartArt Diagrams

In addition to creating a SmartArt diagram from a bulleted list, you can create one from scratch and then add text or pictures to it. Once you create a SmartArt diagram, you can change its layout, add or remove shapes from it, reorder, promote, or demote the shapes, and change the style, color, and shapes used to create the SmartArt. To create a SmartArt diagram, you can click the Insert a SmartArt Graphic button in a content placeholder, or in the Illustrations group on the INSERT tab, click the SmartArt button to open the Choose a SmartArt Graphic dialog box.

REFERENCE

Creating a SmartArt Diagram

- Switch to a layout that includes a content placeholder, and then in the content placeholder, click the Insert a SmartArt Graphic button; or click the INSERT tab on the ribbon, and then in the Illustrations group, click the SmartArt button.
- In the Choose a SmartArt Graphic dialog box, select the desired SmartArt category in the list on the left.
- In the center pane, click the SmartArt diagram you want to use.
- Click the OK button.

Rashad wants you to create a SmartArt diagram on Slide 3 of his marketing presentation. The diagram will list a general overview of the presentation.

To create a SmartArt diagram:

 1. Open the presentation **Marketing**, located in the PowerPoint3 ▸ Tutorial folder included with your Data Files, and then save it as **New Marketing Presentation**.

 2. Display **Slide 3** ("Let Us Plan Your Seminar or Conference") in the slide pane, and then in the content placeholder, click the **Insert a SmartArt graphic** button . The Choose a SmartArt Graphic dialog box opens.

 3. In the List category, click the **Lined List** layout, and then click the **OK** button. A SmartArt diagram containing placeholder text is inserted on the slide, and the SMARTART TOOLS DESIGN tab is selected on the ribbon.

 4. In the Create Graphic group, click the **Text Pane** button. The text pane appears to the left of the diagram. See Figure 3-1. The insertion point is in the first bullet in the text pane.

    Trouble? If the text pane is already displayed, skip Step 4.

| Figure 3-1 | SmartArt inserted on Slide 3 |

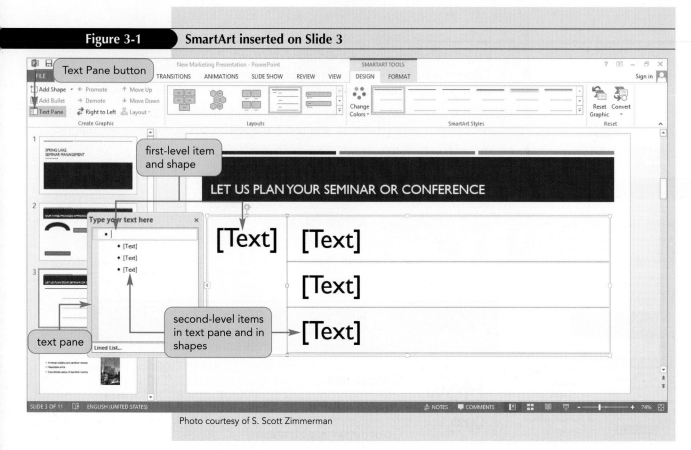

Photo courtesy of S. Scott Zimmerman

Now that you've added the diagram to the slide, you can add content to it. You need to add a first-level item and subitems to the diagram.

To add text to the SmartArt diagram and reorder it:

▶ 1. With the insertion point in the first bulleted item in the text pane, type **How we help**. The text appears in the bulleted list in the text pane and in the leftmost rectangle in the diagram.

▶ 2. In the first subbullet in the bulleted list, click **[Text]**. The placeholder text disappears and the insertion point appears.

▶ 3. Type **Choose site**, and then in the text pane, click the **Close** button ☒.

▶ 4. In the diagram, click the placeholder text in the box under the "Choose site" shape, and then type **Coordinate registration**.

▶ 5. Click the last empty box in the diagram, and then type **Invite speakers**. The "Invite speakers" shape needs to be moved so it is the second shape in the diagram.

▶ 6. Make sure the insertion point is in the Invite speakers shape, and then in the Create Graphic group, click the **Move Up** button. The current shape moves up into the second position in the diagram. You need to add two more shapes to the diagram.

▶ 7. Click in the **Coordinate registration shape**, and then in the Create Graphic group, click the **Add Shape** button. A new shape is added to the bottom of the diagram at the same level as the "Coordinate registration" shape. This shape does not have placeholder text, so you need to reopen the text pane to add the text.

TIP

To switch the order of the shapes, click the Right to Left button in the Create Graphic group on the SMARTART TOOLS DESIGN tab.

▶ **8.** In the Create Graphic group, click the **Text Pane** button. The text pane opens with an additional subbullet below the "Coordinate registration" item.

▶ **9.** Click to the right of the subbullet below the "Coordinate registration" item, and then type **Conduct event**. You need to add one more item to the list.

▶ **10.** With the insertion point after the word "event," press the **Enter** key. A fifth subbullet is created and an additional shape appears in the SmartArt diagram.

▶ **11.** Type **Handle follow-up**. See Figure 3-2.

| Figure 3-2 | SmartArt with text added |

Photo courtesy of S. Scott Zimmerman

Modifying a SmartArt Diagram

There are many ways to modify a SmartArt diagram. For example, you can change the layout of the diagram so the information is presented differently. You can also change the level of items in the diagram. You will change this next.

To change the layout of the SmartArt diagram:

▶ **1.** On the SMARTART TOOLS DESIGN tab, in the Layouts group, click the **More** button. The gallery of layouts in the List category opens.

TIP

To change the shapes in the diagram, select all the shapes, and then click the Change Shape button in the Shapes group on the SMARTART TOOLS FORMAT tab.

2. Click the **Vertical Block List** layout. The layout of the diagram changes to the new layout. Now you need to change the five subbullets to first-level bullets and delete the "How we help" shape.

3. In the text pane, click in the **Choose site** bulleted item.

4. On the SMARTART TOOLS DESIGN tab, in the Create Graphic group, click the **Promote** button. The item is promoted to a first-level item in both the text pane and in the diagram. See Figure 3-3.

Figure 3-3 | **SmartArt after changing the layout and promoting a shape**

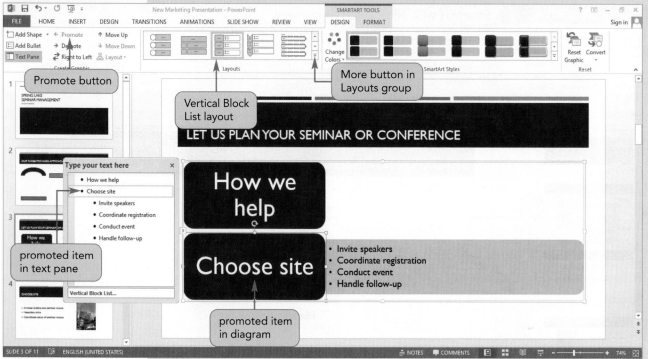

Photo courtesy of S. Scott Zimmerman

5. Promote the other four subbulleted items. All the text in the diagram is now in first-level shapes, and because there are no longer any subbullets, the first-level items are centered in the SmartArt diagram.

6. In the text pane, select **How we help** (the first bulleted item), and then press the **Delete** key. The text and the bullet item are deleted. In the diagram, the first shape is deleted as well.

   Trouble? If there is still a bullet at the top of the text pane and an empty shape above the "Choose site" shape in the diagram, click in the empty line in the text pane, and then press the Delete key.

7. In the text pane, click the **Close** button ☒.

SmartArt diagrams contain multiple objects that are grouped as one object which is then treated as a whole. So when you apply a style or other effect to the diagram, the effect is applied to the entire object. You can also apply formatting to individual shapes within the diagram if you want. You just need to select the specific shape first.

To apply a style to the SmartArt diagram and change its colors:

▶ **1.** On the SMARTART TOOLS DESIGN tab, in the SmartArt Styles group, click the **More** button to open the gallery of styles available for the graphic.

▶ **2.** In the gallery, click the **Inset** style. The style of the graphic changes to the Inset style.

▶ **3.** In the SmartArt Styles group, click the **Change Colors** button. A gallery of color styles opens.

▶ **4.** Under Accent 1, click the **Colored Outline – Accent 1** style. See Figure 3-4.

Figure 3-4	SmartArt with color and style changed

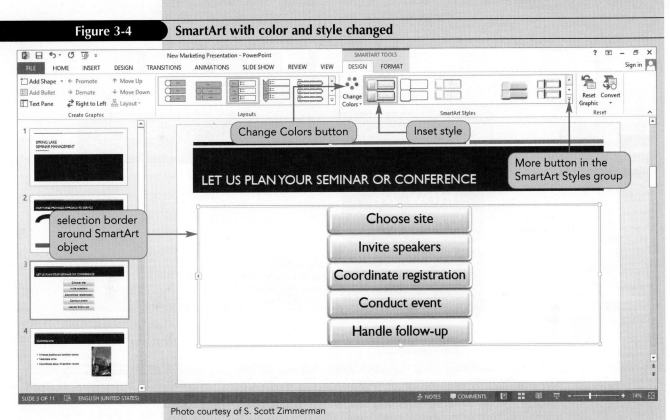

Photo courtesy of S. Scott Zimmerman

▶ **5.** Save your changes.

Animating a SmartArt Diagram

You animate a SmartArt diagram in the same way you animate any object. The default is for the entire object to animate as a single object. But similar to a bulleted list, after you apply an animation, you can use the Effect Options button and choose a different sequence effect. For example, you can choose to have each object animate one at a time.

Rashad wants the shapes in the SmartArt diagram to appear on the slide one at a time during his presentation.

To animate the SmartArt diagram:

▶ **1.** On the ribbon, click the **ANIMATIONS** tab.

▶ **2.** In the Animation group, click the **Appear** animation. The animation previews and the object quickly appears on the slide. One animation sequence icon appears to the left of the diagram object in the Slide pane.

▶ **3.** In the Animation group, click the **Effect Options** button. The selected effect is As One Object.

▶ **4.** Click **One by One**. The animation previews and each shape in the diagram appears one at a time.

▶ **5.** On the status bar, click the **Slide Show** button 🖵. Slide 3 appears in Slide Show view.

▶ **6.** Advance the slide show five times to display each of the shapes on the screen, one at a time.

▶ **7.** Press the **Esc** key to end the slide show.

▶ **8.** Save your changes.

INSIGHT

Converting a SmartArt Diagram to Text or Shapes

You can convert a SmartArt diagram to a bulleted list or to its individual shapes. To convert a diagram to a bulleted list, select the diagram, and then on the SMARTART TOOLS DESIGN tab, in the Reset group, click the Convert button, and then click Convert to Text. To convert a group to its individual shapes, click Convert to Shapes on the Convert menu or use the Ungroup command. In both cases, the shapes are converted from a SmartArt diagram into a set of grouped shapes. To completely ungroup them, you would need to use the Ungroup command a second time. Keep in mind that if you convert the diagram to shapes, you change it from a SmartArt object into ordinary drawn shapes, and you will no longer have access to the commands on the SmartArt Tools contextual tabs.

Adding Audio to Slides

Audio in a presentation can be used for a wide variety of purposes. For example, you might want to add a sound clip of music to a particular portion of the presentation to evoke emotion, or perhaps include a sound clip that is a recording of a customer expressing their satisfaction with a product or service. To add a sound clip to a slide, you use the Audio button in the Media group on the INSERT tab. When a sound clip is added to a slide, a sound icon and a play bar appear on the slide. Similar to videos, the options for changing how the sound plays during the slide show appear on the AUDIO TOOLS PLAYBACK tab. For the most part, they are the same options that appear on the VIDEO TOOLS PLAYBACK tab. For example, you can trim an audio clip or set it to rewind after playing. You can also compress audio in the same way that you compress video.

Inserting an Audio Clip into a Presentation

- Display the slide in which you want to insert the sound in the Slide pane.
- On the ribbon, click the INSERT tab, click the Audio button in the Media group, and then click Audio on My PC.
- In the Insert Audio dialog box, navigate to the folder containing the sound clip, click the audio file, and then click the Insert button.
- If desired, click the AUDIO TOOLS PLAYBACK tab, and then in the Audio Options group:
  - Click the Start arrow, and then click Automatically.
  - Click the Hide During Show check box to select it to hide the icon during a slide show.
  - Click the Volume button, and then click a volume level or click Mute.

Rashad wants you to add a sound clip to the presentation—a recording of a recent customer praising the company. The recorded message is a Windows Media Audio file, which is the most common file format for short sound clips.

To add a sound clip to Slide 3:

1. With **Slide 3** ("Let Us Plan Your Seminar or Conference") displayed in the Slide pane, click the **INSERT** tab on the ribbon.

2. In the Media group, click the **Audio** button, and then click **Audio on My PC**. The Insert Audio dialog box opens.

3. Navigate to the PowerPoint3 ▶ Tutorial folder, click the **Comments** file, and then click the **Insert** button. A sound icon appears in the middle of the slide with a play bar below it, and the AUDIO TOOLS PLAYBACK tab is selected on the ribbon. See Figure 3-5. As with videos, the default start setting is On Click.

Figure 3-5   Sound icon on Slide 2

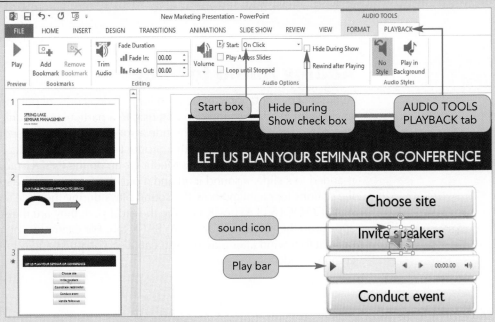

To make it easier to see the sound icon, you can reposition it on the slide.

▶ **4.** Drag the sound icon to the lower-right corner of the slide.

▶ **5.** On the play bar, click the **Play** button ▶. The sound clip plays, which is a comment from a customer complimenting the company on their service. Rashad wants the clip to play automatically after the slide appears on the screen.

▶ **6.** On the PLAYBACK tab, in the Audio Options group, click the **Start box arrow**, and then click **Automatically**. Because the clip will play automatically, there is no need to have the sound icon be visible on the screen during a slide show.

▶ **7.** In the Audio Options group, click the **Hide During Show** check box to select it.

▶ **8.** Save the presentation.

INSIGHT

Playing Music Across Slides

You can add an audio clip to a slide and have it play throughout the slide show. On the AUDIO TOOLS PLAYBACK tab, in the Audio Styles group, click the Play in Background button. When you select this option, the Start timing in the Audio Options group is changed to Automatically, and the Play Across Slides, Loop until Stopped, and Hide During Show check boxes become selected. Also, the Play in Background command changes the trigger animation automatically applied to media to a With Previous animation set to zero so that the sound will automatically start playing after the slide transitions. These setting changes ensure the audio clip will start playing when the slide appears on the screen during a slide show and will continue playing, starting over if necessary, until the end of the slide show.

Adding a Chart to a Slide

The terms "chart" and "graph" often are used interchangeably; however, they do, in fact, have distinct meanings. **Charts** are visuals that use lines, arrows, and boxes or other shapes to show parts, steps, or processes. **Graphs** show the relationship between variables along two axes or reference lines: the independent variable on the horizontal axis and the dependent variable on the vertical axis.

Despite these differences in the definitions, in PowerPoint a chart is any visual depiction of data in a spreadsheet, even if the result is more properly referred to as a graph (such as a line graph). Refer to the Session 3.1 Visual Overview for more information about creating charts in PowerPoint.

Creating a Chart

To create a chart, you click the Insert Chart button in a content placeholder or use the Chart button in the Illustrations group on the INSERT tab. Doing so will open a window containing a spreadsheet with sample data, and a sample chart will appear on the slide. You can then edit the sample data in the window to reflect your own data to be represented in the chart on the slide.

Creating a Chart

- Switch to a layout that includes a content placeholder, and then click the Insert Chart button in the content placeholder to open the Insert Chart dialog box; or click the INSERT tab, and then, in the Illustrations group, click the Chart button to open the Insert Chart dialog box.
- In the list on the left, click the desired chart type.
- In the row of styles, click the desired chart style, and then click the OK button.
- In the spreadsheet that opens, enter the data that you want to plot.
- In the spreadsheet window, click the Close button.

Rashad wants you to create a chart on Slide 10 to illustrate the percentage of each of the costs associated with a typical event that his company organizes. To do this, you'll create a pie chart.

To create a chart on Slide 10:

▶ 1. Display **Slide 10** ("Typical Distribution of Event Costs") in the Slide pane.

▶ 2. In the content placeholder, click the **Insert Chart** button ▮. The Insert Chart dialog box opens. Column is selected in the list of chart types on the left, and the Clustered Column style is selected in the row of styles at the top and shown in the preview area. See Figure 3-6.

Figure 3-6 **Insert Chart dialog box**

selected chart type

Pie chart type

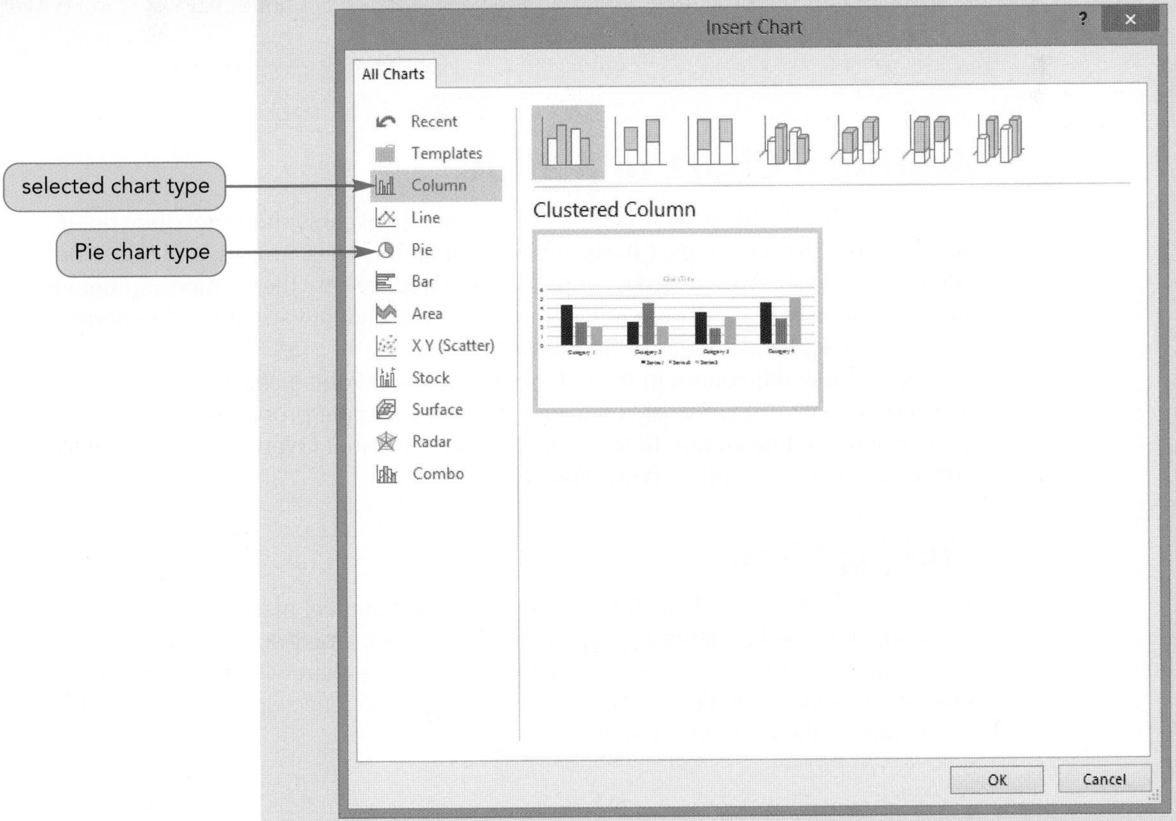

3. In the list of chart types, click **Pie**. The row of chart styles changes to pie chart styles. The Pie style is selected.

4. Click the **OK** button. A sample chart is inserted on Slide 10, and a small spreadsheet (sometimes called a datasheet) opens above the chart, with colored borders around the cells in the spreadsheet indicating which cells of data are included in the chart. See Figure 3-7.

Figure 3-7 | **Spreadsheet and chart with sample data**

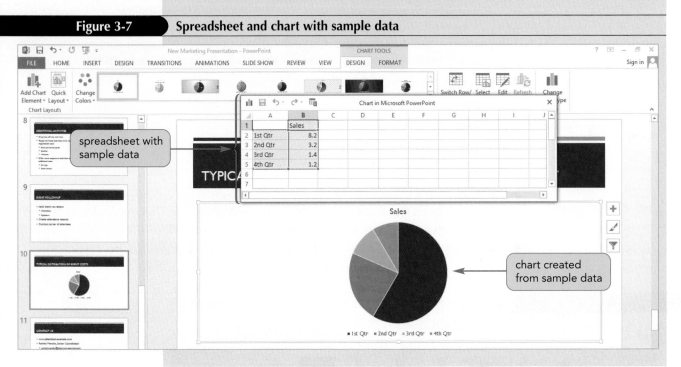

To create the chart for Rashad's presentation, you need to edit the sample data in the spreadsheet. When you work with a worksheet, the cell in which you are entering data is the **active cell**. The active cell has a green border around it.

To enter the data for the chart:

1. In the spreadsheet, click cell **A2**. A green border surrounds cell A2, indicating it is selected.

2. Type **Seminars**, and then press the **Enter** key. Cell A3 becomes the active cell. In the chart, the name in the legend for the blue data series changes to "Seminars".

3. Enter the following in cells **A3** through **A5**:

   Book of Abstracts

   Hotel

   Meals

   Trouble? The text you type in cell A3 will be cut off, but this is not a problem.

TIP

To add or remove a row or column from the chart, drag the corner sizing handles on the color borders.

4. In cell A6, type **Activity**, and then press the **Enter** key. The active cell is cell A7 and the colored borders around the cells included in the chart expands to include row 6. In the chart, a new series (slice) is added to the pie chart.

5. Click in cell **B1** to make it the active cell, type **Cost per Attendee**, and then press the **Enter** key. The active cell is now cell B2.

6. In cell **B2**, type **250**, and then press the **Enter** key. The slice in the pie chart that represents the percentage showing the cost of the Seminars increases to almost fill the chart. This is because the value 250 is so much larger than the sample data values in the rest of the rows in column B. As you continue to enter the data, the slices in the pie chart will adjust as you add each value.

7. In cells **B3** through **B6**, enter the following values:

33

250

180

75

8. Position the pointer on the column divider between the column A and column B headings so that it changes to ↔, and then double-click. Column A widens to fit the widest entry—the text in cell A3.

9. Double-click the column divider between the column B and column C headings to widen column B. See Figure 3-8.

| Figure 3-8 | Spreadsheet and chart after entering formulas in column B |

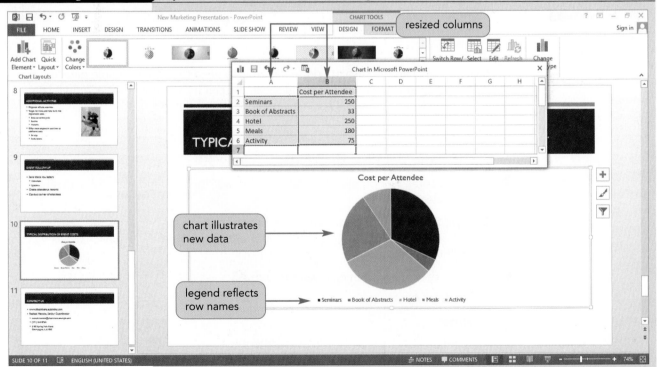

Photo courtesy of Beverly B. Zimmerman

10. In the spreadsheet, click the **Close** button ⊠.

Modifying a Chart

Once the chart is on the slide, you can modify it by changing or formatting its various elements. For example, you can edit the data; apply a style; add, remove, or reposition chart elements; add labels to the data series; and modify the formatting of text in the chart.

You need to make several changes to the chart you created on Slide 10. First, Rashad informs you that some of the data he provided was incorrect, so you need to edit the data.

To change the data used to create the chart:

TIP

To switch to another type of chart, click the Change Chart Type button in the Type group on the CHART TOOLS DESIGN tab.

1. On the CHART TOOLS DESIGN tab, in the Data group, click the **Edit Data** button. The spreadsheet reappears.

2. Click cell **B2**, type **225**, and then press the **Enter** key. The slices in the pie chart adjust to accommodate the new value.

3. Click cell **B5**, type **190**, and then press the **Enter** key. The slices in the pie chart adjust again.

4. Close the spreadsheet.

Rashad also wants you to make several formatting changes to the chart. He wants you to change the chart style. Also, there is no need for a title on the chart because the slide title describes the chart. Finally, Rashad wants you to remove the legend and, instead, label the pie slices with the series name and the percentage value.

To format and modify the chart:

1. On the CHART TOOLS DESIGN tab, in the Chart Styles group, click the **More** button, and then click **Style 12**. The chart is formatted with the selected style.

2. To the right of the chart, click the **Chart Elements** button ![+]. The CHART ELEMENTS menu opens to the left of the chart. See Figure 3-9.

Figure 3-9   **CHART ELEMENTS menu on Slide 9**

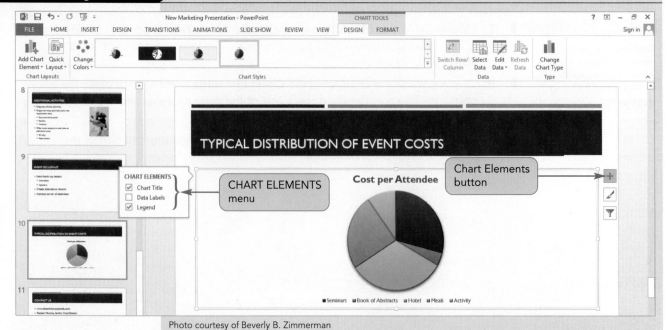

Photo courtesy of Beverly B. Zimmerman

Trouble? If labels appear on the pie slices on your screen, this is not a problem. You will adjust this shortly.

▶ **3.** On the CHART ELEMENTS menu, point to **Data Labels**. A small arrow appears.

▶ **4.** Click the **arrow** ▶ to open the Data Labels submenu. See Figure 3-10.

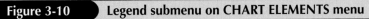

Figure 3-10 **Legend submenu on CHART ELEMENTS menu**

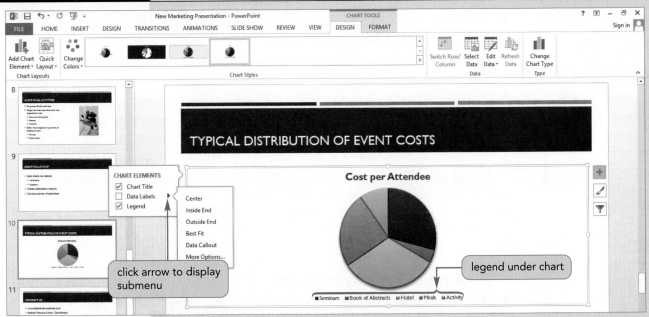

Photo courtesy of Beverly B. Zimmerman

▶ **5.** On the submenu, click **Data Callout**. Callouts containing the series names and percentages appear on the slices in the chart. With the slices labeled, there is no need for the legend.

▶ **6.** On the CHART ELEMENTS menu, click the **Legend** check box to deselect it. The legend is removed from the chart. Now you can remove the chart title.

▶ **7.** On the CHART ELEMENTS menu, click the **Chart Title** check box to deselect it. The chart title is removed from the chart. The font size of the callouts is a little small.

▶ **8.** To the right of the chart, click the **Chart Elements** button ➕ to close the menu, and then in the chart, click one of the callouts. All of the callouts are selected.

▶ **9.** On the ribbon, click the **HOME** tab, and then change the font size of the selected callouts to **18 points**. See Figure 3-11.

TIP

Double-click a chart element to open a task pane containing additional commands for modifying that element.

Figure 3-11   **Final chart on Slide 9**

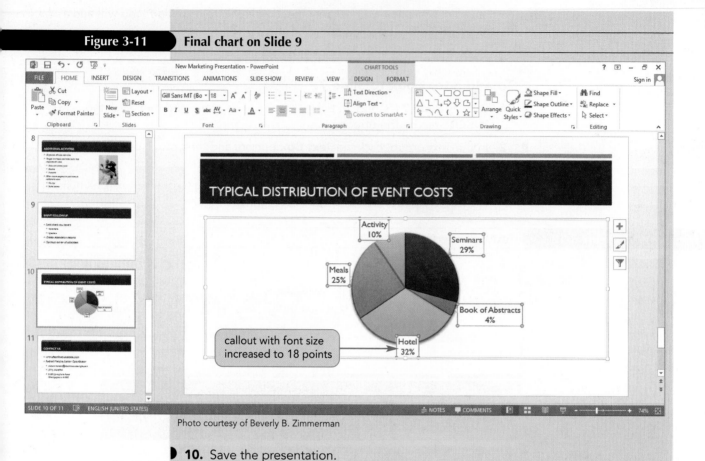

Photo courtesy of Beverly B. Zimmerman

▶ **10.** Save the presentation.

PROSKILLS

Decision Making: Selecting the Correct Chart Type

To use charts effectively, you need to consider what you want to illustrate with your data. Column charts use vertical columns and bar charts use horizontal bars to represent values. These types of charts are useful for comparing the values of items over a period of time or a range of dates or costs. Line charts use a line to connect points that represent values. They are effective for showing changes over time, and they are particularly useful for illustrating trends. Area charts are similar to line charts, but show shading from the line down to the x-axis. Line and area charts are a better choice than column or bar charts when you need to display large amounts of information and exact quantities that don't require emphasis. Pie charts are used to show percentages or proportions of the parts that make up a whole.

Inserting and Formatting Text Boxes

Sometimes you need to add text to a slide in a location other than in one of the text box placeholders included in the slide layout. You could draw any shape and add text to it, or you can add a text box shape. Unlike shapes that are filled with the Accent 1 color by default, text boxes by default do not have a fill. Another difference between the format of text boxes and shapes with text in them is that the text in a text box is left-aligned and text in shapes is center-aligned. Regardless of the differences, after you create a text box, you can format the text and the text box in a variety of ways, including adding a fill, adjusting the internal margins, and rotating and repositioning it.

Rashad wants you to add a description under the photo on Slide 7. You will add a text box to accomplish this.

To add a text box to Slide 7:

1. Display **Slide 7** ("Conduct Event") in the Slide pane, and then click the **INSERT** tab on the ribbon.

2. In the Text group, click the **Text Box** button, and then move the pointer to the slide. The pointer changes to ↓.

3. Position ↓ below the photo, and then click and drag to draw a text box half as wide as the photo and one-half inch high. See Figure 3-12.

Figure 3-12   **Text box inserted on Slide 7**

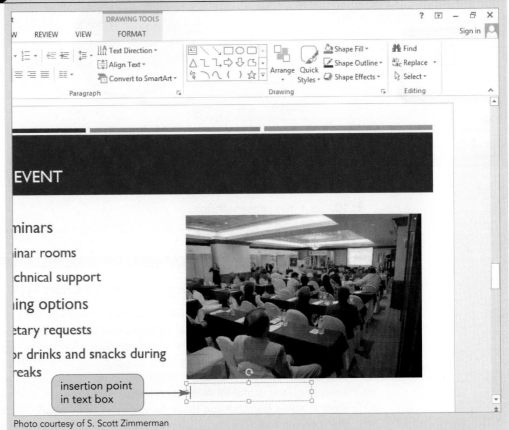

Photo courtesy of S. Scott Zimmerman

Trouble? If your text box is not positioned exactly as shown in Figure 3-12, don't worry. You'll reposition it later.

4. Type **Typical setup for a seminar room**. As you type the text in the text box, the height of the text box changes and the additional text wraps to the next line.

Trouble? If all the text fits on one line, drag the right middle sizing handle to the left until the word "room" appears on the next line so that you can complete the next sets of steps.

The default setting for text boxes you insert is for text to wrap and for the height of the box to resize to accommodate the text you type. This differs from text boxes created from title and content placeholders and shapes with text in them. Recall that text boxes

created from placeholders have AutoFit behavior that reduces the font size of the text if you add more text than can fit. If you add more text than can fit to a shape, the text extends outside of the text box.

The caption under the photo would be easier to read if it were all on one line. You can widen the text box, or if you do not want text to wrap to the next line regardless of how much text is in the text box, you can change the text wrapping option.

To modify and reposition the text box:

▶ **1.** Right-click the text box, and then on the shortcut menu, click **Format Shape**. The Format Shape task pane opens to the right of the Slide pane. At the top, the SHAPE OPTIONS tab is selected. This tab contains categories of commands for formatting the shape, such as changing the fill. See Figure 3-13.

| Figure 3-13 | Format Shape task pane and formatted text box |

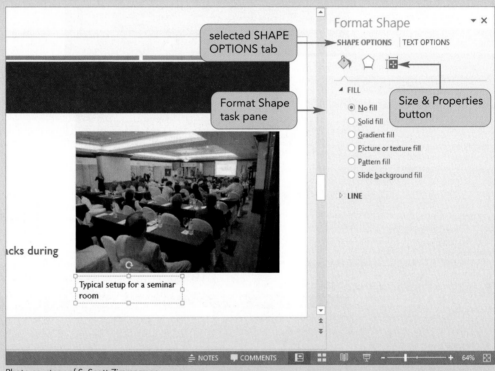

Photo courtesy of S. Scott Zimmerman

▶ **2.** Click the **TEXT OPTIONS** tab. This tab contains commands for formatting the text and how it is positioned.

▶ **3.** Click the **Textbox** button ⬛. The task pane changes to show the TEXT BOX section.

▶ **4.** Click **TEXT BOX**, if necessary, to display commands for formatting the text box. First you want to change the wrap option so the text does not wrap in the text box.

5. Click the **Wrap text in shape** check box to deselect it. The text in the text box appears all on one line. Next, you want to decrease the space between the first word in the text box and the left border of the box. In other words, you want to change the left margin in the text box.

6. Click the **Left margin down arrow**. The value in the box changes to 0" and the text shifts left in the text box.

7. If necessary, drag the text box so its left edge is aligned with the left edge of the photo and its top edge is aligned with the bottom edge of the photo. See Figure 3-14.

Figure 3-14	Format Shape task pane and formatted text box

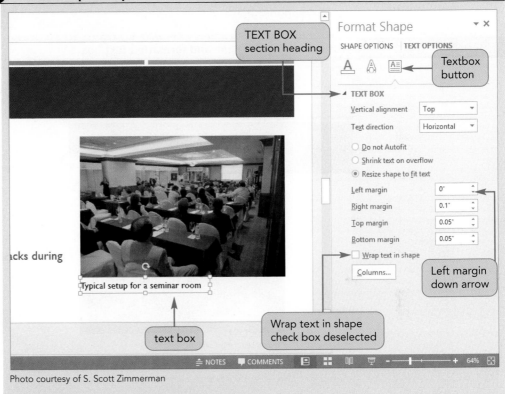

Photo courtesy of S. Scott Zimmerman

8. In the task pane, click the **Close** button ❌ to close the task pane.

9. Save the presentation.

TIP

Clicking any of the Dialog Box Launchers on the DRAWING TOOLS FORMAT tab also opens the Format Shape task pane.

Applying WordArt Styles to Text

WordArt is a term used to describe formatted, decorative text in a text box. WordArt text has a fill color, which is the same as the font color, and an outline color. To create WordArt, you can insert a new text box or format an existing one. You can apply one of the built-in WordArt styles or you can use the Text Fill, Text Outline, and Text Effects buttons in the WordArt Styles group on the DRAWING TOOLS FORMAT tab.

Slide 9 describes services the Spring Lake Seminar Management company provides at the conclusion of an event. Rashad would like you to add a text box that contains WordArt to Slide 9 to reinforce the content on this slide.

To create a text box containing WordArt on Slide 9:

1. Display **Slide 9** ("Event Follow-up") in the Slide pane, and then click the **INSERT** tab on the ribbon.

2. In the Text group, click the **WordArt** button to open the WordArt gallery. See Figure 3-15.

Figure 3-15   WordArt gallery

Photo courtesy of Beverly B. Zimmerman

---

3. Click the **Gradient Fill – Green, Accent 1, Reflection** style. A text box containing the placeholder text "Your text here" appears on the slide, and the DRAWING TOOLS FORMAT tab is selected on the ribbon. The placeholder text is formatted with the style you selected in the WordArt gallery.

4. Type **Thank You!**. The text you typed replaces the placeholder text. You want to change the color used in the gradient fill from green to blue.

5. Click the border of the text box to select the entire object.

6. On the FORMAT tab, in the WordArt Styles group, click the **Text Fill button arrow**, and then click the **Dark Blue, Accent 1** color. Now you need to change this solid fill color to a gradient.

7. Click the **Text Fill button arrow** again, and then point to **Gradient**. The Gradient submenu opens. The gradients on the submenu use shades of the Blue, Accent 1 color.

8. Under Light Variations, click the **Linear Diagonal – Top Left to Bottom Right** gradient.

9. Change the font size of the text in the WordArt text box to **72** points.

10. Drag the text box to position it roughly centered in the white space to the right of the bulleted list.

The shape of text in a text box can be transformed into waves, circles, and other shapes. To do this, use the Transform submenu on the Text Effects menu on the DRAWING TOOLS FORMAT tab. Rashad wants you to change the shape of the WordArt on Slide 9.

To change the shape of the WordArt by applying a transform effect:

▶ **1.** Click the **FORMAT** tab, if necessary.

▶ **2.** In the WordArt styles group, click the **Text Effects** button, and then point to **Transform**. The Transform submenu appears. See Figure 3-16.

Figure 3-16 Transform submenu

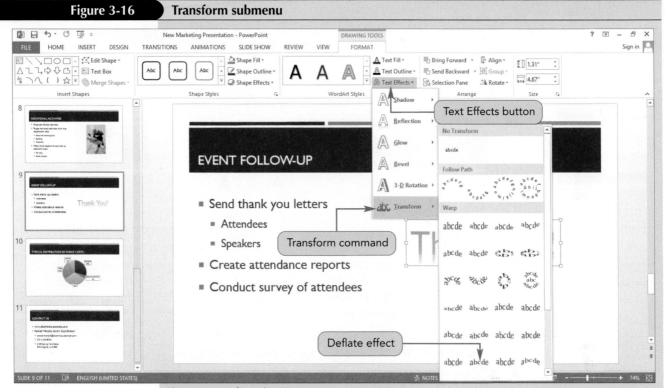

Photo courtesy of Beverly B. Zimmerman

▶ **3.** In the sixth row under Warp, click the **Deflate** effect, and then click a blank area of the slide. See Figure 3-17.

Figure 3-17 | **WordArt after applying Deflate transform effect**

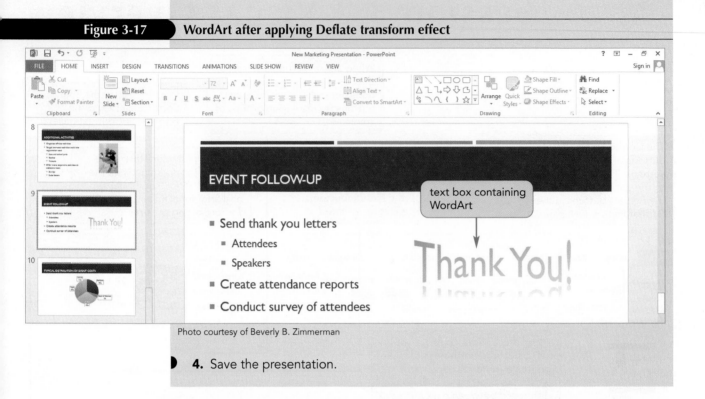

Photo courtesy of Beverly B. Zimmerman

4. Save the presentation.

PROSKILLS

Decision Making: Selecting Appropriate Font Colors

When you select font colors, make sure your text is easy to read during your slide show. Font colors that work well are dark colors on a light background, or light colors on a dark background. Avoid red text on a blue background or blue text on a green background (and vice versa) unless the shades of those colors are in strong contrast. These combinations might look fine on your computer monitor, but they are almost totally illegible to an audience viewing your presentation on a screen in a darkened room. Also avoid using red/green combinations, which color-blind people find illegible.

REVIEW

Session 3.1 Quick Check

1. How do you change the animation applied to a SmartArt diagram so that each shape animates one at a time?
2. What happens when you click the Play in Background button in the Audio Styles group on the AUDIO TOOLS PLAYBACK tab?
3. What is the difference between a chart and a graph?
4. What is a spreadsheet?
5. How do you identify a specific cell in a spreadsheet?
6. What is WordArt?

Session 3.2 Visual Overview:

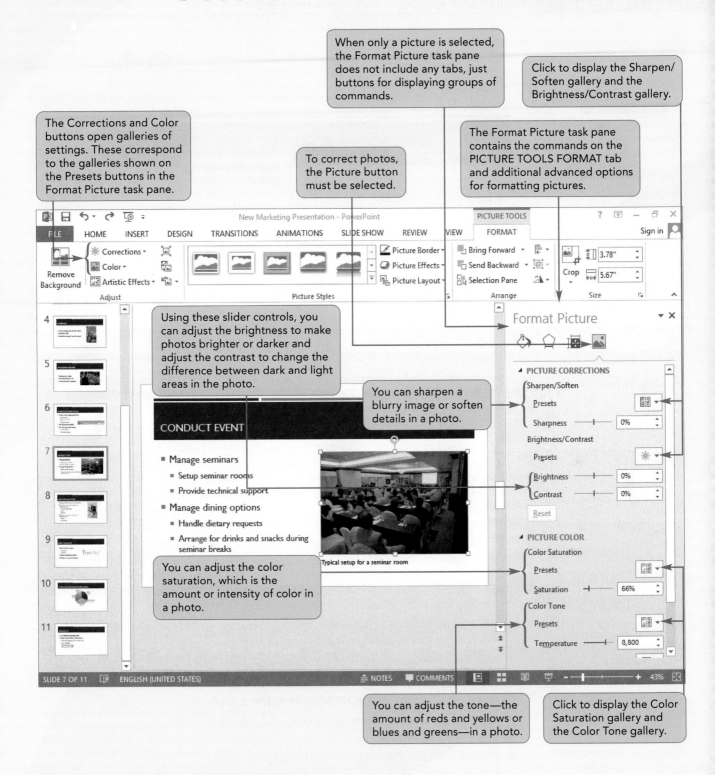

When only a picture is selected, the Format Picture task pane does not include any tabs, just buttons for displaying groups of commands.

Click to display the Sharpen/ Soften gallery and the Brightness/Contrast gallery.

The Corrections and Color buttons open galleries of settings. These correspond to the galleries shown on the Presets buttons in the Format Picture task pane.

To correct photos, the Picture button must be selected.

The Format Picture task pane contains the commands on the PICTURE TOOLS FORMAT tab and additional advanced options for formatting pictures.

Using these slider controls, you can adjust the brightness to make photos brighter or darker and adjust the contrast to change the difference between dark and light areas in the photo.

You can sharpen a blurry image or soften details in a photo.

You can adjust the color saturation, which is the amount or intensity of color in a photo.

You can adjust the tone—the amount of reds and yellows or blues and greens—in a photo.

Click to display the Color Saturation gallery and the Color Tone gallery.

Photos courtesy of Beverly B. and S. Scott Zimmerman and Chabruken/Getty Images

Formatting Shapes and Pictures

To use preset options in the Format Shape task pane, you can use the Shape Fill and Shape Outline buttons.

In task panes, click a tab to display the options on that tab. To create a custom gradient, the SHAPE OPTIONS tab must be selected.

The Format Shape task pane contains the commands on the DRAWING TOOLS FORMAT tab and additional advanced options for formatting shapes.

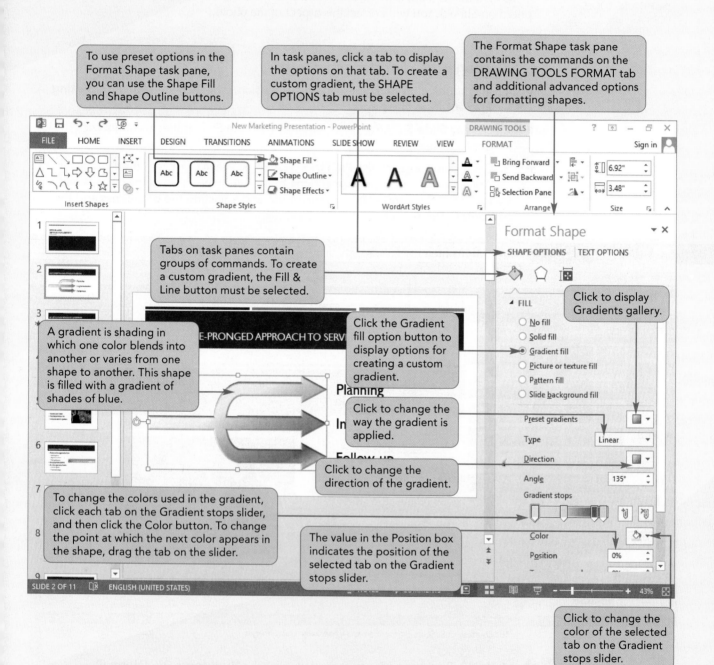

Tabs on task panes contain groups of commands. To create a custom gradient, the Fill & Line button must be selected.

A gradient is shading in which one color blends into another or varies from one shape to another. This shape is filled with a gradient of shades of blue.

Click the Gradient fill option button to display options for creating a custom gradient.

Click to display Gradients gallery.

Click to change the way the gradient is applied.

Click to change the direction of the gradient.

To change the colors used in the gradient, click each tab on the Gradient stops slider, and then click the Color button. To change the point at which the next color appears in the shape, drag the tab on the slider.

The value in the Position box indicates the position of the selected tab on the Gradient stops slider.

Click to change the color of the selected tab on the Gradient stops slider.

Editing Photos

TIP

If you make changes to photos and then change your mind, you can click the Reset Picture button in the Adjust group on the PICTURE TOOLS FORMAT tab.

If photos you want to use in a presentation are too dark or require other fine-tuning, you can use PowerPoint's photo correction tools to correct the photos. These photo correction tools appear on the ribbon and in the Format Picture task pane. Refer to the Session 3.2 Visual Overview for more information about correcting photos and the Format Picture task pane.

Rashad thinks there is too much contrast between the dark and light areas in the photo on Slide 5. You will correct this aspect of the photo.

To change the contrast of a photo:

1. If you took a break after the previous session, make sure the **New Marketing Presentation** file is open.

2. Display **Slide 5** ("Arrange for Speakers") in the Slide pane, and then click the photo to select it.

3. On the ribbon, click the **PICTURE TOOLS FORMAT** tab, and then in the Adjust group, click the **Corrections** button. A menu opens showing options for sharpening and softening the photo and adjusting the brightness and the contrast. See Figure 3-18.

Figure 3-18   Corrections menu

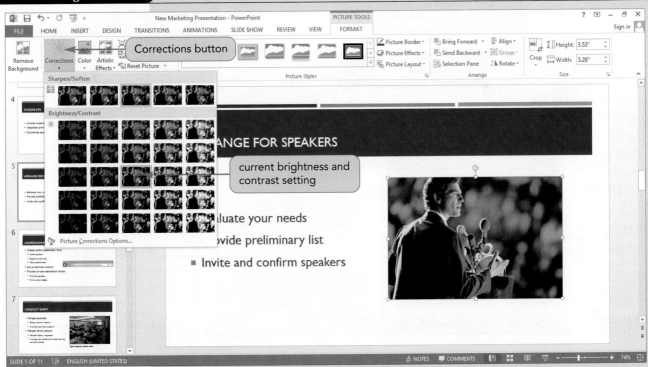

Photos courtesy of S. Scott Zimmerman and Chabruken/Getty Images

TIP

You can also right-click the photo, and then click Format Picture on the shortcut menu to open the Format Picture task pane.

4. In the Brightness/Contrast section, click the **Brightness 0% (Normal) Contrast -20%** style (the third style in the second row). The contrast of the image changes. Because you chose a style with a Brightness percentage of 0%, the brightness of the photo is unchanged.

You want to decrease the contrast just a little more. However, the gallery provides options that change the contrast in increments of 20%, which will be more of an adjustment than you are looking for. For selecting a more precise contrast setting, you need to open the Format Picture task pane.

▶ 5. Click the **Corrections** button again, and then click **Picture Corrections Options**. The Format Picture task pane opens with the Picture button selected and the PICTURE CORRECTIONS section expanded.

▶ 6. Drag the **Contrast** slider to the left until the box next to the slider indicates -30%. The contrast increases slightly.

   Trouble? If you can't position the slider exactly, click the up or down arrow in the box containing the percentage as needed, or select the current percentage and then type -30.

▶ 7. Close the task pane.

Next, Rashad wants you to adjust the saturation and tone of the photo on Slide 7. He wants you to reduce the saturation and increase the tone so the overall photo is a little brighter.

To change the saturation and tone of the photo on Slide 7:

▶ 1. Display **Slide 7** ("Conduct Event") in the Slide pane, click the photo to select it, and then click the **PICTURE TOOLS FORMAT** tab on the ribbon, if necessary.

▶ 2. In the Adjust group, click the **Color** button. A menu opens with options for adjusting the saturation and tone of the photo's color. See Figure 3-19.

Figure 3-19	Color menu

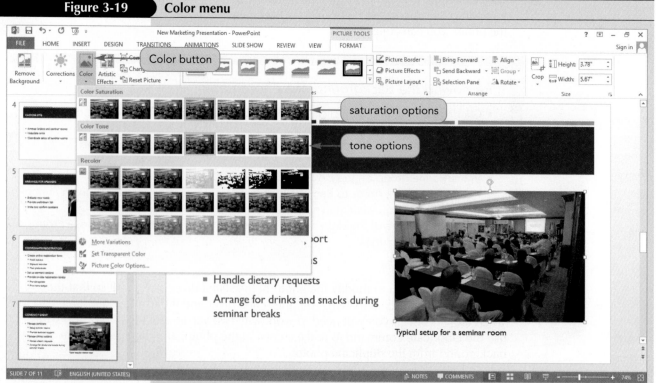

Photos courtesy of S. Scott Zimmerman and Chabruken/Getty Images

TIP

To recolor a photo so it is all one color, click the Color button in the Adjust group on the PICTURE TOOLS FORMAT tab, and then click a Recolor option.

3. Under Color Saturation, click the **Saturation: 66%** option. The colors in the photo are less intense.

4. Click the **Color** button again.

5. Under Color Tone, click the **Temperature: 8800K** option. More reds and yellows are added to the photo.

Finally, Rashad wants you to sharpen the photo on Slide 8 so that the scuba diver and fish are more in focus.

To sharpen the photo on Slide 8:

1. Display **Slide 8** ("Additional Activities") in the Slide pane, click the photo to select it, and then click the **PICTURE TOOLS FORMAT** tab on the ribbon.

2. In the Adjust group, click the **Corrections** button. The options for sharpening and softening photos appear at the top of the menu.

3. Under Sharpen/Soften, click the **Sharpen: 50%** option.

4. Save the presentation.

Removing the Background from Photos

Sometimes a photo is more striking if you remove its background. You can also layer a photo with the background removed on top of another photo to create an interesting effect. To remove the background of a photo, you can use the Remove Background tool. When you click the Remove Background button in the Adjust group on the PICTURE TOOLS FORMAT tab, the photograph is analyzed; part of it is marked to be removed and part of it is marked to be retained. If the analysis removes too little or too much of the photo, you can adjust it.

REFERENCE

Removing the Background of a Photograph

- Click the photo, and then click the PICTURE TOOLS FORMAT tab on the ribbon.
- In the Adjust group, click the Remove Background button.
- Drag the sizing handles on the remove background border to make broad adjustments to the area marked for removal.
- In the Refine group on the BACKGROUND REMOVAL tab, click the Mark Areas to Keep or the Mark Areas to Remove button, and then click or drag through an area of the photo that you want marked to keep or remove.
- Click a blank area of the slide or click the Keep Changes button in the Close group to accept the changes.

Rashad wants you to modify the photo of the scuba diver on Slide 8 so that the background looks like a drawing, but the scuba diver and the fish stay the same. To create this effect, you will need to work with two versions of the photo. You will use the Duplicate command to make a copy of the photo, and then remove the background from the duplicate photo.

To duplicate the photo on Slide 8 and then remove the background from the copy:

1. Make sure the photo is selected on **Slide 8** ("Additional Activities"), and then, on the ribbon, click the **HOME** tab.

2. In the Clipboard group, click the **Copy button arrow**. Because the selected item is an object and not text, there are two available commands on the menu—Copy and Duplicate.

3. Click **Duplicate**. The photo is duplicated on the slide and the duplicate is selected.

4. Point to the selected duplicate photo so that the pointer changes to ✥, and then drag it left to position it to the left of the original photo.

5. With the duplicate photo selected, click the **PICTURE TOOLS FORMAT** tab on the ribbon.

6. In the Adjust group, click the **Remove Background** button. The areas of the photograph marked for removal are colored purple. A sizing box appears around the general area of the photograph that will be retained, and a new tab, the BACKGROUND REMOVAL tab, appears on the ribbon and is the active tab. See Figure 3-20. You can adjust the area of the photograph that is retained by dragging the sizing handles on the sizing box.

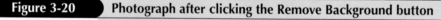

Figure 3-20   Photograph after clicking the Remove Background button

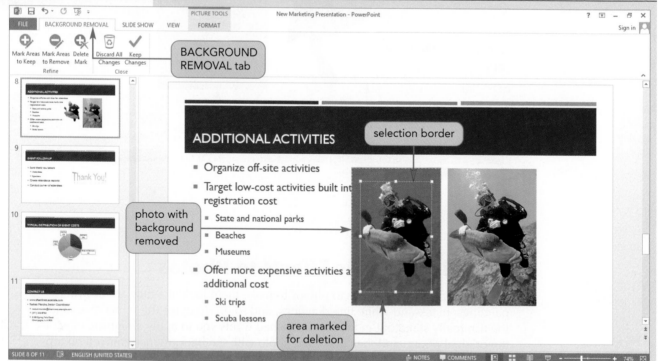

Photo courtesy of Beverly B. Zimmerman

7. Drag the left middle sizing handle to the left edge of the photo. The tail of the fish is colored normally.

8. Drag the bottom middle sizing handle down to the bottom border of the photo. The diver's flipper is colored normally.

   Trouble? If any of the background of the photo is colored normally, click the Mark Areas to Remove button in the Refine group on the BACKGROUND REMOVAL tab, and then drag through the area that should be removed.

9. On the BACKGROUND REMOVAL tab, in the Close group, click the **Keep Changes** button. The changes you made are applied to the photograph, and the BACKGROUND REMOVAL tab is removed from the ribbon. See Figure 3-21.

| Figure 3-21 | Duplicate photo with background removed |

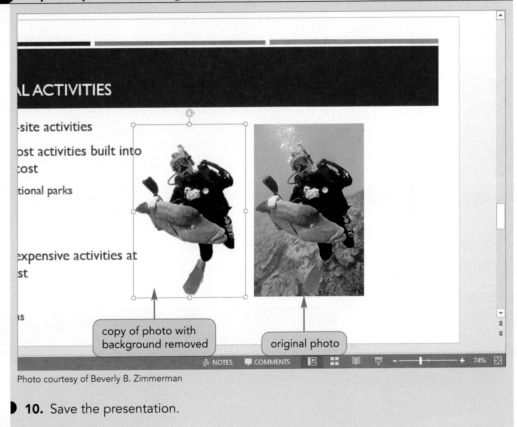

Photo courtesy of Beverly B. Zimmerman

10. Save the presentation.

Applying Artistic Effects to Photos

You can apply artistic effects to photos to make them look like they are drawings, paintings, black-and-white line drawings, and so on. To make the scuba diver and the fish really stand out in the photo, Rashad wants you to apply an artistic effect to the original photo, and then place the photo with the background removed on top of the photo with the artistic effect. You'll do this now.

To apply an artistic effect to the original photo on Slide 8:

1. On **Slide 8** ("Additional Activities"), click the original photo with the background still visible, and then click the **PICTURE TOOLS FORMAT** tab to select it, if necessary.

2. In the Adjust group, click the **Artistic Effects** button. See Figure 3-22.

Figure 3-22   **Artistic Effects menu**

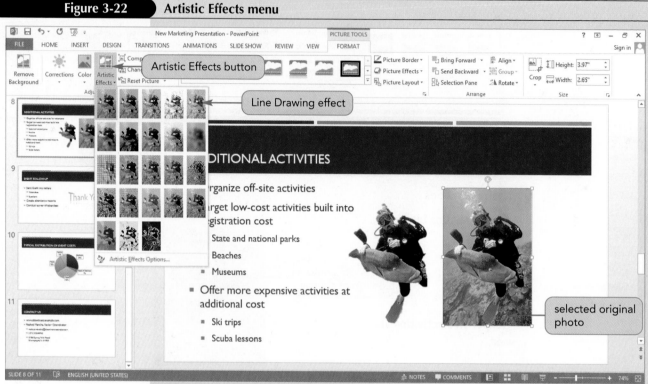

Photo courtesy of Beverly B. Zimmerman

3. Click the **Line Drawing** effect. The photo changes so it looks more like a drawing. Now you will place the photo with the background removed on top of the photo with the artistic effect.

4. Drag the photo with the background removed on top of the photos with the artistic effect applied and position it directly on top of the diver in the photo with the artistic effect applied. See Figure 3-23.

Figure 3-23 | **Final photo on Slide 7**

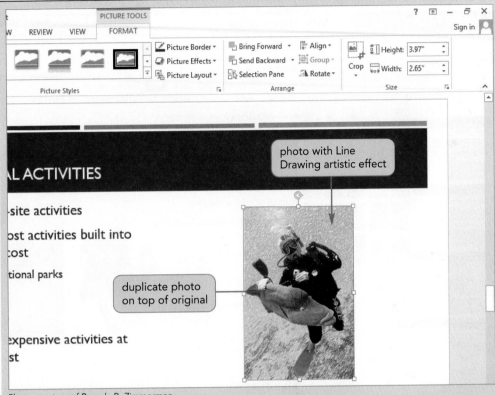

Photo courtesy of Beverly B. Zimmerman

Trouble? If the photo with the background removed seems to move behind the photo with the artistic effect applied, make sure the photo with the background removed is selected, and then in the Arrange group on the PICTURE TOOLS FORMAT tab, click the Bring Forward button.

5. Save your changes.

Creating a Custom Shape

You have learned how to insert and format shapes on slides. In PowerPoint you can also create a custom shape by merging two or more shapes. Then you can position and format the custom shape as you would any other shape.

Rashad wants to illustrate the company's three-pronged approach to service of planning, implementation, and follow-up with a graphic, but none of the SmartArt diagrams matches the idea he has in mind. He asks you to create a custom shape similar to the one shown in Figure 3-24 that illustrates this concept.

Figure 3-24   Rashad's sketch of the logo

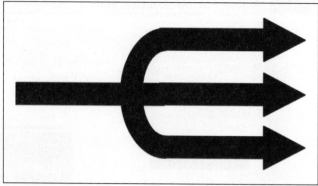

© 2014 Cengage Learning

Using the Adjustment Handle to Modify Shapes

To create the custom shape for Rashad, you will merge several shapes. One of the shapes is an arrow shape. First, you will adjust the arrow so that the arrowhead is longer. You can adjust many shapes using the yellow adjustment handles that appear on a selected shape.

To adjust the arrow shape and duplicate it on Slide 2:

▶ **1.** Display **Slide 2** ("Our Three-Pronged Approach to Service") in the Slide pane.

▶ **2.** Click the **arrow** shape to select it, and then drag the adjustment handle on the top corner of the arrowhead one-half inch to the left so that the arrowhead lengthens and the bottom of the arrowhead is aligned between the "T" and "O" in "TO" in the slide title. See Figure 3-25. You need two more arrow shapes exactly the same size as this one.

Figure 3-25 | **Adjusted arrow shape on Slide 2**

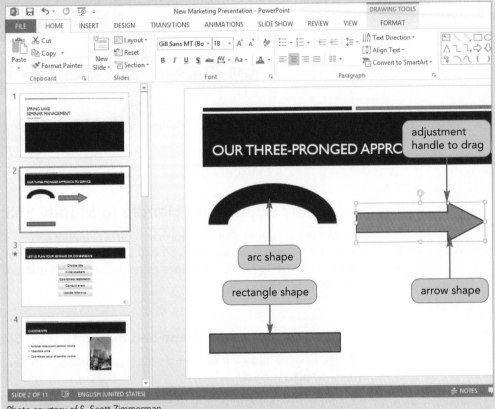

Photo courtesy of S. Scott Zimmerman

> **3.** Duplicate the arrow shape twice.

Aligning Objects

You now have all the shapes on the slide that you need to create the custom shape. First you need to arrange and align the three arrow shapes.

To align the three arrow shapes:

> **1.** Drag the selected arrow down about two inches so it is positioned just above and to the right of the rectangle shape, and then drag the other duplicated arrow down to position it so it is evenly spaced between the top and bottom arrows. There should be approximately one inch between the left ends of each arrow.

> **2.** Click the top arrow, press and hold the **Shift** key, and then click the other two arrows. The three arrows are selected.

> **3.** On the HOME tab, in the Drawing group, click the **Arrange** button, and then point to **Align**. The Align submenu opens. See Figure 3-26.

Figure 3-26   Align menu

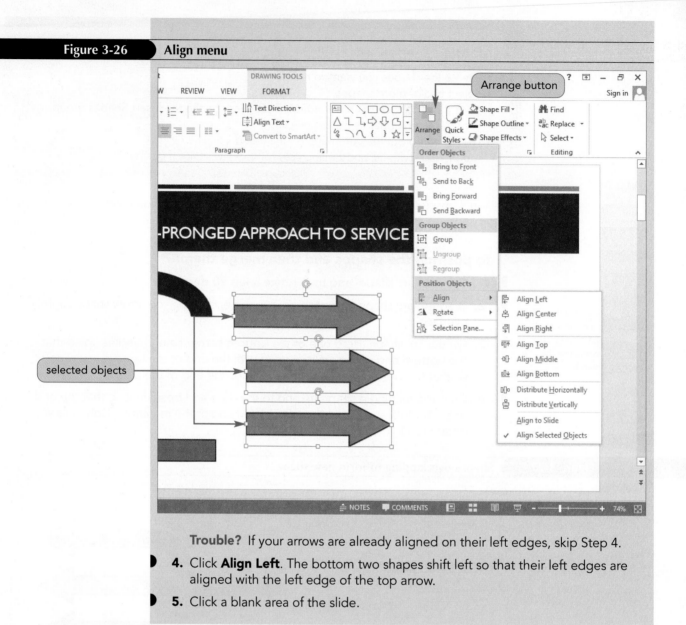

Trouble? If your arrows are already aligned on their left edges, skip Step 4.

4. Click **Align Left**. The bottom two shapes shift left so that their left edges are aligned with the left edge of the top arrow.

5. Click a blank area of the slide.

Merging Shapes

To merge shapes, you need to use the commands on the Merge Shapes menu in the Insert Shapes group on the DRAWING TOOLS FORMAT tab. Each command has a different effect on selected shapes:

- **Union**—Combines selected shapes without removing any portions
- **Combine**—Combines selected shapes and removes the sections of the shapes that overlap
- **Fragment**—Separates overlapping portions of shapes into separate shapes
- **Intersect**—Combines selected shapes and removes everything except the sections that overlap
- **Subtract**—Removes the second shape selected, including any part of the first shape that is overlapped by the second shape

Merging Shapes

- Create the shapes you want to merge.
- Select two or more shapes.
- Click the DRAWING TOOLS FORMAT tab, and then in the Insert Shapes group, click the Merge Shapes button.
- Click the appropriate command on the menu.
- Modify the style, fill, and outline color of the new shape if desired.

You'll position the shapes and then merge them using the Union command.

To position the shapes and then merge them:

1. Click the arc shape, and then rotate it left **90 degrees**.

2. Drag the arc shape and position it so the end of the top arrow shape slightly overlaps the top end of the arc.

Make sure you slightly overlap the arc and arrow shape or the shapes won't merge when you use the Union command.

3. On the arc shape, drag one of the bottom corner sizing handles up so that the bottom end of the arc is aligned with the end of the bottom arrow and so that the bottom arrow slightly overlaps the end of the arc.

4. Drag the rectangle shape up and to the right and position it so that the end of the middle arrow slightly overlaps the end of the rectangle. Compare your screen to Figure 3-27.

Figure 3-27	Shapes overlapping to form new shape

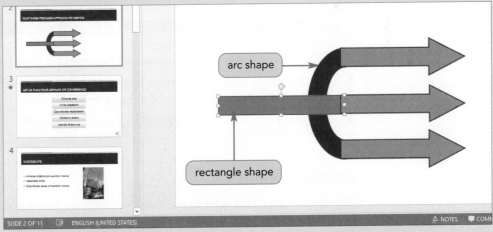

Photo courtesy of S. Scott Zimmerman

5. Click the **DRAWING TOOLS FORMAT** tab. In the Insert Shapes group, the Merge Shapes button is gray and unavailable. At least two shapes need to be selected to use the commands on the Merge Shapes menu.

6. Press and hold the **Shift** key, and then click the middle arrow. The rectangle and the middle arrow shape are now selected, and the Merge Shapes button is now available.

7. In the Insert Shapes group, click the **Merge Shapes** button, and then click **Union**. The two shapes are merged into a new shape formatted the same as the rectangle shape. When you merge shapes that have different formatting, the format of the first shape selected is applied to the merged shape.

8. Click the **arc** shape, press and hold the **Shift** key, click each of the arrow shapes, including the merged shape, and then release the **Shift** key.

9. In the Insert Shapes group, click the **Merge Shapes** button, and then click **Union**. The four shapes are merged into a blue shape, matching the formatting of the first shape selected.

10. Save the presentation.

Applying Advanced Formatting to Shapes

You know that you can fill a shape with a solid color or with a picture. You can also fill a shape with a texture—a pattern that gives a tactile quality to the shape, such as crumpled paper or marble—or with a gradient. You'll change the fill of the custom shape to a texture.

To change the shape fill to a texture:

1. Make sure the custom shape is selected, and then click the DRAWING TOOLS FORMAT tab on the ribbon, if necessary.

2. In the Shape Styles group, click the **Shape Fill button arrow**, and then point to **Texture**. The Texture submenu opens. See Figure 3-28.

Figure 3-28   Texture submenu

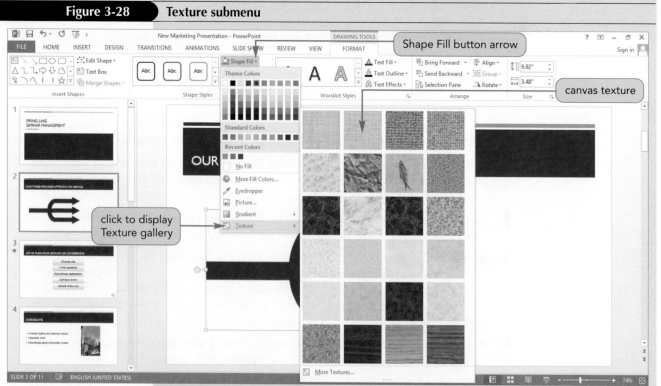

Photo courtesy of S. Scott Zimmerman

3. Click the **Canvas** texture, which is the second texture in the first row. The custom shape is filled with a texture resembling canvas. Rashad doesn't like any of the textures as a fill for the shape. He asks you to remove the texture.

▶ **4.** In the Shapes Styles group, click the **Shape Fill button arrow**, and then click **No Fill**. The texture is removed from the custom shape and only the outline of the custom shape remains.

The texture did not achieve the effect Rashad wanted for the shape. He now asks you to use a gradient to simulate the look of metal or silver. As you have learned, you can apply gradients on the Shape Fill menu that use shades of the Accent 1 color in the theme color palette. You can also create a custom gradient using the options in the Format Shape task pane. To create a custom gradient, you select the colors to use, specify the position in the shape where the color will change, and specify the direction of the gradient in the shape. Refer to the Session 3.2 Visual Overview for more information about using the Format Shape task pane to create a custom gradient.

REFERENCE

Creating a Custom Gradient in a Shape

- Select the shape.
- Click the DRAWING TOOLS FORMAT tab.
- In the Shape Styles group, click the Shape Fill button arrow, point to Gradient, and then click More Gradients to open the Format Shape task pane.
- In the Format Shape task pane, on the SHAPE OPTIONS tab with the Fill & Line button selected, click the Gradient fill option button.
- On the Gradient stops slider, click each tab, click the Color button, and then select a color.
- Drag each tab on the slider to the desired position.
- Click the Type arrow, and then click a type of gradient you want to use.
- Click the Direction button, and then click the direction of the gradient.

You will apply a custom gradient to the custom shape now.

To create a custom gradient fill for the custom shape:

▶ **1.** In the Shape Styles group, click the **Shape Fill button arrow**, and then point to **Gradient**. To create a custom gradient, you need to open the Format Shape task pane.

▶ **2.** Click **More Gradients**. The Format Shape task pane opens with the Fill & Line button 🖌 selected on the SHAPE OPTIONS tab.

▶ **3.** In the FILL section of the task pane, click the **Gradient fill** option button. The commands for modifying the gradient fill appear in the task pane, and the shape fills with shades of light blue. Under Gradient stops, the first tab on the slider is selected, and its value in the Position box is 0%. You will change the position and color of the second tab on the slider.

▶ **4.** On the Gradient stops slider, drag the **Stop 2 of 4 tab** (second tab from the left) to the left until the value in the Position box is **40%**.

Trouble? If you accidentally add a tab to the slider, click it, and then click the Remove gradient stop button 🗑 to the right of the slider.

TIP

Click the Preset gradients button to select from gradients of all six of the accent colors in the theme color palette.

5. With the Stop 2 of 4 tab selected, click the **Color** button. The color palette opens.

6. Click the **Blue-Gray, Accent 4, Lighter 80%** color. Next you need to change the color of the third tab.

7. Click the **Stop 3 of 4 tab**, click the **Color** button, and then click the **Gray-25%, Background 2, Darker 50%** color.

8. Drag the **Stop 4 of 4 tab** to the left until the value in the Position box is **95%**, and then change its color to **Gray-25%, Background 2**. Next you will change the direction of the gradient. Above the Gradient stops slider, in the Type box, Linear is selected. This means that the shading will vary linearly—that is, top to bottom, side to side, or diagonally. You will change the direction to a diagonal.

9. Click the **Direction** button. A gallery of gradient options opens.

10. Click the **Linear Diagonal – Top Left to Bottom Right** direction. The shading in the shape changes so it varies diagonally. See Figure 3-29.

Figure 3-29	Final custom gradient in shape

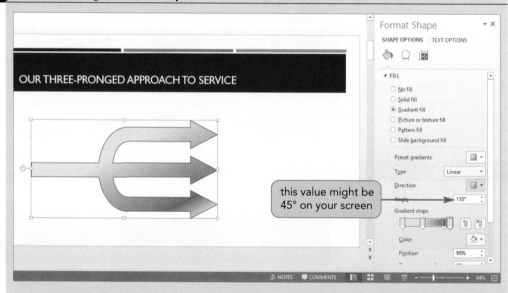

Trouble? If the darker part of the shape isn't in the lower-right as in Figure 3-29, click the Direction button again, and then click the Linear Diagonal–Top Right to Bottom Left direction.

11. In the Format Shape task pane, click the **Close** button **X**.

Now you can finish formatting the shape by changing the outline color and applying a bevel effect.

To finish formatting the custom shape:

1. On the ribbon, click the **DRAWING TOOLS FORMAT** tab, if necessary.

2. In the Shape Styles group, click the **Shape Outline button arrow**, and then click the **Gray-25%, Background 2** color.

3. In the Shape Styles group, click the **Shape Effects** button, point to **Bevel**, and then click the **Circle** bevel.

4. Drag the shape to the left so its left edge aligns with the left edge of the title text box.

Now you need to complete the slide by adding text boxes that list the three elements of the company's service.

To add text boxes to the slide:

1. To the right of the shape's top arrow, draw a text box approximately two inches wide, and then type **Planning**.

2. Duplicate the text box twice, and then position the duplicates to the right of the shape's other two arrows.

3. In the text box to the right of the middle arrow, replace "Planning" with **Implementation**.

4. In the text box to the right of the bottom arrow, replace "Planning" with **Follow-up**.

5. Select all three text boxes, and then change the font size to **40** points.

6. With all three text boxes selected, drag one of the right middle sizing handles to the right until "Implementation" fits on one line.

7. With all three boxes still selected, position them so the Implementation text box is about one-quarter inch to the right of the middle arrow. Compare your screen to Figure 3-30, and make any adjustments if necessary.

Figure 3-30 **Custom shape with final gradient fill**

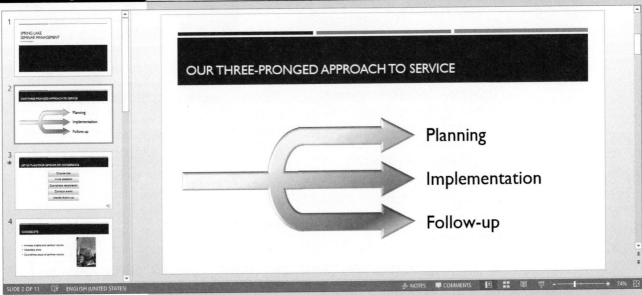

Photo courtesy of S. Scott Zimmerman

8. Save the presentation.

Using the Format Shape and Format Picture Task Panes

Many options are available to you in the Format Shape and Format Picture task panes. Most of the commands are available on the DRAWING TOOLS and PICTURE TOOLS FORMAT tabs on the ribbon, but you can refine their effects in the task panes. For example, you can fill a shape with a color and then use a command in the Format Shape task pane to make the fill color partially transparent so you can see objects behind the shape. Because these task panes are so useful, you can access them in a variety of ways. Once a picture or shape is selected, you can do one of the following to open the corresponding task pane:

- Click any of the Dialog Box Launchers on the DRAWING TOOLS or PICTURE TOOLS FORMAT tab.
- Right-click a shape or picture, and then click Format Shape or Format Picture on the shortcut menu.
- Click a command at the bottom of a menu, such as the More Gradients command at the bottom of the Gradients submenu on the Fill Color menu or the Picture Corrections Options command at the bottom of the Corrections menu.

Making Presentations Accessible

People with physical impairments or disabilities can use computers because of technology that makes them accessible. For example, people who cannot use their arms or hands instead can use foot, head, or eye movements to control the pointer. One of the most common assistive technologies is the screen reader. The screen reader identifies objects on the screen and produces an audio of the text.

Graphics and tables cause problems for users of screen readers unless they have **alternative text**, often shortened to **alt text**. Alt text is text added to an object that describes the object. For example, the alt text for a SmartArt graphic might describe the intent of the graphic.

Adding Alt Text

You can add alt text for any object on a PowerPoint slide. Many screen readers can read the text in title text boxes and bulleted lists, so you usually do not need to add alt text for those objects. For now, you will add alt text for the chart on Slide 10 and the SmartArt diagram on Slide 3 because these graphics contain critical information for understanding the contents of those slides and the presentation overall.

Make sure you select the entire SmartArt object and not just one shape. If you select a shape, the alt text will be available only for that individual shape.

To add alt text for the chart and SmartArt graphic:

1. Display **Slide 3** ("Let Us Plan Your Seminar or Conference") in the Slide pane.

2. Right-click to the right or left of the shapes in the SmartArt graphic to select the entire graphic.

3. On the shortcut menu, click **Format Object**. The Format Shape task pane opens with the SHAPE OPTIONS tab selected.

4. In the task pane, click the **Size & Properties** button 🔲, and then at the bottom of the task pane, click **ALT TEXT** to display the boxes below it. See Figure 3-31.

Figure 3-31   **Options for adding alt text in the Format Chart Area task pane**

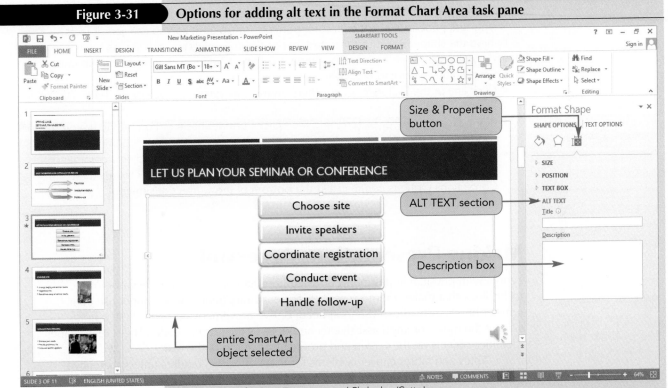

Photos courtesy of S. Scott Zimmerman and Chabruken/Getty Images

5. Under ALT TEXT, click in the **Description** box, and then type **Graphic listing services offered by Spring Lake Seminar Management.** (including the period).

6. Display **Slide 10** ("Typical Distribution of Event Costs") in the Slide pane, and then click the chart.

7. On the ribbon, click the **CHART TOOLS FORMAT** tab.

8. In the Current Selection group, click the **Chart Elements arrow** (the arrow on the top box in the group), and then click **Chart Area.**

9. If necessary, click the **CHART OPTIONS** tab, click the **Size & Properties** button 🔲, and then click **ALT TEXT** to expand the section.

10. Click in the **Description** box, and then type **Pie chart illustrating the distribution of event costs.** (including the period).

11. Close the Format Chart Area task pane.

You could add alt text to each shape in the SmartArt graphic. However, because you identified the entire SmartArt object for a screen reader by adding alt text, someone using a screen reader will know to open the text pane, and many screen readers can read the text in the text pane.

Rashad will add alt text for the rest of the graphics in the presentation later. Next, you need to make sure that the objects on slides will be identified in the correct order for screen readers.

Checking the Order Objects Will Be Read by a Screen Reader

In PowerPoint, most screen readers first explain that a slide is displayed. After the user signals to the screen reader that he is ready for the next piece of information (for example, by pressing the Tab key), the reader identifies the first object on the slide. In PowerPoint, objects are identified in the order that they were added to the slide. For most slides, this means that the first object is the title text box. The second object is usually the content placeholder on the slide. To check the order of objects on the slide, you can use the Tab key or open the Selection task pane. You'll check the order of objects on Slide 8.

To identify the order of objects on Slide 8:

▶ **1.** Display **Slide 8** ("Additional Activities") in the Slide pane, and then click above the bars at the top of the slide. The Slide pane is active, but nothing on the slide is selected.

▶ **2.** Press the **Tab** key. The title text box is selected.

▶ **3.** Press the **Tab** key again. The bulleted list text box is selected next. A screen reader will read the title text first, then the text in the bulleted list.

▶ **4.** Press the **Tab** key once more. The photo is selected. However, remember that there are two photos here, one placed on top of the other. To see which one is selected, you can use the Selection pane.

▶ **5.** On the HOME tab, in the Editing group, click the **Select** button, and then click **Selection Pane**. The Selection task pane opens. See Figure 3-32.

| Figure 3-32 | Selection task pane |

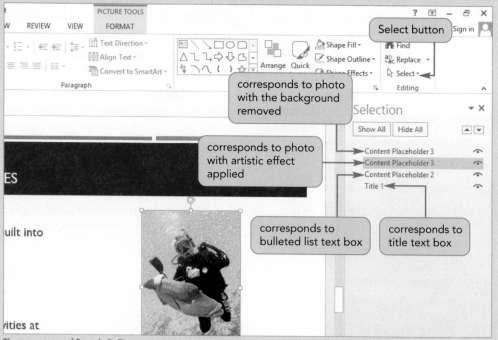

Photo courtesy of Beverly B. Zimmerman

The items are listed in the reverse order they were added to the slide, so the title text box—the first thing selected—appears at the bottom of the list. (The blue box at the bottom of the slide and the three blue bars at the top of the slide aren't listed in the Selection task pane because they are part of the slide background.)

Rashad will examine the order of the objects on the rest of the slides later.

Reordering Objects in the Selection Pane

If an object was in the wrong order in the Selection pane—for example, if the content placeholder was identified first and the title second—you could change this in the Selection pane. To do this, click the object you want move, and then at the top of the task pane, click the Bring Forward ▲ or Send Backward ▼ buttons at the top of the task pane to move the selected object up or down in the list.

Renaming Objects in the Selection Pane

In the Selection task pane for Slide 8, there are two objects with the same name. This is because Slide 8 has the Two Content layout applied, and Rashad added the photo of the scuba diver to the content placeholder on the right. Then you duplicated that photo, so the name in the Selection pane was duplicated as well. To make it clearer which items on slides are listed in the Selection task pane, you can rename each object in the list.

To rename objects in the Selection task pane:

1. In the Slide pane, click the photo, and then drag left. The version of the photo with the background removed moves to the left. The top Content Placeholder 3 is selected in the Selection task pane.

2. In the Selection task pane, click the selected Content Placeholder 3. An orange border appears around the selected item in the task pane. The insertion point appears in the selected text.

3. Press the **Delete** and **Backspace** keys as needed to delete Content Placeholder 3, type **Photo with background removed**, and then press the **Enter** key. The name is changed in the task pane.

4. In the task pane, click **Content Placeholder 3**, click it again, delete the text **Content Placeholder 3**, type **Photo with artistic effect**, and then press the **Enter** key.

5. Drag the photo with the background removed back on top of the photo with the artistic effect applied.

6. Close the Selection task pane.

7. Display **Slide 1** (the title slide) in the slide pane, replace Rashad's name in the subtitle with your name, and then save and close the presentation.

PROSKILLS

Decision Making: Selecting the Right Tool for the Job

Many programs with advanced capabilities for editing and correcting photos and other programs for drawing complex shapes are available. Although the tools provided in PowerPoint for accomplishing these tasks are useful, if you need to do more than make simple photo corrections or create a simple shape, consider using a program with more advanced features or choose to hire someone with skills in graphic design to help you.

You have created and saved a custom shape and used advanced formatting techniques for shapes and photos in the presentation. Rashad is pleased with the presentation. With the alt text you've added, he is also confident that users of screen readers will be able to understand the slides containing the SmartArt and the chart.

REVIEW

Session 3.2 Quick Check

1. What are the five corrections you can make to photos in PowerPoint?
2. What happens when you use the Remove Background command?
3. What are artistic effects?
4. What happens when you merge shapes?
5. How do you create a custom gradient?
6. What is alt text?

ASSESS

SAM Projects

Put your skills into practice with SAM Projects! SAM Projects for this tutorial can be found online. If you have a SAM account, go to www.cengage.com/sam2013 to download the most recent Project Instructions and Start Files.

PRACTICE

Review Assignments

Data Files needed for the Review Assignments: Andes.jpg, Customer.wma, Hiker.jpg, Living.pptx, Paracas Park.jpg

Rashad Menche of Spring Lake Seminar Management was hired by Chasqui International Living in Lima, Peru to manage their annual sales conference. Chasqui International Living builds and manages condominium homes in Lima and Urubamba, Peru. (During the Inca period in Peru, a *chasqui* was a runner who carried news from one city to another.) These homes are specifically targeted to North Americans who are interested in retiring to Peru because of its low cost of living, low taxes, and cultural diversity. One of the jobs they want Rashad to do is to create their presentation for the conference. They also asked him to design a logo for their company. Complete the following:

1. Open the presentation **Living**, located in the PowerPoint3 ▸ Review folder included with your Data Files, add your name as the Slide 1 subtitle, and then save it as **International Living** to the location where you are storing your files.

2. On Slide 9 ("Interested?"), create a SmartArt diagram using the Vertical Picture Accent List layout, which is a List type diagram. Replace the text in the rectangular shapes with **Complete contact sheet**, **Tour model condo**, and **Meet with onsite loan officer**.

3. In the circles in the SmartArt diagram, click the Insert Picture buttons, and then insert the picture **Hiker** in the top circle, insert the picture **Andes** in the second circle, and insert the picture **Paracas Park** in the third circle. All three photos are located in the PowerPoint3 ▸ Review folder.

4. Change the color of the SmartArt diagram to the Colored Outline – Accent 1 style, and then change the style to the Inset style.

5. On Slide 9 ("Interested?"), add the audio clip **Customer**, located in PowerPoint3 ▸ Review folder. Set it to play automatically and hide the icon during the slide show. Position it in the upper-right corner of the slide.

6. On Slide 8 ("Monthly Cost of Living Comparison"), add a clustered bar chart. Use the data shown in Figure 3-33 to create the chart. Expand columns A and B in the data sheet to fit their widest entries.

Figure 3-33   Data for Slide 8

	United States	Lima	Urubamba
Mortgage	2000	1200	700
Condo Fees	185	50	20
Utilities	300	130	60
Groceries	350	175	100
Medical/Dental	200	100	80

7. Remove the chart title, and then move the legend so it appears to the right of the chart.

8. Change the font size of the labels on the x- and y-axes and in the legend to 16 points.

9. Double-click any value on the x-axis to open the Format Axis task pane. At the bottom of the task pane, expand the NUMBER section. Change the Category to Currency, and then change the number of Decimal places to zero.

10. On Slide 6 ("Urubamba Condos, continued"), add a text box approximately two inches wide and one-half inch high. Type **Inca ruins at Machu Picchu**.

11. Change the format of the text box so the text doesn't wrap and so that the left margin is zero.

12. Change the font size of the text in the text box to 24 points, and then align its left edge with the left edge of the photo and its top edge with the bottom edge of the photo.

13. On Slide 6 ("Urubamba Condos, continued"), change the saturation of the photo to 66%, and change the brightness of the photo to 10% and the contrast to -30%.

14. On Slide 7 ("Features of Both Properties"), change the color tone of the photo on the right to Temperature: 4700K.

15. On Slide 10, remove the background of the photo so that the sky is removed.

16. On Slide 10, sharpen the photo by 25%.

17. On Slide 10, insert a WordArt text box using the Fill - Tan, Background 2, Inner Shadow style. Replace the placeholder text with **Enjoy the beauty of Peru!** and change the font size of the text to 48 points. Position the text box so it is aligned with the left and top edges of the slide. Apply the Linear Down gradient style.

18. On Slide 2, on the donut shape, drag the yellow adjustment handle on the left side of the inside circle to the left to change the width of the donut so it is about half as wide.

19. Drag the adjusted donut shape on top of the large circle. Position the donut shape near the top right of the large circle so that smart guides appear indicating that the top and right of the two shapes are aligned. Subtract the donut shape from the larger circle by selecting the shape you want to keep—the large circle—first, and then selecting the shape you want to subtract—the donut shape—before using the Subtract command.

20. Drag the smaller circle on top of the solid circle that was created in the merged shape. Position the smaller circle near the top right of the solid circle in the merged shape without overlapping the edges of the circles, and then subtract this smaller circle from the merged shape.

21. Create a text box approximately two inches wide and one inch high. Type **CIL** in the text box. Change the font to Bernard MT Condensed, and the font size to 48 points. Deselect the Wrap text in shape option, if necessary.

22. Drag the text box to the center of the white circle created when you subtracted the small circle in the merged shape. Select the merged shape first, and then select the text box. Use the Union command to combine the shapes.

23. Fill the merged shape with the From Bottom Left Corner gradient under Dark Variations on the Gradient submenu on the Shape Fill menu, and then customize the gradient by changing the position of the Stop 2 of 3 tab to 40% and changing the color of the Stop 3 of 3 tab to Lime, Accent 1, Lighter 40%. (*Hint:* Make sure you apply the From Bottom Left Corner gradient using the Shape Fill button arrow first or your colors of the tab stops will be different.)

24. Resize the merged shape so it is 2 inches wide and 2.5 inches high.

25. Copy the custom shape, and then paste it on Slide 1 (the title slide). Position the shape to the left of the title. Position it so its left edge is about one-quarter inch from the right edge of the curve graphic on the left edge of the slide, and then use the Align Middle command to vertically center the shape on the slide. Delete Slide 2.

26. On Slide 7 ("Monthly Cost of Living Comparison"), add the following as alt text to the chart: **Chart showing the difference between the cost of living in the U.S. and in Lima and Urubamba, Peru.**

27. On Slide 8 ("Interested?"), add the following as alt text to the SmartArt shape: **SmartArt diagram listing three steps for buying property.**

28. On Slide 8, edit the Content Placeholder 3 name in the Selection Pane to **SmartArt**.

29. Save and close the presentation.

Case Problem 1

Data Files needed for this Case Problem: Description.wma, Testing.pptx

Blue Blazes Testing Centers Sanjiv Jindia is a senior consultant with Blue Blazes Testing Center Services, headquartered in Chattanooga, Tennessee. The company sets up testing centers at colleges and universities throughout the United States and Canada. Sanjiv visits schools to give presentations on the advantages of a testing center and the services offered by Blue Blazes. He asks you to help him create a PowerPoint presentation for his next visit to a local school. Complete the following steps:

1. Open the presentation **Testing**, located in the PowerPoint3 ▶ Case1 folder included with your Data Files, add your name as the subtitle, and then save the presentation as **Testing Centers** to the location where you are storing your files.
2. On Slide 2 ("What Is a Testing Center?"), apply the Film Grain artistic effect to the photo.
3. On Slide 3 ("A Testing Center Saves Time"), change the brightness of the photo to -20% and the contrast to -40%.
4. On Slide 4 ("A Testing Center Saves Money"), change the saturation of the photo to 200% and the tone to a temperature of 5900 K.
5. On Slide 5 ("A Testing Center Provides More Secure Testing"), remove the background of the photo so it shows only the safe and not the green background or the shadow. Rotate the image slightly to the left so it is straighter.
6. On Slide 5, change the saturation of the photo to 33%, change the tone to a temperature of 4700 K, sharpen it by 50%, and then change the brightness to +20% and the contrast to -40%.
7. On Slide 6 ("Are Testing Centers Effective?"), add a pie chart in the content placeholder. Enter the date shown in Figure 3-34 in the spreadsheet to create the chart.

Figure 3-34 Data for chart on Slide 6

	Responses
Highly Effective	385
Effective	292
Moderately Effective	58
Not Effective	19

8. Adjust the width of column A so that you can see all the text in the cells.
9. Change the style of the chart to Style 8, change the colors of the chart to the Color 2 palette, change the font size of the text in the legend to 18 points, and then change the font size of the data labels—the numbers indicating the percentages on the pie slices—to 18 points.
10. Remove the chart title.
11. On Slide 6, insert the audio clip **Description**, located in the PowerPoint3 ▶ Case1 folder. Hide the icon during a slide show and set it to play automatically.
12. Add the following alt text for the chart: **Chart showing that 51% of instructors think that testing centers are effective and only 2% think they are not effective.**
13. On Slide 7 ("About Blue Blazes Testing Centers"), change the sharpness of the photo so it is 50% sharper.
14. Save and close the presentation.

Case Problem 2

Data Files needed for this Case Problem: Accounting.pptx

CHALLENGE

Medical Dental Accounting Services, Inc.   Shaundra Telanicas is an accountant but her mother was a dentist, so Shaundra knew quite a bit about the healthcare industry when she graduated from college with a double major in accounting and business management. After working as a tax accountant for three years, specializing in the medical and dental industries, she realized that healthcare practices often struggle, not because the healthcare service is poor but because the physicians and dentists themselves were not following sound business and financial practices. She founded Medical-Dental Accounting Services, Inc., located in Boise, Idaho. Her company specializes in financial and consulting services for healthcare practices. She needs to give a sales presentation at an upcoming healthcare convention and asked you to help her prepare it. Complete the following steps:

1. Open the file named **Accounting**, located in the PowerPoint3 ▸ Case2 folder included with your Data Files, add your name as the subtitle on Slide 1, and then save it as **Medical Accounting** to the location where you are storing your files.

2. On Slide 2, duplicate the red filled square shape three times. These are the four squares behind the center square in Figure 3-35. Arrange them as shown in Figure 3-35 so that there is about one-quarter inch of space between each square. Merge the four squares using the Union command.

Figure 3-35   **Custom shape for MDAS**

3. Apply the From Center Gradient style (a Light Variations gradient style). Customize this gradient by changing the Stop 1 of 3 tab to the Red, Accent 1 color, changing the Stop 2 of 3 tab to the Red, Accent 1, Darker 50% color, and changing the Stop 3 of 3 tab to Red, Accent 1, Lighter 40% color and changing its position to 80%. Then change the gradient Type to Linear and the direction to Linear Down.

4. Create a text box, type **MD**, press the Enter key, type **AS**. Turn off the Wrap text option if necessary, change the font to Castellar, change the font size to 40 points, and then use the Center button in the Paragraph group on the HOME tab to center the text in the box. Fill the text box shape with White. Apply the Preset 5 shape effect to this square (located on the Presets submenu on the Shape Effects menu).

5. Position the text box so it is centered over the custom shape, using the smart guides to assist you.

⊕ **Explore** 6. Group the custom shape and the text box. (*Hint:* Use the appropriate command on the DRAWING TOOLS FORMAT tab.)

⊕ **Explore** 7. Save the final grouped shape as a picture named **MDAS Logo** to the location where you are storing your files. (*Hint:* Right-click the shape.)

8. Delete Slide 2, and then insert the picture **MDAS Logo** on Slide 1 (the title slide). Resize it, maintaining the aspect ratio, so that it is 2.6 inches square. Position it about one-half inch above the title and so that it is left-aligned with the title text box.

9. Add the following as alt text for the logo: **Company logo**.

10. On Slide 4 ("How We Help You"), change the saturation of the photo to 66%, and sharpen it by 50%.

11. Add the following as alt text for the picture: **Photo of smiling woman at a keyboard**.

12. On Slide 5 ("Financial Concerns of Medical Practices"), insert a SmartArt diagram using the Basic Block List layout (in the List category). Type the following as first-level bullets in the text pane:

- **Planning for tax purposes**
- **Keeping overhead down**
- **Setting up health insurance for employees**
- **Setting up proper billing**
- **Containing office setup costs**

⊕ **Explore** 13. Reverse the order of the boxes in the diagram. (*Hint:* Use a command in the Create Graphic group on the SMARTART TOOLS DESIGN tab.)

14. Change the style of the SmartArt diagram to the Inset style.

15. Animate the SmartArt diagram with the Wipe entrance animation and the From Left effect. Modify this so that each shape appears one at a time.

16. Add the following as alt text for the SmartArt diagram: **SmartArt diagram listing five financial concerns of medical practice owners**.

17. On Slide 8 ("We Are Here for You"), insert the MDAS Logo in the content placeholder on the left, and add the following as alt text for the logo on Slide 8: **Company logo**.

18. Save and close the presentation.

Case Problem 3

Data Files needed for this Case Problem: Properties.pptx

CHALLENGE

Valley Pike Properties Davion Fusilier is co-owner of Valley Pike Properties in Winchester, Virginia. His company acquired two new properties near the end of last year—a luxury apartment building in the city that he is renovating and condos on Silver Creek. He started preselling the properties in January. Both properties are about 80 percent occupied. Davion regularly holds small sales presentations for people interested in purchasing property. He asks you to help him create his final presentation. Complete the following steps:

1. Open the presentation named **Properties**, located in the PowerPoint3 ▶ Case3 folder included with your Data Files, add your name as the subtitle, and then save it as **Valley Pike Properties** to the location where you are storing your files.

2. On Slide 2 ("Two Luxurious Properties"), sharpen the photo on the right by 25%, and then change its tone to a temperature of 7200 K.

3. On Slide 4 ("Living Room"), change the color tone of both photos to a temperature of 5900 K, and change the color saturation of the photo on the right to 66%.

4. On Slide 7 ("Two Styles of Living Rooms"), sharpen the photo on the left by 50%.

5. On Slide 9 ("Available Properties Going Fast!"), insert a clustered column chart using the data shown in Figure 3-36.

Figure 3-36   **Data for chart on Slide 9**

	Briar Hill	Silver Creek
January	0.37	0.31
March	0.46	0.42
June	0.61	0.56
September	0.7	0.82

⊕ **Explore** 6. In the spreadsheet, drag the small blue selection handle in the lower-right corner of cell D5 to the left to cell C5 so that column D is not included in the chart.

7. Change the style of the chart to Style 5.

⊕ **Explore** 8. In the chart, change the chart title to **Percent Occupancy**.

9. Double-click a value on the y-axis to open the Format Axis task pane. At the bottom of the task pane, expand the NUMBER section. Change the Category to Percentage and then change the number of Decimal places to zero.

⊕ **Explore** 10. In the Format Axis task pane, change the maximum value on the y-axis to 100%. (*Hint*: In the AXIS OPTIONS sections at the top of the Format Axis task pane, change the value in the Maximum box under Bounds to 1.)

⊕ **Explore** 11. Change the color of the columns that represent the Briar Hill occupancy percentages to a light green or teal color, and then change the color of the columns that represent the Silver Creek occupancy percentages to a darker green or teal color. (*Hint*: Click one of the columns, use the Shape Fill button in the Shape Styles group on the CHART TOOLS FORMAT tab.)

12. Change the font size of the labels on the y- and x-axis and the legend to 16 points. Change the font size of the title to 20 points.

⊕ **Explore** 13. Animate the chart with the entrance animation Wipe. Modify the animation so that the chart grid animates first and then each category animates one at a time (in other words, so that the two columns showing occupancy rates in January animate together, then the two columns showing occupancy rates in March animate, and so on). Finally, modify the start timing of the chart grid animation so it animates with the previous action.

14. On Slide 10, insert a WordArt text box using the Gradient Fill – Gray-80%, Accent 1, Reflection style. Enter the text, **Thank you for coming!**. Increase the font size of the text in the text box to 66 points.

15. Save and close the presentation.

Case Problem 4

RESEARCH

There are no Data Files needed for this Case Problem.

Bay Area Speech Makers   Bay Area Speech Makers is a club for people who want to become better public speakers. Their goal is to help people gain confidence in speaking in public. They require members to prepare short presentations for the other club members. As a member of the club, you need to prepare a five minute informative presentation consisting of five or six slides about one aspect of a hobby or special interest. For example, you could prepare a presentation about one aspect of hiking, geology, cooking, race cars, or gardening. Keep the presentation focused so that the short

amount of time you have is enough to present your information clearly. Your presentation must contain at least one photo, one SmartArt graphic, and one chart created from factual data. Use the Internet or other sources to find an appropriate photo and research the data. Complete the following steps:

1. Research your topic to find data you can present in a chart. For example, for a presentation about hiking, you could present data showing the number of hikes over 4000 feet in the United States.

2. Decide which information would be clearer or more interesting if it were presented in a SmartArt graphic, and choose the layout you want to use.

3. Plan your presentation slides by writing an outline. Include a title slide and a slide that introduces your topic.

4. Create a new presentation. You can start with a blank presentation and then choose an appropriate theme, or you can create a presentation based on a template from Office.com.

5. Add your name as the subtitle, and then save the presentation with an appropriate name to the location where you are storing your files.

6. Create the slides of your presentation based on your research. Remember to include at least one photo, one SmartArt graphic, and one chart created from factual data. If it would enhance your presentation, consider including a video or audio clip.

7. If you will not be presenting orally, add speaker notes to clarify the information on the slides for your instructor.

8. Add appropriate transitions and animations if they enhance your message.

9. Check the spelling in your presentation and proof it carefully.

10. Save and close the presentation.

OBJECTIVES

Session 4.1
- Add more than one animation to an object
- Set animation triggers
- Use a picture as the slide background
- Create and edit hyperlinks
- Add action buttons
- Create a custom color palette

Session 4.2
- Create a self-running presentation
- Rehearse slide timings
- Record slide timings and narration
- Set options to allow viewers to override timings
- Inspect a presentation for private information
- Identify features not supported by previous versions of PowerPoint
- Save a presentation in other formats

Advanced Animations and Distributing Presentations

Creating an Advanced Presentation for a Wireless Control Systems Company

Case | *Duplantis Control Systems*

Duplantis Control Systems manufactures and installs computer-controlled wireless switches and other devices for monitoring and controlling aspects of electrical systems in buildings. For example, Duplantis has designed a system that can allow remote access and control of thermostats, lights, security systems, and other electrical equipment in commercial buildings such as hotels or office buildings. The company also provides smaller systems to be used in residential homes. Ryder Duplantis, owner of Duplantis Control Systems, has created a PowerPoint presentation about his company's products and services appropriate for his commercial customers. He wants your help in finishing the presentation, which he intends to use at trade shows and conventions. Because he hopes to secure some accounts outside of the United States, he wants to be able to distribute the presentation electronically.

In this tutorial, you will enhance Ryder's presentation by adding multiple animations to objects and setting triggers for animations. You'll also add a picture as the slide background, create links to other slides and customize the color of text links, and create a self-running presentation including narration. Finally, you'll save the presentation in other formats for distribution.

STARTING DATA FILES

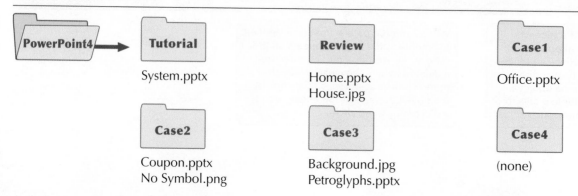

PowerPoint4 → Tutorial
System.pptx

Review
Home.pptx
House.jpg

Case1
Office.pptx

Case2
Coupon.pptx
No Symbol.png

Case3
Background.jpg
Petroglyphs.pptx

Case4
(none)

Session 4.1 Visual Overview:

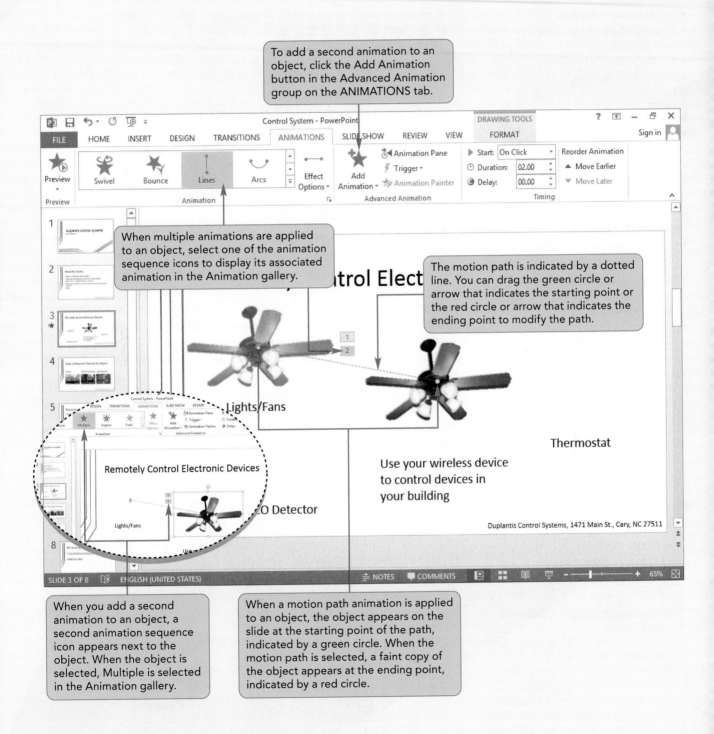

To add a second animation to an object, click the Add Animation button in the Advanced Animation group on the ANIMATIONS tab.

When multiple animations are applied to an object, select one of the animation sequence icons to display its associated animation in the Animation gallery.

The motion path is indicated by a dotted line. You can drag the green circle or arrow that indicates the starting point or the red circle or arrow that indicates the ending point to modify the path.

When you add a second animation to an object, a second animation sequence icon appears next to the object. When the object is selected, Multiple is selected in the Animation gallery.

When a motion path animation is applied to an object, the object appears on the slide at the starting point of the path, indicated by a green circle. When the motion path is selected, a faint copy of the object appears at the ending point, indicated by a red circle.

Understanding Advanced Animations

The list of objects on the "On Click of" submenu corresponds to the objects on the slide. You can also see this list of objects in the Selection pane.

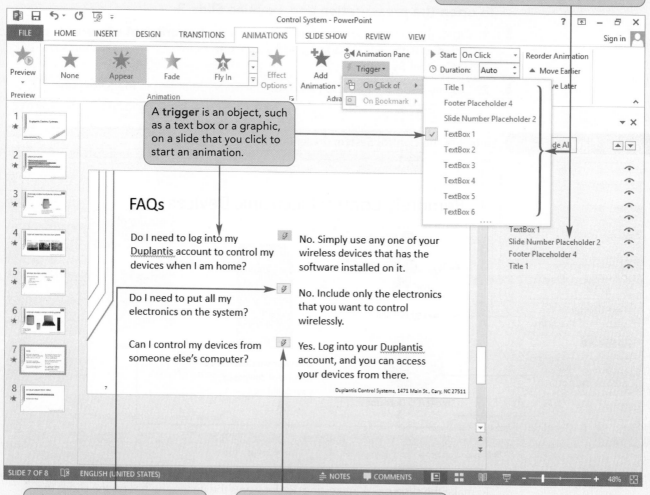

A **trigger** is an object, such as a text box or a graphic, on a slide that you click to start an animation.

When an animation has a trigger, the number in the animation sequence icon is replaced with a lightning bolt. This is because the animation is no longer part of a sequence; it will occur only when the trigger is clicked.

The Play/Pause animation automatically applied to a video when a video is added to a slide is triggered by clicking the video object itself. That is why the animation sequence icon for the Play/Pause animation contains a lightning bolt.

Adding More Than One Animation to an Object

You know how to apply an animation to an object and you can determine how the animation starts, its duration, and its speed. An object can have more than one animation applied to it. For example, you might apply an entrance animation to an object by having it fly into a slide, and then once the object is on the slide, you might want to animate it a second time to further emphasize a bullet point on the slide, or to show a relationship between the object and another object on the slide.

Ryder wants Slide 3 to illustrate the concept of a wireless device, such as a mobile phone, controlling various electronic devices in a building. The slide currently contains text boxes and graphic objects. You will examine this slide now.

To open the presentation and examine Slide 3:

▶ 1. Open the presentation **System**, located in the **PowerPoint4 ▸ Tutorial** folder included with your Data Files, add your name as the subtitle, and then save it as **Control System**.

▶ 2. Display **Slide 3** ("Remotely Control Electronic Devices") in the Slide pane. See Figure 4-1.

Figure 4-1	Slide 3 in the Control System presentation

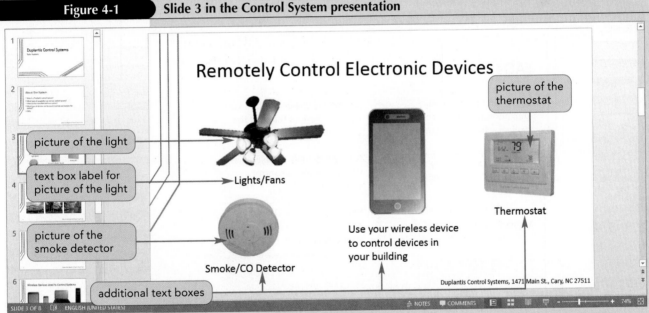

Photos courtesy of S. Scott Zimmerman; Doug Plummer/Getty Images

To make the slide more interesting, Ryder wants the images he has on the slides to appear one at a time in the center of the slide and then move so that they are above their respective text boxes. Then he wants the picture's text box to appear. To create this effect, you will position each picture in the center of the slide and then add two animations to each picture—an entrance animation and then a motion path animation. After you apply and modify the motion path animation to the pictures, you will animate each text box with an entrance animation and modify it so that it appears automatically after the motion path animation is complete.

To add multiple animations to the objects on Slide 3:

1. On **Slide 3** ("Remotely Control Electronic Devices"), drag the picture of the ceiling lights/fan to the center of the slide, on top of the picture of the smartphone. First you need to apply an entrance animation to this image.

2. On the ribbon, click the **ANIMATIONS** tab, and then in the Animation group, click the **Appear** animation. Now you need to add the second animation to the light—the motion path animation. To do this you must use the Add Animation button in the Advanced Animation group; otherwise you will replace the currently applied animation.

3. In the Advanced Animation group, click the **Add Animation** button.

4. Scroll down to locate the Motion Paths section, and then click the **Lines** animation. The animation previews and the light moves down the slide. After the preview, the path appears below the light, and a faint image of the light appears at the end of the path. At the beginning of the path, the green circle indicates the path's starting point, and at the end of the path, the red circle indicates the path's ending point. The second animation sequence icon is selected, and Lines is selected in the Animation group.

5. Click the light to select it. In the Animation gallery, Multiple is selected. This indicates that more than one animation is applied to the selected object.

Make sure you do not click another animation in the Animation group.

The light needs to move to the left instead of down. You can change the basic direction in which an object moves and then fine-tune the path so it ends up in the correct position. Because two animations are applied to the object, you need to make sure that the correct animation sequence icon is selected and the correct animation is selected in the Animation group on the ANIMATIONS tab.

To modify the motion path animation for the light:

1. Click the **2** animation sequence icon to select it. In the Animation gallery, Lines is selected. This is the animation that corresponds to the selected animation sequence icon.

2. In the Animation group, click the **Effect Options** button, and then click **Left**. The motion path changes to a horizontal line, the light moves left across the slide, and the circles at the beginning and end of the motion path change to arrows. You need to reposition the ending of the motion path so that the light ends up above the Lights/Fans text box. First you need to select the motion path.

3. Point to the **motion path** so that the pointer changes to ⛶, and then click. The arrows on the ends of the motion path change to circles and a faint copy of the image appears at the end of the motion path. Now you can drag the start and end points to new locations.

4. Position the pointer on top of the red circle so that it changes to ↗, and then drag the red circle to position it above the Lights/Fans text box. See Figure 4-2.

Figure 4-2 | Repositioned motion path animation

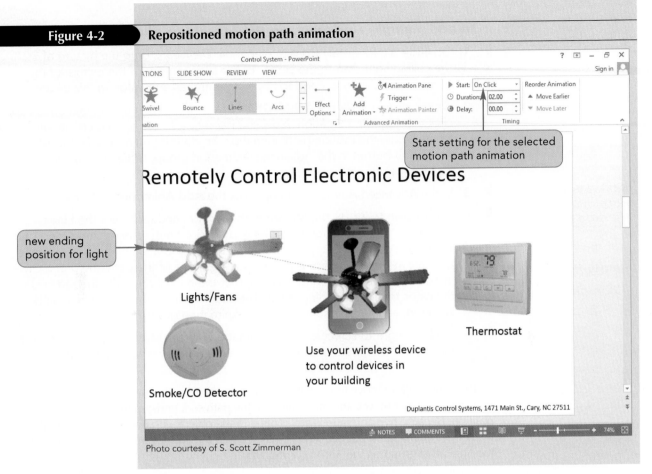

Photo courtesy of S. Scott Zimmerman

Ryder wants the motion path animation to occur automatically after the light appears. The 2 animation sequence icon and the Lines animation in the Animation group are still selected.

To change the start timing of the light's second animation and animate the text box:

1. Make sure the **2** animation sequence icon is selected.

2. In the Timing group, click the **Start** arrow, and then click **After Previous**. Now you need to animate the Lights/Fans text box so it appears automatically after the light finishes moving on the motion path.

3. Click the **Lights/Fans** text box, and then in the Animation group, click the **Appear** animation.

4. In the Timing group, click the **Start** arrow, and then click **After Previous**.

5. In the Preview group, click the **Preview** button. The picture of the light and the Lights/Fans text box disappear from the slide, the picture of the light appears, and then the picture of the light moves from the center of the slide diagonally left. The Lights/Fans text box then appears below the picture of the light.

Now you need to animate the photos of the smoke/CO detector and thermostat and their text boxes in the same manner.

To animate two more photos and their text boxes:

1. Drag the photo of the smoke detector on top of the picture of the lights.

2. Apply the entrance animation **Appear**, and then add the **Lines** motion path animation.

3. Drag the red circle of the motion path so that the picture of the smoke detector ends up above the Smoke/CO Detector text box.

4. If necessary, click the animation sequence icon **3** to select it. In the Animation group on the ANIMATIONS tab, the Lines animation is selected.

5. In the Timing group, click the **Start** arrow, and then click **After Previous**.

6. Click the **Smoke/CO Detector** text box, apply the **Appear** entrance animation to it, and then modify its start timing so that it animates automatically after the previous animation.

7. Drag the picture of the thermostat on top of the picture of the smoke detector, apply the **Appear** entrance animation, and then add the **Lines** animation.

8. Change the Lines animation direction effect so that the picture of the thermostat moves right, and then adjust the end of the motion path as needed so that the picture of the thermostat ends up above the Thermostat text box.

9. Modify the start timing of the Lines animation applied to the thermostat so it starts automatically after the previous animation.

10. Animate the Thermostat text box with the entrance animation Appear, and then modify its start timing so that it animates automatically after the previous animation.

Finally, Ryder wants the photo of a smartphone to appear in the center of the slide, and then for the text box that describes the basic function of the system to appear below the smartphone. The smartphone is below the other three pictures, but you can see the top and bottom of the photo.

To animate the smartphone photo and its text box and view the slide in Slide Show view:

1. Click the picture of the smartphone, and then apply the entrance animation **Appear**.

2. Click the **Use your wireless device...** text box, apply the entrance animation **Appear**, and then change its start timing so that the text box appears automatically after the previous animation. Compare your screen to Figure 4-3.

| Figure 4-3 | Slide 3 with animated objects |

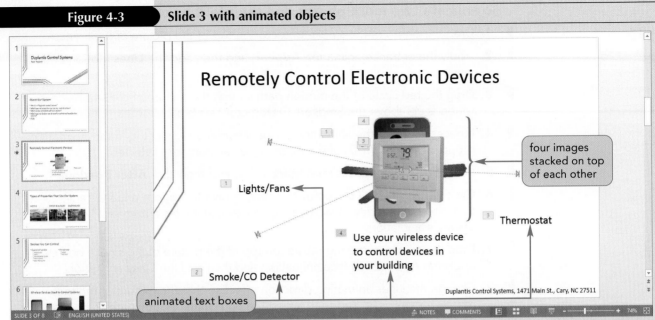

Photos courtesy of S. Scott Zimmerman; Doug Plummer/Getty Images

▶ **3.** On the status bar, click the **Slide Show** button 🖥 to start the slide show from Slide 3. The slide title, the graphic on the left, and the slide number and footer are the only things visible on the slide.

▶ **4.** Press the **spacebar** to advance the slide show. The light appears in the center of the slide, moves up and to the left, and then the Lights/Fans text box appears.

▶ **5.** Press the **spacebar** again, watch the animation of the smoke detector and its text box, and then press the **spacebar** once more to display the thermostat and its text box.

▶ **6.** Press the **spacebar** again. The smartphone appears followed immediately by its text box.

▶ **7.** End the slide show, and then save the changes to the presentation.

Using the Animation Pane

When you apply multiple animations to objects and change the start timings, it can be difficult to locate the animation sequence icon associated with a specific animation. To see a list of all the animations on a slide, you can open the Animation Pane. You'll examine the animations on Slide 3 in the Animation Pane.

To examine the animations in the Animation Pane:

▶ **1.** In the Advanced Animation group, click the **Animation Pane** button. The Animation Pane opens. See Figure 4-4.

Figure 4-4	Animation Pane listing the animations on Slide 3

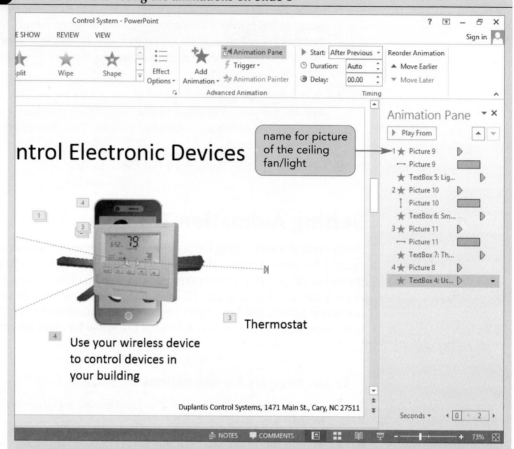

2. In the Animation Pane, point to the first animation in the list, **Picture 9**. The ScreenTip that appears identifies the start timing (On Click), the animation (Appear), and the full name of the object (Picture 9). The picture of the ceiling fan and lights is the first object that is animated on this slide, so you know that Picture 9 identifies that object. The number 1 to the left of the object name is the same number that appears in the animation sequence icon for this animation.

3. In the Animation Pane, point to the second animation in the list, the second **Picture 9**. This is the motion path animation applied to the picture of the ceiling fan and light. There is no number to the left because this animation occurs automatically, not On Click.

4. In the Animation Pane, point to the third animation in the list, **TextBox 5**. The ScreenTip includes the text in the text box, and identifies this object as the Lights/Fans text box. Again, there is no number to the left of the animated item in the list because this animation also occurs automatically.

5. To the right of the first animation in the list, Picture 9, point to the green arrow. The green arrow indicates that the applied animation has no length. This is because the animation is the Appear animation, and this animation does not have a duration that can be adjusted. The ScreenTip also identifies the start time as 0s (zero seconds), which means it starts immediately after the action that causes the animation, in this case, advancing the slide show.

▶ **6.** To the right of the second animation in the list, Picture 9, point to the blue rectangle. Even though this animation is set to start after the previous animation, because the previous animation—Appear—has no length, the ScreenTip indicates that this animation also starts at zero seconds. This animation, however, takes two seconds to complete, so there is an ending time for this animation as well—2s, meaning two seconds.

▶ **7.** To the right of TextBox 5, point to the green arrow. This animation—the Appear animation applied to the Lights/Fans text box—has a start time of 2s because it is set to animate after the previous animation, which ends at the two second mark.

▶ **8.** In the Animation Pane, click the **Close** button ⊠.

Setting Animation Triggers

Ryder created a slide listing FAQs—frequently asked questions—and their answers. Ryder created the content on this slide using separate text boxes for each question and answer, instead of using two text boxes created from content placeholders. He wants to be able to click the question to display its answer. To do this, you need to apply an entrance animation to each text box object containing an answer and then set a trigger for that animation. Refer to the Session 4.1 Visual Overview for more information about triggers.

To set triggers for animations on Slide 7:

▶ **1.** Display **Slide 7** ("FAQs") in the Slide pane, and then on the ribbon, click the **HOME** tab.

▶ **2.** In the Editing group, click the **Select** button, and then click **Selection Pane**. Examine the slide contents. Notice that the slide does not contain a list in a single text box. As you can see in the Selection pane, it contains six text boxes in addition to the slide title and footer text box. You can click each object in the slide to identify its name in the Selection pane. See Figure 4-5.

Figure 4-5   Objects on Slide 7 listed in Selection pane

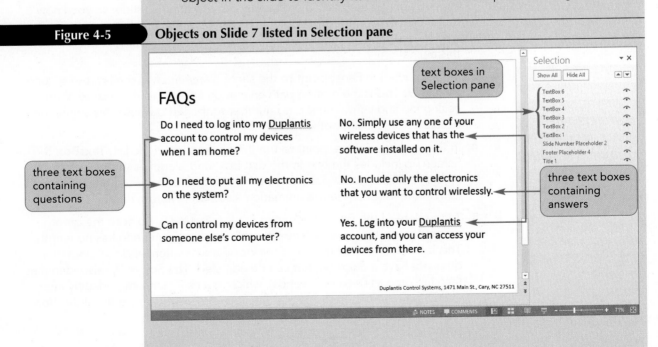

3. On the slide, click the top text box on the left to see that TextBox 1 is selected in the Selection pane, and then click each of the other two text boxes on the left to see their names—TextBox 2 and TextBox 3—selected in the Selection pane.

4. Click the top text box on the right, press and hold the **Shift** key, and then click the two other text boxes on the right. In the Selection pane, TextBox 4, 5, and 6 are selected. You want each of the three text boxes on the right to appear when you click the corresponding text box on the left. First, you need to apply an entrance animation to the text boxes on the right.

5. On the ribbon, click the **ANIMATIONS** tab, and then in the Animation group, click the **Appear** animation. The Appear animation is applied to all three text boxes. Now you need to make the text boxes on the left the triggers for each text box on the right.

6. Next to the top text box on the right, click the **1** animation sequence icon.

7. In the Advanced Animation group, click the **Trigger** button, and then point to **On Click of**. The same list of objects that appears in the Selection pane appears on the submenu.

8. Click **TextBox 1**. The animation sequence icon next to the top right text box changes to a lightning bolt.

9. Next to the middle right text box, click the **0** animation sequence icon, and then set its animation to trigger when you click **TextBox 2**.

10. Next to the bottom right text box, click the **0** animation sequence icon, and then set its animation to trigger when you click **TextBox 3**.

Now you see why Ryder created the slide using six text boxes rather than two lists in two text boxes. If the slide contained only two text boxes, when you clicked any one of the questions on the left, all of the answers in the text box on the right would have appeared at once.

Next you need to test the triggers. You'll view Slide 7 in Slide Show view and click each question to make sure the correct answer appears.

To test the animation triggers in Slide Show view:

1. On the status bar, click the **Slide Show** button 🖵. Slide 7 appears in Slide Show view displaying the slide title and the three text boxes on the left.

2. Click the first question. The text box containing its answer appears on the slide.

3. Click each of the other two questions to display their answers, and then end the slide show.

4. Close the Selection pane, and then save the changes to the presentation.

Changing the Slide Background

The background of a slide can be as important as the foreground when you are creating a presentation with a strong visual impact. To change the background, you use the Format Background task pane. When you change the background, you are essentially changing the fill of the background. The commands are the same as the commands you use when you change the fill of a shape. For example, you can change the color, add a gradient or a pattern, or fill it with a texture or a picture. When you use a picture as the slide background, you can use a picture stored on your computer or network or you can search for one online.

Adding a Picture to the Slide Background

- On the ribbon, click the DESIGN tab.
- In the Customize group, click the Format Background button to open the Format Background task pane.
- With the Fill button selected, click FILL to expand the section, if necessary.
- Click the Picture or texture fill option button.
- To use an image stored on your computer or network, click the File button to open the Insert Picture dialog box, click the image you want to use, and then click the Insert button; or to use an image on Office.com or another location on the Internet, click the Online button, type keywords in the appropriate box, click the Search button, click the image you want to use, and then click the Insert button.
- If the image is too dark, drag the Transparency slider in the Format Background task pane to the right until the image is the desired transparency.
- Click the Apply to All button if you want to apply the background to all the slides in the presentation.

Ryder wants you to use a photo of circuitry as the slide background. You'll search for a photo of circuits on Office.com and use that as the slide background.

To fill the slide background with an online picture:

1. On the ribbon, click the **DESIGN** tab, and then in the Customize group, click the **Format Background** button. The Format Background task pane opens. See Figure 4-6. This task pane has only one button—the Fill button—and one section of commands—the FILL section. It contains the same commands as the FILL section in the Format Shape pane. The Solid fill option button is selected, indicating that the current background has a solid fill.

Figure 4-6   Format Background task pane

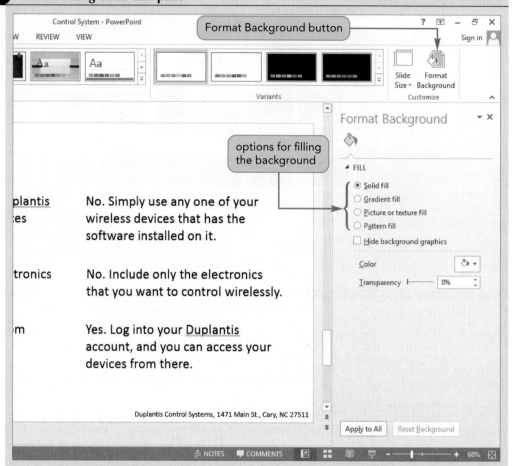

2. Click the **Picture or texture fill** option button. The default texture is applied to the current slide background and the task pane changes to include more commands, including commands for inserting pictures.

3. In the Insert picture from section, click the **Online** button. The Insert Pictures dialog box opens with the insertion point in the Office.com Clip Art box.

4. Type **circuit board chips**, and then click the **Search** button.

5. In the list of results, click the purple picture of a circuit board, as indicated in Figure 4-7.

| Figure 4-7 | Insert Pictures dialog box displaying search results from Office.com |

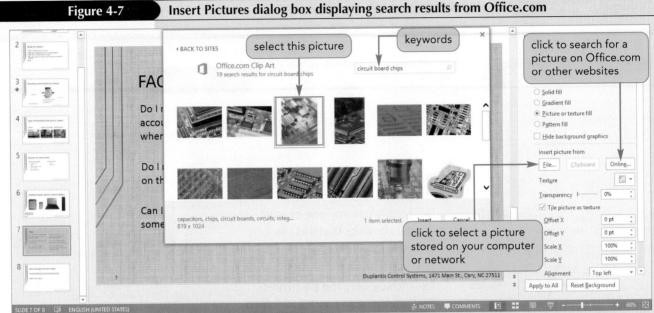

Photos courtesy of S. Scott Zimmerman; Doug Plummer/Getty Images

Trouble? If the picture shown in Figure 4-7 is not available, click any photo of a circuit board with blue or purple colors.

6. Click the **Insert** button. The picture fills the slide background.

You can adjust the position of the photo using the offset options in the task pane. Instead of displaying one image of the picture as the slide background, you can tile it, which means you can make it appear as repeating squares. If you set an image to tile as a background, the four offset options change to offset and scale (size) options. You can adjust the scale of the tiles horizontally (using the Scale X setting) and vertically (using the Scale Y setting). You'll change the picture to tiles.

To change the background picture of the slide to tiles:

1. In the Format Background task pane, click the **Tile picture as texture** check box to select it. The picture changes to a series of tiles on the slide.

2. In the **Scale Y** box, change the value to **75%**, and then press the **Enter** key.

The new background makes it difficult to read the text on the slide. You could adjust the brightness and the contrast of the photo, or you could make the photo more transparent. You'll adjust the transparency of the picture now.

To change the transparency of the background picture:

1. In the Format Background task pane, drag the **Transparency** slider to the right until the value in the Transparency box is **90%**. Now you need to apply this picture background to all the slides.

Trouble? If you can't position the slider so that 90% appears in the Transparency box, click the up or down arrows in the Transparency box as needed to change the value.

2. At the bottom of the task pane, click the **Apply to All** button. Compare your screen to Figure 4-8.

Figure 4-8 | **Picture with transparency adjusted tile as slide background**

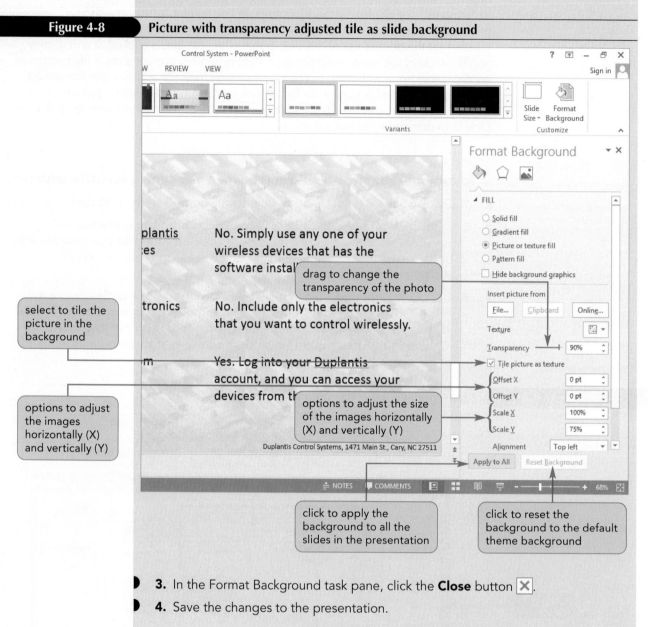

select to tile the picture in the background

options to adjust the images horizontally (X) and vertically (Y)

drag to change the transparency of the photo

options to adjust the size of the images horizontally (X) and vertically (Y)

click to apply the background to all the slides in the presentation

click to reset the background to the default theme background

3. In the Format Background task pane, click the **Close** button ✕.

4. Save the changes to the presentation.

Hiding Background Graphics

INSIGHT

If the theme you are using includes graphics in the background and you need to print the slides in black and white or grayscale, you might want to remove those graphics before printing the slides because the graphic could make the text difficult to read. To hide graphics in the background, select the Hide background graphics check box in the Format Background pane. Note that this will not hide anything you use as a fill for the background, such as the picture you added as the background in this tutorial.

Creating and Editing Hyperlinks

As you know, when you type a web or an email address on a slide, it is formatted as a hyperlink automatically. If you've visited webpages, you've clicked hyperlinks (or links) to "jump to"—or display—other webpages. In PowerPoint, a link on a slide accomplishes the same thing. You can convert any text or object on slide to be a link, and you can set the destination of this link so that when the link is clicked, it will display another slide in the same presentation, a slide in another presentation, a file created in another program, a webpage, or open a new email message addressed to the person whose email address is part of the link. A link can also be set to start a program.

Slide 8 contains a link to Ryder's company's website. You can examine the link more closely to determine the link's destination.

To examine the hyperlink created when you type a website address:

▶ **1.** Display **Slide 8** ("Set Up an Appointment Today!") in the Slide pane.

▶ **2.** Right-click the webpage address hyperlink on the slide. A shortcut menu opens. In addition to the Remove Hyperlink command that you have already used, there are three other commands related to the hyperlink on the shortcut menu.

▶ **3.** Click **Edit Hyperlink**. The Edit Hyperlink dialog box opens. See Figure 4-9. In the Link to list on the left, the Existing File or Web Page option is selected. The web address that is formatted as a hyperlink appears in the Address box at the bottom of the dialog box and also in the Text to display box at the top of the dialog box.

| Figure 4-9 | Edit Hyperlink dialog box for a link to a webpage |

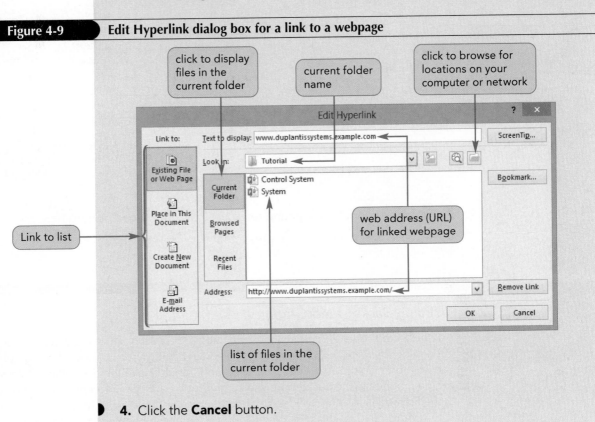

▶ **4.** Click the **Cancel** button.

Creating a Link

You can select any text or object, including graphics or text boxes, and convert them to links. Graphic hyperlinks are visually indistinguishable from graphics that are not hyperlinks, except that when you move the mouse pointer over the object, the pointer changes to 🖑. Text links are usually underlined and a different color than the rest of the text on a slide. After you click a text link during a slide show, the link changes to another color to reflect the fact that it has been clicked, or followed.

Slide 2 in Ryder's presentation is an overview slide. Each bulleted item on this slide describes another slide in the presentation. Ryder wants you to convert each bulleted item to a hyperlink that links to the related slide.

To create a hyperlink to Slide 3 from text on Slide 2:

‣ 1. Display **Slide 2** ("About Our System") in the Slide pane.

‣ 2. Click the first bullet symbol. The text of the first bulleted item is selected.

‣ 3. On the ribbon, click the **INSERT** tab, and then in the Links group, click the **Hyperlink** button. The Insert Hyperlink dialog box opens. In the Link to list on the left, the Existing File or Web Page option is selected. You need to identify the file or location to which you want to link. In this case, you're going to link to a place in the presentation.

‣ 4. In the Link to list on the left, click **Place in This Document**. The dialog box changes to show a Select a place in this document box, listing all the slides in the presentation.

‣ 5. In the Select a place in this document list, click **3. Remotely Control Electron** The Slide preview area on the right side of the dialog box displays Slide 3. This is the slide to which the text will be linked. See Figure 4-10.

| Figure 4-10 | Insert Hyperlink dialog box displaying slides in this presentation |

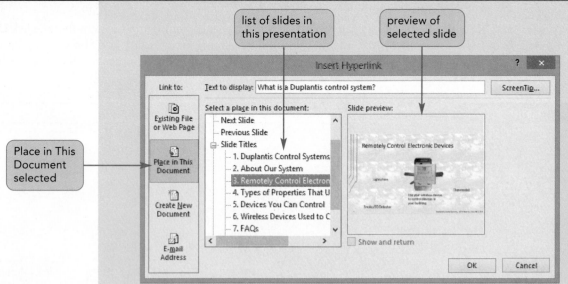

list of slides in this presentation

preview of selected slide

Place in This Document selected

‣ 6. Click the **OK** button, and then click a blank area of the slide to deselect the text. The text of the first bullet is now a hyperlink, and it is now formatted in a teal color and underlined. See Figure 4-11.

Figure 4-11	Slide 2 with a hyperlink to Slide 3

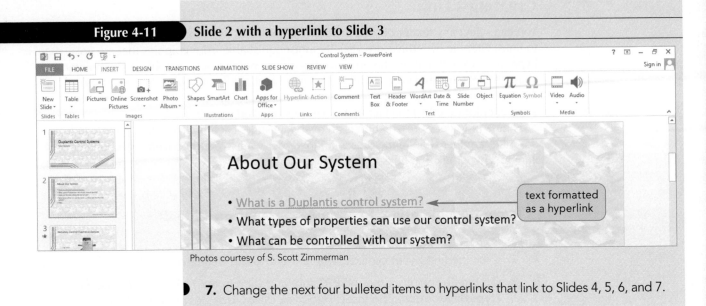

Photos courtesy of S. Scott Zimmerman

▶ **7.** Change the next four bulleted items to hyperlinks that link to Slides 4, 5, 6, and 7.

Now you need to test the links you created. Links are not active in Normal view, so you will switch to Slide Show view.

To test the hyperlinks:

▶ **1.** With Slide 2 ("About Our System") in the Slide pane, on the status bar, click the **Slide Show** button 🖵.

▶ **2.** Click the **What is a Duplantis control system?** hyperlink. Slide 3 ("Remotely Control Electronic Devices") appears in slide show view. (The content of the slide does not appear because you need to advance the slide show to animate the content.)

▶ **3.** Right-click anywhere on the slide, and then on the shortcut menu, click **Last Viewed**. Slide 2 ("About Our System") appears in Slide Show view. The link text in the first bulleted item is now light purple, indicating that the link had been clicked, or was followed. See Figure 4-12.

Figure 4-12	Followed link on Slide 2 in Slide Show view

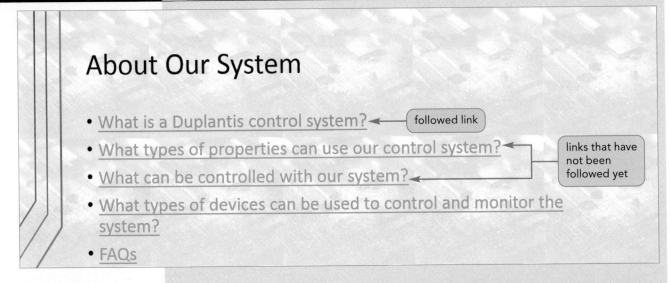

▶ **4.** Click each of the other links to verify that they display the correct slides, using the Last Viewed command on the shortcut menu to return to Slide 2 each time.

▶ **5.** End the slide show.

Adding Action Buttons

An action button is a shape intended to be a link. In the Action Button section in the Shapes gallery, 12 action button shapes are available, such as Action Button: Home or Action Button: Sound. Each action button can link to any slide, presentation file, and so on; the various shapes simply offer variety in the way the buttons look. The default format for each button is to link to the slide or file described by the button name.

REFERENCE

Adding an Action Button

- On the ribbon, click the INSERT tab, and then in the Illustrations group, click the Shapes button.
- In the Action Button section, click an action button shape.
- Drag the pointer on the slide to draw the action button the size you want.
- In the Action Settings dialog box, on the Mouse Click tab, click the desired option button.
- Click the arrow below the selected option button and then click the location to which you want to link, or click the Browse button, click the program you want to run, and then click the OK button.
- Click the OK button in the Action Settings dialog box.
- Resize and reposition the action button icon as desired.

Although Ryder can use the commands on the shortcut menu to return to Slide 2 after clicking a link to another slide, it would be easier for him to navigate during the slide show if you added a link back to Slide 2 on each slide. You'll do this now by adding action buttons on Slides 3 through 7.

To add action buttons to link to Slide 2:

▶ **1.** Display **Slide 3** ("Remotely Control Electronic Devices") in the Slide pane.

▶ **2.** On the INSERT tab, in the Illustrations group, click the **Shapes** button. The gallery of shapes appears. The action buttons are at the bottom of the gallery.

▶ **3.** Scroll down to the bottom of the gallery, and then click the **Action Button: Back or Previous** shape in the Action Button section. The pointer changes to +.

▶ **4.** In the upper-right corner of the slide, drag the pointer to draw an action button about one-half inch high and one inch wide. After you release the mouse button, a blue button containing a left-pointing triangle appears on the slide, and the Action Settings dialog box opens with the Mouse Click tab selected. See Figure 4-13. Because you inserted the Back or Previous action button, "Previous Slide" appears in the Hyperlink to box. This is fine because Slide 2 is the slide before Slide 3.

Figure 4-13   Action button on Slide 3 and Action Settings dialog box

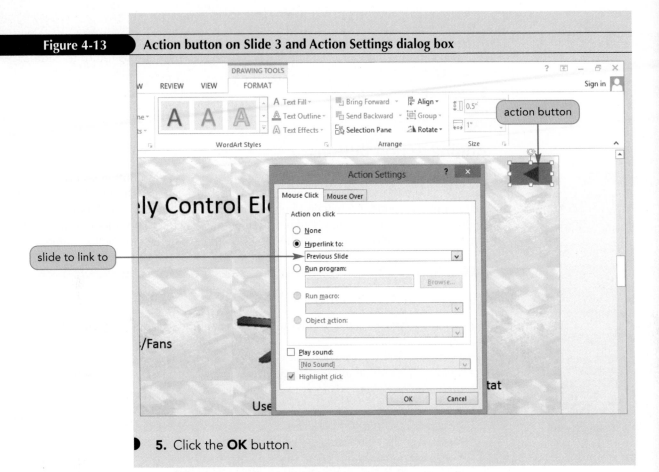

5. Click the **OK** button.

You want the same action button on Slides 4 through 7. You can insert a button on each slide or you can copy the button on Slide 3 and paste it on each slide. You will need to edit the link, however, so that it links to Slide 2 and not the previous slide.

To copy an action button and edit the link:

1. On Slide 3 ("Remotely Control Electronic Systems"), copy the action button to the Clipboard.

2. Display **Slide 4** ("Types of Properties That Use Our System") in the Slide pane, and then paste the contents of the Clipboard to the slide. A copy of the Back or Previous action button appears in the upper-right corner of the slide.

3. Right-click the action button, and then on the shortcut menu, click **Edit Hyperlink**. The Action Settings dialog box opens with the Mouse Click tab selected and Previous Slide selected in the Hyperlink to box.

4. Click the **Hyperlink to** arrow, and then click **Slide**. The Hyperlink to Slide dialog box opens listing the slides in the presentation. See Figure 4-14.

| Figure 4-14 | Hyperlink to Slide dialog box |

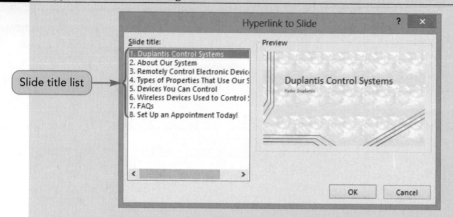

5. In the Slide title list, click **2. About Our System**, and then click the **OK** button. The title of Slide 2 now appears in the Hyperlink to box in the Action Settings dialog box.

6. Click the **OK** button.

7. Copy the action button on Slide 4 to **Slide 5** ("Devices You Can Control"), **Slide 6** (Wireless Devices Used to Control Systems"), and **Slide 7** ("FAQs").

You need to test the action buttons. Again, you must switch to Slide Show view to do this.

To test the action buttons:

1. Display **Slide 2** ("About Our System") in the Slide pane, and then on the status bar, click the **Slide Show** button 🖵.

2. Click the **What is a Duplantis control system?** hyperlink. Slide 3 ("Remotely Control Electronic Systems") appears in Slide Show view.

3. In the upper-right corner of the slide, click the **action button**. Slide 2 ("About Our System") appears on the screen.

4. Click each of the other links to display those slides, and then click the action buttons on each of those slides to return to Slide 2.

5. End the slide show to return to Slide 2 in Normal view.

Finally, you want to add a link on Slide 2 that links to the last slide in the presentation, Slide 8 ("Set Up an Appointment Today!"). Ryder did not add a bulleted item in the overview on Slide 2 for Slide 8 because as the final slide it is meant to display only as the presentation is concluding. You could add another action button, but instead, you will add a shape and convert it as a link.

To create a link from a shape on Slide 2:

1. With Slide 2 ("About Our System") displayed in the Slide pane, on the ribbon, click the **INSERT** tab.

2. In the Illustrations group, click the **Shapes** button, and then in the Rectangles section, click the **Rounded Rectangle** shape.

3. At the bottom of the slide, drag the pointer to draw a rounded rectangle about one-half inch high and four and one-half inches wide.

4. With the shape selected, type **Click to set up an appointment**, and then change the font size of the text in the shape to **24** points.

5. Drag the shape to position it so it is centered in the area below the bulleted list on the slide. See Figure 4-15. Now you need to convert the shape to a link.

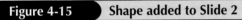

Figure 4-15   **Shape added to Slide 2**

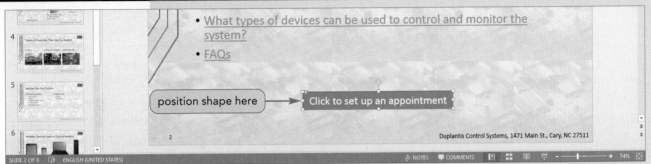

Photos courtesy of S. Scott Zimmerman; Doug Plummer/Getty Images

6. On the ribbon, click the **INSERT** tab, and then in the Links group, click the **Hyperlink** button. The Insert Hyperlink dialog box opens with Place in This Document selected in the Link to list.

7. Scroll the list of slides, click **8. Set Up an Appointment To**, and then click the **OK** button.

Trouble? If the text in the shape changes so it is formatted as a link, the text was selected before you opened the Insert Hyperlink dialog box instead of the entire shape. On the Quick Access Toolbar, click the Undo button, select the entire shape by clicking the shape border, and then repeat Steps 6 and 7.

Now you need to test the new link. Once again, you will switch to Slide Show view.

To test the shape link in Slide Show view:

1. On the status bar, click the **Slide Show** button 🖵. Slide 2 ("About Our System") appears in Slide Show view.

2. Click the **Click to set up an appointment** shape. Slide 8 ("Set Up an Appointment Today!") appears.

3. End the slide show.

INSIGHT

Linking to Another File

You can create a link to another file so that when you click the link during a slide show, the other file opens. The other file can be any file type; it doesn't need to be a PowerPoint file. To create a link to another file, open the Insert Hyperlink dialog box, click Existing File or Web Page in the Link to list, and then click the Browse for File button. To change the link destination of an action button to another file, open the Action Settings dialog box, click the Hyperlink to option button, click the Hyperlink to arrow, and then click Other PowerPoint Presentation or Other File. For either type of link, a dialog box opens in which you can navigate to the location of the file.

When you create a link to another file, the linked file is not included within the PowerPoint file; only the original path and filename to the files on the computer where you created the links are stored in the presentation. Therefore, if you need to show the presentation on another computer, you must copy the linked files to the other computer as well as the PowerPoint presentation file, and then you need to edit the path to the linked file so that PowerPoint can find the file in its new location. To update the path for a text or graphic link, right-click it, and then click Edit Hyperlink on the shortcut menu to open the Edit Hyperlink dialog box. To edit the path of a file linked to an action button, right-click the action button, and then click Hyperlink to open the Action Settings dialog box.

Customizing Theme Colors

As you know, each theme has its own color palette. In addition, you can switch to one of several built-in color palettes. However, sometimes, you might want to customize a palette. You can change one or all of the theme colors.

REFERENCE

Customizing Theme Colors

- On the ribbon, click the DESIGN tab.
- In the Variants group, click the More button, point to Colors, and then click Customize Colors to open the Create New Theme Colors dialog box.
- Click the button next to the theme color you want to customize.
- Click a color in the Theme Colors section or in the Standard Colors section of the palette, or click More Colors, click a color in the Colors dialog box, and then click the OK button.
- Replace the name in the Name box with a meaningful name for the custom palette.
- Click the Save button.

In the Control Systems presentation, the color of both the light blue unfollowed text links and the light purple followed text links makes them a little hard to see on the slide background. To fix that, you will customize the link colors in the color palette.

To create custom theme colors:

1. On the ribbon, click the **DESIGN** tab.
2. In the Variants group, click the **More** button, and then point to **Colors**. A menu of color palettes opens. See Figure 4-16. If you wanted to change the entire color palette, you could select one of these options. You want to change only the color of hyperlinks.

Figure 4-16 Color palettes on Colors submenu

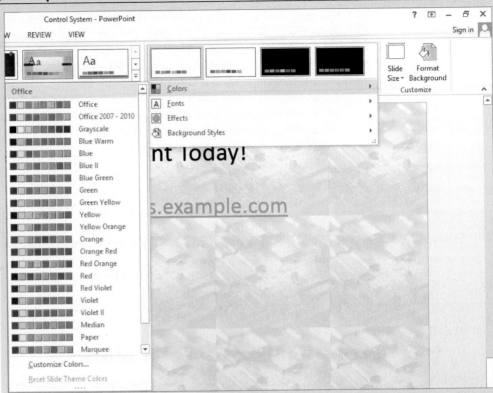

3. At the bottom of the menu, click **Customize Colors**. The Create New Theme Colors dialog box opens. See Figure 4-17. You want to change the color of hyperlinks from light blue to dark blue.

Figure 4-17 Create New Theme Colors dialog box

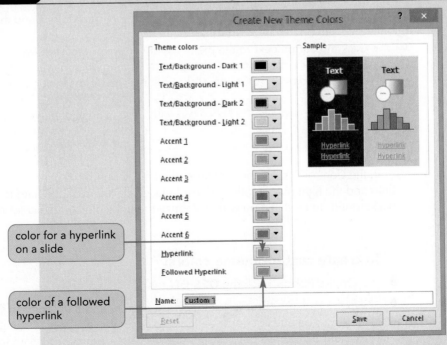

4. Click the **Hyperlink** button to display the complete Theme Colors and Standard Colors palettes.

5. Under Theme Colors, point to the second to last color in the first row. The ScreenTip identifies this as Green, Hyperlink. This is the current color for text hyperlinks.

TIP

Never place dark text on dark background or light text on light background.

6. Under Standard Colors, click the **Dark Blue** color. The Hyperlink color is now the dark blue color you selected, and the top Hyperlink text in the Sample panel in the dialog box is now also dark blue. Next, you'll change the color of the Followed Hyperlinks.

7. Click the **Followed Hyperlink** button to display the color palette. You can choose from additional colors if you open the Colors dialog box.

8. At the bottom of the palette, click **More Colors** to display the Colors dialog box, and then click the **Standard** tab, if necessary.

9. Click the dark purple tile on the right point of the hexagon as shown in Figure 4-18.

Figure 4-18   Standard tab in the Colors dialog box

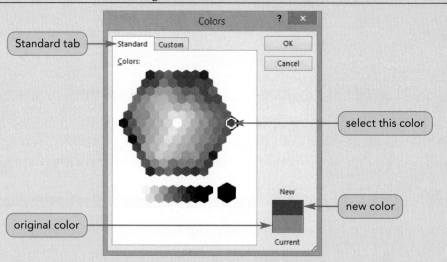

10. Click the **OK** button. The Colors dialog box closes. The Followed Hyperlink color is the dark purple you selected and the bottom Hyperlink text in the Sample panel is dark purple as well. In order to apply the new colors to the presentation, you need to save the new color palette.

11. In the Name box, delete the text Custom 1, and then type **Custom Link Colors**.

12. Click the **Save** button. The dialog box closes and the custom theme colors are applied to the presentation. As you can see in Slide 8 ("Set Up an Appointment Today!"), the link is now dark blue, the color you chose for unfollowed links.

13. Display **Slide 2** ("About Our System") in the Slide pane. The color of the followed links is now dark purple. The followed links will reset to the dark blue of links you haven't followed yet when you close and reopen the presentation. You can also reset the links manually by reapplying the link formatting.

14. Right-click the **What is a Duplantis control system?** link, and then on the shortcut menu, click **Edit Hyperlink**. The Edit Hyperlink dialog box opens. Slide 3 is selected in the list. You don't need to make any changes, so you will simply click the OK button.

Trouble? If a menu of spelling suggestions appears, you right-clicked the word "Duplantis." Right-click any other word in the link.

▶ **15.** Click the **OK** button. The text in the first bullet is reformatted as a link and is colored dark blue. Compare your screen to Figure 4-19.

Figure 4-19	New link colors

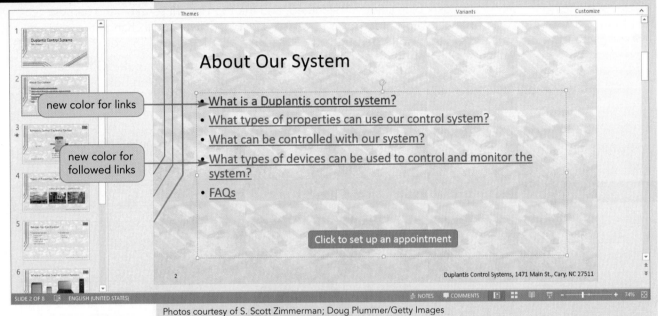

Photos courtesy of S. Scott Zimmerman; Doug Plummer/Getty Images

Now that you have saved the custom theme colors, that color palette is available to apply to any presentation that you create or edit on this computer.

Decision Making: Choosing Custom Theme Colors

When creating custom theme colors, you need to be wary of selecting colors that don't match or make text illegible; for example, red text on a blue background might seem like a good combination, but it's actually difficult to read for an audience at a distance from the screen. It's usually safer, therefore, to select one of the built-in theme color sets and stick with it, or make only minor modifications. If you do create a new set of theme colors, select colors that go well together and that maximize the legibility of your slides.

Deleting Custom Theme Colors

When you save a custom theme color palette, the palette is saved to the computer. If you've applied the custom palette to a presentation, and then saved that presentation, that color palette will still be applied to that presentation even if you delete the custom palette from the hard drive. You'll delete the custom theme color palette you created from the computer you are using.

To delete the custom color palette:

1. On the DESIGN tab, in the Variants group, click the **More** button, and then point to **Colors**. The Custom Link Colors color palette you created appears at the top of the Colors submenu.

2. Right-click the **Custom Link Colors** color palette, and then click **Delete**. A dialog box opens asking if you want to delete these theme colors.

3. Click the **Yes** button to delete the custom theme colors. You can confirm that the color palette was deleted from the hard drive.

4. In the Variants group, click the **More** button, and then point to **Colors**. The Custom Link Colors palette no longer appears on the Colors submenu.

5. Click a blank area of the window to close the menu without making a selection.

6. Save your changes.

Ryder is happy with the modifications you've made to the presentation so far. You applied two animations to pictures and modified motion path animations. You changed the slide background by filling the background with a picture, and then making it somewhat transparent so that you can easily see the text of the slides on top of the picture. You created links using text and a graphic and added action buttons. Finally, you changed the color of linked text so that it can be more easily distinguished on the slides. In the next session, you will create a self-running presentation by setting slide timings. You will then record a narration to accompany the self-running presentation. You also will save the presentation in other formats so it can be more easily distributed.

REVIEW

Session 4.1 Quick Check

1. What happens if you try to add a second animation by using the Animation gallery instead of the Add Animation button?
2. What is a trigger?
3. Describe the five types of fill you can add to a slide background.
4. What items on a slide can be a link?
5. What is an action button?
6. What view do you need to be in to test links?

Session 4.2 Visual Overview:

To set automatic timings manually, select the After check box. During a slide show, the slides will advance automatically after the time displayed in the After box.

When the On Mouse Click check box is selected, the slide show can be advanced manually, even if there are saved slide timings. If the On Mouse Click check box is deselected, the slide show may not be advanced manually, although users can still click links.

One way to set automatic timing is to type the time you want the selected slide to remain on screen during a slide show in the After box on the TRANSITIONS tab. When you select a slide, the exact timing also appears in the After box.

Automatic timings indicate how many seconds a slide will stay on the screen before transitioning to the next screen during a slide show.

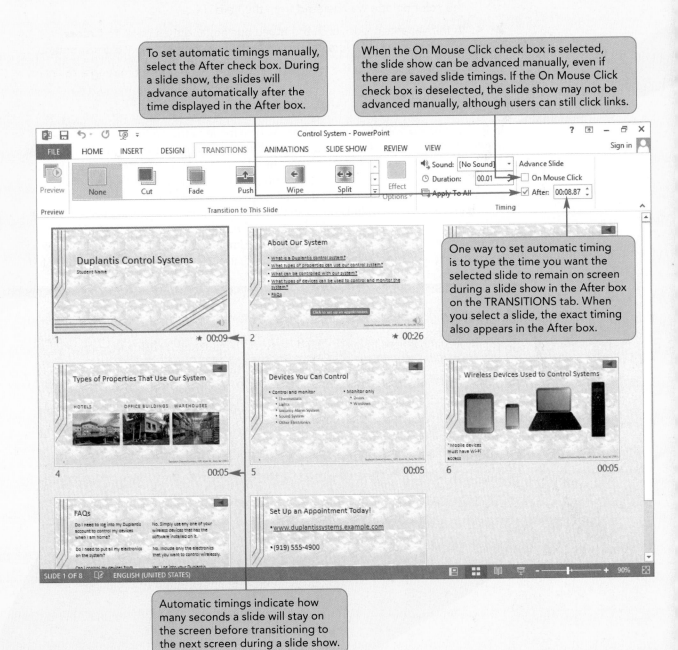

Automatic Slide Timings

A second way to set automatic timings is to click the Rehearse Timings button, and then leave each slide on screen for the desired length of time.

A third way to set automatic timings is to record the slide show, which is similar to rehearsing timings except you have the option to record narrations. When you finish, you can save the narrations only or you can save the narrations and the recorded timings.

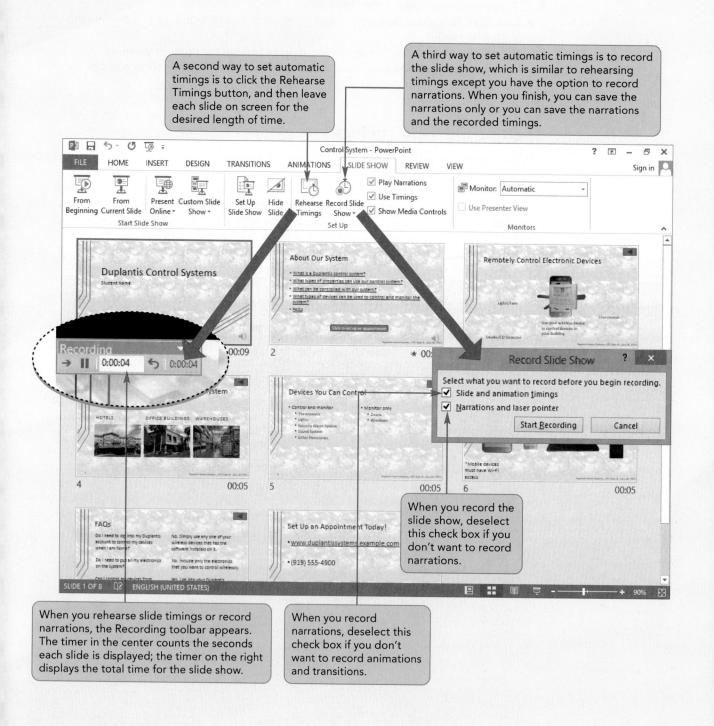

When you rehearse slide timings or record narrations, the Recording toolbar appears. The timer in the center counts the seconds each slide is displayed; the timer on the right displays the total time for the slide show.

When you record narrations, deselect this check box if you don't want to record animations and transitions.

When you record the slide show, deselect this check box if you don't want to record narrations.

Creating a Self-Running Presentation

Ryder intends to use the Control System presentation not only for oral presentations, but also as a self-running presentation on a computer at conventions and exhibitions for contractors. A self-running presentation runs on its own, but it can be set to accept viewer intervention to advance to another slide or return to a previous one. A self-running presentation includes one or more of the following:

- Automatic timing: This feature tells PowerPoint to display slides for a certain amount of time before moving to the next slide.
- Narration: This gives the viewer more information or instructions for overriding the automatic timing.
- Hyperlinks: These allow viewer to speed up or change the order of viewing.
- Kiosk browsing: This feature tells PowerPoint that, when the slide show reaches the last slide, the presentation should start over again at the beginning.

Setting the Slide Timings

When setting up a slide show to be self-running, you need to set the slide timing so the slide remains on the screen for a sufficient amount of time for the viewer to read and comprehend the slide's content. The slide timing might vary for different slides—a slide with only three bullet points might not need to remain on the screen as long as a slide containing six bullet points. PowerPoint allows you to set slide timings in multiple ways to best suit your presentation's content. See the Session 4.2 Visual Overview for more information about setting slide timings.

Ryder asks you to set the timings to five seconds per slide. You'll do this now.

To set the slide timings to five seconds per slide:

1. If you took a break after the last session, make sure the **Control System** presentation you created in Session 4.1 is open in the PowerPoint window in Normal view.

2. On the status bar, click the **Slide Sorter** button ⊞ to switch to Slide Sorter view.

3. Click the **Slide 1** (the title slide) thumbnail, press and hold the **Shift** key, scroll down if necessary, and then click the **Slide 8** ("Set Up an Appointment Today!") thumbnail. All the slides are selected.

4. On the ribbon, click the **TRANSITIONS** tab. In the Timing group, the On Mouse Click check box is selected in the Advance Slide section. This means that the slide show will advance when the viewer does something to advance the slide show.

5. In the Timing group, click the **After** check box. The check box is selected, and 00:00 appears below each slide thumbnail. See Figure 4-20.

Figure 4-20   **TRANSITIONS tab with After box selected**

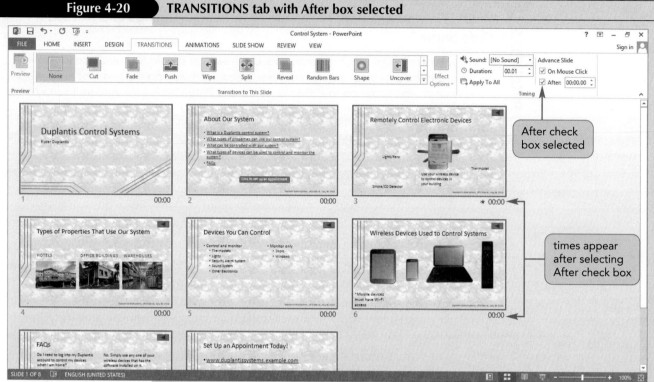

Photos courtesy of S. Scott Zimmerman; Doug Plummer/Getty Images

TIP

If you want to remove slide timings, select all the slides in Slide Sorter view, click the TRANSITIONS tab, and then click the After check box in the Timing group to deselect it.

6. In the Timing group, click the **After** up arrow five times to change the time to five seconds per slide. Under each slide thumbnail, the time changes to 00:05.

7. On the status bar, click the **Slide Show** button ![icon]. Watch as the slide show advances through the first three slides.

   When Slide 3 ("Remotely Control Electronic Devices") appears on the screen, the animations occur automatically, even though some of them were set to start On Click. This is because the automatic timing overrides the On Click start setting for the animation. Slide 3 remains on the screen for as long as it takes to complete all the animations—a little more than six seconds, even though the automatic timing is set to five seconds. Immediately after the last animation occurs, Slide 4 appears.

8. After Slide 4 ("Types of Properties That Use Our System") appears on the screen, press the **spacebar**. Slide 5 ("Devices You Can Control") appears. You are able to advance the slide show manually because you left the On Mouse Click check box selected.

9. Press the **Esc** key to end the slide show, and then save the presentation.

Aa

Verbal Communication: Preparing to Rehearse Timings and Record a Slide Show

Before rehearsing timings or recording a slide show, you should first read and look over each slide in the presentation, watching animations and reading the text. For example, if you want to add narration to a slide on which a bulleted list is animated and you want to comment on each bullet as it appears, plan to time your narration to coincide with the animations. Make sure you take the amount of time that you think a viewer would take to view each slide or bulleted item, and then advance from one slide to the next, according to your desired timing of each item. You should move along at a speed for moderately slow readers. Keep in mind that if you move too slowly, your viewers will become bored or wonder if the slide show is working properly; if you move too quickly, viewers will not have enough time to read and absorb the information on each slide.

Rehearsing the Slide Timings

The timing you set does not give the viewer enough time to read and absorb all the information on the slides. To ensure you have the right slide timing for each slide, you'll rehearse the slide show, and then save the slide timings. When you rehearse a slide show, PowerPoint keeps track of the amount of time each slide is displayed during the slide show. You can then save those times for the self-running slide show. See the Session 4.2 Visual Overview for more information about rehearsing presentations.

You'll set new slide timings by using the Rehearse Timings feature. Read through the next set of steps before completing them so that you are prepared to advance the slide show as needed.

To rehearse the slide timings:

1. On the ribbon, click the **SLIDE SHOW** tab, and then in the Set Up group, click the **Rehearse Timings** button. The slide show starts from Slide 1, and the Recording toolbar appears on the screen in the upper-left corner. The toolbar includes a timer on the left that indicates the number of seconds the slide is displayed, and a timer on the right that tracks the total time for the slide show.

2. Leave Slide 1 on the screen for about five seconds, and then advance the slide show. Slide 2 appears on the screen.

3. Leave Slide 2 on the screen for about five seconds, advance to Slide 3, and then press the **spacebar** to make the first animation occur.

4. After the Lights/Fans text box appears, press the **spacebar** three more times to animate the rest of the objects on the slide.

5. Wait about five seconds after displaying the smartphone and its text box, press the **spacebar** again to display Slide 4. You'll leave Slides 4, 5, and 6 on the screen for about five seconds each.

6. Wait five seconds, press the **spacebar** to display Slide 5, wait five seconds, press the **spacebar** to display Slide 6, wait five seconds, and then press the **spacebar** again. Slide 7 appears on the screen.

7. On Slide 7, click each question to display its answer, waiting a few seconds after each answer appears before clicking the next question, and then press the **spacebar** to display Slide 8.

TIP

Click the Pause Recording button on the Recording toolbar to pause the timer; click the Repeat button to restart the timer for the current slide.

8. Wait five seconds, and then press the **spacebar**. A dialog box opens asking if you want to save the timings.

9. Click the **Yes** button. The timings you rehearsed are saved and the presentation appears in Slide Sorter view. The rehearsed time appears below each slide thumbnail. You can also see the timing assigned to the slides on the TRANSITIONS tab.

10. Click the **TRANSITIONS** tab, and then click the **Slide 1** thumbnail. In the Timing group, the recorded timing to the hundredth of a second for the selected slide appears in the After box. The rehearsed timing replaced the five-second slide timing you set previously.

After you rehearse a slide show, you should run the slide show to check the timings.

To play the slide show using the rehearsed slide timings:

1. On the Quick Access Toolbar, click the **Start from Beginning** button ⬜. The slide show starts and Slide 1 appears on the screen. The slide show advances to Slide 2 automatically after the saved rehearsal timing elapses. When Slide 3 ("Wirelessly Control") appears, the animations occur automatically at the pace you rehearsed them.

2. Continue watching the slide show and evaluate the slide timings. If you feel that a slide stays on the screen for too much or too little time, stop the slide show, click the slide to select it, click the TRANSITIONS tab, and then change the time in the After box in the Timing group.

   Trouble? In PowerPoint 2013, sometimes objects that have triggers do not animate correctly when watching a slide show with rehearsed or recorded timings. If that happens with Slide 7 ("FAQs") in this presentation, continue with the steps and this potential issue will be addressed in the next section. If you create your own presentation and this happens, remove the triggers and then rehearse the slide show again.

3. When the final black slide appears on the screen, advance the slide show to end it, and then save your changes.

Recording Narration

You can record narration to give viewers more information about presentation content. When you add narration, you should prepare a script for each slide so you won't stumble or hesitate while recording.

If you add narration to a slide, you should not read the text on the slide—the viewers can read that for themselves. Your narration should provide additional information about the slides or instructions for the viewers as they watch the self-running presentation so that they know, for instance, that they can click action buttons to manually advance the presentation. Refer to the Session 4.2 Visual Overview for more information about recording narration.

REFERENCE

Recording Narration

- Confirm that your computer has a microphone.
- On the ribbon, click the SLIDE SHOW tab, and then in the Set Up group, click the Record Slide Show button.
- Click the Start Recording button.
- Speak into the microphone to record the narration for the current slide.
- Press the spacebar to go to the next slide (if desired), record the narration for that slide, and then continue, as desired, to other slides.
- End the slide show after recording the last narration; or continue displaying all the slides in the presentation for the appropriate amount of time, even if you do not add narration to each slide, and then end the slide show as you normally would.

When Ryder sets this presentation to be self-running at a convention or exhibition, he wants viewers to have some guidance in navigating through the presentation. You will record narration for Slides 1, 2, and 7 that tells the viewer how to use the hyperlinks, action buttons, and triggers to navigate the presentation. You will also adjust the timing for these three slides to accommodate their accompanying narrations.

First, you'll record narration for Slides 1 and 2.

To record narration for Slides 1 and 2:

1. Make sure your computer is equipped with a microphone.

   Trouble? If your system doesn't have a microphone, find a computer that does, connect a microphone to your computer, or check with your instructor or technical support person. If you cannot connect a microphone to your computer, read the following steps but do not complete them.

2. On the ribbon, click the **SLIDE SHOW** tab, and then in the Set Up group, click the **Record Slide Show** button. The Record Slide Show dialog box opens. You want to record narration and slide timings, so you will not change the default settings.

   When you click the Start Recording button in the next step, the slide show will start and you can begin recording your narration. Be prepared to start talking as soon as each slide appears, without waiting for the animation to finish. When you are finished recording narration for a slide, wait a couple of seconds before advancing the slide show to avoid the end of your sentence being cut off during the slide show.

3. Click the **Start Recording** button. The dialog box closes and the slide show starts from Slide 1. The Recording dialog box appears on the screen in the upper-left corner as it did when you rehearsed the slide timings.

4. Speak the following into the microphone, using a clear and steady voice: **"Thank you for your interest in Duplantis Control Systems. This presentation will advance automatically from one slide to the next."**

5. Press the **spacebar** to advance to Slide 2, and then say into the microphone, **"If you would rather control your progression through the slide show, click the text links on this slide to jump to the slide containing the related information. On other slides, click the blue button in the upper-right corner to return to this slide. To jump to the last slide, click the 'Click to set up an appointment' button at the bottom of this slide."**

6. Wait for a few seconds (to give the viewer time to examine the slide after the narration is finished), and then press the **Esc** key to end the slide show. The timer in the Recording toolbar stops, and then after a moment, Slide Show view closes and you see the newly recorded timings under the thumbnails for Slides 1 and 2 in Slide Sorter view. If you look closely at the thumbnails for these two slides, you will also see a sound icon in the lower-right corner; this is the narration you recorded on each slide.

Trouble? If you advanced the slide show to Slide 3 instead of pressing the Esc key to end it, when Slide Sorter view appears again, first double-click the Slide 3 thumbnail to display it in the Slide pane in Normal view, click the TRANSITIONS tab, and then change the time in the After box to five seconds. Next, click the sound icon in the lower-right corner of Slide 3, and then press the Delete key to delete it. Return to Slide Sorter view.

After recording the narration for Slide 2, you could have continued the recording and simply not said anything to re-record timings for Slides 3 through 6, and then recorded the narration for Slide 7, but if you did, a sound icon would have appeared on each of those slides and the presentation file size would be larger. Instead, you'll record a narration for just Slide 7.

To record narration for Slide 7:

1. Double-click the **Slide 7** ("FAQs") thumbnail to display it in the Slide pane in Normal view.

2. On the SLIDE SHOW tab, in the Set Up group, click the **Record Slide Show button arrow**, and then click **Start Recording from Current Slide**. The Record Slide Show dialog box appears.

3. Click the **Start Recording** button. Slide 7 appears in Slide Show view.

4. Say into the microphone, "**Click a question to display its answer.**", and then press the **Esc** key to end the slide show. The few seconds it took for you to record the sentence on Slide 7 is not enough time for a viewer to click the questions, so you need to adjust the timing on the TRANSITIONS tab.

5. On the ribbon, click the **TRANSITIONS** tab.

6. In the Timing group, click in the **After** box, type **20**, and then press the **Enter** key. The timing for Slide 7 is now 20 seconds.

You'll run the slide show to test the recorded narration and new slide timings for Slides 1, 2 and 7. The slide timings for Slides 3 through 6 and Slide 8 when you rehearsed the presentation previously remain unchanged.

To play the slide show and use the recorded slide timings:

1. On the Quick Access Toolbar, click the **Start from Beginning** button. The slide show starts, you hear the recording that you made for Slide 1, and then the slide show advances to Slide 2 automatically after the recorded time elapses. Notice that you don't see the sound icon on the slide. Several seconds after the recording on Slide 2 finishes playing, the slide show advances automatically to display Slide 3.

TIP
To remove narration on a slide, delete the sound icon, or click the Record Slide Show button arrow in the Set Up group on the SLIDE SHOW tab, point to Clear, and then click Clear Narration on Current Slide.

Trouble? If Slide 1 transitions to Slide 2 before your recorded voice finishes the sentence, display Slide 1 in the Slide pane in Normal view, click the TRANSITIONS tab, in the Timing group, click the up arrow once or twice to add one or two seconds to the slide timing, and then run the presentation again.

2. Click the blue action button in the upper-right corner of the Slide 3. Slide 2 appears again; however the recording does not play again.

3. Click the **FAQs** link. Slide 7 ("FAQs") appears.

4. Click each of the questions on Slide 7, and then wait until the saved time elapses and Slide 8 ("Set Up an Appointment Today!") appears on the screen.

5. Wait approximately five seconds until the black slide that indicates the end of a slide show appears on the screen, and then press the **spacebar**. The presentation appears in Normal view.

6. Display **Slide 1** (the title slide) in the Slide pane.

7. In the lower-right corner of the slide, click the sound icon, and then on the ribbon, click the **AUDIO TOOLS PLAYBACK** tab. Note that the sound is set to play automatically and the icon will be hidden during the slide show. See Figure 4-21.

Figure 4-21 Settings for the recorded sound

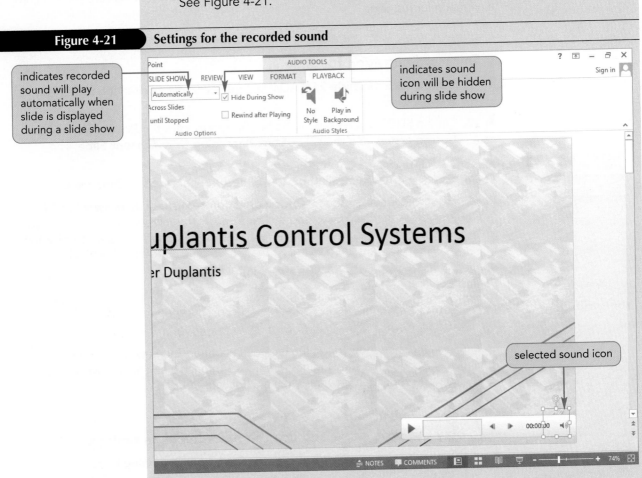

Now that you added sound recordings to the slides, you should optimize the recordings to ensure they will play on any computer.

To optimize the recordings in the presentation:

1. On the ribbon, click the **FILE** tab to display the Info screen in Backstage view.
2. Click the **Optimize Compatibility** button. The Optimize Media Compatibility dialog box opens and a progress bar shows the progress of the optimization.
3. Click the **Close** button in the dialog box. The Optimize Compatibility button no longer appears on the Info screen.
4. At the top of the navigation bar, click the **Back** button ⊙ to exit Backstage view.
5. Save the changes to the presentation.

Next, you'll continue setting up the self-running slide show by setting options to control the slide show manually.

Setting Options for Overriding the Automatic Timings

As you have seen, when a presentation is set to be self-running, you can allow the viewer to override the timings you set. If the On Mouse Click check box is selected in the Timing group on the TRANSITIONS tab, the viewer can advance the slide show using the normal methods of clicking the left mouse button, pressing the spacebar or the Enter key, and so on. To prevent this, you can deselect the On Mouse Click check box. The links in the presentation will continue to function normally, but the viewer will not be able to manually advance the slide show.

To avoid someone accidentally advancing the slide show by clicking the mouse button or pressing a key, Ryder wants you to deselect the On Mouse Click check box. You'll make this adjustment now.

To change the setting so the viewer cannot advance the slide manually:

1. Switch to Slide Sorter view, and then select all the slides.
2. On the ribbon, click the **TRANSITIONS** tab.
3. In the Timing group, click the **On Mouse Click** check box to deselect it. Now viewers will not accidentally override the timings you set by using the ordinary methods of advancing the slide show.

Applying Kiosk Browsing

Now, Ryder wants you to set up the presentation so that in addition to automatically advancing from one slide to another using the saved slide timings, after the last slide it will loop back to the first slide and run again. To do this, you change the settings in the Set Up Show dialog box. In the Set Up Show dialog box, you can set the presentation to loop continuously or you can set the presentation to be browsed at a kiosk, which automatically applies the loop continuously setting. When you set a presentation to be browsed at a kiosk, the normal methods for advancing a slide show are automatically disabled, so even if the On Mouse Click check box is selected in the Timing group on the TRANSITIONS tab, clicking the mouse button or pressing the spacebar or the Enter key will have no effect. However, a viewer can still click hyperlinks on the screen, including action buttons, and can still press the Esc key to end the slide show.

Now, you'll set up the Control System presentation for kiosk browsing.

To set up the presentation for browsing at a kiosk:

▶ 1. On the ribbon, click the **SLIDE SHOW** tab, and then in the Set Up group, click the **Set Up Slide Show** button. The Set Up Show dialog box opens. See Figure 4-22.

| Figure 4-22 | Set Up Show dialog box set for kiosk browsing |

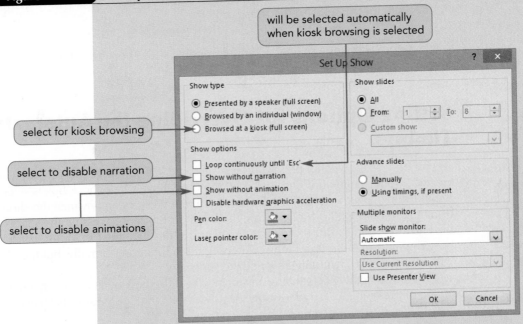

will be selected automatically when kiosk browsing is selected

select for kiosk browsing

select to disable narration

select to disable animations

▶ 2. In the Show type section, click the **Browsed at a kiosk (full screen)** option button. Under Show options, the Loop continuously until 'Esc' check box becomes selected. That option has also changed to light gray, indicating that you cannot deselect it.

▶ 3. Click the **OK** button. The dialog box closes, and the presentation is set up for kiosk browsing.

TIP

To change the resolution of the slide show, click the Slide show monitor arrow, click the monitor you are showing the slide show on, click the Resolution arrow, and then click the resolution you want to use.

When you run the slide show set for kiosk browsing, it will continue to run until someone presses the Esc key. You'll test that setting.

To test the self-running slide show:

▶ 1. Click the **Slide 8** ("Set Up an Appointment Today!") thumbnail, and then on the status bar, click the **Slide Show** button 🖵. This is the final slide in the presentation. After the saved timing for Slide 8 elapses, watch as the slide show automatically starts over with Slide 1.

▶ 2. After Slide 1 (the title slide) appears on the screen, press the **Esc** key to end the slide show.

▶ 3. Save the changes to the presentation.

Using the Document Inspector

The Document Inspector is a tool you can use to check a presentation for hidden data, such as the author's name and other personal information, objects that are in the presentation but are hidden or placed in the area next to a slide instead of on the slide, and speaker notes. Ryder wants you to check the presentation for hidden data.

To check the presentation using the Document Inspector:

▶ **1.** Double-click the **Slide 1** (the title slide) thumbnail to display Slide 1 in the Slide pane in Normal view, and then on the status bar, click the **NOTES** button. Notice that there is a speaker note on this slide that Ryder added before he gave you the presentation to work with.

▶ **2.** On the ribbon, click the **FILE** tab. The Info screen in Backstage view appears. On the right, file properties are listed, including the number of slides in the presentation and the author name. On the left, next to the Check for Issues button, a bulleted list informs you that the presentation contains document properties that you might want to delete, speaker notes, and potential problems for people with vision disabilities. See Figure 4-23.

Figure 4-23	Info screen in Backstage view

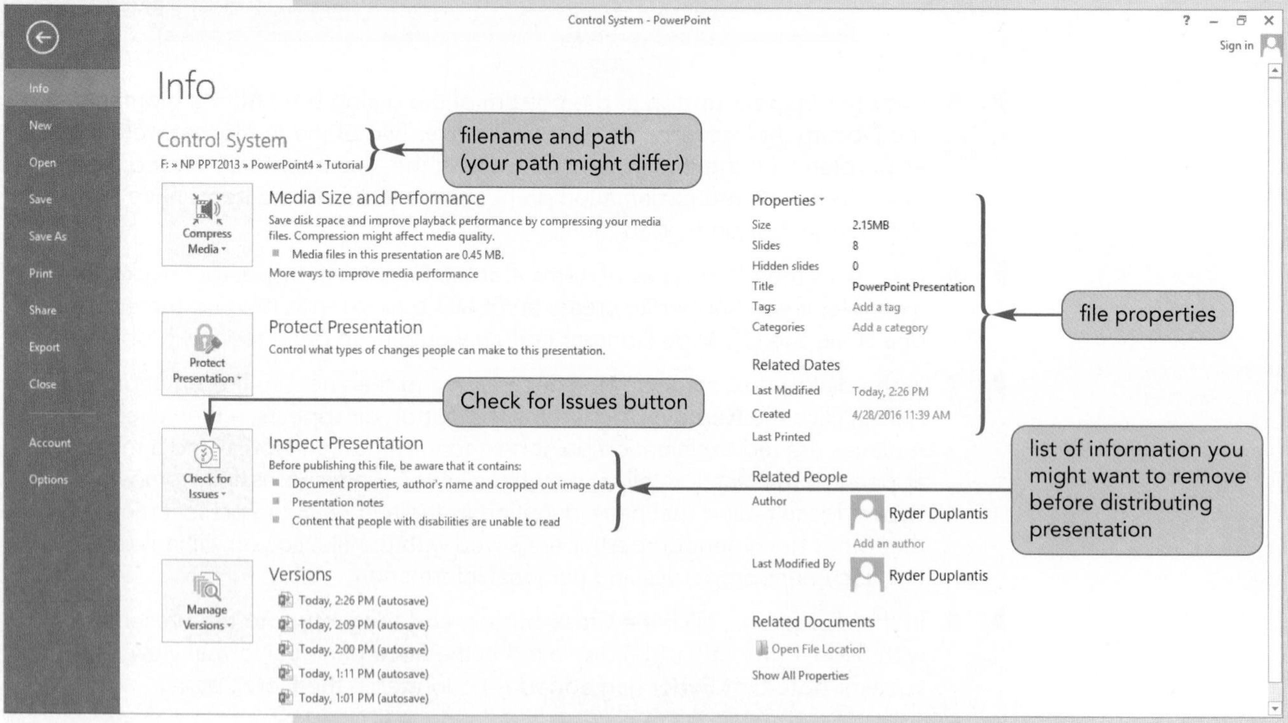

▶ **3.** Click the **Check for Issues** button, and then click **Inspect Document**. The Document Inspector dialog box opens.

Trouble? If a dialog box opens telling you that you need to save the presentation first, click the Yes button to save the presentation.

▶ **4.** Click any of the check boxes in this dialog box that are not checked. See Figure 4-24.

Figure 4-24 **Document Inspector dialog box**

all check boxes should be selected

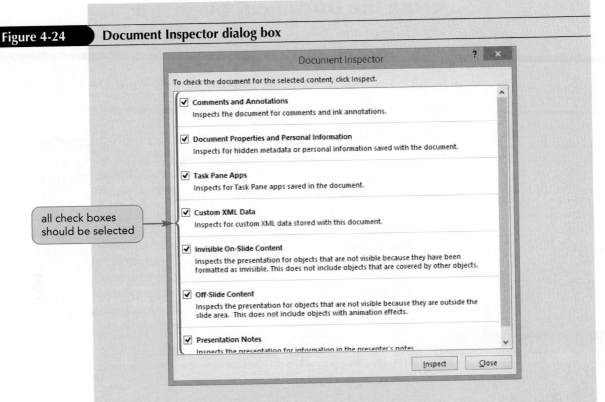

5. Click the **Inspect** button at the bottom of the dialog box. After a moment, the Document Inspector displays the results. Two of the items that were listed as problems on the Info screen are listed in the Document Inspector dialog box and have a red exclamation point next to them. These items have a Remove All button next to them.

6. Look over the other types of items that the Document Inspector checks. For example, if you happen to create an object that extends beyond the edges of a slide, the Off-Slide Content feature would have detected the problem.

7. In the dialog box, scroll down if necessary, and then next to Presentation Notes, click the **Remove All** button. The button disappears, a blue checkmark replaces the red exclamation point next to Presentation Notes, and a message appears in that section telling you that all items were successfully removed. Ryder doesn't mind that he is identified as the author of the presentation or that other document properties are saved with the file, so you will not remove the document properties and personal information.

8. In the dialog box, click the **Close** button, and then return to the presentation with Slide 1 (the title slide) displayed in the Slide pane in Normal view. The speaker note that Ryder had added is no longer in the Notes pane.

9. On the status bar, click the **NOTES** button to close the Notes pane.

10. Save the changes to the presentation.

Save the changes now because you will be saving the presentation in a different format.

Packaging a Presentation for CD

Ryder will present the slide show at various conventions and exhibitions across the country. He plans to bring his own laptop, but he knows it's a good idea to have backups. One way to back up a presentation is to use the Package a Presentation for CD feature. This puts all the fonts and linked files and anything else needed on a CD or in a folder that you can copy to a USB drive or burn to a DVD using a DVD burner program.

To package the presentation for CD:

▶ **1.** Display the Export screen in Backstage view, and then click **Package Presentation for CD**. The right side of the screen changes to display a description of this command.

▶ **2.** Click the **Package for CD** button. The Package for CD dialog box opens. See Figure 4-25.

Figure 4-25   Package for CD dialog box

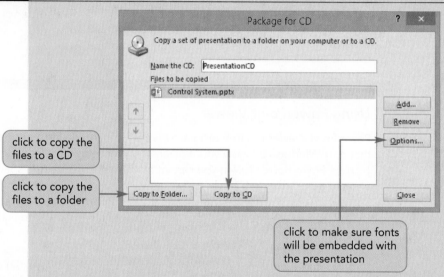

click to copy the files to a CD

click to copy the files to a folder

click to make sure fonts will be embedded with the presentation

▶ **3.** Click the **Options** button. The Options dialog box opens. See Figure 4-26.

Figure 4-26   Options dialog box when packaging a presentation for CD

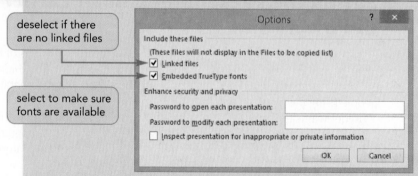

deselect if there are no linked files

select to make sure fonts are available

You will keep the Embed TrueType fonts check box selected to ensure that you will have the fonts used in the presentation available if you run the packaged presentation on another computer. If your presentation contained links to any other files, you would keep the Linked files check box selected to

include those files in the package. However, the presentation file does not contain any linked files, so you will deselect that check box.

▶ 4. Click the **Linked files** check box to deselect it.

▶ 5. Click the **OK** button. The Package for CD dialog box is visible again.

▶ 6. Click the **Copy to Folder** button. The Copy to Folder dialog box opens. The default name for the folder you will create to hold the files of the packaged presentation—PresentationCD—appears in the Folder name box.

Trouble? If you are copying your presentation to a CD, click the Cancel button to close this dialog box, insert a blank CD in the CD drive, click the Copy to CD button, click the No button when the dialog box opens asking if you want to copy the same files to another CD, and then skip to Step 9.

▶ 7. Click the **Browse** button to open the Choose Location dialog box, navigate to the folder where you are storing your files, and then click the **Select** button.

▶ 8. Click the **Open folder when complete** check box to deselect it, if necessary, and then click the **OK** button. A dialog box opens briefly as PowerPoint copies all the necessary files to the PresentationCD folder or disc.

▶ 9. Click the **Close** button in the Package for CD dialog box.

INSIGHT

Using PowerPoint Viewer

PowerPoint Viewer is a free program that you can install and use on any computer that runs Windows to show your PowerPoint presentation in Slide Show view. When you use PowerPoint Viewer, you cannot modify slides and some special effects might not work. To download PowerPoint Viewer, go to www.microsoft.com and use the Search box on the website to search for **PowerPoint Viewer**. In the list of results, click the option to filter the list to show only Downloads, and then click the link for the file with the most recent release date. The file that downloads is an executable file, which means that you double-click it to start the installation process. To be absolutely sure you can show your presentation on another computer, you can download the PowerPoint Viewer executable file and store it on a flash drive to bring with you.

Saving the Presentation in an Earlier Version of PowerPoint

TIP

You can save a presentation in different file types using the options on the Export screen in Backstage view.

You can save a presentation so it is compatible with earlier versions of PowerPoint. Before you do this, it's a good idea to identify features in the presentation that are incompatible with earlier versions of PowerPoint so that you know how the presentation will look for people using the file saved in the earlier format.

Ryder wants to save the presentation as an earlier version of PowerPoint so he can distribute the presentation to potential customers who have not upgraded to PowerPoint 2013. He asks you to check the Control System presentation for features not supported by previous PowerPoint versions.

To check for features not supported by previous versions of PowerPoint:

▶ **1.** On the ribbon, click the **FILE** tab. The Info screen in Backstage view appears.

▶ **2.** Click the **Check for Issues** button, and then click **Check Compatibility**. Backstage view closes, and after a moment, the Microsoft PowerPoint Compatibility Checker dialog box opens listing features that aren't supported by earlier versions of PowerPoint.

▶ **3.** If the Check compatibility when saving in PowerPoint 97-2003 formats check box is not selected, click the **Check compatibility when saving in PowerPoint 97-2003 formats** check box to select it. See Figure 4-27. This ensures that if you save the presentation in the format compatible with PowerPoint versions 97 through 2003, the Compatibility Checker will run automatically.

| Figure 4-27 | Microsoft PowerPoint Compatibility Checker dialog box |

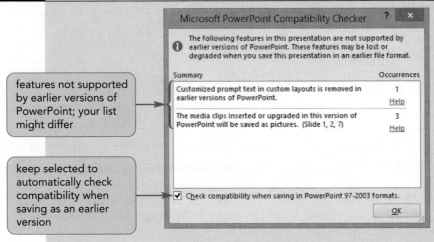

features not supported by earlier versions of PowerPoint; your list might differ

keep selected to automatically check compatibility when saving as an earlier version

▶ **4.** Click the **OK** button.

Now that Ryder understands which features in the Control System presentation are not supported by earlier versions of PowerPoint, he wants you to save the presentation using an earlier version file type. After you do that, he plans to locate a computer that has an earlier version of PowerPoint installed and review the file to see what adjustments he needs to make to ensure that people he sends the file to will be able to see and understand all the content.

To save a presentation in a file format compatible with earlier versions of PowerPoint:

▶ **1.** On the ribbon, click the **FILE** tab. The Info screen in Backstage view appears.

▶ **2.** In the navigation bar, click **Export**. The Export screen appears.

▶ **3.** Click **Change File Type**. Options for changing the file type appear. See Figure 4-28.

Figure 4-28 **Change File Type options on the Export screen**

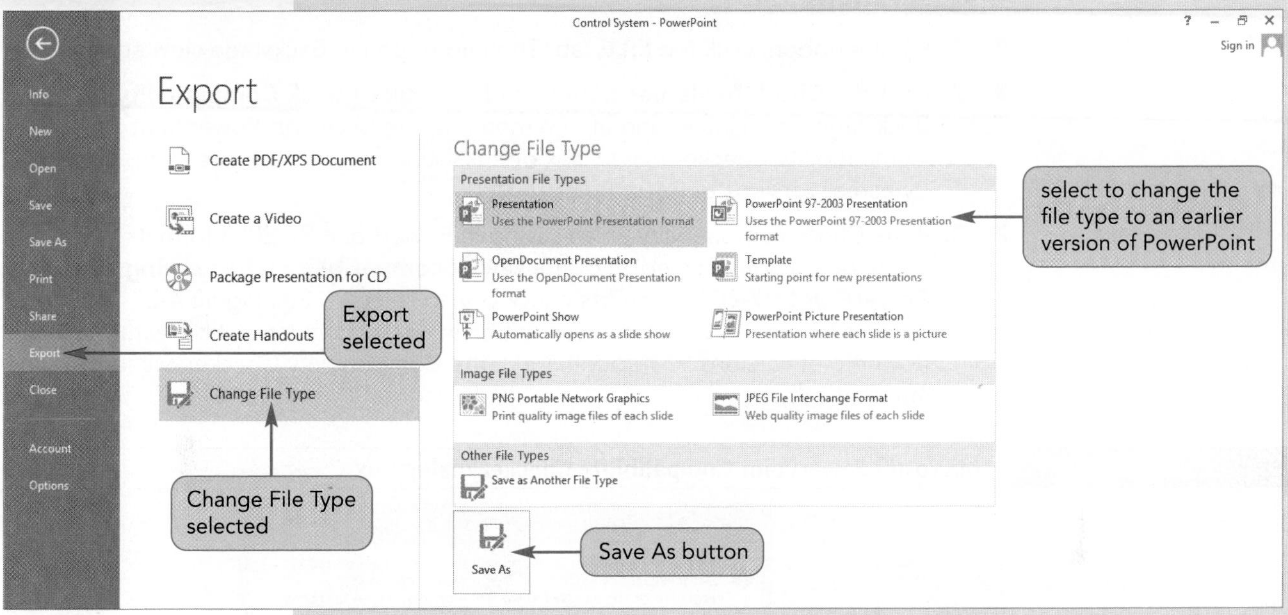

4. Under Change File Type, click **PowerPoint 97-2003 Presentation**, and then click the **Save As** button. The Save As dialog box opens with PowerPoint 97-2003 Presentation in the Save As type box.

5. If necessary, navigate to the location where you are saving your files.

6. Change the name in the File name box to **Control System Earlier Version**, and then click the **Save** button. The Save As dialog box closes and the Microsoft PowerPoint Compatibility Checker dialog box opens. This is because the Check compatibility when saving in PowerPoint 97-2003 formats check box is selected in this dialog box.

7. Click the **Continue** button. In the title bar, "[Compatibility Mode]" appears next to the presentation title, indicating that this file format is an earlier version of PowerPoint.

You have finished the Control System presentation, and ensured that Ryder has the presentation in the formats he needs.

Session 4.2 Quick Check

REVIEW

1. How do you change the amount of time a slide stays on the screen during Slide Show view in a self-running presentation?
2. Do links work in a self-running presentation?
3. How do you prevent viewers from using normal methods of advancing the slide show in a self-running presentation?
4. What does the Document Inspector reveal?
5. Why would you package a presentation to a CD?
6. What does the Compatibility Checker reveal?

ASSESS

SAM Projects

Put your skills into practice with SAM Projects! SAM Projects for this tutorial can be found online. If you have a SAM account, go to www.cengage.com/sam2013 to download the most recent Project Instructions and Start Files.

PRACTICE

Review Assignments

Data Files needed for the Review Assignments: Home.pptx; House.jpg

Ryder Duplantis, owner of Duplantis Control Systems, is expanding his business to include residential homes. He will be attending a home exhibition show, and he wants to bring a self-running presentation that people can watch when they visit his exhibition booth. Complete the following steps:

1. Open the file **Home**, located in the PowerPoint4 ▸ Review folder included with your Data Files, add your name as the subtitle, and then save the presentation as **Home Control Systems**.
2. On Slide 4 ("How Does It Work?"), animate the image of the pointing finger with a motion path animation that ends when it appears as if the finger is on top of the red square.
3. On Slide 4, add the Disappear exit animation to the image of the pointing finger.
4. On Slide 4, click the motion sensors object on the right side of the slide, press and hold the Shift key, and then select the other four objects on the right side of the slide. (Note that each of the five objects on the right side of the slide is a picture and a text box grouped together to form one object.) Apply the Appear entrance animation to the selected objects.
5. Deselect the objects, select the Motion Sensors object, and then change its start timing to With Previous. One at a time, in the following order, change the start timing of the animations applied to the rest of the objects on the right side of the slide to On Click: Wall Speakers, Security Alarms, Porch Light, MP3 Player Docking Station.
6. On Slide 5 ("Typical Device Plan"), select all of the triangles, circles, and the gray rounded rectangle on the floor plan, and then apply the Appear entrance animation.
7. On Slide 5, select only the nine yellow rectangles on the floor plan, and then make the Lights button object the trigger for the animation applied to the triangles. Set the Speakers button object to be the trigger for the animation applied to the three green circles on the floor plan. Set the Thermostat button object to be the trigger for the animation applied to the gray rounded rectangle on the floor plan. Finally, set the Security Alarm button object to be the trigger for the animation applied to the red circle on the floor plan.
8. Add the picture **House**, located in the PowerPoint4 ▸ Review folder, as the slide background. Change the transparency to 85%, and then apply this background to all of the slides. On Slide 1 (the title slide) open the Format Background task pane, and then click the Solid fill option button, to change the background of the title slide back to solid white. Do not apply this change to all the slides.
9. On Slide 2 ("Duplantis Smart Home Features"), convert the "Click to see a typical setup" shape to a link to Slide 5 ("Typical Device Plan"). (*Hint*: Make sure the entire shape is selected before you add the link.)
10. On Slide 2, convert the first bulleted item to a link to Slide 4 ("How Does It Work?").
11. On Slide 4 ("How Does It Work?"), add a Return action button about one-half inch high and three-quarters of an inch wide in the lower left corner and link it to Slide 2 ("Duplantis Smart Home Features"). Copy this action button to Slide 5.
12. On Slide 3 ("What Do I Need?"), convert the "Get a quote" shape to a link to Slide 6 ("Get a Free Quote Today!").

13. Customize the color palette so that the color of hyperlinks is the Indigo, Accent 1 theme color and the color of followed links is the light brown color on the Standard tab of the Colors dialog box (the second color in the second to last row of colors in the color hexagon). Save the custom palette as **Link Colors** to apply the new colors, and then delete the custom palette.

14. Rehearse the slide timings as follows: Leave Slide 1 on the screen for about five seconds and Slides 2 and 3 on the screen for about 10 seconds. On Slide 4, remember to advance the slide show to animate the pointing finger, and then advance the slide show five times to display the rest of the objects on the slide. Wait a few seconds after the last object appears, and then advance to Slide 5. Click each button to trigger the animations, waiting a few seconds between each click. Display Slide 6 for about 5 seconds.

15. Record the following narration for Slide 1: **"This is a self-running presentation. If you want, you can click buttons on each slide to control the presentation."** Press the Esc key to end the slide show after recording this.

16. Optimize the media.

17. Use a command on the TRANSITIONS tab to prevent viewers from advancing the slide show using the ordinary methods (pressing the spacebar or the Enter key and so on).

18. Set up the presentation for kiosk browsing.

19. Save the changes to the presentation, inspect the presentation for hidden information, and then have the Document Inspector remove speaker notes.

20. Save the changes to the presentation.

21. Save the presentation in a format compatible with PowerPoint 97-2003. Name the file **Home Control Systems Earlier Version**.

22. Use the Package Presentation for CD command to package the presentation to a folder named **Duplantis Home**. Do not include linked files (there aren't any) and make sure to embed fonts.

23. Close the file, saving changes if prompted.

Case Problem 1

APPLY

Data Files needed for this Case Problem: Office.pptx

Virtual Office   Dessa Sobieski writes a column titled "The Entrepreneur" in the Park City, Utah newspaper the *Wasatch Mountain Times*. Recently she wrote a column about the "virtual office" a new type of service that provides many benefits to home businesses and smaller companies such as phone answering service, accounting, re-ordering supplies, and other clerical services. Some virtual office companies also offer physical office space on an as-needed basis. Because of her article, Dessa was invited by the Salt Lake City Area Home Business Association to give a presentation at one of their monthly meetings about virtual office services. She has asked you to help her prepare the presentation. Complete the following steps:

1. Open the presentation **Office**, located in the PowerPoint4 ▶ Case1 folder included with your Data Files, and then save the presentation with the filename **Virtual Office**. Add your name as a footer on all the slides. (Do not add your name as the subtitle.)

2. On Slide 1 (the title slide), drag the picture to the center of the slide. Apply the entrance animation Shape to the picture, and change its effect to Out. Add the motion path animation Lines and adjust the path as needed so that the picture ends up on the right side of the slide. Change the start timing of the motion path animation to After Previous.

3. On Slide 1, apply the Split entrance animation to the title, and then change its start timing to After Previous.

4. On Slide 1, set the photo as the trigger for the title animation.

5. On Slide 2 ("Types of Services Provided"), convert the items in the bulleted list to links to Slides 3 through 7.

6. Customize the color palette so that the color of hyperlinks is the White, Text 1 theme color and the color of followed links is the Tan, Accent 1 theme color. Save the custom palette as Office Links, and then delete the Office Links color palette.

7. On Slide 2, in the lower-left corner of the slide, draw an Action Button: End shape about one-half inch high and three-quarters of an inch wide. Keep the default link to the last slide in the presentation.

8. On Slide 3 ("Phone Answering Service"), in the lower-left corner of the slide, draw an Action Button: Back or Previous shape about one-half inch high and three-quarters of an inch wide. Keep the default link to the previous slide.

9. Copy the action button on Slide 3, and then paste it on Slide 4 ("Accounting"). Edit the link destination so it links to Slide 2.

10. Copy the action button on Slide 4 and paste it on Slide 5 ("Website Management"), Slide 6 ("Meeting Spaces"), and Slide 7 ("Professional Address").

11. Use the Document Inspector to remove speaker notes. Save the changes to the presentation.

12. Save the presentation in a format compatible with PowerPoint 97-2003. Name the file **Virtual Office Earlier Version**.

13. Use the Package Presentation for CD command to package the presentation to a folder named **Virtual Office Package**, making sure to embed fonts and without including linked files.

14. Close the presentation, saving changes if prompted.

Case Problem 2

Data Files needed for this Case Problem: Coupons.pptx, No Symbol.png

Kritikos Koupons App   Peter Kritikos works full time for a large computer company, but on the side, he creates apps for smartphones and tablets. His most recent app is a coupon app that allows users to find and download coupons for products they want to buy and provides barcodes so that the coupon can be scanned directly from the smartphone or table by the cashier. Peter markets his product online and in person at various consumer events, such as trade shows. He asked you to help him create a self-running PowerPoint presentation. Complete the following steps:

1. Open the presentation **Coupon**, located in the PowerPoint4 ▸ Case2 folder included with your Data Files, add your name as the subtitle, and then save the presentation with the filename **Coupon App**.

2. On Slide 1 (the title slide), change the slide background to a gradient fill. Apply the Medium Gradient – Accent 1 style from the Preset gradients gallery. Change the type to Linear, if necessary, and the direction to Linear Down. Do not apply the background to all the slides (in other words, only Side 1 has the gradient fill background).

⚙ **Troubleshoot** 3. On Slide 1, make any adjustments needed so the text is readable.

4. On Slide 2 ("Save Time and Money"), move the images of the scissors and the finger with a string tied around it so they are out of the way, and then position the stack of newspapers in the center of the space to the right of the text boxes. Apply the Appear entrance animation to the top text box ("No more stacks of newspapers!"). Apply the Appear entrance animation to the picture of the newspaper stacks, and change its start timing to With Previous so that it appears at the same time as the text box.

5. On Slide 2, insert the picture No Symbol, located in the PowerPoint4 ▸ Case2 folder, and position it on top of the newspapers. Apply the entrance animation Appear to the No Symbol picture, change its start timing to After Previous so that it appears after the picture of the newspapers appears, and set a delay of one second.

6. On Slide 2, apply the entrance animation Appear to the middle text box ("No more clipping coupons!").

7. Select the picture of the newspapers (make sure the newspapers picture is selected and not the No Symbol image), and then add the exit animation Disappear as a second animation to the picture of the newspapers. Change the start timing of this animation to With Previous so that it disappears when the middle text box appears.

8. Add the exit animation Disappear as a second animation to the No Symbol picture, and then change the start timing of this animation to With Previous so that it disappears with the newspapers picture.

9. Apply the entrance animation Appear to the picture of the scissors and change its start timing to With Previous so that it appears at the same time as the other two pictures disappear.

10. Select the No Symbol picture and add the Appear animation as a third animation. Change the start timing of this animation to After Previous so it appears after the picture of the scissors appears, and set a delay of one second.

11. Apply the Appear animation to the bottom text box ("No more forgetting coupons at home!"). Add the Disappear animation to the scissors as a second animation, changing its start timing to With Previous. Apply the Appear animation to the picture of the finger with the string tied around it, changing its start timing to With Previous. And add the Disappear animation to the No Symbol picture, changing its start timing to With Previous.

12. Drag the picture of the scissors to the No Symbol picture. It will slide behind the No Symbol picture. Drag the picture of the finger with string tied around it to the No Symbol picture.

⚙ **Troubleshoot** 13. View Slide 2 in Slide Show view, and then add the additional animation needed to the No Symbol picture so it appears one second after the picture of the finger with the string tied around it.

14. On Slide 4 ("Using the Kritikos Koupon App"), apply the Appear animation to the top left text box ("Touch to return to Home screen"), and then add the Disappear animation to that text box.

15. Apply the Appear animation to the second text box on the left, and then add the Disappear animation to that text box.

⚙ **Troubleshoot** 16. Each time you advance the slide show, you want a new callout to appear and the one that was already visible on the slide to disappear at the same time. View Slide 4 in Slide Show view, and then adjust the animations to the second callout as needed to achieve this.

17. Apply the animations and timing that you applied to the second text box to the third and then the fourth text box on the left, and then to the top two text boxes on the right, starting from the top. Apply the Appear animation to the bottom text box on the right, and change its start timing to With Previous. (You don't need the last callout to disappear before the slide show transitions to the next slide.)

18. On Slide 5 ("Start Saving Today!"), apply the Lines motion path animation to the logo so that it moves to the right and ends up to the right of the bulleted list. Change its start timing to After Previous and set a delay of one-half second.

19. On Slide 5, apply the Fly In animation to the bulleted list, change its sequence effect so it animates as one object, and then change its start timing to After Previous.

20. Rehearse and save the timings for the presentation, leaving each slide on the screen a reasonable amount of time and pausing after each animation.

21. Save the changes to the presentation, and then use the Document Inspector to remove document properties and the author's name.

22. Save the changes, and then close the file.

Case Problem 3

Data Files needed for this Case Problem: Background.jpg, Petroglyphs.pptx

CHALLENGE

Kennedy Elementary School   David Stark is a travel writer for a television studio in Tulsa, Oklahoma. He recently reported on his travels to national parks in the Southwest. In his report, he described petroglyphs, which are carvings in rock found in many parts of the world. They first appeared about 12,000 years ago and continued among some cultures up to the 20th century. The principal of Kennedy Elementary School saw his report and asked him to give a presentation to the students at the school. He asked you to help him complete his presentation. Complete the following steps:

1. Open the presentation **Petroglyphs**, located in the PowerPoint4 ▸ Case3 folder included with your Data Files, add your name as the subtitle, and then save the presentation with the filename **Native American Petroglyphs**.

2. Add the picture **Background**, located in the PowerPoint4 ▸ Case3 folder, as the slide background on all slides. Tile the picture as texture, change the vertical offset (Y) to **-100** points, and change the scale in both directions to **60%**.

3. On Slide 1 (the title slide), change the color of the title and subtitle text to White, Background 1.

4. On Slide 3 ("Petroglyph Locations in the Southwest"), draw a rectangle large enough to cover Utah on the map on the slide.

5. Apply the Lines motion path animation to the Canyonlands text box (on top of the top left picture), and adjust it so that the text box ends up below the top-left picture.

6. Animate the rectangle shape you drew so that it disappears at the same time as the text box moves.

7. Animate the top-left picture with the Wheel entrance animation so that it appears after the text box has finished moving.

8. Draw a rectangle on top of Arizona on the slide, and then animate the Chaco Culture text box (on top of the bottom-left picture), the second rectangle you drew, and the picture in the same manner as you did for the first three objects.

9. Draw a rectangle on top of New Mexico on the slide, and then animate the Petrified Forest text box (on top of the picture on the right), the third rectangle you drew, and the picture in the same manner.

⊕ **Explore** 10. Fill the rectangle shapes with the orange color of the wide band behind the images, and remove their outlines. (*Hint*: Use the Eyedropper tool on the Shape Fill menu to match the color.)

11. On Slide 5 ("Examples of Images"), apply the Appear entrance animation to all of the text boxes under the images, and then set the pictures above each text box as a trigger for that text box's animation.

⊕ **Explore** 12. On Slide 4 ("Newspaper Rock, Utah"), start recording from the current slide. In Slide Show view, before you start speaking, right-click to display the shortcut menu, and then change the pointer to a laser pointer. Keep the laser pointer off to the side while saying the first sentence, and then use it to circle the bulleted item "Tse' Hane" while you say the second sentence. Because you need to turn on the laser pointer, there will be silence at the beginning of the recording.

   "There are other newspaper rocks in many other locations around the world. The Navajo word for this rock translates to 'Rock that tells a story.' "

⊕ **Explore** 13. On Slide 4, trim off the silence at the beginning of the audio clip. If there is any at the end of the clip, trim that as well.

14. Optimize the media in the presentation.

15. Save the changes to the presentation, and then close the presentation.

CREATE

Case Problem 4

There are no Data Files needed for this Case Problem.

Bucket List   A "bucket list" is a list of goals that you want to achieve before you die. The term comes from the idiom "kick the bucket." You need to create a self-running PowerPoint presentation that illustrates your real or imaginary bucket list. Your presentation should include at least one slide with recorded narration, one object with multiple animations applied to it, and at least one object with a motion path animation applied to it. Make your presentation attractive and interesting so that viewers want to watch the whole thing. Complete the following steps:

Note: Please be sure not to include any personal information of a sensitive nature in the documents you create to be submitted to your instructor for this exercise. Later on, you can update the documents with such information for your own personal use.

1. Decide what you are going to include as your goals. If you need inspiration to come up with life goals, use a search engine and the search expression "popular life goals bucket lists."
2. Find graphics that illustrate each of your goals. Use your own pictures or search for pictures on Office.com or other site on the Internet.
3. Create a new presentation. Apply an appropriate theme. If you don't want to use one of the installed themes, look at the templates on Office.com.
4. Title the presentation Bucket List, add your name as the subtitle, and then save the presentation as **Bucket List** to the location where you are saving your files.
5. Create at least eight slides in addition to the title slide. Add photos and other illustrations as needed. Remember to keep the presentation content interesting so that viewers will want to watch the entire slide show.
6. Remember to include at least one slide with recorded narration, one object with multiple animations applied to it, and at least one object with a motion path animation applied to it. Any slide that does not have recorded narration must contain enough information to help a viewer understand the slide content. Do not include any links or triggers for animations.
7. Add any other animations you think will add interest. Add transitions if appropriate.
8. Check the spelling in your presentation and proof it.
9. Add timings to the slides using any method so that the presentation is self-running. Prevent viewers from using the mouse or keyboard to advance the slide.
10. Save and close the presentation.

Teamwork

What Is a Team?

The American Heritage Dictionary describes a team as a "group organized to work together." More than just people thrown together, teams consist of individuals who have skills, talents, and abilities that complement each other and, when joined, produce synergy—results greater than those a single individual could achieve. It is this sense of shared mission and responsibility for results that makes a team successful in its efforts to reach organizational goals.

Characteristics of Teams

Have you ever heard someone described as a "team player"? Members on a team get to know how the others work, so they can make contributions where they'll count most. On a football team, not everyone plays the role of quarterback; the team needs other positions working with the quarterback if touchdowns are to be scored. However, before the first play is ever made, the members bring their skills to the team and spend time learning each others' moves so they can catch the pass, block, or run toward the goal line together. Similarly, in a professional environment, the best teams have members whose background, skills, and abilities complement each other.

Managing Workflow on a Team

When team members collaborate on a project, someone needs to manage the workflow. This is especially important if team members are all contributing to a shared file stored on a server or a shared folder on the Internet. Some businesses have the capability to allow team members to co-author a presentation stored on a server. If this capability is not available, however, the team will need to create a strategy for managing the file to make sure that one person's changes do not get overwritten.

One way to manage workflow is to create an ordered list of team members assigned to work on a presentation file, and have team members access and edit the file only after the person preceding them on the list is finished with it. Another way is to allow anyone to access the presentation, but to have each team member save their version of the presentation with a different name—for example, they can add their initials to the end of the filename—and then each person can make their version available for the team member who has been designated to compare all the presentations to create one final version.

PROSKILLS

Create a Collaborative Presentation

Many people volunteer for a program that requires them to work collaboratively. For example, you might be a coach of a youth sports program, a Boy Scout leader, or a member of a local historical society. Often, volunteer groups require their members to meet occasionally to share ideas and information. PowerPoint is a useful tool for collecting notes, data, and images that you can then show everyone all at once. One way to do this could be to create a presentation for the group, post it to a shared folder on the World Wide Web, such as on your SkyDrive, and each person in the group can add slides containing the information they want to share. In this exercise, you'll use PowerPoint to create a presentation for an upcoming meeting for a group of which you are a member, using the skills and features presented in Tutorials 3 and 4.

Note: Please be sure not to include any personal information of a sensitive nature in the documents you create to be submitted to your instructor for this exercise. Later on, you can update the documents with such information for your own personal use.

1. Start a new, blank PowerPoint presentation, and save it with an appropriate name.
2. On Slide 1, type an informative title for your presentation, and add the name of the group as a subtitle.
3. Apply a theme appropriate for the group and the presentation content.
4. Modify the slide background and theme colors to match the colors used by your group or association.
5. Add the group's logo or a photo appropriate to the group to the title slide. Consider creating a logo by creating a custom shape.
6. Create a slide that lists the group members who will contribute to the presentation.
7. Create at least six slides for the presentation. Consider the purpose of the group as well as the purpose of the upcoming meeting. If you know others have information to share, add slides with titles to help guide them.
8. Add SmartArt and charts to the slides to help clarify the content. Add text boxes if needed to help describe the content.
9. Add photos to add interest to your slides. Edit the photos if needed using PowerPoint's photo editing tools.
10. Create an overview slide with a bulleted list corresponding to the other slides in the presentation. Convert the text of each bullet to be a link to the appropriate slide. Add any other links the group thinks are necessary.
11. Add alt text as needed to make the presentation more accessible.
12. Decide whether the presentation should be self-running or given orally. If it will be self-running, decide the best way to set the timings.
13. Save the presentation in at least one other format.
14. Save and close the file.

GLOSSARY/INDEX

improvement over the original version of third normal form. AC A19

broken link A reference to a file that has been moved since the link was created. EX 365

browser A program, such as Internet Explorer, that is designed to display webpages. WD 393
 viewing webpages, WD 403–405

bubble diagram A diagram that graphically shows a table's functional dependencies and determinants. Also known as a data model diagram or a functional dependency diagram. AC A12–A13

building block Reusable content in Word; includes all of the ready-made items that can be inserted into a document via a gallery, such as headers, preformatted text boxes, and cover pages. WD 287

Building Blocks Organizer dialog box, WD 290–291

Building Blocks template A special template that contains all the building blocks installed with Word on your computer, as well as any Quick Parts you save to it. WD 287

C

calculated column A column in an Excel table in which a formula entered or edited in one cell of the column is automatically copied into to all cells in that column. EX 465
 inserting in Excel tables, EX 467

calculated control A control that displays a value that is the result of an expression. The expression usually contains one or more fields, and the calculated control is recalculated each time any value in the expression changes. AC 326, AC 356–364
 adding to main form, AC 358–360
 adding to subform's form footer section, AC 356–358
 enhancing information, AC 367
 formatting, AC 360–364
 moving, AC 361–364
 resizing, AC 361–364

calculated field A field that you create with an expression that displays the results of the expression in a datasheet, form, or report, but does not exist as a field in the database.
 conditional values, AC 245–249

calculated field, PivotTable reports, EX 316

Can Grow property A property that controls the appearance of a control or section in a form or report when viewed, printed, or previewed. When you set the property to Yes, the control or section expands vertically to print or preview all the data within the control or section. When you set the property to No, the data that doesn't fit within the fixed size of the control or section isn't visible, printed, or previewed. AC 414, AC 415

candidate key A column, or a collection of columns, whose values are non-changing and whose values uniquely and minimally identify each row of a table, but that has not necessarily been chosen as the primary key. AC A3

caption, labels, changing, AC 338–340

cascades A referential integrity option in which the DBMS, when you change a primary key value, automatically changes the matching foreign key values to the new primary key value, and when you delete a record, automatically deletes the matching foreign key rows. AC A11

category One series of data represented in a chart or graph. PPT 139

Category field A field that groups the values in a PivotTable; appears in a PivotTable as a row label, a column label, and a report filter. EX 298

CD, packaging presentations for, PPT 229–230

cell The intersection of a row and a column. PPT 138, WD 373–374
 active, PPT 149–150
 content. *See* cell content
 defined names. *See* defined name
 locking and unlocking, EX 420–421
 in other worksheets, referencing, EX 339–341

cell range (range) A group of cells in a rectangular block.
 defined names. *See* defined name
 in other worksheets, referencing, EX 339–341

cell reference The column and row location that identifies a cell within a worksheet.
 external, EX 350

character spacing The space between individual characters. WD 258–260

character style A style with formatting options that affect individual characters, including font style, font color, font size, bold, italic, and underline. WD 260

chart (Access)
 embedding in forms, AC 474–480
 selecting type, AC 474–475

chart (PowerPoint) A visual that uses lines, arrows, and boxes or other shapes to show parts, steps, or processes. PPT 138–139, PPT 147–153
 creating, PPT 147–150
 formatting, PPT 151–153
 selecting type, PPT 153

chart object An Excel chart that is linked to or embedded in a Word document. WD 370
 linked, modifying, WD 383–385
 linking, WD 380–387

Chart Type dialog box, AC 477–478

chevrons In mail merge, the set of angled brackets (<< >>) that enclose a merge field in the main document. WD 300

Circle Invalid Data command, EX 419

clearing To remove the data from a row or column but leaves the blank row or column in the worksheet; also to remove, such as a filter. EX 281

collaborating, WD 415–416

color
 fonts, selecting, PPT 159
 report rows, AC 415–416
 themes, WD 252–253, WD 254
 themes, customizing, PPT 211–215

Colors dialog box, PPT 213

column
 freezing in worksheets, EX 262–263
 newspaper-style (snaking), AC 433
 reports, resizing and renaming in layout view, AC 406–407

column header A unique label that describes the contents of the data in a column; also called a field name. EX 259

COLUMNS area, PivotTables, EX 303

Combine The Word feature that allows you to merge the contents of two separate documents and to see which reviewers made which changes; designed for documents that do contain tracked changes. WD 362–366

combo box A control that provides the features of a text box and a list box; you can choose a value from the list or type an entry. AC 304
 adding to forms, AC 336–342
 to find records, AC 348–355
 modifying in Design and Layout views, AC 340–342
 using for foreign keys, AC 336

Combo Box tool A tool you use in Design view to add a combo box to a form. AC 336

comma-separated value (CSV) file A text file in which each paragraph contains one record, with the fields separated by commas; can have a .txt or .csv file extension. WD 340

comma-separated values. *See* CSV

comment A text box that is attached to a specific cell in a worksheet in which you can enter notes. EX 409, EX 425–427

Compare The Word feature that allows you to merge the contents of two separate documents and to quickly spot the differences between two copies of a document; designed for documents that do not contain tracked changes. WD 362–366

Compatibility Checker A dialog box that alerts you to any features that are not supported by earlier versions of Excel when you save a workbook in an earlier format. EX A17–A18

I

IF function The logical function that tests a condition and then returns one value if the condition is true and another value if the condition is false. EX 467–470

IF Function Arguments dialog box, EX 404

IFERROR function A function that can determine if a cell contains an error value and then display the message you choose rather than the default error value. EX 482, EX 500–502

IIf (Immediate If) function A function that test a condition and returns one of two values based on whether the condition being tested is true or false. AC 235, AC 245–248

Import Objects dialog box, AC 455

importing A process that allows you to copy the data from a source, without having to open the source file, and to add the imported data in an Access table, form, report, for field. AC 473
    file formats, AC 463
    saving and running import specifications, AC 457–460
    tables from Access databases, AC 454–455
    XML files as Access tables, AC 456

In comparison operator A comparison operator that defines a condition with a list of two or more values for a field. If a record's field value matches one value from the list of defined values, then Access selects and includes that record in the query results. AC 240

input mask A field property used to define a predefined format to enter and display data in a field. AC 269
    when to use, AC 281

Input Mask Wizard An Access tool that guides you in creating a predefined format for a field. AC 276–281

input message A message that appears when the cell becomes active; can be used to specify the type of data the user should enter in that cell. EX 408
    creating, EX 413–414

Insert Address Block dialog box, WD 335–336

Insert Chart dialog box, PPT 148

Insert Hyperlink dialog box, EX 368, EX 370–371, PPT 205

Insert Merge Field menu, WD 314

Insert Pictures dialog box, PPT 202

insertion anomaly The inability to add a record to a table because you do not know the entire primary key value. AC A14

insignificant zero A zero whose omission from a number does not change the number's value. EX A14

integrating Access with other programs, AC 472–474. *See also* embedding; exporting; importing; linking

integration The process of sharing information among the Office programs via object linking and embedding; you can integrate information by either embedding or linking. WD 370

integrity A database has integrity if its data follows certain rules, known as integrity constraints. AC A11

integrity constraint A rule that must be followed by data in a database. AC A11

intelligent key. *See* natural key

Internet Explorer, viewing HTML documents, AC 448

intersection table A table that connects two other tables having a many-to-many relationship; its primary key is a composite key, consisting of the primary keys of the other two tables. AC A6

IsNull function A function that tests a field value or an expression for a null value; if the field value or expression is null, the result is true; otherwise, the result is false. AC 235

J

junction table. *See* intersection table

K

Keep lines together A setting in the Paragraph dialog box that ensures that the lines of a multiline heading paragraph will never be separated by a page break. WD 274

Keep Together property A property for a group in a report to keep parts of the group together on the same page. Settings for the property are "do not keep together on one page" (default), "keep whole group together on one page" (prints the group header, detail, and group footers on the same page), and "keep header and first record together on one page" (prints the group header on a page only if it can also print the first detail record). For a section, this property specifies whether the section starts printing on a new page if the entire section doesn't fit entirely on the current page. AC 409–410

Keep with next A setting in the Paragraph dialog box that ensures that a heading is never separated from the paragraph that follows it. WD 274

key
    artificial, AC A21–A23
    foreign, AC A4–A5
    natural (logical, intelligent), AC A21
    primary. *See* primary key
    surrogate (synthetic), AC A23–A25

kiosk browsing, PPT 225–226

L

label An unbound control that displays text. AC 326
    changing caption, AC 338–340

label (mailing), AC 430–434

Label Options dialog box, WD 333–334

Label Wizard An Access tool that asks you a series of questions, and then creates a mailing label report based on your answers. AC 430–434

Last function, AC 256

layout
    PivotTables, EX 305–306
    reports, EX 306
    stacked, AC 302
    tabular, AC 302

layout (PowerPoint) The arrangement of placeholders on the slide; in SmartArt, the arrangement of the shapes in the diagram.
    SmartArt diagrams, changing, PPT 142–143

Layout view The Access view in which you can make design changes to a form or report while it is displaying data so that you can immediately see the effects of changing the design.
    modifying combo boxes, AC 340–342
    modifying reports, AC 388–395
    modifying split forms, AC 315–319
    resizing and renaming columns, AC 406–407

left angle bracket (<)
    input mask character, AC 279
    merge fields, WD 300

LEFT function A text function that returns a specified number of characters from the beginning of a specified string. EX A4–A6

LEN function A text function that returns the number of characters (length) of a specified string. EX A4–A6

Like comparison operator A comparison operator that selects records by matching field values to a specific pattern that includes one or more wildcard characters. AC 237

line
    adding to forms, AC 367–368
    adding to reports, AC 416–417
    horizontal, inserting, WD 399–401

line break, reviewing in Reveal Formatting pane, WD 274–275

Line tool A tool in Design view that you use to add a line to a form or report. AC 346

link A connection between files that allows data to be transferred from one file to another. EX 350
    broken, EX 365
    linking workbooks, EX 352–361
    managing, EX 365–367

Link Spreadsheet dialog box, AC 488

link table. *See* intersection table

linked file, storing, WD 382

linked style A style that contains both character and paragraph formatting options. WD 260–261

linking (Access) Creating a connection in a destination program to an original file maintained by a source

TASK REFERENCE

TASK	PAGE #	RECOMMENDED METHOD
Advanced filter, clear	EX B7	On the DATA tab, in the Sort & Filter group, click the Clear button
Advanced filter, create	EX B4	On the DATA tab, in the Sort & Filter group, click the Advanced button, set filter options, data, and criteria ranges, click OK
All Markup view, switch to	WD 357	Click REVIEW tab, click the Display for Review arrow in the Tracking group, click All Markup
Alternate row color, set and remove in a report	AC 415	In Design view, select the Detail section, click the FORMAT tab, in the Background group, click Alternate Row Color
Animation, apply a second animation	PPT 193	Click ANIMATIONS tab, in Advanced Animation group click Add Animation, click animation
Animation pane, open	PPT 196	Click ANIMATIONS tab, in Advanced Animation group click Animation Pane
Application Part, create	AC 481	Click the FILE tab, click Save Database As, click Template, click Save As, click enter a name and description, click Application Part, click OK
AutoFilter, use in a table or query datasheet	AC 242	Click the arrow on the column heading, click one or more filter options, click OK
Blog post, create	WD 405	Click FILE tab, click New, click Blog post, click the Create button
Bookmark, create	WD 389	Select text, click INSERT tab, click the Bookmark button in the Links group, type bookmark name, click Add
Built-in functions, use in a query	AC 246	Display the query in Design view, right-click a blank field, click Build, double-click Functions, click Built-In Functions, select a category, double-click a function, replace any placeholders, click OK
Caption, change for a form's navigation bar	AC 470	Click the form selector, open the Property Sheet, type the value in the Navigation Caption box, press Enter
Cells, reference in other worksheets	EX 339	Enter a reference in the format =*SheetName!CellRange*
Cell or range, select by their defined name	EX 397	Click the Name box arrow, click a defined name
Chart, create	PPT 148	*See* Reference box: Creating a Chart
Chart, edit data	PPT 151	Click CHART TOOLS DESIGN tab, in Data group, click Edit Data
Chart, edit with Microsoft Graph	AC 476	In Design view, right-click the chart's edge, point to Chart Object, click Open, make desired changes, click File, click Exit & Return
Chart, embed in a form or report	AC 474	*See* Reference box: Embedding a Chart in a Form or Report
Chart element, add or remove	PPT 151	To right of chart, click Chart Elements button, click element check box or point to element, click arrow, click element
Chart style, change	PPT 151	Click CHART TOOLS DESIGN tab, in Chart Styles group, click More button, click style
Chart Wizard, start	AC 474	In Design view, on the DESIGN tab, in the Controls group, click the More button, click the Chart tool
Color, change an object's background	AC 371	Click the object, click the 🎨▾ arrow, click the desired color
Comment, delete	EX 429	Click a cell with a comment, on the Review tab, in the Comments group, click the Delete button
Comment, show or hide	EX 428	Click a cell with a comment, the Show/Hide Comment button

TASK	PAGE #	RECOMMENDED METHOD
Control, apply a special effect to	AC 370	Select the control, open the Property Sheet, set the Special Effect property
Control, delete	AC 334	Right-click the control, click Delete
Control layout, remove control from a form	AC 317	In Layout view, right-click the control, point to Layout, click Remove Layout
Control tip property, set for a form control	AC 361	In Layout view, right-click the control, click Properties, click Other tab, type the tip in the ControlTip Text property box, press Enter
Controls, align selected	AC 332	Right-click one of the selected controls, point to Align, click desired alignment
Controls, move and resize in a form or report	AC 413	Select controls, click the ARRANGE tab, click Size/Space, click desired setting
Crosstab query, edit column headings	AC 261	In Design view, right-click the Field box, click Zoom, edit the value or expression, click OK
Database, back up	AC 292	Click the FILE tab, click Save As, click Back Up Database, click Save As, navigate to desired location, click Save
Date field, insert	WD 302	Click INSERT tab, click the Date & Time button in the Text group, click a Date format, click OK
Defined name, edit or delete	EX 399	On the FORMULAS tab, in the Defined Names group, click the Name Manager button (or press Ctrl+F3), select a name, click Edit and modify or click Delete, click OK, click Close
Developer tab, display or hide on the ribbon	EX 432	Click the FILE tab, click Options in the navigation pane, click Customize Ribbon, check or uncheck Developer check box, click OK
Excel table, add a record	EX 268	Click the row below the Excel table, type values for the new record, pressing Tab to move from field to field
Excel table, apply a style	EX 267	On the TABLE TOOLS DESIGN tab, in the Table Styles group, click the More button, click a table style
Excel table, create	EX 264	On the INSERT tab, in the Tables group, click the Table button, verify the range of data, click OK
Excel table, delete a record	EX 270	Select a record, on the HOME tab, in the Cells group, click the Delete button arrow, click Delete Table Rows
Excel table, filter using a slicer	EX 286	Click a slicer button on the slicer
Excel table, find and replace a record	EX 269	Click in the Excel table, on the HOME tab, in the Editing group, click the Find & Select button, use the Find and Replace dialog box
Excel table, modify	EX 267	On TABLE TOOLS DESIGN tab, in the Table Style Options group, check or uncheck options
Excel table, rename	EX 266	Click in the Excel table, on the TABLE TOOLS DESIGN tab, in the Properties group, select the name in the Table Name box, type a name, press Enter
Export steps, save	AC 463	In the Export dialog box, click the Save export steps check box, enter a description, click Save Export
Field, add to a form or report	AC 327	In Design view, on the DESIGN tab, in the Tools group, click Add Existing Fields, click the record source, double-click the field
Filter, clear from a column	EX 281	Click the filter button, click Clear Filter From "column"
Filter, clear from an Excel table	EX 285	On the DATA tab, in the Sort & Filter group, click the Clear button
Filter, select multiple items	EX 282	Click the filter button, check two or more items, click OK

TASK	PAGE #	RECOMMENDED METHOD
Filter, specify complex criteria	EX 283	Click the filter button, point to Number Filters, Text Filters, or Date Filters, specify the filter criteria, click OK
Filter, use multiple columns	EX 280	Filter for one column, repeat to filter for additional columns
Filter, use one column	EX 278	Click a filter button, deselect the (Select All) check box, click the item to filter by, click OK
Filter buttons, display or hide	EX 278	On the DATA tab, in the Sort & Filter group, click the Filter button
Form, create using the Datasheet tool	AC 311	Select the record source in the Navigation Pane, click the CREATE tab, in the Forms group, click More Forms, click Datasheet
Form, create using the Multiple Items tool	AC 313	Select the record source in the Navigation Pane, click the CREATE tab, in the Forms group, click More Forms , click Multiple Items
Form, create using the Split Form tool	AC 314	Select the record source in the Navigation Pane, click the CREATE tab, in the Forms group click More Forms, click Split Form
Form, select in Design view	AC 348	Click the form selector
Format Shape task pane, open	PPT 155	Right-click shape, click Format Shape
Formula results, copy and paste as values	EX A6	Copy the range with formula results, click the first cell in the paste location, on the HOME tab, in the Clipboard group, click the Paste button arrow, click the Values button
Formula with an external reference, create	EX 356	Click a cell in the destination file, type =, click a cell in the source file, complete the formula as usual
Go To, use to find document elements	WD 247	Click HOME tab, click the Find button arrow in the Editing group, click a document element in the Go to what box, click Next or Previous
Horizontal line, insert	WD 399	Click HOME tab, click in the Paragraph group, click Horizontal Line
Hyperlink, create	PPT 205	Select object or text, click INSERT tab, in Links group, click Hyperlink, click option in Link to list, click link destination, click OK
Hyperlink, edit	EX 377	Right-click the cell with the hyperlink, click Edit Hyperlink, make edits in the Edit Hyperlink dialog box, click OK
Import steps, save	AC 458	In the Get External Data dialog box, click the Save import steps check box, enter a description, click Save Import
Input Mask Wizard, start	AC 276	Click the field's Input Mask box, click , specify your choices in the Input Mask Wizard dialog boxes
Invalid data, circle	EX 421	On the DATA tab, in the Data Tools group, click the Data Validation button arrow, click Circle Invalid Data
Kiosk browsing, set up	PPT 226	Click SLIDE SHOW tab, in Set Up group, click Set Up Slide Show, click Browsed at a kiosk (full screen) option button, click OK
Label Wizard, start	AC 431	Click the CREATE tab, in the Report group, click Labels
Links, manage	EX 365	On the DATA tab, in the Connections group, click the Edit Links button, select an option, click OK
Long Text field, change properties of	AC 289	Display the table in Design view, select the Long Text field, change the value in the Text Format box or in the Append Only box
Lookup field, create	AC 272	Click the Data Type arrow, click Lookup Wizard, specify your choices in the Lookup Wizard dialog boxes
Lookup field, change to a Text field	AC 305	Display the table in Design view, select the field, click the Lookup tab, set the Display Control property to Text Box

TASK	PAGE #	RECOMMENDED METHOD
Macro button, move or resize	EX 450	Right-click the macro button, press Esc, drag the button by its selection box to new location or drag a sizing handle
Mail merge, finish by merging to new document	WD 319	Click MAILINGS tab, click the Finish & Merge button in the Finish group, click Edit Individual Documents, click OK
Mail merge, finish by merging to printer	WD 319	Click MAILINGS tab, click the Finish & Merge button in the Finish group, click Print Documents, click OK
Mail merge, insert merge fields in main document for	WD 313	Click REVIEW tab, click the Insert Merge Field button arrow in the Write & Insert Fields group, click a merge field
Mail merge, preview merged document for	WD 317	Click MAILINGS tab, click the Preview Results button in the Preview Results group
Mail merge main document, select type of	WD 304	Click MAILINGS tab, click the Start Mail Merge button in the Start Mail Merge group, click a main document type
Media, optimize	PPT 226	Click FILE tab, on Info screen click Optimize Compatibility, click Close
Motion path animation, adjust	PPT 193	Click motion path, drag red or green circles at ends of the path
Not logical operator, use in a query	AC 241	In Design view, click the Criteria box for a field, open the Zoom dialog box, type Not, press the spacebar, type the criteria
Object, duplicate	PPT 165	Click HOME tab, in Clipboard group, click Copy button arrow, click Duplicate
Object, rename in Selection Pane	PPT 180	Click HOME tab, in Editing group, click Select, click Selection Pane, in Selection Pane click object name twice, edit name
Object dependencies, identify	AC 282	Click the DATABASE TOOLS tab, in the Relationships group, click the Object Dependencies button, click the object, click ▷
Object order on slide, identify	PPT 179	Click HOME tab, in Editing group, click Select, click Selection Pane
Objects, align	PPT 170	Select objects, click HOME tab, in Drawing group, click Arrange, point to Align, click alignment command
Padding, change in a form control	AC 316	In Layout view, click the control, click the ARRANGE tab, in the Position group, click Control Padding, click the desired setting
Page margins, setting in a report	AC 412	Click the PAGE SETUP tab, click Margins, click an option
Pattern match, use in a query	AC 239	In Design view, in the Criteria box for a field, type Like, press the spacebar, type the text to match enclosed in quotes
PDF, create from report	AC 485	Right-click the name of the report in the Navigation pane, click Export, click PDF or XPS, navigate to the appropriate location, enter a name in the File name box, click Publish
Photo, color saturation and tone, change	PPT 163	Click PICTURE TOOLS FORMAT tab, in Adjust group, click Color, click option under either Color Saturation or Color Tone
Photo, sharpen or soften	PPT 163	Click PICTURE TOOLS FORMAT tab, in Adjust group, click Corrections, click option under Sharpen/Soften
Photo artistic effects, apply	PPT 166	Click PICTURE TOOLS FORMAT tab, click Artistic Effects, click style
Photo brightness and contrast, change	PPT 162	Click PICTURE TOOLS FORMAT tab, in Adjust group, click Corrections, click option under Brightness/Contrast
PivotChart, create	EX 316	On the PIVOTTABLE TOOLS ANALYZE tab, in the Tools group, click the PivotChart button, select a chart, click OK
PivotTable, create	EX 301	See Reference box: Creating a PivotTable

TASK	PAGE #	RECOMMENDED METHOD
PivotTable, create recommended	EX 314	Click in an Excel table, on the INSERT tab, in the Tables group, click the Recommended PivotTables button, select a PivotTable, click OK
PivotTable, rearrange	EX 306	In the PivotTable Fields pane, drag field buttons between the ROWS, COLUMNS and FILTERS areas
PivotTable, refresh	EX 312	On the PIVOTTABLE TOOLS ANALYZE tab, in the Data group, click the Refresh button
PivotTable field, filter	EX 309	Click a filter arrow, click a filter item, click OK
PivotTable Fields pane, show or hide	EX 311	Click in the PivotTable, on the PIVOTTABLE TOOLS ANALYZE tab, in the Show group, click the Field List button
PivotTable report, filter	EX 308	Drag a field button from PivotTable Fields pane to FILTERS area or drag a field button from ROWS or COLUMNS area to FILTERS area
PivotTable Row and Column field items, filter	EX 309	In the PivotTable, click the Column Labels or Row Labels filter button, check or uncheck items, click OK
PivotTable style, apply	EX 307	On the PIVOTTABLE TOOLS DESIGN tab, in the PivotTable Styles group, click the More button, click a style
PivotTable value fields, format	EX 307	In the VALUES area of the PivotTable Fields pane, click the button, click the Value Field Settings button, click the Number Format button, select a format, click OK
Presentation, check for hidden information	PPT 226	Click FILE tab, on Info screen, click Check for Issues, click Inspect Document, click Inspect, click Remove All next to data you want to remove, click Close
Property sheet, open or close for a field or control	AC 248	Select the field or control, click the DESIGN tab, in the Show/Hide group click the Property Sheet button
Quick Part, delete from Building Blocks template	WD 291	Click INSERT tab, click the Quick Parts button in the Text group, click Building Blocks Organizer, click a Quick Part in the Building blocks list, click Delete
Report, create a custom	AC 405	Click the CREATE tab, click Blank Report
Report, filter in Report view	AC 385	Right-click the value to filter, point to Text Filters, click a filter option
Report, select and copy data in Report view	AC 387	Click the top of the selection, drag to the end of the selection, click the HOME tab, in the Clipboard group, click 📋
Reveal Formatting pane, open	WD 272	Click ✍ at the bottom of Styles pane, click 🔍 in Style Inspector
Row(s) and column(s), freeze	EX 263	Click the cell below and to the right of row(s) and column(s) to freeze, on the VIEW tab, in the Window group, click the Freeze Panes button, click an option
Row(s) and column(s), unfreeze	EX 263	On the VIEW tab, in the Window group, click the Freeze Panes button, click Unfreeze Panes
Saved export, run	AC 464	Click the EXTERNAL DATA tab, in the Export group, click Saved Exports, click the saved export, click Run
Saved import, run	AC 458	Click the EXTERNAL DATA tab, in the Import & Link group, click Saved Imports, click the saved import, click Run
Shape, adjust	PPT 169	Select shape, drag yellow adjustment handle
Shape, fill with texture	PPT 173	Click DRAWING TOOLS FORMAT tab, in Shape Styles group click Shape Fill button arrow, point to Texture, click texture

TASK	PAGE #	RECOMMENDED METHOD
Shape effect, apply	PPT 176	Click DRAWING TOOLS FORMAT tab, in Shape Styles group click Shape Effects, point to a style category, click style
Shape outline, change	PPT 175	Click DRAWING TOOLS FORMAT tab, in Shape Styles group click Shape Outline button arrow, click color
Simple Markup view, switch to	WD 361	Click REVIEW tab, click the Display for Review arrow in the Tracking group, click Simple Markup
Slicer, create for a PivotTable	EX 310	ON the PIVOTTABLE TOOLS ANALYZE tab, in the Filter group, click the Click Insert Slicer button, click a field check box, click OK
Slicer, create for an Excel table	EX 285	On the TABLE TOOLS DESIGN tab, in the Tools group, click the Insert Slicker button, select one or more field check boxes, click OK
Slicer, format	EX 285	On the SLICER TOOLS OPTONS tab, set the slicer's size and style
Slide background, set picture as tiles	PPT 202	In Format Background task pane, select Tile picture as check box
Slide show, prevent viewer from advancing	PPT 225	Click TRANSITIONS tab, in Timing group deselect On Mouse Click check box
Slide timings, rehearse	PPT 220	Click SLIDE SHOW tab, in Set Up group, click Rehearse Timings, advance slide show, click Yes to save rehearsed timings
Slide timings, set	PPT 218	Select slide thumbnails, click TRANSITIONS tab, in Timing group click After check box, change value in After box to desired timing
SmartArt diagram colors, change	PPT 144	Click SMARTART TOOLS DESIGN tab, in SmartArt Styles group, click Change Colors, click color style
SmartArt diagram layout, change	PPT 142	Click SMARTART TOOLS DESIGN tab, in Layouts group, click More button, click layout
SmartArt diagram style, change	PPT 144	Click SMARTART TOOLS DESIGN tab, in SmartArt Styles group, click More button, click style
Sort, one column	EX 271	Click in the column to sort, on the DATA tab, in the Sort & Filter group, click ⬆A/Z or ⬇Z/A
Spacing, change in a form control	AC 316	In Layout view, click the control, click the ARRANGE tab, in the Position group, click Control Margins, click the desired setting
Style Inspector, open	WD 270	Click ⬛ at the bottom of the Styles pane
Style Set, select	WD 256	Click DESIGN tab, click the More button in the Document Formatting group, click a style set
Styles pane, change way styles are displayed in	WD 269	Click Options in the bottom-right corner of the Styles pane, select style pane options, click OK
Styles pane, open	WD 261	Click HOME tab, click the Dialog Box Launcher in the Styles group
Subform, open in a new window	AC 356	Right-click the subform border, click Subform in New Window
Subform/Subreport Wizard, start	AC 352	Click the DESIGN tab, in the Controls group, click More, make sure ⬛ is selected, click ⬛, click in the grid where the upper-left corner of the subform/subreport should be placed
Subtotal Outline view, use	EX 295	Click an outline button to show or hide the selected outline level
Subtotals, remove	EX 296	ON the DATA tab, in the Outline group, click the Subtotal button, click the Remove All button
Synonym, replace selected word or text with	WD 249	Right-click a word or selected text, point to Synonyms, click synonym
Tab Control, add to a form	AC 468	Click the DESIGN tab, in the Controls group, click ⬛, click in the grid at the location of the upper-left corner for the tab control

TASK	PAGE #	RECOMMENDED METHOD
Tab order, change in a form	AC 364	In Design view, click the DESIGN tab, in the Tools group, click Tab Order, drag the rows into the desired order, click OK
Tab Stop property, change for a form control	AC 361	In Layout view, right-click the control, click Properties, click the Other tab, set the Tab Stop property
Tabs, clear all from document	WD 338	Click HOME tab, click the Dialog Box Launcher in the Paragraph group, click Tabs, click Clear All, click OK
Table, analyze	AC 453	Select the table, click DATABASE TOOLS tab, in the Analyze group, click Analyze Table
Table, create from Application Part	AC 483	Click the CREATE tab, click the Application Parts button, click the application part template, click the appropriate relationship option button, click Create
Table, convert to text	WD 340	Click in the table, click the TABLE TOOLS LAYOUT tab, click Convert to Text in the Data group, select a separator character, click OK
Table of Contents, add text to	WD 282	Select text, click REFERENCES tab, click the Add Text button in the Table of Contents group, click a level
Table relationships, view	AC 306	Click the DATABASE TOOLS tab, click Relationships
Template from Office.com, create a new document from	WD 244	Click FILE tab, click New, click in the Search for online templates box, type a keyword, click a template, click the Create button
Template saved to Templates folder, create new document from	WD 287	Click FILE tab, click New, click PERSONAL, click template
Text box, insert	PPT 154	Click INSERT tab, in Text group, click Text Box, drag pointer on slide, type text
Text box margins, change	PPT 156	Right-click text box, click Format Shape, click TEXT OPTIONS, click Textbox button, click TEXT BOX, change values in margin boxes
Text box wrapping option, change	PPT 155	Right-click text box, click Format Shape, click TEXT OPTIONS, click Textbox button, click TEXT BOX, select or deselect Wrap text in shape check box
Theme, create a custom	WD 254	Click DESIGN tab, click the Themes button in the Document Formatting group, click Save Current Theme, navigate to a new location if necessary, type a theme name in the File name box, click the Save button
Theme colors, customize	WD 254	Click DESIGN tab, click the Colors button in the Document Formatting group, click Customize Colors, select theme colors, type a name for the new set of colors in the Name box, click Save
Theme colors, select	WD 252	Click DESIGN tab, click the Colors button in the Document Formatting group, click a set of theme colors
Theme fonts, select	WD 253	Click DESIGN tab, click the Fonts button in the Document Formatting group, click a set of theme fonts
Thesaurus, use to find synonyms	WD 249	Right-click a word or selected text, point to Synonyms, click synonym
Title, add to a form or report	AC 343	On the DESIGN tab, in the Header/Footer group, click Title, type the title, press Enter
Top values query, create	AC 267	On the DESIGN tab, in the Query Setup group, in the Return (Top Values) box, enter the number of or percentage of records to select